THE ESSENTIAL HISTORY OF LIVERPOOL

FOREWORD BY IAN CALLAGHAN

ALEX MURPHY AND ERIC DOIG

WH S

This book is dedicated to Steve McLean, Red forever. And to Patrick McLean, the next generation.

First published in 2003
by Headline Book Publishing
for WHSmith, Greenbridge Road, Swindon SN3 3LD

10 9 8 7 6 5 4 3 2 1

ISBN 0 7553 1268 6

Design by designsection, Frome, Somerset

All photographs supplied by Colorsport except page 9 Liverpool Record Office; pages 13, 29 Popperfoto; page 24; and page 28 GDF Cartophily

The authors would like to thank: David Bull, Ian Callaghan, Jimmy Case, Adrian Chiles, Phil Chisnall, Ian Cook, Peter Cormack, David Fairclough, Tony Hateley, Mel Henderson, Emlyn Hughes, David Johnson, Mark Lawrenson, Ronnie Moran, Richard Murphy, Phil Neal, Micky Payne, Ivan Ponting, Jo Riches, Ian St John, John Wark and Adrian Whitfield. Eric Doig thanks his colleague, Jonny Stokkeland, a Norwegian Supporters Branch statistician whose dedication, and enthusiasm for all matters concerning LFC has greatly assisted the researching of club history over the last decade.

Printed and bound in Great Britain by Clays Ltd, St Ives PLC, Bungay, Suffolk

HEADLINE BOOK PUBLISHING
A division of Hodder Headline
338 Euston Road
London NW1 3BH

www.headline.co.uk
www.hodderheadline.com

Contents

Foreword
By Ian Callaghan

I feel enormously proud that for 20 years I was a player for Liverpool Football Club. All through my playing days, and in the years since I stopped being a player and became a supporter again, that pride has grown as Liverpool have developed from a middling Second Division side into one of the biggest clubs in Europe.

My association with the club started when I was a little lad, watching my heroes, players like Billy Liddell, from the boys' pen at Anfield. It was a dream come true when Liverpool wanted to sign me, and the great Bill Shankly himself persuaded my mum and dad to let me join the club. In due course I became a first-team player, and it was an enormous honour that the man whose place in the team I inherited was the marvellous Billy Liddell.

That was in the early days of Bill Shankly's time at Anfield, and he was terrific to me, a real father figure. Under Bill Liverpool really began to realise the potential that had been untapped for years. Bill brought success back to the club, but he brought other things too. He was the first man to really create a bond between the supporters and the players, and that link has never been broken. All the qualities of the man were reflected in his teams: hard work, the importance of team work, and a dash of inspiration and charisma which captured fans' imagination.

I was lucky to be a member of the team that won promotion back to the First Division, won two League Championships in the mid-1960s and, in 1965, the FA Cup for the first time in the club's history. Shankly built another team which dominated English football in the early 1970s, and brought the first European trophy

Ian Callaghan impressing in training as a youngster in 1963.

The experienced Ian Callaghan in action against Ipswich Town in 1975.

to the club – the UEFA Cup. To be the first to achieve something as wonderful as that is a fantastic feeling. It was a feeling that was repeated after Bob Paisley took over from Bill and we won the European Cup for the first time in 1977.

Under Bob the success kept coming. His great achievement was ensuring stability at Liverpool, which meant that there were never any great changes. Year after year Liverpool had the strongest team in the land, and the club stayed at its trophy-winning peak.

In the last 10 years or so the trophies have arrived less frequently but the spirit of the club remains the same. With Gerard Houllier as manager the supporters still remain passionate about their club, and that bond between the team and the fans endures. Every time I go to Anfield now as a spectator, I feel the belief the Liverpool public has in its team, and I share it. I am convinced Liverpool remain the greatest club there is, and it is only a matter of time before the Reds are Champions again.

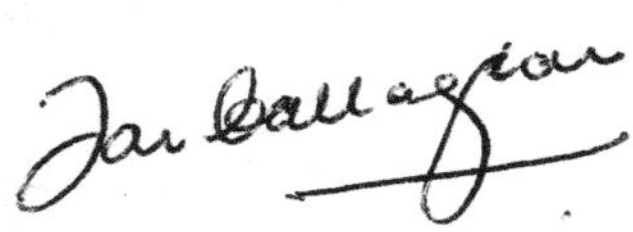

Introduction

At times this book reads like the battle honours of a conquering army. Especially in the later chapters, Liverpool's success is a litany of championships, cups, doubles and trebles. But the story of Liverpool is not a tale of conquest for its own sake. The glory of Liverpool Football Club lies not just in the honours they have won, but in the happiness they have given people.

When I think of what the club means I think of my late grandad, Richard Murphy, who worked on the docks in the week and spent Saturday afternoons on the Kop. In his later years when he couldn't face the crowds any more, he took to his bed to listen on the radio when the Reds were playing. All over Europe he followed them, a faithful fan of the airwaves, the dim light from the radio display blinking in the darkened bedroom. He'd leave the door open, and bellow match summaries and score flashes downstairs to my grandmother: 'Mary, 1-0, Keegan'. It was a big feature of his love for Liverpool that he hated to see them let in goals. Of course, he didn't mind Liverpool scoring at the other end. On Saturday nights we'd watch the games on *Match of the Day*, and every time Liverpool put the ball in the net, he'd say the same thing: 'Ping!' Whenever I see a Liverpool goal now, Grandad's voice goes off in my head: 'Ping!'

As is often the way in the city, Grandad's devotion was not shared by his son, my dad, an Evertonian. When I was little they waged a none-too-subtle war for my allegiance. But in the early years there was no contest. Liverpool were invincible, and they had Bill Shankly, with all his earthy glamour and colourful one-liners. It sounds odd to talk about a crop-headed bantam-cock Scotsman in terms of glamour, but that's what Shankly had. He dripped charisma, and half a city owes him boundless thanks for everything he did to raise the club and its supporters from a pit of depression in the 1950s. Within a few years he had got them back in the First Division, won the championship and took them into Europe. He told Liverpudlians: 'This is your team. This is who you are. You are mighty.' The people loved him for it. I know Grandad did.

I'm writing this while the TV news is showing highlights of Liverpool's victory against Manchester United in the 2003 League Cup final. Michael Owen has just scored, triggering a noise in my head something like the one a microwave oven makes when your shepherd's pie is ready.

'Ping!'

Chapter One: 1892-1919
The Birth of Liverpool

It should be a romantic story. The tale of how Liverpool came into existence should set the tone for the glorious deeds that were to follow. Perhaps, like Celtic, the club might have been built by the city's poor immigrants, subscribing pennies from their meagre funds to create something of their own in an alien city. Or it might have been brought into being by a benign millionaire, consumed with a mission to leave an immortal sporting legacy for the city which made his fortune.

The truth is sadly more prosaic. The club which went on to become the most successful in Britain was born out of a tawdry row over the rent on a scrubby patch of waste ground in the poor Anfield district of Liverpool.

It was 1892, and the strongest football club on Merseyside – indeed, one of the most powerful clubs in the country – was a team named Everton. Their president was a local brewing tycoon called John Houlding, whose vision and cash had done much to turn Everton from a church side playing in parks into a professional club, one of the founder members of the Football League, and the champions of England just the year before.

A schism opened up when Houlding bought Everton's home ground, at Anfield Road, and demanded a rent rise from £100 a year to £250. Houlding was, after all, a tough businessman as well as an enthusiastic sportsman, and he was determined to reap a dividend from all the money he had pumped into Everton. Houlding reasoned that the club could well afford the increase: they were collecting good gate money from attendances averaging over 10,000, and they could clearly afford to pay stars like centre forward Fred Geary as much as £3 per week.

As well as the extra rent, Houlding insisted that the only ale on sale at the ground should come from his brewery. Most Everton members were furious with Houlding's plan, and civil war split the club in two.

The anti-Houlding majority within the club came back with a compromise deal to carry on playing at Anfield, but Houlding turned it down. Most of Everton's players and members soon found a new ground a few hundred yards from Anfield, at Goodison Park. Houlding had met his match in George Mahon, a former organist from St Domingo Church, who pulled out all the stops in a campaign to loosen Houlding's stranglehold on Everton.

In truth, the marriage between Houlding and Everton Football Club had always been based on shaky foundations. Everton had begun life as St Domingo FC, a Methodist Church Sunday School side, in 1878. The club was built according to strict non-conformist principles, and many of its members were active in the Temperance movement, which identified lax licensing laws and chronic alcoholism as society's major ills.

Houlding, by contrast, was a leading figure in Liverpool's politically influential beerage. From poor beginnings he had worked his way up to become a rich brewery owner, famous for his Everton Beacon Ale, and kept several pubs in the city. At Houlding's insistence, Everton Football Club used one of his hostelries close to Anfield – the Sandon Hotel – as its base.

'King John', as he was nicknamed in the local press, was also a freemason, a prominent Orangeman and a Conservative politician, a trinity of interests that left him with little in common with the average Everton member.

In the end Houlding fell into a classic trap which still ensnares football benefactors today. Running Everton was good for his standing in the city and good for profits, yet he wanted to be loved as well. In classic playground style, Houlding had the ball, but none of the other boys wanted to play with him. He now found himself the proud owner of a football ground, with no team to play there.

That was swiftly remedied when Houlding rallied the rump of his followers to form a new club. After some debate they chose a new name, and after a difficult labour, Liverpool Football Club was given life on 15 March 1892 – but only after the Football Association had vetoed Houlding's plan to keep the name 'Everton'.

Empty Teamsheet

A minor snag was that the fledgling Liverpool side did not have enough players to fill 11 jerseys. Only a few – Andrew Hannah, Pat Gordon and Duncan McLean – had resisted the clarion call from the Everton loyalists, and recruitment was placed in the hands of an Irish immigrant named John McKenna, an acquaintance of Houlding's from the Orange Order.

He set off on a tour of Scotland, an especially fertile source of talent for English clubs in those days, and McKenna came home with enough players to field a team of immense promise.

The newly founded club's application to join the Football League was immediately turned down, and so Liverpool's first-ever season was spent in the Lancashire League, where they came up against sides like Heywood Central and Southport.

Liverpool, playing in Blackburn Rovers-style blue-and-white quarters, won the league with ease thanks to their complement of Scottish professionals (they were nicknamed 'The Team of Macs'), and in the summer of 1893 the club's second application to become members of the Football League was successful.

John Houlding, architect of both Liverpool and Everton football clubs.

They kicked off their first season in the Second Division, along with fellow new boys Woolwich Arsenal, and won the championship at the first attempt. After winning their first game, 2-0 away to Middlesbrough Ironopolis, they went on to win a total of 22 games out of 28. The final hurdle to promotion was a 'Test Match', a forerunner of the modern play-offs, against Newton Heath, from the bottom of the First Division. Liverpool won 2-0 against the club that was soon to be renamed Manchester United, and just two years after the club was born, Liverpool found themselves – alongside Everton – in the First Division.

The long-awaited first league derby match took place in October 1894 at Goodison, which had already been hailed as the finest football ground in the country. Compared to other clubs' arenas, which were still at the primitive stage of development, Goodison's banked terracing and covered areas were opulent. The ground was nicknamed 'Toffeeopolis', and even though it had been constructed hastily after the flight from Houlding's Anfield, facilities were far superior to the old place. Goodison even had dressing rooms on site, while Liverpool and their opponents were still changing in a room at the Sandon and walking from the pub to the ground. The *Football Echo* in August 1892 reported pointedly after the new Goodison had opened, 'The players will not have to parade themselves through the public street as was the case at Anfield Road, in all their "war paint", and what is of more importance, visiting teams will not have to run the gauntlet through a crowd of incensed partisans whom they might probably have displeased in some manner on the field.'

John McKenna, whose successful Scottish recruitment tour led to 'The Team of Macs'.

Over 44,000 spectators paid their sixpences to cram in for the game, and thousands more were left outside as the 'Ground Full' notices went up well before kick-off. Everything pointed to an Everton victory: they were the city's senior club, and came into the match on the back of six victories. Liverpool had failed to win any of their first eight league games. The form worked itself out, and Everton won 3-0.

The return match at Anfield a month later was drawn 2-2, but by then Liverpool were heading for relegation after just one season in the First Division. Liverpool finished second from bottom of the table, then lost a Test Match 1-0 against Bury.

Undeterred by this setback, Liverpool set about regaining their place in the First Division, and McKenna went shopping for new players, once again plundering Scotland for likely lads.

Record Signing Pays Back

It worked. Liverpool sprinted to the 1895-96 Second Division Championship, scoring a club-record 106 goals in the season. Jimmy Ross, the Edinburgh forward who McKenna had lured from Preston North End, scored 23 of them. Those goals showed why the club were prepared to risk their biggest-ever transfer fee to buy him. Liverpool had shelled out all of £75 for Ross.

The Test Match format had been expanded, so Liverpool still had to overcome Small Heath and West Bromwich Albion in two-legged, home and away matches, before promotion was achieved. They skated through those games, only losing away at West Brom, and were back in Division One, this time intent on a longer stay.

By now Liverpool were on the verge of consolidating their status as one of England's most important clubs. In their first season, Anfield had drawn crowds of around 2,000 for Lancashire League games, but by the time they

Record signing Jimmy Ross, scorer of 23 goals in the 1895-96 Division Two Championship-winning season.

were winning the Second Division Championship in 1895-6, big games were attracting five-figure attendances. The club were ready to take the next step forward and challenge the game's elite – sides like Aston Villa, Sunderland and Everton. To do that John McKenna had to make his most important signing to date – and it wasn't a player.

Audacious Move

It was an audacious move that clearly announced Liverpool's ambition to be England's top club. Just as he had convinced so many players before, John McKenna persuaded Sunderland's Tom Watson – the most successful manager in the country – that his future lay on Merseyside. The lavish salary probably helped, but there is no doubt that the honey-tongued McKenna must also have tempted Watson with a beguiling picture of what could be achieved at Anfield.

Whatever the clinching reasons, Watson took over team affairs from a grateful McKenna for the first season back in Division One in August 1896, and his arrival heralded the first glory years at Anfield. Watson's 19-year reign, which ended with his death in 1915, saw the club's first two championships, as well as a maiden FA Cup final appearance.

Liverpool's development into a club of consequence matched the onward march of the city itself. The greatest port in the Empire, it housed four of the world's eight largest shipping lines, and every day you could wander down to the dockside and watch the greatest ships in the world sail in and out of the harbour. Outside the noxious slums, where thousands of Irish immigrants lived out pitiful existences, a current of confidence was running through the place.

Watson, only 37 when he started his work at Anfield, was a man out of his time. Until he came along, the modern concept of a football manager had not been invented. Clubs employed secretaries to take care of administration, teams were usually picked by committees and playing matters and tactics, if

50 Greatest Players

HARRY BRADSHAW Winger

Joined Liverpool: 1893 **From:** Northwich Victoria

Debut: 28 October 1893 v Woolwich Arsenal (a), Division Two – won 5-0

Appearances: 138 **Goals:** 53

Left Liverpool: 1898 **For:** Tottenham Hotspur

Honours won with Liverpool: Division Two championship 1894, 1896; 1 England cap

Bradshaw holds the distinction of being the first-ever Liverpool player to win an England cap. He appeared in a 6-0 victory against Ireland at Trent Bridge, Nottingham, on 20 February 1897, his speedy wing play helping Aston Villa centre forward Frederick Wheldon to score a hat-trick on his debut. Despite the promising start Bradshaw never played for his country again and died of consumption in 1899 aged just 26.

Bradshaw scored in his first game for Liverpool, and scored a total of eight goals in Liverpool's Second Division-winning season of 1893-94. He added 17 when Liverpool were relegated the following year, then notched another 11 as they came back up as champions in 1896.

He left Liverpool to play for Tottenham in the Southern League in 1898, then had a spell with Thames Ironworks, the forerunners of West Ham United.

applicable, were largely left in the hands of the captain. But when Watson was 'secretary' of Sunderland, he took a decisive role in all footballing matters. His special area of expertise was in training and the physical conditioning of players, and under his guidance Sunderland became the fittest and best-prepared team in the country. He also took a controlling interest in players' diets, going as far as issuing weekly menus which players were obliged to follow. Watson's revolutionary approach worked. Sunderland won the championship three times in the early 1890s, and he soon began to have a similarly uplifting effect at Liverpool.

In his first season the team finished fifth in the First Division, and enjoyed their best-ever FA Cup campaign, losing 3-0 against Aston Villa in a semi-final at Sheffield United's ground. Watson was building a team capable of challenging for the biggest prize, and Liverpool – by now wearing a more familiar red strip – finished league runners-up behind Villa in 1899. They went one better when they became the first champions of the new century in 1901.

To win their first title, Liverpool had to usurp Villa who were the undisputed kings of the English game. The Midlanders had won five of the

The FA Cup semi-final 1899. A Sheffield United attack is cleared by a Liverpool defender in the 2-2 draw at Nottingham.

previous seven championships, but 1900-01 proved to be one of their off-seasons. Even without Villa to reckon with, Liverpool looked destined to end the campaign behind the leading pack, until an away win against front-runners Sunderland in February triggered an extraordinary late burst. Liverpool went unbeaten in their last 12 games, and when they won 1-0 at West Bromwich on the last day of the season the title was secured.

Conquering Heroes Welcomed Home

Even in those less demonstrative times, Liverpool's success created a stir in the city. When the team's train arrived back in Liverpool from the Black Country on the night of 29 April it was almost midnight, but thousands thronged the streets to welcome the conquering heroes home. They were cheered every mile of the way as their carriages travelled from the station to Anfield, led by a drum and fife band.

50 Greatest Players

MATT McQUEEN Winger/Utility player

Joined Liverpool: 1892 **From:** Leith Athletic

Debut: 2 September 1893 v Middlesbrough (a), Division Two – won 2-0

Appearances: 103 **Goals:** 7

Left Liverpool: 1899-1900 (retired)

Honours won with Liverpool: Division Two championship 1894, 1896; 2 Scotland caps

McQueen was nothing if not versatile. He played in every position for the club, including goalkeeper. As well as being a pioneering member of 'The Team of Macs', he later returned to Anfield, first as a director in 1918, and then as manager in 1923. McQueen stepped in after David Ashworth resigned, and steered the team to the First Division Championship.

He made his Scotland debut in a 5-0 win over Wales in March 1890 while he was a Leith Athletic player. McQueen made his second and last international appearance in March 1891 in a 4-3 win against Wales at the Racecourse Ground, Wrexham. He ended his Anfield playing days to become a league referee. McQueen lived at 32 Kemlyn Road, the site of which has since been swallowed up by Anfield.

Liverpool's spell at the top was destined to be short-lived, but their precipitous fall could be blamed on outside forces. For just as Watson was preparing to build a new dynasty on Merseyside to rival the one he had created on Wearside, his championship-winning team was sabotaged.

The Football League introduced a new regulation limiting players' wages to £4 a week. The country's poorer clubs had complained that their best players were being siphoned off by richer sides, and they could no longer compete fairly. The League accepted their point of view, and imposed the wage cap summarily. It came as a body blow to Liverpool, who were paying their best players £10 a week. Watson was faced with a mass defection as players decided that they could make better wages outside football. Or, if they could only earn £4 a week, they might as well return to their home towns and pick their wages up there. For Liverpool, who relied on imported players for their success, it was a disaster.

Before the new season Watson was reduced to advertising for players to fill the gaps in his squad. A notice in the *Athletic News* read: 'Liverpool Football Club. Wanted. Players for all positions for next season: maximum wage paid to class men. Apply by letter to Tom Watson, Anfield Road, Liverpool.' Liverpool had to use all their ingenuity to keep hold of their most valuable players, and risked breaking the rules to do so. Alex Raisbeck, a classy and commanding Scottish centre half – a luxuriantly moustachioed Alan Hansen-type figure – was given a job on top of his playing duties to supplement his wages. He became Anfield's official Bill Inspector, which in theory meant he had to check that the advertising hoardings around the pitch were in good order. It is unclear how much inspecting of bills he did, but the job helped to secure his future with the club.

Predictably, Liverpool suffered that season. Shorn of some of the players who had brought the championship to the club, the Reds only just managed to avoid relegation in 1902, finishing two points clear of the drop.

Houlding Dies

There was more sadness at Anfield that year as the club mourned the death of John Houlding. The grand patriarch was recovering from illness in Nice in March when his condition took a turn for the worse. Just a few months earlier the streets of Liverpool had been crowded with cheering supporters honouring the great team that Houlding helped to create. Now the same streets were filled with silent mourners, as Houlding's coffin was borne by Liverpool players. Officials and supporters of Everton also paid their respects to a towering pioneer of Merseyside football, old feuds long since forgotten.

The Liverpool FC squad prior to the 1905-06 championship season

With Watson unable to recruit enough high-quality players to arrest the decline, Liverpool were relegated in 1904. Once again, though, they returned at the first attempt, and Watson used the season's sojourn in the Second Division to build another team capable of challenging for the title. He set about the task pragmatically, beefing up the defence and starting with the goalkeeping position.

His old keeper at Sunderland, Ned Doig, joined the club and immediately stiffened the Reds' defensive backbone. The successful Division Two Championship campaign was built around strong defence, with Doig resolute between the sticks.

Watson's new-look team then astounded everyone by winning the First Division in their first season back. The revitalised Reds became the first side ever to take the title the season after winning promotion, carrying off the championship in 1906 by four points from Preston North End.

Liverpool had done themselves no favours by losing their first three games, but they finished with a flourish, winning nine – including a key victory at Deepdale against their closest rivals Preston in March –

50 Greatest Players

JACK COX Winger

Joined Liverpool: 1898 **From:** Blackpool

Debut: 12 March 1898 v Notts County (h), Division One – won 2-0

Appearances: 361 **Goals:** 81

Left Liverpool: 1909 **For:** Blackpool (player/manager)

Honours won with Liverpool: Division One champions 1901 and 1906; Division Two champions 1905; 3 England caps

A tricky winger with a devastating turn of speed, Cox was comfortable playing on either flank, but he also contributed valuably as a goalscorer. In the Division One Championship season of 1900-01 he scored 10 times, and another 10 when Liverpool won the Second Division title in 1905. He scored nine goals as the Division One title came back to Anfield in 1906.

He made his England debut as a 24-year-old in March 1901 as England beat Ireland 2-0 at the Dell, Southampton, and played again the following May at Villa Park as the Scots were defeated 3-2. His final international appearance came against Scotland in April 1903. Scotland won 2-1 on that occasion at Bramall Lane, Sheffield.

In 1909 he returned to his former club Blackpool as player-manager after 11 years at Anfield. After retiring from football, he had some success as a bowls player.

Two Reds heroes from the glory seasons of 1905 and 1906. Left: veteran keeper Ned Doig. Above: Billy Dunlop.

and drawing one of their last 10 matches. The goals flowed, with Joe Hewitt scoring 24, and the defence remained impregnable. Watson, showing a ruthlessness that would be the trademark of later Liverpool managers, brought in Sam Hardy from Chesterfield to replace the veteran Doig early in the season.

Hardy had caught Watson's eye the previous season, even though Chesterfield had lost 6-1 at Anfield. He proved to be a shrewd buy. The only worry he ever caused Watson was on Christmas Day, 1909. when he sent the directors a telegram shortly before kick off to say he was 'unfit' for that afternoon's league match against Bolton at Anfield. Bradley, normally a left half, took Hardy's place and received an ovation at the end for playing his part in a 3-0 victory.

The real heroes of that 1906 title-winning effort were the players who had kept faith with the club since the 1901 championship triumph, right through the maximum wage debacle and relegation. Left back Billy Dunlop, Raisbeck, outside left Jack Cox and centre forward Sam Raybould were all survivors from that first great side.

50 Greatest Players

ALEX RAISBECK Centre half

Joined Liverpool: 1898 **From:** Stoke City

Debut: 3 September 1898 v The Wednesday (h), Division One – won 4-0

Appearances: 341 **Goals:** 20

Left Liverpool: 1909 **For:** Partick Thistle

Honours won with Liverpool: Division One championship 1901, 1906; Division Two championship 1905; 8 Scotland caps

The Scot was Liverpool's first great captain, and the first to lift the Division One Championship. Before joining Liverpool he was a Stoke player, but homesickness made him flee the Potteries. Liverpool persuaded him to give it another chance south of the border, and Merseyside was more to his taste. Over the next decade he became synonymous with Liverpool.

Raisbeck finally headed home to play for Partick Thistle, then Hamilton Academicals. He also managed Bristol City, Halifax, Chester and Bath City. Raisbeck returned to Liverpool as a scout, and died in the city in 1949.

He made his international debut in April 1900 as Scotland beat England 4-1 at Celtic Park, Glasgow. His final cap came in April 1907 at St James' Park, Newcastle, when England and Scotland drew 1-1.

The only blight on the season was an FA Cup semi-final defeat against Everton at Villa Park. The Toffees went on to beat Newcastle 1-0 in the final at Crystal Palace, making it a clean sweep of trophies for Merseyside.

The architecture of Anfield began to take on its distinctive character in the second championship season. It had become clear to the club that the ground's capacity needed to be raised, as Anfield was now regularly drawing crowds exceeding 20,000. The answer was a vast, uncovered banking of cinders, which provided the best view in the ground and became known across the world as 'the Kop'. It was named by Ernest Edwards, sports editor of the *Liverpool Daily Post*, in respect to the hundreds of Lancashire Fusiliers who had died in the battle of Spion Kop, a 1900 Boer War bloodbath, still fresh in the minds of many.

Watson's second championship-winning Reds side could not repeat the feat. The players were ageing together, and were no match for up-and-coming sides like Newcastle United, Manchester United and Blackburn Rovers. The club suffered a succession of mediocre seasons, and Watson's last hurrah as Liverpool manager was the club's first FA Cup final appearance in 1914.

Great Matches

FA CUP FINAL **Crystal Palace, 25 April 1914**
Attendance: 72,778

Liverpool 0 **Burnley 1**
Freeman

In the buttonhole of the suit of King George V sat the red rose of Lancashire, a well-received gesture to the two teams from the north-west who had fought their way to the final. It was the first FA Cup final to be granted a Royal attendance, a sign that football had finally dispersed across every social strata of the country. The match had also outgrown its host stadium; hundreds watching from outside the bowl swelling the attendance figure to around 100,000. Moreover, it was Liverpool's first FA Cup final. At a time when the league was still the poor relation to this prestigious tournament, 20,000 people flocked down from Merseyside to cheer on Tom Watson's team.

Liverpool came into the game on the back of four successive defeats and morale could not have been boosted on the morning of the match when skipper Harry Lowe failed a fitness test. Donald Mackinlay deputised and Robert Ferguson took the captaincy.

The next day's *Daily Mirror* reported: 'Liverpool were generally the aggressors in the first half, and Taylor (Burnley's left back) was knocked out temporarily with a shot from Nicholl (Liverpool's outside left), which would have gone through had not Burnley's left back got his head in the way.

'Lacey (Liverpool's inside left) did a lot of very clever things, and with Nicholl formed the most effective wing. Lacey tested Sewell once with a tremendous shot, which Burnley's reserve keeper saved splendidly, and then Miller (Liverpool's centre forward) had the goal at his mercy, but just shot wide of the post.

'Generally speaking Liverpool dominated the game in this half, and the Burnley defence could not be described as great. They got the ball away somehow or other, and Liverpool missed many grand openings.' Even at a distance of nearly a century, you can taste the frustration of the Reds' players and supporters that day.

They would rue such missed opportunities when a second-half volley from Burnley's Bert Freeman screamed past Liverpool's keeper Kenny Campbell. Despite concerted efforts by the Reds they could not break down the claret and blue defence and it was the Burnley captain who had the privilege of collecting the cup from the King.

Liverpool: Campbell, Longworth, Pursell, Fairfoul, Ferguson, Mackinlay, Sheldon, Metcalfe, Miller, Lacey, Nicholl

Burnley: Sewell, Bamford, Taylor, Halley, Boyle, Watson, Nesbitt, Lindley, Freeman, Hodgson, Mosscrop

Referee: H.S. Bamlett

The Anfield Four (clockwise from top right): Tom Fairfoul, Thomas Miller, Bob Purcell and Jackie Sheldon.

Liverpool had beaten Barnsley, Gillingham, West Ham, Queen's Park Rangers and Aston Villa in the semi-final at White Hart Lane to reach the final, where their opponents were Burnley. The Reds lost 1-0 in front of a crowd of over 77,000 at the Crystal Palace in London.

The next season kicked off under a darkening cloud, as Britain declared war on Germany on 14 August 1914. Other sports cancelled their fixture lists, but the football authorities vowed to finish the 1914-15 season as scheduled. After all, the fighting would be over by Christmas...

Murmurs of discontent swelled to a cacophony as the fighting intensified. Football matches became recruiting fairs and Liverpool, like all clubs, saw their crowds tail off as the season went on and thousands of fans headed off to war. By March 1915 it was clear there was little appetite for football in the country, and the 1915-16 season was cancelled.

An Anfield era came to an end with double sadness. On Good Friday 1915, just as football was about to close down for the duration, four Liverpool players were implicated in a betting conspiracy.

The Anfield Four

The four – Bob Purcell, Tommy Miller, Jackie Sheldon and Tom Fairfoul – met four United players in a Manchester pub and hatched a plan to fix the game between the teams on 2 April. They agreed that the game would end 2-0 to United. Bookmakers began to smell a rat when bets started piling on for that scoreline and their suspicions were confirmed on the day of the game, when Liverpool turned in an abject display and duly lost 2-0. An element of farce crept into proceedings when Liverpool players clearly berated their centre forward, Jack Pagnam, when he nearly scored late in the game.

The unsubtle scam was blown open. The Football League inquiry found the Anfield Four guilty, and together with the United four, they were banned from the game for life. Seven of the bans were rescinded at the end of the war, to honour the men's services for King and Country. One of the players, United's Sandy Turnball, was granted clemency posthumously. He had died in the fighting at Arras in France in 1917. The only one of the eight whose ban remained in force was United's Enoch West. He protested his innocence all along but was not cleared to play again until 1945. He was 62 by then, a little late to revive his truncated career.

Great Managers – 1896-1915

TOM WATSON

Watson was an instantly recognisable figure, with his impressive walrus moustache and flamboyant bow ties. He was an affable Geordie, and a man who provoked laughter rather than fear in the players under his command. Yet beneath the easy-going exterior was a fierce determination to succeed. He did exactly that at Sunderland in the 1890s, creating the greatest club side in Britain, and winning the championship three times with a side that became known as 'The Team of All Talents'.

Liverpool's chairman John McKenna persuaded Watson to leave Roker Park, and the tobacconist's shop he managed in the town, with a sufficiently generous salary. The new boss applied his tried and trusted methods at Liverpool – a more scientific training regime, the wholesale import of Scottish players, strict discipline and stricter diets. Watson was obsessive about nutrition a century before Arsène Wenger inflicted his broccoli fixation on the English game. The results were astonishing.

Watson's 21 years at Anfield featured two championships in 1901 and 1906, with relegation and a Second Division Championship in between. The only disappointment of his management career was never winning the FA Cup. The nearest he came was in 1914 when Liverpool lost 1-0 to Burnley in the final at the Crystal Palace.

50 Greatest Players

ARTHUR GODDARD Winger

Joined Liverpool: 1902 **From:** Glossop North End

Debut: 8 March 1902 v Wolverhampton (a), Division One – lost 3-1

Appearances: 415 **Goals:** 77

Left Liverpool: 1914 **For:** Cardiff City

Honours won with Liverpool: Division Two championship 1905; Division One championship 1906

Goddard came from Stockport and played his early League football with Glossop North End. Liverpool manager Tom Watson identified him as a player who could inject some pace and trickery into his team, and Goddard didn't let him down. He quickly became a first-team regular, and racked up over 400 games before leaving the club to join Cardiff City on the outbreak of the First World War. He won Division One and Two championship winners' medals with Liverpool, but was unlucky never to win international honours. He was, though, selected to play for Football League representative sides on three occasions.

His longevity saw him play in more Merseyside Derbies than any other pre-Second World War Liverpool player. He appeared in 25 of the matches.

Amid the carnage of Flanders, the peaceful death of a middle-aged man might have gone unnoticed in 1915. But followers of Liverpool paused to remember a fine servant of the club when Tom Watson died on the afternoon of Thursday 6 May. He was 56. On 11 May an honour guard of great Liverpool players, including Raisbeck and Doig, carried his coffin for burial in the city he had grown to know and love. His grave in Anfield Cemetery, at general section 4, Plot 1463, is unmarked.

Watson might have been Geordie born and bred, but he died a Liverpudlian, and the sorrow at his passing in the city was deeply felt.

Finally an exhausted continent laid aside its arms. The city of Liverpool had played a pugnacious role in the conflict. They had raised the first battalion of Kitchener's army, suffered a siege as the port was closed by enemy submarine action and countless men and women had given their lives – among them Liverpool players Joe Dines, Wilfrid Bartrop and Tom Gracie.

Chapter Two: 1919-39
The Inter-War Years

It was always going to be impossible for the Liverpool board to find a man to match the stature of Tom Watson. And they didn't try.

Liverpool's first great leader had been a charismatic, ebullient character, whose personality and drive did much to drag the club to the pinnacle of the English game. His replacement was his opposite in every way.

David Ashworth took over at Liverpool in December 1919, after earning some success as Oldham Athletic's manager. Where Watson had been a large-framed man, Ashworth was tiny, standing just five feet tall. He was nicknamed 'Little Dave', and his fastidious appearance, complete with bowler hat and tidy waxed moustache, made him a curious figure. Even in those more formal times he looked more like an assistant bank manager than the boss of a First Division football club. Yet for all that, David Ashworth knew his business.

Where previous managers had used imported players to win success, Ashworth set about constructing a side largely from Liverpudlian components. His teams were full of players from the city of Liverpool itself, from the neighbouring areas of Bootle or Birkenhead, or from St Helens or Widnes in the city's hinterland. The club's Scottish accent was still there, it was just slightly less marked than it had been pre-war. It was a combination that eventually gelled – after a couple of seasons of steady improvement the Reds landed their third championship success.

The 1921-22 title campaign was, again, founded on a solid defence. Ashworth had unearthed another wonderful goalkeeper in Irishman Elisha Scott, and he conceded a parsimonious 36 goals that season in an era when goals were abundant. The Kop readily took to Scott, who in typical goalkeeper's fashion arrived with a full set of idiosyncrasies. In the winter he insisted on wearing long johns under his shorts, and protected his knees with bulky, protective pads. He wore thick woolly gloves, and the ensemble was completed with never fewer than three jumpers. Scott of Anfield could have been mistaken for Scott of the Antarctic.

With Scott in stubborn form, international defenders in Longworth, Mackinlay and Bromilow and goal-hungry forwards in 'Smiler' Chambers, Forshaw and Lacey, the Reds enjoyed a 30-match spell with just a single defeat. After dealing out a 5-1 thrashing to Cardiff, the championship was

Liverpool's 1921-22 League championship was based on a sound defence which featured goalkeeper Elisha Scott (back row, fourth from left), and full backs Ephraim Longworth and Donald Mackinlay (middle row third and fourth from left).

wrapped up with a 2-1 victory over the title-holders, Burnley, at Anfield – with three games still left to play. Ashworth had won the league with a team that cost virtually nothing, and had won in style.

The *Athletic News* of 24 April 1922 trumpeted: 'The supreme event in the Eastertide football was the decision of the League Championship. When Liverpool had the honour of defeating last season's winners Burnley, and on the same day Oldham Athletic overcame Tottenham Hotspur at Boundary Park, the premiership of the First Division was beyond argument, for the North London club, which alone threatened to wrest the prize from Liverpool, could not do so even if they won all their matches and Liverpool finished their programme in absolute ignominy.'

The season ended ignominiously for Liverpool, with defeats against Cardiff and West Bromwich, but that did not dispel the mood of triumph around Anfield. Then, just as Little Dave was beginning to challenge Big Tom's place in the pantheon of great Liverpool managers, Ashworth sensationally quit.

It was January 1923, and his team looked set fair to retain their title. Bizarrely, he chose to turn his back on Anfield and rejoin his old club, Oldham, who were at the bottom of the First Division. The big question around Liverpool was: why?

Shock Departure

Ashworth's decision was the first in a series of shock departures by Liverpool managers down the years. His successors, Bill Shankly in 1974, and Kenny Dalglish in 1991, both left suddenly and unexpectedly for reasons that have never quite made complete sense. Ashworth, like Shankly and Dalglish after him, was close to the height of his powers and the team was at or near its peak. It is likely that Ashworth's reason was simple and cash-related – Oldham offered him more money. It was, though, a decision that backfired. Oldham were relegated, and Ashworth's career never again approached the peaks it had reached with Liverpool.

Life went on at Anfield and Matt McQueen, a club director who had been a Scotland international and a Liverpool player in the 1890s, took over as manager in February 1923. The Reds stuttered towards the season's end, but hung on to keep the championship trophy at Anfield.

Great Managers – 1919-23

DAVID ASHWORTH

Ashworth was a fastidious little Irishman, standing just 5ft (1.22m) tall below his trademark bowler hat, but his achievement at Anfield was mighty. After moving to Liverpool from Oldham Athletic he set about building a team good enough to win the championship, and duly won it in 1921-22, only his second full season in charge. His team, which featured legendary names such as Elisha Scott, Ephraim Longworth, Dick Forshaw, Don Mackinlay and Harry Chambers, finished a comfortable six points in front of Tottenham Hotspur.

Ashworth's side was well on its way to a second title the following season when he resigned in January 1923 to rejoin his former club, Oldham. Apparently the Latics board, desperate to avoid relegation, offered him a bigger salary to return – but the gamble failed. He took Oldham down to the Second Division, while Matt McQueen led the Liverpool team Ashworth had built to the First Division title. Ashworth was sacked by Oldham in 1927, and thereafter his management career dwindled away at Manchester City, Walsall, Caernarvon Town and Llanelli. He ended his working life scouting for Blackpool, and died in the town in March 1947, aged 79.

This second championship of the 1920s was achieved with more style than the first. They won 28 matches and lost only 8 – only one of which was at Anfield against Newcastle. Goals were more plentiful – the team scored 70 during the season – rumbustious England inside left Harry Chambers top-scored with 22, inside right Dick Forshaw, who later won a championship with Everton, chipped in with 19 and Dick Johnson contributed another 14 goals.

They gorged on a stream of crosses and passes from outside left Fred Hopkin. Ephraim Longworth and the team captain, Don Mackinlay, were commanding presences at full back, and left half Tom Bromilow was one of the finest playmakers in the country. The good times couldn't last, though, and the league triumph of 1923 proved to be the club's last trophy for 24 years, the longest silverless span in the Reds' history. McQueen did a valuable job stepping in after Ashworth left, but he was not the man to take the club forward. Liverpool ended his first full season as manager in May 1924 in 12th position.

50 Greatest Players

EPHRAIM LONGWORTH Full back

Joined Liverpool: 1910 **From:** Leyton

Debut: 19 September 1910 v Sheffield United (a), Division One – lost 2-0

Appearances: 371 **Goals:** 0

Left Liverpool: 1928 (became club coach)

Honours won with Liverpool: Division One championship 1922, 1923; 5 England caps

Longworth played in Liverpool's first-ever FA Cup final, when they lost 1-0 to Burnley at the Crystal Palace in 1914. He kept his place in the side after war was over, and played in their championship sides of the early 1920s, as captain in 1921-22. He also became the first Liverpool player to captain England. He was one those rare players who improve with age, and didn't even make his international debut until he was 32. It was an appearance worth waiting for, as England came back from 4-2 down to beat Scotland 5-4 at Hillsborough in April 1920. Longworth also captained England against Belgium at Highbury in March 1923, leading his team to a 6-1 win.

The full back was easy to spot on the field with a floppy lock of hair always hanging over his forehead. His partnership with Don Mackinlay helped Liverpool win consecutive championships in the 1920s. The Lancastrian played until he was 40 years old and then took a job on the coaching staff at Anfield after his playing days were over. He worked for the club beyond the Second World War and died in 1968.

Liverpool's giant South African keeper Arthur Riley prepares to launch the ball upfield against West Bromwich Albion in 1926.

Offside Law Changed

By then Huddersfield Town's manager, Herbert Chapman, was moulding the Yorkshire club into an irresistible force, capable of winning three titles on the trot. McQueen, whose footballing philosophies had been formed in the previous century, could find no answer to the new ideas sweeping the game. In 1925-26 a change in the offside law which reduced from three to two the number of defenders who could put an attacker offside transformed football, making it a faster, more open spectacle than it had been. More goals were being scored, and sides had to adapt quickly. Liverpool were slower to change than most, and a series of mediocre league placings followed.

McQueen could take credit for one of the club's greatest signings of the early 20th century. Gordon Hodgson was a key figure in the Springbok team that toured Britain in 1925 and McQueen was quick to snap him up. The South African scored his first two goals for the club in a 3-3 draw at Manchester United on 10 March 1926, was Liverpool's leading scorer for seven of his 11 seasons at the club and still holds the record for hat-tricks in a Liverpool career, with 17. At the same time he managed to play a leading role for Lancashire as a fast bowler. At a time when Dixie Dean was breaking all scoring records for Everton, Hodgson gave Liverpool fans a hero of their own, even if the team was no longer challenging for honours.

Keep it in the Family

McQueen soldiered on until 1928, when he lost a leg in a car crash and had to resign. Not for the first time, and certainly not for the last, the club looked within the Liverpool family for a new manager, and they appointed George Patterson, Watson's assistant more than a decade earlier.

Patterson stayed in the job for eight years, but these were doleful times at Anfield. The club were mediocre and had to look up from a succession of mid-table finishes while sides like Arsenal, Sheffield Wednesday, Everton, Manchester City and Sunderland dominated the First Division.

One bright spot for Liverpool came at the start of Patterson's time as manager, in August 1928, when one of Anfield's most enduring landmarks

50 Greatest Players

DON MACKINLAY Half back

Joined Liverpool: 1910 **From:** Newton Villa

Debut: 20 April 1910 v Nottingham Forest (h), Division One – won 7-3

Appearances: 434 **Goals:** 34

Left Liverpool: 1929 **For:** Prescot Cables

Honours won with Liverpool: Division One championship 1922, 1923; 2 Scotland caps

The Glaswegian was spotted by Liverpool's all-seeing Scottish scouting network, and went on to serve the club for two decades. Mackinlay was captain when Liverpool won the title in 1922-23. He also played in Liverpool's first-ever FA Cup final against Burnley in 1914, taking the place of the injured Harry Lowe. Mackinlay shared in the disappointment of the Reds' 1-0 defeat.

He played for Scotland twice in 1922, in a 2-1 defeat away to Wales in Wrexham and in a 2-1 win over Ireland at Celtic Park. Mackinlay deserved many more caps, only Scotland's stubborn policy of choosing home-based men over exiled players keeping him out of the team on a regular basis.

Liverpool goalkeeper Elisha Scott saves from Arsenal's David Jack (left) and Jack Lambert (right) in the league match at Highbury in 1931. The high-flying Gunners won the match 3-1.

was redeveloped. Before kick-off in the league game against Bury, John McKenna led a procession around the pitch from the players' tunnel to the corner of the ground where the club's flag was unfurled to signify the opening of the newly-roofed Kop – after which a huge crowd of 40,000 saw the Reds win 3-0 with goals from Miller, who scored twice, and Whitehurst. Liverpudlians were hugely proud of the new stand, and in later years it would accommodate 28,000 boisterous fans. It became home to some of the most passionate supporters anywhere, and their songs and their fervour made the Kop the most famous stand in world football.

That was one of the last official functions McKenna carried out for the club he served so steadfastly. As well as the work he did with Houlding in Liverpool's pioneer days, he was chairman of the club from 1909 to 1914 and again from 1917 to 1919. McKenna also served as the Football League president for a total of 26 years, and was a vice president of the Football Association. He died on 22 March 1936, aged 82.

Patterson Stands Down

A bout of ill-health obliged Patterson to stand down in 1936, to be replaced by George Kay, a Mancunian who had captained West Ham to defeat against Bolton in the 1923 White Horse FA Cup final at Wembley. He had managed Luton Town and Southampton at lower levels, but Liverpool, with their First Division status, was a step up for him. His first task was to safeguard the club's jealously held place in Division One.

Kay had the character for a scrap. He had been through hell in the trenches of the First World War and it was an experience which forged his tough, fearless character – exactly what Liverpool needed at that time.

The club was at a low ebb throughout the 1930s, mirroring the economic depression which had hit Liverpool's inhabitants. Cotton, tobacco and flour kept the docks working, but the mass of the population missed out on the benefits of trade. At a time when Reds fans looked to their club to provide

50 Greatest Players

ELISHA SCOTT Goalkeeper

Joined Liverpool: 1912

From: Broadway United (Belfast)

Debut: 1 January 1913 v Newcastle (a), Division One – drew 0-0

Appearances: 468

Left Liverpool: 1934 **For:** Belfast Celtic

Honours won with Liverpool: Division One championship 1922, 1923; 27 Northern Ireland caps

The 17-year-old Belfast boy arrived on Merseyside to have a trial with Everton. Elisha had been recommended by his older brother, Billy, who played in goal for the Blues in the early years of the century but the Goodison management turned Elisha down on the grounds that he was too small. Liverpool, though, had no qualms about his stature and snapped him up.

Scott took Kenny Campbell's place as Liverpool's first-choice keeper after the First World War and went on to enjoy a long career at Anfield. He was at the top of his form when Liverpool were winning titles in the early 1920s and was still a formidable performer into the 1930s. So much so that Everton tried to buy him in 1934 – more than 20 years after they had shown him the door.

50 Greatest Players

GORDON HODGSON Inside right/Centre forward

Joined Liverpool: 1925

From: Transvaal

Debut: 27 February 1926 v Manchester City (a), Division One – drew 1-1

Appearances: 377 **Goals:** 241

Left Liverpool: 1936 **For:** Aston Villa

Honours won with Liverpool: 3 England caps

Until Roger Hunt came along to smash every scoring record in sight, the South African was Liverpool's most prolific forward of all time. He was snapped up by Liverpool after impressing on a tour of England with his club, and for 11 seasons he entertained the Anfield crowd during some lean years. His best season was 1930-31 when he scored 36 league goals – a club best until Hunt took it from him. He was the club's leading league scorer for eight consecutive seasons. Although he was South African by birth, Hodgson's parents were English, and he represented England three times in 1930 and 1931. He scored his only international goal against Wales in a 4-0 win at Wrexham in November 1930.

Hodgson, a natural all-round athlete, also found time to bowl quickly for Lancashire CC in the summers. He died on 14 June 1951, aged 47.

a distraction from the troubles of everyday life, all they saw was a reflection of their own sorry plight.

Kay steadied the ship, but Liverpool failed to make much impression in the years of his tenure. He at least started to stamp his own ideals on the club – introducing stricter codes of discipline, sequestering the squad for nights before matches, and making training more rigorous. He led by example, too. Kay was utterly devoted to his job, and punished himself with work. In the end, his labours were to kill him.

Kay's first steps at rebuilding put the accent on attack. His own playing career was largely spent as a centre half, but he wanted to watch his teams going forward. A clever wing half named Matt Busby was signed from Manchester City in the first days of Kay's Anfield career, giving the side more guile in the middle of the field. Another significant recruit, although he didn't make his debut until 1940, was a promising half back named Bob Paisley.

50 Greatest Players

JIMMY McDOUGALL Left half

Joined Liverpool: 1928 **From:** Partick Thistle

Debut: 25 August 1928 v Bury (h), Division One, won 3-0

Appearances: 356 **Goals:** 12

Left Liverpool: 1938 **For:** South Liverpool (player/manager)

Honours won with Liverpool: 2 Scotland caps

Another figure in the long line of great Scottish leaders who have worn the Red with distinction. McDougall captained Liverpool in the 1930s as well as Scotland.

He played his early football as a forward, but at Liverpool he was converted into a highly effective half back, where he played alongside another craggy Scot, Matt Busby. Their partnership flourished at a time when success was scarce for Liverpool.

McDougall only won two Scottish caps, but he was captain on both occasions. In May 1931 he led the team in two European tour matches – a 5-0 defeat against Austria in Vienna, followed by a 3-0 defeat against the Italians in Rome.

Best of all, a newly signed Scottish teenager called Billy Liddell arrived in 1939. Shortly after he settled into his new lodgings at the home of Ned Doig's widow in Miriam Road, Anfield, Football League fixtures were abandoned for the duration. To many, he was to become the finest Liverpool player ever to kick a football.

When Liddell travelled from his home town of Dunfermline to sign for the club, he was just 17. But he would be no teenage star – the first six years of his career spent as an RAF navigator. He did, however, turn out for Liverpool 150 times in wartime regional competitions, a welcome source of entertainment for the blitzed and war-weary Liverpool faithful.

When Liddell made his full Liverpool debut in January 1946, he was already almost 24. But before long his importance to the side had earned him an enduring nickname – Liddellpool.

Chapter Three: 1946-59
Champions Humbled

The all-clear sounded in 1945, but it would be another year before Football League fixtures kicked off again. It took that long to reconstruct the game's fractured infrastructure, and gather back the players who had been sent to every corner of the world in the country's service. Some, like Bob Paisley, came back with hard-won battle-honours. The wing half had fought valiantly as an artilleryman with Monty's Desert Rats in North Africa, took part in the invasion of Italy and helped liberate Rome. Others did not return to Anfield. Club captain Tom Cooper was among the dozens of professional footballers killed in the war.

Where playing football had been frowned upon as an unpatriotic act in 1914-18, the sport was encouraged by the government during the Second World War. Clubs participated in highly competitive regional competitions, Liverpool among them. The Reds were Northern Region champions in 1943 – just ahead of Lovells Athletic, a sweet factory works team.

Billy Liddell (left) in action against Wolves in Liverpool's 2-1 victory at the end of the 1946-47 season. The win proved enough to bring the league title back to Anfield.

A glance at team photographs of the immediate post-war period suggest the privations people had suffered. The players are thin, shirts hanging off bony shoulders. As food shortages still gripped Britain, Liverpool's chairman, William McConnell, along with Kay, came up with the brainwave of taking the team on a tour of North America. The United States and Canada were lands of plenty, and the Liverpool party spent the summer of 1946 eating their way across the continent, gorging themselves on the kind of meals that had become a fond memory back home. When they weren't demolishing North American soccer teams (played 10, won 10, goals for 70, goals against 10) the Liverpool players shifted huge amounts of steak, eggs, chicken and fresh fruit and vegetables. It was a much healthier and heavier Liverpool party which headed back to Blighty from the gaunt group which had trooped down the gangplank of the *Queen Mary* at the start of the trip.

The Great Freeze

The extra insulation did Liverpool's players no harm in the first season after the war, as the country drifted into its most severe winter for decades. The Reds started steadily, winning 13 of their first 23 matches up to the New Year. Then the frost bit and snow settled in for weeks.

The freeze lasted from the middle of January into March, and the fixture list was laid waste. The government banned the Football League from rescheduling matches in midweek to save energy and the games which were played took place on treacherous icy pitches.

When the ice age abated, Liverpool set off on a determined run to reel in the Division One leaders Wolves, who at one stage enjoyed an 11-point advantage over the chasing pack. As Wanderers caved in towards the end of the season, Liverpool grew stronger, winning seven and drawing one of their last eight games. Fittingly, Liverpool travelled to Molineux on 31 May for their last match, needing a win to take them to the top of the table.

Now Britain was moving into one of the hottest summers on record, and Wolves' ground sweltered in the sun. It was the home team who wilted, and Liverpool won 2-1 thanks to goals from Balmer and Stubbins. Even then, Liverpool could still have lost the title to Stoke City. The Potters had one match left, thanks to the backlog, and faced Sheffield United away. A victory would have given City the championship, but United won the match, and the First Division trophy was on its way back to Anfield after 24 years.

Not for the last time, Liverpool had won the title with a win away to Wolves, and it was fitting that the match-winners should be Balmer and Stubbins. Balmer was a link with the earlier pre-Kay era, and had been with

Great Matches

FOOTBALL LEAGUE DIVISION ONE — **Molineux, 31 May 1947**
Attendance: 50,078

Wolverhampton Wanderers 1
Dunn

Liverpool 2
Balmer
Stubbins

Temperatures were reaching 90 degrees in the stadium, but supporters of both sides had other reasons to sweat. The Wolves needed just a point to secure the league title; Liverpool had to win to stay in the race.

Thousands of Liverpool fans had travelled to the Midlands – perhaps as much in hope as expectancy, but their team produced a deadly performance. Wolves threw everything at them but, time after time, their ex-keeper Cyril Sidlow kept them at bay. Meanwhile Liverpool began to put together some moves of their own and in a marvellous exhibition of passing football, Balmer got on the end of a six-man move to open the visitors' account.

They did not have to wait too long for the second – a magnificent individual effort from Albert Stubbins, who, according to the *Liverpool Echo,* 'covered the half-field in record time with the ball at his toe'. Wolves did manage to pull one back, but by that time the away supporters were clearing their throats to sing their way home to Merseyside.

Liverpool had done the hard work in depriving the great Stan Cullis, playing in his last game, of a championship medal, but they still had a nervous wait. If Stoke won their match-in-hand against Sheffield United, they would be champions. If Reds fans needed something to take their minds off it in that anxious fortnight before that game, Balmer, Stubbins and Co. had given them plenty of thrills to relive on this sweltering afternoon.

Wolverhampton Wanderers: Williams, Mclean, Crook, Alderton, Cullis, Wright, Hancocks, Dunn, Pye, Forbes, Mullen

Liverpool: Sidlow, Harley, Lambert, Jones, Hughes, Spicer, Watkins, Balmer, Stubbins, Liddell, Priday

the club since 1935. Stubbins was one of the fresh talents imported by Kay post-war, having joined from Newcastle for £13,000 at the start of the season. He had been a star of wartime football, scoring over 240 goals in the period, and Liverpool were lucky to land him. Everton chased Stubbins as well, and the player tossed a coin to decide where his future lay. Those two goals at Molineux meant Balmer and Stubbins ended the season as joint top scorers with 24 each. They owed much to the peerless service provided by Liddell on the wing and Paisley from half back.

There was one other man to whom Liverpool owed a debt of gratitude for their title: Stoke manager Bob McGrory. Before City's crucial last game McGrory sold Stanley Matthews to Blackpool for £11,500, at a stroke robbing his team of its best player and turning the supporters against him.

For a while it looked like Liverpool might achieve their first League and Cup Double in 1947. They began their best run in the FA Cup competition for three decades away to Walsall of Division Three (South) in the third round, two goals from Balmer setting up a 5-2 win. In the fourth round the Reds beat Grimsby, a mid-table First Division side, 2-0 at Anfield. Then Balmer was the match-winner again in the fifth round, as Derby from Division One were dispatched 1-0 at Anfield, earning Liverpool their first quarter-final tie since they reached the final in 1914. Stubbins scored a hat-trick and Balmer also netted in a 4-1 victory over Second Division Birmingham at Anfield. But the Reds fell one game short of Wembley. Burnley, the team who had beaten them in their last final, would bar the way again, as the Second Division side won 1-0 in a semi-final replay at Maine Road, watched by 72,000.

Liverpool could not reach the same heights in ensuing seasons. Kay, suffering ill-health brought on by years of heavy smoking and hard work, became less of an influence, but his team had one last tilt at a trophy before his reign was brought to an end. It came in the 1949-50 FA Cup, when the Reds reached their first final for 36 years.

On Wembley Way

The Reds were enduring another mediocre season in the league when they embarked on a Cup campaign to quicken the pulse, beginning with a 0-0 draw at Blackburn of Division Two in the third round. Rovers were defeated 2-1 in the replay. Exeter City from Division Three (South) lost 3-1 at Anfield in the fourth round. Stockport was the Reds' destination for the fifth round, and Stubbins scored in a 2-1 win. By now Wembley was in every Liverpudlian's sights, and a feverish Anfield crowd of over 50,000 saw the Reds reach the semi-finals with a 2-1 win over fellow First Division side Blackpool. Liverpool were paired with rivals Everton in the semi-finals, dashing hopes of the first-ever all-Merseyside FA Cup final. They met at Maine Road, and goals from Paisley and Liddell sent the Reds to Wembley with a 2-0 win.

Liverpool were favourites to win the final. They had already beaten their opponents, Arsenal, twice that season in the league, but they were never at their best at Wembley. In any case, their chances of victory had been sabotaged by a capricious team selection which robbed them of one of their most important players.

At this time Kay was at the mercy of a committee of directors when it came to picking a team, and before the final they decided to replace the influential

Great Managers – 1936-51

GEORGE KAY

Kay was a workaholic Mancunian who led Liverpool to the championship immediately after the Second World War.

That the Reds were in good enough shape to take that first title was due largely to Kay. He kept the club together from 1939-45, and ensured football continued to be played at Anfield in spite of everything Hitler's U-boats and Luftwaffe could throw at the city.

By the time league football kicked off again Liverpool were readier than most, thanks in large part to a summer tour of North America which allowed the undernourished squad to eat themselves back to rude health. The Reds took the 1946-47 title a point ahead of Manchester United and Wolverhampton Wanderers. Kay's triumphant side included great names like Liddell, Nieuwenhuys, Balmer, Stubbins and Done.

Kay also led Liverpool to the FA Cup final in 1950, where they lost 2-0 to Arsenal. By then he was a sick man, his constitution wrecked by hard work and cigarettes, and doctors advised him to quit. He did so in February 1951 and died three years later.

Paisley with Laurie Hughes, who had just come back from an injury. Kay wanted Paisley in the side but lost the vote, and Liverpool lost the match.

Reg Lewis scored the Gunners' first goal after 18 minutes, but Liverpool still fancied themselves in the second half against an ageing Arsenal team. The game was played in torrential rain, and the Reds reckoned that the heavy surface might mean heavy legs on the other side. Arsenal's outside left, the great Middlesex and England cricketer Denis Compton, was one of the thirtysomething Londoners feeling the pace. But he gulped down a restorative tumbler of brandy at half-time and skipped out for the restart as frisky as a spring lamb. His pass set up Lewis's second killer goal and the Reds still had another 15 years to wait for their first FA Cup triumph.

Kay's days as Liverpool manager were nearly through. Clearly diminished by illness, he stood down on doctors' advice in February 1951. He died at his home, 13 St James Close, on 18 April 1954, aged 62.

That summer Hughes also gained the favour of the England selectors, as he went to Brazil with the World Cup squad. He made his international debut in the 2-0 group win over Chile, and also played in England's most embarrassing defeat ever, as Walter Winterbottom's side went down 1-0 against the USA. Hughes played in England's third and final match of the tournament, a 1-0 defeat by Spain, and never won another cap.

Kay's replacement could not have been a bigger contrast. Where Kay was a man of few words, and kept himself rather distant from his players, Don Welsh was a laugh-a-minute zany. His party piece was walking on his hands, a trick he performed whatever the surroundings and whenever the fancy took him – in dressing rooms or directors' boxes, coming down grandstand steps or through hotel dining rooms watched by startled guests. A former army physical training instructor, Welsh at least knew how to get the players fit – but what of his other qualities?

He arrived at Anfield from the Brighton and Hove Albion manager's job, but he was better known as a player. He had captained Charlton Athletic to a 1947 FA Cup final win over Burnley, and the Liverpool board associated him with success. Precious little of that commodity came the club's way in the five years Welsh was in charge.

A young full back on Liverpool's books at the time, Ron Moran, was immediately taken with the new manager. 'He was 30 years ahead of his

50 Greatest Players

JACK BALMER Inside forward

Joined Liverpool: 1935 **From:** Everton

Debut: 21 September 1935 v Leeds (a), Division One – lost 1-0

Appearances: 312 **Goals:** 111

Left Liverpool: 1952 (retired)

Honours won with Liverpool: Division One championship 1947

Balmer was an amateur with Everton, where his uncles William and Robert were accomplished players, but he moved across to Anfield when his chances of becoming a first-team regular looked slim. He went on to become a prolific goalscorer for the Reds, his 24 in 1946-47 doing much to bring the championship to Anfield. That was also the season when Balmer became the first player to score hat-tricks in three consecutive matches, at the start of a goal streak which saw him net 15 in seven matches. Despite his fine record for his home-town club, Balmer was never capped by England, although he appeared in wartime internationals.

Billy Liddell (left) shoots past Tottenham Hotspur's Bill Nicholson in a 2-2 draw at Anfield in 1954.

time,' said Moran. 'He was so enthusiastic and keen for the job, but he didn't have the players. You can have the best tactics, but unless you have the players who want to work and win, it doesn't do any good. There were perhaps too many players in their 30s.'

Expectations were high around Anfield when Welsh began his work. Although he inherited a side that needed fresh blood, there was money in the transfer kitty, and gates were booming. Everything seemed in place for the Reds to challenge the top sides of the day; the likes of Tottenham, Manchester United, Arsenal and Wolves, who all won the championship in the first years of the 1950s. In these hopeful days Anfield recorded its biggest-ever crowd, 61,905 turning up to see the Reds beat Wolves 2-1 in an FA Cup fourth round tie on 2 February 1952.

The Old Number-switch Trick

Moran said: 'They had a players' pen in the ground, where you watched the game when you weren't playing. I was in there that day, because I wasn't in the side, and I remember it was a huge crowd. We got the better of Wolves by switching Billy Liddell to centre forward.' Liddell retained his number 11 jersey, throwing Wolves into confusion, with defenders unsure who to mark. Moran recalled: 'Billy Wright was the captain and the centre half of Wolves,

50 Greatest Players

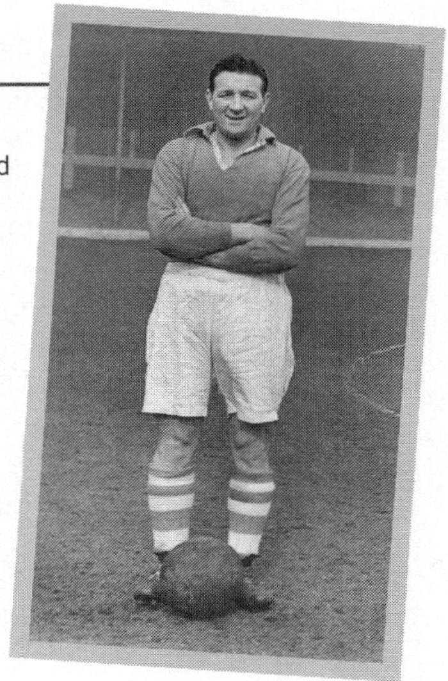

BOB PAISLEY Half back

Joined Liverpool: 1939 **From:** Bishop Auckland

Debut: January 1946 v Chester City (a), FA Cup – won 2-0

Appearances: 277 **Goals:** 12

Left Liverpool: 1954 (joined staff)

Honours won with Liverpool: Division One championship 1947

The early years of his career were swallowed up by war, during which Paisley served with valour in the North African desert and in Italy. When football resumed he played a big part in Liverpool's 1947 championship triumph. He was primarily a defensive player, but among the goals he scored was an FA Cup semi-final winner against Everton at Maine Road in 1950. It was the big regret of Paisley's playing days that he was dropped for the final to make way for Laurie Hughes. Many felt Liverpool's defeat at the hands of Arsenal would not have happened if the tough Paisley, who had done so much to get them to Wembley, had been in the starting line-up.

and you could tell he didn't know how to react or what to do. We had won the game before it had even kicked off.'

Despite the occasional happy day such as that win over Wolves, Welsh's team generally failed to shine, and after his first full season in charge they finished in 11th place. The following season was even worse, with a 17th place in the league, and a disastrous defeat in the third round of the FA Cup, 1-0 away to Gateshead of Division Three (North).

The 1953-54 season was the worst in Liverpool's history. They ended up last in the table, winning just nine matches, conceding 97 goals. From mid-December 1953 they went 14 matches without a win, starting with losses to Portsmouth, Manchester United and West Bromwich Albion, letting in five goals each time. On 10 April the coup de grâce came with a 3-0 defeat at Highbury. After half a century in the First Division, Liverpool were relegated.

Moran said: 'Now, after all my years coaching, I can see what was wrong. It's simple. The players weren't good enough. It doesn't matter who the manager is then, you are going to get relegated. Even when Mr Shankly came in, he still needed new players to change the club's fortunes.'

An early return for the Reds looked unlikely soon after the new season kicked off. In consecutive weeks in December they lost 9-1 at Birmingham City, the club's record defeat, and 4-1 away to Doncaster Rovers. Now Liverpool were facing a second relegation to the fathomless depths of Division Three (North). Their form improved marginally after the New Year and they survived to finish in mid-table, despite a 6-1 defeat away to Rotherham United on the last day of the season. Amid the wreckage of a dispiriting season, the Reds humiliated Everton 4-0 at Goodison Park in an FA Cup fourth round tie – no small comfort as the Toffeemen had gained promotion and were now Merseyside's top team.

A crowd of over 72,000 at Goodison Park saw Liddell score the first. Winger Alan A'Court thumped in the second, and John Evans added a third, then a fourth as the Reds easily came out on top. There wouldn't be another league or cup derby for seven years, so Liverpool fans at least had that memory to keep them warm in the long, dark Second Division days. Their promising Cup run that season, though, ended at home to Huddersfield in the next round.

50 Greatest Players

ALBERT STUBBINS Forward

Joined Liverpool: 1946 **From:** Newcastle United

Debut: 14 September 1946 v Bolton (a), Division One – won 3-1

Appearances: 178 **Goals:** 83

Left Liverpool: 1953 **For:** Ashington

Honours won with Liverpool: Division One championship 1947

The Geordie's Liverpool career flowered just briefly, his best seasons coming immediately after he had signed for the club from Newcastle. Liverpool had won his services in a duel with Everton, and they shelled out a club-record £12,500 to seal the deal. He paid them back in the first year scoring 24 goals as Liverpool won the First Division championship. But his form dwindled along with the team's and he was never quite the same force again. Stubbins earned immortality later on as the only footballer to feature on the cover of The Beatles' *Sergeant Pepper* album, on the insistence of Paul McCartney, just above Marlene Dietrich and below Karl Marx.

Liverpool just missed promotion the following season, ending up in third place behind the promoted sides Sheffield Wednesday and Leeds. The supporters largely kept faith with Welsh and his players, and gates regularly topped 40,000. But the board had seen enough, Anfield was ripe for change, and in May 1956 Welsh became the first manager in the club's history to be shown the door.

The new face wasn't a new face at all. It was Phil Taylor, a long-serving Liverpool player who had moved on to the club's coaching staff at the end of his career. Taylor was a Bristolian, and played for Bristol Rovers before joining Liverpool in 1936. He won a First Division Championship medal with the Reds in 1947, but he could never recreate those halcyon days as a manager.

Moran said: 'He never really wanted the job. He did it out of duty and loyalty. In fact, I don't think he was ever officially given the manager's job on a permanent basis. He was always the "acting manager".'

In Taylor's three seasons in charge the Reds went close to promotion every time. In 1957 they finished third again, a point behind promoted Nottingham Forest. They were fourth in 1958, in touching distance of champions West Ham, promoted Blackburn and third-placed Charlton.

There was at least some reflected glory for the Reds as Alan A'Court was chosen to play for England in the 1958 World Cup in Sweden. With Tom Finney ruled out through injury, A'Court played in two group games, a 0-0 draw with eventual winners, Brazil, and a 2-2 draw with Austria. The winger set up England's opening goal against the Austrians, as Johnny Haynes followed up his blocked shot to score. A'Court also played in a qualification play-off as Walter Winterbottom's team lost 1-0 against the USSR.

But 1959 saw the nadir of a desolate decade for Liverpool. They came a respectable fourth in the table, although a distance behind second-placed Fulham. But they suffered a 2-1 defeat in the third round of the Cup away to amateur side, Worcester City. It was a candidate for the most embarrassing loss in the club's entire history. Moran said: 'I played in that one, and it was a shock to lose. For a professional it's always a shock to lose, but especially against a non-league side.

'The match was played on a Wednesday, because the pitch was too icy on the Saturday. It hadn't got much better four days later. In those conditions some players want to fight it out and win. Some don't.'

By November 1959 Taylor felt he had done all he could, and resigned from a job which he never really had. After years of disappointment and underachievement, Liverpool didn't really need a new manager. They needed a miracle worker. He arrived over the Pennines from Huddersfield in an Austin A40 motor car.

Chapter Four: 1959-65
Shankly: The Early Years

Bill Shankly arrived at Anfield in 1959, unproven, but with all the qualities of a great manager.

When Liverpool began the search for a new boss, they had no obvious candidate in mind. The board was so bereft of ideas they recruited the England coach, Walter Winterbottom, to help with their hunt. Winterbottom told the directors they needed a man of vigour and enthusiasm, somebody with plenty of experience, preferably an ex-player. There was one name at the top of his short-list: Bill Shankly, the manager of Huddersfield Town.

Shankly fitted Winterbottom's ideal to the letter. The nuggety little Scot had played with distinction for Preston North End, winning a cup-winner's medal with them, before moving into management after the war. He started at Carlisle United, before moving on to Grimsby, Workington and lastly Huddersfield. He had no trophies to show for his work, but possessed a reputation for making scarce resources go a long way. Liverpool's directors judged he was the man to get them back into the First Division, and crucially for them, without costing the club a fortune.

Liverpool's chairman Tom Williams set off for Huddersfield, and put his cards on the table. Rather unrealistically, he asked Shankly, 'How would you like to manage the best club in England?' 'Why?' Shankly answered archly. 'Is Matt Busby packing in at Manchester United?'

Before agreeing to the move, Shankly insisted on a few ground rules. As well as a salary of £2,500, he wanted complete control over team selection, transfers and all playing matters. Until then, a cabal of directors still had a major say in who played and who didn't, and they had total power in player recruitment and sales. Shankly demanded nothing less than a revolution in the way the team was run. Yet the directors desperately wanted promotion, and Shankly looked their best bet to get it. They gave in, and Shankly was officially appointed Liverpool's new manager on 14 December 1959.

Shankly had come very close to becoming manager of Liverpool eight years before, when Kay left. He was then a promising young manager at Carlisle in Division Three (North), making a name for himself as a footballing alchemist, working wonders with ordinary players and not much money. Shankly had also become well known as a genius at public relations, before public relations had even been invented. His messages over the Tannoy to the Brunton Park public before games, explaining decisions, opening up the running of the team to supporters' scrutiny, were famous. Liverpool's directors wanted Shankly to replace Kay, but then the board baulked at Shankly's demands for full control over footballing affairs and appointed Don Welsh instead. Eight years later they were prepared to bend to Shankly's will. Up to a point.

Ramshackle Eyesore

He must have wondered why he'd bothered after his first game in charge, a numbing 4-0 defeat against Cardiff City at Anfield, watched by 27,291 largely depressed supporters. It wasn't just the team that needed major corrective surgery. Anfield had degenerated into a ramshackle eyesore, and as Shankly remarked, the training ground at Melwood was fit only for for people to walk their dogs. The practice pitches were bumpy and bare, except for weeds. There was one pristine rectangle of emerald turf; a staff member told him: 'That's kept for cricket in the summer, boss'. The cricket field was quickly commandeered for football and Shankly set about turning Melwood into a base fit for professional athletes. Right from the start, Shankly showed the club that he meant to have the best for his players.

One of his first actions was to call a meeting of the existing coaching staff. Shankly quickly reassured them that their jobs were safe – he did not intend to bring in his own back-room people. He recognised the experience and expertise of people like Bob Paisley, Reuben Bennett and Joe Fagan. Although they had been associated with the failed regimes of the past, Shankly put his faith in them and they became the nucleus of the fabled Anfield Bootroom for the next 30 years.

His impact on the players was immediate. A teenage Ian Callaghan had signed for Liverpool as an amateur in 1958 and was trying to break into the first team when Shankly took over. 'It was clear as soon as you met him that he was a special man,' Callaghan said. 'You got the feeling immediately that

50 Greatest Players

BILLY LIDDELL Centre forward

Joined Liverpool: 1938

From: Lochgelly Violet

Debut: January 1946 v Chester City (a), FA Cup – won 2-0

Appearances: 534 **Goals:** 228

Left Liverpool: 1961 (retired)

Honours won with Liverpool: Division One championship 1947; 28 Scotland caps

For the immediate post-war generation, Billy Liddell was Liverpool. The Scot was the best player in the side which won the championship in 1947, and he remained the club's best player right through the 1950s. The team struggled in that decade, but the crowds still flocked to worship Liddell, who remained loyal to the club and at the top of his game even during the grim Second Division days. He was best known as a winger, but could also play through the middle as an orthodox centre forward.

Word had already began to spread about the 17-year-old prodigy when George Kay signed Liddell after a tip-off from Matt Busby. Even though the war saw his football being played in Regional League matches, Billy soon confirmed early impressions, making his debut for Scotland before enlisting and playing for Bomber Command.

Liddell was unleashed on to the league defences a few games into the 1946-47 season, providing the steel, guile and skills that helped the side to the league championship. And although the quality of the players around him began to diminish, his talents continued to light up Anfield.

Despite opportunities to join more successful clubs, Billy remained loyal to Liverpool. He played his last league game in August 1960 just before his 39th birthday and was seen regularly at the club right up until his death in 2001. Later Reds followers may sing the praises of the likes of Dalglish, but there can never have been a greater Liverpool player than Billy Liddell.

here was a person who could transform the club. He was so enthusiastic, and the most charismatic person you would ever meet.'

In hindsight it is easy to imagine that Shankly, the man of destiny, was bound to succeed at Anfield. His legend has been burnished so brightly, you might think that success ran on iron rails right from the day he arrived at the club. Yet that is far from the truth. Shankly had to combat a deep-seated inertia at Liverpool, and for the first months he felt as if he was fighting a losing battle against the dead hand of directors who did not share his ambition, and could not be made to appreciate the work that was needed to turn the club around. Every advance, he had to struggle for. Every penny needed to improve the team, he had to gouge out of the board. Anfield itself was falling down, and the playing surface was atrocious. Shankly was horrified when the groundsman told him there was no water supply to irrigate the rutted pitch. After a row he eventually extracted £3,000 to rectify the matter.

Only the Best

'Bill always wanted the best for the players,' said Callaghan. 'Whether it was the best training kit, or the best training facilities, he fought to get them. There is no comparison between Melwood when he took charge, and what it became in later years. It was not very good. Run-down, you might say. But he changed all that. The facilities at Melwood were terrible, so we got a bus back to Anfield after training, and we had a bath and changed there. In the bad weather we'd be on the bus covered in mud. It was stupid, really.'

Kevin Lewis. Although often seen as a reserve, his goals were essential in Shankly's team's climb to the top.

Shankly was worn out with arguments over transfers. The going rate for a decent player was £30,000 plus. The board wanted him to shop in the sales for £10,000 players. Shankly bid £18,000 for Leeds United's Jack Charlton; Leeds wanted slightly more. The Liverpool board got cold feet and to the manager's fury, refused to sanction the deal. He had been prepared to cut costs and lower his sights in his earlier jobs – there would always be a limit to the ambition of clubs like Carlisle, or Workington, after all. But at Anfield, Shankly knew what could be achieved, and his board didn't see it.

After Shankly's first five months as manager Liverpool had finished third in the Second Division. Once again, they had gone close to promotion, but fell away behind Villa and Cardiff. By now

Shankly had a clear idea of what needed doing to the team. He had inherited a squad of nearly 40 players, and had identified the men he wanted to keep, and the ones who could leave. Within a year, 24 players were gone.

The Reds faced one more frustrating season in the Second Division. In 1960-61 – for the fourth time in six seasons – they finished third, missing promotion behind Ipswich and Sheffield United. Shankly spent the summer of 1961 arranging the key signings who would help transform Liverpool from a failing Second Division side into the best team in England.

Just at the right time Shankly found an ally in the boardroom to fight on his behalf. His name was Eric Sawyer, who became a director at the behest of John Moores, the Littlewoods Pools tycoon who owned major stakes in Everton and Liverpool. Sawyer wasn't a football man, but he soon recognised that Shankly needed and deserved the board's full backing. Thanks to Sawyer's influence, Bill Shankly soon found funds more forthcoming. His relationship with some directors would never be classed as warm, but the wearying struggles of his first months were largely over. Shankly called Sawyer, 'A man of vision, a director who would only be associated with success and who was sick and tired of sitting in the pigsty we called a ground'.

The players could sense that the club was on the up. 'It was clear promotion was coming, and we were on the verge of greater things,' said Callaghan. 'Bill could see the potential from the start, and his ambition passed on to the players. He could see that Liverpool was a great city, and a football-daft city, and it deserved two great teams. He had this burning desire to raise Liverpool up again. I grew up as a Liverpool fan, when players like Billy Liddell caught my imagination, and I knew how the club had been in the doldrums in the 50s. That was the only reason I signed for Liverpool. Everton wanted me, but I signed for Liverpool, even though they were the poor relations at the time. He set about changing that. It wasn't just a job for him. It was a mission, really.'

The March Begins

Thanks to Shankly's insistence and Sawyer's cajoling, a team capable of winning promotion took shape. The board bankrolled the signing of centre forward Ian St John from Motherwell for £37,500, and centre half Ron Yeats from Dundee United for £30,000, before the start of the 1961-62 season. For the first time, Shankly felt he was getting somewhere. He said: 'St John and Yeats were really the cornerstone, the beginning of the big march'.

When Liverpool finally put Division Two behind them they said farewell in style. Shankly's men scorched their way to the title, scoring 99 goals, and finished the season with an eight-point gap over second-placed Leyton Orient.

They looked likely champions by Bonfire Night, after winning 10 and drawing one of their first 11 games. Goals flew in from every position on the field, but the Reds' real destroyer was Roger Hunt, by now the finished article as a goal-scorer, aged 23. The centre forward scored 13 in that first ferocious burst of form, and went on to set the club's record for goals in a season with 41. He formed a formidable partnership with Ian St John, who scored 18. At the back, Ron Yeats was the immovable object that Shankly had promised he would be.

It was the season Shankly's creed of keeping the game simple was shown at its most effective. He didn't tinker with his team. Week after week, the names stayed the same: Slater, Byrne, White or Moran, Milne, Yeats, Leishman, Callaghan, St John, Hunt, Melia and A'Court. In all, 17 players were used to win the Second Division title, but some of the reserves only played a handful of games.

Callaghan said: 'He knew his best 11, and we stayed fit throughout the season. We were a very good team, with lots of very good players. People talk about the spine of the team and how important it was to Bill to get that right, and it's true. We had Ronnie Yeats at the back, and nothing got past him. We called him the Giant. And Bill's other big signing, Ian St John, scored so many important goals, and gave us so much up front. Roger Hunt was up there with him, and he was a wonderful player. Everywhere you looked on the field there were great players.'

Good Enough for Finney...

It was no fluke that the team remained largely injury-free. Shankly's training regime was designed to reduce wear and tear on players to a minimum. He oversaw the pre-season training, which got the players super-fit to start with. After that, sessions were tailored to keep the players in condition. There were few slogging cross-country runs, never much in the way of repetitive routines to build lung capacity. Shankly concentrated on dynamic, intensive sessions, shaped to keep his players fresh and their skills razor-keen.

When he was a player at Preston, Shankly had been impressed by the way Tom Finney, his favourite footballer of all time, spent hours kicking a ball against the wall of the stand, controlling it, dribbling, and shooting again, to perfect his craft. If it was good enough for Finney, Shankly thought, it was good enough for Liverpool. Five-a-sides were a favoured way of compressing all the techniques needed for a match into a short space of time. There would be no heavy legs in Shankly's teams. The serious physical exertion was saved for Saturday afternoons or Wednesday nights.

Ian Callaghan said: 'It was never laborious. We would come in at 10 and we'd be finished by 12, but it was highly organised. We would work on set things every day, and everybody knew what they were doing. It was all short, sharp work. But don't get the idea that it was easy. We were very, very fit.'

Shankly, too, made Melwood a happy place to come to work. His love for the game was infectious, and spread to his players. In the filthiest weather, Shankly would say, 'Great to be alive, boys. All you need is the green grass and a ball.' Put like that, how could anyone disagree?

And so Liverpool made stately progress through their last Second Division season. Hunt scored five hat-tricks, and by the time Southampton visited Anfield on 21 April 1962, the Reds needed a win to guarantee promotion back to Division One after eight mainly miserable years.

It was a carnival. If by any mischance Liverpool slipped up, there were still five matches left to rectify the position, so the Kop could relax and savour the occasion. And savour it they did, as a 2-0 victory sent them back to the big league at last. Kevin Lewis, deputising for the injured St John, scored them both.

The 1961-61 Second Division championship campaign was a model of consistency. Only 17 players were used all season. Goals came from every position but the chief destroyers were Ian St John (middle row, second from left) and Roger Hunt (front row, second from left).

Great Matches

FOOTBALL LEAGUE DIVISION TWO **Anfield, 21 April 1962**
Attendance: 40,410

Liverpool 2 **Southampton 0**
Lewis 2

This was the match that ensured Liverpool would return to the First Division after eight desolate seasons in the Second Division. It sticks in the memory as an occasion rather than a football match – but what an occasion.

Both goals were scored by Kevin Lewis, a 21-year-old winger on the fringes of the first team who was only in the side because Ian St John was injured, and thousands of supporters stayed inside Anfield after the final whistle to sing their songs and acclaim their team. They chanted for the players to come out of the dressing room and take a bow, refusing to budge until they had had a chance to hail their heroes. Eventually they did so, some still wet from the bath and draped in towels. Shankly had insisted all along that Liverpool Football Club belonged to the people; and there would be no divide between player and Kopite on this day. Shankly's dream was to see players and supporters marching forward together for the greater glory of Liverpool. This was one of the first great demonstrations of the spirit Shankly was creating.

Ian Callaghan said: 'I remember the sheer relief of it. After so long, we were back in the First Division. I had lived through it as a supporter and as a player, and when we finally went up it felt great.'

Liverpool: Furnell, Byrne, Moran, Milne, Yeats, Leishman, Callaghan, Hunt, Lewis, Melia, A'Court

Southampton: Godfrey, Patrick, Traynor, Wimshurst, Knapp, Huxford, Paine, Clifton, Reeves, Mulgrew, Penk

Callaghan said: 'We went up into the directors' box to greet the crowd after the match, and the supporters were going mad. It was a marvellous sight to see. I think most Liverpudlians were looking forward to derby matches again, and the chance to beat Everton. It really felt like the start of something big. All along, I knew we would go up. With Bill in charge, and with people like Bob Paisley, Joe Fagan and Reuben Bennett at the club as well, it was unthinkable that we wouldn't.'

Even now, Shankly felt that some in the club were content with promotion, and would have settled for consolidation. But the manager did not want to settle for consolidation. He didn't just want to play on the same pitch as Everton – he wanted to play them off it, and to win the championship.

At a presentation ceremony the promotion-winning players each received a silver cigarette box in recognition of their efforts. The choice of gift typified the chasm between the people at the top and the manager. Shankly was a health fanatic who extolled the virtues of fresh air, early nights, temperance, good food and clean living. He cut through the mood of self-congratulation with a typically abrasive speech. He said: 'We got promotion, but you don't think that is satisfactory, do you? Next time we come back here for presents we will have won the big league. The First Division.'

Shankly had earned the gratitude of the board for returning the club to the First Division, but it wasn't the end of the spats between manager and directors. In August 1962 the winger Johnny Morrissey, a crowd favourite, was sold behind Shankly's back. Worse, he was sold to Everton for £10,000, and went on to play a leading role in the Blues' championship victory of 1962-63. Shankly was furious and resolved to resign. The heroine of the piece for Liverpudlians was Shankly's wife, Nessie. She told her husband that he could move if he wanted to; she was staying put. Nessie informed her husband that it was time they put down some roots, and she wasn't moving again. Her pleas worked, and Shankly vowed to battle on.

Back to Goodison

Life back at the top didn't come easily to Liverpool. Where last season the Reds had failed to win just one of their first 11 games, now they could only win three over the same period. But at least they didn't lose the match all Merseyside had anticipated since the mid-50s: the first derby for seven years.

The game on 22 September 1962 at Goodison was watched by over 72,000, and Liverpool needed a last-minute goal from Hunt to save face in a 2-2 draw. Roy Vernon had given Everton the lead with a penalty, but Kevin Lewis had levelled the scores. One or two directors may have shifted uneasily in their seats as Morrissey gave Everton a 2-1 lead, but Liverpool's frantic attempts to save the game paid off at the end as Hunt conjured up the equaliser. Defeat in this match of all matches would have been unthinkable.

The Reds' league position was improved by a run of nine consecutive victories from mid-November and they ended the season in a respectable eighth position, but the real excitement came in the FA Cup.

Liverpool battled through to the last four after wins over Wrexham, Burnley, Arsenal and West Ham, but they lost to Leicester in the semi-finals. The match at Hillsborough ended 1-0 to City, even though the Reds battered Gordon Banks's goal for most of the afternoon. From this day superstitious supporters judged Leicester to be Liverpool's bogey team; but Shankly rated

Roger Hunt powers a late face-saving strike past Gordon West in the long-awaited Merseyside derby at Goodison Park in 1962.

them as the best side in the First Division at that stage. Knowing Shankly, that may have been a back-handed swipe at the champions, Everton.

Liverpool had enjoyed a solid season back in the First Division, but they were not treading water. Shankly was improving his team as he went along. Tommy Lawrence, a young Scottish goalkeeper, was fast-tracked into the first team, and Willie Stevenson was imported from Rangers to beef up the midfield. In the summer of 1963 Shankly added the final ingredient: Peter Thompson, a winger who switched from Preston for £40,000.

The 1963-64 season got off to a dubious start for the Reds. They lost their first three home games, against Nottingham Forest, Blackpool and West Ham United, and looked anything but champions in waiting. Fortress Anfield turned into open house for visiting sides to Liverpool. Ian St John said: 'Shanks came out with a famous quote at that time, "I assure you, Liverpool will win at home before the season is over."

'It was still a transitional period for us,' he said. 'We had bought Peter Thompson, who was a wonderful dribbler and such a special talent, and it took us a while to work out how to get the best out of him. And he had to get used to playing with us.'

But a 6-0 spree against Wolves at Anfield heralded a leap forward in form, and from then on the Reds battled Manchester United and Everton all the way for the title. Liverpool's peerless fitness told in the final stretch, and they won seven matches on the trot from the end of March to pull away from the others.

The club's FA Cup jinx continued, with defeat at home against Swansea Town (they weren't even a City yet). Liverpool lost 2-1 in the quarter-finals against the Second Division side, and St John said: 'It was an awful day, the worst.

'Ronnie Moran missed a penalty which would have taken it to a replay, and they had an Irishman in goal named Noel Dwyer who saved everything. He was better than Gordon Banks that afternoon. I was completely out of it for the whole of the second half. I'd got concussion, and there were no concessions to substitutes then. You just stayed on, and I was walking around in a cloud. Back then that was just the way it was.'

Shankly Delivers

The Reds' league form remained irresistible, and on 18 April 1964 they faced Arsenal at home, knowing victory would bring the championship trophy back to Anfield after 17 years. Roared on by a fervent crowd of over 48,000, Liverpool won 5-0. Shankly had delivered on his promise.

'It was a beautiful day, typical end-of-season weather, and it was a great day for the club,' St John recalled. 'George Eastham missed a penalty for them, and everything smiled on us. Alf Arrowsmith scored one of the goals, and it was one of the last he did score for the club. He did his knee in the Charity Shield against West Ham the next season and he was finished. It was a terrible tragedy. He was not a footballer, he was a natural goalscorer who scored goals for fun. He could put them in from anywhere.'

The 21-year-old Arrowsmith had added extra impetus to Liverpool's title challenge by scoring 14 goals in the second half of the season after replacing the injured Jimmy Melia. St John dropped back into Melia's midfield role, and Arrowsmith moved up front alongside Hunt. After his injury Arrowsmith stayed at Anfield for four years before moving on to Bury and Rochdale, but he was never the same force.

St John said the happiness of the afternoon typified that era at the club. 'It was so much fun,' he said. 'To be able to participate in it all was brilliant. There was a great spirit between the supporters and the players. They were

Great Matches

FOOTBALL LEAGUE DIVISION ONE

Anfield, 18 April 1964
Attendance: 48,623

Liverpool 5 — **Arsenal 0**

St John
Arrowsmith
Thompson 2
Hunt

Liverpool needed to win this match to capture the league championship for the first time in 17 years, and they pulled it off with some style.

The football Liverpool played graced the proceedings, proving them worthy champions. An early strike by Ian St John settled the nerves and got them underway and they were 2-0 ahead by half-time when Alf Arrowsmith – ostensibly a callow reserve striker, but one who had scored 15 goals in the season – beat Furnell in the Arsenal goal.

The second half saw the Reds go into exhibition mode as Peter Thompson crashed two more past the hapless keeper before Roger Hunt rose to head home a cross after Thompson had once again made mincemeat of the Gunners' defence.

After playing Arsenal off the Anfield pitch the Reds embarked on a lap of honour around it, but they started the parade empty-handed. Even though a title-clinching Liverpool display could have been predicted with some confidence, the Football League hadn't sent the First Division trophy for post-match presentation. St John said: 'It didn't matter. A man in the crowd gave Yeatsy a cup made out of cardboard, and we ran around with that. It was a marvellous atmosphere, everyone had been waiting so long to win the league again.'

Liverpool: Lawrence, Byrne, Moran, Milne, Yeats, Stevenson, Callaghan, Hunt, St John, Arrowsmith, Thompson

Arsenal: Furnell, Magill, McCulloch, Neill, Ure, Sneddon, Skirton, Strong, Baker, Eastham, Armstrong

the first fans to really sing and chant at matches, the whole pop music scene was taking off in Liverpool, and the supporters reflected that in their songs. It felt like we were doing our stuff on the pitch, and they were doing their bit as supporters. It was carnival time every week at Anfield.'

A landmark season in Liverpool history kicked off in Iceland, as the Reds played in European competition for the first time. They had been drawn away to Reykjavic in the first round, and it was with some trepidation that the Liverpool party set off for the fringes of the Arctic Circle for their debut match. There were no charter planes from Speke

Ian St John slots home the first goal and the championship is on the way back to Anfield for the first time in 17 years.

Airport in those days. An arduous coach journey took them up to Prestwick Airport in Scotland to catch a scheduled flight to Iceland. One member of the Liverpool party with experience of European football was Phil Chisnall, who had joined the Reds from Manchester United in the summer for £25,000 – the last player to transfer directly between the two clubs. Chisnall's other major claim to fame is that he was the first man ever to kick a ball on *Match of the Day*, kicking off for Liverpool against Arsenal on 22 August 1964.

Chisnall said: 'It was a step into the unknown, because Liverpool hadn't been in Europe. But there was no fear, because we weren't expecting much from the opposition. Teams like Reykjavic in those days weren't as good as they would be now. We knew it would be easier than a league game.'

The journey was more taxing than the match, as Liverpool cantered to a 5-0 victory. Roger Hunt and Gordon Wallace scored two each and Chisnall also scored. He said: 'It was one of the best goals I ever scored. The ball came over from a corner and cleared the heads of the centre halves. I was waiting outside the box and hit it on the half-volley. It screamed into the top of the net so sweet. If I tried for 20 years to repeat it, I would never do it. It was the perfect strike.'

In the return leg the Kop amused themselves on Anfield's first European night by cheering the opposition players and aiming good-natured boos at their own team. With the Reds ambling to an 11-1 aggregate win, they could afford to be generous to the Icelandic amateurs.

Belgian champions Anderlecht proved tougher opponents in the next round. Their team was full of internationals and seasoned European campaigners. Liverpool, for all their ability and domestic success, were novices in the two-legged continental game, but they need not have worried. They beat Anderlecht 3-0 at home in the first leg, and looked old hands playing away in the second leg, defending cagily and winning 1-0. Against Anderlecht they also unveiled a new all-red strip, which Shankly believed made his men look even more formidable.

In those days the European Cup was not an over-blown, drawn-out affair like the modern Champions League. It was a straight knockout, which made the route to the final shorter, but more perilous. One slip-up and you were out. So it was that after just two ties, Liverpool found themselves in the quarter-finals, taking on the German champions, Cologne. Both legs ended 0-0, largely due to the spectacular performance of the German keeper Schumacher, and a replay was ordered at neutral Rotterdam. Ian St John and Roger Hunt both scored, but the third game ended all-square again at 2-2. With penalty shoot-outs still a twinkle in UEFA minds, the match had to be settled on the toss of a disc, red on one side for Liverpool, white on the other for Cologne.

Stuck in the Mud

The referee called the two captains together in the middle of the pitch and span the disc. To ratchet up the tension another notch, the disc stuck on its side in the mud. The referee, both captains, the two teams, the entire stadium and millions watching on television right across Europe peered at the disc, to see if it would fall one way or the other. Eventually, the sheepish ref fished it out of the mire and span again; it went Yeats's way. The Reds were in the European Cup semi-finals.

At their first attempt, they had equalled Manchester United and Tottenham's exploits in reaching the last four of the European Cup. The question was, could they go that one step further? Their opponents could not have been more formidable: Internazionale of Milan, the holders, who had beaten the great Real Madrid 3-1 in the previous year's final.

While the European Cup story was unfolding, Liverpool were also advancing in the FA Cup, a competition which they still had never won. Some supporters were beginning to wonder if they ever would.

Ronnie Moran lurks behind West Ham's Bobby Moore in the 2-2 draw with West Ham at Anfield in October 1964.

They started off at West Bromwich Albion, then a middle-ranking power in the First Division, where goals from Hunt and St John set up a 2-1 win. The fourth round almost turned out to be another of the embarrassments which had scarred the Reds' recent cup history. They were drawn to play Stockport County, bottom of the Fourth Division, at Anfield.

It would be wrong to suggest that Liverpool were complacent about the outcome of the tie. Nevertheless, Shankly decided his team didn't need him

Liverpool meet Cologne in the European Cup quarter-final at Anfield in March 1965. Man of the match, Cologne goalkeeper, Toni Schumacher, makes another fine save from Willie Stevenson, forcing a replay in Rotterdam.

for a home match against Stockport and he left the shop in Bob Paisley's hands while he went to Germany to scout on Cologne prior to the European Cup tie. For an excruciating 50 minutes it looked like the Reds would lose as County scored early on, and attacked Liverpool's goal fearlessly. But for liberal supplies of luck, the match might have been beyond the Reds' reach when Gordon Milne dredged up an equaliser to take the tie to Edgeley Park. Shankly was told the result by a porter at Euston Station on his way home from Germany, and you would not have wanted to be the passenger in the next seat as he fumed all the way to Lime Street.

There was no mistake in the replay, two goals from Hunt wrapping up a 2-0 win. Bolton Wanderers, who were pressing for promotion from the Second Division, were waiting in the fifth round, and Callaghan's goal decided another nervy encounter to see the Reds through 1-0.

In a Liverpool cup run of that era it was as certain as death and taxes that Leicester City would crop up sooner or later. The teams were pitched together in the quarter-finals, and Gordon Banks produced his customary brilliance to keep the Reds out at Filbert Street. If there were two teams that seemed always to bring the best out of Banks, they were Brazil and Liverpool. But the jinx was laid at Anfield, Hunt scoring the only goal of the match.

Liverpool found themselves in the odd position of being second favourites for their semi-final with Chelsea at Villa Park. Even though the Reds were reigning champions, and had been working wonders on the foreign stage, Liverpool had been struggling in the league while a confident Chelsea were troubling the First Division leaders. But Liverpool were in no mood to waste yet another opportunity to lift the elusive cup. Peter Thompson sent a fulminating shot past Peter Bonetti to put the Reds in front. Then Willie Stevenson put the lid on proceedings with a cool penalty after Ron Harris had chopped St John in the box. The Reds were back at Wembley for the first time in 15 years. A city held its breath, desperate for victory.

Doctor's Note

The week before the cup final, Liverpool had to honour a league fixture away to Wolves. Shankly was reluctant to risk any of his first-choice team in the firing line, so fielded a reserve side. The Football League ordered an inquiry, but Liverpool were able to produce a doctor's note for every missing player. Liverpool's reserves won the match 3-1, in any case. The club's medic had certainly earned a bonus – not only for proving efficient at his paperwork, but also for making sure that every one of the stricken players was cured in time to face Leeds five days later.

Liverpool might have travelled south for the final free of illness, but they were not without injuries. The most serious centred on Gordon Milne, who had hurt his knee in the semi-final. Geoff Strong and Chisnall were in reserve, and when Milne failed a fitness test, Strong got the jersey. Chisnall spent the match sitting on the bench next to Shankly.

The final was played on May Day, and Wembley was doused by an unseasonal downpour as the Reds marched out to face Leeds United. The match might not have been a spectacle for the neutral, but as Liverpool supporters may have observed at the time, what are neutrals doing at the cup final anyway? It was a particularly sore point that year, as Liverpool's ticket allocation from the Football Association was a paltry 15,000 out of 100,000. Thousands of loyal fans, who had been desperately waiting for this day, were left to the tender mercies of the touts.

The Liverpool fans with tickets witnessed an epoch-making afternoon as the cup was finally captured. Hunt's and St John's goals, won the day as Liverpool triumphed 2-1 after extra time.

Great Matches

FA CUP FINAL

Wembley, 1 May 1965
Attendance: 100,000

Liverpool 2
Hunt
St John

Leeds United 1*
Bremner

***after extra time**

The splash headline in that night's *Football Echo* told the story: 'Ee-Aye-Addio, the Reds have won the Cup!' After 73 years of hurt the prize which had tormented Liverpool players and supporters for so long was heading for Anfield. And one man above all others deserved the credit: full back Gerry Byrne.

Leeds United's diddy but dangerous Scots midfielder, Bobby Collins, clattered into Byrne in the early minutes, and Liverpool's trainer, Bob Paisley, raced on to apply first aid. Byrne got up holding his shoulder gingerly, but carried on playing. There could be no substitute in those days to relieve the casualty.

There was no indication then that Byrne had broken his collarbone, or that he was in agony as the two ends of the fractured bone rubbed against each other. The full back stayed on the field all through the 90 minutes, as Leeds happily played unambitious, negative football, content to let Liverpool make the play and then thwart them in the final third.

And so the match went into the extra half-hour for the first time since 1947. Even now, Byrne did not go missing. Weary players drooped from the effort of ploughing up

Liverpool's cup. Above: Roger Hunt puts Liverpool ahead.

Ian St John's fabulous extra-time header takes the cup to Merseyside.

and down a wet Wembley, which grew heavier by the minute as the rain pelted down. Yet, in the third minute of extra time, in response to some fine play by Willie Stevenson, Byrne found the grit to make one more run forward, got to the byline and crossed for Roger Hunt to meet the low centre with his head to score the Reds' opener. Leeds looked sunk, but just seven minutes later Billy Bremner, with a panache lacking in the rest of their approach, slotted the ball past Lawrence for Leeds' equalizer.

Still Shankly's super-fit Liverpool scented blood. Ian Callaghan crossed for Ian St John to thud the winning header past Gary Sprake. Only nine minutes of play remained and with the stuffing knocked out of Don Revie's side, the Reds turned on the style forcing a couple of great saves from Gary Sprake. As the final whistle blew Wembley resounded to Liverpudlian anthems that lasted long after the team's extended lap of honour had passed. The joy and relief of Liverpool's fans was obvious, the long wait was over and at last the red ribbons of Liverpool were tied on to the Football Association Challenge Cup.

Liverpool: Lawrence, Lawler, Byrne, Strong, Yeats, Stevenson, Callaghan, Hunt, St John, Smith, Thompson

Leeds United: Sprake, Reaney, Bell, Bremner, Charlton, Hunter, Giles, Storrie, Peacock, Collins, Johanneson

Referee: W. Clements

Ron Yeats is masterful in the air, as ever, as Liverpool take on Arsenal in August 1964.

Chisnall said: 'It's funny the things you remember. We all wore new club suits for the day, and Shanks somehow got whitewash on his off the tunnel wall, and it bothered him all through the game. He was trying to brush paint off his trousers when Ian St John scored. Shanks missed it. "Who scored, son?" he asked me, and I told him, "It's Ian St John, boss". All he said was, "These bleeding pants". '

The players and their wives were treated to dinner at the Savoy that night. The chairman, Sidney Reakes, gave a speech, naming the victorious players in turn. Chisnall said: 'This is how much that fellow knew. Two of the players he mentioned were Robert Hunt and Tommy Lawrenson. The boys cracked up at that.'

Holy Grail

The half-million crowd which jammed the city streets to greet the winners showed what the FA Cup meant to the people of the city. The silver trophy had become a Holy Grail on Merseyside: it had been 32 years since Everton had won it, and the Reds never had. Liverpool had never seen an outpouring of joy like this, and the masses in the streets outnumbered those for VE Day.

The players did not have long to indulge in parties or to shake off hangovers. Internazionale were travelling to Anfield for the first leg of the European Cup semi-final three days after Wembley, and were ready to provide the stiffest challenge of a long and testing 60-match season.

Internazionale were coached by Helenio Herrera, the high priest of 'catenaccio', the defensive system that had been invented by the Swiss and elevated into an art form by the Italians. Herrera's brand of ultra-defensive anti-football was frighteningly effective, but seldom pretty. Shankly's team was never cavalier for the sake of it; it was built on a stern defence and a strict work ethic. But it also overflowed with invention and attacking verve. Shankly never sent his men out to squeeze the life from a game. For Herrera, football was a war of attrition.

Yet Shankly had one or two tricks to confound the Italians. The first weapon in his armoury was the Liverpool crowd. Fuelled by the adrenaline of the Cup win, and by the emotion-charged civic procession, Anfield was mad with passion and noise... but still not noisy enough for Shankly. As the Internazionale players were warming up on the pitch, already quailing before the wall of sound, Shankly sent out Byrne and Milne to parade the newly-won Cup around Anfield. The din shook the concrete under the Kop, reverberated around the stands, and poured over the pitch in a tidal wave of decibels. Shankly cackled to himself as the Italians visibly blanched.

50 Greatest Players

RONNIE MORAN Left back

Joined Liverpool: 1952 **From:** School

Debut: 22 November 1952 v Derby County (a), Division One – lost 3-2

Appearances: 379 **Goals:** 17

Left Liverpool: 1968 (joined staff)

Honours won with Liverpool: Division One championship 1964; Division Two championship 1962

Moran was a sturdy and reliable full back in the unsuccessful Liverpool sides of the 1950s, but he played long enough to enjoy the trophies of the 1960s. He made 35 appearances in the 1963-64 title-winning season, a fitting reward for the selfless years playing his heart out without glory in the Second Division. His last season was 1964-65, when he deputised for injured team-mates in the European Cup semi-finals against Internazionale. It was no fault of Moran's immensely capable performances that the Reds went out.

He made an even greater contribution after his playing days, when he joined the Liverpool coaching staff and served the club for another 35 years as wise lieutenant to the likes of Shankly and Paisley.

What followed was a pedigree performance by Liverpool, an exhibition of the pass-and-move philosophy drummed into the players by Shankly and his cohorts, and it made for an occasion that has been hailed as Anfield's greatest European night. Hunt, Callaghan and St John scored in Liverpool's 3-1 victory, and hopes were sky-high for the return in northern Italy a week later.

Liverpool learnt many lessons on that trip to Milan. The problems began as soon as they reached their hotel hard by the shores of Lake Como. The Liverpool party had not been warned about the bells from the neighbouring church which tolled throughout the night disturbing the players' sleep.

Chisnall said: 'There was a monastery up the hill from the hotel, and the bells rang every hour. Shanks was always very observant, and as soon as we arrived at the hotel he cocked an ear for these bells and knew they were going to keep us awake. He marched straight up the hill to see the head monk, and asked if they could stop the bells at night. I don't think any of these Franciscan friars had ever seen or heard a Scotsman before, and they didn't know what to make of Shanks. The abbot said, "Mr Shankly, these bells have been ringing for 1,000 years. We cannot stop them for your football team."' Liverpool were absorbing the black arts of European competition very quickly.

On the evening of the game Liverpool were rocked by the fervour of close to 100,000 fanatical Milanese in the San Siro, who welcomed the visiting team with a fusillade of coins, flares and smoke bombs. Events turned sour once the game kicked off, with a sequence of mysterious refereeing decisions going in the home team's favour. The Italians struck an indirect free-kick into the net, and a goal was allowed. An Italian striker kicked the ball out of Tommy Lawrence's grasp and into the net. Again, a goal was given. A third goal was enough to end Liverpool's first European Cup campaign.

Some Liverpool players were convinced they had been robbed. Tommy Smith tested the Spanish referee's impartiality in the best way he knew how – booting him as hard as he could as they made their way down the tunnel after the match. The official limped away as quickly as he could to the safety of his dressing room.

Chisnall said: 'There was a lot more ducking and diving with referees then, funny things going on. We all felt sick. I know Tommy had a go at the referee, but to be honest Tommy would sometimes kick the ref after we'd won 6-0, so that was only to be expected. That was Tommy.'

Years later, a *Sunday Times* investigation found evidence to suggest corruption, which Bill Shankly and the team had always suspected.

Chapter Five: 1965-74
Days of Glory

In the mid-1960s Liverpool's critics said they were a mechanical side. It is true, there was something relentless about the way in which Shankly's men rolled over opponents, playing a brand of football that laid the stress on perpetual movement and fantastic fitness. They were a hard team too, without being dirty. Shankly had built a side which could out-play its rivals, and look after itself too if it came to that. Shankly did not like the word 'mechanical', though. He preferred 'methodical'. However you describe Liverpool's style of play at that time, there was certainly something chilling about they way in which they powered their way to a second championship in three years.

Week after week during 1965-66 the same players swept aside all-comers, finally recapturing the title, which they had ceded to Manchester United for a season, with a 2-1 win at home against Chelsea. Along the way Shankly used just 14 players, and two of those were reserves who played four games between them. Best of all, the Reds saved one their most emphatic victories for a match against Everton, winning 5-0 at Anfield in September. They hit the top of the table in November and never looked like being caught, eventually finishing six points ahead of the decade's perennial also-rans, Leeds United.

It was also a season when Liverpool furthered their European education. The Reds played in the European Cup-Winners' Cup, making the final after battling through a series of ties which were just as hard, perhaps harder, than the ones they had faced in the European Cup two years earlier.

There was no gentle warm-up against an amateur outfit in this continental odyssey. Juventus came first, and the Reds progressed 2-1 on aggregate after winning the second leg 2-0 at Anfield. Belgian side Standard Liege were next, and Liverpool won home and away to fix up a quarter-final against the dangerous Hungarians of Honved. After a 0-0 draw away from home, goals from full back Chris Lawler and St John took Liverpool through to the semi-finals, and the toughest task so far.

Liverpool were drawn to play Jock Stein's Celtic, and a crowd of over 80,000 greeted the Reds at Parkhead for the first leg. The Bhoys had most of the play, but Liverpool restricted them to a single Bobby Lennox goal. Liverpool won the return 2-0 at Anfield, with Tommy Smith thundering in a long-range free-kick, and Geoff Strong finding the winner. The Scots felt cheated when the referee chalked off a Lennox goal for offside, and Tommy Lawrence bore the brunt of their ire as whisky bottles rained into his penalty area.

Liverpool returned to Glasgow for their first-ever European final, and Borussia Dortmund were their opponents at Hampden Park on a night when the Reds strangely failed to reproduce anything like their best form. The half-fit Hunt scored but the game went into extra-time, and it was the Germans who produced a winner. Liverpool still had eight years to wait for their first European trophy.

It was not obvious at the time, but 1966 proved to be the highwater mark of Shankly's first championship-winning side. You wouldn't have described it as an old team, but nothing the Class of '66 did in the next half-dozen years quite matched the virtuosity of the mid-60s period.

That summer Liverpool players did their bit for England when the World Cup was won. Roger Hunt, who had been with England to the 1962 World Cup in Chile but never played, was an effective foil for Geoff Hurst in the final against West Germany. Hunt played all six of England's games, scoring three goals.

Willie Stevenson in ballet mode at Goodison Park in August 1966. Liverpool went down 1-3 to their rivals.

Ian Callaghan played in the last group match, against France, and crossed for Hunt to score in the 2-0 win which took England into the quarter-finals. But Alf Ramsey dispensed with wingers for the knockout stages, and Callaghan spent the rest of the tournament watching from the bench along with Gerry Byrne, who was in the squad but never got a game.

After three years of constant success, the 1966-67 season came as something of a let-down for Liverpool fans. The team could manage only fifth place in the First Division as Manchester United won the title again, and the Reds' FA Cup effort came off the rails at Goodison in the fifth round, as Everton won 1-0. In the European Cup Ajax of Amsterdam underlined how much the Reds still had to learn about continental competition. Johann Cruyff and his friends took Liverpool apart, winning 5-1 in the first leg in Amsterdam. The Reds held the Dutch side to a 2-2 draw in the return, but the signs were there for all to see: Liverpool were still some way off being a European super-power.

Shankly Takes a Scalpel to his Team

By now Shankly began to see that changes needed to be made to his beloved team, but he took a surgeon's scalpel to the squad rather than a butcher's cleaver. Shankly was not a sentimental man when it came to football, but he felt a large measure of loyalty to the players who had dominated English football in the preceding years. It was too soon for a mass clear-out, but some old favourites disappeared from the scene.

In May 1967 30-year-old Gordon Milne, who had been Shankly's first significant signing, had been eased out to Blackpool. Milne's partner in the middle of the field, 29-year-old Willie Stevenson, was sold to Stoke City in December 1967. Their places were taken by St John, who was given a more withdrawn midfield role, and Shankly's new £65,000 signing from Blackpool, a bullocking 19-year-old powerhouse named Emlyn Hughes.

Shankly also set out to give his forward line more height and aggression by signing Tony Hateley, a strapping centre forward, from Chelsea for £96,000. The way in which Shankly landed his man says a lot about his methods. Once he had identified a likely recruit he stopped at nothing to bring him to Anfield. Hateley said: 'I had gone on holiday with the kids, and we were on the beach at Yarmouth eating ice creams. Nobody knew where we were, I thought. Then these two policemen came up to me. I wondered what was up, when one says, "Bill Shankly wants to talk to you". I had to phone him up, and he told me to catch the next train out and meet him. I did, and I didn't take any persuading to sign.

Tony Hateley, an Anfield success, but it was not enough for Shankly.

'I liked Bill Shankly. He was a very funny man, but I felt Bob Paisley was the power behind him. Shankly was strong on the discipline. Early nights, no drinking after Thursdays. He used to come round to your house on a Thursday night and check your car was still in the driveway.'

The new striker got the Kop on his side straight away by scoring a hat-trick in his second home game as the Reds demolished Newcastle 6-0. But although Hateley kept scoring, Liverpool could not quite match the pace set by the 1967-68 champions, Manchester City, and the Reds finished in third place three points adrift.

Fun in the Fog

That season also saw Liverpool reach the FA Cup quarter-finals, losing 2-1 to West Brom in a second replay at Maine Road. The Cup run saw Hateley have fun in the fog against Walsall at Anfield in the fourth round, scoring four as Liverpool won 5-2. But the mist was so thick most of the crowd saw little more than the nearest touchline. The Anfield Road End kept the rest of the ground informed as the goals flew in.

In the Inter-City Fairs Cup, the Reds reached the quarter-finals with little difficulty, putting eight goals past TSV München at Anfield in the second round. But Liverpool's lack of expertise in two-legged competition was evident again as they lost both matches to Ferencvaros of Hungary 1-0.

50 Greatest Players

ROGER HUNT Striker

Joined Liverpool: 1959 **From:** Stockton Heath

Debut: 9 September 1959 v Scunthorpe United (h), Division Two – won 2-0

Appearances: 492 **Goals:** 286

Left Liverpool: 1969 **For:** Bolton Wanderers

Honours won with Liverpool: Division One championship 1964, 1966; Division Two championship 1962; FA Cup winner 1965; 34 England caps

One of the greatest goalscorers in English football history. Until Rush came along he had scored more goals than any other Red, and still holds the record for most goals in a season. In 1961-62 he netted 41 as Liverpool won the Second Division. Hunt continued to score heavily once Liverpool had reclaimed their place in the First Division, and his strike partnership with Ian St John paved the way for two championships and the FA Cup. History has painted him as the man who kept Jimmy Greaves out of the 1966 World Cup final, but that is inaccurate as well as unfair. Hunt played every game in that tournament, while Hurst only broke into the side for the quarter-final against Argentina when Greaves was injured. The choice for Alf Ramsey was between Greaves and Geoff Hurst – Hunt was always going to be in his side. He recognised the qualities of a great centre forward and selfless team man.

Anyone who remembered the desperate pre-Shankly days at Anfield would have regarded this season as a success; but the Reds had raised the bar and the crowd craved trophies. An early casualty was Hateley, shipped out to Coventry City for £80,000 just after the start of the 1968-69 season.

The Reds had been obliged to change their playing style when Hateley came into the side. When the line was led by St John, scarcely 5ft 8in (1.63m), and Hunt, a shade above 5ft 9in (1.66m), the emphasis was on passes to feet in and and around the penalty area. St John was a terrific header of the ball, with an astonishing ability to leap above the tallest of defenders, and Hunt also used his head to good effect. But the rhythm of the team had to be disrupted by the presence of Hateley, who was not as adept as the other two on the deck, and thrived on balls in the air.

Hateley said: 'I took the number nine jacket off Saint, which was a big honour, because he was a terrific player. He wore the ten shirt and played deeper, and I played up front with Roger Hunt. The team scored 90-odd goals that 1967-68 season, Roger got about 30 and I scored about 26. It was well over 50 between us, and most seasons it would have been enough to win the championship. We had Callaghan and Thompson on the wings throwing the ball over, and I made a lot of goals for Roger winning balls in the air. We had a very good team. We were unlucky to go out of the Cup when Jeff Astle of West Brom scored with a left-footer to knock us out. It must have been the only left-footed goal in his whole career.'

Hateley was replaced by Alun Evans, who became Britain's first £100,000 teenager when he joined from Wolves. 'Shanks said I was injury prone, and I didn't want to stay where I wasn't wanted,' Hateley said.

The 19-year-old new boy made an early impact but 1968-69 turned out to be another frustrating season at Anfield. Liverpool finished second in the table, six points behind Leeds, and there was no joy in the cups. Leicester City (of course) knocked them out of the FA Cup 1-0 in a fifth round replay at Anfield. And just to show that luck evens itself out over time, the Reds lost to Athletic Bilbao in the first round of the Fairs Cup – on the toss of a coin.

Liverpool had now endured three seasons without success, and they lurched further into decline in 1969-70. Finally, in February 1970, when the Reds lost an FA Cup quarter-final 1-0 away to Watford, a side from the lower reaches of the Division Two, Shankly set about dismantling his first great team. The nightmare on Vicarage Road changed everything.

50 Greatest Players

GERRY BYRNE Full back

Joined Liverpool: 1955 **From:** School

Debut: 28 September 1957 v Charlton (a), Division Two – lost 5-1

Appearances: 333 **Goals:** 4

Left Liverpool: 1969 (retired)

Honours won with Liverpool: Division One championship 1964, 1966; Division Two championship 1962; FA Cup winner 1965; 2 England caps

Byrne's finest hour was the 1965 FA Cup final. When he broke his collarbone in the early minutes it seemed inevitable that his game was over. In those pre-substitute days, the Reds would surely have lost to Leeds. Yet Byrne stayed on the field, right through the 90 minutes of normal time and the 30 minutes of extra time. All the while the broken bones were rubbing against each other, yet so stoically did Byrne bear the pain his Leeds opponents did not even realise he was injured. Liverpool won 2-1 and Bill Shankly said: 'They should give all the medals to Gerry Byrne.' It is odd to think that when Shankly first arrived at Anfield, Byrne was on the transfer list, his career floundering. He emerged to be a key Liverpool player throughout the 1960s.

Youth Has its Chance

Hunt had been sold to Bolton the previous December. Tommy Lawrence, Yeats, St John, Thompson and Strong soon lost their places. Into the side came talented youngsters like keeper Ray Clemence, who had been in the reserves since signing from Scunthorpe for £18,000 in 1967; Alec Lindsay, a left back who arrived from Bury for £67,000; Brian Hall, a Glaswegian midfielder; Steve Heighway, an old-school winger who had been playing for Skelmersdale United; John Toshack, a Welsh international centre forward who came from Cardiff for £110,000; and Larry Lloyd, a hulking Bristolian who had moved from Bristol Rovers for £50,000 in April 1969.

In laying the foundations for a glorious new era at Anfield, Shankly knew breaking up the old team was the right thing to do. He would have liked to have kept the old gang together for another couple of years, but in the end results forced his hand. The only doubt for Shankly was whether the new team he was putting together could match the exploits of the old one.

He knew that the fresh players he was introducing were fine footballers, but he still worried about the team's fate, and whether they could ever live up to the Yeatses, St Johns and Hunts. He confided in Tommy Smith, one of the players along with Callaghan and Lawler who survived the post-Watford

50 Greatest Players

TOMMY LAWRENCE Goalkeeper

Joined Liverpool: 1957 **From:** Warrington Town

Debut: 27 October 1962 v West Brom (a), Division One – lost 1-0

Appearances: 390

Left Liverpool: 1971 **For:** Tranmere Rovers

Honours won with Liverpool: Division One championship 1964, 1966; FA Cup winner 1965; 3 Scotland caps

'The Flying Pig' is not the most flattering nickname a goalkeeper has ever attracted, but Tommy Lawrence was a popular man at Anfield and his nickname was meant admiringly. Lawrence was a heavy man with a big, broad chest, and not especially tall. But he was also a fearless acrobat, and flung himself across the goal with the agility of a gymnast. Liverpool's success in the 1960s was based on a solid back-four, and Lawrence was a formidable final barrier. Lawrence was also known for his speed off his line, and the Reds' defence pushed up together knowing that Lawrence would deal with any long balls played in behind them, playing as an auxiliary sweeper. It was a system learned and perfected by Lawrence's willing understudy, Ray Clemence.

putsch, that his first aim was to avoid relegation in 1970-71. Just as it had been when he started building his first team, Shankly's priority was defence. 'You can add the frills later,' he reasoned. Shankly told Smith: 'Don't let any goals in. I don't care if we don't score any, I don't want to let any in. That way we'll get 42 points and we won't be relegated.'

The Reds were slightly more expansive than that, but not by much. The back line based on Clemence in goal, Lawler, Lloyd, Smith and Lindsay let in just 24 goals that season as Liverpool finished fifth. They only scored 42 themselves.

Liverpool also enjoyed a lengthy run in the Fairs Cup, beating their old rivals Ferencvaros, as well as Dinamo Bucharest, Hibernian and the powerful Bayern Munich on the way to the semi-finals, where they lost the tightest of contests with Leeds 1-0 on aggregate to a Billy Bremner goal at Anfield.

It was in the FA Cup that the Reds made significant strides. They beat Fourth Division Aldershot, Swansea of Division Three, Southampton from the First Division and Spurs in a replay to reach the semi-finals. Again hopes were high for the first-ever all-Merseyside Cup final, until the Reds were drawn to play Everton at Old Trafford in the semi-final.

Harry Catterick's team were the reigning League champions, but goals by Alun Evans and Brian Hall won the match for Liverpool after Alan Ball had given Everton the lead. Heighway showed he was the true heir to Peter Thompson by tormenting Everton down both wings to set up the goals.

Just as in 1950 Liverpool faced Arsenal at Wembley. The match was a typically tense affair, goalless after 90 minutes and exploding into life in extra-time, as Heighway shot Liverpool into the lead after two minutes. Arsenal, who had won the championship the previous Monday night, were a resilient side, though. They equalised through Eddie Kelly, then Charlie George let fly with a long-range winner to give the Gunners the Double.

Defeat did not shame Liverpool. Arsenal were a side at the zenith of their powers, while the Reds were a young team in the first stage of development. Shankly had seen enough to dream that his emerging team could equal their illustrious predecessors.

Emlyn Hughes said: 'That cup final was the start of another great period for Liverpool. It was an achievement for such a young and inexperienced team to have reached the final at all, and it showed we were heading the right way. The basis was there, and you had a team that had absorbed so much footballing wisdom, not just from people like Bill Shankly, Bob Paisley and Ronnie Moran, but from the older players, like St John, Yeats and Hunt. There was a sense of passing from one generation to the next that really began with the cup defeat at Watford.'

Larry Lloyd outjumps Arsenal's Peter Storey in the 1971 FA Cup final. Arsenal won the match 2-1 after extra time.

FA Cup final week of 1971 was also significant because it saw one of the key Liverpool signings of all time. Kevin Keegan, a little 20-year-old striker from Scunthorpe United, arrived at Anfield a few days before the match, and despite all the distractions Shankly found the time to recruit a player who had been watched and highly recommended by Fagan and Paisley.

It had taken less than five minutes to conclude the business. Shankly offered the boy £45 per week. Keegan took a deep breath, said he was on £35 at Scunthorpe (an exaggeration) and asked for £50. Shankly gave him the £50, and also promised £100 per match if he made the first team. It did not take long for Keegan to start earning his bonuses.

He caught the eye on a pre-season trip to Scandinavia, throwing everything he had into matches which other players treated as gentle warm-up games. He was also the most dedicated trainer any of the Liverpool staff had ever seen, and in the end Keegan gave Shankly little option: he had to pick him for the opening match of the 1971-72 season against Nottingham Forest. For

50 Greatest Players

IAN ST JOHN Forward

Joined Liverpool: 1961 **From:** Motherwell

Debut: 19 August 1961 v Bristol Rovers (a), Division Two – won 2-0

Appearances: 425 **Goals:** 118

Left Liverpool: 1971 **For:** Coventry City

Honours won with Liverpool: Division One championship 1964, 1966; Division Two championship 1962; FA Cup winner 1965; 14 Scotland caps

St John's arrival at Anfield marked the start of the club's rise to pre-eminence in English football. He was the attacking spark the team had been looking for. The Scottish striker formed a prolific partnership with Roger Hunt and Saint scored 18 as the Reds won the Second Division in his first season. He added 21 as Liverpool won the League in 1963-64. In later seasons St John played a deeper midfield role, giving him a platform to show his all-round skills, and he was a fount of attacking ideas for the rest of the 1960s. If he is remembered for one goal, it has to the header in May 1965 which beat Leeds in the FA Cup final.

£33,000, Shankly had bought the player who would take his solid new side up to the next level of achievement. He had found his frills.

Keegan's impact was immediate. In that first match against Forest at Anfield he scored the opener in a 3-1 victory. After that he was an automatic choice and went on to score nine league goals that season. Toshack, with whom Keegan formed a fabled partnership, top scored with 13 as Liverpool entered the last month vying with Leeds, Derby, Manchester City and Manchester United for top spot.

It came down to the last day of the season. Brian Clough's Derby had finished their matches and had gone on holiday to Majorca with 58 points in the bag. Liverpool could steal the title from them as long as they beat Arsenal at Highbury and fellow-challengers Leeds lost at Wolves.

Wolves did Liverpool a favour by beating Don Revie's side, but Liverpool plugged away against the Gunners and could not find the goal to win the title. Then with two minutes left Toshack burst the net. The Reds began celebrating the most dramatic conclusion to a season the Football League had ever seen only for the goal to be ruled out for offside. The match finished 0-0, and Clough had won the First Division while sitting in a bar in Spain.

At a cost of £33,000, Kevin Keegan's six years at Anfield made him one of Shankly's greatest signings.

Hughes said: 'It was an incredible finish to the season. With half-a-dozen games to go any one of five teams could have won the title. On the last day it was down to three, and when Tosh put the ball in against Arsenal, we thought we'd done it. But the referee disallowed it. The ref was Fitzpatrick, who had this habit of scooting away from you backwards after he'd made a decision you didn't agree with. He scooted half the length of the pitch, with me chasing him and calling him a fat little bastard. I couldn't catch him.

'Although we'd lost the title we had become the team to beat again. All the pieces in the jigsaw were in place.'

Liverpool put matters right the very next season, holding off a challenge from Arsenal to win Shankly's third championship. Again, continuity played a huge part in the team's effectiveness. Only 16 players were used, reserve keeper Frankie Lane playing just once and utility defender Trevor Storton only four times. Callaghan, Lawler and Lloyd were ever-present, and Clemence, Heighway, Hughes, Keegan and Lindsay all played at least 37

50 Greatest Players

RON YEATS Centre half

Joined Liverpool: 1961 **From:** Dundee United

Debut: 19 August 1961 v Bristol Rovers (a), Division Two – won 2-0

Appearances: 454 **Goals:** 16

Left Liverpool: 1971 **For:** Tranmere Rovers

Honours won with Liverpool: Division One championship 1964, 1966; Division Two championship 1962; FA Cup winner 1965; 2 Scotland caps

Occasionally, the outrageous Shankly stories are true. It is a fact that after Yeats had just signed for Liverpool, the gentlemen of the Press were invited into the dressing room to take a walk around the hulking new centre half. The tale shows how proud Shankly was of his recruit. Yeats was to be the defensive rock on which Shankly built a winning team. Along with St John, the arrival of Yeats at Anfield marked the end of a miserable chapter in the Reds' history and the start of the glory days. Yeats' strengths were not subtle, but were priceless to Shankly. He was a physically commanding presence, brave as a lion and a fine captain.

games. It was a feature of the team that goals flew in from all positions. Keegan and Toshack were joint top-scorers with 13, but Peter Cormack, Phil Boersma, Hughes and Heighway all chipped in. Barring mathematical miracles, Liverpool wrapped up the championship with a 2-0 win over Leeds at Anfield, with Cormack and Keegan getting the goals that brought the First Division trophy back to the club after seven years. And they weren't finished yet. Liverpool were closing in on their first-ever European trophy.

All season long they had been battling through a trans-continental assault course known as the UEFA Cup. Shankly rated it a tougher competition than even the European Cup, and not just because there were more games to play. He reasoned that the sides who competed in it tended to be improving, hungry teams eager to prove themselves in continental competition. To reach the final the Reds had to slog their way to Germany and back three times, and also faced trips to Greece and north London.

European Blueprint

After their overseas disappointments in the 1960s a European trophy had become something of an obsession for Shankly. He was haunted by memories of Milan in 1965, when a rogue referee cost him the chance of beating his mate Jock Stein in becoming the first British manager to win the European Cup. Now his team began perfecting a style of play that provided the blueprint for triumph after triumph on foreign fields.

A feature of the 1972-73 UEFA Cup campaign was the assurance of the team's displays away from home. They became masters at slowing games down, playing keep-ball, calming the crowd, and taking the heat out of matches. Liverpool dispatched Eintracht Frankfurt, AEK Athens, Dinamo Berlin and Dinamo Dresden without losing an away leg, and conceded just one away goal.

The semi-final pitted them against Tottenham, and Alec Lindsay's solitary goal at Anfield looked a tenuous advantage to take to White Hart Lane for the second leg. The lead was wiped out by Martin Peters in the second half, and as waves of white shirts poured towards Clemence's goal, Liverpool looked in danger of losing their place in the final. Then Heighway broke away to score, and even though Peters grabbed a second to give Spurs a 2-1 win on the night the Reds were through on away goals.

50 Greatest Players

PETER THOMPSON Winger

Joined Liverpool: 1963 **From:** Preston North End

Debut: 24 August 1963 v Blackburn (a), Division One – won 2-1

Appearances: 415 **Goals:** 54

Left Liverpool: 1973 **For:** Bolton Wanderers

Honours won with Liverpool: Division One championship 1964, 1966; FA Cup winner 1965; 16 England caps

When he signed from Preston for £40,000 Thompson became the club's record buy, but Shankly knew exactly what he was getting for his money. There was almost certainly never a better exponent of the dribbler's art at Liverpool than Peter Thompson. Bill Shankly used to say that if the team needed a rest they could give it to Thompson, and the winger would dribble it round the opposition for the rest of the match if necessary. But Thompson was more than a footballing variety act. He used his ability to hurt defenders, and rounded off his work with crosses which created dozens of goals for the likes of Hunt and St John. He was a key weapon in the Reds' attacking armoury which dominated English football in the mid-1960s.

Tosh Dropped

Their opponents in the final were yet another German side, Borussia Mönchengladbach. The UEFA Cup final was played over two legs in those days, and when Liverpool hosted the first game their preparation was far from smooth. Shankly decided that John Toshack's power in the air would be superfluous against the Germans, and chose to play Brian Hall up front with Keegan instead. Toshack was not happy about missing out on a European final, had cross words with Shankly, and stormed out.

The match kicked off amid driving rain and the pitch quickly became waterlogged. The referee had no option but to postpone the match until the next evening. Even though he had only seen 25 minutes of action, Shankly decided that his team selection was wrong. He spotted a weakness in the German defence's ability to deal with crosses, and resolved to play Toshack the next day. The Welshman was brooding at home when Shankly phoned him late that night. By now Toshack had made his mind up to demand a transfer, and was about to give Shankly both barrels when the manager told him he was back in the team.

Spurs' Martin Peters watches Tommy Smith take control in Liverpool's 2-1 win at White Hart Lane in November 1972.

That wasn't the end of the disharmony. Although he had told Toshack he was playing, Shankly forgot to tell Hall he wasn't, until shortly before kick off. Now it was Hall's turn to feel aggrieved. Yet despite all the ructions behind the scenes Shankly's instincts proved correct. Liverpool won the first leg 3-0, Keegan scoring two and Lloyd soaring above the German defence to head another.

The key moment came when Borussia were awarded a penalty, and their star striker, Jupp Heynckes, stepped up for the chance to score an important away goal. Ray Clemence saved it.

Clemence said: 'I watched Heynckes take a penalty in the semi-final on television and decided to dive the same way. It was a reward for my homework.'

'It was a great occasion,' said Hughes. 'Toshack and Keegan murdered them. We were in a great position for the second leg.' Even with that handy lead Liverpool spent the first-half of the second leg on the ropes. Borussia battered them from the off, and went in at half-time 2-0 up. If they kept it up in the second half, the Reds' lead would surely be obliterated.

Hughes said: 'We came off at half-time panting like dogs, and Shanks said to us, "Don't worry, boys. You've won. They've blown themselves out." And he was right. We didn't cruise in the second half because you never can in a football match, but we held on well enough to win 3-2 on aggregate. It was such an honour to be in the first Liverpool team ever to win a European trophy.

'It was a superb time to be a Liverpool player. You were part of a great team that was on the verge of dominating Europe. The 60s side had given us the basis of how to play. They showed us you had to play in a different way

Action from the 1973 UEFA Cup final first leg as Chris Lawler connects with a high volley and Gunter Netzer (Borussia Mönchengladbach) tries to intercept.

in Europe. It was different from the league, where it's all about getting the ball forward quickly, huffing and puffing and fighting and scratching. We learned to play nice and easy, especially away from home, putting the home crowd to sleep, and accepting that 0-0 was a great result. The lessons we were learning paved the way not just for the greatest era in Liverpool's history, but for the greatest era of any side in the history of English football.'

Leeds Set the Pace

Liverpool's burgeoning expertise in continental competition could not save them from an early European Cup exit at the hands of Red Star Belgrade in 1973-74. In the league, too, the Reds struggled, failing to keep up with Leeds who set a new record by reeling off 29 matches before their first defeat of the season. By the time Stoke beat Revie's side in February Liverpool were nine points behind, and although towards the end Leeds faltered and Liverpool chased them hard, there was an inevitability about Leeds's championship victory.

Peter Cormack, who had joined the club from Nottingham Forest in the summer of 1972, said: 'Leeds had built up a huge lead at one point, but we got it back to about three points at one stage. We lost it one night in April at Sheffield United. We outplayed them, just couldn't score, and lost 1-0. That finished us.

'Every pre-season Shanks used to say whoever finished ahead of Leeds would win the title. They had a great side, a great manager, and they always seemed to come second or thereabouts.'

Liverpool had better fortune in the FA Cup, beginning with a third round victory against Keegan's home-town club, Doncaster Rovers. The south Yorkshire side were average even by Fourth Division standards, and at the end of the season they had to apply for re-election to the Football League. But they fought Liverpool valiantly at Anfield, and a 2-2 draw was harsh on Rovers. Keegan's two goals saved Liverpool's skins, and Kopites with good memories might have recalled a similar Cup tie against Stockport nine years earlier, when a lower-league side outplayed Liverpool at Anfield before succumbing in a replay. Liverpool duly won the rematch in Yorkshire, only to come up against more cussed opposition at Anfield in the Fourth Round.

Second Division Carlisle, Shankly's old club, held the Reds 0-0 before goals from Phil Boersma and Toshack at Brunton Park set up a fifth round tie at home to Ipswich Town. Hall and Keegan scored the goals which took Liverpool within two games of Wembley. The quarter-final was at Second Division Bristol City, where a Toshack goal was enough to take the Reds into the last four. Now they faced their old nemeses, Leicester City, at Old Trafford, where the teams drew 0-0. Liverpool turned on the style in the replay at Villa Park, Hall, Keegan and Toshack all scoring in one of the great Liverpool cup performances.

Supermac Eats his Words

The Reds were favourites to win the final against Newcastle United, who had suffered a mediocre season in the First Division. Most of the pre-match buzz centred on the Geordies' garrulous centre forward, Malcolm 'Supermac' Macdonald, who entertained anyone in ear-shot with lurid descriptions of the mayhem he was about to visit on the Liverpool back-four. In the event he barely got a kick as Liverpool swept to a 3-0 victory, playing the kind of perpetual motion passing game that was Shankly's ideal. By the end of the game the manager was conducting the massed Red choirs in the stands as his team put on an exhibition.

Cormack said: 'That was the highlight of my career. It gave me so much satisfaction to have a cup winner's medal. The whole week was unforgettable, and I didn't know what pressure meant until then. It built up all week, and just took over everything. There was so much going on in and around the game. We even made an LP!

'It all boiled up to the moment when we walked out of the tunnel for the match, and to see all the supporters there, and to feel their expectation, it really hits you. I can understand how people freeze in that atmosphere.

'In terms of the match, I'd say that the final was the easiest game of the whole cup run. We could have gone out at home to Doncaster, when one of their players hit the bar with five minutes to go. But that was a year when the best team won the cup. That team played some lovely passing football. No disrespect to Larry Lloyd, but Phil Thompson had come in to play centre half with Emlyn Hughes, and we were passing the ball out from defence more than ever, and there were good passers all over the field. It was a pleasure to play in that side.'

Of all the numerous civic receptions Liverpool teams have enjoyed down the years, the one in May 1974 when Shankly's team came back with a second FA Cup stands out. It was the occasion when Shankly uttered one of his most famous one-liners. Before going out onto the balcony of St George's Hall with his players, Shankly took Brian Hall to one side. 'Son, who's that Chinaman? The one with the sayings and the book'. Hall, imagining that the old boy was beginning to lose his grip, answered, 'Chairman Mao, boss?' 'Aye, that's the fellow,' Shankly said. Moments later Shankly surveyed the

Great Matches

FA CUP FINAL

Wembley, 4 May 1974
Attendance: 100,000

Liverpool 3 — **Newcastle United 0**
Heighway
Keeagn 2

This was the model Liverpool performance, reserved for what was destined to be Bill Shankly's last competitive game as manager. He retired two months after his team's clinical dissection of Newcastle United.

The run-up to the game was all about how, in one of the more infuriating footballing cliches, 'Newcastle's name was on the Cup.' It is true, the Geordies enjoyed outrageous amounts of luck to reach Wembley. They had scraped through replays against Scunthorpe and non-League Hendon. They were even given a chance, ludicrously, to replay their quarter-final against Nottingham Forest, who were leading 3-1 when the game was abandoned after a pitch invasion by Geordie fans. Once they reached the final, Newcastle's centre forward Malcolm Macdonald wasted no opportunity to explain exactly what he was going to do to the Liverpool defence. So many empty words.

Liverpool dominated from first kick to last, although it took them until the second half to open the scoring. It looked like Alec Lindsay had broken the deadlock soon after the break but the effort was disallowed, but only 13 minutes had passed before a Tommy Smith cross brushed off Brian Hall's boot only to end up on the end of Kevin Keegan's. He duly thumped in a right foot shot past the despairing McFaul. Liverpool were rampant. Steve Heighway scored a second, running on to John Toshack's flick from Ray Clemence's monster clearance and then with two minutes left, a mesmerising 12-pass move including flicks, deft passes and one-twos, ended with the ball reaching Keegan on the far post. He obliged with a simple side-footed strike. Shankly spent the last minutes urging his team to put on an exhibition of the passing football he loved to see, and also conducting the Liverpool supporters in the stands. The loudest chant of all: 'Supermac, Superstar, how many goals have you scored so far?'

Before Phil Thompson tucked his winner's medal in his pocket he had to remove the Newcastle number nine from it first. That is where Malcolm Macdonald had spent his Saturday afternoon.

Liverpool: Clemence, Smith, Lindsay, Thompson, Cormack, Hughes, Keegan, Hall, Heighway, Toshack, Callaghan

Newcastle United: McFaul, Clark, Kennedy, McDermott, Howard, Moncur, Smith (Gibb), Cassidy, Macdonald, Tudor, Hibbitt

Referee: G. Kew

vast crowd assembled in the city, held out his arms for silence, and a hush descended. Shankly intoned, 'Chairman Mao has never seen such a display of Red power.' The roars of acclaim could be heard in Manchester.

'They were some amazing sights when we got back to Liverpool with that cup,' said Cormack. 'There were patients being pushed out of hospitals still in their beds, all decorated with red, to wave to us. People were coming out with their dogs dressed in red shirts and scarves.'

Even on that day, amid all the adulation, Shankly was harbouring a secret. He had decided to resign. The news broke on an unsuspecting city on 12 July 1974, when club chairman John Smith addressed a press conference, which newspapermen thought had been called to announce the signing of Ray Kennedy. Smith announced: 'It is with great regret that as chairman of the board I have to inform you that Mr Shankly has intimated to us that he wishes to retire.'

Liverpool without Shankly was unimaginable. Cormack said: 'I was driving back from a trip to the Lakes, and heard the news on the radio. I could not believe it. To the players he was a legend, the best manager in the world. He had the respect of the whole city, and he was a big part of my life.'

Why?

After the truth of it had sunk in, people's first question was: why? Shankly said that after 15 years in the job he was tired and wanted a rest. His wife,

Steve Heighway tucks away Liverpool's second and the cup is Anfield-bound.

Ness, had been ill, and he wished to spend more time with her. Shankly knew that it can't have been much fun being a football widow for so long, and she deserved more of his time. He counted up the number of occasions when he had taken his wife out in the previous years, and the figure he came up with was two: once to the theatre, once to a garden fete.

It is true, in that last 1973-74 season Shankly looked every one of his 60 years, but people read into his resignation more than a simple desire to spend more time at home. It was suggested that Shankly was unhappy with the direction in which the club was moving. When Smith took over as chairman he began clawing back power that Shankly had fought for – the power to run the club his way, with total control of transfers in and out.

It was fitting that Shankly's resignation was announced on the day that Ray Kennedy joined the club. It was a deal largely carried out by Smith, not Shankly. Kennedy was a player Shankly admired, but he was used to making all the running in transfer deals. Now Smith had usurped his position as the main mover in player recruitment. The chairman demanded that the board should have a right of veto over any player Shankly wanted to buy. Shankly did not make trouble over this stipulation, but it is unlikely he was sanguine about the state of affairs. If Shankly feared that directors would dabble increasingly in team affairs, he was justified. When Bob Paisley took over, his sphere of influence did not extend much further than Melwood. Transfers were handled by the board. For Shankly, it was turning the clock back two decades. It was not as it had been.

Worse indignities were to follow for Shankly once Paisley had been installed as his successor. The club didn't know what to do with Shankly, and Shankly didn't know what to do with himself.

He was offered a nebulous role of general manager at the club, the kind of sinecure which his great friend Matt Busby was given at Old Trafford. Shankly turned it down; it was too soon, and he really did want a break. It has been suggested that he later regretted his decision to reject the position, and would have liked a formal role at the club. But the post was not offered twice. Likewise, he was never given the option of becoming a director: he had been the scourge of the species throughout his career, and they weren't about to let him become one of them now.

As the 1974-75 season got underway, Shankly could not help turning up to Melwood every day, to go for a run and to see his players. But the players still called him 'Boss', and with Paisley now in charge, that situation could not be tolerated. Shankly was told he could train at Melwood in the afternoons when everyone had gone home. Unsurprisingly, Shankly

Great Managers – 1959-74

BILL SHANKLY

Bill Shankly won more than mere trophies in his 15-year spell as Liverpool manager (although heaven knows he won enough of those). He won the hearts of an entire city.

Right from the first day he nosed his Austin A40 through the gates of Melwood, Shankly put his whole being into turning the club around and making it the mightiest in Britain. Although the European Cups came after he had retired, Shankly laid the foundations for Liverpool to become the greatest club on the continent.

When you look at what Shankly achieved, it is no wonder the supporters loved him. He took a failing Second Division outfit with a crumbling ground to the First Division championship inside five years. The club's first FA Cup followed in 1965, and the title was recaptured a year later. Shankly had the energy and ability to break up that team when it was on its last legs, to build another great side which took the League title, another FA Cup and the UEFA Cup in the 1970s. By sheer force of will and strength of character he had transformed Liverpool Football Club and made it one of the greatest sporting institutions in the world.

Shankly, (upper picture) as a young manager at a mediocre Liverpool and (lower picture) saying farewell to fans of the giant football club he had created.

nurtured a bitter resentment at the treatment he received from the club he rightly felt he had raised to greatness.

To be fair to the club, the slights Shankly suffered had more to do with insensitivity on Liverpool's part than with malice. They appeared to see him as just another ex-employee, who could be packed off with a thank-you. His parting gift from the club, although generous enough in its way, typified the gulf that separated them. He was given a Ford Capri, a flashy motor car for the least flashy man in Liverpool. They did not seem to appreciate that Liverpool was always more than just a job to Shankly. It was his life, and he couldn't cut his ties with the club overnight.

He found a warmer welcome at Bellefield, Everton's training ground near his home, and he started going there most days for a cup of tea and a chat with friends like Mick Lyons and Howard Kendall. How ironic that after a career baiting Evertonians he should find a haven among them in his later years. Shankly also did some work for other clubs as a consultant, helping Ron Yeats and John King at Tranmere and John Toshack at Swansea among many. He even gave a team talk for Tommy Docherty at Manchester United.

Cormack said: 'His departure could have been handled a bit better. The club could have made him honorary president or something like that, but then maybe they thought that was unfair on Bob Paisley, to have Shanks overseeing him. My feelings are that the club would have done anything for him, but I've no doubts that it helped bring his life to an end early. Liverpool was his routine, it was his whole life and he had nothing to replace it. I don't think he could cope after giving up the thing he loved doing.'

For all Paisley's later success, there is no doubt that the nature of the club changed with Shankly's departure. European Cups and Doubles came the club's way, but some remained nostalgic for the days of Shankly. Keegan, perhaps the greatest Shankly signing of them all, said in his autobiography: 'As much as I liked Bob Paisley, the club died a little when Shanks left... Something very big had gone for me when Shanks walked out of the door.'

Chapter Six: 1974-77
Kings of Europe

The first match of a new age at Anfield was not a happy occasion. Liverpool played Leeds in the Charity Shield at Wembley, and although they won the match on penalties the game came to be remembered for a punch-up between Keegan and the Leeds captain Billy Bremner. They were both sent off.

As the disgraced flyweights left the pitch they removed their jerseys and threw them on the ground. Perhaps they felt embarrassed about the girlish slaps they had exchanged, a flurry of ineffectual wafts which shamed Bremner especially. He was the so-called hardman. Keegan, at least, was an effete striker and could be excused his lack of a decent right hand. Whatever, the shirt-throwing action was deemed to be incendiary in the extreme particularly as this was the first Charity Shield to be broadcast live on television. Millions watched Bremner and Keegan's petulant, though hardly malevolent, conduct. The full majesty of the Football Association disciplinary committee was

Referee Mr Matthewson restrains Kevin Keegan after his bust-up with Billy Bremner in the 1974 FA Charity Shield against Leeds United.

brought to bear on the unlucky players, and each was fined £500. Even harsher, they were both banned for 11 matches. It was a sad departure for Shankly, who had been allowed to lead his team out one last time at Wembley.

Paisley was livid at the treatment Keegan received. A campaign had been waged in the press to make an example of Bremner and Keegan, and questions about the matter had even been raised in parliament. The new Liverpool manager felt the FA were over-reacting to outside pressure. 'People who don't know how to run the country are trying to run football, which they know even less about,' he said.

Paisley's first season did not improve once the real action kicked off. Larry Lloyd transferred to Coventry City, and for the first time in living memory the team suffered a rash of injuries. From November until March they could only win four games out of 20 in the league, and the Reds also lost in the FA Cup away to Ipswich in the fourth round. The Cup-Winners' Cup campaign also ground to a halt against their old Hungarian rivals, Ferencvaros.

The season, however, would not be a complete write-off. All the time Paisley was bedding in new players, subtly changing the team he had inherited. Phil Neal replaced Chris Lawler at right back. And he began to

50 Greatest Players

CHRIS LAWLER Full Back

Joined Liverpool: 1959 **From:** School

Debut: 20 March 1963 v West Brom (h), Division One – drew 2-2

Appearances: 549 **Goals:** 61

Left Liverpool: 1975 **For:** Portsmouth

Honours won with Liverpool: Division One championship 1966, 1973; FA Cup winner 1965; UEFA Cup winner 1973; 4 England caps

Liverpool-born Lawler spanned the generations between the first great Shankly side of the 1960s and the fine side which emerged in the 1970s. His breakthrough came in the FA Cup-winning season of 1965, and he barely missed a match for the next eight years. He was a quiet man off the pitch and undemonstrative on it, but Shankly relied on his unflappable presence at right back season after season. He was a solid defender, and also a surprisingly regular goalscorer – in 1969-70 he hit a remarkable 10 League goals from open play.

reshape the midfield, with Terry McDermott arriving from Newcastle and Jimmy Case coming through from the reserves to make his debut on the last day of the season. Paisley also had the idea of putting Ray Kennedy into the midfield. The ex-Arsenal man had lost some of his sharpness up front, but Paisley admired his passing ability and skill on the ball, and knew he could still do a job for the team. Other managers might have eased Kennedy out of the club. Paisley resuscitated his flagging career. By the end of Paisley's first season Liverpool's form had improved so much that they ended up in second place behind Derby County.

Three-cornered Fight

The following season turned up one of the most exciting duels for the championship in years. For much of 1975-76 it was a three-cornered fight between Liverpool, Tommy Docherty's resurgent Manchester United, and Dave Sexton's attractive Queens Park Rangers. In the final weeks it culminated in a battle down the stretch between the Reds and Rangers.

All season long people had been waiting for Rangers' challenge to blow up. The team was stuffed with entertainers like Stan Bowles, Gerry Francis, Don Givens and Dave Thomas, but they didn't seem to be the kind of team who could grind out results over a 42-match season. Yet after they played their final game the west Londoners found themselves one point clear of Liverpool. The Reds, though, still had another game to play, 10 days later, away to Wolves, who faced relegation if they lost it.

It must have been an excruciating week and a half for Rangers, who had never won the title. All that time they were champions-in-waiting – waiting for Liverpool to slip up. They must have been even more on edge on the night the Reds played the championship decider at Molineux.

In the crucial game Wolves took the lead and were still leading as the match ebbed into the final 15 minutes. The championship was heading for Loftus Road. Jimmy Case said: 'We heard later that the Rangers lads were drinking champagne and had the cigars on the go'. But Wolves' world collapsed over the closing stages as goals by Keegan, Toshack and Kennedy gave Paisley his first championship as manager.

'When Ray Kennedy tucked his goal away we knew we'd done it, and the celebrations started,' said Case. 'There were amazing scenes all the way up the M6 back to Liverpool with red and white everywhere. There was a huge party going on. The fans had been incredible all night. So many turned up that they couldn't all get into the ground and when we were getting changed for the match you could see them, all these Liverpool fans still waiting to get

The Liverpool players celebrate winning the league championship at Molineux in May 1976. From left: Tommy Smith, Ray Kennedy, Ian Callaghan, David Fairclough, Phil Thompson, Phil Neal, Emlyn Hughes, Jimmy Case and Kevin Keegan.

in. Phil Thompson and Terry McDermott opened the dressing room door which led to the outside, and they all started filing through. The supporters walked through the dressing room, through the other door right on to the terraces. It was so funny, and you just felt, "How can we not win for these people?" That sort of thing is illegal now, but it used to go on then.'

The Reds' campaign wasn't finished yet. All season long they had been picking their careful way though a hazardous UEFA Cup campaign, which featured wins over Hibernian, Real Sociedad, Slask Wroclaw from Poland and Dinamo Dresden on the way to the semi-finals. There, the Reds faced Barcelona in the first leg away from home, days before the decisive Wolves match.

Cruyff and Neeskens

The Catalan side looked a frightening proposition, with players like Cruyff and Neeskens in their ranks. Case said: 'Neeskens was a powerhouse in midfield. Cruyff was the best player I ever played against. I'd always admired him. He was the fastest thing you have even seen over the first few yards, and you had to think hard how to stop him.

'I was playing right-midfield, so as often as not I was up against him, and you just had to do your best to stop him getting the ball. Every time it even edged his way, I'd get close to Cruyff. But not too close, because if he got the ball he'd get away from you and be at the by-line before you'd breathed. It's occasions like that which tax your football brain. It was exciting playing against him.'

Case and his team-mates must have done reasonably well because the unflustered Reds won in the Camp Nou, managing a 1-0 win through Toshack's goal. It was a performance which showed why Liverpool were such a good side, Case said. 'The whole team had the technique, the passing, the movement, the control of the ball and we could play at a reasonable tempo,' he said. 'But you need more. You also need strength of thought, to do the right things when the match becomes a game of chess. You have to out-think the opposition as well as out-play them. That Liverpool side knew exactly what it was doing, and we had the players to put it into practice.'

Victory in Barcelona was also a tribute to a masterful Paisley team talk. Case said: 'We had our team meeting in the chapel which they have in the ground there, because it was the only quiet room in the whole place. Bob

Tommy Smith beats Barcelona's Johan Cruyff to the ball in the UEFA Cup semi-final second leg. The game at Anfield finished 1-1, but the Reds went through after a win 1-0 in the Camp Nou.

started talking about their winger, and he couldn't pronounce his name. He had a few goes at it, then gave up, and said, "Anyway, you have to watch him. He's not that fast, but he's quite nippy." That was Bob. To an outsider it might have sounded like he was talking in code, but we knew what he meant.'

In the second leg a 1-1 draw at Anfield, which came courtesy of a rare Phil Thompson goal, was enough to take Liverpool through to the final against Bruges.

The first leg was at Anfield, and the newly-crowned Belgian champions rocked Liverpool by racing 2-0 up inside the first quarter of an hour. 'At that point we were just trying to retrieve anything we could to take into the second leg,' said Case. Liverpool fought a rearguard action, gradually asserted control over the game, and flooded forward in the second half to win the leg 3-2. Case scored the second.

'Somebody had a shot, and I could see the ball was going to hit the post,' Case said. 'The posts weren't perfectly round, and it was hard to predict where the ball was going to bounce out to, so all the while I was watching the ball and trying to adjust my feet. The ball came straight to me, and I was able to jump and flick it in.'

The second leg was played a fortnight after the title-decider at Wolves, and Liverpool were in no mood to let a League and UEFA Cup double slip away. The Belgians scored from the spot, but Keegan crashed in a free-kick that was enough to recapture the trophy.

Jimmy Case scores Liverpool's second goal in the UEFA Cup final first leg against Bruges in April 1976.

After taking a year to settle in to his new job, Paisley had clearly got Liverpool back on track. His victory speech was typically self-effacing. 'Bill Shankly set such a high standard,' he said. 'Liverpool have been geared to this sort of thing for 15 years. I have just helped things along.'

It was a typical Paisley comment. Case said: 'He was such a modest bloke. Some managers are flamboyant. They like to go in front of the cameras and talk, but Bob was the opposite. When we travelled away you would see him in the hotel, queuing up for breakfast wearing his slippers. It's hard to imagine George Graham doing that. You couldn't meet anyone more down to earth than Bob.'

Liverpool had served a long apprenticeship in European competition, and 1976-77 was destined to be the season all the years of hard work and hard knocks paid off. The European Cup was finally captured in May 1977, and that victory over Borussia Mönchengladbach might so easily have crowned a glorious treble. The only obstacle between Liverpool and that achievement turned out to be Jimmy Greenhoff's back.

Fortress Anfield

The Reds retained their championship largely thanks to impregnable home form. Of the 21 league matches they played at Anfield, 18 were won, three drawn, and not a single one lost. Ipswich and Manchester City chased them for much of the season but Liverpool went into the penultimate match, at home to West Ham, needing just a draw for the title. The game finished 0-0, and the first leg of the treble was safe.

One week later Liverpool played Manchester United in the FA Cup final, after a run to Wembley that was not without alarms. In round three Liverpool beat Third Division Crystal Palace 3-2 in a replay after being held 0-0 at Anfield. Then the Reds enjoyed three straight home wins to reach the semi-finals: 3-0 against Carlisle United, who were on their way to relegation from the First Division; 3-1 against Oldham Athletic of the Second Division; and 2-0 against First Division Middlesbrough. Now came the toughest test of all: Everton in the semi-finals.

The game was played at Maine Road, and still rankles in the minds of Evertonians, who have never forgiven the Welsh referee, Clive Thomas, who disallowed Bryan Hamilton's late 'winner'. Terry McDermott lobbed Liverpool into the lead, then Everton's Duncan McKenzie equalised. Jimmy Case headed the Reds back in front, only for Bruce Rioch to make the score 2-2. In the last moments Hamilton diverted the ball past Ray Clemence, seemingly with his hip, for what looked like a good goal – but Thomas blew up. He refused to say why Hamilton's effort had been struck out: handball, offside? Thomas wasn't saying, and the game ended all square. The replay, also at Maine Road, was clear cut. Neal rammed in a penalty, Case made it two and Ray Kennedy sealed the 3-0 win which took the Reds to Wembley.

Kevin Keegan takes on Manchester United captain Martin Buchan in the 1977 FA Cup final. Liverpool lost 2-1 and hopes of a treble disappeared.

By their own admission, Liverpool did not play at their best against Tommy Docherty's United. The champions were favourites, but they could not find a way past Alex Stepney in the United goal, and half-time came with the score 0-0. All the goal action was compressed into a five-minute spell early in the second half. First Stuart Pearson planted a shot past Clemence to put United ahead. Then Case, the man of the match, controlled an awkward high ball on the edge of the box before swivelling and lifting a volley over Stepney for one of the great FA Cup final goals. But all the luck was with United. Lou Macari aimed a shot which was heading wide until it struck Jimmy Greenhoff on the back. The ball span goalwards, eluding Clemence and Joey Jones before crossing the line. The hopes of a treble were lost.

But Liverpool could not afford to spend time moping about what might have been. Four days later they faced the biggest game in the club's history: the European Cup final in Rome's Stadio Olimpico.

The European Cup run had begun quietly enough for Liverpool the previous September, when the Irish champions, Crusaders, visited Anfield for the first round, first leg. A crowd of just 22,442 saw Neal and Toshack score to set the Reds on their way. The return leg was even easier, a 5-0 procession, with David Johnson twice, Keegan, McDermott and Heighway getting goals.

The second round proved far trickier. Liverpool travelled to Trabzonspor, Turkey, in the first leg, and were thankful to survive food poisoning, hostile surroundings and a 'one-eyed' ref to escape with a 1-0 defeat. That deficit was turned around in the home leg, with Heighway, Johnson and Keegan securing a 3-0 win. That set up one of the most memorable ties in Liverpool's European history, against the champions of France, St Etienne, in the quarter-finals.

Introducing 'Supersub'

Liverpool were away for the first leg and were taken aback by the quality of the opposition. They boasted wonderful players like Bathenay and Rocheteau in their side, and as the French zipped the ball around the park and rained shots in on Ray Clemence's goal, it looked like St Etienne might wrap the tie up on their own ground. A series of fine saves kept the score down to 1-0, but against opposition as good as this, Liverpool knew they faced a tough task at home. It turned out to be one of the greatest nights Anfield has seen, and was especially memorable for David Fairclough, the Reds' striker and boyhood Liverpudlian.

After a couple of minutes Kevin Keegan had scored with a good piece of fortune. He lobbed the keeper who was slightly indecisive and the breeze took it in. That put the tie level overall, and Liverpool attacked frantically, desperate for a winner, but could not break through the St Etienne defence. Half-time came and went with the tie still poised at 1-1. Then Liverpool were rocked back when Bathenay launched a 40-yarder past Clemence. Liverpool now needed two goals to reach the semi-finals. Tired from their efforts, and stymied by the quality and discipline of the opposition, it looked all over.

'There was a sensation that it had gone then,' said Fairclough. 'We hadn't looked like scoring one, never mind two. It looked out of our reach. I was told to warm up with 20 minutes to go, and then Ray Kennedy scored. Bob Paisley just said to me, "Get out there and see if you can get a piece of the action." It was the general order he issued, see if you can get on the end of something.' With eight minutes left, Fairclough did just that.

'Ray Kennedy played it forward, I wrestled the ball off Lopez about 35 yards out and had a clear run on goal,' he said. 'Then I was just making sure I hit the target. The keeper came roaring out. I'd learned that if you hit it close to the keeper he struggled to get down to block it. It might have seemed that it wasn't the best-hit shot but it was placed under his body.

'I was quite cool until the noise hit me. Then I realised I'd done something special. When you're playing it's like you go deaf, or you're under water. You concentrate that hard, and all you're aware of is a kind of buzz around you. But after I scored I wheeled in front of the Kop, they were going berserk and Jimmy Case caught hold of me.

50 Greatest Players

KEVIN KEEGAN Striker

Joined Liverpool: 1971 **From:** Scunthorpe United

Debut: 14 August 1971 v Nottingham Forest (h), Division One – won 3-1

Appearances: 323 **Goals:** 100

Left Liverpool: 1977 **For:** Hamburg

Honours won with Liverpool: European Cup winner 1977; League Division One championship 1973, 1976, 1977; FA Cup winner 1974; UEFA Cup winner 1973, 1976; 28 England caps

Shankly plundered the ranks of Scunthorpe United once again to find the most important player of Liverpool's early 1970s renaissance. While Keegan's Old Showground forerunner, Ray Clemence, kept a tight ship at the back, Keegan was a fertile source of attacking inspiration at the other end. With Toshack he formed one of the best striking double-acts British football has seen. He took a leap into the unknown with Hamburg in 1977, and left behind a glorious memory: his last match for Liverpool was the 3-1 win over Mönchengladbach in Rome, a night when Keegan tormented his opposite number, Berti Vogts, and did much to win the club's first European Cup.

Keegan wins the penalty that sealed the European Cup for Liverpool in 1977.

'Once the final whistle went I just felt relief. Some of the older players went mad, because they knew what it all meant. I was younger, I thought this happened all the time. It was quite late, and I wasn't a big drinker, but I said to my pal, "Shall we go for a pint?" So we went past this pub where we used to go, the Bulldog. It was half past 10, and it was absolutely packed. We didn't think we'd get a drink. We thought Ted would have put the towels up. So I just went home and watched the match on telly with my mum. It was only later I realised I probably would have got a pint. Someone said, "That night the whole of Liverpool was yours." But I didn't realise what I'd done.'

By comparison, the semi-final against Switzerland's top team, Zurich, was a gentle workout. The Reds won 3-1 away, with two goals from Neal and one from Heighway, then reached the final by completing a 6-1 aggregate victory at Anfield in front of 50,611, with two goals from Case and one from Keegan.

Top-quality Internationals

Their opponents in the final, Borussia Mönchengladbach, did not have the glamour or the history of their German rivals, Bayern Munich, but they were nevertheless a dangerous side. They had top-quality internationals like Berti Vogts, Rainer Bonhof and Uli Stielike in the side, as well as the European Player of the Year, Denmark's Allan Simonsen, up front. But Liverpool always looked the better team on the night, and were deserved winners.

Jimmy Case said: 'That result showed the strength of that Liverpool team, because of the build-up to the game. We had lost four days earlier in the FA Cup final to Manchester United, a game we should have won, and that left us devastated. But you can have all the technique in the world, you still need the temperament to succeed, and that's what we had. When the night of the European Cup final arrived we were ready.'

After the match the Liverpool players headed for a party at Rome's Holiday Inn to celebrate the greatest triumph in the club's history. It turned into a joyous free-for-all, as what seemed like the entire travelling contingent of 26,000 Liverpudlians piled into the hotel to join in the festivities. Again, on a night which marked the culmination of the work begun by Bill Shankly 18 years earlier, there were no barriers between players and supporters. It was a victory shared by all Liverpudlians, whoever they were.

There were even wilder scenes when Liverpool arrived home with the cup. 'It really hit me what we'd done when the plane landed back at Speke, and we came out of the airport, and saw the thousands of people waiting for us,' said Case.

'I never knew what that phrase meant, about the hairs on the back of your neck standing up, until that day. As we went past fire stations, they sounded

Great Matches

EUROPEAN CUP FINAL — **Olympic Stadium, Rome, 25 May 1977**
Attendance: 57,000

Liverpool 3
McDermott
Smith
Neal (penalty)

Borussia Mönchengladbach 1
Simonsen

Liverpool midfielder Jimmy Case said: 'Looking back, what I remember about the evening was that it was a perfect summer's night, and what a sight it was to look around and see our fans filling the stadium. We walked out and saw them there, and we'd heard the stories of how they'd got there – selling all their stuff, hitch-hiking to Italy, the whole works – and we wanted to win it for them.'

And win it they did. Liverpool took the lead through Terry McDermott in the first half, before Allan Simonsen equalised for the Germans early in the second half. But Steve

Tommy Smith rises to meet Steve Heighway's corner and launches a fierce header to put Liverpool back in front.

Phil Neal doesn't share his team-mates anxiety as his penalty goes in off the post to give Liverpool breathing space with a 3-1 lead.

Heighway planted a corner kick on Tommy Smith's meaty forehead and Liverpool were back in front. Then Keegan, who had given Berti Vogts the runaround all night, lured the Borussia captain into a rash tackle, and Phil Neal smacked the penalty in off the post. Liverpool were Champions of Europe.

Case said: 'For a local lad like me it meant everything. Just making my debut for Liverpool would have been enough for me, just to say you had played for Liverpool. But to be there, playing, when we won the European Cup was something else.'

Liverpool: Clemence, Neal, Jones, Smith, R. Kennedy, Hughes, Keegan, Case, Heighway, McDermott, Callaghan

Borussia Mönchengladbach: Kneib, Vogts, Klinkhammer, Wittkamp, Bonhof, Wohlers (Hannes), Simonsen, Wimmer (Kulik), Stielike, Schafer, Heynckes

Referee: Mr Wurtz (France)

the sirens on the engines, and the hairs on the back of my neck were standing up then all right.'

The sense of achievement around Anfield was enormous, but Paisley still had work to do that summer to keep the show on the road for the following season. Most importantly of all, he had a yawning gap in his European Cup-winning team which needed to be filled. That night in Rome was Keegan's last competitive game as a Liverpool player.

Keegan Goes Continental

Keegan had told the Anfield hierarchy a year earlier that he wanted to move abroad, and Real Madrid showed early signs of interest. Liverpool were reluctant to lose their best striker, and the chairman, John Smith, did a deal with him. Stay one more year, Smith told Keegan, then you can leave for a maximum of £500,000. That suited both parties: it gave Keegan an extra season to try to win the European Cup with Liverpool, and it gave the club another season to plan for a replacement.

In the end Real's interest in Keegan cooled, and it was Hamburg who came up with the best offer. Keegan agreed to join them for a salary of £100,000 a year – four times what he was on at Anfield – and Liverpool collected the £500,000 transfer, vowing to the fans that they would spend it on players.

Paisley was not impressed with the idea of English footballers moving to other countries. Like Shankly before him, he nursed a deep suspicion of the continent. 'I wouldn't play a man for England if he is with a foreign club,' said Paisley. 'We have to fight against this trend of losing our best players.'

His mistrust of foreign parts did not quite match Shankly's paranoia, though. On trips behind the Iron Curtain it was not unusual to find Shankly standing on a chair in his hotel room, peering up at the lightbulb looking for hidden cameras, certain that spies were watching his every move.

Paisley initially identified Ipswich Town striker David Johnson as the man to take Keegan's place. Liverpool spent £200,000 on the ex-Evertonian, but the manager then set his sights on perhaps the greatest striking talent in the British game: Celtic's Kenny Dalglish.

It cost Liverpool a British-record £440,000 to land the Scotland international, but the deal was done with little fuss and as the 1977-78 season swung into action, Liverpool had moved into a new age with as little disruption as possible. One great talent had departed. Another world-class performer had slipped into the club – one who would dominate its fortunes for the next 14 years.

Chapter Seven: 1977-80
Kenny's From Heaven

The first season in the Age of Dalglish saw Liverpool join an elite group of clubs: they became the sixth side after Real Madrid, Benfica, Internazionale, Ajax and Bayern Munich to retain the European Cup. It was just as well that the Reds ended the season on a high with a win over Bruges in the final at Wembley, because on the home front their form fell several notches below their European displays, and Paisley's team were eclipsed by Nottingham Forest.

Brian Clough's Forest had only just been promoted after finishing third in the Second Division, but they began life in the First Division with some style. They reeled off three straight victories to head the early table, and although surprising teams invariably find themselves top of the league in September, rarely are they still there by Hallowe'en.

Kenny Dalglish celebrates his goal as Liverpool beat Benfica in the European Cup quarter-final in March 1978.

Forest, though, proved themselves immune to fluctuations of form, and while the rest of the country was talking about bubbles bursting sooner or later, Forest continued to grind out victories. By Christmas only Everton were within shouting distance of Forest: Liverpool had fallen back during a five-match winless run as autumn turned to winter. By the New Year, Forest were five points clear of the field. Some bubble.

The Reds, though, were having more joy in Europe. East Germany's champions, Dinamo Dresden, came to Anfield for the first leg of Liverpool's first game in the defence of the European Cup, and the Reds put on a bravura performance to win 5-1. On the face of it the return should have been a stroll, but it turned out to be the exact opposite: Liverpool spent 90 minutes haring around a field in East Germany as super-charged opponents gave them the chasing of their lives.

Men Possessed

David Fairclough said: 'They came out of the traps like nothing you have ever seen. We had grave doubts about what we were seeing. None of us had ever seen footballers run around like this before. They played the game at a tempo we had never experienced, and we didn't think was possible. They were like men possessed, and we were convinced they were all on something that night. At that time there were rumours that athletes were having complete blood transfusions to improve their performances, and that's one of the explanations we came up with for their behaviour.'

The use of drugs was hardly unknown in East German sport around that time, and it was later revealed that the country's elite athletes were chemically enhanced in a programme run by officially-sanctioned scientists. Abuse of drugs was wholesale. There is no evidence to prove that the Dinamo Dresden players were high as kites that night: perhaps they were simply on a decent bonus. Whatever the truth, Fairclough and his team-mates insist the Germans were fuelled with something more potent than sauerkraut and pumpernickel.

Liverpool, dizzy from Dresden's onslaught, quickly found themselves 2-0 down. If anything, the home team looked favourites to overturn the deficit from the first leg. Somehow they clung on to reach half-time still two goals ahead on aggregate.

Fairclough had started the game on the bench, and Paisley threw him on for the second half in an attempt to reverse the tide. His mission was to run at Dresden and turn the defence: anything to give Liverpool some respite from the crazed waves of human dynamos which were crashing towards

50 Greatest Players

JOHN TOSHACK Centre forward

Joined Liverpool: 1970 **From:** Cardiff City

Debut: 14 November 1970 v Coventry (h), Division One – drew 0-0

Appearances: 246 **Goals:** 96

Left Liverpool: 1978 **For:** Swansea City

Honours won with Liverpool: Division One championship 1973, 1976, 1977; FA Cup winner 1974; UEFA Cup winner 1973, 1976; 26 Wales caps

The big Welshman had a square-shouldered gait that made it look like he had forgotten to remove the clothes hanger before donning his shirt. But it did not stop him being one of the finest headers of the ball in Liverpool history. His ability to rise above defenders and propel the ball with fearsome power helped earn him his impressive goals total. He flowered in combination with Kevin Keegan, and it was their punch up front which as much as anything helped Liverpool recover from the late-1960s barren period. Toshack's best season came in 1975-76, when he scored 23 goals in all competitions as Liverpool pulled off a League and UEFA Cup double.

their goal. Paisley's tactic worked: Fairclough set up Steve Heighway to score, and the away goal scuppered Dresden's chances. Liverpool were through to face Benfica.

Liverpool went to the Portuguese side's stately Stadium of Light for the first leg of the quarter-finals (thanks to a champions' bye, the Reds were already in the last eight) and after winning 2-1 on a rainy night in Lisbon they had just about guaranteed themselves a place in the last four.

Fairclough said: 'That was a great test of character against Benfica, because we played in a torrential downpour, and the conditions were terrible. The stadium was completely open, no roof, and all you could see as you looked around you was thousands and thousands of umbrellas.

'Benfica were a team full of Portuguese internationals, and they were a good side, and to win on their ground in those circumstances was a tremendous achievement.' Liverpool won the second leg 4-1, and that set up a semi-final with their opponents from the 1977 European Cup final, Borussia Mönchengladbach.

The first leg was played in Germany, and Liverpool had David Johnson to thank for a reasonable result. He scored a hugely important away goal as the home side edged the tie 2-1. The Germans came to Anfield with grim purpose, determined to hold their lead. Liverpool won 3-1 thanks to goals from Ray Kennedy, Dalglish and Case. In the end, for all it was a European Cup semi-final, Fairclough rated it the easiest tie of the lot.

By now the League Championship had been settled. Forest went unbeaten from November to the end of the season, and won the title by seven points from Liverpool. Clough had built a title-winning team that looked as if it had been modelled on Liverpool lines. As well as having a solid defence, Forest played a crisp, short-passing game that relied on a high degree of team-work and industry. Clough did not encourage the star mentality at his club, and you could not say that any of his players stood out as individuals. Some of them – like pudgy winger John Robertson – did not even look like footballers, but they certainly could play.

Liverpool finished the season with a 12-game unbeaten run to take the runners-up spot. The Reds had to bend the knee to Forest in the League Cup as well, as they lost in their first appearance in the competition's final.

In that final at Wembley Liverpool worried away at Forest's goal for most of the match, but 18-year-old Chris Woods, playing in place of the cup-tied Shilton, saved everything. Forest won the replay 1-0 at Old Trafford with a Robertson penalty, awarded after Phil Thompson committed a foul which he insisted was closer to the centre circle than the 18-yard box.

Keegan's Boys Hammered

Liverpool fared better in the Super Cup, a newly-invented contest between the previous season's European Cup winners, and the winners of the European Cup-Winners' Cup. The Reds won it by smashing Keegan's Hamburg 6-0 at Anfield. But the real thing was the European Cup final against Bruges. 'They had some very good players,' said Fairclough, 'and they were coached by Ernst Happel, a very clever coach technically.

'At first it was just a huge relief to be picked in the starting line-up. The previous season I had been on the bench for the final in Rome, and Bob Paisley had promised to put me on towards the end of the game. But when the second goal by Smithy went in, all that changed and I never got on. So to be picked for the game against Bruges was a great feeling, even though I was really annoyed that Bob Paisley would even contemplate not picking me. I had been playing well and deserved my place on merit. Even up to the last minute he was deciding between me and Stevie Heighway.'

Paisley had other selection dilemmas too. Tommy Smith pulled out of the game when he dropped a pickaxe on his foot in a domestic accident. Even the

Anfield Iron had to admit defeat when his foot was impaled and crushed by half a hundredweight of pointed steel. Young Scottish prospect Alan Hansen was drafted into central defence, and Emlyn Hughes moved out to left back. But as events panned out, the make-up of the defence was the last thing Liverpool had to worry about. They could have played Gladys Knight and the Pips in the back four and still won. Bruges settled into an ultra-defensive, offside trap-obsessed game, and barely threatened the Reds goal all night. The only difficulty for Liverpool was how to break down the white wall in front of them.

Fairclough said: 'They were a better team than their tactics indicated. Ernst Happel was obviously worried about our speed going forward, and played these offside tactics to catch us breaking forward. It worked to an extent: I was caught offside a number of times. But in the end we managed to get through them.'

Kenny's Invention

The goal came in the 65th minute. Another Liverpool new boy, Graeme Souness, found Dalglish in the area with a precise pass but the striker seemed to have no kind of angle with which to fashion a telling shot. But Dalglish found a way. Fairclough said: 'Kenny invented that chip shot. I don't think any of us had ever seen him score like that before. I think in that instant he made it up, and from then on he used it in one-on-ones with goalkeepers. Wait for them to make a move, then lift the ball.' That one goal was enough. Liverpool were still Champions of Europe.

It was typical of Paisley's skills as a team-builder that the Reds had pulled off a second European Cup victory while his side was evolving. There would be no lull for Liverpool while the new players bedded in. Transformation was seamless. Hansen, just 22, began to emerge as a defender of uncommon ability. In the midfield Souness, who joined in January 1978 from Middlesbrough, was already showing immense talent and character.

Fairclough said: 'You saw Alan and straight away knew he was going to be a great player. I first noticed him playing in central midfield, he was such a powerful runner. He was strong, and had great ability on the ball. You didn't always see that when he played centre half, but it was there. And Graeme gave us a completely new dimension in midfield. Strong tackling and a great passer.'

By now Ian Callaghan and Tommy Smith were ready to step sideways after giving 35 years' service between them. Paisley had prepared well for the moment of their departure.

You could argue for days about the best Liverpool side of all time. Was it Shankly's 1966 champions? The early 70s team which won the League, FA

Great Matches

EUROPEAN CUP FINAL **Wembley, 10 May 1978**
Attendance: 92,000

Liverpool 1 **FC Bruges 0**
Dalglish

Kenny Dalglish stole all the glory with his exquisite goal, but Liverpool's second European Cup was also a night of fulfilment for Emlyn Hughes, who became the first English captain to hoist the gargantuan Champions Cup trophy twice.

He was adaptable enough to switch from his central defensive role to play at left back in the final. Tommy Smith had lost an argument with a pickaxe on the eve of the match (the pickaxe was a write-off), and Hughes took his place. He played a perfect game, showing the leadership qualities which made him one of the great Liverpool skippers. David Fairclough said: 'He epitomised everything that was good about that Liverpool team. He possessed a huge will to win, and he showed every member of the team they had to be winners.'

Wembley was so full of Liverpudlians, perhaps Bruges mistook it for Anfield. Whatever the reason, they came to defend and might have succeeded if not for King Kenny. The hour mark had come and gone with Liverpool going nowhere fast. Latching on to a Souness pass on the edge of the area, Dalglish waited for his moment before coolly despatching his shot past the already committed Bruges keeper Jensen. As simple as that – Bruges had nothing to offer in return and the trophy would stay at Anfield.

Liverpool: Clemence, Neal, R. Kennedy, Hughes, Thompson, Hansen, Dalglish, Case (Heighway), Fairclough, McDermott, Souness
Bruges: Jensen, Bastijns, Maes (Volders), Krieger, Leekens, Cools, De Cubber, Vandereycken, Simeon, Ku (Sanders), Sorensen
Referee: Mr Corver (Holland)

and UEFA Cups? The Double winners of 1986? One thing is sure: no Liverpool team has ever dominated a Division One season like Bob Paisley's side did in 1978-79.

For once, the stats tell no lie. They only conceded 16 goals all season, and Ray Clemence kept 28 clean sheets. They were unbeaten at Anfield, conceding just two points, and their goal difference at home read: For 51, Against 4. Week after week, the team sheet read the same: Clemence, Neal, Hansen, Thompson, Alan Kennedy, Case, McDermott, Souness, Ray Kennedy, Dalglish and either Johnson or Heighway.

While supporters might favour sides from other eras as the best ever to wear the red, one man remained convinced that this team was peerless: he was Bob Paisley.

Kenny Dalglish scores the deciding goal of the 1978 European Cup final at Wembley.

Jimmy Case said: 'Someone once asked Bob Paisley to name a greatest team from all the players he had been involved with during his time at Liverpool. He didn't pick Roger Hunt from one era, and John Barnes from later years, and Alan Hansen, and mix them all up. He just named the team which won the League in 1978-79, because it was such a strong unit. We only used 15 players all season.' Of those 15, Fairclough started three games and Sammy Lee just one. 'Bob was able to pick the same team because we had no injuries or suspensions,' Case said. 'And that was no accident.

'We avoided injuries because of the way we played the game. Every time you got the ball there would be two or three options to move it on, the movement in the team was that good. And we could move it quickly because the technique of everyone in the team was excellent. It's when you dwell on

50 Greatest Players

TOMMY SMITH Defender/midfielder

Joined Liverpool: 1962 (as trainee)

Debut: 8 May 1963 v Birmingham (h), Division One – won 5-1

Appearances: 638 **Goals:** 49

Left Liverpool: 1978 **For:** Swansea City

Honours won with Liverpool: European Cup winner 1977; Division One championship 1966, 1973, 1976, 1977; FA Cup winner 1965, 1974; UEFA Cup winner 1973, 1976; 1 England cap

Bill Shankly used to insist that Smith had never been a boy, that he was 30 years old when he was born. One look at Smith's boxer's visage and brawny frame and you could see what he meant. Yet Smith was always more than the hardman of popular legend. He could play, too. Shankly wouldn't have let him near his team if he couldn't. But it is also true that football in the 1960s was a more physical game than it became in later years. It is doubtful whether Smith's uncompromising tackles would see him stay on the field longer than 10 minutes now. He might have made his name as the Anfield Iron, a formidable obstacle between the opposition and Liverpool's goal, but he could score goals as well. Who can ever forget the thumping header in the 1977 European Cup final, a fairytale ending to a fine Liverpool career.

Tommy Smith (left) and Ian Callaghan parade the European Cup. It was a fitting finale to two great Liverpool servants. Just over a year later both had left the club.

50 Greatest Players

IAN CALLAGHAN Winger/midfielder

Joined Liverpool: 1959 **From:** School

Debut: 16 April 1960 v Bristol Rovers (h), Division Two – won 4-0

Appearances: 857 **Goals:** 69

Left Liverpool: 1978 **For:** Swansea City

Honours won with Liverpool: European Cup winner 1977; Division One championship 1964, 1966, 1973, 1976, 1977; Division Two championship 1962; FA Cup winner 1965, 1974; UEFA Cup winner 1973, 1976; 4 England caps

The only Liverpool player to make the journey from the Second Division to the European Cup final, Callaghan's Anfield career spanned nearly 18 years from his debut as a 17-year-old until his final match in the semi-final of the European Cup against Borussia Mönchengladbach in March 1978.

Brought in as a flying right winger, he was an ever-present during the two years in the 60s when Liverpool won the league championship, and earned a place in the 1966 World Cup squad. He played in the early stages of that tournament before Sir Alf decided that flank men were supernumerary. When Shankly's rebuilding brought another League title to Anfield in 1973 after a seven-year absence, Ian was one of three men (the others being Chris Lawler and Larry Lloyd) to play in every single league game. In 1974, Ian was honoured by the football writers as their Player of the Year and earned an England recall under Don Revie in 1977 in his adopted central midfield role.

In September 1978 he signed for Swansea City under his former colleague John Toshack and was to play several dozen League games for the Welsh club, helping them win promotion into the Second Division in the process.

A crowd favourite for his skill and endeavour, Callaghan showed incredible consistency and fitness – he only missed a handful of matches during the 15 years when he was a regular in the first team. His appearance record for the club will probably never be beaten – a fitting tribute to Liverpool FC's greatest servant.

the ball you give your opponent a chance to dive in, and that's when you get your injuries. And we passed it around with a purpose too. We weren't taking the mick out of the opposition, because if you do that they'll kick you, and you get more injuries that way.'

The pattern for the season was set early on. They won their first six league matches, and remained unbeaten until October. In the midst of the run came a 7-0 annihilation of Tottenham Hotspur – including recent World Cup winners Ardiles and Villa – at Anfield in September 1978. Phil Neal said: 'We set out to prove a point to Ardiles and Villa. We wanted to say, "Hey, pal, you might have won the World Cup, but here's a little taste of what British football can be like…" The day before in training there was a buzz about the place, and I knew we were going to put on a performance. Never in my wildest dreams did I think we would hit them for seven.'

The only impediment to the Reds' serene progress came in the European Cup, when Nottingham Forest knocked them out 2-0 on aggregate. Forest won 2-0 at the City Ground, and put on a Liverpool-esque display at Anfield to come away with a 0-0 draw. Clough's team went on to keep the trophy in England.

Immune to Defeat

In the league, Liverpool settled into a steady rhythm which saw them collect shoals of points. Neal said: 'It was a wonderful team to play in. There was such a bond between all the players, that we went out every week feeling immune to defeat. We felt we could walk on water.

'I always used to think that team could run itself. Some days you didn't need a manager. There were that many leaders in the team, everyone was a skipper. We all knew what we were doing, and had complete faith and trust in our team-mates.'

As the season went on and the title looked a foregone conclusion, the Reds set their own milestones. A national newspaper had offered £50,000 to any team which could score 84 league goals in the season, and Liverpool closed in on the cash. Before the last match of the season at Leeds the Reds were stuck on 82 goals. David Johnson struck to take them within one goal of the jackpot, and the tension mounted as Liverpool pressed for the next.

Neal said: 'Jimmy Case put the ball in the net, and it was disallowed. None of us could see why, and we went mad at the ref and the linesman. My goodness, we swore at them.' But the newly crowned champions added two more goals through Johnson and Case to capture the prize. Neal said: 'Sir John Smith, who was the club's chairman, came into the dressing room after the game when we were all celebrating. He said, "Well done, boys. That money will do the club some good." The players just looked at each other. Then we had to battle the Inland Revenue for years to get the money, but we got it in the end and shared it out among the staff and everyone.'

Liverpool's hopes of a first-ever League and Cup double were dashed when they lost 1-0 to Manchester United in a semi-final replay at Goodison, but it had been a memorable season to commemorate Paisley's 40th anniversary as an employee of Liverpool Football Club. Neal said: 'The team showed the quality of the man. Everything was right about it: the balance, the organisation, the way everybody knew their job, everybody attacked and everybody defended. It just showed that Bob Paisley knew the lot about footballers and football teams.'

Champions Again

The team barely changed the following season. The only difference was that Johnson cemented his place as Dalglish's strike partner. There was no change in the destination of the title either as the Reds once again laid waste to the rest of the First Division. They put together a run of 16 league matches without defeat, hit the top by Christmas and led all the way to the line, winning the title ahead of Manchester United with a game to spare.

Once again their European Cup campaign was over before it had begun. In their first game Liverpool were drawn to play the Georgian Champions Dinamo Tbilisi, and goals from Johnson and Case gave them a 2-1 win in the first leg at Anfield. The second leg was a rout. Neal said: 'We got battered. It was a hostile atmosphere, they were a competent side, and they played really well. They scored three, but they should really have won by six. That's how much better than us they were on the day.'

Liverpool had more luck in the domestic cup competitions, and for much of the season they gamely chased a treble of League, League Cup and FA Cup. In the League Cup the Reds brushed past Tranmere, Chesterfield, Exeter and Norwich before meeting Nottingham Forest, again, in the semi-finals. Neal said: 'For a couple of years around that time it seemed as if Forest had a voodoo hold over us. They beat us with all kinds of outrageous refereeing decisions.' The Reds lost 1-0 away in the first leg, and could only draw the home leg 1-1 despite playing an ultra-attacking line-up and swarming all over the Forest area for long periods.

Their experiences in the FA Cup were even more excruciating. They beat Grimsby easily enough in the third round, 5-0 at Anfield with Johnson scoring a hat-trick. They even managed to put the Forest jinx on hold for an afternoon, winning 2-0 at the City Ground in the fourth round. Bury were dispatched 2-0 at Anfield in the fifth round, and Terry McDermott scored a satisfying winner to beat Spurs in London in the quarter-finals. That set up one of the most exhausting, nerve jangling cup marathons in their history.

The Arsenal saga began with a 0-0 draw at Hillsborough. In the first replay four days later at Villa Park Fairclough gave Liverpool the lead, only for Alan Sunderland to equalise. The second replay took place 12 days later, again at Villa. This time Sunderland gave the Gunners the lead after

50 Greatest Players

EMLYN HUGHES Midfielder/Defender

Joined Liverpool: 1967 **From:** Blackpool

Debut: 4 March 1967 v Stoke (h), Division One – won 2-1

Appearances: 665 **Goals:** 62

Left Liverpool: 1979 **For:** Wolverhampton Wanderers

Honours won with Liverpool: European Cup winner 1977, 1978; Division One championship 1973, 1976, 1977, 1979; FA Cup winner 1974; UEFA Cup winner 1973, 1976; 59 England caps

Hughes can never be displaced in the Anfield hall of fame as the first Liverpool captain ever to lift the European Cup, which he did on that fabled night in Rome in 1977. For good measure he was skipper again the following year when the Reds retained the trophy at Wembley. As a player he began as a rampaging wing half at Blackpool, and even as a raw teenager it was clear he was going to be a force in the game. Bill Shankly practically kicked the down door at Bloomfield Road to sign the kid the Kop were soon calling 'Crazy Horse'. Later in his career he switched to central defence, and with Phil Thompson created one of the most constructive central-defensive partnerships the English game had seen. The only major honour he never won at Anfield was the League Cup, and he captained Wolves to that elusive prize the season after leaving Liverpool.

15 seconds, but Dalglish levelled in injury time. The third replay was played at Coventry City, and the only goal came in the 12th minute of the match. It went to Arsenal, when the former Gunner, Ray Kennedy, slipped on the ball in his own penalty area, allowing Frank Stapleton to cross for Brian Talbot to score with his head. It had taken four matches and seven hours of football to find a winner. For good measure the two sides drew 1-1 in the league at Anfield in the midst of it all, and by the end of it all the two sets of players knew each other better than their own families.

The long wait for a Liverpool double went on.

Chapter Eight: 1980-83
We'll Always Have Paris

Liverpool had endured a couple of unhappy seasons in the European Cup, falling at the first fence twice since winning the trophy in 1978. Yet in 1980-81 the Reds looked certain to win at least one match: they were drawn to play Finnish amateurs Oulu Palloseura in the first round.

The first leg was away from home, and the Reds again displayed early-season jitters as they faltered to a 1-1 draw, only McDermott's goal saving them from a mortifying defeat. Yet Liverpool announced they were back in European business in the second leg, winning 10-1 at Anfield.

The second round threw up the tie everyone in Britain wanted to see: Liverpool v Alex Ferguson's exciting Scottish champions, Aberdeen. The Reds travelled north for the first leg and put on a master class in playing away from home in Europe. Liverpool striker David Johnson said: 'We played it just right, and when Terry McDermott scored the only goal, we felt the tie was wrapped up there and then.

'That goal was typical of Terry. He made a long run from midfield, and I stuck him through for the goal. It was something he did so often. I remember I complained to him once that I'd made a long run and not been given the pass. Terry said, "Try doing it 10 times without getting the ball." And that was true, he made so many runs, but you only noticed every tenth occasion when the ball would get to him and he'd score.' At Anfield Liverpool won 4-0 with some comfort to reach the last eight.

The quarter-finals provided exactly the kind of opposition that had caused Liverpool trouble in Europe down the years – CSKA Sofia, a well-organised Eastern Bloc side backed by a fanatical support in an intimidating Stalinist concrete khazi of a stadium. This time Liverpool were able to draw the sting out of such a fraught trip by winning the first leg 5-1 at Anfield to all-but ensure a place in the last four of the competition. Souness was in especially destructive form at Anfield, scoring a hat-trick, and there were goals too from the prolific McDermott and for a Scouse midfielder who was just breaking into the side, Sammy Lee.

Even so, Liverpool went to Bulgaria with some apprehension. Johnson said: 'We had scored five against them at home, but they were still a good side, and when we got there it was one of those bleak places which made you

One of a hat-trick of goals for Graeme Souness against CSKA Sofia in the European Cup quarter-final.

think it was going to be an awkward time. Then we went out for the game, and it was some atmosphere in the ground, with 65,000 in there all screaming their heads off.' But Johnson put the tie beyond Sofia by scoring the only goal of the game. 'It wasn't a great goal,' Johnson said, 'but it was a goal, and we were through.'

That set up a semi-final against one of European football's great powers, Bayern Munich. Johnson said: 'That was always going to be the hardest game so far, because year after year Bayern have a great side, and they were especially good that season. The side was packed with household-name German internationals.

'The first leg was at Anfield, and it was 0-0. They played very well to get what for them was a great result. To them, it was job done. They had never been beaten in the Olympic Stadium in European competition, and they were very, very confident of going through. They all spoke perfect English, and as we were walking off the pitch at Anfield, the things they were saying to us suggested they were full of confidence for the next match. In their own minds they were through.'

50 Greatest Players

STEVE HEIGHWAY Winger

Joined Liverpool: 1970 **From:** Skelmersdale United

Debut: 29 August 1970 v West Brom (a), Division One – drew 1-1

Appearances: 475 **Goals:** 76

Left Liverpool: 1981 **For:** Minnesota Kicks

Honours won with Liverpool: European Cup winner 1977, 1978; Division One championship 1973, 1976, 1977, 1979; FA Cup winner 1974; UEFA Cup winner 1973, 1976; 33 Republic of Ireland caps

Heighway was the latest in a long line of exciting Liverpool wingers which had included the likes of Liddell, Callaghan and Thompson. He emerged from amateur football a fully formed First Division player, and his speed and control down the wings made him an instant crowd favourite. Heighway was a big occasion player, and scored goals in the 1971 and 1974 FA Cup finals, and also set up Terry McDermott's opener in the 1977 European Cup final. It sounds odd to say it considering the honours he won in a rich 10-year playing career, but his most valuable work for the club might have come more recently as a hugely influential leader of Liverpool's academy, and nurturer of the players of the future.

Nothing which happened in the fortnight before the second leg did anything to shake the Germans' conviction. Liverpool, who had suffered an unusually heavy injury load all season, found their squad further reduced by a catalogue of bumps, tweaks and strains. Paul Breitner, the great West German full back, went on television and wrote off the Reds' chances, claiming the British players were technically inferior to their German opponents, an opinion Paisley passed on to the Liverpool dressing room.

Paisley's pre-match team talk was also made easier thanks to a brazen display of chutzpah on Bayern Munich's part on the day of the game. The home supporters were handed flyers on their way into the ground with travel and ticket information for the final. By this time the Liverpool players were seething and desperate to turn over their presumptuous hosts. Johnson said: 'It brought out the fighting spirit within us. We were the underdogs, and being British we loved that. Everything was stacked against us. The injuries had been terrible all year, and they got worse in the run up to that second leg. We went over there with a skeleton crew, really.

'No disrespect to these players, but Colin Irwin and Richard Money came into the side from the reserves, and Bob Paisley had to name Jimmy Case as a sub even though he was coming back from injury and barely fit.'

Howard Gayle was treated to an appalling torrent of racist abuse from the home fans in Liverpool's European Cup semi-final against Bayern Munich in Germany.

Liverpool's luck did not improve once the match kicked off. Johnson said: 'After ten minutes Dalglish went over on his ankle and had to come off. That looked like it then, all these problems and then your star player goes off after ten minutes, it just looks like it's not meant to happen for you.

'Howard Gayle came on for Kenny, and Howard was a lad with loads of bottle and loads of pace, but he got lots of stick from the crowd because he was black, and the Bayern players singled him out for a bit of treatment because he was a young lad. They wanted to test him. Howard reacted with aggression and he was flying into tackles. He was booked in the first half for a foul, and should in all honesty have been sent off.'

Sub the Sub

'Bob Paisley tried to calm Howard down, but in the end it looked like he was going to be dismissed, so Bob had to sub the sub. That meant Jimmy Case went on, who was only 50 per cent fit at best.' Still, Liverpool hung on and the game remained goalless until deep into the second half. Then Liverpool suffered another cruel blow.

'My hamstring went,' said Johnson. 'I told the bench what had happened, but they couldn't do anything about it. We were only allowed two subs, and we had used both of them, so I had to stay on. I hobbled over to the wing to get out of the way and just limped up and down the touchline.

'There were all these coppers walking around the ground with Alsatians and rifles, and Roy Evans told me later that Bob asked one of them to lend him his gun. He wanted to shoot me because I was useless.' But it was a good job Paisley didn't put Johnson out of his misery. 'With a few minutes to go Ray Clemence cleared the ball and it came straight to me,' Johnson said. 'I controlled it first time, and with my second touch crossed it to Ray Kennedy running through the middle, and he scored.'

Karl-Heinz Rummenigge equalised in the last minute, but a 1-1 draw was enough to see Liverpool through on away goals. It was perhaps the greatest away win in Liverpool's four decades of European competition. 'It was a team performance,' said Johnson. 'We had our backs to the wall and we reacted well. We dug in and never admitted we were beaten.'

50 Greatest Players

RAY KENNEDY Midfielder

Joined Liverpool: 1974 **From:** Arsenal

Debut: 31 August 1974 v Chelsea (a), Division One – won 3-0

Appearances: 393 **Goals:** 72

Left Liverpool: 1982 **For:** Swansea City

Honours won with Liverpool: European Cup winner 1977, 1978, 1981; Division One championship 1976, 1977, 1979, 1980, 1982; UEFA Cup winner 1976; League Cup winner 1981; 17 England caps

The last signing of the Shankly era played a key role in the days of Paisley. He joined as 22-year-old striker, but made his name at Anfield as a left-sided midfield player, from where he played a huge part in Liverpool's first conquests of Europe. His unselfish support play helped the likes of Graeme Souness and Terry McDermott shine, and his disciplined performances were hugely valuable in European ties. He never lost his knack for goal, and chipped in with numerous vital strikes. In the 1981 European Cup semi-final Liverpool were on their way out in the second leg against Bayern Munich when Kennedy materialised late on to score a decisive away goal.

While Liverpool were making their mark in Europe, they were enduring their most disappointing league season for ten years. In January they lost 2-1 at home to Leicester, which ended an incredible run of 86 home matches without defeat. Aston Villa were the new champions, playing with an attacking swagger that jarred strangely with the character of their grimly taciturn manager, Ron Saunders. The Reds' FA Cup campaign ended at Goodison in the fourth round, as Imre Varadi scored the decisive goal in Everton's 2-1 win.

Liverpool did manage to capture the League Cup for the first time, though. After beating Bradford, Swindon, Portsmouth, Birmingham and Manchester City, Liverpool met Second Division West Ham at Wembley. Liverpool were favourites to win the match but the Hammers were a dangerous side, one of the best teams to play in English football's second flight for many years. They had an effective mix of experienced internationals, long-serving stalwarts and richly talented young performers with lashings of promise: any First Division manager would have been happy to see the likes of Brooking, Devonshire, Goddard, Lampard, Martin, Stewart, Parkes and Billy Bonds in their squad.

Alan Kennedy (out of picture, right) shoots past Phil Parkes to score Liverpool's opener against West Ham United in the 1981 League Cup final at Wembley.

As Phil Neal looks on, Graeme Souness takes on Real Madrid's Laurie Cunningham in the 1981 European Cup final.

West Ham proved their worth at Wembley, and were good value for a 1-1 draw. Alan Kennedy scored for the Reds and Stewart equalised from the spot late on. Liverpool looked in trouble in the replay at Villa Park when Goddard scored early, but Dalglish levelled the scores, and Alan Hansen popped up with the winner. The League Cup was welcome enough, but the main focus of the season was still the European Cup.

Camp Kop

An estimated 15,000 Liverpudlians travelled over to Paris for the final, and most of them arrived in the French capital days early to enjoy the sights and soak up the atmosphere. A tented town full of Scousers sprang up in the Bois de Boulogne, an enclave which was quickly nicknamed Camp Kop. The final at the Parc des Princes they had waited for so eagerly turned out to be disappointing as a spectacle, but the result was all they wished.

Johnson said: 'On paper it was a classic final, Liverpool against Real Madrid, with all their history in the competition. It didn't really turn out that

Great Matches

EUROPEAN CUP FINAL — **Parc des Princes, Paris, 27 May 1981**
Attendance: 48,360

Liverpool 1 — **Real Madrid 0**
A Kennedy

Alan Kennedy's strike that won the European Cup.

The 1981 final against Real Madrid was not a classic, but it was resolved by a classic goal. With eight minutes left Alan Kennedy mooched forward from his left back position to collect a throw-in from Ray Kennedy, and his momentum took him further and further up the field as he looked for another red shirt to pass to. Madrid's defenders backed off him, discounting the threat posed by the moustachioed full back, until the man the Kop called 'Barney Rubble' found himself within shooting distance. After skinning the right back, Cortes, he crashed it past Agustin at the near post to seal Liverpool's third European crown.

The match had widely been anticipated as a classic confrontation between Liverpool, the dominant force in European football for the previous few years, against the six-time winners, Real Madrid. But as so often, expectations were confounded. The game was largely disjointed and formless, wrecked by nerves. You could say it was absorbing rather than exciting.

As the 90 minutes went by, it became apparent that in a battle of attrition like this, Liverpool were more likely to emerge the victors. So it proved, thanks to Alan Kennedy – the man for the hour. The Reds became the fourth team to win the European Cup three times (after Real Madrid, Ajax and Bayern Munich). It was also a personal triumph for the self-effacing Bob Paisley. He was the first manager to win the trophy for a third time. More than anybody, Phil Thompson drew enormous satisfaction from the victory. The boy from Kirkby, a Reds fan from boyhood, was Liverpool's captain on the night, and no prouder man ever lifted the trophy.

Liverpool: Clemence, Neal, A. Kennedy, R. Kennedy, Thompson, Hansen, Dalglish (Case), Lee, Johnson, McDermott, Souness

Real Madrid: Agustin, Garcia Cortes (Pineda), Camacho, Angel, Sabido, Garcia Navajas, Juanito, Del Bosque, Santillana, Stielike, Cunningham

Referee: Mr Palotai (Hungary)

way, though. You couldn't say it was a great game. That was partly because of the conditions. The pitch was a rugby field really, and it was bobbly. The white lines were all raised about an inch above the grass, so the ball bounced up every time it rolled over one.'

The two teams cancelled each other out so that only an outrageous intervention or error looked likely to produce a goal. In the end, Alan Kennedy turned out to be the hero. He collected Ray Kennedy's throw in, ran on and on towards the Real Madrid penalty area before thumping a shot past the Spaniards' startled keeper. Johnson said: 'As soon as he scored, he took off and ran behind the goal, and I was running after him.

'There was a moat running around the pitch, and I grabbed hold of him and was ready to throw him in it. I said, "Why didn't you pass you greedy bastard?" I was unmarked on the penalty spot waiting for Alan to pull it back. Alan just said to me, "Dave, if I'd passed to you we'd still be playing".

'It was such a good night for so many reasons. First of all, obviously, because we'd won the European Cup for a third time. And it was extra

50 Greatest Players

RAY CLEMENCE Goalkeeper

Joined Liverpool: 1967 **From:** Scunthorpe United

Debut: 25 September 1968 v Swansea Town (h), League Cup – won 2-0

Appearances: 665

Left Liverpool: 1981 **For:** Tottenham Hotspur

Honours won with Liverpool: European Cup winner 1977, 1978, 1981; Division One championship 1973, 1976, 1977, 1979, 1980; UEFA Cup winner 1973, 1976; FA Cup winner 1974; League Cup winner 1981; 56 England caps

Was Clemence Bill Shankly's greatest-ever signing? It must be a toss up between him and Keegan. Liverpool paid Scunthorpe £18,000 for the 19-year-old keeper, which was good value for a man who became in many judges' eyes the best in the world. He learned his trade in the reserves until Shankly decided he was ready to replace Tommy Lawrence and quickly proved himself a master of all the goalkeeper's arts: he was a wonderful shot-stopper, he could produce acrobatic saves when necessary, and possessed a finely honed positional sense. He would have won many more international caps but for the presence of Peter Shilton, who different England managers at different times preferred to Clemence.

Souness, Dalglish and Hansen celebrate on a glorious night in Paris.

special for me personally because I'd been on the bench in 1977 and injured in 1978, so to play the game was an honour.

'But there was one more reason why it was such a great night. Whenever Bob Paisley made a tactical substitution, history showed that it was either me or Terry McDermott who came off. If he wanted to throw somebody on to hold a lead, one of us would be off. But that night we were 1-0 up, and I saw Jimmy Case warming up on the touchline, and somebody was digging around in the box where they kept the numbers which showed who was coming off. Nobody was injured, so I was waiting to see if me or Terry was going off. Then they held the number seven up, Kenny Dalglish's number. Me and Terry Mac were checking our shirts to see if we were wearing the right numbers, but it was Kenny who went off. That meant so much to me, because Kenny was easily the best footballer I ever played with or against, and for Bob Paisley to leave me on and take Kenny off was such a big honour.'

Liverpool's victory over Real Madrid sparked some of the wildest celebrations Paris had seen since Liberation. Johnson said: 'The president of the French FA had organised a table for us at the Lido nightclub, and we took the European Cup down there. It was an incredible place, you've never seen anything like it in your life. There were waterfalls in there, even elephants, and they had the Bluebell girls, these 6ft 3in topless dancers. The club was saucer shaped, and as we walked down towards the stage with the cup the spotlights shone on us, the show stopped and everybody in the place stood up and applauded us. It was the kind of night you never forget.'

A Great Man

Bill Shankly died at 1.20am on Tuesday, 29 September 1981. He was 67.

After suffering a heart attack the previous Saturday Shankly had been rushed to Broadgreen Hospital, where his condition improved so quickly he was admitted to an open ward. Doctors looked forward to the patient making a speedy recovery, but on the Monday he suffered a second attack, and he died in the hospital's intensive care unit.

A torrent of sorrow swept over the city, and the early editions of that day's Liverpool *Daily Post* provided the first of the thousands of tributes which poured in to one of the most popular football men of all time. Ron Yeats, the skipper of his first championship-winning side, said: 'He was like a second father to me. He will be missed more than I can say. He was a great man. His motivation could move mountains.' Ian Callaghan said: 'He's a

50 Greatest Players

JIMMY CASE Midfielder

Joined Liverpool: 1972 **From:** South Liverpool

Debut: 26 April 1975 v Queens Park Rangers (h), Division One – won 3-1

Appearances: 269 **Goals:** 46

Left Liverpool: 1981 **For:** Brighton & Hove Albion

Honours won with Liverpool: European Cup winner 1977, 1978 and 1981; Division One championship 1976, 1977, 1979, 1980; UEFA Cup winner 1976; League Cup winner 1981

When local boy Case broke into the first team, his all-round dynamism provoked almost the same excitement that the young Keegan had a few years earlier. He loved to burst forward from midfield, and when he scored they were often spectacular efforts which exploded from his right boot. He was also assiduous in his defensive duties and a tidy passer. Alongside the likes of Graeme Souness and Terry McDermott, he was a vital cog in one of the best-ever Liverpool engine rooms. One of his best goals was reserved for a losing cause, a dipping volley against Manchester United in the 1978 FA Cup final. One question hangs over his Anfield career: why, at a time when England were not good enough to qualify for the World Cup, was Case not thought to be good enough for England?

one-off. There has never been anyone like him. They broke the mould when they made him.'

On the day of Shankly's funeral an honour guard of ex-Liverpool players including Emlyn Hughes, Ray Clemence, Ron Yeats and John Toshack served as pallbearers for their departed leader. As the cortege passed by Everton's training ground, yards from Shankly's home in Bellefield Avenue, the club's players lined the pavement in respect, heads bowed. Crowds stood at the side of the road as Shankly's body was driven to St Mary's Church, West Derby, where a requiem service was held. The small church was packed to overflowing with mourners, including representatives from every one of the 92 League clubs, and hundreds more stood outside. Many more lined the route as the funeral cars made their way to Priory Road Crematorium, close to Liverpool's ground.

United in Mourning

The first match at Anfield after Shankly's death was against John Toshack's Swansea City side. Mark Lawrenson, who had just signed for Liverpool from Brighton, said: 'It was as if a member of your family had died. There was this atmosphere about the place of everybody being united in mourning. The minute's silence was eerie, and after it the crowd were singing, "Shankly, Shankly".'

If Shankly's death marked the passing of an epoch at Anfield, Paisley's European Cup-winning side was also undergoing change. Liverpool supporters had grown used to seeing their sides evolve over the years, but Paisley acted ruthlessly to pep up the team during the 1981-82 season. Some of the changes were forced upon him. After a dozen years spent harvesting winners' medals at Anfield, Ray Clemence decided to move on, and he was transferred to Tottenham for £300,000. That gave ambitious Zimbabwean Bruce Grobbelaar the chance he craved.

The season also saw the departures of other players who had won the lot with the Reds, but who in Paisley's view were reaching the end of their useful lives at Liverpool. Ray Kennedy went to Swansea, Jimmy Case to Brighton and David Johnson to Everton. Phil Thompson lost the captaincy to Graeme Souness. Into their places stepped a number of outstanding young players: Craig Johnston, a midfielder from Middlesbrough, made his first appearances; Mark Lawrenson, the club's £900,000 record signing from Brighton, won a first-team place; Ian Rush began to find his form after initially struggling following his move from Chester; and Irishman Ronnie Whelan emerged as a left-sided midfielder of rare class.

Lawrenson said: 'After I joined from Brighton I came into the side straight away at left back, which I was thrilled about because I expected to have my 18 months in the reserves. Bruce played from the start of the season too, because Clem had gone, but the other new lads had to wait their turn. When Bob changed the rest of the team, he did it all in one go.'

Lost Patience

In an incident which had echoes of the post-Watford clear-out in 1970, the Liverpool management lost their patience after one specific match: this time it was a league game at Maine Road, on Boxing Day 1981.

Lawrenson said: 'We lost 3-1, the pitch had been awful and we were worse. We got back in the dressing room, and Joe Fagan let us have it. He only lost his temper once a year, and this was it. He tore into us, saying we weren't pulling our weight, we'd had six months to turn it around, and it stops here. The next match was away to Swansea in the cup, and everybody had us down to lose. That's when Bob changed things. We won that game 4-0 and went on a run, then. That was the death-knell of a few Liverpool careers right there.

Ronnie Whelan celebrates scoring for Liverpool against Tottenham Hotspur in the 1982 League Cup final.

50 Greatest Players

TERRY McDERMOTT Midfielder

Joined Liverpool: 1974 **From:** Newcastle United

Debut: 16 November 1974 v Everton (a), Division One – drew 0-0

Appearances: 329 **Goals:** 81

Left Liverpool: 1982 **For:** Newcastle United

Honours won with Liverpool: European Cup winner 1977, 1978, 1981; Division One championship 1977, 1979, 1980, 1982; League Cup winner 1981, 1982; 25 England caps

If he had done nothing else in his career, McDermott would deserve his place in history for the goal he scored in the 1977 European Cup final. His crisp finish to a flowing Liverpool move was unforgettable, and typical of McDermott's attacking midfield style.

The Kirkby-born McDermott came to Anfield late, arriving after spells at Bury and Newcastle United. But his Liverpool career did not progress smoothly. It took him a while to fit into the system, but once he did he made up for lost time, slotting into a brilliant quartet that also featured Souness, Ray Kennedy and Jimmy Case.

'The only clue I had that the team was changing for that game at Swansea was when Bob came up to me in the hotel reception on the morning of the game. He did it in his own special way. He said to me, "Can you do that left one?" I asked him what he meant, and he said, "Can you do that left-sided one?" I said, "You mean play left back?" and he said, "No, that left midfield one." So then I knew he wanted me to play left midfield, and he was changing the team around. But that was Bob. He had his own language, and in that north east accent he wasn't always the easiest to understand.'

The new-look team's first success came in the League Cup. After defeating Exeter, Middlesbrough, Arsenal, Barnsley and Ipswich, the Reds faced Tottenham in the final at Wembley. Steve Archibald's goal looked like it had given Clemence and Co. a deserved victory, but Whelan curled in an equaliser to take the match into extra-time, when an unstoppable Whelan strike and a Rush tap-in secured the trophy.

Liverpool's involvement in the European Cup ended at the hands of CSKA Sofia in the quarter-finals. Lawrenson said: 'We lost 2-0 away, but it was one of those games where you couldn't remember them having a shot, but they scored two goals. It was a real pipe and slippers job for our back four. How they won I'll never know. I got sent off, too.

'I tackled one of their players, and he collapsed as if he'd just got a Tomahawk missile up his jacksy. It was a real Hamlet moment. The crowd went ballistic, and the ref sent me off. He reported that I was sent off for striking an opponent, but I had never done that in my career. We tried to get a recording off the Bulgarian FA so I could plead my innocence in an appeal, but of course no tape was forthcoming.'

Ian Rush, Liverpool's leading scorer every season from 1981-88 (except 1984-85 when he was beaten by John Wark).

Unfamiliar League Position

After the European setback Liverpool's league form grew more and more formidable. Shankly's passing had cast a gloomy shadow over the club for the first months of the season, and Paisley's team did not play with the panache of old. They kicked off the New Year in an unfamiliar position in the bottom half of the table. The defence looked shaky without the reassuring presence of Clemence, and Grobbelaar's flamboyant antics and occasional clangers did not inspire confidence.

Refreshed by Paisley's amendments to the line-up, the Reds shook off the depression and by March they had climbed into the top six. Their form in the springtime was irresistible and 11 wins in a row took them right to the top. When Liverpool finally clinched a 13th championship – their fifth in seven seasons – Paisley said: 'I'm proudest of this one because there was so much to do'. In the end the Reds won the title by four points from Ipswich Town.

Their top scorer in 1981-82 with 17 league goals was Ian Rush, who had emerged from his early crisis of confidence to forge a devastating striking partnership with Dalglish. Rush had been ready to walk out on the club because Paisley would not pick him. Paisley's answer was simple: score goals, and you'll be in the team. Rush simmered down, took his manager at his word, and the goals began to fly in.

Great Managers – 1974-83

BOB PAISLEY

Quite simply, Bob Paisley is the most successful manager in the history of British football. His roll call of honours is unlikely ever to be bettered: three European Cups, six championships, three League Cups and a UEFA Cup.

He was not a natural leader of men, and he begged Shankly not to stand down in 1974. But when Shankly insisted on going the Liverpool board asked Paisley to take over, and out of a sense of duty he agreed.

Paisley was never a personality manager like Shankly, but he had one advantage which set him apart from the crowd: he knew more about football and footballers than any man alive. Surely there was never a better judge of a player than he. And underneath the kindly uncle image lurked a ruthless streak the width of the Mersey.

In the nine years Paisley was manager Liverpool took a stranglehold on the First Division and extended that grip to Europe, winning the greatest continental prize of all in 1977, 1978 and 1981. Yet despite all that, precious few Paisley stories do the rounds. There is practically an industry of Shankly anecdotes, yet Paisley left no legacy of one-liners. In time-honoured fashion he let his teams talk for him, and in Paisley's era Liverpool roared.

The next season was a landmark in Liverpool's history: it was Paisley's last as manager. After 42 years at Anfield the boss was coming up to retirement age, and he announced in the summer that he would go at the end of the 1982-83 season. If anyone expected him to take it easy in his last few months, they were in for a shock. Paisley threw himself into his work with the vim of a new boy with something to prove, and the team which had taken shape the previous season looked even stronger.

Their slick early-season form was typified by a 5-0 trouncing of Everton at Goodison, a match in which boyhood Toffee Rush put four past his mate Neville Southall. Lawrenson said: 'Everybody remembers Rushie scoring four, but they forget who got the fifth. It was me, a tap-in from 18 yards.'

The Reds' recent poor record in the FA Cup went on as they lost 2-1 to Brighton in the fifth round, but Liverpool continued to treat the League Cup

By 1983, Alan Hansen had established himself as a Liverpool great. Here he is in action against Athletic Bilbao in the European Cup second round, first leg in 1983.

as their own personal property. After getting past Ipswich, Rotherham, Norwich, West Ham and Burnley, they played Manchester United in the final. Norman Whiteside put United ahead, but Alan Kennedy's spectacular goal took the match into extra time. Whelan scored his by now customary League Cup final decider, and the Reds had won the competition for the third successive time. As Liverpool prepared to receive the trophy Souness urged Paisley to climb the steps to the Royal Box to take the cup himself. The Liverpool players had to man-handle their modest manager up the steps, but Paisley deserved his moment in the spotlight.

Once again Liverpool fell to eastern European opposition in the European Cup, as Polish champions Widzew Lodz beat them 4-3 on aggregate. But they made the League Championship all their own. At one point Liverpool had a lead of 16 points over their nearest challengers, Watford, and by the end of the season they were champions by 11 points. 'We'd won the title by about March, and we hardly won another game. We went on our holidays early and got the Ambre Solaire out,' Lawrenson said.

Since taking over from Shankly in 1974, Paisley had filled nine seasons with six championships, three European Cups, three League Cups and a UEFA Cup. It wasn't a bad record for a man who didn't want the job in the first place. In less than a decade he had made himself the most successful manager in the history of British football. Strange to recall that when he quit as a player in 1954 he had dithered between getting a job on a building site or opening a shop. In the end he found a position as Liverpool's trainer, having had the foresight to take a physiotherapy course when he was still playing. Even then he feared that football might not give him a living for long: when Shankly took the Liverpool boss's job in 1959 Paisley dreaded that the new man might bring in his own staff. But Shankly was shrewd enough to recognise Paisley as a rare repository of footballing wisdom. It was the start of a partnership that proved to be incalculably valuable to Liverpool.

'He was fantastic,' said Lawrenson. 'He knew everything there was about players and systems, and he never missed a thing. He'd come to Melwood and sit in his little office there, and he knew everything that was going on everywhere in the club. He didn't say a great deal, and in a year I might have two or three conversations with him. That meant you were doing what he wanted, and he didn't need to say anything else.'

But now he was going, the Liverpool board faced the same problem they had in 1974 when Shankly quit: how to replace the irreplaceable?

Chapter Nine: 1983-89
A Matter of Life and Death?

Older fans of the TV science fiction series *Doctor Who* will recognise the scenario: the old Doctor miraculously morphs into the new before your eyes. His features change, but the spirit of the person remains the same, his powers remain intact. So it was with Liverpool managers. Shankly went, and Paisley took his place. Now Paisley went only to be replaced by another long-serving denizen of the Bootroom, Joe Fagan. The moment had been prepared for.

Fagan was 62 when he took over in the summer of 1983, and had already spent a lifetime steeped in football. He was born in Liverpool, and an unremarkable playing career as a centre half began with amateur side Earlestown Bohemians before he signed for Manchester City in 1938. His League debut was delayed by war, and it would be fair to say that it never reached the heights once it did get underway. After leaving City he played for Bradford Park Avenue and Altrincham before moving into management with the Lancashire amateur club, Nelson, in 1951.

Like Paisley, Fagan had a spell as a trainer and wielded the magic sponge for Rochdale, then joined the Liverpool staff a year before Bill Shankly arrived. He stayed on to work for Shankly, and became Paisley's assistant in 1974. Although he was a valued member of Liverpool's back-room think tank he never showed any inclination to take the top job. Again like Paisley before him, he was reluctant to become manager, but in the end his sense of loyalty prevailed and he agreed to do it.

His team got off to a sluggish start by their own standards in the 1983-84 season, and results were patchy. At their best the Reds were still taking sides apart, like on the day in October when Luton were beaten 6-0 and Ian Rush helped himself to five goals. But there were inexplicable lapses too, such as an afternoon in mid-December when they lost 4-0 at Coventry. But by this time Liverpool had garnered enough points to hit the top of the table, and by the time they travelled to Notts County in May they only needed a point for their 15th title. A 0-0 draw was not their best result of the season (as well as lashing Luton, they had put five past County at Anfield, smashed another five against Coventry at home and West Ham were hit for six) but it was good enough to give them a third championship in successive years. The last side to do that had been Arsenal in the 1930s.

Fagan had stressed the time-honoured Liverpool virtues of continuity and simplicity, and they paid off for him. It was still largely Paisley's team, playing in the same old way. The only regular new face in the side early in the season was Mick Robinson, a £200,000 signing from Brighton, who played up front with Rush when Dalglish was withdrawn into a deeper midfield role. He made a useful contribution – after all, Fagan had learned a thing or two about bringing in new players without disrupting the balance of the side. Fagan joked: 'Our methods are so easy sometimes players just don't understand them at first.' It also helped Liverpool's title-winning cause that Rush enjoyed the season of his life, scoring 32 League goals.

Fagan had moved to strengthen the side in the title run-in, beefing up the midfield by signing Ipswich's free-scoring Glaswegian, John Wark, for £450,000. The switch came as a massive culture shock for Wark. He had been used to winning European trophies and challenging at the top of the table with his old club, but it was immediately clear to him that Liverpool was a step up.

'At Ipswich, we only had a squad of 14 first-team players, so you were assured of your place,' Wark said. 'At Liverpool you were looking around at 18 or 20 internationals all competing for a shirt. You were looking over your shoulder all the time, worried about your place in the team. You had to be on your toes all the time, even in training.

'I was lucky. They slotted me in the team straight away in place of Craig Johnston, but it wasn't easy. In one of my first games I hit a 30-yard pass, and was standing admiring it when I heard Ronnie Moran's voice over the crowd. "Move your flaming bum," he shouted, or something like that. You had to learn the Liverpool way very quickly, or you were out. It was pass and move, pass and move. There was no time for standing still watching the ball.'

Father Figure

It was typical that it was Ronnie Moran's shrill pipes that Wark heard above the throng. Wark said that Fagan left all the training and the discipline to Moran, preferring to play more of an overseer's role. 'When he went mad you knew about it,' said Wark. 'But generally Joe was more of a father figure.'

Wark played all the way through the final run-in to the title and made nine League appearances. It was a good effort, and he gave the team extra impetus at a crucial time when the sheer volume of games in a season can leave sides exhausted and prone to injuries. Even so, strictly speaking he was not entitled to a League Championship winner's medal because he hadn't quite played enough games. The club fought to get him one, and he duly received it. 'That was typical Liverpool,' said Wark. 'It was all about the team, and the spirit of playing for each other. They felt I deserved a medal, and they got me one.

'That's why I signed for Liverpool, to improve myself as a player and to win the Championship. I had the chance to join Manchester United but turned it down. I'm glad I made the decision I did and I never regretted it.

'It was an amazing feeling to join that side because every time you went out you felt like you were going to win. Especially at Anfield around that time, teams were scared to play us. That was the power Liverpool had over the others.'

Days before Wark signed for the Reds, Fagan had presided over Liverpool's first appearance in an all-Merseyside cup final. It might not have been the FA Cup showdown the city had craved for nearly a century, but the Milk Cup was good enough.

The Reds had reached the final in exhausting fashion. After beating Brentford over two legs in their first tie, they needed replays to get past Fulham, Birmingham and Sheffield Wednesday, before meeting Walsall in a two-legged semi-final.

Chilling Omen

Third Division Walsall were not expected to push Liverpool over the two matches, but they earned an ovation from the Kop after playing with enormous heart and attacking verve to draw 2-2 in the first leg at Anfield. Liverpool won the second leg at Fellows Park with goals from Rush and Whelan, but the victory was marred by an incident which provided a chilling omen of events to come.

As Whelan scored the second goal the crowd surged forward, in the way that football crowds do, and a low wall behind the goal crumbled under the weight. Many supporters at the front of the terracing were buried by other fans falling on top of them. The game was stopped, and the players raced to help lift trapped fans to safety, some of them children. There were no serious injuries, and after the rubble was cleared away, the referee restarted the game. No one seemed too concerned.

The Liverpool v Everton League Cup final at Wembley hardly lived up to pre-match expectations: it was scrappy, nervy and goalless. Both sets of players and fans breathed a collective sigh of relief at the final whistle, as neither of them had lost the most significant cup match between the teams since they had begun playing each other in 1894.

Craig Johnson with the Milk Cup after Liverpool had beaten Everton in the replay in 1984.

The match was played in driving rain for the most part, and goal-scoring chances were rare. Alan Hansen might have considered himself lucky to survive a penalty shout when he appeared to be playing basketball in his own penalty area, but 0-0 was a fair scoreline. The replay three days later at Maine Road was more to Liverpool's satisfaction, as Souness settled it with a powerful long-range left-foot shot.

Fourth Successive League Cup

Liverpool's fourth successive League Cup win was worth celebrating – and it was also their 39th match without defeat in the competition. But there was just a whiff of anti-climax about the occasion. Perhaps the words of former Everton player Duncan McKenzie were true: 'Who wants to win a cup final on a Wednesday night?' If you discount European Cup finals, he might have been right.

Liverpool's attempt to recapture the European Cup after two undistinguished seasons in the competition had begun in September, with a straightforward victory over Danish champions, Odense. The hardest game on the way to the final came next, against Athletic Bilbao from Spain, who threw an impenetrable defensive blanket over Liverpool at Anfield to draw 0-0, and looked forward to playing the Reds on their own ground, roared on by their fanactical Basque following. But Liverpool were at their assured best in the away leg, soaking up all the Spaniards could throw at them before Rush's header put them through. By contrast, the Benfica side Liverpool faced in the quarter-finals was a pale imitation of its great predecessors, and after a 1-0 win at Anfield, Liverpool swept to a 4-1 win in Portugal.

Their opponents in the semi-final, Dinamo Bucharest, were a rough old bunch. They were planets behind Liverpool when it came to playing football, but world class when it came to sly practice and off-the-ball skullduggery. Their inflammatory antics were bad enough at Anfield, where Sammy Lee's goal gave the Reds another 1-0 win. But on their own ground Dinamo set

50 Greatest Players

PHIL THOMPSON Centre half

Joined Liverpool: 1971 (as trainee)

Debut: 3 April 1972 v Manchester United (a), Division One – won 3-0

Appearances: 477 **Goals:** 13

Left Liverpool: 1985 **For:** Sheffield United

Honours won with Liverpool: European Cup winner 1978, 1981; Division One championship 1973, 1976, 1977, 1979, 1980, 1982, 1983; UEFA Cup winner 1976; FA Cup winner 1974; League Cup winner 1981, 1982; 42 England caps

Liverpool's emergence as a European superpower in the mid to late-1970s can be traced back to Phil Thompson's introduction into the first team. He established a central defensive partnership with Emlyn Hughes that changed the way the Reds played. The pair strived to play the ball out of defence, and their constructive approach was the bedrock of the possession game which Liverpool mastered. Thompson was also an awkward man for strikers to deal with: sharp of knee and elbow, he was a hard tackler and took an over-my-dead-body approach to defending Liverpool's goal. In 1981 he captained Liverpool to their European Cup final triumph over Real Madrid in Paris.

out to boot anything that moved. The Romanians managed to score, but two goals from Rush put Liverpool in the final, bruised but relieved.

The venue for the final was Rome's Stadio Olimpico, where four years earlier they had beaten Borussia Mönchengladbach to win the European Cup for the first time. But it was just Liverpool's fortune that the team they faced for this match knew the place even better then them. They would have to play Roma – home ground, the Stadio Olimpico!

That made for a much different atmosphere from the one which Liverpool enjoyed on their last visit. That night, over 26,000 Reds fans had turned Rome into a suburb of Liverpool as the Eternal City was painted a deep shade of crimson, and Scouse voices echoed around St Peter's, the Spanish Steps and the Trevi Fountain. Now, the Reds were far more subdued as Romans decorated their own city to hail their team, and prepared to celebrate their first-ever triumph in the competition.

It was not simply home advantage that made the Italians favourites to win the game. They had a cosmopolitan line-up featuring the wonderful Brazilian

Great Matches

EUROPEAN CUP FINAL | **Stadio Olimpico, Rome, 30 May 1984**
Attendance 69,693

AS Roma 1 | **Liverpool 1***
Pruzzo | **Neal**
***after extra time, Liverpool won 4-2 on pens**

Liverpool entered the Colosseum for their fourth European Cup final, and their chances of pulling off a result in front of 60,000 fanatical Romans seemed on a par with the Christians' hopes of grabbing a score draw against the gladiators a thousand years earlier. Yet that is precisely what they managed to achieve, holding the home team to 1-1 after extra time, then keeping their nerve to win 4-2 on penalty kicks. That they were able to retain their self-belief in such a hostile environment was largely down to the leadership qualities of the third and last Liverpool skipper to hoist the European Cup, Graeme Souness.

Bruce Grobbelaar does enough to make Bruno Conti sky his penalty.

Ian Rush recalled in his autobiography: 'Every man-jack in the team ran his heart out that night to prevent the Italians being able to settle into their rhythm.'

The tactics paid off when Phil Neal scored in the first half. Pruzzo equalised just before half-time, and there were no more goals before the end of extra time. That meant penalties.

Steve Nicol took the first kick – and missed. Roma scored their first to take the lead. Souness scored his, and Roma missed theirs to make the score level after two kicks each. Phil Neal converted his kick, and Roma made it 2-2. Then Ian Rush netted to make the score 3-2, and the Italian international Bruno Conti missed his kick. Now Liverpool only needed Alan Kennedy to score the next penalty to win the Cup. It was never in doubt as Kennedy blasted the ball past Tancredi.

Liverpool: Grobbelaar, Neal, A. Kennedy, Lawrenson, Whelan, Hansen, Dalglish (Robinson), Lee, Rush, Johnston (Nicol), Souness

AS Roma: Tancredi, Nappi, Bonetti, Righetti, Falcao, Nela, Conti, Toninho, Cerezo (Strukely), Pruzzo (Chierico), Di Bartolomei, Graziani

Referee: Mr Fredriksson (Sweden)

Falcao, as well as sublimely gifted local players like Conti and Graziani. As match night rolled around, it would have been easy for Liverpool to feel like a team under siege. But the resilience of this Liverpool side would not be cowed by a partisan crowd. Led by Souness, the captain, they faced the massed ranks of howling Roma *tifosi* with indifference, and by the time the Reds were marching down the tunnel for the start of the match singing the team's favourite song, it was the Italians' turn to feel nervous.

Liverpool started with more assurance and deserved the lead Phil Neal gave them after a quarter of an hour. But Roma, yelled onwards by the hostile home support, came at Liverpool and found an equaliser just before half time. No more goals came in normal time or extra time, and so the match became the first-ever European Cup final to go to penalties. Fagan's advice to his team was characteristically avuncular and understated. He said: 'Whatever happens I'm proud of what you have done.'

The stage was set for Alan Kennedy to take the decisive kick, and no one in the ground was less fussed by the prospect than he. After all, he had already scored a European Cup final-winning goal before, in Paris three years earlier. Kennedy was the course and distance specialist, and he duly planted the ball past Tancredi. Later, he made the process sound as simple as booting the ball into a practice goal at Melwood. 'I was confident,' he said. 'I took a penalty in training and put it in the same spot. Just like that.' Fagan might have been press-ganged into the job, but he had become the first manager in England to win three major trophies in one season.

Deadly Stampede

For all it matters, Liverpool reached the 1985 European Cup final in magisterial fashion. In more comfortable style than ever, they had cruised through the earlier rounds, and even looked capable of beating Michel Platini's formidable Juventus. But as history shows, Liverpool fans inside the Heysel Stadium, Brussels, charged into a section of Juventus fans before kick off and triggered a deadly stampede. Panic-stricken Italian fans fled in the face of the rioting Liverpudlians and, in the chaos that ensued, a wall collapsed. Dozens of people were crushed by masonry and the bodies of their fellow supporters. Thirty-nine were killed and over 400 injured.

Of course, the excuses have been lined up. Yes, Heysel was unfit to stage a game of this magnitude. It was already falling to bits, and the Brussels city authorities admitted it had not received a safety check for half-a-century. It is true security was non-existent, and supporters were able to walk through the turnstiles into the ground with tickets unchecked. Dozens simply hopped

50 Greatest Players

GRAEME SOUNESS Midfielder

Joined Liverpool: 1978 **From:** Middlesbrough

Debut: 14 January 1978 v West Brom (a), Division One – won 1-0

Appearances: 359 **Goals:** 56

Left Liverpool: 1984 **For:** Sampdoria

Honours won with Liverpool: European Cup winner 1978, 1981, 1984; Division One championship 1979, 1980, 1982, 1983, 1984; League Cup winner 1981, 1982, 1983, 1984; 37 Scotland caps

If you were picking an all-time Liverpool team, you would have to find a place for Graeme Souness – it would be difficult telling him he wasn't in the side. As a midfield player he had the lot. He was a ferocious tackler, a sumptuous passer of the ball and a dangerous sniper on the edge of the box. He could play like an angel, but was also a master of the footballing black arts. Souness was good, he knew he was good, and that arrogance and assurance did much to intimidate any opponents with a scintilla of self-doubt. As a captain he was peerless, his leadership skills especially valuable on the night Liverpool faced down Roma in their own back yard to win the European Cup in 1984.

over a low wall to watch the European Cup final for nothing. True, also, that Liverpool fans were segregated from Juventus fans by thin strands of wire and the Belgian police did nothing to separate the two camps. Yet none of that excuses why Liverpool fans swarmed into the neighbouring section of terracing, causing mayhem and fatalities.

It is probably correct to say that they did not intend to kill any Italians. But they certainly weren't intending to shake hands with them either. The hooligan two-step everybody had seen a hundred times before – the pathetic ritual dispute over 'territory' inside a ground, with pushing and shoving and the mouthing of threats – now ended in a dance of death.

There are so many aspects of that night which are still difficult to absorb even years later. Perhaps most difficult to comprehend is how it was considered right to play the game at all. It was claimed that an abandonment would have created more trouble inside the ground, but that does not ring true. Of more pressing concern may have been the lucrative television contracts which had to be observed – no football, no fee. So after the corpses had been carried out of the stadium and lain in a makeshift tented mortuary, the European Cup final kicked off 90 minutes late.

The players knew much of what had gone on, but not the full extent of it, and they were numbed by the experience. The match was beamed live to millions of television viewers all around Europe, treated like any normal European Cup final, as if it still mattered who won. One country decided not to broadcast the dishonourable spectacle, and that was West Germany. Did the lives of those Italians mean so little that the entertainment could commence as soon as their bodies had been removed from the arena?

UEFA Ban

The days that followed showed English football in an even shabbier light, if that was at all possible. The day after the carnage all British clubs were banned from playing in Belgium. The day after that, the FA voluntarily withdrew all English clubs from European competition for a year, which was also fair enough. But it did not go far enough for European football's governing body, UEFA. It placed an open-ended ban on English teams in Europe, and added a rider that Liverpool's ban would continue for another three years after the other teams were readmitted. To their shame, the English clubs affected by the ban objected to the ruling. This was surely a time for English football to make an act of contrition, to swallow hard and accept whatever an outraged Europe handed out. Tough on Everton, who had just won the Cup-Winners' Cup and qualified for the European Cup by winning the League Championship in some style. But not quite as tough as going to watch a football match and ending up dead.

A period of silence and humility was called for on the part of English football, yet Everton slunk to the High Court along with Manchester United, Norwich and Southampton in search of a legal loophole to get around the ban. On 21 June Liverpool joined in the tawdry cavilling and launched an appeal against their ban. Only Tottenham, who had qualified for the UEFA Cup, refused to join in the grubby process.

Amid all this Joe Fagan left Liverpool, shocked by the brutal farewell football had handed him after so many years in the game. Fagan had told the directors he intended to quit at the season's end, and now he carried out that intention. The good old man must have wondered where all the joy had gone.

Liverpool had already lined up his replacement, and the identity of the new manager came as a surprise. As usual Liverpool kept the appointment in-house, but everyone had expected the new boss to emerge from the Bootroom, not the dressing room. There was even more surprise when

Kenny Dalglish announced he was going to combine his new job with his playing duties to become player-manager.

Phil Neal said: 'People everywhere, whether they worked for a newpaper or the railway, were wondering. It was a subject of conversation, and it was the same for us, no more and no less than anybody else. We had a lot on our plates trying to win matches.

'It was a surprise when they named Kenny as the manager, but the club were very good at that. They were very good at keeping their business close to themselves. It was quickly overshadowed because they announced it on the afternoon of the game at Heysel and quite soon there were more important things to worry about than who was going to be manager the next season.'

Dalglish gave the side a new look during the 1985-86 season, partly by choice and partly by necessity. Graeme Souness had moved to Sampdoria for £500,000, so the midfield needed to be reshaped. He replaced one tough nut with another, Steve McMahon joining from Aston Villa for £350,000. McMahon, another in a series of boyhood Evertonians to end up wearing the red, slotted straight into central midfield. Later in the season McMahon

Great Managers – 1983-85

JOE FAGAN

Smokin' Joe had the difficult job of taking over after the purple Paisley years, but if anyone imagined the Liverpool machine might miss a beat they were wrong. In his first season Fagan took the club to its first-ever treble, winning the League Cup, the First Division Championship, and the European Cup on an emotional night in Rome.

Fagan turned 65 the season after, and wanted a rest. He had been the ultimate back-room boy at Anfield for over 20 years, and the top job did not really suit his temperament. Fagan had been a valued member of the Bootroom brains trust, first as a lieutenant to Bill Shankly, then as Paisley's number two, and he did not enjoy being the focus of attention. Like Paisley before him, he served out of loyalty and a sense of responsibility.

In his second and last season as manager Liverpool finished runners-up in the League behind Everton and lost to Manchester United in the FA Cup semi-finals. His last match should have been a glorious farewell, the European Cup final against Juventus in Brussels. It will be remembered not as a valedictory for a decent man and faithful servant of Liverpool, but as a requiem for 39 people.

competed with a Fagan signing, Kevin MacDonald, who had arrived from Leicester, for a place in the side. Dalglish began to coax the best out of Danish international Jan Molby, who Fagan had signed from Ajax, and also had the imagination to play him in a deep-lying sweeper's role. On his day the Dane's passing ability eclipsed anybody else's in the British game.

At right back quiet Scot Steve Nicol came in for Phil Neal, who left in December 1985 to manager Bolton Wanderers. Neal said: 'I was nearly 35 then and took advice off my great mentor, Bob Paisley, about my next move. I had had 12 great years at Liverpool and had won so much, and I would have loved to have stayed another 12 years, but you have to move on.

'I had the utmost respect for Kenny, and the dignity he demonstrated after Heysel and Hillsborough showed the person he was. He helped to bring Liverpool and Juventus together after Heysel, and he was so good with the families who had suffered from Hillsborough. It was hard dealing with all those people who had lost loved ones, and that was a lot for one person to

50 Greatest Players

ALAN KENNEDY Full back

Joined Liverpool: 1978 **From:** Newcastle United

Debut: August 1978 v Queens Park Rangers (h), Division One – won 2-1

Appearances: 359 **Goals:** 21

Left Liverpool: 1985 **For:** Sunderland

Honours won with Liverpool: European Cup winner 1981, 1984; Division One championship 1979, 1980, 1982, 1984, 1986; League Cup winner 1981, 1982, 1983, 1984; 2 England caps

Not all that many full backs score winning goals in European Cup finals. The man the Kop called 'Barney Rubble' did it twice. The first came against the mighty Real Madrid in Paris in 1981. Late in the game the score stood at 0-0 when Alan received a throw-in from Ray Kennedy down Real's right flank. Alan ran with the ball, and kept running. The Madrid defence didn't appear to have an answer to a left back bearing down on their goal-line, and as they waited for him to cross, the defender cut into the area and lifted a shot over the keeper. The whooping scorer never stopped sprinting until he had reached the Red fans behind the goal. In the 1984 final against Roma, Kennedy took the decisive penalty in the shoot-out and rifled home nervelessly.

cope with, but he did it. He was one of many wonderful people I knew in my time at Liverpool, and I still love the place and care a great deal about the club.'

On the other flank elegant Irish left back Jim Beglin took Alan Kennedy's place, and Dalglish's surgery extended to his own position in the team. He picked ex-Luton striker Paul Walsh instead of himself in the first months of the season before returning to the side for the run-in.

Slow Burn

If Dalglish began the 1985-86 season in a hurry, so did Manchester United. Ron Atkinson's team won their first ten League matches, and they had a 10-point lead over Liverpool before autumn had barely begun.

After United's charge ground to a halt, Everton forged ahead. They opened up an 11-point lead over Liverpool in the New Year, and looked favourites for their second title in consecutive seasons. But Liverpool's slow-burn title challenge exploded over the closing stages. Dalglish brought himself back into the side and played some of the best football of his life as Liverpool finished the season by winning 11 and drawing one of their last 12 games. The last match was at Stamford Bridge, and fittingly, Dalglish scored the only goal of the game to secure Liverpool's eighth championship in 11 years.

By now the Reds were aiming for their first-ever League and FA Cup Double. Seven days after winning the championship, Liverpool faced Everton at Wembley in the match that had been anticipated by generations of fans: the first all-Merseyside FA Cup final.

The run to Wembley had begun with a 5-0 tune-up against Norwich City, who were on their way to winning the Second Division title. They beat Chelsea 2-1 away in the fourth round, setting up a tricky encounter with Third Division York City. The Reds escaped with a 1-1 draw from the first game at Bootham Crescent, where but for a Molby penalty they would have been out. Then they needed extra time to win the replay 3-1 at Anfield. Their quarter-final opponents were Graham Taylor's cussed Watford side, who defended stoically to earn a 0-0 draw at Anfield. Again, Liverpool needed extra time to win the replay 2-1 at Vicarage Road. White Hart Lane was the venue for Liverpool's semi-final with Southampton, and extra time was necessary again, as the score was poised at 0-0 after 90 minutes. But Rush scored twice to set up the final against Everton.

After such anticipation, the match could so easily have gone horribly wrong for Liverpool. Everton settled into their rhythm quicker than the Reds, and deserved it when they took the lead through Gary Lineker. Everton's midfield appeared to have an iron grip on the game, and

50 Greatest Players

PHIL NEAL Full back

Joined Liverpool: 1974

From: Northampton Town

Debut: 16 November 1974 v Everton (a), Division One – drew 0-0

Appearances: 650 **Goals:** 60

Left Liverpool: 1985 **For:** Bolton Wanderers

Honours won with Liverpool: European Cup winner 1977, 1978, 1981, 1984; Division One championship 1976, 1977, 1979, 1980, 1982, 1983, 1984; League Cup winner 1981, 1982, 1983, 1984; UEFA Cup winner 1976; 50 England caps

Neal has won more medals than any other player in the history of English football. Quite some achievement when you consider that before joining Liverpool he had played seven anonymous seasons for Northampton Town in the Fourth Division and by the time he moved to Anfield had already played over 200 games for the Cobblers. Yet nothing he did at the County Ground suggested he would go on to win four European Cups, seven championships and a half-century of England caps.

He hardly ever missed a game, and was an irreplaceable component of the Reds defence for the most successful decade in the club's history. Neal was also a deadly penalty taker, never more assured than on the night in May 1977 when he scored from the spot in Rome to give Liverpool a decisive lead in the European Cup final.

Grobbelaar was fighting with Beglin. From who knows where Liverpool dredged up a revival around the hour. Rush equalised, Craig Johnston fired Liverpool ahead, and Rush made the match safe in the closing minutes. Liverpool had won their first-ever League and Cup Double, and they had begun to expunge the disgrace of Heysel.

It was always going to be impossible for Liverpool to match the feats of the Double-winning season, and in 1986-87 they suffered one of their increasingly rare trophy-less seasons. After the New Year Liverpool looked likely title winners as they put together a run of 12 matches without defeat, including 10 victories. But they finished the season with five defeats in their last nine matches and Everton ran away with League. The Reds went down to Luton in the third round of the Cup, and they even lost a League Cup final, against Arsenal, something they were not used to doing. To put the

Great Matches

FA CUP FINAL

Wembley, 10 May 1986
Attendance: 98,000

Liverpool 3	**Everton 1**
Rush 2	**Lineker**
Johnston	

After waiting for it to come around for nearly a century, the first all-Merseyside FA Cup final was everything Liverpool hoped it would be. It did not begin auspiciously, though. Everton started much the better side, and it was no surprise when they took the lead. Peter Reid played a through-ball for Gary Lineker to chase, and the England centre forward burnt off the chasing Alan Hansen before shooting. Grobbelaar saved the first attempt, but Lineker pounced on the rebound to score.

Ian Rush rounds Bobby Mimms to score Liverpool's first goal.

Everton might have finished a below par Liverpool off, but the Reds finally sprang into life on the hour. First Molby set up Ian Rush for the equaliser. Then five minutes later Craig Johnston side-footed home a cross that fizzed across the box to put Liverpool ahead. Late on Whelan crossed for Rush to grab number three.

'I have so many great memories of that day,' Mark Lawrenson said. 'People were desperate to watch the match, and I saw fans shinning up to the third floor at Wembley and climbing in through a window. We hadn't played well in the first half, and when we came in at half time, Ronnie Moran tore into us. Ronnie could be fierce, but this time he went off the Richter Scale. We turned it around in the second half, and won the match. We went back in the dressing room, celebrating and drinking champagne out of the cup, when we heard these voices from the big baths they had in there. There were three of our supporters in the water, fully clothed. They just looked at us and said: "Come on in fellers, the water's lovely".'

Liverpool: Grobbelaar, Lawrenson, Beglin, Nicol, Whelan, Hansen, Dalglish, Johnston, Rush, Molby, MacDonald

Everton: Mimms, Stevens (Heath), Van Den Hauwe, Ratcliffe, Mountfield, Reid, Steven, Lineker, Sharp, Bracewell, Sheedy

Referee: A. Robinson

50 Greatest Players

MARK LAWRENSON Centre half

Joined Liverpool: 1981

From: Brighton & Hove Albion

Debut: 29 August 1981 v Wolves (a), Division One lost 1-0

Appearances: 356 **Goals:** 18

Left Liverpool: 1988 **For:** Oxford United

Honours won with Liverpool: European Cup winner 1984; Division One championship 1982, 1983, 1984, 1986, 1988; FA Cup winner 1986; League Cup winner 1982, 1983, 1984; 24 Republic of Ireland caps

Lawrenson became Liverpool's record signing when Paisley snapped him up from Brighton for £900,000, but the manager knew it was cash well spent. The Ireland international was already a classy performer, and he thrived at Anfield. After replacing Phil Thompson at the heart of the Reds' defence, Lawrenson formed a perfect double act with Alan Hansen. His best attributes were athleticism and the split-second timing of his tackles. It was his misfortune to play for Ireland when they were a relatively minor footballing power, otherwise his claim to being one of the world's best defenders would have been unanswerable.

finishing touch to a miserable season Liverpool waved farewell to Ian Rush, who went to Juventus. The Welshman had scored his 200th goal for the Reds against QPR on 18 March 1987.

Liverpool did not want to lose Rush, but the Italians made them an offer they couldn't refuse: £3.2m was simply too much money to turn down. The good news was that the avalanche of lira allowed Kenny Dalglish to embark on an overhaul of his squad, and he didn't waste the opportunity. He squeezed every last drop out of the windfall, and if he was going to lose a player of Rush's quality he could console himself with the calibre of players he was able to buy with the proceeds: John Barnes signed from Watford for £900,000; John Aldridge came from Oxford for £750,000; Peter Beardsley was a £1.8m buy from Newcastle; and shortly after the season started Ray Houghton followed Aldridge from Oxford for £825,000.

The fresh infusion of exciting talent transformed Liverpool, and they surged to the top of the table playing a style of attacking football that had rarely, if ever, been seen in English club football. They lost just two matches all season and scored 87 goals in the the 40-match programme. Rush's replacement, Aldridge, was the top scorer in the the country, with 26. By Christmas they were already 10 points clear of their nearest challengers, Nottingham Forest, and it was March before they lost a League game. Their 29-match unbeaten trot equalled the record set by Leeds in 1973-74.

The High-water Mark

In April a 5-0 home win against Nottingham Forest came to be seen as the pinnacle of the Dalglish era, a performance that has been hailed by the finest ever served up by a Liverpool side in a league game. No less an authority than Shankly's hero, Tom Finney, told *The Times*: 'I've never seen skill at that pace'. In a eulogy that gives a fair impression of that great Reds side, he went on: 'In all my time as a player and as a spectator, that was the finest exhibition of football I've seen. Everybody will have left believing they had seen something that will never be bettered. The execution of the moves was tremendous. They have great individual players and they all support each other. The number of times defenders came through to join the attack, it could have been seven or eight quite easily.'

When a 1-0 home win over Spurs on 23 April gave the Reds their 17th championship, with four matches still to play, Liverpool were advancing on their second Double in two years. Only a rag-tag outfit from south London stood in their way. Wimbledon were their opponents in the FA Cup final, and the Reds were the shortest-priced favourites to win the trophy since Leeds played Second Division Sunderland in 1973. And everybody knows what happened then. In hindsight, perhaps it was rash to write off Wimbledon so carelessly. They did, after all, finish the season seventh in the First Division. Mugs don't win cups.

If Liverpool wondered whether Wimbledon might shelve their rough-and-ready approach for the sake of Wembley and the billions watching worldwide on television, they quickly found out. In the tunnel before the match the Dons' prime merchant of mayhem, Vinnie Jones, leaned over

John Barnes played a major part in Liverpool's polished performances in the 1980s and 1990s.

Liverpool players and staff celebrate winning the 1988 League Championship.

to Dalglish and announced: 'I am going to rip your ear off and spit in the hole.' Now Kenny is a tough Glaswegian and had seen a hundred cut-price gangsters in the Jones mould down the years, and he was probably not over-worried by Jones's lurid threat. But at least he knew that Wimbledon weren't at Wembley to play pat-ball. The Beautiful Game would have the day off.

Predictably Liverpool had the best of the play, and Beardsley put the ball in the net only for the referee to disallow it because he had blown up for an earlier foul. And even when Lawrie Sanchez gave Wimbledon the lead after heading in a Dennis Wise free kick, the Reds were still fancied to win. But as the minutes ticked by and Wimbledon's doughty defence stood firm, anxiety grew. Liverpool's best chance came on the hour, when Aldridge was awarded a penalty. He had already scored 11 from the spot that season, but to the striker's eternal mortification, Wimbledon's keeper, Dave Beasant, punched this one clear.

Aldridge said: 'I took a lot on my shoulders, but it wasn't a bad penalty. It was a good height for Dave Beasant, though, that was the thing. He'd done his homework and made the goal smaller. He spread himself on the side where I put most of my kicks. It wasn't a penalty in the first place, though. It was a good tackle. The lad got the ball but I went over. I was surprised when it was given.'

50 Greatest Players

KENNY DALGLISH Striker

Joined Liverpool: 1977 **From:** Celtic

Debut: August 1977 Charity Shield v Manchester United (Wembley) drew 0-0

Appearances: 515 **Goals:** 172

Left Liverpool: 1991 **For:** Management

Honours won with Liverpool: European Cup winner 1978, 1981, 1984; Division One championship 1979, 1980, 1982, 1983, 1984, 1986; FA Cup winner 1986; League Cup winner 1981, 1982, 1983, 1984; 55 Scotland caps

Dalglish is a candidate for the greatest Liverpool player of all time, perhaps only Billy Liddell challenging him for that honour. At times he raised football to the sublime, yet for all that he was not a flashy player. He scored goals of audacious brilliance, but was also happy to stick them away in the six-yard box. Not for him the showmanship of a Cantona, who professed he only wanted to score 'beautiful goals'. Dalglish just wanted to score; it just so happens that on so many occasions he had to resort to magicianship to conjure a goal. He could play so many roles to perfection. As a targetman to hold the play up, you could never get the ball off him. As a play-maker, his passing was incisive and flawless. As a finisher he was imaginative, and deadly. The chip to beat Bruges in the 1981 European Cup final was Dalglish distilled.

Kenny Dalglish with the 1986 FA Cup trophy.

It was the first-ever penalty save in a Wembley final, and it cost Liverpool their Double. Despite that setback, Liverpool fans could still look back on a memorable season which had seen their team win the championship playing football of matchless quality. Nobody could have dreamt that it would turn into the cruellest of times of all for every Liverpudlian.

Century of Crimes

One phrase more than any other has become associated with Bill Shankly: 'football isn't a matter of life and death – it's more important than that'. How those words have rung false since 15 April 1989. Perhaps the only comfort to be derived from that bleakest of days was that Shankly was not alive to witness the tragedy of Hillsborough.

While Heysel could be blamed on the criminality of supporters, Hillsborough was the culmination of a century of crimes against football supporters. The deaths of 96 spectators was an accident waiting to happen, and it could have taken place at just about any ground in the country on any match day. The root cause of 96 deaths was the casual contempt with which fans had been treated for decades by the football authorities and the police.

No one was ever held to account for the mis-allocation of tickets on the day of that FA Cup semi-final between Liverpool and Nottingham Forest. It was a typically crass error which set in train a lethal chain of events. Liverpool, with an average crowd of over 40,000, were allowed to sell 24,000 tickets for the match, and they were given the smaller Leppings Lane end of Sheffield Wednesday's ground. Forest, average crowd about 17,000, were given 30,000 tickets, and Hillsborough's massive Kop terrace. Liverpool's secretary, Peter Robinson, complained about the administrative blunder, but his appeals were ignored.

The events of the day itself are almost too horrid to rehearse. Roadworks delayed the arrival of thousands of Liverpool fans, and long queues built up outside the turnstiles at the Leppings Lane end. The kick-off could have been delayed to make sure everybody was admitted safely, but the criminal decision was taken to relieve congestion outside the ground by opening a gate, letting fans pour into an enclosure which was already full to capacity. People at the front of the terrace were condemned to death when that gate was opened. They were crushed against the steel fencing which separated pitch from terrace, with no chance of escape.

Bruce Grobbelaar was defending the goal at the Leppings Lane end and he grew aware of the distress of the supporters behind him. 'Bruce, they're killing us,' somebody shouted. Grobbelaar tried to keep one eye on the game while begging police officers to unlock a gate in the fence to relieve the crush. Liverpool went close with an attempt on goal, drawing excited gasps from all around the ground, and making the crush to get inside more frantic. Dozens more died in that surge.

Eventually, it dawned that there was real trouble in the Leppings Lane end, and the referee took the teams off, and the grim battle to save lives began.

It took a cold-eyed, hard-hitting report from someone who had nothing to do with football to put Hillsborough in its proper context. Officially-sanctioned reports, such as the one Lord Justice Taylor compiled after the tragedy at Sheffield Wednesday, are usually couched in dispassionate language. Lord Taylor's report was coolly and diplomatically written, but it scarcely concealed a real anger over the circumstances which led to so many deaths.

The Taylor Report

His 104-page report was published in January 1990, and made 76 recommendations. He insisted that supporters should no longer be crammed in behind steel fences, treated in Taylor's words like 'prisoners of war'. He recommended the immediate removal of the kind of fences which had proved fatal at Hillsborough. He also criticised the police for failing to control the crowd outside the ground. In a coruscating attack on the culture that for decades had required supporters to risk their lives for the sake of watching football, he said: 'The years of patching up grounds, of having periodic disasters and narrowly avoiding many others by muddling through on a wing and a prayer, must be over.'

Even while writing his report in the aftermath of Hillsborough, Taylor did not seem convinced that football was ready to put its house in order. He observed with a jaundiced eye that his report was the ninth to examine safety at football grounds. Similar studies had been commissioned after the 1923 FA Cup final at Wembley when a crowd of over 125,000 swarmed dangerously into the new Wembley; after Burnden Park in 1946 when three fans were crushed to death; after Ibrox Park in 1971 (just the worst in a string of disasters at Rangers' ground) when 66 died; after Valley Parade in 1985 when 56 were burnt to death. After all that, Taylor could not believe how so many people, 'could die from overcrowding before the very eyes of those controlling the event'.

As soon as the report was published the government announced, in line with Taylor's recommendation, that terracing at First and Second Division grounds should be all-seater by August 1994, and at every League ground by 1999. It was at least a start. After so many futile deaths, it finally looked as though there had been a decisive tilt towards treating football supporters like fully paid up citizens and members of the human race, and away from the mindset that treated them like potential terrorists.

The days and weeks that followed were unbearably sad, as the city and the football club tried to face up to their loss. To their eternal credit Kenny Dalglish, his players and their wives, did all they could to comfort the bereaved, drawing up a rota of funerals to attend, and hospitals to visit. In these blackest days of all the club drew together, drawing strength and succour from the spirit of togetherness. Anfield disappeared under flowers as thousands filed past a makeshift monument to the dead.

At that grief-filled time it was hard to imagine that one day Liverpool Football Club would have to think about its future. Could they bear to complete their fixtures for the season? Should they simply write off the rest of the season as a mark of respect to the dead? Gradually, the feeling among supporters and the majority of the bereaved was that the game must go on. They would draw more comfort from seeing the Reds on the park than they would in seeing the season consigned to history.

Defeaning Silence

So on 3 May 1989 Liverpool played Everton in a league match at Goodison Park. Merseyside's football fraternity came together, and never in all the years since the schism of 1892 had the two clubs been closer in spirit. The pre-match minute's silence was deafening in its eloquence. The result was 0-0, but that never mattered. Liverpool had played their first game post-Hillsborough, and it was like a huge sigh of relief.

Now they had resolved to play on, Liverpool had a duty to win the FA Cup. On a raw night of emotion they beat Forest 3-1 at Old Trafford in the rescheduled semi-final. Victory meant everything to John Aldridge, the Kopite turned Liverpool player, who had been rocked to his soul by Hillsborough. Aldridge, who scored twice in the game, said: 'That was probably the biggest club game in my career because of what it meant and what it stood for. It meant even more to me than the Wembley game, thinking of all the people that died.'

The final brought Liverpool back into a neighbourly embrace with Everton, and against all the odds the two teams laid on the most entertaining FA Cup final for years. Aldridge put Liverpool ahead in the fourth minute, only for Stuart McCall to equalise in the closing seconds. Rush, the man who had returned to Anfield in a cut-price deal after a disillusioning year in Italy, shot the Reds back into the lead early in extra time. McCall volleyed his second to put the game level again, only for Rush to head in John Barnes's winner to capture the trophy.

It was turning into the kind of season that, in other circumstances, would be revered as one of the most exciting of all time. After the high drama of the FA Cup final came the closest conclusion to a championship duel the Football League had ever seen.

The last match of the season pitted leaders Liverpool against second in the table Arsenal. At one stage, in February, Liverpool had trailed the Gunners by 19 points, but the Reds launched a spring offensive which brought George Graham's team within range, and as the season drew to a close Arsenal inexplicably began to shed points with abandon. By the time the League's last act was played out, Arsenal needed to win by two goals to deprive Liverpool of the title, and their second Double.

At half time and with the score 0-0, Liverpool seemed safe. Even when Alan Smith scored for Arsenal early in the second half, Liverpool were confident. The match drained away to the final seconds, when Lee Dixon humped a despairing ball forward. It reached Smith, who helped it into the path of Michael Thomas, breaking from midfield. He held off two challenges and dabbed the ball past Grobbelaar. Arsenal were Champions, and they were cheered to the echo by the home crowd. Football still mattered. But not as much as it had done before 15 April.

Tributes left at the Kop End goal at Anfield after the Hillsborough tragedy.

Chapter Ten: 1989-94
The Souness Era

The first post-Hillsborough season began with the departure of one of the Kop's favourite players. Dalglish, unable to promise John Aldridge an automatic starting position with Rush and Beardsley in the squad, accepted an offer of £1m for him from Spanish side Real Sociedad. There was a commonly-held theory around the time that Rush and Aldridge were not suited to playing in the same team, and Dalglish appeared to share it.

In the brutal environment of professional football, the manager must act decisively for what he sees as the good of the team, and Dalglish did that now. Aldridge was on his way out, and when Liverpool agreed terms with Real Sociedad, he was on his way. Aldridge went on to enjoy one of the happiest periods of his career and life in northern Spain, but leaving Anfield was a huge wrench for him. He had taken his time to reach the top level, and scoring goals for Liverpool was all he ever wanted to do. Now the thing he loved had been snatched from him, he was certain to feel disappointed. He was also convinced that an Aldridge-Rush front-running partnership could have carried on working.

'People said me and Rush couldn't play alongside each other but it was totally unfair,' Aldridge argued. 'Whenever we played either he scored or I did, and I don't think we lost in any of those games. Saying we couldn't play together was a fallacy. We could have, and should have been given the chance, but Kenny didn't see it that way. I was a bit older and got shown the door.' He was at least allowed a sentimental leave-taking. On the night Liverpool destroyed Crystal Palace 9-0 at Anfield in September 1989, Aldridge started the game on the bench. When Ronnie Whelan was fouled in the area and the referee awarded a penalty, Dalglish sent Aldridge on in Beardsley's place to take it. He duly scored his last Liverpool goal in his last appearance for the team.

Palace gained mighty revenge the following April when the two sides met in the FA Cup semi-finals. The match at Villa Park was one of the most exciting Cup ties Liverpool have ever been involved with, although you would never have guessed it would turn out to be a classic when Rush shot Liverpool into the lead after a quarter of an hour and Liverpool still looked comfortable as they went in at half time still 1-0 up. But Palace stormed into

50 Greatest Players

JOHN ALDRIDGE Centre forward

Joined Liverpool: 1987 **From:** Oxford United

Debut: 21 February 1987 v Aston Villa (a), Division One – drew 2-2

Appearances: 104 **Goals:** 63

Left Liverpool: 1989 **For:** Real Sociedad

Honours won with Liverpool: Division One championship 1988; FA Cup winner 1989; 19 Republic of Ireland caps

It took this boyhood Kopite a few years and a few clubs before he found his way home. After scoring heavily for Newport County and Oxford United, he signed for his beloved Liverpool, and the goals just kept on coming. He was drafted as the replacement for Ian Rush, who had departed for Juventus, and went on to match the great Welshman's strike rate. In a team lit up by the extravagant talents of Peter Beardsley and John Barnes, Aldridge was the unfussy finisher who converted so many of their brilliant ideas into goals. He was not the kind of player who captured the popular imagination, but the Anfield crowd recognised a kindred spirit. His sorrow over missing the penalty in the 1988 FA Cup final defeat against Wimbledon was deep and sincere. Kenny Dalglish, the manager who had signed him from Oxford, eventually decided Aldridge and Rush weren't suited to play alongside each other, and the Irish international was sold to Real Sociedad.

attack from the restart and equalised through Mark Bright. The south London side went ahead with Gary O'Reilly's goal with 20 minutes left, but the Reds were not finished. As the match ticked into the last 10 minutes Steve McMahon made it 2-2, then John Barnes scored a penalty after Steve Staunton had been fouled inside the area. Incredibly, Palace scored again with two minutes left, Andy Gray climbing above Liverpool's inattentive defence to take the tie into extra time. Palace's Alan Pardew made it 4-3 early in the extra period, and then held out to reach Wembley, where they lost 1-0 in a replay to Manchester United.

History turns on such moments. United's FA Cup triumph was Alex Ferguson's first trophy as the club's manager, and there was a feeling that this might be his last chance after five unsuccessful years at Old Trafford. His emerging team might have fared less well against Liverpool and defeat could easily have spelt the end for the man who went on to build a dynasty which eclipsed Liverpool in the last decade of the 20th century.

That galling defeat against Palace cost Liverpool the chance of another League and Cup Double, because while the cup run was unfolding the Reds were charging to the title.

Ian Rush, back at Liverpool and back in the goals. He picked up two more in this 5-2 thrashing of Chelsea at Stamford Bridge in December 1989.

Attacking Trident

Inspired by an attacking trident formed by Barnes, Beardsley and Rush, Liverpool set a devastating pace all season, and nobody else posed a convincing threat. Liverpool surged to the championship over the closing stages, helped in large measure by an inspired Dalglish loan signing. The manager introduced Israeli Ronny Rosenthal, on loan from Standard Liege, for the last few matches, and his return of seven goals in eight games was decisive in the run-in.

Under the gruff Glaswegian exterior of Kenny Dalglish lurks a showman with an eye for drama, and the 39-year-old chose the moment of his last appearance as a Liverpool player carefully. After the title was safely won, Dalglish came on as a substitute in the final minutes of the last home match of the season against Derby. After the final whistle, which heralded a 1-0 victory on the day, he showed the venerable First Division trophy to all four corners of Anfield amidst wild acclaim, and took his bow as a Liverpool footballer.

After winning their 18th championship in style, a handy nine points ahead of Aston Villa in second place, it seemed like Liverpool's place at the summit of English football was secure for the foreseeable future. Who could have guessed back in the summer of 1990 that a new century would dawn and Liverpool would still be waiting for their 19th title.

It looked like business as usual the following season as Liverpool sprinted into February as league leaders and were safely in the last 16 of the FA Cup. They were in prime position as springtime loomed: perfectly poised for a super-charged late burst to burn off their rivals. Surely, more glory was at hand. No one expected Dalglish to throw the club into disarray on 22 February 1991 by tendering his resignation.

His timing was curious. Just two days earlier Liverpool had played out a thrilling 4-4 draw with Everton in an FA Cup fifth round replay at Goodison, and the second replay was five days away. But at the press conference to announce his decision, Dalglish insisted he could not go on for another day. He had nothing left to give. The pressure of match days, said Dalglish, 'made his head explode'. A look at Dalglish's drawn face, and the dull monotone with which he expressed himself during these dark days, made his point for him. He had been worn down by the demands of managing England's leading club for five years, and the added emotional burdens of first Heysel, then Hillsborough, had taken their toll. The club's directors begged him to stay, but it would have been cruel to keep him in his job. Dalglish had earned a break, and owed nobody anything.

Great Managers – 1985-91

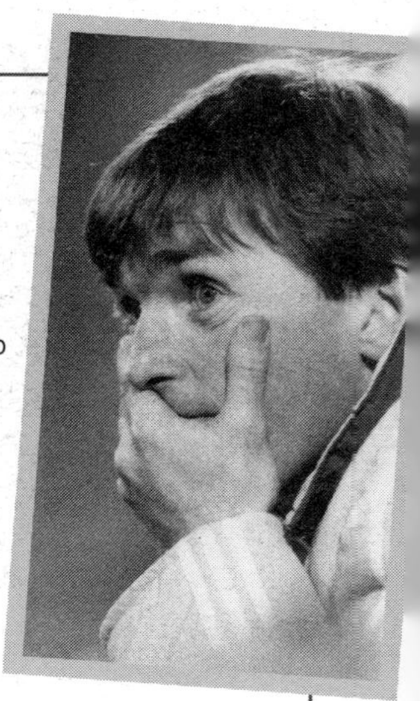

KENNY DALGLISH

Dalglish was the imaginative choice to replace Joe Fagan as Liverpool manager, and what an inspired decision it turned out to be.

The Glaswegian was still close to the peak of his playing powers as a 33-year-old in 1985, so it was natural for Dalglish to become player-manager. The dual responsibility did him no harm. In his first season he became the first Liverpool manager to win the League and FA Cup Double, and the first player-manager from any club to achieve that feat. For good measure, the FA Cup was captured when the Reds beat Everton 3-1 in the long-awaited, first-ever all-Merseyside final.

Dalglish was changed forever by the horror of Hillsborough in 1989, and the Liverpool manager's job seemed to lose some of its savour afterwards. He left in 1991, saying the pressure of match-days 'was making my head explode'. In happier times his Liverpool teams had won three championships and two FA Cups, playing some of the most exciting football in the club's history.

50 Greatest Players

ALAN HANSEN Centre half

Joined Liverpool: 1977 **From:** Partick Thistle

Debut: 24 September 1977 v Derby County (h), Division One – won 1-0

Appearances: 620 **Goals:** 14

Left Liverpool: 1990 (retired)

Honours won with Liverpool: Division One championship 1979, 1980, 1983, 1984, 1986, 1988, 1990; FA Cup winner 1986, 1989; 26 Scotland caps

Hansen was never your typical centre half. For a start, he jokingly claims he avoided heading the ball at all costs, preferring to leave that hazardous activity to a string of partners who included Phil Thompson, Mark Lawrenson, Gary Gillespie and Glenn Hysen. And there was never the blood-and-thunder, fist-clenching, up-and-at-'em mentality that marks the breed. Instead Hansen retained his composure at all times, and would have supporters and managers covering their eyes as he dribbled out from the back, rather than launching the ball into Row X when the heat was on. Hansen was not the fastest defender who ever drew breath, but his speed of thought and footballing nous were matchless. These are qualities that he now puts to great use as a compelling expert on BBC television.

Liverpool appointed Ronnie Moran as caretaker-manager, and in the usual Anfield way of things he would have been favourite to get the job permanently. He was the next in line from a Bootroom lineage which was slowly fading away: Shankly was dead, Paisley and Fagan retired.

Moran was 57, but fitter than most men half his age, and his appointment would have given Liverpool another seamless transition of power in the Anfield mould. But Moran didn't want the job. The board had been able to persuade Bob Paisley and Joe Fagan to take the manager's position against their inclinations, but Ronnie Moran was adamant. For the first time in over 30 years, Liverpool looked beyond their own staff for a new manager. Just before the end of the 1990-91 season, which had been a frustrating experience for everyone at the club and which had seen the Reds lose to Everton in the fifth round of the FA Cup after two replays and fall behind Arsenal in the hunt for the championship, they found their man.

Liverpool manager Graeme Souness and his assistant Roy Evans watch Liverpool's 3-0 victory over Norwich City in April 1991.

Biggest Mistake of His Life?

He was hardly a new face around Anfield: with the promise of a five-year contract worth £350,000 a year Liverpool lured Graeme Souness south from his job as Rangers' manager, and he took over on 16 April 1991. His chairman at Ibrox, David Murray, said: 'I think he is making the biggest mistake of his life. Time will tell.' In the final analysis it could be said that the mistake was on the part of Liverpool's directors for hiring a manager so out of step with the club's greatest traditions. Souness's short era turned out to be fractious, and damaging to the club's long-term interest. It might be said that Liverpool are still paying for the mistakes made in those three years.

It was a time when English football was undergoing a financial revolution, with the advent of the Premier League, and a massive rise in the amount of cash television was prepared to pay to screen matches. Never before had a top league position mattered so much to a club's prosperity, and it was at this crucial juncture that Liverpool took their eye off the ball and let Manchester United, then Arsenal, forge ahead. The rest of the decade, and the early years of the 21st century, was the story of how Liverpool fought to regain their position at the top of English football. It would be a sterner task even than the one Shankly faced in the 1960s.

Souness threw himself into the Liverpool job like it was a 50:50 ball. There was to be no shirking, no gentle settling-in period. He was a man on a mission, and his mission was to overhaul a Liverpool team he didn't think was strong enough to win the league. The directors had promised him liberal funds for re-building, and Souness set about spending it. In two days in July 1991 he laid out over £5m on two Derby County players. Welsh striker Dean Saunders joined for a British-record £2.9m, and Mark Wright arrived for £2.2m as a replacement for Alan Hansen, who had retired the previous season. Souness also made changes to the coaching staff and brought his own assistant with him from Rangers, Phil Boersma. Boersma was a former Liverpool striker of the 1970s, best remembered for walking out on the club in a fit of pique before the 1974 FA Cup final, after Shankly had picked Chris Lawler as substitute instead of him.

Ian Rush wrote in his autobiography that Souness also ditched Liverpool's carefully honed pre-season training programme, a move which the striker claimed left the team with a string of injuries which hung around all season. Rush complained that Souness put the players through a sequence of

50 Greatest Players

PETER BEARDSLEY Striker

Joined Liverpool: 1987 **From:** Newcastle United

Debut: 15 August 1987 v Arsenal (a), Division One – won 2-1

Appearances: 175 **Goals:** 59

Left Liverpool: 1991 **For:** Everton

Honours won with Liverpool: Division One championship 1988, 1990; FA Cup winner 1989; 34 England caps

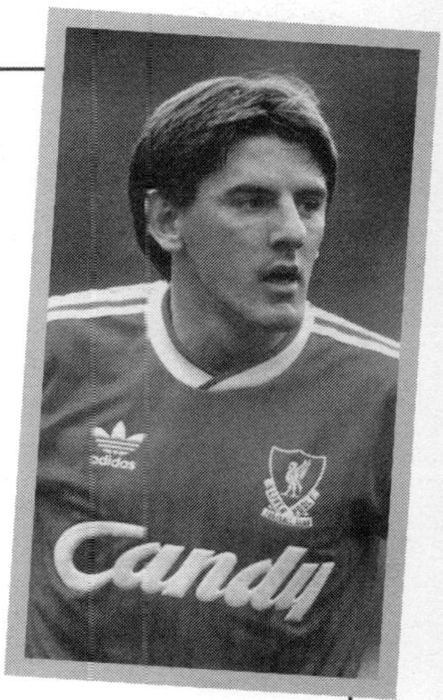

Beardsley was a footballer from another age. Previous generations of football supporters would have recognised him as the perfect inside forward, providing the craft and guile from deep positions, a creator before a taker of chances, but a canny penalty area operator when the opportunity arose. His partnerships with Rush and Aldridge, and with Gary Lineker for England, became shining examples of what coaching jargon came to call the split-striker's role. In his later days at Anfield he was often left out of the team as Dalglish rejigged the line-up. When Graeme Souness came in as manager he was dispensed with altogether. It is testimony to the high regard in which he was held by Liverpool fans that they never held the identity of his new club against him.

punishing running drills on the first day back in training, which was not the Liverpool way. 'He ripped up the tried and trusted formula that had produced so much success since Shankly's era and he tried to run the club his own way,' he wrote. 'We had just had our summer break, and I don't believe that the limbs and muscles of the players had been hardened sufficiently for such strenuous work. It produced an incredible series of injuries to the lads, before a single ball had even been kicked.'

Top Player Cull

Souness may just have been unlucky with the high casualty rate his side suffered, and his training methods might have had nothing to do with the slew of injuries Liverpool suffered throughout the season. But whatever the reason, the absence of so many players at different times wrecked the side's rhythm. It is certainly true that Souness did not help himself by forcing through a cull of top players who still had much to offer. Beardsley, McMahon and Houghton all fell out of favour. To Souness's credit, he brought on youngsters like Steve McManaman, Rob Jones, Jamie Redknapp and Robbie Fowler in due course, but some of his signings were disastrous.

Rob Jones promised so much for Liverpool and England, but his football career was cruelly terminated by injury.

While he was Rangers manager Souness had been much taken with the talents of a Hungarian international midfielder, Istvan Kozma, who played for Dunfermline in the Scottish Premier League. Souness brought Kozma down to Anfield for £300,000 in January 1992, convinced he was the ball-playing midfielder who could transform his ailing side. Alas, Kozma started just three games for the Reds and was released on a free transfer when the Department of Employment withdrew his work permit.

Steve McMahon was transfer-listed by Graeme Souness at a time when many thought he was playing the best football of his career.

Liverpool ended Souness's first full season in sixth place, their worst showing since 1965. The title was won by Leeds United, whose closing games were inspired by Eric Cantona. The title should have gone to the resurgent Manchester United, but a miserable end to the season saw them win just four of their last 14 matches.

Dalglish Back

While Liverpool supporters muttered about the decline in their team's league status, they might have cast a rueful glance at Blackburn Rovers. They were now managed by Dalglish, who had broken off his sabbatical to manage a club transformed by Jack Walker's millions. Dalglish coaxed his new team into the First Division play-offs, and after beating Leicester in the final at Wembley looked forward to meeting Liverpool in the first-ever Premiership season. Dalglish said: 'Seven months ago football was not the most important thing in my life. I'd had enough and needed to recharge my batteries. The time is right to come back.'

A troubled season took a turn for the worse when Peterborough knocked the Reds out of the League Cup, and their return to European competition ended in meek defeat against Italian side, Genoa. But the FA Cup salvaged much pride.

The run began with an undemanding 4-0 win at Fourth Division Crewe, but from then on the Reds stumbled all the way to Wembley. They needed a replay before beating Second Division Bristol Rovers 2-1 at Anfield in the fourth round. Then Division Two champions in waiting, Ipswich, held Liverpool to a 0-0 draw at Portman Road before the Reds sneaked through 3-2 at home.

Mark Wright argues with Bruce Grobbelaar during Liverpool's nervous display in the FA Cup semi-final against Portsmouth in 1992.

Michael Thomas, who, perhaps deciding Anfield was his lucky ground, had joined the Reds, scored the only goal of the quarter-final against Aston Villa at home, the only time Liverpool faced a top flight side in the whole Cup run.

Semi-final Shoot-out

Portsmouth from the Second Division were their opponents in the semi-final at Highbury, where Liverpool were lucky to escape with a 1-1 draw. Darren Anderton scored a late goal to put Pompey ahead, only for Whelan to grab an even later goal to force a replay. After 120 minutes of football in the re-match at Villa Park the score was 0-0, and the Reds faced a shoot-out. Portsmouth went to pieces, missing three of their first four kicks, and Liverpool went through to the final.

Minutes after that first game against Portsmouth, Souness had told his players he was having a triple heart bypass operation the next morning. The surgery was a success, but the manager's standing with Liverpool's fans received a mortal blow thanks to an unsavoury PR stunt Souness engineered during his convalescence. He sold an exclusive story about his ordeal to the *Sun*. That same paper had accused Liverpool supporters of looting corpses and urinating on members of the emergency services at Hillsborough under a splash headline which screamed: 'The Truth'. Not surprisingly, the paper has been reviled on Merseyside ever since. To compound Souness's crass actions, the interview, complete with pictures of Souness canoodling with his lover, appeared on the third anniversary of Hillsborough. Rush wrote: 'From then on his relationship with many fans was never quite the same.' Souness later made a donation to the Alder Hey children's hospital in Liverpool as an act of good faith, but the damage had been done.

Concerned Medics

Against medical advice Souness dragged himself to Wembley for the final with Second Division Sunderland, who had enjoyed a tub-thumping jaunt to the final, beating three top flight sides along the way. Ronnie Moran was nominally in charge of the Liverpool side, and Souness was flanked by concerned medics, whose job was to make sure he didn't get too excited.

As events turned out, there was precious little to get worked up about, as the Reds controlled the match from the first whistle and won 2-0 with some aplomb. It was a day when the young McManaman came to the fore, playing in place of the injured Barnes. He ripped up and down both wings, teasing Sunderland's defence at every opportunity, and crossed for Michael Thomas to volley the first goal. Thomas then set up Rush for the clincher.

Even now, Liverpool were nearly deprived of their hard-earned winners' medals. For once the losers went up the 39 steps to the Royal Box first, and were mistakenly handed Liverpool's medals, and the Reds were handed Sunderland's. They swapped them over later. And on a day of trophy mishaps, a member of the Liverpool party put a dent in the FA Cup as they got on their coach on the way out of Wembley. It was a brand new trophy, the fourth in the competition's 120-year history, and had been commissioned by the FA to replace the old one which had been in service since 1911. Liverpool had been in possession of the pot for less than an hour and it already needed repairing.

The Reds had ended the season in customary, trophy-winning fashion, but there was something missing. They didn't quite look like a Liverpool team. Perhaps it had something to do with the new kit. The all-red shirt, designed by Shankly to make his men look like giants, had been altered by the addition of Adidas-inspired diagonal white stripes. It made the players look as if they had dish-cloths draped over their shoulders.

Birth of the Premier League

English football kicked off a new era in 1992-93 with the birth of the FA Premiership. The top-flight teams had finally cut loose from their lowlier brethren to form a shiny new made-for-TV elite competition. The game was well on its way to becoming a plutocracy where the richest clubs thrived, while the poor relations lived off the crumbs. As a sign of the new order, Aldershot, a harmless-enough Fourth Division club, went to the wall in March 1992 for the sake of a few thousand quid. Meanwhile the new Premiership clubs were sharing out the first instalment of the £304 million the BBC and BSkyB had paid to screen the first five seasons of the new league. Apart from the bigger clubs getting more money, there seemed to be only one difference between the old First Division and the new Premier League: the refs wore green instead of black.

This was Liverpool's centenary season, but there was little joy in 1992-93 as the Reds endured their worst season since the 1950s. The recriminations began as early as pre-season, when Souness sacked Anfield loyalist Phil Thompson, the reserve team coach, after a disagreement. Souness swung the axe elsewhere during the

Steve McManaman was man-of-the-match in the 1992 FA Cup final against Sunderland.

season, sending the former club skipper, Glenn Hysen, back to Sweden. Saunders was sold at a loss to Villa in September after just a year at Anfield. Ray Houghton, whose face had not fitted in Souness's regime, was also sold to Villa. New faces were coming in, and among Souness's early-season signings were Paul Stewart from Spurs for £2.3m, promising young Watford keeper David James for £1m, Danish defender Torben Piechnik from BK Copenhagen for £500,000 and Norwegian full back Stig-Inge Bjornebye from Rosenborg for £600,000.

The stylish Jan Molby was one of the few survivors from Dalglish's reign.

Rush's Records

Still, a winning blend eluded Liverpool. Injuries continued to plague the squad, and the Reds plummeted down the Premier League table. The only bright points were the scoring exploits of Rush, who broke records while the side crumbled around him. In October against Manchester United he scored his 286th goal for Liverpool, beating Roger Hunt's all-time club record. A month later against Middlesbrough he scored his 200th league goal for Liverpool.

Despite Rush's good form, Liverpool found themselves in the unlikely position of 16th after 12 matches of the season, just one win above the drop zone. Trepidation gave way to outright crisis in November, December and January. First Spartak Moscow beat the Reds home and away to knock them out of the Cup-Winners' Cup 6-2 on aggregate. Then relegation-bound Crystal Palace knocked Liverpool out of the League Cup.

To end the calamitous run of cup defeats, Bolton Wanderers of the new Second Division beat Liverpool 2-0 at Anfield in the FA Cup. It wasn't so much the result against Wanderers that alarmed Liverpool supporters, it was the manner in which it was achieved. The side from two divisions below Liverpool blasted the Reds off the park; Anfield was no longer a fortress. Liverpool's home used to be a place where other teams feared to tread. Now it was just another ground.

By now Liverpool's league challenge was in tatters. They had been thrashed 5-1 by Coventry the week before Christmas, and Liverpool put together a run of seven matches without a win. In February they began another run of six matches without a win, and absenteeism in the injury-ravaged club had reached such epidemic proportions that 34-year-old Liverpool coach, Sammy Lee, was called into the squad for the league match at Crystal Palace.

Rudimentary Discipline

The team lacked rudimentary discipline, and in that game at Palace Souness himself was ordered from his dug-out, accused of swearing at a linesman. A 3-2 defeat at Oldham Athletic, when Don Hutchison became the sixth Liverpool player to be sent off in the season, triggered an emergency board meeting to discuss Souness's position. The word around Anfield was that the manager was on his way out. That suspicion seemed to be confirmed when he missed Liverpool's last match of the season, a 6-2 win over Tottenham at Anfield, which featured Rush's 300th goal in all competitions for the Reds. Souness went to watch Coventry play Leeds instead.

The familiar running style of Ronnie Rosenthal.

When Liverpool called a press conference for the next day it seemed certain that Souness's sacking would be announced. Yet to the disbelief of everybody in the room chairman David Moores declared, in the face of all the recent speculation, that Souness was staying on to complete his contract. By now Liverpool supporters had grown desperate for change and the news that Souness had survived the boardroom machinations left them feeling even more deflated.

Undeterred by his scrape with the sack, Souness pressed on with his rebuilding. In the summer of 1993 he paid Nottingham Forest £2.27m for Nigel Clough, a striker admired for his ability on the ball, but not for his pace or strike rate. Centre half Neil Ruddock joined from Spurs for £2.5m and Liverpool fans were aghast when West Ham left back Julian Dicks arrived in September, in exchange for gifted young midfielder Mike Marsh and promising full back David Burrows. Dicks, a walking disciplinary time-bomb, was as far away from being a typical Liverpool footballer as you could get. Many accustomed to seeing the likes of Hansen, Dalglish and even Souness in the famous red were quick to express surprise at such signings.

By now, Souness could do little right in the eyes of supporters. There was ill-feeling in the dressing room too, as even long-serving players like Rush were treated in a cavalier fashion by Souness, who tinkered desperately with the line-up to find a winning formula. Rush was dropped from the team, brought back, made club

50 Greatest Players

RONNIE WHELAN Midfielder

Joined Liverpool: 1979 **From:** Home Farm

Debut: 3 April 1981 Division One v Stoke City (h) won 3-0

Appearances: 493 **Goals:** 73

Left Liverpool: 1994 **For:** Southend United

Honours won with Liverpool: Division One championship 1982, 1983, 1984, 1986, 1988, 1990; FA Cup winner 1986, 1989; League Cup winner 1982, 1983, 1984; 51 Republic of Ireland caps

Whelan was that priceless commodity, a player who never seemed to have an off-day. Whatever the circumstances, the Irishman could be relied upon to give his customary impeccable performance in the Reds' midfield. He started out on the left side, from where he would link up with the attack. When he scored they were often spectacular long-range efforts, as against Spurs in a memorable League Cup final display at Wembley in 1982. Later in his Anfield career, when John Barnes made the left wing his own, Whelan moved inside and was just as effective as ever. He captained Liverpool to their 1989 FA Cup final win over Everton.

Nigel Clough came with the usual Forest ball-playing reputation and had already made his debut for England. Here he is in action against Brazil in the summer of 1993.

captain, dropped again, and seriously considered leaving the club even in his testimonial year. The squad was riven with dissent, and it came to a head during a 2-0 defeat at Everton in September 1993. Grobbelaar and McManaman came to blows on the pitch as Liverpool players fought among themselves. Team spirit had never been lower.

Liverpool's season was over by January. They had been knocked out of the League Cup on penalties by Wimbledon, they were miles off the pace in the league, and the last act came against Bristol City in an FA Cup replay at Anfield after a 1-1 draw at Ashton Gate. Just as they had against Bolton the year before, Liverpool let lower league opponents humiliate them, and City won 1-0 in some comfort. It was the end of the road for Souness, and three days later he agreed to resign with 27 months of his contract left to run. David Moores commented pointedly: 'Liverpool Football Club is all about winning things and being a source of pride to our fans. It has no other purpose.' It was time to bring the pride back.

Chapter Eleven: 1994-98
The Evans Years

After the bumpy experience of Souness's time in charge of the club the appointment of Roy Evans as the new boss came as balm to a bruise.

The man from Bootle was a lifelong Liverpool fan who had paid his dues as a player and a coach in a quarter of a century at Anfield. He made his debut as a full back under Shankly in 1970, but never quite had the class to command a regular place in the first team. Although he never grabbed attention as a player, the Reds' hierarchy spotted in him a thoughtful footballing brain and he had an organisational ability that marked him out as a potential coach. In 1974, at the age of 25, he was offered the chance to quit playing to take a job on the staff instead. With a heavy heart, Evans realised his long-term future was better served by attending the Paisley University of Football Management, rather than struggling on as an average left back, perhaps in the lower leagues.

He worked his way up to reserve team coach at a time when Liverpool took the Central League very seriously indeed. Evans won the competition seven times in nine seasons, until he was promoted to first team duties in 1983. He was passed over for the top job in 1991 when Souness became manager, but when the Scot's years of misrule came to an end Evans was the best and the only man for the role. At the age of 45 he was ready for biggest challenge of his life.

It was too late to change Liverpool's sliding fortunes in the 1993-94 season, and the campaign ended with a symbolic break with the past. The home game against Norwich on 30 April 1994 was the last before the Kop was demolished. From the following season Liverpool had to make their ground all-seater, and it was time to sing 'Auld Lang Syne' to the most famous standing terrace in the world. Over 16,000 supporters packed the enclosure one last time, and sang their songs throughout the match, and for hours after the final whistle. The fervour in the stands might have been the same as ever, but once again the Liverpool team failed to match the occasion. Norwich won 1-0 as the Reds put on an oddly lacklustre display. Liverpool ended the season in eighth place, 32 points behind Champions Manchester United, their worst finish since they were promoted in 1962-63. Anfield was rotten ripe for change, and Evans acted decisively during the summer to arrest the decline.

Future Reds Oyvind Leonhardsen of Norway (right) and Phil Babb of the Republic of Ireland meet in the 1994 World Cup finals in the USA.

His first purchases were defensive. He had learned enough from Shankly to know that team building starts from the back, and Evans began acquiring defenders. In September 1994 he picked up two: Phil Babb, who caught the eye playing for Ireland in the World Cup, joined from Coventry for £3.75m, and John Scales arrived from Wimbledon for £3.5m. Evans played the new men in an enterprising 3-5-2 formation which flew in the face of Liverpool's favoured 4-4-2, but Evans's Liverpool principles remained rock-solid. The emphasis was thrown back on to short passing and plenty of movement. Evans belied his reputation for softness by showing many underperforming or troublesome players the door. Torben Piechnik, Dicks, Clough and Hutchison were on their way out.

The team had already begun to show signs of improvement, as Crystal Palace were thrashed 6-1 at Selhurst Park on the first day of the season. The second match was even more extraordinary, as Robbie Fowler scored a hat-trick against Arsenal in only four and a half minutes in a 3-0 win at Anfield. Despite their speed out of the blocks the Reds struggled to keep a title challenge on track. They stayed in the top six all season, and after beating Manchester City 2-0 at Anfield after Christmas they went third, but the championship developed into a duel between Manchester United and Dalglish's Blackburn.

Football has a habit of throwing up strange quirks of fate, and it seemed written in the stars that Kenny should land the Premiership title at Anfield. He brought his team to his old ground for the last match of the season needing a victory to make sure of the championship. Liverpool won the game 2-1, but United's failure to win at West Ham the same afternoon meant Blackburn were champions anyway. Anfield cheered Dalglish as if he had won the championship for them.

The League Cup at least gave Evans the chance to adorn his first full season with a trophy. It had been 11 years since the Reds had won the competition they once monopolised, so success was overdue. They closed in on the final by beating Burnley, Stoke, Blackburn, Arsenal and Palace before meeting First Division Bolton in the final. Once again McManaman showed his best form in the big match, scoring twice in Liverpool's 2-1 win.

Grobbelaar Accused

As if to prove that there is nothing new in football, one of Liverpool's former players became embroiled in a match-fixing scandal that stained the club's reputation. Eight decades earlier, the Anfield Four had been banned from football for life after rigging the result of a match against Manchester United. Now Bruce Grobbelaar, who had joined Southampton in the summer of 1994, was accused of taking part in a conspiracy to throw a series of Liverpool games.

A newspaper sting operation captured Grobbelaar on video boasting about the cash he had collected from Asian businessmen in return for letting goals in. It was claimed that Grobbelaar had been paid £40,000 for his part in a 3-0 defeat against Newcastle at Anfield in November 1993. The Zimbabwean complained on the video that he had 'accidentally' made two saves against Manchester United in January 1993 which cost him a £125,000 pay-day.

Grobbelaar was eventually cleared in a second crown court trial, but a judge subsequently set aside his libel claim, openly doubting the jury's decision and issuing a withering verdict on the ex-Liverpool keeper's actions.

Stan Collymore in action for England against Japan in 1995.

Best Football Since 1990

The 1995-96 season began with optimism at Anfield higher than it had been for years. The side had shown a huge improvement the season before, and Evans's bold move in spending a British-record £8.5m on Nottingham Forest striker, Stan Collymore, showed that the club's ambition was boundless. When local lad Jason McAteer joined in September 1995 from Bolton for £4.5m, there was a feeling that Evans was constructing a side that would play football the Liverpool way and was perhaps capable of winning the championship.

Their form in the autumn was impressive, especially in a 5-2 home win over Bolton and a rousing 6-0 rout of Manchester City, and the football the team was playing was the best fans had seen since 1990. But their hopes of a realistic championship tilt went up in smoke after Bonfire Night when Liverpool went five matches without a win and slipped to seventh. They had already ceded too much ground to the eventual champions, Manchester United. They were out of the UEFA Cup, having lost 1-0 on aggregate to Danish side Brondby, and Newcastle put them out of the League Cup, so Liverpool's only hope was the FA Cup.

They set off in pursuit of Wembley by taking Third Division Rochdale apart at Anfield, Collymore scoring a hat-trick in a 7-0 win. Collymore scored again at Shrewsbury in the fourth round as the Reds won 4-0, and he also scored the winner as Liverpool beat Charlton 2-1 at home in the fifth round. The toughest test so far came at Leeds in the quarter-finals, and the Reds were relieved to get a 0-0 draw to force a replay. McManaman scored twice and Fowler got the third as a 3-0 win took the Reds into the semi-final against Aston Villa at Old Trafford. Villa were enjoying an impressive season in the Premier League, and Liverpool needed to be at their best to win 3-0. That set up the most enticing FA Cup final for years, against Manchester United who had already won the league and were chasing a second Double in two seasons.

The match was featureless and largely depressing for Liverpool supporters. All season long the Reds had been playing their attractive passing game with some panache, but they chose this day to go into their shells. Their expansive, flowing football was nowhere to be seen as both teams were content to constrict the other's space and keep a clean sheet. Fear ruled, and it took a deflected shot late on from Eric Cantona to win the match. What sticks in many people's minds is the appearance of the Liverpool team before the game.

No cup final is ever settled in the gents' outfitters the week before the match, but the white suits and sunglasses the Liverpool players sported at Wembley chimed with a suspicion that they were more interested in flash than football. It might have been a false impression, but they did not project the image of men who had turned up to work. As they preened on the Wembley pitch before kick off the players looked like they were about to star in a Bacardi ad, not play in the most important game of recent seasons. It obviously doesn't matter what the players wear before a game, but perception is everything, and from that day the Liverpool team were stuck with their damaging 'Spice Boys' tag, and it was their own fault.

Paisley Dies

The 1995-96 season also saw the death of Paisley, aged 77, after a long illness. Supporters and players paid tribute to a remarkable man who was easily the most successful British manager of all time. Steve McLean, a fan who revered Paisley, wrote a supporter's tribute in the next issue of *Total Football* magazine: 'I was lucky enough to meet him on a few occasions. There were always the stories – how the players would crease up at team talks over his quaint pronunciation of opposing players' names in that lovely, warm laconic Geordie lilt. But he had well-hidden steel running through him.

'One day I made the trip back to Anfield from Sheffield. Bob had agreed that he and the players would make a cassette tape to help a young Reds fan who was in a coma. Her parents reckoned that the Liverpool squad's voices would help their daughter through her ordeal.

'His tiny office was remarkably bare. A desk with three telephones, a couple of chairs and a clock that ran backwards. Cassette tapes, the operation of them at least, were a mystery to Bob. He couldn't get it right, and it was like helping an inept child who didn't know how to button his coat. But he persevered and finally recorded his message in that slow, croaky way of his. As soon as he stepped outside, though, players who had been larking about like kids stopped, halted by just a glance and that familiar half-smile. It was an expression that contained love, but a certain hardness too. Above all the nickname, Uncle Bob, said it all. He was a lovely man with a huge, extended family built up over five decades.'

David Fairclough said: 'His wartime experiences as a Desert Rat taught him there can be humour even in desperate circumstances. In Rome for the 1977 European Cup final he focused our attention on the job by saying: "Don't think you're here on holiday. There's nothing to see. I should know – I tore the place down in the war".'

After more signs of improvement Liverpool looked ready to make a real breakthrough in 1996-97. The time when they could look Manchester United in the eye at the top of the table was overdue.

50 Greatest Players

IAN RUSH Striker

Joined Liverpool: 1980 and 1988 **From:** Chester City and Juventus
Debut: 13 December 1980
v Ipswich (a), Division One – drew 1-1
Appearances: 660 **Goals:** 348
Left Liverpool: 1987 and 1996 **For:** Juventus and Leeds United
Honours won with Liverpool: European Cup winner 1984; Division One championship 1982, 1983, 1984, 1986, 1990; FA Cup winner 1986, 1989, 1992; League Cup winner 1981, 1982, 1983, 1984, 1995; 67 Wales caps

Rush is he greatest goalscorer in Liverpool's history. When he arrived from Chester City for £330,000 as a gangling teenager, he didn't look like a man about to carve his name in the club's annals. It took him a year in the reserves before he got his chance and even then he found scoring difficult. But once he got his eye in, the goals came in floods. He broke nearly every goalscoring record around: 44 FA Cup goals – five of them in finals; 49 League Cup goals (equal with Geoff Hurst), 28 goals for Wales and a club record of 47 goals in a season in 1983-84. And to all Reds fans' delight, he saved a few for Everton, the team he had supported as a boy, scoring a record 25 derby goals. In 1984 he was rewarded with both the Footballer of the Year and the PFA Player of the Year awards.

Liverpool could not resist the £3.2m Juventus offered for Rush in 1987, but after a year he returned and emerged a better all-round player. As well as an intuitive knack for finishing, Rush's best feature was his speed. He won more international caps while at Liverpool than any other Red.

After leaving Liverpool, Rushie joined Leeds and then Wrexham before moving into coaching, instilling youngsters with the knowledge that made him one of the game's most potent strikers.

Evans's big new summer signing, Czech winger Patrik Berger, lit up the team at at the start of the season, and the two goals he scored in a 3-0 win at Leicester put them in pole position in mid-September. Their cause was helped when United suffered a cataclysmic run of defeats in October and November, and for the first time in years the title looked like Liverpool's to lose. By January they were clear at the head of the Premiership, but remorselessly United clawed back the deficit, and when Ferguson's side won

3-1 at Anfield in April, the Premier League trophy was heading for Old Trafford again. Liverpool could only win one of their last five matches, and what had been a season of rich promise ended in a disappointing fourth-place finish.

Scrawny 17-year-old Scores on Debut

The penultimate match of the season did at least herald a brighter future. A scrawny 17-year-old kid called Michael Owen came off the bench at Selhurst Park and scored in Liverpool's 2-1 defeat against Wimbledon. He was the youngest player ever to score for the Reds.

Liverpool could also draw some comfort from having made progress in Europe. They reached the the Cup-Winners' Cup semi-finals after overcoming MyPa47 of Finland, Swiss side Sion and Brann Bergen of Norway. The Reds faced Paris St Germain in the first leg away from home, and David James endured a horrible night between the sticks as the French won 3-0. The Reds

Patrik Berger gets an early taste of Anfield glory for the Czech Republic in Euro 1996.

50 Greatest Players

JOHN BARNES Winger

Joined Liverpool: 1987 **From:** Watford

Debut: 15 August 1987 v Arsenal (a), Division One – won 2-1

Appearances: 407 **Goals:** 110

Left Liverpool: 1997 **For:** Newcastle United

Honours won with Liverpool: Division One championship 1988, 1990; FA Cup winner 1989; League Cup winner 1995; 48 England caps

For many people's money, Barnes was the most exciting footballer Liverpool have had in the modern era. His ability to destroy defenders down the left wing was breathtaking, his skill with a ball at his feet as good as anyone's in the English game over the last 30 years. He also possessed the physique and eye for goal of a centre-forward, and starred in the great Liverpool side of the late 1980s that bristled with attacking intent. Barnes impressed too with his dignity under fire. More than any other player of his generation he was subjected to sick taunts from spectators, yet Barnes rose above the hatred and never showed a flicker of concern.

won the return leg 2-0, but there was no way back. Liverpool were having to learn all over again the hard lessons of European competition.

Evans' Fresh Talent

Evans had spent the summer bringing in fresh talent. The most prominent newcomer was the ex-Manchester United enforcer Paul Ince who arrived from Internazionale for £4.2m. He was joined by another midfielder, Oyvind Leonhardsen, who came from Wimbledon for £4.5m, and ageing German striker Karl-Heinz Riedle, a £1.8m buy from Borussia Dortmund.

Collymore was sold to Villa, after a brief Anfield career that saw more gripes than goals. On several occasions he had broken the solemn code of omerta which prevails among pros and criticised his club and his manager in public. He routinely refused to play in the reserves when Evans felt he needed a run-out to tune up his game, and called into question his commitment to Liverpool by continuing to live in the Midlands instead of moving nearer Merseyside. In the end, he was more trouble than he was worth. And when you remember that he was worth £8.5m, that is a lot of trouble. It was also time for John Barnes' distinguished Liverpool career to end, as the veteran winger moved to Newcastle on a free transfer.

In theory the new men looked like shrewd additions to the squad but results never matched expectations. After a slow start, which could have been due to new players bedding into the side, Liverpool forged ahead in December and January. They went eight games undefeated, winning six, and by the start of March they were second in the table. But it was too late to make any impression on United, who had been top since October, and they went on to win their fifth title in the 1990s.

Again, Liverpool slumped over the closing stages to finish third. Most importantly, it meant they missed out once again on a place in the increasingly important Champions League. Only the emergence of the teenaged Owen as a striker of real class dispelled the gloom. His 18 league goals made him easily the team's top scorer.

The Reds could find no consolation in the cups either that season. They went out of the League Cup to Middlesbrough in the semi-finals while the FA Cup proved an even more barren exercise, as Coventry won 3-1 at Anfield in the third round. Europe, too, proved to be another journey into oblivion. After an entertaining joust with their old Glaswegian friends

50 Greatest Players

MARK WRIGHT Centre half

Joined Liverpool: 1991 **From:** Derby County

Debut: 17 August 1991 v Oldham (h), Division One – won 2-1

Appearances: 210 **Goals:** 9

Left Liverpool: 1998 (retired)

Honours won with Liverpool: FA Cup winner 1992; 5 England caps

At the peak of his career, there was no more elegant defender in British football. He was at his most impressive emerging from defence with the ball at his feet, foraging into the opposition half like an English Beckenbauer. Graeme Souness bought him from Derby for £2.2m, but Wright struggled in his early months and found himself in the reserves. Injuries hit him too, but Wright battled back and ended up as an inspiring captain, lifting the FA Cup in 1992.

After Souness left the club, Wright ran into trouble with the new boss Roy Evans. Wright was perceived to have an attitude problem, and a transfer looked imminent. Once again, Wright redoubled his efforts, fought his way back into the side, and played his best football until more cruel injuries hastened the end of his playing days.

and rivals Celtic, which Liverpool won 2-2 on away goals, they slunk out for the second year running against French opposition. This time it was Strasbourg who won 3-0 on their own ground before closing the deal at Anfield.

By now it was clear face that the Reds needed fresh impetus. Roy Evans had restored stability after the stormy days of Souness, but Liverpool could not put up with many more nondescript seasons. It remained Liverpool's ambition to get back among European football's super powers, and to do that the directors injected some fresh European ideas. In an imaginative, forward-thinking move they hired a man with a French passport and the heart and soul of a true Liverpudlian. Gérard Houllier joined the club as joint manager in the summer of 1998.

Who, me? Liverpool directors turned to French football thinker, Gérard Houllier in 1998.

Chapter Twelve: 1998-2003
Hou Let The Reds Out

Houllier had been a Liverpool fan since the 1960s, when as a young teacher he worked at Alsop Secondary School in the city and spent his Saturdays on the Kop. He revelled in the unique community spirit of the Anfield crowd, admired the team ethos and attacking verve of Shankly's sides, and knew that this was how football should be played. Partly inspired by what he had seen on Merseyside, he went on to become a brilliant coach. Gaining a fine reputation in French domestic football, he then served as assistant to the national team manager, Michel Platini, before taking over the side himself. He was closely connected with the planning programme which produced the World Cup-winning side of 1998, and was technical director of that triumphant side.

Houllier had a unique mix of footballing beliefs: he had never forgotten the team ethic and the importance of local pride, and he had grafted this on to a respect for English football, a deep technical knowledge and a matchless understanding of the European game. He was the perfect choice for Liverpool.

Michael Owen on his way to becoming a household name by scoring for England against Argentina in the 1998 World Cup finals in France.

Emile Heskey made his debut for England a month before joining the Reds.

Evans Quits

For a few uneasy months Houllier and Evans worked side by side as joint managers, but by November Evans decided to quit and give his friend a clear run at the job. Evans left with dignity and the sincere thanks of the Liverpool supporters and directors. His record as manager was respectable, but the Reds needed to move up a level to tackle the Manchester United monolith.

Improvements came slowly. The first season Houllier was at the club, 1998-99, wrought little discernible advancement. The team finished a depressing seventh in the Premiership, and they lost to Tottenham and Manchester United in the early rounds of the League and FA Cups. They began brightly enough in the UEFA Cup with an 8-0 aggregate win over Slovakian side Kosice, and enjoyed their best European result in years against Valencia in the second round. The Spanish side earned a 0-0 draw at Anfield, but a late fightback in the Mestalla saw Liverpool go through. Valencia led 2-0 with 10 minutes left when McManaman and Berger scored to send the Reds through on away goals. But it was hasta la vista to Liverpool's cup run in the next round, as they lost 3-1 away to Celta Vigo in the first leg and 1-0 at home.

By the beginning of 1999-2000 Houllier was putting his own stamp on the club. Without being overbearing, he had introduced a stronger work ethic at Melwood and discipline was tighter. Much of the credit for that was given to Phil Thompson, installed as Houllier's Number Two. They made a perfect good gendarme/bad cop double act.

Shampoo Salesman

The playing staff was overhauled too, with several players discovering that the urbane Houllier could be ruthless. Part-time shampoo salesman McAteer and Armani mannequin David James were moved on to further their modelling careers elsewhere, and other players who had fallen slightly short of Houllier's standards were allowed to leave. To rejuvenate the team Houllier went on a spending spree, recruiting German midfielder Dietmar Hamann from Newcastle for £8m, keeper Sander Westerveld for £4m and Czech winger Vladimir Smicer from Lens for £4.5m. Crucially, too, for the club's future, Houllier bought Sami Hyypia from Dutch club Willem II for £2.5m and Stephane Henchoz from Blackburn for £3.5m. That central defensive partnership gave him the foundations on which he could build a side.

Sami Hyypia, the new rock of Anfield, was recruited in time for the start of the 1999-2000 season.

It turned out to be a year of frustration in the League as a poor start gave way to a hot streak of form in mid-season before another inexplicable loss of form in the closing stages robbed the Reds of a more respectable final placing. Over those closing stages Manchester United won their last 11 matches on the spin to take yet another title while Liverpool failed to score a goal in any of their last five matches, lost three of them, and slipped from second to fourth. The way in which Liverpool's challenge crumpled, added to early League and FA Cup defeats against Southampton and Blackburn, left Houllier distraught. The kind of steadiness which won championships seemed as far away as ever.

As the Reds embarked on the 2000-01 season it quickly became obvious that success in the League would remain out of their reach, but Liverpool proved unbeatable in all other competitions. Houllier's emerging side pulled off a feat that none of their illustrious Anfield forebears had managed: a cup treble.

It was achieved on the back of a massive pre-season investment in new players. Once again the board backed Houllier all the way with cash, and the manager spent it wisely. Towards the end of the previous season Leicester striker Emile Heskey had become the club's biggest-ever buy at £11m. Middlesbrough wing back Christian Ziege came for half that, and Everton's Nick Barmby hopped across the city for £6m.

Other reinforcements came cheaper. German defender Markus Babbel was a Bosman free transfer. Steven Gerrard, Jamie Carragher and Danny Murphy, who had all emerged from the Liverpool youth system, continued to mature.

50 Greatest Players

STEVE McMANAMAN Midfielder

Joined Liverpool: 1987 (as trainee)

Debut: 25 December 1990 v Sheffield United (h), Division One – won 2-0

Appearances: 364 **Goals:** 66

Left Liverpool: 1999 **For:** Real Madrid

Honours won with Liverpool: Honours won with Liverpool: FA Cup 1992; League Cup 1995; 24 England caps

The loss of McManaman to Real Madrid was one of the most serious blows to hit Liverpool in recent times. It was a bitter disappointment to lose a home-grown player who for several seasons had been the heartbeat of the team's attack. Just as he was reaching the height of his powers he moved to Spain, courtesy of a Bosman free transfer, leaving behind a rich fund of memories: of the goals he scored, which were often spectacular if infrequent; and of the days when he was on song and could take teams apart – like in 1995 when as a coltish 23-year-old he ran Bolton ragged at Wembley and scored twice to win the League Cup.

Their development gave Houllier plenty of pride, because along with the likes of Owen and Fowler they gave the squad the local identity which the Frenchman craved. Shrewdest of all, and perhaps the signing of the season anywhere in the country, was Scottish international midfielder Gary McAllister, who joined from Coventry for a negligible fee. But while the freedom of contract revolution may have helped Liverpool, it cost them too. When McManaman's contract ended he was able to leave Anfield and join Real Madrid.

First Taste

The first trophy to come to Anfield was the League Cup. While other top sides treated the competition as a distraction, Liverpool gave it their full attention and were in pulverising mood all the way. They beat Chelsea 2-1 at Anfield, Stoke City 8-0 away, Fulham 3-0 at home and Palace 6-2 on aggregate in the semi-finals. That sent the Reds through to the final at the striking Millennium Stadium in Cardiff, to play First Division Birmingham City. It was Liverpool's first glimpse at the ground's famous retractable roof. Frustratingly, the Blues' defence did not slide open so easily and the Reds were in for a tough afternoon.

Liverpool took the lead through Fowler, and as the match ebbed into injury time it looked enough to win the cup. But Birmingham were given a penalty after Henchoz fouled in the area, and Darren Purse's kick took the game into extra time. No more goals came in the next half hour, and the final went to penalties. After five kicks each the score was tied at 4-4. Sudden death came into play. Icy Carragher scored with the first, and when Westerveld stopped Andy Johnson's attempt, Liverpool had won the first leg of the treble.

Less than three months later Liverpool were back at Cardiff for the FA Cup final. It had been a largely trouble-free run to the final, with only Second Division Wycombe Wanderers giving the Reds much of a scare in a tight semi-final at Villa Park. Their opponents at the Millennium Stadium were Arsenal, who were chasing another double and slight favourites to win the game. It was billed as a shoot-out between England's Michael Owen and the Premiership's top scorer, Thierry Henry. Owen won, turning on one of his best performances to score twice as Liverpool captured their first FA Cup for nine years.

Shrewd observers recognised that Owen was going to be a good 'un even while he was still playing for Mold Alexandra Under 10s. He thrived under the watchful gaze of Liverpool's youth coaches and it was no surprise to them when he was called up for first-team action aged just 17. He scored that day at Selhurst Park, and has been scoring ever since. Top scorer in the Premiership, two World Cups with England, a cup treble with Liverpool and European Player of the Year – and still in his early 20s, no other English striker came close to matching his ability.

Houllier had shown canny foresight in beefing up his squad because he needed every pair of legs at his disposal as the Reds slogged through the two domestic cups, as well as the most exhausting UEFA Cup campaign yet devised.

European competition never used to be like this. When Liverpool won the European Cup in 1978, they only had to play seven matches including the final. By the time they had beaten Alavés in the UEFA Cup final in 2001, they had played 13 ties in a six-month route-march which took them to Romania, the Czech Republic, Greece, Italy, Portugal, Spain and Germany again.

The Liverpool of Old

Like the Liverpool of old, Houllier's team found that the key to success on the continent lay in carving out results away from home. The new-look Reds were quickly becoming masters of the counter-attacking style of play, and the system proved ideally suited to Europe. In their first match, against a willing though limited Rapid Bucharest side playing in front of a small crowd, the Reds stuck to their task and came away with a 1-0 win thanks to Barmby's well-taken goal. A 0-0 draw at Anfield took the Reds through.

50 Greatest Players

ROBBIE FOWLER Striker

Joined Liverpool: 1990 (as trainee)

Debut: 22 September 1993 v Fulham (a), League Cup – won 3-1

Appearances: 330 **Goals:** 173

Left Liverpool: 2001 **For:** Leeds United

Honours won with Liverpool: UEFA Cup winner 2001; FA Cup winner 2001; League Cup winner 1995, 2001; 18 England caps

Not since Greaves has English football seen such an instinctive finisher as Robbie Fowler. He was the natural heir to Ian Rush, and burst into the first team with goals pouring from his boots – especially the lethal left one. He showed his gluttony for goals in an early League Cup outing against Fulham, where he pulverised the Cottagers with five strikes. After a blistering start Fowler went off the boil, but when Stan Collymore was signed, Fowler felt the pressure and raised his game again. Injury and some ill-judged nocturnal adventures soured his last months at Anfield, and it was with a spirit of regret and missed opportunities that the Toxteth boy left the club for Leeds.

In the next round Liverpool could only eke out a 1-0 lead against Slovan Liberec at Anfield, but they showed resilience as well as attacking potency in the second leg to win 3-2 on the night. Liverpool's opponents were becoming increasingly difficult, and in the last 32 they came up against dangerous Greek side Olympiakos, who had been eliminated from the Champions League. In the teeth of a rabid Greek chorus of over 40,000 voices, Liverpool came away from the first leg with a valuable 2-2 draw. At Anfield, Barmby scored his fourth goal of the competition so far to help the Reds win 4-2 on aggregate.

Old adversaries Roma were next up, and Houllier's men put up one of their best displays in Europe since the ban had been lifted to win 2-0. Liverpool drew the sting from Roma's swarming attackers before two deadly Owen strikes gave them what appeared to be an unassailable lead. On a night of rare drama at Anfield, the Italian side fought all the way, scored one goal, and had loud shouts for a penalty turned down as Liverpool hung on to win 2-1 over the two legs. Another copybook away display gave Liverpool a 0-0 draw in the first leg of the quarter-final against Porto, and Danny Murphy and Michael Owen scored the goals at Anfield to take them into the last four.

The ultimate test came in the first leg of the semi-final, when Liverpool braved a 90,000 crowd at the Camp Nou as well as a Barcelona side stuffed with great names. They looked an especially formidable outfit going forward and the Reds had their hands full coping with the majestic Rivaldo, speedy Overmars and lethal Patrick Kluivert. But yet again Liverpool proved durable competitors in the most unpromising circumstances. They flew home delighted with a 0-0 draw, and took full advantage in the home leg in which the influence of McAllister in midfield proved cruical, and his penalty was the only goal of the game. After 16 years Liverpool were back in the final of a European competition.

On their way to the final in Dortmund the Reds had beaten some of European football's true aristocrats. Now they came up against one of Spain's lesser-known sides. Alavés were devoid of the stellar names Barcelona could muster, but they had surged to the final on the back of some impressive performances including victories over Internazionale and Kaiserslautern.

Despite Alavés' commanding goal rate in the earlier rounds, a tight low-scoring final was widely predicted. It was anything but, as Liverpool emerged victorious from one of the greatest European finals ever played. Goals have seldom been more golden that the one in extra time which gave the Reds a 5-4 win after 117 minutes of spellbinding football.

Liverpool fans had been yearning for a season such as this for over a decade, and to put the final flourish on it they qualified for the following season's Champions League by coming third in the Premier League. For once the Reds' league form was white-hot in the run-in, and they won six and drew one of their last seven matches to earn entry into the Champions League for the first time. Houllier's standing at Liverpool was sky-high, and the way looked clear for the Reds to elbow their way back in to the continent's elite after a long, unsatisfying absence.

Champions League

If the UEFA Cup effort seemed like an ordeal at the time, it was a gentle warm-up compared to the Reds' first Champions League drive in 2001-02. After an easy qualifying win over Finnish side FC Haka, the Reds plunged into a first group stage with Borussia Dortmund, Boavista and Dynamo Kiev. But as the Reds' first foray into the competition got underway, Gérard Houllier was stricken with a heart condition which almost claimed his life.

On the day of Liverpool's league game with Leeds at Anfield in October 2001, Houllier was rushed to hospital for emergency heart surgery. After 10 hours in theatre, the operation was declared a success, but the manager needed rest to recuperate from his illness, and was ordered to stay away from football for the foreseeable future. Phil Thompson took over as interim

Great Matches

UEFA CUP FINAL **Westfalenstadion, Dortmund, 16 May 2001**
Attendance: 65,000

Liverpool 5	**Alavés 4***
Babbel	**Alonso**
Gerrard	**Javi Moreno 2**
McAllister (pen)	**Cruyff**
Fowler	
Geli o.g.	

***after extra time and golden goal**

'The good thing about this team,' Houllier said after a match that many hailed as one of the greatest ever played, 'is that you never feel there is a split or a lack of togetherness when something goes wrong. That is a major improvement.' Houllier had got it right. After too many years when there was a lack of cohesion or a clear sense of purpose about the club the old spirit came flooding back on an inspiring night in the Westfalenstadion.

It took just four minutes to confound sceptics who had predicted a dull 0-0 draw, as Babbel's firm header put Liverpool 1-0 up. They went further ahead after a quarter of an hour when Gerrard collected Owen's pass and finished emphatically. But Alavés had not started playing yet, and they looked a different side when substitute Ivan Alonso came on. It took him just five minutes to score, and the first-half glut of goals continued as McAllister scored a penalty awarded for a foul on Owen.

With a two-goal lead at the break, Liverpool may have felt they had seen the last of the Spanish resistance, but it was not so. Early in the second half Javi Moreno scored twice to level the match. Houllier sent on Fowler in place of Heskey with 15 minutes left, and he produced a typically instinctive strike to put the Reds ahead once more. Just as it seemed as if the drama was over for the night, Alavés' ex-Manchester United player, Jordi Cruyff, put a header past Westerveld, forcing golden goal extra time.

Chances came and went until with just a couple of minutes left before penalties came into play, McAllister powered a free kick into the box. The unlucky Delfi Geli deflected it into the net, and it was all over. The 20,000-strong Liverpool contingent hailed their modern heroes, and remembered the old ones who had paved the way for nights such as this: 'Gérard, Gérard, Gérard... Shankly in disguise' they sang.

Liverpool: Westerveld, Babbel, Henchoz (Smicer), Hyypia, Carragher, Gerrard, McAllister, Hamann, Murphy, Owen (Berger), Heskey (Fowler)
Alavés: Herrera, Eggen (Ivan Alonso), Karmona, Tellez, Contra, Tomic, Desio, Astudillo (Magno), Geli, Cruyff, Javi Moreno
Referee: G. Veissiere (France)

manager, and it was to his and the players' credit that results stayed on track. Liverpool emerged undefeated and top of the group, which in the interminable processes of the overblown Champions League meant they went straight into another four-team mini-league. Now they found themselves among a quartet that looked murderously difficult: Barcelona, Roma and Galatasaray completed the line up. Liverpool went into the last match needing to beat Roma by two goals to reach the quarter-finals, and showed once again that they had the strength to gouge out a result when it mattered most. Jari Litmanen, the Finnish striker who had been an inspired acquisition by Houllier, scored an early penalty and Heskey made the match safe on the hour. To make the night even more special, it marked the return to Anfield of Houllier, who was afforded a movingly warm welcome by the adoring home crowd.

They were drawn to play German side Bayer Leverkusen in the knockout stages, and Hyypia scored the only goal of the game at Anfield in the first leg. It was not enough. Leverkusen swept the Reds away on their own patch to win 4-2, and Liverpool's first step into the Champions League was at an end. Back on the home front Liverpool suffered a dip in fortunes in the cups, but the team's league form showed promise. After topping the table at the end of the year, Liverpool kept in touch with the leaders, and put together an irresistible run in the last weeks to take the runners-up spot seven points behind Arsenal. The Reds lost just once in their last 17 matches, winning 13 of them, but Arsenal didn't lose a match after Christmas, and won their last

50 Greatest Players

SAMI HYYPIA Centre half

Joined Liverpool: 1999 **From:** Willem II

Debut: 7 August 1999 v Sheffield Wednesday (a), Premier League – won 2-1

Appearances: 213 **Goals:** 16

Honours won with Liverpool: UEFA Cup winner 2001; FA Cup winner 2001, 2003; League Cup winner 2001; 53 Finland caps

The big Finn was little known before making a £2.6m move from Dutch football, but Reds manager Gérard Houllier knew his business. And when Houllier followed the signing of Hyypia with the capture of Swiss star Stephane Henchoz from Blackburn Rovers, he had put together an indomitable central defensive partnership.

Hyypia quickly imposed himself on Anfield, and Houllier had found a captain as well as an accomplished defender. The Reds had discovered a silk-and-steel central defender in the best Anfield traditions of ball-playing centre backs such as Alan Hansen and Phil Thompson.

50 Greatest Players

STEVEN GERRARD Midfielder

Joined Liverpool: 1995 (as trainee)

Debut: 29 November 1998 v Blackburn (h), Premier League – won 2-0

Appearances: 193 **Goals:** 22

Honours won with Liverpool: UEFA Cup winner 2001; FA Cup winner 2001; League Cup winner 2001, 2003; 17 England caps

The best is yet to come from Gerrard, but already he has shown enough talent to suggest he will be one of the great Liverpool midfielders. The Liverpool lad clearly has the full range of qualities for the position: an eye for a killer pass, an appetite for hard work, the hunger to win the ball, and the ability to break forward and shoot with power. The big occasion hasn't fazed him either, as he showed on the night of one of his best performances to date: for England when they demolished Germany 5-1 in Munich. So much of what was good about England that night flowed from the precocious Gerrard. He was already being spoken about as one of his country's most important players alongside more established internationals like Michael Owen and David Beckham.

13 games. Arsène Wenger's team had shown Liverpool how much they still had to do to win the championship, the prize they craved more than any other.

Liverpool kicked off the 2002-03 season with a fresh-looking squad pepped up with two recruits from Senegal's swashbuckling World Cup side. Houllier spent £15m on Salif Diao from Sedan and El-Hadji Diouf from Lens, while Nick Barmby moved on to Leeds for £2.75m and club captain Jamie Redknapp went to Spurs on a free transfer.

The new-look Reds plunged into their Champions League group with enormous optimism, but it soon became clear that Houllier still work to do when it came to fashioning a team capable of mixing it with the top sides in Europe. The Reds began by losing 2-0 in Valencia, and when they could only draw their second game against Basle at Anfield, qualification was always going to be a struggle. In the end it proved beyond them, and after they drew the final game of the group 3-3 away to the Swiss side, the Reds were faced with the consolation prize of entry into the UEFA Cup.

After comfortable victories in that competition against Vitesse Arnhem and Auxerre, the draw threw up one of British football's most evocative fixtures: Liverpool v Celtic. The Reds did well to hold the Hoops to a 1-1 draw at Parkhead, but in the home leg Houllier's team were out-thought, out-fought and out-played by Martin O'Neill's side.

The FA Cup was also a wash-out, as Liverpool lost to Crystal Palace. But the Reds drew more pleasure from a League Cup run which ended with a dissection of Manchester United in the final in Cardiff, a match which showed that Liverpool were still capable of beating the best in British football on their day. In the League, it turned out to be another unhappy season. The Reds fell out of touch with the leading trio of United, Arsenal and Newcastle months before the campaign ended, and on the last day of the season they missed Champions League qualification by losing at Chelsea. Houllier's signings had not done the trick for him, and Steven Gerrard's sending off in that game highlighted a worrying indiscipline that had crept into their make-up. But Houllier vowed the club was on the right track. 'There will be no clear-out,' he told critics who suggested his team needed a major overhaul.

While the Reds were reflecting on defeat at Stamford Bridge, up at Goodison Park Manchester United were celebrating their eighth title in 11 seasons. Sir Alex Ferguson's dynasty looked stronger than ever; invincible

50 Greatest Players

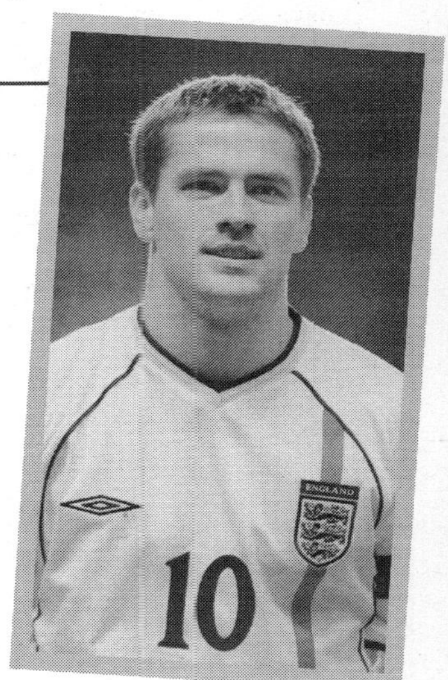

MICHAEL OWEN Striker

Joined Liverpool: 1996 (as trainee)

Debut: 6 May 1997 v Wimbledon (a), Premier League – lost 2-1

Appearances: 259 **Goals:** 139

Honours won with Liverpool: FA Cup winner 2001; League Cup winner 2001, 2003; UEFA winner Cup 2001; 50 England caps

In 2001 Michael Owen became the first ever Liverpool player to be voted European Footballer of the Year. It was just one more significant landmark in a career that has already delivered so much.

Owen has made a habit of breaking new ground. He was the youngest player ever to score for Liverpool when he was just 17, and also the youngest man to play for England in the 20th century. Before his 23rd birthday he had already been a star at two World Cups. His game has been built on express speed of thought and deed, as well as an unerring instinct for the location of the goal. The future looks bright for Michael Owen.

A series of stunning peformances for Senegal in the 2002 World Cup brought El-Hadji Diouf to the attention of Houllier and Thompson.

even. Yet history shows us that even the mightiest empires crumble in the end. Liverpool know that better than anybody.

At the start of this book I wrote that the glory of Liverpool Football Club lies in the pleasure it has given millions of people. Players and managers come and go, but the supporters remain, hearts full of hope even in the darkest hours. In the summer of 2002 I sat down to watch Brazil play Turkey in the semi-final of the World Cup on TV with my friend Steve McLean. He was in the advanced stages of cancer, but as we watched the game he talked about the Reds' chances for the following season. We talked about the great sides of the past; and inevitably about legendary Reds players. As he recounted the deeds of Dalglish, his eyes shone with satisfaction, any thoughts of mortality banished. Then almost as an aside, he said he hoped for two years. Just long enough, he said, for Liverpool to win the championship again. To anybody who has never loved a football club as much as Liverpudlians love theirs, it sounds maudlin, yet for Steve it was simple statement of fact.

As it turned out he didn't have two years; he had just two weeks, and when he died there was a signed Liverpool shirt at the foot of his bed, sent by the club after a request from Steve's workmates. It was a small symbol that the family spirit fostered by Shankly years before was still alive. And perhaps the old man was half right after all. Football might not really be a matter of life and death, but it gives us cause to rejoice while we're here. Especially Liverpudlians.

THE ESSENTIAL HISTORY OF

LIVERPOOL

CLUB STATISTICS

The Liverpool Directory

Club Information

- Address: Anfield Road, Liverpool, L4 0TH
- Official Website : http://www.liverpoolfc.tv
- General Enquiries: 0151 263 2361
- Ticket Enquiries phone: 0151 260 8680
- Ticket Enquiries fax: 0151 261 1416
- 24-hour Information Service: 0151 260 9999
- Tickets Credit Card Bookings: 0151 263 5727
- Museum and Tour Centre : 0151 260 6677
- Formed: 1892
- Nickname: the Reds or the Pool

League and Premiership Record

- 1893 Elected to Division Two
- 1894-95 Division One
- 1895-96 Division Two
- 1896-1904 Division One
- 1904-05 Division Two
- 1905-54 Division One
- 1954-1962 Division Two
- 1962-92 Division One
- 1992 Founder members of FA Premier League

Honours

- League Division One Champions: 1900-01, 1905-06, 1921-22, 1922-23, 1946-47, 1963-64, 1965-66, 1972-73, 1975-76, 1976-77, 1978-89, 1979-80, 1981-82, 1982-83, 1983-84, 1985-86, 1987-88, 1989-90
- League Division One runners-up: 1898-99, 1909-10, 1968-69, 1973-74, 1974-75, 1977-78, 1984-85, 1986-87, 1988-89, 1990-91, 2001-02
- Division One (Two) Champions: 1992-93
- League Division Two Champions: 1893-94, 1895-96, 1905-05, 1961-62
- FA Cup winners: 1965, 1974, 1986, 1989, 1992, 2001
- FA Cup runners-up: 1914, 1950, 1971, 1977, 1988, 1996
- League Cup winners: 1981, 1982, 1983, 1984, 1995, 2001, 2003
- League Cup runners-up: 1978, 1987 1969
- Charity Shield winners: 1966, 1974, 1976, 1979, 1980, 1982, 1988, 1989, 2001
- Charity Shield joint-winners: 1964, 1965, 1977, 1986, 1990

European Record

- European Cup winners: 1977, 1978, 1981, 1984
- European Cup runners-up: 1985
- European Cup-Winners' Cup runners-up: 1966
- UEFA Cup winners: 1973, 1976, 2001
- Super Cup winners: 1977, 2001
- World Club Championship runners-up: 1981, 1984

Records

- Record victory: 11-0 v Stromsgodset (h) European Cup-Winners' Cup first round first leg – 17 September 1974
- Record defeat: 1-9 v Birmingham City (a) Football League Division Two – 11 December 1954
- Most points in a season: 90 in 1987-88
- Most goals in a season: 106 in 1895-96
- Most league appearances for club: Ian Callaghan (640)
- Most league goals for club: Roger Hunt (245)
- Most goals by one player in a game: 5 – Andy McGuigan v Stoke (h) 4 January 1902;

John Evans v Bristol Rovers (h) 15 September 1954;
Ian Rush v Luton (h) 29 October 1983

- Youngest player: Max Thompson (17 years and 128 days)
- Most capped player: Ian Rush (67 caps for Wales)
- Record transfer fee paid: £11m to Leicester for Emile Heskey, March 2000
- Record transfer fee received: £12.5m from Leeds for Robbie Fowler, November 2001

Anfield

- On 30 September 1997, Liverpool banked a record £604,048 when Celtic visited Anfield in the UEFA Cup
- The ground's modern capacity is 45,362
- Anfield was chosen as a host stadium for the Euro '96 tournament
- The ground used to be the home of Everton FC, before a split saw the Toffees move to Goodison Park in 1892. The new Liverpool FC stayed at Anfield
- In 1889 Anfield staged an international between England and Ireland
- Liverpool's first game at Anfield was a 7-1 friendly win over Rotherham on 1 September 1892
- A vast new standing bank was built behind one goal in 1906. It was quickly nicknamed the Spion Kop, in memory of a bloody battle in the Boer War in which a number of soldiers from a local regiment were killed
- In 1928, the Kop was roofed and extended
- Liverpool installed floodlights in 1957
- In the summer of 1994, the Kop was demolished to make way for a new all-seater stand in line with the Taylor Report
- In 1982, the Shankly Gates were erected in memory of the club's legendary manager

Anfield's world famous Kop end in full song.

50 Greatest Players

This list is not intended to be definitive. Indeed there are many gifted players who have missed the cut and few supporters would agree on the same choice of the 50 greatest players ever to have pulled on the famous red shirt. The players listed are my choice, taking into consideration their respective performances, their achievements as players and their dedication to the club. All of them have contributed to making Liverpool FC the world famous club it is today.

No. 1 Billy Liddell (Winger/Centre forward) – 534 appearances, 228 goals. Liddell practically carried Liverpool through the post-war period. Showed selfless devotion to the team, and was a sublime ball-player, dribbler and finisher (see page 45).
No. 2 Kenny Dalglish (Striker) – 515 appearances, 172 goals. A magician with a football, and a striker who had every attribute. Indisputably the greatest Liverpool player of the last 40 years (see page 148).
No. 3 Kevin Keegan (Striker/Midfielder) – 323 appearances, 100 goals. Determined and skilful, he provided the attacking spark which gave life to Bill Shankly's second great Liverpool side (see page 96).
No. 4 Elisha Scott (Goalkeeper) – 468 appearances. The Belfast boy broke into the Reds side in the 1920s and held his place until well into the 1930s, winning a reputation as a larger-than-life character and shot-stopper supreme (see page 30).
No. 5 Ian Rush (Striker) – 660 appearances, 348 goals. A genius in the penalty area, simply the most lethal goalscorer Liverpool have ever had (see page 174).
No. 6 Roger Hunt (Centre forward) – 492 appearances, 286 goals. Roger was a goalscoring phenomenon throughout the 1960s, and holder of every Liverpool scoring record going – until Rush began breaking them (see page 69).
No. 7 Alex Raisbeck (Centre half) – 341 appearances, 20 goals. The elegant Scot was Liverpool's first great leader on the pitch, and helped them win the league in 1901 and 1906 (see page 18).
No. 8 Ray Clemence (Goalkeeper) – 665 appearances. The rock of the Liverpool rearguard as they dominated at home and conquered Europe (see page 121).
No. 9 Ian Callaghan (Winger/Midfielder) – 857 appearances, 69 goals. Played for Liverpool more times than anybody else, swapped positions and hardly had a bad game (see page 109).
No. 10 Alan Hansen (Centre half) – 620 appearances, 14 goals. Unflappable defender who injected class into the defence in a golden era (see page 157).
No. 11 Gordon Hodgson (Inside right/Centre forward) – 377 appearances, 241 goals. The South African was a prodigious goalscorer in the inter-war years, and set many club striking records (see page 31).
No. 12 John Barnes (Midfielder) – 407 appearances, 110 goals. One of the most exciting talents ever to play for Liverpool, and helped form one of the most dangerous attacking spearheads Anfield has ever seen (see page 176).
No. 13 Gerry Byrne (Full back) – 333 appearances, 4 goals. The ultimate club man, Byrne was prepared to run through brick walls for his team-mates, as shown in the 1965 FA Cup final when he played on with a smashed collarbone (see page 70).
No. 14 Graeme Souness (Midfielder) – 359 appearances, 56 goals. A leader on the field without equal, his compelling combination of artistry and aggression meant his mere presence intimidated the opposition and inspired the Reds (see page 138).
No. 15 Ian St John (Forward) – 425 appearances, 118 goals. More than just a goalscorer, St John had the guile to create countless chances for team-mates. A brilliant header of the ball for a striker of below average height (see page 74).
No. 16 Michael Owen (Striker) – 259 appearances, 139 goals. Tipped for great things when he was still a boy, Owen has never stopped scoring goals since breaking into the first team as a teenager (see page 189).
No. 17 Albert Stubbins (Forward) – 178 appearances, 83 goals. His efforts up-front made an great contribution to Liverpool's first post-war title (see page 41).
No. 18 Ron Yeats (Centre half) – 454 appearances, 16 goals. Signed as the final piece in Shankly's 1960s jigsaw. He was a huge physical presence and a born captain (see page 76).
No. 19 Phil Neal (Full back) – 650 appearances, 60 goals. A richly decorated defender who was quietly effective in defence, a useful addition to the attack, and scorer of more goals than any full back has a right to claim (see page 143).
No. 20 John Aldridge (Striker) – 104 appearances, 63 goals. He didn't have the longest Anfield career, but his goals ratio proved him to be among them finest forwards Liverpool have had (see page 154).
No. 21 Jack Balmer (Inside forward) – 312 appearances, 111 goals. Everton missed out on a prolific scorer. The first player ever to score three hat-tricks in successive appearances (see page 38).

No. 22 Steve McManaman (Midfielder) – 364 appearances, 66 goals. His class and ability on the ball him made him a huge local favourite (see page 182).
No. 23 Peter Thompson (Winger) – 415 appearances, 54 goals. As a tricky wideman, Thompson had no equal in the English game throughout the 1960s and was unlucky to not win more England caps (see page 77).
No. 24 Mark Lawrenson (Centre half) – 356 appearances, 18 goals. With Hansen he formed half of the best central defensive duos in Liverpool history (see page 145).
No. 25 Bob Paisley (Half back) – 277 appearances, 12 goals. One of the outstanding players of the post-war years (see page 40).
No. 26 Peter Beardsley (Striker) – 175 appearances, 59 goals. A craftsman and an artist when it came to making chances for others, and scored an abundance of beautiful goals (see page 159).
No. 27 Robbie Fowler (Striker) – 330 appearances, 173 goals. One of the greatest instinctive finishers ever to wear the red jersey (see page 184).
No. 28 Ephraim Longworth (Full back) – 371 appearances, 0 goals. Captained the title-winning Liverpool team of 1921-22 and also became the first Red to skipper England (see page 26).
No. 29 Emlyn Hughes (Midfielder/Defender) – 665 appearances, 62 goals. One of Shankly's most significant signings, and an inspirational captain the first two times the Reds won the European Cup (see page 112).
No. 30 Chris Lawler (Full back) – 549 appearances, 61 goals. Season after season he never let the Reds down, and scored a huge number of goals for a non-penalty taking full back (see page 88).
No. 31 Terry McDermott (Midfielder) – 329 appearances, 81 goals. An effective passer, handy goalscorer and a wonderfully gifted athlete who would run all day in the Liverpool cause (see page 126).
No. 32 Ronnie Moran (Left back) – 379 appearances, 17 goals. A faithful club man who played solidly throughout the dog-days of the 1950s, and helped in the club's 1960s renaissance (see page 63).
No. 33 Ronnie Whelan (Midfielder) – 493 appearances, 73 goals. Abundant natural ability, and a key figure in the Reds' midfield for over a decade (see page 167).
No. 34 Tommy Lawrence (Goalkeeper) – 390 appearances. Unkindly nicknamed 'the Flying Pig', but Shank's first title-winning team at Anfield was built on his ability between the sticks (see page 71).
No. 35 Tommy Smith (Defender/midfielder) – 638 appearances, 49 goals. In 15 years of service to Liverpool, his hard-tackling, no-nonsense style made the 'Anfield Iron' a legend (see page 108).
No. 36 Don Mackinlay (Half back) – 434 appearances, 34 goals. The Glaswegian captained Liverpool to the championship in 1922-23 (see page 28).
No. 37 Jimmy Case (Midfielder) – 269 appearances, 46 goals. Ludicrously underrated, and desperately unlucky never to win an England cap (see page 123).
No. 38 Steven Gerrard (Midfielder) – 193 appearances, 22 goals. Already made a massive impact for Liverpool and England, with more to come (see page 188).
No. 39 Sami Hyypia (Left half) – 213 appearances, 16 goals. The cornerstone of the contemporary Liverpool defence (see page 187).
No. 40 Matt McQueen (Winger/Utility Player) – 103 appearances, 7 goals. The Scot was the ultimate utility player, turning out in every position for the Reds including goalkeeper (see page 14).
No. 41 Alan Kennedy (Left back) – 359 appearances, 21 goals. An exciting, attacking full back, and scorer of two of the most important goals in Liverpool's history (see page 141).
No. 42 Jack Cox (Winger) – 361 appearances, 81 goals. Adaptable enough to play on either flank or as centre forward for a Liverpool team which won First and Second Division Championships before the First World War (see page 16).
No. 43 Ray Kennedy (Midfielder) – 393 appearances, 72 goals. Arrived at Anfield as a proven striker, and after years of sterling service to the Reds, left as with a reputation as a classy midfielder (see page 117).
No. 44 Harry Bradshaw (Winger) – 138 appearances, 53 goals. He was the first Liverpool player ever to win an England cap, and helped the Reds win two Second Division championships in the 1890s (see page 12).
No. 45 Steve Heighway (Winger) – 475 appearances, 76 goals. His unorthodox style allied to great pace and trickery down the flanks helped set up Liverpool's success in the 1970s (see page 115).
No. 46 Arthur Goddard (Winger) – 415 appearances, 77 goals. His skill on the wing lit up Anfield in the Edwardian era, and he helped the Reds to a First Division title (see page 22).
No. 47 Phil Thompson (Centre half) – 477 appearances, 13 goals. Astonishingly mature as a young FA Cup finalist, he developed into a teak-tough defender who led the Reds with distinction (see page 135).
No. 48 John Toshack (Centre forward) – 246 games, 96 goals. The Welsh international was one of the best headers of a football Liverpool have had, and a perfect foil for Kevin Keegan (see page 103).
No. 49 Jimmy McDougall (Left half) – 356 games, 12 goals. The Scot was a great Liverpool captain of the 1930s, and forged a formidable half back pairing with Matt Busby (see page 32).
No. 50 Mark Wright (Centre half) – 210 games, 9 goals. An outstanding FA-Cup winning captain in the Souness era. His ball-playing skills were allied to a fierce competitive streak (see page 177).

Results and Tables 1892-2003

The following pages include details of every official match played by Liverpool FC. Each season has its own page and is dated at the top. The opponents played at home are written in capital letters and appear in upper and lower case for away games. The date of the match, the score, the Liverpool goalscorers and the match attendance are also included. Full league and cup appearances and the goalscorers are featured separately. The final league table is included at the bottom of each page as well as a Fact File which notes particularly interesting facts and figures for the season as well as any notable transfers.

The results of matches played during the war years, 1914-18 and 1939-45, are regarded as unofficial and are included in a separate section starting on page 296.

In both the League & Cup Appearances and Goalscorers tables the category 'other' includes matches in the FA Charity Shield, World Club Championship, Screen Sport Super Cup, European Super Cup, Football League Centenary Cup and Test Matches.

Key: QR – qualifying round; Rd – round; R – replay; 2nd R – second replay; L – leg; 1L – first leg; F – final; SF – semi-final; SF/2L – semi-final second leg; QF – quarter-final; P – Phase; G – Group, i.e. (P1/GE) – Phase 1/Group E.

Season 1892-93

Lancashire League

DATE	OPPONENTS	SCORE	GOALSCORERS	ATTENDANCE
Sep 3	HIGHER WALTON	W 8-0	Smith 2, McQue 2, Cameron 2, McVean, McBride	200
Sep 24	BURY	W 4-0	Miller 2, McVean, Cameron	4,000
Oct 1	WEST MANCHESTER	W 3-1	Wyllie, Smith, Miller	3,000
Oct 22	Higher Walton	W 5-0	Miller 3, Wyllie 2	150
Nov 5	Blackpool	L 0-3		3,000
Nov 12	Fleetwood R	W 4-1	McVean 2, Miller, Smith	2,000
Nov 26	Rossendale United	W 2-0	Miller, McBride	1,500
Dec 3	FLEETWOOD R	W 7-0	Miller 5, McVean, McQueen M	1,000
Dec 12	BLACKPOOL	L 0-2		4,000
Dec 24	South Shore	W 1-0	Wyllie	2,000
Dec 31	HEYWOOD CENTRAL	W 6-2	Wyllie 2, McVean 2, McQueen M, Miller	1,000
Jan 2	Fairfield	W 4-1	Miller, Wyllie, McQueen H, Cameron	3,000
Jan 7	Heywood Central	W 2-1	Wyllie, McBride	1,000
Jan 14	West Manchester	D 0-0		2,000
Feb 11	Bury	L 0-3		8,000
Feb 18	Nelson	W 3-2	Miller 2, McVean	1,500
Feb 25	SOUTHPORT CENTRAL	W 2-0	McBride, McQueen M	1,500
Mar 4	NELSON	W 3-0	McQueen M 2, McQueen H	2,000
Mar 16	FAIRFIELD	W 5-0	Miller 2, McLean, Wyllie, McQueen H	2,000
Mar 18	SOUTH SHORE	W 4-1	Wyllie, Miller 2, McVean	2,000
Mar 25	ROSSENDALE UNITED	W 2-1	Smith, Wyllie	1,200
Apr 15	Southport Central	D 1-1	Miller	1,500

FA Cup

DATE	OPPONENTS	SCORE	GOALSCORERS	ATTENDANCE
Oct 15	Nantwich	(QR1) W 4-0	Miller 3, Wyllie	700
Oct 29	NEWTOWN	(QR2) W 9-0	Wyllie 3, McVean 2, McCartney, McQueen H Cameron, Townsend o.g.	4,000
Nov 19	Northwich Victoria	(QR3) L 1-2	Wylie	1,000

League & Cup Appearances

PLAYER	LEAGUE	CUP COMPETITION FA CUP	TOTAL
Cameron	7	2	9
Hannah	22	3	25
Kelly	3		3
Kelso	1		1
Kelvin	4	2	6
McBride	20	3	23
McCartney	18	2	20
McLean	22	3	25
McOwen	1		1
McQue	18	2	20
McQueen H	16	1	17
McQueen M	16	1	17
McVean	21	3	24
Miller	21	3	24
Pearson	1		1
Richardson	1		1
Ross	18	3	21
Smith	10	2	12
Wyllie	22	3	25

Goalscorers

PLAYER	LEAGUE	CUP COMPETITION FA CUP	TOTAL
Miller	22	3	25
Wyllie	11	5	16
McVean	9	2	11
Cameron	4	1	5
McQueen M	5		5
Smith	5		5
McBride	4		4
McQueen H	3	1	4
McQue	2		2
McCartney		1	1
McLean	1		1
Opps' o.gs.		1	1

Final Lancashire League Table

	P	W	D	L	F	A	PTS	GAV.
1 LIVERPOOL	22	17	2	3	66	19	36	3.4
2 BLACKPOOL	22	17	2	3	82	31	36	2.6
3 BURY	22	17	1	4	83	24	35	
4 FLEETWOOD RANGERS	22	10	5	7	47	51	25	
5 WEST MANCHESTER	22	10	4	8	68	55	24	
6 HEYWOOD CENTRAL	22	11	1	10	54	60	23	
7 ROSSENDALE	22	8	2	12	46	55	18	
8 SOUTHPORT CENTRAL	22	7	2	13	33	44	16	
9 FAIRFIELD	22	5	6	11	34	53	16	
10 SOUTH SHORE	22	5	6	11	46	66	16	
11 NELSON	22	4	2	16	54	73	10	
12 HIGHER WALTON	22	3	3	16	28	110	9	

LIVERPOOL CALEDONIANS – DISBANDED, RECORD EXPUNGED.

NOTE: AT THIS TIME, POSITIONS WERE DECIDED BY GOAL AVERAGE E.G. GOALS FOR DIVIDED BY GOALS AGAINST.

Fact File

Liverpool won the Lancashire League and the Liverpool Senior Cup, beating Everton in the final, in the club's first season. Both cups were stolen and had to be replaced at a cost of £130.

MANAGER: John McKenna and WE Barclay
CAPTAIN: Andrew Hannah
TOP SCORER: John Miller 25 (22 league)
BIGGEST WIN: 9-0, 29 October 1892, v Newtown (H), FA Cup
HIGHEST ATTENDANCE: 8,000, 11 February 1893, v Bury (A), League

Season 1893-94

Football League Division Two

DATE	OPPONENTS	SCORE	GOALSCORERS	ATTENDANCE
Sep 2	Middlesbrough	W 2-0	McVean, McQue	2,000
Sep 9	LINCOLN CITY	W 4-0	McBride 2, Gordon, McVean	5,000
Sep 16	Ardwick	W 1-0	Stott	6,000
Sep 23	SMALL HEATH	W 3-1	Stott 2, Henderson D	8,000
Sep 30	Notts County	D 1-1	McQueen H	6,000
Oct 7	MIDDLESBROUGH	W 6-0	McLean D, Stott 3, Henderson D, McQueen H	6,000
Oct 14	Small Heath	W 4-3	Gordon, Stott, Henderson D, McQueen H	8,000
Oct 21	Burton Swifts	D 1-1	McVean	3,000
Oct 28	Woolwich Arsenal	W 5-1	McLean D, McQueen M, McCartney, Stott, Bradshaw	7,000
Nov 4	NEWCASTLE UNITED	W 5-1	Stott, Gordon 2, Bradshaw, Dick	8,000
Nov 11	Walsall Town Swifts	D 1-1	Bradshaw	5,000
Nov 18	NOTTS COUNTY	W 2-1	Gordon, Henderson D	8,000
Nov 25	Newcastle United	D 0-0		2,000
Dec 2	ARDWICK	W 3-0	Stott, McQueen H, Henderson D	4,000
Dec 9	WALSALL TOWN SWIFTS	W 3-0	McVean 3	5,000
Dec 28	Crewe Alexandra	W 5-0	Gordon, Bradshaw, McQueen H, McVean Henderson D	4,000
Dec 30	GRIMSBY TOWN	W 2-0	Bradshaw, Henderson D	3,000
Jan 1	WOOLWICH ARSENAL	W 2-0	McBride, McVean	5,000
Jan 6	Rotherham Town	W 4-1	Stott 2, Henderson D, McQueen H	500
Jan 13	ROTHERHAM TOWN	W 5-1	McQueen H 1, Bradshaw 2, Henderson D 2	4,000
Feb 3	NORTHWICH VICTORIA	W 4-0	McLean D (pen), Stott 2, Bradshaw	3,000
Mar 3	BURTON SWIFTS	W 3-1	Worgan 2, McLean D (pen)	8,000
Mar 17	Lincoln City	D 1-1	Givens	4,000
Mar 24	CREWE ALEXANDRA	W 2-0	Dick, McQueen H	3,000
Mar 28	Northwich Victoria	W 3-2	Givens, McQueen H, McLean D	3,000
Mar 31	Grimsby Town	W 1-0	Givens	4,000
Apr 7	Burslem Port Vale	D 2-2	McVean, McQueen M	5,000
Apr 14	BURSLEM PORT VALE	W 2-1	Hannah, McQue	5,000

FA Cup

Jan 27	GRIMSBY TOWN	(Rd1) W 3-0	Bradshaw 2, McQue	8,000
Feb 10	PRESTON NORTH END	(Rd2) W 3-2	Henderson D 2, McVean	18,000
Feb 24	Bolton Wanderers	(Rd3) L 0-3		20,000

Test Match

Apr 28	NEWTON HEATH	W 2-0	Gordon, Bradshaw	5,000

League & Cup Appearances

PLAYER	LEAGUE	CUP COMPETITION FA CUP	OTHER	TOTAL
Bradshaw	14	3	1	18
Dewhurst	1			1
Dick	11			11
Givens	5			5
Gordon	21	3	1	25
Hannah	24	3	1	28
Henderson D	20	2	1	23
Henderson J	1			1
Hughes	1			1
McBride	25	2	1	28
McCartney	17	1	1	19
McLean D	27	3	1	31
McOwen	23	3		26
McQue	26	3	1	30
McQueen H	27	2	1	30
McQueen M	27	3	1	31
McVean	22	3	1	26
Stott	15	2		17
Worgan	1			1

Goalscorers

PLAYER	LEAGUE	CUP COMPETITION FA CUP	OTHER	TOTAL
Stott	14			14
Henderson D	10	2		12
Bradshaw	8	2	1	11
McVean	9	1		10
McQueen H	9			9
Gordon	6		1	7
McLean D	5			5
Givens	3			3
McBride J	3			3
McQue J	2	1		3
Dick D	2			2
McQueen M	2			2
Worgan	2			2
Hannah	1			1
McCartney	1			1

Fact File

Liverpool were known as 'The Team of Macs', frequently the only player who wasn't Scottish was William McOwen, who was English.

MANAGER: John McKenna and WE Barclay
CAPTAIN: Andrew Hannah
TOP SCORER: Jimmy Stott 14 (league)
BIGGEST WIN: 6-0, 7 October 1893, v Middlesbrough (H), League
HIGHEST ATTENDANCE: 20,000, 24 February 1894, v Bolton Wanderers (A), FA Cup
RECORD: 28 league games without defeat and a win in a test match to secure promotion to Division One

Final Division Two Table

		P	W	D	L	F	A	Pts
1	Liverpool	28	22	6	0	77	18	50
2	Small Heath	28	21	0	7	103	44	42
3	Notts Co	28	18	3	7	70	31	39
4	Newcastle United	28	15	6	7	66	39	36
5	Grimsby T	28	15	2	11	71	58	32
6	Burton Swifts	28	14	3	11	79	61	31
7	Burslem Port Vale	28	13	4	11	66	64	30
8	Lincoln C	28	11	6	11	59	58	28
9	Woolwich Arsenal	28	12	4	12	52	55	28
10	Walsall T Swifts	28	10	3	15	51	61	23
11	Middlesbrough I	28	8	4	16	37	72	20
12	Crewe Alex	28	6	7	15	42	73	19
13	Ardwick	28	8	2	18	47	71	18
14	Rotherham T	28	6	3	19	44	91	15
15	Northwich V	28	3	3	22	30	98	9

Season 1894-95

Football League Division One

DATE	OPPONENTS	SCORE	GOALSCORERS	ATTENDANCE
Sep 1	Blackburn Rovers	D 1-1	Bradshaw	12,000
Sep 3	Burnley	D 3-3	Gordon, Bradshaw, McQueen H	10,000
Sep 8	ASTON VILLA	L 1-2	Bradshaw	20,000
Sep 13	BOLTON WANDERERS	L 1-2	Ross	6,000
Sep 15	West Bromwich Albion	L 0-5		6,000
Sep 22	BLACKBURN ROVERS	D 2-2	McVean, McQueen H	14,000
Sep 29	Wolverhampton Wanderers	L 1-3	Ross (pen)	4,000
Oct 6	SHEFFIELD UNITED	D 2-2	Kerr, Bradshaw	12,000
Oct 13	Everton	L 0-3		44,000
Oct 20	STOKE	W 2-0	Ross 2	8,000
Oct 27	Aston Villa	L 0-5		5,000
Nov 3	BURNLEY	L 0-3		8,000
Nov 10	Stoke	L 1-3	Kerr	4,000
Nov 17	EVERTON	D 2-2	Hannah D, Ross (pen)	30,000
Nov 24	Sunderland	L 2-3	McVean, Hannah D	8,000
Dec 1	WOLVERHAMPTON WANDERERS	D 3-3	Bradshaw 2, McVean	7,000
Dec 8	Sheffield United	D 2-2	Bradshaw 2	8,000
Dec 15	SMALL HEATH	W 3-1	Bradshaw 2, Hannah D	7,000
Dec 25	Bolton Wanderers	L 0-1		8,000
Dec 29	Small Heath	L 0-3		5,000
Jan 1	WEST BROMWICH ALBION	W 4-0	Bradshaw 2, Ross, Hannah D	12,000
Jan 5	The Wednesday	L 0-5		10,000
Jan 9	Derby County	W 1-0	Ross	6,000
Jan 12	NOTTINGHAM FOREST	W 5-0	McVean 2, Ross, McQue, Hannah D	5,000
Mar 2	DERBY COUNTY	W 5-1	Bradshaw, Kerr, Ross 2, Hannah D	12,000
Mar 25	SUNDERLAND	L 2-3	Ross, Becton	20,000
Mar 30	THE WEDNESDAY	W 4-2	Bradshaw 2, Becton 2	6,000
Apr 6	Nottingham Forest	L 0-3		4,000
Apr 12	Preston North End	D 2-2	Ross, Becton	10,000
Apr 20	PRESTON NORTH END	L 2-5	Bradshaw 2	20,000

FA Cup

Feb 12	Barnsley St Peters	(Rd1) W 2-1*	McVean, Ross	4,000
Feb 11	BARNSLEY ST PETERS	(R) W 4-0	Bradshaw, Drummond, McVean, McQueen H	4,000
Feb 16	NOTTINGHAM FOREST	(Rd2) L 0-2		5,000

*Match counted as draw after Barnsley protest. After extra time. Score at 90 mins 1-1.

Test Match

Apr 27	Bury**	L 0-1		5,000

**Played at Blackburn.

League & Cup Appearances

PLAYER	LEAGUE	CUP COMPETITION FA CUP	OTHER	TOTAL
Becton	5			5
Bradshaw	30	3	1	34
Cameron	4			4
Cleland			1	1
Curran	14	3	1	18
Drummond	14	3	1	18
Dunlop	4		1	5
Givens	5			5
Gordon	5			5
Hannah A	16			16
Hannah D	17	1		18
Henderson	2			2
Kerr	12			12
McBride	5			5
McCann	15	2		17
McCartney	28	3		31
McLean D	24	2		26
McLean J	18	2	1	21
McQue	29	3		32
McQueen H	12	2		14
McQueen M	23	3	1	27
McVean	20	3	1	24
Neill			1	1
Ross	27	3	1	31
Whitehead			1	1
Worgan	1			1

Goalscorers

PLAYER	LEAGUE	CUP COMPETITION FA CUP	OTHER	TOTAL
Bradshaw	17	1		18
Ross	12	1		13
McVean	5	2		7
Hannah D	6			6
Becton	4			4
Kerr	3			3
McQueen H	2	1		3
Drummond		1		1
Gordon	1			1
McQue	1			1

Fact File

Liverpool's colours until 1898 were blue and white quarters.

MANAGER: John McKenna & WE Barclay

CAPTAIN: Andrew Hannah

TOP SCORER: Harry Bradshaw 18 (17 League)

BIGGEST WIN: 5-0, 12 January 1895, v Nottingham Forest (H), Division One

HIGHEST ATTENDANCE: 44,000, 13 October 1894, v Everton (A), Division One

Final Division One Table

	P	W	D	L	F	A	Pts
1 Sunderland	30	21	5	4	80	37	47
2 Everton	30	18	6	6	82	50	42
3 Aston Villa	30	17	5	8	82	43	39
4 Preston NE	30	15	5	10	62	46	35
5 Blackburn R	30	11	10	9	59	49	32
6 Sheffield U	30	14	4	12	57	55	32
7 Nottingham F	30	13	5	12	50	56	31
8 The Wednesday	30	12	4	14	50	55	28
9 Burnley	30	11	4	15	44	56	26
10 Bolton W	30	9	7	14	61	62	25
11 Wolverhampton W	30	9	7	14	43	63	25
12 Small Heath	30	9	7	14	50	74	25
13 WBA	30	10	4	16	51	66	24
14 Stoke	30	9	6	15	50	67	24
15 Derby Co	30	7	9	14	45	68	23
16 Liverpool	30	7	8	15	51	70	22

Season 1895-96

Football League Division Two

DATE	OPPONENTS	SCORE	GOALSCORERS	ATTENDANCE
Sep 7	Notts County	W 3-2	Ross, McQue, Bradshaw	7,000
Sep 14	NEWCASTLE UNITED	W 5-1	Ross 3, Becton, Bradshaw	8,000
Sep 21	Loughborough Town	W 4-2	Ross, Allan, Hannah D 2	3,500
Sep 28	BURSLEM PORT VALE	W 5-1	Allan 4, Hannah D	5,000
Sep 30	Burton Wanderers	W 4-1	Bradshaw 2, Becton 2	3,000
Oct 5	Newcastle United	L 0-1		12,000
Oct 7	CREWE ALEXANDRA	W 6-1	Allan 2, Ross 2, Geary 2	3,000
Oct 12	NEWTON HEATH	W 7-1	Becton 2, Bradshaw 2, Geary 2, Ross	10,000
Oct 19	Grimsby Town	L 0-1		5,000
Oct 21	Burslem Port Vale	L 4-5	Becton 3, Geary	1,000
Oct 26	NOTTS COUNTY	W 3-0	Bradshaw, Geary, Ross	8,000
Nov 2	Newton Heath	L 2-5	Becton, Ross.	10,000
Nov 9	LEICESTER FOSSE	W 3-1	Geary 2, Wilkie	7,000
Nov 16	Woolwich Arsenal	W 2-0	Bradshaw, Geary	10,000
Nov 23	DARWEN	D 0-0		3,000
Nov 30	Leicester Fosse	L 0-2		8,000
Dec 7	LOUGHBOROUGH TOWN	W 1-0	Becton	1,000
Dec 14	Darwen	W 4-0	McQue, Becton, Geary, McVean	2,000
Dec 21	Lincoln City	W 1-0	Allan	3,000
Jan 1	MANCHESTER CITY	W 3-1	Ross 2, McVean	20,000
Jan 4	Rotherham	W 5-0	Allan 3, Ross, Bradshaw	2,000
Jan 11	WOOLWICH ARSENAL	W 3-0	Ross 2, McQue	7,000
Jan 25	LINCOLN CITY	W 6-1	Ross 2, Bull, Geary, Becton Allan	4,000
Feb 18	ROTHERHAM	W10-1	Allan 4, McVean 3, Ross 2, Becton	2,000
Feb 22	GRIMSBY TOWN	W 3-1	Allan 2, Becton	10,000
Feb 29	Burton Swifts	W 7-0	McCartney, Ross 3, Becton 3	1,500
Mar 7	Burton Wanderers	L 1-2	Allan	2,000
Mar 21	BURTON SWIFTS	W 6-1	Bradshaw 2, Allan 2, Ross, McQue	4,000
Mar 28	Crewe Alexandra	W 7-1	Allan 3, McVean 2, McQue, Becton	3,000
Apr 3	Manchester City	D 1-1	Allan	25,000

FA Cup

Feb 1	MILLWALL	(Rd1)	W 4-1	Ross, Becton, Allan, Bradshaw	10,000
Feb 15	Wolverhampton Wanderers	(Rd2)	L 0-2		15,000

Test Matches

Apr 18	SMALL HEATH	W 4-0	Allan 2, McCartney, Bradshaw	20,000
Apr 20	Small Heath	D 0-0		5,000
Apr 25	WEST BROMWICH ALBION	W 2-0	Bradshaw, Allan	20,000
Apr 27	West Bromwich Albion	L 0-2		6,000

League & Cup Appearances

PLAYER	LEAGUE	CUP COMPETITION FA CUP	OTHER	TOTAL
Allan G	20	2	4	26
Battles	2		3	5
Becton	24	2	4	30
Bradshaw	26	2	4	32
Bull	1			1
Curran	6			6
Cleghorn	3		4	7
Dunlop	13			13
Geary	19	2	1	22
Goldie	22	2	4	28
Hannah	11			11
Holmes	17	2		19
Keech	6			6
McCartney	22	2	4	28
McLean J	8			8
McQue	26	2	4	32
McQueen	22			22
McVean	24		3	27
Ross	25	2	4	31
Storer	11	2	4	17
Whitehead	2			2
Wilkie	20	2	1	23

Goalscorers

PLAYER	LEAGUE	CUP COMPETITION FA CUP	OTHER	TOTAL
Allan	25	1	3	29
Ross	23	1		24
Becton	18	1		19
Bradshaw	11	1	2	14
Geary	11			11
McVean	7			7
McQue	5			5
Hannah	3			3
McCartney	1		1	2
Bull	1			1
Wilkie	1			1

Fact File

Liverpool won the championship, scoring 106 league goals in only 30 games, to return to the First Division.

MANAGER: John McKenna & WE Barclay
CAPTAIN: Jimmy Ross
TOP SCORER: George Allan 29 (25 league)
BIGGEST WIN: 10-1, 18 February 1896, v Rotherham (H), Division Two (Still a record league win)
HIGHEST ATTENDANCE: 25,000, 3 April 1896 v Manchester City (A), Division Two
MAJOR TRANSFERS IN: George Allan from Leith Athletic

Final Division Two Table

	P	W	D	L	F	A	PTS
1 Liverpool	30	22	2	6	106	32	46
2 Manchester C	30	21	4	5	63	38	46
3 Grimsby T	30	20	2	8	82	38	42
4 Burton W	30	19	4	7	69	40	42
5 Newcastle United	30	16	2	12	73	50	34
6 Newton Heath	30	15	3	12	66	57	33
7 Woolwich Arsenal	30	14	4	12	58	42	32
8 Leicester Fosse	30	14	4	12	57	44	32
9 Darwen	30	12	6	12	72	67	30
10 Notts Co	30	12	2	16	57	54	26
11 Burton Swifts	30	10	4	16	39	69	24
12 Loughborough	30	9	5	16	40	66	23
13 Lincoln C	30	9	4	17	53	75	22
14 Burslem Port Vale	30	7	4	19	43	78	18
15 Rotherham T	30	7	3	20	34	97	17
16 Crewe Alex	30	5	3	22	30	95	13

Season 1896-97

Football League Division One

DATE	OPPONENTS	SCORE	GOALSCORERS	ATTENDANCE
Sep 1	The Wednesday	W 2-1	Allan 2	2,000
Sep 5	Blackburn Rovers	L 0-1		7,000
Sep 7	BOLTON WANDERERS	L 0-2		15,000
Sep 12	DERBY COUNTY	W 2-0	Methven o.g., Bradshaw	16,000
Sep 19	Bury	W 2-1	McVean, Allan	7,000
Sep 26	WEST BROMWICH ALBION	D 0-0		14,000
Oct 3	Everton	L 1-2	Ross	45,000
Oct 10	NOTTINGHAM FOREST	W 3-0	Michael, McVean, Bradshaw	10,000
Oct 17	Sunderland	L 3-4	Goldie, Gow o.g., Allen	6,000
Oct 19	Sheffield United	D 1-1	Bradshaw	6,000
Oct 24	BLACKBURN ROVERS	W 4-0	Allan 2, Ross, Michael	10,000
Oct 31	West Bromwich Albion	W 1-0	Allan	5,000
Nov 7	SUNDERLAND	W 3-0	Hannah D 2, McVean	10,000
Nov 14	Preston North End	D 1-1	Michael	10,000
Nov 21	EVERTON	D 0-0		30,000
Nov 28	Nottingham Forest	L 0-2		6,000
Dec 12	BURY	W 3-1	Allan 2, McVean	7,000
Dec 19	Derby County	L 2-3	Michael, Neill	10,000
Dec 25	ASTON VILLA	D 3-3	Becton 2 (1 pen), Allan	15,000
Dec 25	Burnley	L 1-4	Becton	9,000
Jan 1	Bolton Wanderers	W 4-1	Allan 2, Geary, McCartney	20,000
Jan 2	SHEFFIELD UNITED	D 0-0		15,000
Jan 9	Wolverhampton Wanderers	W 2-1	Allan, Geary	2,000
Jan 16	STOKE	W 1-0	Allan	10,000
Feb 16	Stoke	L 1-6	Allan	7,000
Mar 4	WOLVERHAMPTON WANDERERS	W 3-0	Becton, Bradshaw, Allan	4,000
Mar 13	Aston Villa	D 0-0		18,000
Mar 27	BURNLEY	L 1-2	Neill	12,000
Apr 3	THE WEDNESDAY	D 2-2	Michael, Becton (pen)	6,000
Apr 10	PRESTON NORTH END	D 0-0		12,000

FA Cup

Jan 30	BURTON SWIFTS	(Rd1)	W 4-3	Hannah, Allan, Cleghorn, Ross	4,000
Feb 13	West Bromwich Albion	(Rd2)	W 2-1	McVean, Neill	16,000
Feb 27	NOTTINGHAM FOREST	(Rd3)	D 1-1	Becton	15,000
Mar 3	Nottingham Forest	(R)	W 1-0	Allan	10,000
Mar 20	Aston Villa*	(SF)	L 0-3		30,000

*Played at Bramall Lane.

League & Cup Appearances

PLAYER	LEAGUE	CUP COMPETITION FA CUP	TOTAL
Allan	29	5	34
Becton	20	5	25
Bradshaw	25	3	28
Cleghorn	17	5	22
Donnelly	6	2	8
Dunlop	5	2	7
Geary	8	3	11
Goldie	29	5	34
Hannah	3	1	4
Holmes	13		13
Jowitt	1		1
McCartney	30	5	35
McCowie	2		2
McQue	8	1	9
McQueen	1		1
McVean	23	2	25
Michael	19	4	23
Neill	22	4	26
Ross	21	2	23
Storer	23	3	26
Wilkie	25	3	28

Goalscorers

PLAYER	LEAGUE	CUP COMPETITION FA CUP	TOTAL
Allan	16	2	18
Becton	5	1	6
McVean	4	1	5
Michael	5		5
Bradshaw	4		4
Hannah	2	1	3
Neill	2	1	3
Ross	2	1	3
Geary	2		2
Cleghorn		1	1
Goldie	1		1
McCartney	1		1
Opps' o.gs.	2		2

Fact File

Harry Bradshaw became the first Liverpool player to win a cap for England v Ireland on 20 February 1897; and George Allan was the first Liverpool player capped for Scotland v England on 3 April 1897.

MANAGER: Tom Watson
CAPTAIN: Jimmy Ross
TOP SCORER: George Allan 18 (16 league)
BIGGEST WIN: 4-0, 24 October 1896, v Blackburn Rovers (H), Division One
HIGHEST ATTENDANCE: 45,000, 3 October 1896, v Everton (A), Division One
MAJOR TRANSFERS OUT: Malcolm McVean and Jimmy Ross to Burnley

Final Division One Table

		P	W	D	L	F	A	Pts
1	Aston Villa	30	21	5	4	73	38	47
2	Sheffield U	30	13	10	7	42	29	36
3	Derby Co	30	16	4	10	70	50	36
4	Preston NE	30	11	12	7	55	40	34
5	Liverpool	30	12	9	9	46	38	33
6	The Wednesday	30	10	11	9	42	37	31
7	Everton	30	14	3	13	62	57	31
8	Bolton W	30	12	6	12	40	43	30
9	Bury	30	10	10	10	39	44	30
10	Wolverhampton W	30	11	6	13	45	41	28
11	Nottingham F	30	9	8	13	44	49	26
12	WBA	30	10	6	14	33	56	26
13	Stoke	30	11	3	16	48	59	25
14	Blackburn R	30	11	3	16	35	62	25
15	Sunderland	30	7	9	14	34	47	23
16	Burnley	30	6	7	17	43	61	19

Season 1897-98

Football League Division One

DATE	OPPONENTS	SCORE	GOALSCORERS	ATTENDANCE
Sep 4	Stoke	D 2-2	Becton, Walker.	5,000
Sep 11	PRESTON NORTH END	D 0-0		20,000
Sep 18	The Wednesday	L 2-4	Walker, Becton	8,000
Sep 25	EVERTON	W 3-1	Cunliffe, McQue, Becton	30,000
Oct 2	Preston North End	D 1-1	Bradshaw	8,000
Oct 9	STOKE	W 4-0	Cunliffe 2, Bradshaw, Becton	12,000
Oct 16	Everton	L 0-3		40,000
Oct 23	DERBY COUNTY	W 4-2	McQue, Cunliffe, Marshall 2	12,000
Oct 30	Aston Villa	L 1-3	Bradshaw	25,000
Nov 6	NOTTINGHAM FOREST	L 1-2	Cunliffe	10,000
Nov 13	West Bromwich Albion	L 1-2	Becton	10,000
Nov 20	WOVERHAMPTON WANDERERS	W 1-0	Finnerhan	12,000
Nov 27	Nottingham Forest	W 3-2	McCowie, Lumsden	8,000
Dec 11	Wolverhampton Wanderers	L 1-2	Bradshaw	8,000
Dec 18	BLACKBURN ROVERS	L 0-1		5,000
Dec 25	Bolton Wanderers	W 2-0	Cunliffe, McCowie	8,000
Dec 27	SUNDERLAND	L 0-2		30,000
Dec 29	Sheffield United	W 2-1	McCowie, Hartley	8,000
Jan 1	WEST BROMWICH ALBION	D 1-1	McCartney	12,000
Jan 8	Blackburn Rovers	L 1-2	Ball o.g.	6,000
Jan 22	Sunderland	L 0-1		9,000
Feb 5	SHEFFIELD UNITED	L 0-4		18,000
Mar 12	NOTTS COUNTY	W 2-0	Becton, Cox	8,000
Mar 19	BOLTON WANDERERS	D 1-1	Bradshaw	7,000
Mar 26	Bury	W 2-0	McCowie, Becton	2,000
Mar 31	BURY	D 2-2	Geary, McCowie	3,000
Apr 2	Notts County	L 2-3	McCowie, Becton	8,000
Apr 11	THE WEDNESDAY	W 4-0	Morgan, Becton 2, Robertson	7,000
Apr 12	Derby County	L 1-3	Walker	3,500
Apr 16	ASTON VILLA	W 4-0	Robertson, Walker, Morgan, Becton	20,000

FA Cup

Jan 29	HUCKNALL ST JOHN'S	(Rd1) W 2-0	Becton, McQue	8,000
Feb 12	Newton Heath	(Rd2) D 0-0		12,000
Feb 16	NEWTON HEATH	(R) W 2-1	Wilkie, Cunliffe	6,000
Feb 26	Derby County	(Rd3) D 1-1	Bradshaw	20,000
Mar 2	DERBY COUNTY	(R) L 1-5	Becton (pen)	15,000

League & Cup Appearances

PLAYER	LEAGUE	CUP COMPETITION FA CUP	TOTAL
Battles	1		1
Becton	21	5	26
Bradshaw	23	3	26
Cleghorn	30	5	35
Colvin	3		3
Cox	2		2
Cunliffe	14	4	18
Dunlop	20	5	25
Finnerhan	5	3	8
Geary	11		11
Goldie	28	4	32
Goldie	4		4
Hartley	7	5	12
Holmes	12		12
Howell	1		1
Lumsden	6	2	8
Marshall	17	1	18
McCartney	27	5	32
McCowie	19	2	21
McQue	14	5	19
McQueen	2		2
Morgan	4		4
Robertson	3		3
Storer	30	5	35
Walker J	3		3
Walker W	12		12
Wilkie	10	1	11
Wilson	1		1

Goalscorers

PLAYER	LEAGUE	CUP COMPETITION FA CUP	TOTAL
Becton	11	2	13
Cunliffe	6	1	7
Bradshaw	5	1	6
McCowie	6		6
McQue	2	1	3
Lumsden	2		2
Marshall	2		2
Morgan	2		2
Robertson	2		2
Walker J	2		2
Walker W	2		2
Cox	1		1
Finnerhan	1		1
Geary	1		1
Hartley	1		1
McCartney	1		1
Wilkie		1	1
Opps' o.gs.	1		1

Fact File

Only one of the 28 players this season scored more than 10 goals, 16 others accounted for the rest.

MANAGER: Tom Watson
CAPTAIN: John McCartney
TOP SCORER: Frank Becton 13 (11 league)
BIGGEST WIN: 4-0, 9 October 1897, v Stoke City (H), Division One; 4-0, 11 April 1898, v The Wednesday (H), Division One
HIGHEST ATTENDANCE: 40,000, 16 October 1897, v Everton (A), Division One
MAJOR TRANSFERS IN: Jack Cox from Blackpool, D Cunliffe and R Marshall from Leith Athletic, W Walker from Scotland
MAJOR TRANSFERS OUT: John McCartney to New Brighton Tower

Final Division One Table

		P	W	D	L	F	A	PTS
1	Sheffield U	30	17	8	5	56	31	42
2	Sunderland	30	16	5	9	43	30	37
3	Wolverhampton W	30	14	7	9	57	41	35
4	Everton	30	13	9	8	48	39	35
5	The Wednesday	30	15	3	12	51	42	33
6	Aston Villa	30	14	5	11	61	51	33
7	WBA	30	11	10	9	44	45	32
8	Nottingham F	30	11	9	10	47	49	31
9	Liverpool	30	11	6	13	48	45	28
10	Derby Co	30	11	6	13	57	61	28
11	Bolton W	30	11	4	15	28	41	26
12	Preston NE	30	8	8	14	35	43	24
13	Notts Co	30	8	8	14	36	46	24
14	Bury	30	8	8	14	39	51	24
15	Blackburn R	30	7	10	13	39	54	24
16	Stoke	30	8	8	14	35	55	24

Season 1898-99

Football League Division One

DATE	OPPONENTS	SCORE	GOALSCORERS	ATTENDANCE
Sep 3	THE WEDNESDAY	W 4-0	Morgan, Walker, Robertson Goldie W	18,000
Sep 10	Sunderland	L 0-1		30,000
Sep 17	WOLVERHAMPTON WANDERERS	W 1-0	Cox	15,000
Sep 24	Everton	W 2-1	McCowie 2 (1 pen)	45,000
Oct 1	NOTTS COUNTY	D 0-0		12,000
Oct 8	Stoke City	L 1-2	Cox	8,000
Oct 15	ASTON VILLA	L 0-3		20,000
Oct 22	Burnley	L 1-2	Morgan	10,000
Oct 29	SHEFFIELD UNITED	W 2-1	McCowie (pen), Allan	10,000
Nov 5	Newcastle United	L 0-3		20,000
Nov 12	PRESTON NORTH END	W 3-1	Morgan 2, Allen	12,000
Nov 19	Bury	L 0-3		6,000
Nov 26	Nottingham Forest	W 3-0	McCowie, Morgan, Walker	12,000
Dec 3	BOLTON WANDERERS	W 2-0	Morgan, McCowie	12,000
Dec 10	Derby County	L 0-1		6,000
Dec 17	WEST BROMWICH ALBION	D 2-2	Walker, Morgan	18,000
Dec 24	Blackburn Rovers	W 3-1	Robertson 2, Cox	6,000
Dec 26	West Bromwich Albion	W 1-0	Morgan	10,000
Dec 27	Notts County	D 1-1	Allan	16,000
Dec 31	The Wednesday	W 3-0	Massey o.g., Walker, Allan (pen)	4,000
Jan 2	Sheffield United	W 2-0	Walker, Cox	12,000
Jan 7	SUNDERLAND	D 0-0		20,000
Jan 14	Wolverhampton Wanderers	D 0-0		7,000
Jan 21	EVERTON	W 2-0	Walker, Robertson	30,000
Feb 4	STOKE CITY	W 1-0	Goldie W	
Feb 18	BURNLEY	W 2-0	Allan, Robertson	12,000
Mar 11	Preston North End	W 2-1	Morgan, Allan	9,000
Mar 25	NOTTINGHAM FOREST	L 0-1		14,000
Apr 1	Bolton Wanderers	L 1-2	Morgan	15,000
Apr 3	NEWCASTLE UNITED	W 3-2	Cox, Walker, Allan	12,000
Apr 8	DERBY COUNTY	W 4-0	Raisbeck, Walker 3	15,000
Apr 20	BURY	W 1-0	Walker	10,000
Apr 22	BLACKBURN ROVERS	W 2-0	Allan, Robertson	20,000
Apr 29	Aston Villa	L 0-5		41,357

FA Cup

DATE	OPPONENTS	ROUND	SCORE	GOALSCORERS	ATTENDANCE
Jan 28	BLACKBURN ROVERS	(Rd1)	W 2-0	Cox, Allan	14,000
Feb 11	NEWCASTLE UNITED	(Rd2)	W 3-1	Morgan, Raisbeck, Higgins o.g.	7,000
Feb 25	West Bromwich Albion	(Rd3)	W 2-0	Morgan, Robertson	17,124
Mar 18	Sheffield United*	(SF)	D 2-2	Allan, Morgan.	35,000
Mar 23	Sheffield United**	(R)	D 4-4	Walker, Allan, Boyle o.g., Cox	20,000
Mar 30	Sheffield United†	(2nd R)	L 0-1		20,000

*Played at Nottingham. **Played at Bolton. †Played at Derby.

League & Cup Appearances

PLAYER	LEAGUE	CUP COMPETITION FA CUP	TOTAL
Allan	30	6	36
Cleghorn	6		6
Cox	27	6	33
Dunlop	33	6	39
Geary	1		1
Goldie A	25	5	30
Goldie W	27	6	33
Howell	30	6	36
Marshall	3		3
McCowie	12		12
McQueen	2	1	3
Morgan	32	6	38
Perkins	5		5
Raisbeck	32	6	38
Robertson	33	6	39
Stevenson	8	1	9
Storer	27	5	32
Walker	32	6	38
Wilkie	2		2
Wilson	7		7

Goalscorers

PLAYER	LEAGUE	CUP COMPETITION FA CUP	TOTAL
Morgan	10	3	13
Walker	11	1	12
Allan	8	3	11
Cox	5	2	7
Robertson	6	1	7
McCowie	5		5
Goldie W	2		2
Raisbeck	1	1	2
Opps' o.gs.	1	2	3

Fact File

The marathon FA Cup semi-final v Sheffield United also included an abandoned game on 27 March when Liverpool were winning 1-0. Liverpool FC team colours changed to the famous red shirts.

MANAGER: Tom Watson
CAPTAIN: Harry Storer
TOP SCORER: Hugh Morgan 13 (10 league)
BIGGEST WIN: 4-0, 3 September 1898, v The Wednesday (H), Division One; 4-0, 8 April 1899, v Derby County (H), Division One
HIGHEST ATTENDANCE: 45,000, 24 September 1898, v Everton (A), Division One

Final Division One Table

		P	W	D	L	F	A	PTS
1	Aston Villa	34	19	7	8	76	40	45
2	Liverpool	34	19	5	10	49	33	43
3	Burnley	34	15	9	10	45	47	39
4	Everton	34	15	8	11	48	41	38
5	Notts Co	34	12	13	9	47	51	37
6	Blackburn R	34	14	8	12	60	52	36
7	Sunderland	34	15	6	13	41	41	36
8	Wolverhampton W	34	14	7	13	54	48	35
9	Derby Co	34	12	11	11	62	57	35
10	Bury	34	14	7	13	48	49	35
11	Nottingham F	34	11	11	12	42	42	33
12	Stoke	34	13	7	14	47	52	33
13	Newcastle U	34	11	8	15	49	48	30
14	WBA	34	12	6	16	42	57	30
15	Preston NE	34	10	9	15	44	47	29
16	Sheffield U	34	9	11	14	45	51	29
17	Bolton W	34	9	7	18	37	51	25
18	The Wednesday	34	8	8	18	32	61	24

Season 1899-1900

Football League Division One

DATE	OPPONENTS	SCORE	GOALSCORERS	ATTENDANCE
Sep 2	Stoke	L 2-3	Hunter, Raisbeck	10,000
Sep 9	SUNDERLAND	L 0-2		20,000
Sep 16	West Bromwich Albion	L 0-2		10,000
Sep 23	EVERTON	L 1-2	Robertson	30,000
Sep 30	Blackburn Rovers	L 0-2		7,000
Oct 5	Notts County	L 1-2	Cox	10,000
Oct 7	DERBY COUNTY	L 0-2		12,000
Oct 14	Bury	L 1-2	Walker	6,000
Oct 21	NOTTS COUNTY	W 3-1	Raisbeck, Robertson, Walker	10,000
Oct 28	Manchester City	W 1-0	Robertson	20,000
Nov 4	SHEFFIELD UNITED	D 2-2	Hunter, Robertson	20,000
Nov 11	Newcastle United	D 1-1	Walker	8,000
Nov 18	ASTON VILLA	D 3-3	Morgan, Walker, Raisbeck	20,000
Nov 25	WOLVERHAMPTON WANDERERS	D 1-1	Walker	12,000
Dec 2	Burnley	L 1-2	Walker	5,000
Dec 9	PRESTON NORTH END	W 1-0	Walker	7,000
Dec 16	Nottingham Forest	L 0-1		5,000
Dec 23	GLOSSOP NORTH END	W 5-2	Hunter 3, Satterthwaite 2	5,000
Dec 25	Derby County	L 2-3	Hunter, Robertson	10,000
Dec 30	STOKE	D 0-0		5,000
Jan 6	Sunderland	L 0-1		3,000
Jan 13	WEST BROMWICH ALBION	W 2-0	Morgan 2	6,000
Jan 20	Everton	L 1-3	Raybould	30,000
Feb 3	BLACKBURN ROVERS	W 3-1	Cox 2, Robertson	6,000
Mar 3	MANCHESTER CITY	W 5-2	Raybould 2 (1 pen), Walker, Satterthwaite, Cox	20,000
Mar 10	Sheffield United	W 2-1	Raybould, Satterthwaite	15,000
Mar 17	NEWCASTLE UNITED	W 2-0	Robertson, Walker	18,000
Mar 24	Aston Villa	L 0-1		15,000
Mar 31	Wolverhampton Wanderers	W 1-0	Robertson	7,000
Apr 7	BURNLEY	L 0-1		10,000
Apr 9	BURY	W 2-0	Raybould 2	5,000
Apr 14	Preston North End	W 3-1	Satterthwaite, Raybould, Cox	5,000
Apr 21	NOTTINGHAM FOREST	W 1-0	Robertson (pen)	10,000
Apr 28	Glossop North End	W 2-1	Goldie W, Walker	2,000

FA Cup

Jan 27	Stoke	(Rd1)	D 0-0		8,000
Feb 1	STOKE	(R)	W 1-0	Hunter	10,000
Feb 17	WEST BROMWICH ALBION	(Rd2)	D 1-1	Cox	15,000
Feb 21	West Bromwich Albion	(R)	L 1-2	Robertson	13,000

League & Cup Appearances

PLAYER	LEAGUE	CUP COMPETITION FA CUP	TOTAL
Cox	25	4	29
Dunlop	34	4	38
Foxall	1		1
Goldie A	21	4	25
Goldie W	25	4	29
Howell	26	2	28
Hunter J*	20	4	24
Hunter TJ**	1		1
Kyle	4	1	5
Morgan	23	3	26
Parkinson	1		1
Perkins	23	4	27
Raisbeck	32	4	36
Raybould	11		11
Robertson	34	4	38
Satterthwaite	18		18
Stevenson	13		13
Storer	11		11
Walker	27	4	31
Wilson C	22	2	24
Wilson D	2		2

*Known as Sailor
**Known as Jack

Goalscorers

PLAYER	LEAGUE	CUP COMPETITION FA CUP	TOTAL
Robertson	9	1	10
Walker	10		10
Hunter J*	6	1	7
Raybould	7		7
Cox	5	1	6
Satterthwaite	5		5
Morgan	3		3
Raisbeck	3		3
Goldie W	1		1

Fact File

It was reported that Scottish international centre forward, George Allen, was too ill for pre-season training. He died of tuberculosis on 17 October 1899. He was 24 years of age.

MANAGER: Tom Watson
CAPTAIN: Alex Raisbeck
TOP SCORER: John Walker 10 (league), Tom Robertson 10 (9 league)
BIGGEST WIN: 5-2, 23 December 1899, v Glossop (H), Division One; 3 March 1900, v Manchester City (H), Division One
HIGHEST ATTENDANCE: 30,000, 23 September 1899, v Everton (H) and 20 January 1900 (A)
TRANSFERS IN: John (Sailor) Hunter from Abercorn, Sam Raybould from New Brighton Tower, Charlie Satterthwaite from Burton Swifts
TRANSFERS OUT: Archie Goldie to New Brighton Tower, Hugh Morgan to Blackburn Rovers

Final Division One Table

		P	W	D	L	F	A	Pts
1	Aston Villa	34	22	6	6	77	35	50
2	Sheffield U	34	18	12	4	63	33	48
3	Sunderland	34	19	3	12	50	35	41
4	Wolverhampton W	34	15	9	10	48	37	39
5	Newcastle U	34	13	10	11	53	43	36
6	Derby Co	34	14	8	12	45	43	36
7	Manchester C	34	13	8	13	50	44	34
8	Nottingham F	34	13	8	13	56	55	34
9	Stoke	34	13	8	13	37	45	34
10	Liverpool	34	14	5	15	49	45	33
11	Everton	34	13	7	14	47	49	33
12	Bury	34	13	6	15	40	44	32
13	WBA	34	11	8	15	43	51	30
14	Blackburn R	34	13	4	17	49	61	30
15	Notts Co	34	9	11	14	46	60	29
16	Preston NE	34	12	4	18	38	48	28
17	Burnley	34	11	5	18	34	54	27
18	Glossop	34	4	10	20	31	74	18

Season 1900-01

Football League Division One

DATE	OPPONENTS	SCORE	GOALSCORERS	ATTENDANCE
Sep 1	BLACKBURN ROVERS	W 3-0	Robertson T, Satterthwaite, Raybould	20,000
Sep 8	Stoke	W 2-1	Robertson T, Raybould	10,000
Sep 15	WEST BROMWICH ALBION	W 5-0	Goldie, Walker, Raybould 2, Robertson T	18,000
Sep 22	Everton	D 1-1	Raybould	50,000
Sep 29	SUNDERLAND	L 1-2	Wilson	20,000
Oct 6	Derby County	W 3-2	Robertson T 2, Walker	8,000
Oct 13	BOLTON WANDERES	W 2-1	Cox, Satterthwaite	12,000
Oct 20	Notts County	L 0-3		18,000
Oct 27	PRESTON NORTH END	W 3-2	McGuigan, Cox, Raybould	12,000
Nov 3	Wolverhampton Wanderers	L 1-2	Walker	12,000
Nov 10	ASTON VILLA	W 5-1	Raybould 2, McGuigan, Walker 2	18,000
Nov 17	The Wednesday	L 2-3	Raybould, Raisbeck	10,000
Nov 24	Newcastle United	D 1-1	Cox	17,000
Dec 1	SHEFFIELD UNITED	L 1-2	Satterthwaite	15,000
Dec 8	Manchester City	W 4-3	Raybould, Cox, Robertson T, McGuigan	20,000
Dec 15	BURY	W 1-0	Cox	14,000
Dec 22	Nottingham Forest	D 0-0		6,000
Dec 25	DERBY COUNTY	D 0-0		18,000
Dec 29	Blackburn Rovers	L 1-3	Raybould	8,000
Jan 1	STOKE	W 3-1	Robertson T, Cox, McGuigan	15,000
Jan 19	EVERTON	L 1-2	Cox	18,000
Feb 16	Bolton Wanderers	L 0-1		8,000
Feb 23	Sunderland	W 1-0	Cox	11,249
Mar 2	Preston North End	D 2-2	Satterthwaite, Raybould	1,500
Mar 9	WOLVERHAMPTON WANDERERS	W 1-0	Raybould	15,000
Mar 16	Aston Villa	W 2-0	McGuigan, Hunter S	14,000
Mar 23	THE WEDNESDAY	D 1-1	Raybould	12,000
Mar 30	NEWCASTLE UNITED	W 3-0	Hunter S 2, Raybould	10,000
Apr 8	NOTTS COUNTY	W 1-0	Raybould	15,000
Apr 13	MANCHESTER CITY	W 3-1	Robertson T 2, Cox	14,000
Apr 20	Bury	D 0-0		8,000
Apr 22	Sheffield United	W 2-0	Raybould, Satterthwaite	6,000
Apr 27	NOTTINGHAM FOREST	W 2-0	Cox, Goldie	20,000
Apr 29	West Bromwich Albion	W 1-0	Walker	4,000

FA Cup

Jan 5	West Ham United	(QR)	W 1-0	Raybould	6,000
Feb 9	Notts County	(Rd1)	L 0-2		15,000

League & Cup Appearances

PLAYER	LEAGUE	CUP COMPETITION FA CUP	TOTAL
Cox	32	2	34
Davies	1		1
Dunlop	33	2	35
Glover	10		10
Goldie	34	2	36
Howell	2		2
Hunter J*	8	1	9
Hunter TJ**	2		2
McGuigan	14	2	16
Parry	8		8
Perkins	34	2	36
Raisbeck	31	2	33
Raybould	31	2	33
Robertson J	25	2	27
Robertson T	34	2	36
Satterthwaite	21		21
Walker	29	1	30
Wilson	25	2	27

*known as 'Sailor'
** known as 'Jack'

Goalscorers

PLAYER	LEAGUE	CUP COMPETITION FA CUP	TOTAL
Raybould	17	1	18
Cox	10		10
Robertson T	9		9
Walker	6		6
McGuigan	5		5
Satterthwaite	5		5
Hunter J*	3		3
Goldie	2		2
Raisbeck	1		1
Wilson	1		1

*Known as Sailor

Fact File

Liverpool were Division One champions for the first time. All the games were cancelled on 2 February due to Queen Victoria's funeral.

MANAGER: Tom Watson

CAPTAIN: Alex Raisbeck

TOP SCORER: Sam Raybould 18 (17 league)

BIGGEST WIN: 5-0, 15 September 1900, v West Bromwich Albion (H), Division One

HIGHEST ATTENDANCE: 50,000, 22 September 1900, v Everton (A), Division One

TRANSFER IN: Andrew McGuigan from Hibernian, John Robertson from Stoke City, Maurice Parry from Brighton

Final Division One Table

		P	W	D	L	F	A	Pts
1	Liverpool	34	19	7	8	59	35	45
2	Sunderland	34	15	13	6	57	26	43
3	Notts Co	34	18	4	12	54	46	40
4	Nottingham F	34	16	7	11	53	36	39
5	Bury	34	16	7	11	53	37	39
6	Newcastle U	34	14	10	10	42	37	38
7	Everton	34	16	5	13	55	42	37
8	The Wednesday	34	13	10	11	52	42	36
9	Blackburn R	34	12	9	13	39	47	33
10	Bolton W	34	13	7	14	39	55	33
11	Manchester C	34	13	6	15	48	58	32
12	Derby Co	34	12	7	15	55	42	31
13	Wolverhampton W	34	9	13	12	39	55	31
14	Sheffield U	34	12	7	15	35	52	31
15	Aston Villa	34	10	10	14	45	51	30
16	Stoke	34	11	5	18	46	57	27
17	Preston NE	34	9	7	18	49	75	25
18	WBA	34	7	8	19	35	62	22

Season 1901-02

Football League Division One

DATE	OPPONENTS	SCORE	GOALSCORERS	ATTENDANCE
Sep 2	Small Heath	D 0-0		10,000
Sep 7	Stoke	L 0-1		10,000
Sep 14	EVERTON	D 2-2	White, Raybould	30,000
Sep 21	Sunderland	D 1-1	Cox	16,000
Sep 28	SMALL HEATH	W 3-1	Raybould 2, Robertson T (pen)	20,000
Oct 5	Derby County	D 1-1	RobertsonT	8,000
Oct 12	THE WEDNESDAY	L 1-2	Robertson T	15,000
Oct 19	Notts County	D 2-2	S Hunter, Cox	10,000
Oct 26	BOLTON WANDERERS	D 1-1	McGuigan	16,000
Nov 2	Manchester City	W 3-2	Robertson T, Satterthwaite, Cox	20,000
Nov 9	WOLVERHAMPTON WANDERERS	W 4-1	Satterthwaite, Robertson T (pen), McGuigan 2	16,000
Nov 23	Newcastle United	L 0-1		18,000
Nov 30	ASTON VILLA	W 1-0	Raybould	18,000
Dec 7	Sheffield Utd	L 1-2	Raybould	12,000
Dec 14	NOTTINGHAM FOREST	L 0-2		12,000
Dec 26	SUNDERLAND	L 0-1		20,000
Dec 28	BLACKBURN ROVERS	W 1-0	McGuigan	12,000
Jan 4	STOKE	W 7-0	McGuigan 5, Raybould 2	10,000
Jan 11	Everton	L 0-4		25,000
Feb 1	Bury	D 0-0		7,000
Feb 15	NOTTS COUNTY	L 0-1		10,000
Feb 22	Bolton Wanderers	L 0-1		10,000
Mar 1	MANCHESTER CITY	W 4-0	Cox, Raybould 3	20,000
Mar 8	Wolverhampton Wanderers	L 1-3	Raybould	6,000
Mar 15	Grimsby Town	D 1-1	Goddard	6,000
Mar 22	NEWCASTLE UNITED	L 0-1		12,000
Mar 29	Aston Villa	W 1-0	Fleming	20,000
Apr 1	The Wednesday	D 1-1	Raybould	15,000
Apr 5	SHEFFIELD UNITED	W 1-0	Raybould	5,000
Apr 12	Nottingham Forest	D 1-1	Goddard	5,000
Apr 14	DERBY COUNTY	L 0-2		12,000
Apr 19	BURY	W 1-0	Raybould	12,000
Apr 21	GRIMSBY TOWN	D 2-2	Raybould 2	12,000
Apr 26	Blackburn Rovers	D 1-1	Walker	2,000

FA Cup

Jan 25	EVERTON	(Rd1)	D 2-2	Robertson T (pen), Hunter	25,000
Jan 30	Everton	(R)	W 2-0	Raisbeck, Hunter	20,000
Feb 8	Southampton	(Rd2)	L 1-4	Fleming	20,000

League & Cup Appearances

PLAYER	LEAGUE	CUP COMPETITION FA CUP	TOTAL
Bowen	2		2
Cox	31	3	34
Davies	6	1	7
Dunlop	33	3	36
Fleming	24	2	26
Glover	18		18
Goddard	11		11
Goldie	34	3	37
Green	4		4
Hunter J*	9	3	12
Hunter TJ**	2		2
Marshall	1		1
McGuigan	18	3	21
Morris	3		3
Parry	13		13
Perkins	33	3	36
Raidsbeck	26	3	29
Raybould	29		29
Robertson J	17	3	20
Robertson T	22	3	25
Satterthwaite	6		6
Walker	18		18
White	6		6
Wilson	8	3	11

*Known as Sailor
**Known as Jack

Goalscorers

PLAYER	LEAGUE	CUP COMPETITION FA CUP	TOTAL
Raybould	16		16
McGuigan	9		9
Robertson T	5	1	6
Cox	4		4
Hunter J*	1	2	3
Fleming	1	1	2
Goddard	2		2
Satterthwaite	2		2
Raisbeck		1	1
Walker	1		1
White	1		1

Fact File

Andy McGuigan scored five goals in a 7-0 win over Stoke City in January.

MANAGER: Tom Watson
CAPTAIN: Alex Raisbeck
TOP SCORER: Sam Raybould 16 (league)
BIGGEST WIN: 7-0, 4 January 1902, v Stoke City (H) Division One
HIGHEST ATTENDANCE: 30,000, 14 September 1901, v Everton (H), Division One
TRANSFER IN: Arthur Goddard from Glossop North End

Final Division One Table

		P	W	D	L	F	A	Pts
1	Sunderland	34	19	6	9	50	35	44
2	Everton	34	17	7	10	53	35	41
3	Newcastle U	34	14	9	11	48	34	37
4	Blackburn R	34	15	6	13	52	48	36
5	Nottingham F	34	13	9	12	43	43	35
6	Derby Co	34	13	9	12	39	41	35
7	Bury	34	13	8	13	44	38	34
8	Aston Villa	34	13	8	13	42	40	34
9	The Wednesday	34	13	8	13	48	52	34
10	Sheffield U	34	13	7	14	53	48	33
11	Liverpool	34	10	12	12	42	38	32
12	Bolton W	34	12	8	14	51	56	32
13	Notts Co	34	14	4	16	51	57	32
14	Wolverhampton W	34	13	6	15	46	57	32
15	Grimsby T	34	13	6	15	44	60	32
16	Stoke	34	11	9	14	45	55	31
17	Small Heath	34	11	8	15	47	45	30
18	Manchester C	34	11	6	17	42	58	28

Season 1902-03

Football League Division One

DATE	OPPONENTS	SCORE	GOALSCORERS	ATTENDANCE
Sep 6	BLACKBURN ROVERS	W 5-2	Raybould 2, Cox 2, Livingstone	20,000
Sep 13	Sunderland	L 1-2	Raybould (pen)	20,000
Sep 20	STOKE	D 1-1	Roose o.g.	20,000
Sep 27	Everton	L 1-3	Raybould (pen)	40,000
Oct 4	THE WEDNESDAY	W 4-2	Raybould 2 (pen), Livingstone, Goddard	17,000
Oct 11	West Bromwich Albion	W 2-1	Raybould 2	20,000
Oct 18	NOTTS COUNTY	L 0-2		16,000
Oct 25	Bolton Wanderers	D 1-1	Raybould	8,000
Nov 1	MIDDLESBROUGH	W 5-0	Raybould 3, Chadwick, Cox	15,000
Nov 8	Newcastle United	W 2-1	Raybould, Goddard	5,000
Nov 15	WOLVERHAMPTON WANDERERS	W 4-1	Livingstone, Cox, Goddard, Raybould	15,000
Nov 22	Derby County	L 1-2	Chadwick	10,000
Nov 29	Sheffield United	L 0-2		7,000
Dec 6	GRIMSBY TOWN	W 9-2	Livingstone, Raybould 4 (1 pen), Chadwick 2, Goddard 2	5,000
Dec 13	Aston Villa	W 2-1	Goddard, Raybould	20,000
Dec 20	NOTTINGHAM FOREST	W 2-1	Goddard, Cox	16,000
Dec 25	BOLTON WANDERERS	W 5-1	Wilson 2, Raybould (pen), Chadwick, Cox	20,000
Dec 27	Bury	L 1-3	Raybould	11,000
Jan 1	WEST BROMWICH ALBION	L 0-2		25,000
Jan 3	Blackburn Rovers	L 1-3	Green	5,000
Jan 17	Stoke	L 0-1		5,000
Jan 31	The Wednesday	L 1-3	Goddard	15,000
Feb 14	Notts County	W 2-1	Goddard 2	7,000
Feb 28	Middlesbrough	W 2-0	Raybould, Chadwick	15,000
Mar 7	NEWCASTLE UNITED	W 3-0	Raybould 2, Raisbeck	15,000
Mar 23	DERBY COUNTY	W 3-1	Goldie, Raybould, Cox	8,000
Mar 28	SHEFFIELD UNITED	L 2-4	Cox, Raybould	15,000
Mar 30	SUNDERLAND	D 1-1	Raybould	3,000
Apr 4	Grimsby Town	L 1-3	Chadwick	6,000
Apr 10	EVERTON	D 0-0		28,000
Apr 11	ASTON VILLA	W 2-1	Goddard, Raybould	15,000
Apr 18	Nottingham Forest	L 0-1		3,000
Apr 25	BURY	W 2-0	Raybould 2	10,000
Apr 27	Wolverhampton Wanderers	W 2-0	Raybould, Cox	8,000

FA Cup

Feb 7	Manchester United (Rd1)	L 1-2	Raybould	15,000

Fact File

Sam Raybould set a club record by scoring 31 league goals in a season.

MANAGER: Tom Watson
CAPTAIN: Alex Raisbeck
TOP SCORER: Sam Raybould 32 (31 league)
BIGGEST WIN: 9-2, 6 December 1902, v Grimsby Town (H), Division One
HIGHEST ATTENDANCE: 40,000, 27 September 1902, v Everton (A), Division One
TRANSFERS IN: Edgar Chadwick from Southampton, George Livingstone from Celtic
TRANSFERS OUT: Andy McGuigan to Middlesbrough

League & Cup Appearances

PLAYER	LEAGUE	CUP COMPETITION FA CUP	TOTAL
Carlin	1		1
Chadwick	29	1	30
Cox	29	1	30
Davies	2		2
Dunlop	28	1	29
Fleming	4		4
Glover	30	1	31
Goddard	33	1	34
Goldie	34	1	35
Green	3		3
Livingstone	31	1	32
McCallum	2		2
Morris	11		11
Parry	31	1	32
Perkins	12	1	13
Platt	22		22
Raisbeck	27	1	28
Raybould	33	1	34
Wilson	12		12

Goalscorers

PLAYER	LEAGUE	CUP COMPETITION FA CUP	TOTAL
Raybould	31	1	32
Goddard	11		11
Cox	9		9
Chadwick	7		7
Livingstone	4		4
Wilson	2		2
Goldie	1		1
Green	1		1
Raisbeck	1		1
Opps' o.gs.	1		1

Final Division One Table

		P	W	D	L	F	A	Pts
1	The Wednesday	34	19	4	11	54	36	42
2	Aston Villa	34	19	3	12	61	40	41
3	Sunderland	34	16	9	9	51	36	41
4	Sheffield U	34	17	5	12	58	44	39
5	Liverpool	34	17	4	13	68	49	38
6	Stoke	34	15	7	12	46	38	37
7	WBA	34	16	4	14	54	53	36
8	Bury	34	16	3	15	54	43	35
9	Derby Co	34	16	3	15	50	47	35
10	Nottingham F	34	14	7	13	49	47	35
11	Wolverhampton W	34	14	5	15	48	57	33
12	Everton	34	13	6	15	45	47	32
13	Middlesbrough	34	14	4	16	41	50	32
14	Newcastle U	34	14	4	16	41	51	32
15	Notts Co	34	12	7	15	41	49	31
16	Blackburn R	34	12	5	17	44	63	29
17	Grimsby T	34	8	9	17	43	62	25
18	Bolton W	34	8	3	23	37	73	19

Season 1903-04

Football League Division One

DATE	OPPONENTS	SCORE	GOALSCORERS	ATTENDANCE
Sep 5	Nottingham Forest	L 1-2	Smith	12,000
Sep 12	THE WEDNESDAY	L 1-3	Cox	18,000
Sep 19	Sunderland	L 1-2	Dunlop	17,000
Sep 26	WEST BROMWICH ALBION	L 1-3	Cox	18,000
Oct 1	Notts County	L 2-4	Cox, Fleming (pen)	10,000
Oct 3	Small Heath	W 2-1	Parkinson, Fleming (pen)	10,000
Oct 10	EVERTON	D 2-2	Morris 2	30,000
Oct 17	Stoke	L 2-5	Cox, Fleming	8,000
Oct 24	DERBY COUNTY	W 3-1	Goddard, Morris, Parkinson	13,000
Oct 31	Manchester City	L 2-3	Goddard, Parkinson	30,000
Nov 7	NOTTS COUNTY	W 2-1	Hughes, Prescott o.g.	10,000
Nov 14	Sheffield United	L 1-2	Goddard (pen)	12,000
Nov 21	NEWCASTLE UNITED	W 1-0	Morris	5,000
Nov 28	Aston Villa	L 1-2	Parkinson	12,000
Dec 12	WOLVERHAMPTON WANDERERS	L 1-2	Parkinson	15,000
Dec 19	Bury	D 2-2	Cox 2	5,000
Dec 25	Derby County	L 0-2		16,000
Dec 26	BLACKBURN ROVERS	L 1-2	Buck	20,000
Dec 28	Wolverhampton Wanderers	L 2-4	Parkinson, Raisbeck	10,000
Jan 2	NOTTINGHAM FOREST	D 0-0		14,000
Jan 9	The Wednesdsay	L 1-2	Raybould	13,000
Jan 16	SUNDERLAND	W 2-1	Cox, Raybould	20,000
Jan 23	West Bromwich Albion	D 2-2	Hughes, Carlin	12,000
Jan 30	SMALL HEATH	L 0-2		15,000
Feb 13	STOKE	D 0-0		10,000
Feb 22	MIDDLESBROUGH	W 1-0	Robinson	15,000
Feb 27	MANCHESTER CITY	D 2-2	Robinson, Raybould	15,000
Mar 12	SHEFFIELD UNITED	W 3-0	Robinson, Goddard, Hewitt J	20,000
Mar 19	Newcastle United	D 1-1	Goddard	20,000
Mar 26	ASTON VILLA	D 1-1	Robinson	14,000
Apr 1	Everton	L 2-5	Robinson, Parry	40,000
Apr 2	Middlesbrough	L 0-1		12,000
Apr 16	BURY	W 3-0	West (pen), Cox, Fleming	10,000
Apr 23	Blackburn Rovers	W 3-2	Raybould, Cox, Goddard	4,000

FA Cup

Feb 6	Blackburn Rovers	(Rd1)	L 1-3	Raybould	10,000

Fact File

Liverpool were relegated to the Second Division for the third time.

MANAGER: Tom Watson
CAPTAIN: Alex Raisbeck
TOP SCORER: Jack Cox 9 (league)
BIGGEST WIN: 3-0, 16 April 1904, v Bury (H), Division One
HIGHEST ATTENDANCE: 40,000, 1 April 1904, v Everton (A), Division One
TRANSFERS IN: Jack Parkinson (local), Robert Robinson and Joe Hewitt from Sunderland, Alf West from Barnsley
TRANSFERS OUT: John Glover to Small Heath, C Satterthwaite to Woolwich Arsenal

League & Cup Appearances

PLAYER	LEAGUE	CUP COMPETITION FA CUP	TOTAL
Buck	13		13
Carlin	5		5
Chadburn	2		2
Chadwick	14	1	15
Cotton	12		12
Cox	33	1	34
Craik	1		1
Dunlop	21	1	22
Fleming	18		18
Goddard	33	1	34
Hewitt	10		10
Hoare	7		7
Hughes	31	1	32
McLean	4		4
Morris	17	1	18
Parkinson	18		18
Parry	29	1	30
Platt	22	1	23
Raisbeck	30	1	31
Raybould	15	1	16
Robinson	9		9
West	24	1	25
Smith	2		2
Wilson	4		4

Goalscorers

PLAYER	LEAGUE	CUP COMPETITION FA CUP	TOTAL
Cox	9		9
Goddard	6		6
Parkinson	6		6
Raybould	4	1	5
Robinson	5		5
Fleming	4		4
Morris	4		4
Hughes	2		2
Buck	1		1
Carlin	1		1
Dunlop	1		1
Hewitt	1		1
Parry	1		1
Raisbeck	1		1
Smith	1		1
West	1		1
Opps' o.gs.	1		1

Final Division One Table

		P	W	D	L	F	A	Pts
1	The Wednesday	34	20	7	7	48	28	47
2	Manchester C	34	19	6	9	71	45	44
3	Everton	34	19	5	10	59	32	43
4	Newcastle U	34	18	6	10	58	45	42
5	Aston Villa	34	17	7	10	70	48	41
6	Sunderland	34	17	5	12	63	49	39
7	Sheffield U	34	15	8	11	62	57	38
8	Wolverhampton W	34	14	8	12	44	66	36
9	Nottingham F	34	11	9	14	57	57	31
10	Middlesbrough	34	9	12	13	46	47	30
11	Small Heath	34	11	8	15	39	52	30
12	Bury	34	7	15	12	40	53	29
13	Notts Co	34	12	5	17	37	61	29
14	Derby Co	34	9	10	15	58	60	28
15	Blackburn R	34	11	6	17	48	60	28
16	Stoke	34	10	7	17	54	57	27
17	Liverpool	34	9	8	17	49	62	26
18	WBA	34	7	10	17	36	60	24

Season 1904-05

Football League Division Two

DATE	OPPONENTS	SCORE	GOALSCORERS	ATTENDANCE
Sep 1	BURTON UNITED	W 2-0	Robinson 2	10,000
Sep 3	GLOSSOP NORTH END	D 2-2	Goddard, Hewitt	12,000
Sep 10	Chesterfield	D 1-1	Goddard	5,000
Sep 17	BRADFORD CITY	W 4-1	Morris, Parry, Cox 2	15,000
Sep 24	Lincoln City	W 2-0	Raybould 2	5,000
Oct 1	LEICESTER FOSSE	W 4-0	Robinson 4	12,000
Oct 8	Barnsley	W 2-0	Robinson, Carlin	5,000
Oct 15	WEST BROMWICH ALBION	W 3-2	Robinson, Parkinson 2	15,000
Oct 22	Burnley	W 2-0	Robinson, Cox	9,000
Oct 29	GRIMSBY TOWN	W 5-0	Chorlton 2, Raybould 2, Robinson	12,000
Nov 5	Blackpool	W 3-0	Parkinson, Robinson 2	8,000
Nov 12	Burslem Port Vale	W 2-1	Mullineux o.g., Raybould	3,000
Nov 19	Gainsborough Trinity	W 2-1	Raybould, Parkinson (pen)	4,000
Dec 3	Bolton Wanderers	L 0-2		30,000
Dec 17	BRISTOL CITY	W 3-1	Raisbeck, Parkinson 2	12,000
Dec 24	Manchester United	L 1-3	Parkinson	40,000
Dec 26	BARNSLEY	W 2-1	Robinson, Raybould	25,000
Dec 31	Glossop North End	W 2-0	Parkinson, Goddard	9,000
Jan 7	CHESTERFIELD	W 6-1	Robinson, Raisbeck, Goddard, Parry, Raybould 2	10,000
Jan 21	LINCOLN CITY	D 1-1	Robinson	7,000
Jan 28	Leicester Fosse	W 3-0	Robinson, West, Goddard	12,000
Feb 11	West Bromwich Albion	W 2-0	Raybould, Parkinson	9,000
Feb 25	Grimsby Town	W 1-0	Parkinson	6,000
Mar 4	BLACKPOOL	W 5-0	Parkinson 3, Robinson, Goddard	6,000
Mar 7	Bradford City	W 4-2	Parkinson 2 (1 pen), Raybould, Robinson	10,000
Mar 11	Doncaster Rovers	W 4-1	Robinson 2, Cox, Dunlop	5,000
Mar 18	GAINSBOROUGH TRINITY	W 6-1	Parkinson 2, Raybould 3, Goddard	14,000
Mar 25	Burton United	L 1-2	Cox	3,000
Apr 1	BOLTON WANDERERS	D 1-1	Chorlton (pen)	25,000
Apr 8	BURSLEM PORT VALE	W 8-1	Parkinson 3, Robinson 2, Cox 2, Raybould	13,000
Apr 15	Bristol City	W 1-0	Cox	5,000
Apr 21	DONCASTER ROVERS	W 1-0	Raybould	20,000
Apr 22	MANCHESTER UNITED	W 4-0	Cox, Raybould 3	28,000
Apr 29	BURNLEY	W 3-0	Parkinson, Robinson, Cox	10,000

FA Cup

Feb 4	EVERTON	(Rd1)	D 1-1	Parkinson	28,000
Feb 8	Everton	(R)	L 1-2	Goddard	40,000

League & Cup Appearances

PLAYER	LEAGUE	CUP COMPETITION FA CUP	TOTAL
Carlin	4	1	5
Chorlton	12		12
Cox	32	2	34
Doig	34	2	36
Dunlop	32	2	34
Fleming	29	2	31
Garside	1		1
Goddard	28	2	30
Hewitt	9		9
Hughes	4		4
Lathom	1		1
Morris	7		7
Murray	12		12
Parkinson	21	2	23
Parry	30	2	32
Raisbeck	33	2	35
Reybould	32	2	34
Robinson	32	1	33
West	16	2	18
Wilson	5		5

Goalscorers

PLAYER	LEAGUE	CUP COMPETITION FA CUP	TOTAL
Robinson	23		23
Parkinson	21	1	22
Raybould	19		19
Cox	10		10
Goddard	7	1	8
Chorlton	3		3
Parry	2		2
Raisbeck	2		2
Carlin	1		1
Dunlop	1		1
Hewitt	1		1
Morris	1		1
West	1		1
Opps' o.gs.	1		1

Fact File

Liverpool won promotion to First Division at the first attempt, and set a record for being the first club to do this three times.

MANAGER: Tom Watson
CAPTAIN: Alex Raisbeck
TOP SCORER: Robert Robinson 23 (league)
BIGGEST WIN: 8-1, 8 April 1905, v Burslem Port Vale (H), Division Two
HIGHEST ATTENDANCE: 40,000, 24 December 1904, v Manchester United (A), Division Two
TRANSFERS IN: J Edward (Teddy) Doig from Sunderland, Sam Hardy from Chesterfield Town

Final Division Two Table

	P	W	D	L	F	A	Pts
1 Liverpool	34	27	4	3	93	25	58
2 Bolton W	34	27	2	5	87	32	56
3 Manchester U	34	24	5	5	81	30	53
4 Bristol C	34	19	4	11	66	45	42
5 Chesterfield T	34	14	11	9	44	35	39
6 Gainsborough T	34	14	8	12	61	58	36
7 Barnsley	34	14	5	15	38	56	33
8 Bradford C	34	12	8	14	45	49	32
9 Lincoln C	34	12	7	15	42	40	31
10 WBA	34	13	4	17	56	48	30
11 Burnley	34	12	6	16	43	52	30
12 Glossop	34	10	10	14	37	46	30
13 Grimsby T	34	11	8	15	33	46	30
14 Leicester Fosse	34	11	7	16	40	55	29
15 Blackpool	34	9	10	15	36	48	28
16 Burslem Port Vale	34	10	7	17	47	72	27
17 Burton U	34	8	4	22	30	84	20
18 Doncaster R	34	3	2	29	23	81	8

Season 1905-06

Football League Division One

DATE	OPPONENTS	SCORE	GOALSCORERS	ATTENDANCE
Sep 2	Woolwich Arsenal	L 1-3	Robinson	20,000
Sep 9	BLACKBURN ROVERS	L 1-3	Cox	15,000
Sep 11	Aston Villa	L 0-5		15,000
Sep 16	Sunderland	W 2-1	Raybould 2	16,000
Sep 23	BIRMINGHAM	W 2-0	Robinson, Hewitt	20,000
Sep 30	Everton	L 2-4	Hewitt 2	40,000
Oct 7	DERBY COUNTY	W 4-1	Cox 2, Robinson, Goddard	20,000
Oct 14	The Wednesday	L 2-3	Robinson, Hewitt	15,000
Oct 21	NOTTINGHAM FOREST	W 4-1	Hewitt, Cox, Raybould, Robinson	15,000
Oct 28	Manchester City	W 1-0	Hewitt	25,000
Nov 4	BURY	W 3-1	Carlin, Robinson 2	14,000
Nov 11	Middlesbrough	W 5-1	Hewitt 3, Carlin 2	18,000
Nov 18	PRESTON NORTH END	D 1-1	Hewitt	15,000
Nov 25	Newcastle United	W 3-2	West 2 (2 pens), Raybould	30,000
Dec 2	ASTON VILLA	W 3-0	Cox, Hewitt, Spence o.g.	25,000
Dec 9	WOLVERHAMPTON WANDERERS	W 4-0	Hewitt 2, Raybould, Goddard	10,000
Dec 16	Sheffield United	W 2-1	Parry, Cox	15,000
Dec 23	NOTTS COUNTY	W 2-0	Robinson, Hewitt	10,000
Dec 25	BOLTON WANDERERS	D 2-2	Hewitt, Goddard	25,000
Dec 26	Stoke	L 1-2	Hewitt	20,000
Dec 30	WOOLWICH ARSENAL	W 3-0	Raisbeck, Goddard, Raybould	15,000
Jan 1	STOKE	W 3-1	Raybould 2, Hewitt	25,000
Jan 6	Blackburn Rovers	D 0-0		10,000
Jan 20	SUNDERLAND	W 2-0	Hewitt, Carlin	12,000
Jan 27	Birmingham	L 0-1		15,000
Feb 10	Derby County	W 3-0	Hewitt, Raybould, Robinson	3,000
Feb 17	THE WEDNESDAY	W 2-1	Cox 2	20,000
Mar 3	MANCHESTER CITY	L 0-1		25,000
Mar 14	Nottingham Forest	W 2-1	Hewitt 2	6,000
Mar 17	MIDDLESBROUGH	W 6-1	Parkinson, Carlin 2, Hewitt, Cox, Goddard	18,000
Mar 21	Notts County	L 0-3		8,000
Mar 24	Preston North End	W 2-1	Chorlton, Hewitt	20,000
Apr 2	Bury	D 0-0		10,000
Apr 9	NEWCASTLE UNITED	W 3-0	Parkinson 2, Raybould	10,000
Apr 13	EVERTON	D 1-1	West (pen)	33,000
Apr 14	Wolverhampton Wanderers	W 2-0	Hewitt, Goddard	10,000
Apr 16	Bolton Wanderers	L 2-3	Parkinson 2	25,000
Apr 21	SHEFFIELD UNITED	W 3-1	Parkinson 2, Robinson	10,000

FA Cup

Jan 13	LEICESTER FOSSE	(Rd1)	W 2-1	Raybould, Goddard	12,000
Feb 3	BARNSLEY	(Rd2)	W 1-0	West	10,000
Feb 24	BRENTFORD	(Rd3)	W 2-0	Hewitt, Goddard	20,000
Mar 10	SOUTHAMPTON	(Rd4)	W 3-0	Raybould 3	20,000
Mar 31	Everton*	(SF)	L 0-2		37,000

*Played at Villa Park, Birmingham.

Sherrif of London's Charity Shield

Apr 28	Corinthians**	W 5-1	Goddard 2, Hewitt 2, o.g.	20,000

**Played at Craven Cottage.

League & Cup Appearances

PLAYER	LEAGUE	CUP COMPETITION FA CUP	OTHER	TOTAL
Bradley	31	5	1	37
Carlin	14	2		16
Chorlton	6			6
Cox	28	4	1	33
Doig	8			8
Dunlop	31	5	1	37
Fleming	4			4
Garside	4			4
Goddard	38	5	1	44
Gorman	1			1
Griffiths	1			1
Hardy	30	5	1	36
Hewitt	37	5	1	43
Lathom	5	1		6
Murray	3			3
Parkinson	9	1	1	11
Parry	36	5	1	42
Raisbeck	36	4	1	41
Raybould	25	4	1	30
Robinson	34	4		38
West	37	5	1	43

Goalscorers

PLAYER	LEAGUE	CUP COMPETITION FA CUP	OTHER	TOTAL
Hewitt	24	1	2	27
Reybould	10	4		14
Goddard	6	2	2	10
Robinson	10			10
Cox	9			9
Parkinson	7			7
Carlin	6			6
West	3	1		4
Chorlton	1			1
Parry	1			1
Raisbeck	1			1
Opps' o.gs.	1		1	2

Fact File

The Reds became the first team to win both Second and First Division titles in successive seasons.

MANAGER: Tom Watson
CAPTAIN: Alex Raisbeck
TOP SCORER: Joe Hewitt 27 (24 league)
BIGGEST WIN: 6-1, 17 March 1906, v Middlesbrough (H), Division One
HIGHEST ATTENDANCE: 40,000, 30 September 1905, v Everton (A), Division One
TRANSFERS IN: Jimmy Bradley from Stoke City
TRANSFERS OUT: Richard Morris and David Murray to Leeds City

Final Division One Table

		P	W	D	L	F	A	Pts
1	Liverpool	38	23	5	10	79	46	51
2	Preston NE	38	17	13	8	54	39	47
3	The Wednesday	38	18	8	12	63	52	44
4	Newcastle U	38	18	7	13	74	48	43
5	Manchester C	38	19	5	14	73	54	43
6	Bolton W	38	17	7	14	81	67	41
7	Birmingham	38	17	7	14	65	59	41
8	Aston Villa	38	17	6	15	72	56	40
9	Blackburn R	38	16	8	14	54	52	40
10	Stoke	38	16	7	15	54	55	39
11	Everton	38	15	7	16	70	66	37
12	Woolwich Arsenal	38	15	7	16	62	64	37
13	Sheffield U	38	15	6	17	57	62	36
14	Sunderland	38	15	5	18	61	70	35
15	Derby Co	38	14	7	17	39	58	35
16	Notts Co	38	11	12	15	55	71	34
17	Bury	38	11	10	17	57	74	32
18	Middlesbrough	38	10	11	17	56	71	31
19	Nottingham F	38	13	5	20	58	79	31
20	Wolverhampton W	38	8	7	23	58	99	23

Season 1906-07

Football League Division One

DATE	OPPONENTS	SCORE	GOALSCORERS	ATTENDANCE
Sep 1	STOKE	W 1-0	Hewitt	30,000
Sep 8	Blackburn Rovers	D 1-1	Cox	18,000
Sep 10	BURY	D 2-2	Raybould, Hewitt	10,000
Sep 15	SUNDERLAND	L 1-2	Hewitt	30,000
Sep 22	Birmingham	L 1-2	Cox	10,000
Sep 29	EVERTON	L 1-2	Parkinson	40,000
Oct 6	Woolwich Arsenal	L 1-2	McPherson	25,000
Oct 13	THE WEDNESDAY	L 1-2	Raybould	15,000
Oct 20	Bury	W 3-1	Robinson, Raybould 2	10,000
Oct 27	MANCHESTER CITY	W 5-4	Robinson 3, Raybould, McPherson	20,000
Nov 3	Middlesbrough	W 1-0	Raybould	18,000
Nov 10	PRESTON NORTH END	W 6-1	Raisbeck 2, Raybould 2, McPherson 2	15,000
Nov 17	Newcastle United	L 0-2		35,000
Nov 24	ASTON VILLA	W 5-2	Robinson 2, Raybould, Goddard, Raisbeck (pen)	25,000
Dec 1	Derby County	W 1-0	Hewitt	10,000
Dec 8	Bristol City	L 1-3	Robinson	14,000
Dec 15	NOTTS COUNTY	W 5-1	Robinson, McPherson, Raybould 2, Raisbeck (pen)	5,000
Dec 22	Sheffield United	L 0-1		14,000
Dec 25	Manchester United	D 0-0		20,000
Dec 26	BOLTON WANDERERS	L 0-2		25,000
Jan 1	Bolton Wanderers	L 0-3		20,000
Jan 5	BLACKBURN ROVERS	L 0-2		18,000
Jan 19	Sunderland	D 5-5	Parkinson 3, Raybould, Cox	20,000
Jan 26	BIRMINGHAM	W 2-0	Parkinson, McPherson	15,000
Feb 9	WOOLWICH ARSENAL	W 4-0	Parkinson 2, McPherson, Cox	25,000
Feb 16	The Wednesday	W 3-2	McPherson, Raybould, Cox	12,000
Mar 2	Manchester City	L 0-1		20,000
Mar 11	Stoke	D 1-1	Hewitt	3,000
Mar 16	Preston North End	L 1-3	Cox	10,000
Mar 23	NEWCASTLE UNITED	W 4-1	Goddard, Cox, Bradley, Hewitt	25,000
Mar 29	Everton	D 0-0		45,000
Mar 30	Aston Villa	L 0-4		26,000
Apr 1	MANCHESTER UNITED	L 0-1		20,000
Apr 6	DERBY COUNTY	W 2-0	Hewitt 2	6,000
Apr 13	BRISTOL CITY	L 2-4	McPherson, Raybould	10,000
Apr 17	MIDDLESBROUGH	L 2-4	Goddard, Blanthorne	10,000
Apr 20	Notts County	L 0-2		1,000
Apr 27	SHEFFIELD UNITED	D 2-2	Raybould, McPherson	10,000

FA Cup

Jan 12	BIRMINGHAM	(Rd1) W 2-1	Raybould 2	20,000
Feb 2	Oldham Athletic	(Rd2) W 1-0	McPherson	21,500
Feb 23	BRADFORD CITY	(Rd3) W 1-0	Cox	18,000
Mar 9	The Wednesday	(Rd4) L 0-1		30,000

League & Cup Appearances

PLAYER	LEAGUE	CUP COMPETITION FA CUP	TOTAL
Blanthorne	2		2
Bradley	36	4	40
Carlin	8		8
Chorlton	14	1	15
Cox	25	4	29
Doig	4		4
Dunlop	23	4	27
Goddard	35	4	39
Gorman	9	3	12
Griffiths	4		4
Hardy	34	4	38
Hewitt	23		23
Hughes	4		4
Lathom	9		9
Lipsham	3		3
McKenna	1		1
McPherson	28	4	32
Parkinson	9	4	13
Parry	19		19
Raisbeck	27	1	28
Raybould	35	4	39
Robinson	28	4	32
Rogers	1		1
Saul	33	3	36
West	4		4

Goalscorers

PLAYER	LEAGUE	CUP COMPETITION FA CUP	TOTAL
Raybould	15	2	17
McPherson	10	1	11
Cox	7	1	8
Hewitt	8		8
Robinson	8		8
Parkinson	7		7
Raisbeck	4		4
Goddard	3		3
Blanthorne	1		1
Bradley	1		1

Fact File

Sam Hardy, the first Liverpool goalkeeper to get international recognition, gained the first three of his 14 caps against the three 'home' countries.

MANAGER: Tom Watson
CAPTAIN: Alex Raisbeck
TOP SCORER: Sam Raybould 17 (15 league)
BIGGEST WIN: 6-1, 10 November 1906, v Preston North End (H), Division One
HIGHEST ATTENDANCE: 45,000, 29 March 1907, v Everton (A), Division One
TRANSFERS IN: Billy McPherson from St. Mirren
TRANSFERS OUT: Sam Raybould to Woolwich Arsenal

Final Division One Table

		P	W	D	L	F	A	PTS
1	Newcastle U	38	22	7	9	74	46	51
2	Bristol C	38	20	8	10	66	47	48
3	Everton	38	20	5	13	70	46	45
4	Sheffield U	38	17	11	10	57	55	45
5	Aston Villa	38	19	6	13	78	52	44
6	Bolton W	38	18	8	12	59	47	44
7	Woolwich Arsenal	38	20	4	14	66	59	44
8	Manchester U	38	17	8	13	53	56	42
9	Birmingham	38	15	8	15	52	52	38
10	Sunderland	38	14	9	15	65	66	37
11	Middlesbrough	38	15	6	17	56	63	36
12	Blackburn R	38	14	7	17	56	59	35
13	The Wednesday	38	12	11	15	49	60	35
14	Preston NE	38	14	7	17	44	57	35
15	Liverpool	38	13	7	18	64	65	33
16	Bury	38	13	6	19	58	68	32
17	Manchester C	38	10	12	16	53	77	32
18	Notts Co	38	8	15	15	46	50	31
19	Derby Co	38	9	9	20	41	59	27
20	Stoke	38	8	10	20	41	64	26

Season 1907-08

Football League Division One

DATE	OPPONENTS	SCORE	GOALSCORERS	ATTENDANCE
Sep 2	Nottingham Forest	L 1-3	Hewitt C	10,000
Sep 7	Manchester United	L 0-4		20,000
Sep 14	BLACKBURN ROVERS	W 2-0	Goddard 2	20,000
Sep 16	Sheffield United	D 0-0		7,000
Sep 21	Bolton Wanderers	W 4-0	Bradley, Hewitt J 2, Robinson	15,000
Sep 28	BIRMINGHAM	L 3-4	Hewitt J, Robinson, Goddard	20,000
Oct 5	Everton	W 4-2	Hewitt J, Raisbeck, Cox, Hewitt C	40,000
Oct 12	SUNDERLAND	W 1-0	Fitzpatrick	20,000
Oct 19	Woolwich Arsenal	L 1-2	Hewitt J	25,000
Oct 26	THE WEDNESDAY	W 3-0	Fitzpatrick, Hewitt J, Hewitt C	20,000
Nov 2	Bristol City	L 0-2		12,000
Nov 9	NOTTS COUNTY	W 6-0	McPherson, Hewitt C, Hewitt J 3, Robinson	18,000
Nov 16	Manchester City	D 1-1	McPherson	25,000
Nov 23	PRESTON NORTH END	L 1-2	Hewitt C	14,000
Dec 7	ASTON VILLA	W 5-0	Robinson 2, Parkinson 2, Goddard	18,000
Dec 14	NEWCASTLE UNITED	L 1-5	Parkinson	20,000
Dec 21	Middlesbrough	L 1-3	Parkinson	14,000
Dec 25	CHELSEA	L 1-4	Hewitt J	25,000
Dec 28	SHEFFIELD UNITED	W 3-0	Hewitt J, Saul, Robinson	5,000
Jan 1	NOTTINGHAM FOREST	D 0-0		20,000
Jan 18	BOLTON WANDERERS	W 1-0	Parkinson	20,000
Jan 25	Birmingham	D 1-1	Hewitt J	15,000
Feb 8	Sunderland	L 0-1		30,000
Feb 15	WOOLWICH ARSENAL	W 4-1	Hewitt J 3, Bradley	25,000
Feb 29	BRISTOL CITY	W 3-1	Hewitt J 2, Bradley	15,000
Mar 7	Notts County	D 2-2	Parkinson, Raisbeck (pen)	10,000
Mar 9	The Wednesday	W 2-1	Robinson, Hewitt J	5,000
Mar 14	MANCHESTER CITY	L 0-1		10,000
Mar 21	Preston North End	L 0-3		15,000
Mar 25	MANCHESTER UNITED	W 7-4	Hewitt J 2, McPherson 3, Robinson 2	10,000
Mar 28	Bury	L 1-3	Hewitt C	8,000
Apr 4	Aston Villa	L 1-5	Orr	18,000
Apr 6	Blackburn Rovers	W 3-1	Orr, Hewitt J, Cox	8.000
Apr 11	Newcastle United	L 1-3	Orr	30,000
Apr 17	EVERTON	D 0-0		35,000
Apr 18	MIDDLESBROUGH	L 0-1		10,000
Apr 20	Chelsea	W 2-0	Chorlton, Parkinson	35,000
Apr 27	BURY	W 2-1	Orr 2	10,000

FA Cup

Jan 11	DERBY COUNTY	(Rd1)	W 4-2	Cox, Gorman, Bradley, Parkinson	15,000
Feb 1	BRIGHTON & HOVE ALBION	(Rd2)	D 1-1	Cox	36,000
Feb 5	Brighton & Hove Albion	(R)	W 3-0	Bradley 2, Cox	10,000
Feb 22	Newcastle United	(Rd3)	L 1-3	Saul	45,987

League & Cup Appearances

PLAYER	LEAGUE	CUP COMPETITION FA CUP	OTHER	TOTAL
Berry	1			1
Bowyer	4	1		5
Bradley	34	4		38
Chorlton	7			7
Cox	35	4		39
Doig	5			5
Dunlop	2			2
Fitzpatrick	4			4
Goddard	35	4		39
Gorman	9	1		10
Griffin	3			3
Griffiths	1			1
Hardy	33	4		37
Harrop	8			8
Hewitt C	16			16
Hewitt J	36	4		40
Hignett	1			1
Hughes	4	1		5
Lathom	3			3
McPherson	20	3		23
Orr	7			7
Parkinson	8	2		10
Parry	21	3		24
Raisbeck	23	3		26
Robinson	24	2		26
Rogers	12	1		13
Saul	27	4		31
Uren	2			2
West	33	3		36

Goalscorers

PLAYER	LEAGUE	CUP COMPETITION FA CUP	TOTAL
Hewitt J	21		21
Robinson	9		9
Parkinson	7	1	8
Bradley	3	3	6
Hewitt C	6		6
Cox	2	3	5
McPherson	5		5
Orr R	5		5
Goddard	4		4
Fitzpatrick	2		2
Raisbeck	2		2
Saul	1	1	2
Chorlton	1		1
Gorman	1		1

Fact File

'Honest' John McKenna, first manager and club founder with John Houlding, was elected Vice President of the Football League.

MANAGER: Tom Watson

CAPTAIN: Alex Raisbeck

TOP SCORER: Joe Hewitt 21 (league)

BIGGEST WIN: 6-0, 9 November 1907, v Notts County (H), Division One

HIGHEST ATTENDANCE: 40,000, 5 October 1907, v Everton (A), Division One

TRANSFERS IN: Ronald Orr from Newcastle United

TRANSFERS OUT: Billy McPherson decided to return to Scotland, signed for Glasgow Rangers, Teddy Doig, released

Final Division One Table

		P	W	D	L	F	A	Pts
1	Manchester U	38	23	6	9	81	48	52
2	Aston Villa	38	17	9	12	77	59	43
3	Manchester C	38	16	11	11	62	54	43
4	Newcastle U	38	15	12	11	65	54	42
5	The Wednesday	38	19	4	15	73	64	42
6	Middlesbrough	38	17	7	14	54	45	41
7	Bury	38	14	11	13	58	61	39
8	Liverpool	38	16	6	16	68	61	38
9	Nottingham F	38	13	11	14	59	62	37
10	Bristol C	38	12	12	14	58	61	36
11	Everton	38	15	6	17	58	64	36
12	Preston NE	38	12	12	14	47	53	36
13	Chelsea	38	14	8	16	53	62	36
14	Blackburn R=	38	12	12	14	51	63	36
14	Woolwich Arsenal=	38	12	12	14	51	63	36
16	Sunderland	38	16	3	19	78	75	35
17	Sheffield U	38	12	11	15	52	58	35
18	Notts Co	38	13	8	17	39	51	34
19	Bolton W	38	14	5	19	52	58	33
20	Birmingham	38	9	12	17	40	60	30

Season 1908-09

Football League Division One

DATE	OPPONENTS	SCORE	GOALSCORERS	ATTENDANCE
Sep 1	ASTON VILLA	W 3-2	Hewitt, Chorlton (pen), Robinson	14,000
Sep 5	CHELSEA	W 2-1	Orr 2	20,000
Sep 12	Blackburn Rovers	L 0-1		25,000
Sep 14	Sheffield Utd	W 2-0	Orr 2	13.000
Sep 19	BRADFORD CITY	W 4-0	Orr, Parkinson, Hewitt 2	25,000
Sep 26	Manchester United	L 2-3	Cox, Raisbeck (pen)	25,000
Oct 1	Nottingham Forest	L 1-5	Bowyer	10,000
Oct 3	EVERTON	L 0-1		40,000
Oct 10	Leicester Fosse	L 2-3	Orr 2	12,000
Oct 17	WOOLWICH ARSENAL	D 2-2	Orr, Hewitt	18,000
Oct 24	Notts County	W 2-1	Parkinson, Orr	10,000
Oct 31	NEWCASTLE UNITED	W 2-1	Orr, Cox	20,000
Nov 7	Bristol City	L 0-1		10,000
Nov 14	PRESTON NORTH END	W 2-1	Hewitt, Robinson	18,000
Nov 21	Middlesbrough	L 0-1		15,000
Nov 28	MANCHESTER CITY	L 1-3	Bowyer	12,000
Dec 5	The Wednesday	W 3-2	Hewitt, Bowyer, Orr	10,000
Dec 12	Bury	L 1-2	Hewitt	10,000
Dec 19	SHEFFIELD UNITED	W 2-1	Orr 2	10,000
Dec 25	Aston Villa	D 1-1	Orr	20,000
Dec 26	NOTTINGHAM FOREST	D 1-1	Orr	25,000
Jan 1	Sunderland	W 4-1	Hewitt 3, Goddard	20,000
Jan 2	Chelsea	L 0-3		25,000
Jan 9	BLACKBURN ROVERS	D 1-1	Robinson	20,000
Jan 23	Bradford City	W 2-0	Hewitt, Orr	20,000
Jan 30	MANCHESTER UNITED	W 3-1	Goddard, Chorlton (pen), Hewitt	30,000
Feb 13	LEICESTER CITY	W 4-1	Bradley, Goddard 2, Bowyer	10,000
Feb 20	Wollwich Arsenal	L 0-5		15,000
Feb 27	NOTTS COUNTY	D 1-1	Robinson	12,000
Mar 13	BRISTOL CITY	L 1-2	Chorlton (pen)	5,000
Mar 20	Preston North End	L 0-2		15,000
Mar 27	MIDDLESBROUGH	L 1-2	Harrop	12,000
Apr 3	Manchester City	L 0-4		18,000
Apr 9	Everton	L 0-5		45,000
Apr 10	THE WEDNESDAY	L 1-2	Robinson	20,000
Apr 12	SUNDERLAND	W 3-0	Orr (pen), Parkinson, Raisbeck	20,000
Apr 17	BURY	D 2-2	Orr 2	15,000
Apr 30	Newcastle United	W 1-0	Orr	30,000

FA Cup

Jan 16	LINCOLN CITY	(Rd1) W 5-1	Orr 3, Hewitt, Parkinson	8,000
Feb 6	NORWICH	(Rd2) L 2-3	Cox, Robinson	25,000

League & Cup Appearances

PLAYER	LEAGUE	CUP COMPETITION FA CUP	TOTAL
Allman	1		1
Berry	2		2
Bowyer	14		14
Bradley	34	2	34
Chorlton	33	2	35
Cox	28	2	30
Crawford	7		7
Dunlop	13	1	14
Goddard	36	2	38
Goode	6		6
Griffin	1		1
Hardy	32	2	34
Harrop	30	1	31
Hewitt	33	2	35
Hughes	2		2
Hunter	1		1
Orr	33	2	35
Parkinson	17	1	18
Parry	20	2	22
Peake	1		1
Raisbeck	15	1	16
Robinson	21	1	22
Rogers	6		6
Saul	15	1	16
Sloan	6		6
Uren	1		1
West	10		10

Goalscorers

PLAYER	LEAGUE	CUP COMPETITION FA CUP	TOTAL
Orr	20	3	23
Hewitt	12	1	13
Robinson	5	1	6
Bowyer	4		4
Goddard	4		4
Parkinson	3	1	4
Chorlton	3		3
Cox	2	1	3
Raisbeck	2		2
Bradley	1		1
Harrop	1		1

Fact File

Two wins and a draw in the last three games meant that Liverpool avoided relegation by two points.

MANAGER: Tom Watson
CAPTAIN: Alex Raisbeck
TOP SCORER: Ronald Orr 23 (20 league)
BIGGEST WIN: 4-0, 19 September 1908, v Bradford City (H), Division One
HIGHEST ATTENDANCE: 45,000, 9 April 1909 v Everton (A), Division One
TRANSFERS IN: Robert Crawford from Arthurlie

Final Division One Table

	P	W	D	L	F	A	Pts
1 Newcastle U	38	24	5	9	65	41	53
2 Everton	38	18	10	10	82	57	46
3 Sunderland	38	21	2	15	78	63	44
4 Blackburn R	38	14	13	11	61	50	41
5 The Wednesday	38	17	6	15	67	61	40
6 Woolwich Arsenal	38	14	10	14	52	49	38
7 Aston Villa	38	14	10	14	58	56	38
8 Bristol C	38	13	12	13	45	58	38
9 Middlesbrough	38	14	9	15	59	53	37
10 Preston NE	38	13	11	14	48	44	37
11 Chelsea	38	14	9	15	56	61	37
12 Sheffield U	38	14	9	15	51	59	37
13 Manchester U	38	15	7	16	58	68	37
14 Nottingham F	38	14	8	16	66	57	36
15 Notts Co	38	14	8	16	51	48	36
16 Liverpool	38	15	6	17	57	65	36
17 Bury	38	14	8	16	63	77	36
18 Bradford C	38	12	10	16	47	47	34
19 Manchester C	38	15	4	19	67	69	34
20 Leicester Fosse	38	8	9	21	54	102	25

Season 1909-10

Football League Division One

DATE	OPPONENTS	SCORE	GOALSCORERS	ATTENDANCE
Sep 4	Chelsea	L 1-2	Hewitt	25,000
Sep 6	Bolton Wanderers	W 2-1	Parkinson 2	20,000
Sep 11	BLACKBURN ROVERS	W 3-1	Stewart, McDonald, Parkinson	25,000
Sep 18	Nottingham Forest	W 4-1	Parkinson 3, Orr	15,000
Sep 25	SUNDERLAND	L 1-4	Hewitt	30,000
Oct 2	Everton	W 3-2	Goddard, Stewart, Parkinson	45,000
Oct 9	MANCHESTER UNITED	W 3-2	Parkinson 2, Stewart	30,000
Oct 16	Bradford City	W 2-1	Bowyer, Stewart	25,000
Oct 23	THE WEDNESDAY	W 3-1	Stewart, Parkinson 2	30,000
Oct 30	Bristol City	W 1-0	Robinson	8,000
Nov 6	BURY	D 2-2	Parkinson, Goddard	25,000
Nov 13	Tottenham Hotspur	L 0-1		25,000
Nov 20	PRESTON NORTH END	W 2-0	Goddard, Stewart	20,000
Nov 27	Notts County	L 1-3	Harrop	5,000
Dec 4	NEWCASTLE UNITED	W 6-5	Stewart, Parkinson 2, Orr 2, Goddard	22,000
Dec 11	MIDDLESBROUGH	D 0-0		25,000
Dec 18	Aston Villa	L 1-3	Parkinson (pen)	18,000
Dec 25	BOLTON WANDERERS	W 3-0	Parkinson (pen), Orr, Goddard	25,000
Dec 27	Woolwich Arsenal	D 1-1	Parkinson	15,000
Dec 28	Sheffield United	L 2-4	Goode, McDonald	15,000
Jan 1	WOOLWICH ARSENAL	W 5-1	Parkinson 3 (1 pen), Bowyer 2	25,000
Jan 8	Chelsea	W 5-1	Stewart 3, Parkinson 2	25,000
Jan 22	Blackburn Rovers	D 1-1	Stewart	15,000
Feb 12	Everton	L 0-1		40,000
Feb 19	Manchester United	W 4-3	Goddard 2, Stewart 2	45,000
Feb 26	BRADFORD CITY	W 1-0	Goddard	15,000
Mar 5	The Wednesday	L 0-3		12,000
Mar 12	BRISTOL CITY	L 0-1		20,000
Mar 19	Bury	W 2-1	Bowyer, Goddard	10,000
Mar 25	SHEFFIELD UNITED	D 0-0		30,000
Mar 26	TOTTENHAM HOTSPUR	W 2-0	Parkinson, Stewart	20,000
Mar 28	Sunderland	L 1-2	Stewart	20,000
Apr 2	Preston NORTH END	L 0-2		4,000
Apr 9	NOTTS COUNTY	W 2-1	Stewart, Parkinson	15,000
Apr 16	Newcastle United	W 3-1	Goddard 2 (1 pen), Stewart	20,000
Apr 20	NOTTINGHAM FOREST	W 7-3	Parkinson 4, Bowyer 2, Stewart	5,000
Apr 23	Middlesbrough	D 2-2	Parkinson, Goddard	8,000
Apr 30	ASTON VILLA	W 2-0	Orr, Parkinson	30,000

FA Cup

Jan 15	Bristol City	(Rd1) L 0-2		10,000

League & Cup Appearances

PLAYER	LEAGUE	CUP COMPETITION FA CUP	TOTAL
Beeby	5		5
Bowyer	12	1	13
Bradley	30		30
Chorlton	38	1	39
Crawford	20		20
Goddard	35	1	36
Goode	1		1
Hardy	32	1	33
Harrop	32	1	33
Hewitt	4		4
Mackinlay	1		1
McConnell	13	1	14
McDonald	34	1	35
Orr	31		31
Parkinson	31	1	32
Peake	3		3
Robinson	37	1	38
Rogers	17	1	18
Speakman	2		2
Stewart	37	1	38
Uren	3		3

Goalscorers

PLAYER	LEAGUE	CUP COMPETITION FA CUP	TOTAL
Parkinson	30		30
Stewart	18		18
Goddard	12		12
Bowyer	6		6
Orr	5		5
Hewitt	2		2
McDonald	2		2
Goode	1		1
Harrop	1		1
Robinson	1		1

Fact File

A transitional season, in which several players were released and new ones bought, saw the club finish in second place in the league.

MANAGER: Tom Watson

CAPTAIN: Arthur Goddard

TOP SCORER: Jack Parkinson 30 league

BIGGEST WIN: 7-3, 20 April 1910, v Nottingham Forest (H), Division One

HIGHEST ATTENDANCE: 45,000, 2 October 1909, v Everton (A) and 19 February 1910, v Manchester United (A), Division One

TRANSFERS IN: John McDonald from Rangers, Don Mackinlay from Newton Villa, James Stewart from Motherwell

TRANSFERS OUT: Alex Raisbeck to Partick Thistle, Jack Cox to Blackpool

Final Division One Table

		P	W	D	L	F	A	PTS
1	Aston Villa	38	23	7	8	84	42	53
2	Liverpool	38	21	6	11	78	57	48
3	Blackburn R	38	18	9	11	73	55	45
4	Newcastle U	38	19	7	12	70	56	45
5	Manchester U	38	19	7	12	69	61	45
6	Sheffield U	38	16	10	12	62	41	42
7	Bradford C	38	17	8	13	64	47	42
8	Sunderland	38	18	5	15	66	51	41
9	Notts Co	38	15	10	13	67	59	40
10	Everton	38	16	8	14	51	56	40
11	The Wednesday	38	15	9	14	60	63	39
12	Preston NE	38	15	5	18	52	58	35
13	Bury	38	12	9	17	62	66	33
14	Nottingham F	38	11	11	16	54	72	33
15	Tottenham H	38	11	10	17	53	69	32
16	Bristol C	38	12	8	18	45	60	32
17	Middlesbrough	38	11	9	18	56	73	31
18	Woolwich Arsenal	38	11	9	18	37	67	31
19	Chelsea	38	11	7	20	47	70	29
20	Bolton W	38	9	6	23	44	71	24

Season 1910-11

Football League Division One

DATE	OPPONENTS	SCORE	GOALSCORERS	ATTENDANCE
Sep 3	BRADFORD CITY	L 1-2	Stewart	20,000
Sep 10	Blackburn Rovers	W 2-1	Parkinson 2	20,000
Sep 17	NOTTINGHAM FOREST	L 2-3	Brough, Orr	23,000
Sep 19	Sheffield United	L 0-2		8,000
Sep 24	Manchester City	W 2-1	Gilligan, Parkinson	20,000
Oct 1	EVERTON	L 0-2		40,000
Oct 8	The Wednesday	L 0-1		10,000
Oct 15	BRISTOL CITY	W 4-0	Brough, Harrop, Parkinson 2	15,000
Oct 22	Newcastle United	L 1-6	Peake	20,000
Oct 29	TOTTENHAM HOTSPUR	L 1-2	Brough	20,000
Nov 5	Middlesbrough	D 2-2	Goddard, Bowyer	20,000
Nov 12	PRESTON NORTH END	W 3-0	Orr, Parkinson, Bowyer	8,000
Nov 19	Notts County	L 0-1		10,000
Nov 26	MANCHESTER UNITED	W 3-2	Goddard (pen), Parkinson, Stewart	12,000
Dec 3	Oldham Athletic	L 1-3	Goddard	8,000
Dec 10	Bury	L 0-3		6,000
Dec 17	SHEFFIELD UNITED	W 2-0	Parkinson, Stewart	10,000
Dec 24	Aston Villa	D 1-1	Stewart	16,000
Dec 26	SUNDERLAND	L 1-2	Goddard (pen)	35,000
Dec 27	Everton	W 1-0	Parkinson	51,000
Dec 31	Bradford City	W 3-1	Bowyer, Parkinson 2	17,000
Jan 2	Sunderland	L 0-4		12,000
Jan 7	BLACKBURN ROVERS	D 2-2	Parkinson, Goddard	6,000
Jan 21	Nottingham Forest	L 0-2		12,000
Jan 28	MANCHESTER CITY	D 1-1	Bowyer	16,000
Feb 11	THE WEDNESDAY	W 3-0	Parkinson 3	12,000
Feb 18	Bristol City	D 1-1	Parkinson	6,000
Feb 27	NEWCASTLE UNITED	W 3-0	Gilligan 2, Parkinson	8,000
Mar 4	Tottenham Hotspur	L 0-1		20,000
Mar 11	MIDDLESBROUGH	W 3-0	Parkinson, Gilligan, Goddard	20,000
Mar 18	Preston North End	L 1-2	Orr	2,000
Mar 25	NOTTS COUNTY	W 2-1	Goddard 2	10,000
Apr 1	Manchester United	L 0-2		12,000
Apr 8	OLDHAM ATHLETIC	W 1-0	Gilligan	13,000
Apr 14	Woolwich Arsenal	D 0-0		15,000
Apr 15	BURY	W 2-0	Peake 2	10,000
Apr 17	WOOLWICH ARSENAL	D 1-1	Parkinson	20,000
Apr 29	ASTON VILLA	W 3-1	Orr 2, McDonald	25,000

FA Cup

Jan 14	GAINSBOROUGH TRINITY (Rd1)	W 3-2	Bowyer 2, Goddard	15,000
Feb 4	Everton (Rd2)	L 1-2	Parkinson	50,000

League & Cup Appearances

PLAYER	LEAGUE	CUP COMPETITION FA CUP	TOTAL
Beeby	11		11
Bowyer	13	1	14
Bradley	4		4
Brough	11		11
Chorlton	7		7
Crawford	31	2	33
Gilligan	15		15
Goddard	31	2	33
Hardy	27	2	29
Harrop	34	2	36
Leavey	5		5
Longworth	33	1	34
Mackinlay	2		2
McConnell	29	2	31
McDonald	25	1	26
Orr	30	2	32
Parkinson	33	2	35
Peake	8		8
Robinson	38	2	40
Rogers	2		2
Speakman	2		2
Stewart	11	1	12
Uren	12	1	13
West	4	1	5

Goalscorers

PLAYER	LEAGUE	CUP COMPETITION FA CUP	TOTAL
Parkinson	19	1	20
Goddard	8	1	9
Bowyer	4	2	6
Gilligan	5		5
Orr	5		5
Stewart	4		4
Brough	3		3
Peake	3		3
Harrop	1		1
McDonald	1		1

Fact File

Jack Parkinson scored his 100th league goal v Woolwich Arsenal on 17 April 1911. The fixture was a benefit game for Sam Hardy.

MANAGER: Tom Watson
CAPTAIN: Arthur Goddard
TOP SCORER: Jack Parkinson 20 (19 league)
BIGGEST WIN: 4-0, 15 October 1910, v Bristol City (H), Division One
HIGHEST ATTENDANCE: 50,000, 4 February 1911, v Everton (A), FA Cup
TRANSFERS IN: Kenny Campbell from Cambuslang Rovers, Sam Gilligan from Bristol City

Final Division One Table

		P	W	D	L	F	A	Pts
1	Manchester U	38	22	8	8	72	40	52
2	Aston Villa	38	22	7	9	69	41	51
3	Sunderland	38	15	15	8	67	48	45
4	Everton	38	19	7	12	50	36	45
5	Bradford C	38	20	5	13	51	42	45
6	The Wednesday	38	17	8	13	47	48	42
7	Oldham Ath	38	16	9	13	44	41	41
8	Newcastle U	38	15	10	13	61	43	40
9	Sheffield U	38	15	8	15	49	43	38
10	Woolwich Arsenal	38	13	12	13	41	49	38
11	Notts Co	38	14	10	14	37	45	38
12	Blackburn R	38	13	11	14	62	54	37
13	Liverpool	38	15	7	16	53	53	37
14	Preston NE	38	12	11	15	40	49	35
15	Tottenham H	38	13	6	19	52	63	32
16	Middlesbrough	38	11	10	17	49	63	32
17	Manchester C	38	9	13	16	43	58	31
18	Bury	38	9	11	18	43	71	29
19	Bristol C	38	11	5	22	43	66	27
20	Nottingham F	38	9	7	22	55	75	25

Season 1911-12

Football League Division One

DATE	OPPONENTS	SCORE	GOALSCORERS	ATTENDANCE
Sep 2	Woolwich Arsenal	D 2-2	McConnell, Gilligan	12,000
Sep 4	Bolton Wanderers	L 1-2	Parkinson	15,000
Sep 9	MANCHESTER CITY	D 2-2	Parkinson, Orr	25,000
Sep 16	Everton	L 1-2	Parkinson	40,000
Sep 23	WEST BROMWICH ALBION	L 1-3	Parkinson	18,000
Sep 30	Sunderland	W 2-1	McDonald, Robinson	12,000
Oct 7	BLACKBURN ROVERS	L 1-2	Harrop	30,000
Oct 14	The Wednesday	D 2-2	Gilligan, Parkinson	12,000
Oct 21	BURY	D 1-1	Gilligan	10,000
Oct 28	Middlesbrough	L 2-3	Uren, Gilligan	13,720
Nov 4	NOTTS COUNTY	W 3-0	Bovill 2, Goddard	15,000
Nov 11	Tottenham Hotspur	L 0-2		20,000
Nov 18	Manchester United	W 3-2	Parkinson, Bovill 2	15,000
Nov 25	PRESTON NORTH END	L 0-1		10,000
Dec 2	Aston Villa	L 0-5		16,000
Dec 9	NEWCASTLE UNITED	L 0-1		20,000
Dec 16	Sheffield United	L 1-3	Parkinson	12,000
Dec 23	OLDHAM ATHLETIC	W 1-0	Gilligan	10,000
Dec 25	BOLTON WANDERERS	W 1-0	Parkinson	25,000
Dec 30	WOOLWICH ARSENAL	W 4-1	Parkinson 2, Bovil 2	16,000
Jan 1	BRADFORD CITY	W 1-0	Uren	40,000
Jan 6	Manchester City	W 3-2	Parkinson, Bovill, Stuart	15,000
Jan 20	EVERTON	L 1-3	Gilligan	35,000
Jan 27	West Bromwich Albion	L 0-1		15,000
Feb 10	Blackburn Rovers	L 0-1		15,000
Feb 17	THE WEDNESDAY	D 1-1	Robinson	15,000
Feb 24	Bury	D 2-2	Gracie, Stewart	8,000
Mar 2	MIDDLESBROUGH	D 1-1	Miller	25,000
Mar 9	Notts County	D 0-0		15,000
Mar 16	TOTTENHAM HOTSPUR	L 1-2	Lacey	20,000
Mar 23	Manchester United	D 1-1	Parkinson	12,000
Mar 30	Preston North End	L 1-2	Gilligan	9,000
Apr 5	SUNDERLAND	W 2-1	Lowe, Gilligan	30,000
Apr 6	ASTON VILLA	L 1-2	Gilligan	30,000
Apr 8	Bradford City	W 2-0	Speakman, Gilligan	10,000
Apr 13	Newcastle United	D 1-1	Stewart	15,000
Apr 20	Sheffield United	W 2-0	Stewart, Goddard (pen)	25,000
Apr 27	Oldham Athletic	W 1-0	Gilligan	8,000

FA Cup

Jan 13	LEYTON ORIENT	(Rd1) W 1-0	Parkinson	33,000
Feb 3	Fulham	(Rd2) L 0-3		30,000

League & Cup Appearances

PLAYER	LEAGUE	CUP COMPETITION FA CUP	TOTAL
Bovill	23	2	25
Bowyer	2		2
Campbell	7		7
Crawford	15		15
Gilligan	23		23
Goddard	28	1	29
Gracie	6		6
Hardy	31	2	33
Harrop	29	2	31
Lacey	11		11
Lester	1		1
Longworth	37	2	39
Lowe	28	2	30
Mackinlay	7		7
McConnell	8		8
McDonald	19	1	20
Miller	8		8
Orr	7		7
Parkinson	25	2	27
Peake	8		8
Pursell	24	2	26
Robinson	31	2	33
Scott	4		4
Speakman	3		3
Stewart	6		6
Stuart	3	2	5
Uren	24	2	26

Goalscorers

PLAYER	LEAGUE	CUP COMPETITION FA CUP	TOTAL
Parkinson	12	1	13
Gilligan	11		11
Bovill	7		7
Stewart	3		3
Goddard	2		2
Robinson	2		2
Uren	2		2
Gracie	1		1
Harrop	1		1
Lacey	1		1
Lowe	1		1
McConnell	1		1
McDonald	1		1
Miller	1		1
Orr	1		1
Speakman	1		1
Stuart	1		1

Fact File

Robert (Whitey) Robinson – signed in February 1904 – played his 250th league game on 16 March 1912.

MANAGER: Tom Watson

CAPTAIN: Arthur Goddard

TOP SCORER: Jack Parkinson 13 (12 league)

BIGGEST WIN: 3-0, 4 November 1911, v Notts County (H); 4-1, 30 December 1911, v Woolwich Arsenal (H), Division One

HIGHEST ATTENDANCE: 40,000, 16 September 1911, v Everton (A) and 1 January 1912, v Bradford City (H), Division One

TRANSFERS IN: Bill Lacey with Tom Gracie in exchange for Harold Uren from Everton, Robert Pursell from Queens Park

TRANSFERS OUT: Sam Hardy to Aston Villa, Tom Chorlton to Manchester United, Ronald Orr to Raith Rovers

Final Division One Table

		P	W	D	L	F	A	PTS
1	Blackburn R	38	20	9	9	60	43	49
2	Everton	38	20	6	12	46	42	46
3	Newcastle U	38	18	8	12	64	50	44
4	Bolton W	38	20	3	15	54	43	43
5	The Wednesday	38	16	9	13	69	49	41
6	Aston Villa	38	17	7	14	76	63	41
7	Middlesbrough	38	16	8	14	56	45	40
8	Sunderland	38	14	11	13	58	51	39
9	WBA	38	15	9	14	43	47	39
10	Woolwich Arsenal	38	15	8	15	55	59	38
11	Bradford C	38	15	8	15	46	50	38
12	Tottenham H	38	14	9	15	53	53	37
13	Manchester U	38	13	11	14	45	60	37
14	Sheffield U	38	13	10	15	63	56	36
15	Manchester C	38	13	9	16	56	58	35
16	Notts Co	38	14	7	17	46	63	35
17	Liverpool	38	12	10	16	49	55	34
18	Oldham Ath	38	12	10	16	46	54	34
19	Preston NE	38	13	7	18	40	57	33
20	Bury	38	6	9	23	32	59	21

Season 1912-13

Football League Division One

DATE	OPPONENTS	SCORE	GOALSCORERS	ATTENDANCE
Sep 4	OLDHAM ATHLETIC	W 2-0	Tosswill, Miller	20,000
Sep 7	WOOLWICH ARSENAL	W 3-0	Peart o.g., Goddard 2	30,000
Sep 9	Chelsea	W 2-1	Goddard, Gracie	16,000
Sep 14	Bradford City	L 0-2		20,000
Sep 21	MANCHESTER CITY	L 1-2	Lacey	25,000
Sep 28	West Bromwich Albion	L 1-3	Miller	20,000
Oct 5	EVERTON	L 0-2		46,000
Oct 12	The Wednesday	L 0-1		20,000
Oct 14	Sheffield United	L 1-4	Metcalf	3,000
Oct 19	BLACKBURN ROVERS	W 4-1	Metcalf 2, Ferguson, Goddard (pen)	20,000
Oct 26	Derby County	L 2-4	Metcalf 2	6,000
Nov 2	TOTTENHAM HOTSPUR	W 4-1	Mackinlay, Goddard, Parkinson 2	20,000
Nov 9	Middlesbrough	W 4-3	Miller, Metcalf 2, Parkinson	11,973
Nov 16	NOTTS COUNTY	D 0-0		15,000
Nov 23	Manchester United	L 1-3	Mackinlay	14,000
Nov 30	ASTON VILLA	W 2-0	Mackinlay, Miles o.g.	30,000
Dec 7	Sunderland	L 0-7		14,000
Dec 14	Bolton Wanderers	D 1-1	Mackinlay	12,000
Dec 21	SHEFFIELD UNITED	D 2-2	Parkinson, Metcalf	20,000
Dec 26	NEWCASTLE UNITED	W 2-1	Miller 2	35,000
Dec 28	Woolwich Arsenal	D 1-1	Peake	15,000
Jan 1	Newcastle United	D 0-0		20,000
Jan 4	BRADFORD CITY	W 2-1	Parkinson, Mackinlay	20,000
Jan 18	Manchester City	L 1-4	Stewart	20,000
Jan 25	WEST BROMWICH ALBION	W 2-1	Miller 2	20,000
Feb 8	Everton	W 2-0	Parkinson 2	40,000
Feb 10	Oldham Athletic	W 1-3	Metcalf	25,000
Feb 15	THE WEDNESDAY	W 2-1	Metcalf, Miller	25,000
Mar 1	DERBY COUNTY	W 2-1	Welfare, Lacey	18,000
Mar 8	Tottenham Hotspur	L 0-1		15,000
Mar 10	Blackburn Rovers	L 1-5	Mackinlay	4,000
Mar 15	MIDDLESBROUGH	W 4-2	Peake, Lowe, Metcalf, Parkinson	15,000
Mar 22	Notts County	L 0-3		7,000
Mar 24	CHELSEA	L 1-2	Lacey	25,000
Mar 29	MANCHESTER UNITED	L 0-2		12,000
Apr 5	Aston Villa	W 3-1	Goddard, Parkinson, Metcalf	25,000
Apr 12	SUNDERLAND	L 2-5	Metcalf 2	28,000
Apr 19	BOLTON WANDERERS	L 5-0	Metcalf, Parkinson 3, Goddard	15,000

FA Cup

Jan 15	BRISTOL CITY	(Rd1) W 3-0	Goddard (pen), Peake, Lacey	15,000
Feb 1	Woolwich Arsenal	(Rd2) W 4-1	Metcalf 3, Lacey	8,653
Feb 22	NEWCASTLE UNITED	(Rd3) D 1-1	Lacey	37,903
Feb 26	Newcastle United	(R) L 0-1		45,000

League & Cup Appearances

PLAYER	LEAGUE	CUP COMPETITION FA CUP	TOTAL
Berry	1		1
Bovill	1		1
Campbell	37	4	41
Crawford	22	4	26
Dines	1		1
Ferguson	38	4	42
Gilligan	2		2
Goddard	33	4	37
Gracie	13	1	14
Holden	1		1
Lacey	21	4	25
Lester	1		1
Longworth	36	3	39
Lowe	34	4	36
Mackinlay	22	1	23
Metcalf	28	4	32
Miller	30	4	34
Parkinson	24	2	26
Peake	26	4	30
Pursell	20	1	21
Scott E	1		1
Scott J	6		6
Speakman	1		1
Stewart	4		4
Tosswill	11		11
Welfare	4		4

Goalscorers

PLAYER	LEAGUE	CUP COMPETITION FA CUP	TOTAL
Metcalf	15	3	18
Parkinson	12		12
Goddard	7	1	8
Miller	8		8
Lacey	3	3	6
Mackinlay	6		6
Peake	2	1	3
Ferguson	1		1
Gracie	1		1
Lowe	1		1
Stewart	1		1
Tosswill	1		1
Welfare	1		1
Opps' o.gs.	2		2

Fact File

Arthur Goddard, right winger and a club captain, played his 400th game on 24 March 1913. He had scored 75 goals in those games.

MANAGER: Tom Watson
CAPTAIN: Ephraim Longworth
TOP SCORER: Arthur Metcalf 18 (15 league)
BIGGEST WIN: 5-0, 19 April 1913, v Bolton Wanderers (H), Division One
HIGHEST ATTENDANCE: 46,000, 5 October 1912, v Everton (A), Division One
TRANSFERS IN: Robert Ferguson from Third Lanark, Elisha Scott from Broadway United (Belfast)
TRANSFERS OUT: Sam Gilligan to Gillingham as player/manager

Final Division One Table

		P	W	D	L	F	A	Pts
1	Sunderland	38	25	4	9	86	43	54
2	Aston Villa	38	19	12	7	86	52	50
3	The Wednesday	38	21	7	10	75	55	49
4	Manchester U	38	19	8	11	69	43	46
5	Blackburn R	38	16	13	9	79	43	45
6	Manchester C	38	18	8	12	53	37	44
7	Derby Co	38	17	8	13	69	66	42
8	Bolton W	38	16	10	12	62	63	42
9	Oldham Ath	38	14	14	10	50	55	42
10	WBA	38	13	12	13	57	50	38
11	Everton	38	15	7	16	48	54	37
12	Liverpool	38	16	5	17	61	71	37
13	Bradford C	38	12	11	15	50	60	35
14	Newcastle U	38	13	8	17	47	47	34
15	Sheffield U	38	14	6	18	56	70	34
16	Middlesbrough	38	11	10	17	55	69	32
17	Tottenham H	38	12	6	20	45	72	30
18	Chelsea	38	11	6	21	51	73	28
19	Notts Co	38	7	9	22	28	56	23
20	Woolwich Arsenal	38	3	12	23	26	74	18

Season 1913-14

Football League Division One

DATE	OPPONENTS	SCORE	GOALSCORERS	ATTENDANCE
Sep 1	Derby County	D 1-1	Miller	7,000
Sep 6	Blackburn Rovers	L 2-6	Miller 2	30,000
Sep 13	SUNDERLAND	L 1-3	Gracie	25,000
Sep 20	Everton	W 2-1	Lacey 2	40,000
Sep 27	WEST BROMWICH ALBION	D 0-0		25,000
Oct 4	The Wednesday	L 1-4	Crawford (pen)	25,000
Oct 11	BOLTON WANDERERS	W 2-1	Miller 2	15,000
Oct 18	Chelsea	L 0-3		40,000
Oct 25	OLDHAM ATHLETIC	L 0-3		25,000
Nov 1	Manchester United	L 0-3		20,000
Nov 8	BURNLEY	D 1-1	Lacey	18,000
Nov 15	Preston North End	W 1-0	Mackinlay	12,000
Nov 22	NEWCASTLE UNITED	D 0-0		20,000
Nov 29	TOTTENHAM HOTSPUR	W 2-1	Dawson, Miller	25,000
Dec 6	Aston Villa	L 1-2	Sheldon (pen)	15,000
Dec 13	MIDDLESBROUGH	W 2-1	Miller, Gracie	25,000
Dec 20	Sheffield United	W 1-0	Miller	10,000
Dec 25	MANCHESTER CITY	W 4-2	Lacey, Sheldon 2, Gracie	30,000
Dec 26	Manchester City	L 0-1		25,000
Dec 27	BLACKBURN ROVERS	D 3-3	Dawson, Miller, Lacey	30,000
Jan 1	BRADFORD CITY	L 0-1		35,000
Jan 3	Sunderland	W 2-1	Sheldon, Parkinson	15,000
Jan 17	EVERTON	L 1-2	Metcalf	35,000
Jan 24	West Bromwich Albion	W 1-0	McDougall	10,000
Feb 7	THE WEDNESDAY	L 1-2	Lacey	20,000
Feb 14	Bolton Wanderers	L 1-2	Miller	20,000
Feb 28	Oldham Athletic	D 2-2	Nicholl, Metcalf	12,000
Mar 14	Burnley	L 2-5	Banks, Nicholl	16,000
Mar 18	CHELSEA	W 3-0	Banks 2, Miller	12,000
Mar 23	PRESTON NORTH END	W 3-1	Miller 2, Nicholl	25,000
Apr 1	Newcastle United	W 2-1	Sheldon, Miller	18,000
Apr 4	Tottenham Hotspur	D 0-0		25,000
Apr 10	DERBY COUNTY	W 1-0	Banks	30,000
Apr 11	ASTON VILLA	L 0-1		40,000
Apr 13	Bradford City	L 0-1		20,000
Apr 15	MANCHESTER UNITED	L 1-2	Dawson	28,000
Apr 18	Middlesbrough	L 0-4		15,000
Apr 27	SHEFFIELD UNITED	W 2-1	Miller 2	7,000

FA Cup

Jan 10	BARNSLEY	(Rd1)	D 1-1	Lacey	33,000
Jan 15	Barnsley	(R)	W 1-0	Lacey	23,999
Jan 31	GILLINGHAM	(Rd2)	W 2-0	Lacey, Ferguson	42,045
Feb 21	West Ham United	(Rd3)	D 1-1	Miller	15,000
Feb 25	WEST HAM UNITED	(R)	W 5-1	Lacey 2, Miller 2, Metcalf	43,729
Mar 7	QUEENS PARK RANGERS	(Rd4)	W 2-1	Sheldon, Miller	43,000
Mar 28	Aston Villa*	(SF)	W 2-0	Nicholl 2	27,474
Apr 25	Burnley**	(F)	L 0-1		72,778

*Played at White Hart Lane, London. **Played at Crystal Palace, London.

League & Cup Appearances

PLAYER	LEAGUE	CUP COMPETITION FA CUP	TOTAL
Banks	9		9
Bovill	3		3
Campbell	34	8	42
Crawford	7		7
Dawson	13	1	14
Fairfoul	38	8	46
Ferguson	36	7	43
Goddard	11		11
Gracie	14		14
Grayer	1		1
Holden	1		1
Lacey	35	8	43
Longworth	27	7	34
Lowe	29	5	34
Mackinlay	16	6	22
McDougall	6	1	7
Metcalf	10	5	15
Miller	32	8	40
Nicholl	14	5	19
Parkinson	5	2	7
Peake	5		5
Pursell	26	8	34
Scott	4		4
Sheldon	22	8	30
Speakman	14	1	15
Staniforth	3		3
Stewart	3		3

Goalscorers

PLAYER	LEAGUE	CUP COMPETITION FA CUP	TOTAL
Miller	16	4	20
Lacey	6	5	11
Sheldon	5	1	6
Nicholl	3	2	5
Banks	4		4
Dawson	3		3
Gracie	3		3
Metcalf	2	1	3
Crawford	1		1
Ferguson		1	1
Mackinlay	1		1
McDougall	1		1
Parkinson	1		1

Fact File

In a poor league season, Liverpool reached the FA Cup final for the first time. The final, played at Crystal Palace, was also the first at which a reigning monarch, King George V, was present.

MANAGER: Tom Watson
CAPTAIN: Harry Lowe
TOP SCORER: Tom Miller 20 (16 league)
BIGGEST WIN: 4-2, 25 December 1913, v Manchester City (H), Division One
HIGHEST ATTENDANCE: 72,778, 25 April 1914, v Burnley, FA Cup Final at Crystal Palace
TRANSFERS IN: Jackie Sheldon from Manchester United
TRANSFERS OUT: Jimmy Stewart to Hamilton Academicals, John Bovill to Linfield

Final Division One Table

		P	W	D	L	F	A	Pts
1	Blackburn R	38	20	11	7	78	42	51
2	Aston Villa	38	19	6	13	65	50	44
3	Middlesbrough	38	19	5	14	77	60	43
4	Oldham Ath	38	17	9	12	55	45	43
5	WBA	38	15	13	10	46	42	43
6	Bolton W	38	16	10	12	65	52	42
7	Sunderland	38	17	6	15	63	52	40
8	Chelsea	38	16	7	15	46	55	39
9	Bradford C	38	12	14	12	40	40	38
10	Sheffield U	38	16	5	17	63	60	37
11	Newcastle U	38	13	11	14	39	48	37
12	Burnley	38	12	12	14	61	53	36
13	Manchester C	38	14	8	16	51	53	36
14	Manchester U	38	15	6	17	52	62	36
15	Everton	38	12	11	15	46	55	35
16	Liverpool	38	14	7	17	46	62	35
17	Tottenham H	38	12	10	16	50	62	34
18	The Wednesday	38	13	8	17	53	70	34
19	Preston NE	38	12	6	20	52	69	30
20	Derby Co	38	8	11	19	55	71	27

Season 1914-15

Football League Division One

DATE	OPPONENTS	SCORE	GOALSCORERS	ATTENDANCE
Sep 2	BOLTON WANDERERS	W 4-3	Sheldon, Lacey, Metcalf, Nicholl	15,000
Sep 5	NOTTS COUNTY	D 1-1	Metcalf	15,000
Sep 12	Sunderland	D 2-2	Sheldon (pen), Metcalf	14,000
Sep 19	THE WEDNESDAY	W 2-1	Miller 2	25,000
Sep 21	Blackburn Rovers	W 2-4	Metcalf, Nicholl	15,000
Sep 26	West Bromwich Albion	L 0-4		15,000
Oct 3	EVERTON	L 0-5		32,000
Oct 10	Chelsea	L 1-3	Pagnam	30,000
Oct 17	BRADFORD CITY	W 2-1	Miller 2	20,000
Oct 24	Burnley	L 0-3		18,000
Oct 31	TOTTENHAM HOTSPUR	W 7-2	Pagnam 4, Sheldon 2, Banks	20,000
Nov 7	Newcastle United	D 0-0		25,000
Nov 14	MIDDLESBROUGH	D 1-1	Pagnam	25,000
Nov 21	Sheffield United	L 1-2	Pagnam	6,000
Nov 28	ASTON VILLA	L 3-6	Nicholl 2, Miller	15,000
Dec 5	Manchester City	D 1-1	Nicholl	8,000
Dec 12	Bradford Park Avenue	L 0-1		8,000
Dec 19	OLDHAM ATHLETIC	L 1-2	Pagnam	10,000
Dec 25	Bolton Wanderers	W 1-0	Lacey	15,000
Dec 26	MANCHESTER UNITED	D 1-1	Pagnam	25,000
Jan 2	Notts County	L 1-3	Miller	8,000
Jan 16	SUNDERLAND	W 2-1	Miller, Pagnam	17,000
Jan 23	The Wednesday	L 1-2	Pagnam	12,000
Feb 6	Everton	W 3-1	Sheldon, Nicholl, Pagnam	30,000
Feb 13	Chelsea	D 3-3	Pagnam 3	14,000
Feb 27	Burnley	W 3-0	Sheldon (pen), Nicholl 2	22,000
Mar 6	Tottenham Hotspur	D 1-1	Sheldon	12,000
Mar 10	Bradford City	L 2-3	Metcalf, Pagnam	5,000
Mar 13	MANCHESTER CITY	W 3-2	Pagnam, Metcalf, Miller	20,000
Mar 20	Middlesbrough	L 0-3		6,000
Mar 24	WEST BROMWICH ALBION	W 3-1	Pagnam 2, Mackinlay	20,000
Mar 29	NEWCASTLE UNITED	D 2-2	Miller, Pagnam	3,000
Apr 2	Manchester United	L 0-2		12,000
Apr 3	Aston Villa	L 2-6	Sheldon (pen), Miller	12,000
Apr 5	BLACKBURN ROVERS	W 3-0	Miller, Nicholl, Sheldon	30,000
Apr 12	SHEFFIELD UNITED	W 2-1	Pagnam, Sheldon (pen)	4,000
Apr 17	BRADFORD PARK AVENUE	W 2-1	Pagnam, Banks	20,000
Apr 24	Oldham Athletic	W 2-0	Pagnam 2	5,000

FA Cup

Jan 9	STOCKPORT COUNTY	(Rd1)	W 3-0	Pagnam 2, Metcalf	10,000
Jan 30	Sheffield United	(Rd2)	L 0-1		25,000

League & Cup Appearances

PLAYER	LEAGUE	CUP COMPETITION FA CUP	TOTAL
Banks	17		17
Bartrop	3		3
Bratley	13		13
Campbell	15		15
Crawford	6		6
Fairfoul	24	1	25
Ferguson	18		18
Hafekost	1		1.
Lacey	32	1	33
Longworth	35	2	37
Lowe	26	2	28
Mackinlay	20	2	22
McDougall	1		1
Metcalf	14	2	16
Miller	33	2	35
Nicholl	38	2	40
Pagnam	29	2	31
Pursell	27	2	29
Scott	23	2	25
Sheldon	35	2	37
Speakman	7		7
Wadsworth	1		1

Goalscorers

PLAYER	LEAGUE	CUP COMPETITION FA CUP	TOTAL
Pagnam	24	2	26
Miller	11		11
Sheldon	10		10
Nicholl	9		9
Metcalf	6	1	7
Banks	2		2
Lacey	2		2
Mackinlay	1		1

Fact File

All the players in the squad donated 12.5 per cent of their salaries to the war effort and 18 footballs were sent to the troops at the front.

MANAGER: Tom Watson (died May 1915)
CAPTAIN: Harry Lowe
TOP SCORER: Fred Pagnam 26 (24 league)
BIGGEST WIN: 7-2, 31 October 1914, v Tottenham Hotspur (H), Division One
HIGHEST ATTENDANCE: 32,000, 3 October 1914, v Everton (H), Division One
TRANSFERS IN: Fred Pagnam from Blackpool

Final Division One Table

		P	W	D	L	F	A	Pts
1	Everton	38	19	8	11	76	47	46
2	Oldham Ath	38	17	11	10	70	56	45
3	Blackburn R	38	18	7	13	83	61	43
4	Burnley	38	18	7	13	61	47	43
5	Manchester C	38	15	13	10	49	39	43
6	Sheffield U	38	15	13	10	49	41	43
7	The Wednesday	38	15	13	10	61	54	43
8	Sunderland	38	18	5	15	81	72	41
9	Bradford PA	38	17	7	14	69	65	41
10	WBA	38	15	10	13	49	43	40
11	Bradford C	38	13	14	11	55	49	40
12	Middlesbrough	38	13	12	13	62	74	38
13	Liverpool	38	14	9	15	65	75	37
14	Aston Villa	38	13	11	14	62	72	37
15	Newcastle U	38	11	10	17	46	48	32
16	Notts Co	38	9	13	16	41	57	31
17	Bolton W	38	11	8	19	68	84	30
18	Manchester U	38	9	12	17	46	62	30
19	Chelsea	38	8	13	17	51	65	29
20	Tottenham H	38	8	12	18	57	90	28

Season 1919-20

Football League Division One

DATE	OPPONENTS	SCORE	GOALSCORERS	ATTENDANCE
Aug 30	Bradford City	W 3-1	Lewis, Chambers, Pearson	25,000
Sep 1	ARSENAL	L 2-3	Chambers, Pagnam	12,000
Sep 6	BRADFORD CITY	W 2-1	Pagnam, Mackinlay	30,000
Sep 8	Arsenal	L 0–1		25,000
Sep 13	ASTON VILLA	W 2-1	Pagnam, Mackinlay	28,000
Sep 20	Aston Villa	W 1-0	Forshaw	30,000
Sep 27	NEWCASTLE UNITED	D 1-1	Pagnam	40,000
Oct 4	Newcastle United	L 0-3		40,000
Oct 11	Chelsea	L 0-1		40,000
Oct 18	CHELSEA	L 0-1		40,000
Oct 25	Burnley	W 2-1	Chambers 2	15,000
Nov 1	BURNLEY	L 0-1		30,000
Nov 8	Bradford Park Avenue	W 2-1	Chambers, Lacey	15,000
Nov 15	BRADFORD PARK AVENUE	D 3-3	Forshaw 2, Pearson	30,000
Nov 22	Preston North End	L 1-2	Chambers	14,000
Nov 29	PRESTON NORTH END	L 1-2	Lewis	12,000
Dec 6	Middlesbrough	L 2-3	Lewis, Pearson	20,000
Dec 13	MIDDLESBROUGH	W 1-0	Chambers	30,000
Dec 20	Everton	D 0-0		40,000
Dec 25	SUNDERLAND	W 3-2	Lacey, Hobson o.g., Miller T	30,000
Dec 26	Manchester United	D 0-0		45,000
Dec 27	EVERTON	W 3-1	Lewis, Miller T 2	49,662
Jan 1	MANCHESTER UNITED	D 0-0		30,000
Jan 3	Sheffield United	L 2-3	Miller T 2	25,000
Jan 17	SHEFFIELD UNITED	W 2-0	Miller T, Lewis	35,000
Jan 24	Bolton Wanderers	W 3-0	Lacey, Miller T, Bromilow	20,000
Feb 4	BOLTON WANDERERS	W 2-0	Lewis 2	30,000
Feb 7	Blackburn Rovers	W 2-0	Miller T 2	20,000
Feb 14	BLACKBURN ROVERS	W 3-0	Chambers 2, Bamber	30,000
Feb 26	Notts County	L 0-1		12,000
Feb 28	NOTTS COUNTY	W 3-0	Pearson, Sheldon, Miller T	30,000
Mar 10	THE WEDNESDAY	W 1-0	Chambers	15,000
Mar 13	The Wednesday	D 2-2	Forshaw, Mackinlay	12,000
Mar 20	MANCHESTER CITY	W 1-0	Chambers	35,000
Mar 27	Manchester City	L 1-2	Chambers (pen)	40,000
Apr 2	Oldham Athletic	D 1-1	Miller T	23,000
Apr 3	DERBY COUNTY	W 3-0	Forshaw 3	28,000
Apr 5	OLDHAM ATHLETIC	D 2-2	Chambers 2	30,000
Apr 10	Derby County	L 0-3		14,000
Apr 17	WEST BROMWICH ALBION	D 0-0		40,000
Apr 24	West Bromwich Albion	D 1-1	Mackinlay	40,000
May 1	Sunderland	W 1-0	Chambers	30,000

FA Cup

Jan 10	South Shields	(Rd1)	D 1-1	Lewis	10,000
Jan 14	SOUTH SHIELDS	(R)	W 2-0	Lewis, Sheldon	40,000
Jan 31	Luton Town	(Rd2)	W 2-0	Lacey 2	12,640
Feb 23	BIRMINGHAM	(Rd3)	W 2-0	Sheldon, Miller T	50,000
Mar 6	Huddersfield Town	(Rd4)	L 1-2	Miller T	44,248

League & Cup Appearances

PLAYER	LEAGUE	CUP COMPETITION FA CUP	TOTAL
Armstrong	1		1
Bamber	24	5	29
Bennett	1		1
Bromilow	23	5	28
Campbell	32	5	37
Chambers	34		34
Forshaw	23		23
Jenkinson	13		13
Johnson	1		1
Lacey	32	5	37
Lewis	23	5	28
Longworth	27	5	32
Lowe	5		5
Lucas	16		16
Mackinlay	41	5	46
Matthews	1		1
McNab	2		2
Miller J	8		8
Miller T	20	5	25
Pagnam	8		8
Pearson	33	5	38
Pursell	2		2
Scott	9		9
Sheldon	37	5	42
Speakman	4		4
Wadsworth H	9		9
Wadsworth W	33	5	38

Goalscorers

PLAYER	LEAGUE	CUP COMPETITION FA CUP	TOTAL
Chambers	15		15
Miller T	11	2	13
Lewis	7	2	9
Forshaw	7		7
Lacey	3	2	5
Mackinlay	4		4
Pagnam	4		4
Pearson	4		4
Sheldon	1	2	3
Bamber	1		1
Bromilow	1		1
Opps' o.gs.	1		1

Fact File

For the first time, two goalkeepers from the same club were selected to oppose each other in an international match; Kenny Campbell for Scotland and Elisha Scott for Ireland, 13 March 1920.

MANAGER: David Ashworth

CAPTAIN: Ephraim Longworth/Don Mackinlay

TOP SCORER: Harry Chambers 15 (league)

BIGGEST WIN: 3-0, 24 January 1920, v Bolton Wanderers (A); 3-0, 14 February 1920, v Blackburn Rovers (H); 3-0, 28 February 1920, v Notts County (H); 3-0, 3 April 1920, v Derby County (H), Division One

HIGHEST ATTENDANCE: 49,662, 27 December 1919, v Everton (H), Division One

TRANSFERS IN: Bill Jenkinson from Golborne United, Bert Pearson from Port Vale

Final Division One Table

		P	W	D	L	F	A	Pts
1	WBA	42	28	4	10	104	47	60
2	Burnley	42	21	9	12	65	59	51
3	Chelsea	42	22	5	15	56	51	49
4	Liverpool	42	19	10	13	59	44	48
5	Sunderland	42	22	4	16	72	59	48
6	Bolton W	42	19	9	14	72	65	47
7	Manchester C	42	18	9	15	71	62	45
8	Newcastle United	42	17	9	16	44	39	43
9	Aston Villa	42	18	6	18	75	73	42
10	Arsenal	42	15	12	15	56	58	42
11	Bradford PA	42	15	12	15	60	63	42
12	Manchester U	42	13	14	15	54	50	40
13	Middlesbrough	42	15	10	17	61	65	40
14	Sheffield U	42	16	8	18	59	69	40
15	Bradford C	42	14	11	17	54	63	39
16	Everton	42	12	14	16	69	68	38
17	Oldham Ath	42	15	8	19	49	52	38
18	Derby Co	42	13	12	17	47	57	38
19	Preston NE	42	14	10	18	57	73	38
20	Blackburn R	42	13	11	18	64	77	37
21	Notts Co	42	12	12	18	56	74	36
22	The Wednesday	42	7	9	26	28	64	23

Season 1920-21

Football League Division One

DATE	OPPONENTS	SCORE	GOALSCORERS	ATTENDANCE
Aug 28	MANCHESTER CITY	W 4-2	Mackinlay, Miller T 2, Wadsworth W	45,000
Sep 1	West Bromwich Albion	D 1-1	Miller T	30,000
Sep 4	Manchester City	L 2-3	Chambers, Wadsworth W	40,000
Sep 6	WEST BROMWICH ALBION	D 0-0		35,000
Sep 11	OLDHAM ATHLETIC	W 5-2	Johnson 2, Chambers, Sheldon, Bamber	30,000
Sep 18	Oldham Athletic	D 0-0		20,000
Sep 25	PRESTON NORTH END	W 6-0	Chambers, Wadsworth H, Johnson 3, Forshaw	40,000
Oct 2	Preston North End	W 3-2	Chambers, Forshaw, Wadsworth H	28,000
Oct 9	SHEFFIELD UNITED	D 2-2	McKinney, Johnson	40,000
Oct 16	Sheffield United	W 1-0	Chambers	20,000
Oct 23	EVERTON	W 1-0	Forshaw	50,000
Oct 30	Everton	W 3-0	Johnson, Chambers 2	55,000
Nov 6	BRADFORD PARK AVENUE	L 0-1		35,000
Nov 13	Bradford Park Avenue	W 3-1	Chambers, Forshaw 2	12,000
Nov 20	Newcastle United	L 0-2		50,000
Nov 27	NEWCASTLE UNITED	L 0-1		40,000
Dec 4	BURNLEY	D 0-0		35,000
Dec 11	Burnley	L 0-1		30,000
Dec 18	ASTON VILLA	W 4-1	Johnson 2, Lewis, Mackinlay (pen)	35,000
Dec 25	Chelsea	D 1-1	Johnson	45,000
Dec 27	CHELSEA	W 2-1	Wadsworth W, Chambers	50,000
Jan 1	Aston Villa	W 2-0	Johnson, Chambers	30,000
Jan 15	SUNDERLAND	D 0-0		30,000
Jan 22	Sunderland	L 1-2	Chambers	18,000
Feb 5	Manchester United	D 1-1	Chambers	30,000
Feb 9	MANCHESTER UNITED	W 2-0	Lewis, Chambers	35,000
Feb 12	BRADFORD CITY	W 2-1	Chambers 2	35,000
Feb 19	Bradford City	D 0-0		28,000
Feb 26	HUDDERSFIELD TOWN	W 4-1	Wadsworth W, Chambers 2, Forshaw	35,000
Mar 5	Huddersfield Town	W 2-1	Chambers, Johnson	18,000
Mar 12	MIDDLESBROUGH	D 0-0		40,000
Mar 19	Middlesbrough	W 1-0	Chambers (pen)	25,000
Mar 25	TOTTENHAM HOTSPUR	D 1-1	Forshaw	40,000
Mar 26	Blackburn Rovers	D 1-1	Forshaw	25,000
Mar 28	Tottenham Hotspur	L 0-1		35,000
Apr 2	BLACKBURN ROVERS	W 2-0	Chambers, Wadsworth H	35,000
Apr 9	Derby County	D 0-0		10,000
Apr 16	DERBY COUNTY	D 1-1	Chambers	28,000
Apr 23	Bolton Wanderers	L 0-1		25,000
Apr 30	BOLTON WANDERERS	L 2-3	Johnson, Lacey	30,000
May 2	Arsenal	D 0-0		17,000
May 7	ARSENAL	W 3-0	Chambers, Forshaw, Wadsworth W	27,000

FA Cup

Jan 8	MANCHESTER UNITED	(Rd1)	D 1-1	Chambers	36,000
Jan 12	Manchester United	(R)	W 2-1	Lacey, Chambers	29,189
Jan 29	Newcastle United	(Rd2)	L 0-1		61,400

Fact File

Ephraim Longworth became the first Liverpool player to captain England, v Belgium, on 21 May 1921.

MANAGER: David Ashworth

CAPTAIN: Ephraim Longworth

TOP SCORER: Harry Chambers 24 (22 league)

BIGGEST WIN: 6-0, 25 September 1920, v Preston North End (H), Division One

HIGHEST ATTENDANCE: 61,400, 29 January 1921, v Newcastle United, FA Cup

TRANSFERS IN: Bill Cunningham from Blyth Spartans, Ted Parry from Colwyn Bay

TRANSFERS OUT: Bert Pearson, back to Port Vale, Bill Jenkinson to Wigan Borough

League & Cup Appearances

PLAYER	LEAGUE	CUP COMPETITION FA CUP	TOTAL
Bamber	30	3	33
Bromilow	40	3	43
Chambers	40	3	43
Cunningham	2		2
Forshaw	27		27
Harrington	4		4
Johnson	26	1	27
Lacey	22	2	24
Lewis	17	3	20
Longworth	24		24
Lucas	29	3	32
Mackinlay	35	3	38
Matthews	1		1
McKinney	3		3
McNab	1		1
McNaughton	1		1
Miller T	4		4
Mitchell	15		15
Parry	2		2
Pearson	10	3	13
Penman	1		1
Scott	26	3	29
Sheldon	35	3	38
Wadsworth H	25		25
Wadsworth W	42	3	45

Goalscorers

PLAYER	LEAGUE	CUP COMPETITION FA CUP	TOTAL
Chambers	22	2	24
Johnson	13		13
Forshaw	9		9
Wadsworth W	5		5
Miller	3		3
Wadsworth H	3		3
Lacey	1	1	2
Lewis	2		2
Mackinlay	2		2
Bamber	1		1
McKinney	1		1
Sheldon	1		1

Final Division One Table

		P	W	D	L	F	A	Pts
1	Burnley	42	23	13	6	79	36	59
2	Manchester C	42	24	6	12	70	50	54
3	Bolton W	42	19	14	9	77	53	52
4	Liverpool	42	18	15	9	63	35	51
5	Newcastle United	42	20	10	12	66	45	50
6	Tottenham H	42	19	9	14	70	48	47
7	Everton	42	17	13	12	66	55	47
8	Middlesbrough	42	17	12	13	53	53	46
9	Arsenal	42	15	14	13	59	63	44
10	Aston Villa	42	18	7	17	63	70	43
11	Blackburn R	42	13	15	14	57	59	41
12	Sunderland	42	14	13	15	57	60	41
13	Manchester U	42	15	10	17	64	68	40
14	WBA	42	13	14	15	54	58	40
15	Bradford C	42	12	15	15	61	63	39
16	Preston NE	42	15	9	18	61	65	39
17	Huddersfield T	42	15	9	18	42	49	39
18	Chelsea	42	13	13	16	48	58	39
19	Oldham Ath	42	9	15	18	49	86	33
20	Sheffield U	42	6	18	18	42	68	30
21	Derby Co	42	5	16	21	32	58	26
22	Bradford PA	42	8	8	26	43	76	24

Season 1921-22

Football League Division One

DATE	OPPONENTS	SCORE	GOALSCORERS	ATTENDANCE
Aug 27	Sunderland	L 0-3		40,000
Aug 31	MANCHESTER CITY	W 3-2	Forshaw, Matthews 2	27,000
Sep 3	SUNDERLAND	W 2-1	Matthews, Forshaw	40,000
Sep 7	Manchester City	D 1-1	Chambers	25,000
Sep 10	Sheffield United	W 1-0	Bromilow	30,000
Sep 17	SHEFFIELD UNITED	D 1-1	Chambers	30,000
Sep 24	Chelsea	W 1-0	Matthews	35,000
Oct 1	CHELSEA	D 1-1	Forshaw	35,000
Oct 8	Preston North End	D 1-1	Beadles	20,000
Oct 15	PRESTON NORTH END	W 4-0	Chambers, Forshaw, Lucas (pen), Beadles	38,000
Oct 22	Tottenham Hotspur	W 1-0	Beadles	31,593
Oct 29	TOTTENHAM HOTSPUR	D 1-1	Lewis	40,000
Nov 5	Everton	D 1-1	Shone	52,000
Nov 12	EVERTON	D 1-1	Forshaw	50,000
Nov 19	MIDDLESBROUGH	W 4-0	Shone 3, Lucas (pen)	35,000
Nov 26	Middlesbrough	L 1-3	Shone	24,000
Dec 3	Aston Villa	D 1-1	Chambers	30,000
Dec 10	ASTON VILLA	W 2-0	Shone, Forshaw	40,000
Dec 17	MANCHESTER UNITED	W 2-1	Lacey, Chambers	40,000
Dec 24	Manchester United	D 0-0		30,000
Dec 26	NEWCASTLE UNITED	W 1-0	Chambers	40,000
Dec 27	HUDDERSFIELD TOWN	W 2-0	Chambers 2	40,000
Dec 31	Bradford City	D 0-0		18,000
Jan 2	Newcastle United	D 1-1	Forshaw	50,000
Jan 14	BRADFORD CITY	W 2-1	Chambers, Forshaw	15,000
Jan 21	Huddersfield Town	W 1-0	Chambers	20,000
Feb 4	Birmingham	W 2-0	Chambers 2	15,000
Feb 11	BIRMINGHAM	W 1-0	Forshaw	30,000
Feb 25	ARSENAL	W 4-0	Forshaw 3, Turnbull o.g.	40,000
Mar 4	Blackburn Rovers	D 0-0		35,000
Mar 11	BLACKBURN ROVERS	W 2-0	Mackinlay, Forshaw	35,000
Mar 18	BOLTON WANDERERS	L 0-2		30,000
Mar 22	Arsenal	L 0-1		12,000
Mar 25	Bolton Wanderers	W 3-1	Forshaw 2, Chambers	30,000
Apr 1	OLDHAM ATHLETIC	W 2-0	Chambers, Gilhespy	30,000
Apr 8	Oldham Athletic	L 0-4		12,000
Apr 14	Burnley	D 1-1	Chambers	30,000
Apr 15	CARDIFF CITY	W 5-1	Bromilow, Chambers 3, McNab	50,000
Apr 17	BURNLEY	W 2-1	Chambers, Forshaw	50,000
Apr 22	Cardiff City	L 0-2		30,000
Apr 29	WEST BROMWICH ALBION	L 1-2	Beadles	45,000
May 6	West Bromwich Albion	W 4-1	Forshaw, Beadles 2, McNab	15,000

FA Cup

Jan 7	Sunderland	(Rd1)	D 1-1	Forshaw	30,000
Jan 11	SUNDERLAND	(R)	W 5-0	Forshaw 2, Chambers 2, Wadsworth W	46,000
Jan 28	WEST BROMWICH ALBION	(Rd2)	L 0-1		50,000

Charity Shield

May 10	Huddersfield Town*	L 0-1		20,000

*Played at Old Trafford.

Fact File

The League Championship trophy and medals were presented to the team by John McKenna, President of the Football League, after the Charity Shield match against Huddersfield at Old Trafford in May.

MANAGER: David Ashworth
CAPTAIN: Don Mackinlay
TOP SCORER: Harry Chambers 21 (19 league)
BIGGEST WIN: 5-0, 11 January 1922, v Sunderland (H), FA Cup
HIGHEST ATTENDANCE: 52,000, 5 November 1921, v Everton (A), Division One
TRANSFERS IN: Fred Hopkin from Manchester United, Cyril Gilhespy from Sunderland, Harry Beadles from local league football

League & Cup Appearances

PLAYER	LEAGUE	CUP COMPETITION FA CUP	OTHER	TOTAL
Bamber	8			8
Beadles	11		1	12
Bromilow	40	3	1	44
Chambers	32	3	1	36
Checkland	5			5
Cunningham	1			1
Forshaw	42	3	1	46
Gilhespy	2			2
Hopkin	42	3	1	46
Lacey	39	3	1	43
Lewis	19	3		22
Longworth	26		1	27
Lucas	27	3		30
Mackinlay	29	3	1	33
Matthews	7			7
McNab	29	3	1	33
Mitchell	3			3
Parry	7			7
Scott	39	3	1	43
Shone	15			15
Wadsworth H	1			1
Wadsworth W	38	3	1	42

Goalscorers

PLAYER	LEAGUE	CUP COMPETITION FA CUP	OTHER	TOTAL
Chambers	19	2		21
Forshaw	17	3		20
Beadles	6			6
Shone	6			6
Matthews	4			4
Bromilow	2			2
Lucas	2			2
McNab	2			2
Gilhespy	1			1
Lacey	1			1
Lewis	1			1
Mackinlay	1			1
Wadsworth W		1		1
Opps' o.gs.	1			1

Final Division One Table

	P	W	D	L	F	A	Pts
1 Liverpool	42	22	13	7	63	36	57
2 Tottenham H	42	21	9	12	65	39	51
3 Burnley	42	22	5	15	72	54	49
4 Cardiff C	42	19	10	13	61	53	48
5 Aston Villa	42	22	3	17	74	55	47
6 Bolton W	42	20	7	15	68	59	47
7 Newcastle United	42	18	10	14	59	45	46
8 Middlesbrough	42	16	14	12	79	69	46
9 Chelsea	42	17	12	13	40	43	46
10 Manchester C	42	18	9	15	65	70	45
11 Sheffield U	42	15	10	17	59	54	40
12 Sunderland	42	16	8	18	60	62	40
13 WBA	42	15	10	17	51	63	40
14 Huddersfield T	42	15	9	18	53	54	39
15 Blackburn R	42	13	12	17	54	57	38
16 Preston NE	42	13	12	17	42	65	38
17 Arsenal	42	15	7	20	47	56	37
18 Birmingham	42	15	7	20	48	60	37
19 Oldham Ath	42	13	11	18	38	50	37
20 Everton	42	12	12	18	57	55	36
21 Bradford C	42	11	10	21	48	72	32
22 Manchester U	42	8	12	22	41	73	28

Season 1922-23

Football League Division One

DATE	OPPONENTS	SCORE	GOALSCORERS	ATTENDANCE
Aug 26	ARSENAL	W 5-2	Johnson 3, Bromilow, Chambers	40,962
Aug 30	Sunderland	L 0-1		36,000
Sep 2	Arsenal	L 0-1		20,000
Sep 6	SUNDERLAND	W 5-1	Forshaw, Chambers 2, Johnson, Mackinlay	30,000
Sep 9	Preston North End	W 3-1	Wadsworth W, Johnson, Chambers	34,000
Sep 16	PRESTON NORTH END	W 5-2	Chambers, Forshaw 3, Bromilow	36,000
Sep 23	BURNLEY	W 3-0	Chambers, Forshaw 2	45,000
Sep 30	Burnley	L 0-2		25,000
Oct 7	EVERTON	W 5-1	Chambers 3, McNab, Bromilow	54,368
Oct 14	Everton	W 1-0	Johnson	52,000
Oct 21	CARDIFF CITY	W 3-1	Gilhespy, Forshaw, Wadsworth W	35,000
Oct 28	Cardiff City	L 0-3		40,000
Nov 4	Tottenham Hotspur	W 4-2	Chambers 2, Forshaw, Gilhespy	45,000
Nov 11	TOTTENHAM HOTSPUR	D 0-0		30,000
Nov 18	ASTON VILLA	W 3-0	Mackinlay, Chambers, Johnson	32,000
Nov 25	Aston Villa	W 1-0	Chambers	40,000
Dec 2	NEWCASTLE UNITED	L 0-2		30,000
Dec 9	Newcastle United	W 1-0	Chambers	35,000
Dec 16	NOTTINGHAM FOREST	W 2-1	Johnson, Mackinlay	25,000
Dec 23	Nottingham Forest	W 3-1	Johnson, Forshaw 2	20,000
Dec 25	Oldham Athletic	W 2-0	Mackinlay, Johnson	20,166
Dec 26	OLDHAM ATHLETIC	W 2-1	Mackinlay, Forshaw	40,000
Dec 30	Chelsea	D 0-0		40,000
Jan 6	CHELSEA	W 1-0	Lacey	25,000
Jan 20	Middlesbrough	W 2-0	Chambers, Johnson	25,000
Jan 27	MIDDLESBROUGH	W 2-0	Chambers, Johnson	40,000
Feb 7	WEST BROMWICH ALBION	W 2-0	Forshaw, Johnson	28,000
Feb 10	West Bromwich Albion	D 0-0		18,000
Feb 17	BLACKBURN ROVERS	W 3-0	Forshaw 3	25,000
Mar 3	BOLTON WANDERERS	W 3-0	Forshaw, Johnson, Hopkin	25,000
Mar 12	Blackburn Rovers	L 0-1		30,000
Mar 17	Manchester City	L 0-1		40,000
Mar 24	MANCHESTER CITY	W 2-0	Chambers, Forshaw	25,000
Mar 30	SHEFFIELD UNITED	W 2-1	Chambers 2	40,000
Mar 31	Birmingham	W 1-0	Chambers	30,000
Apr 2	Sheffield United	L 1-4	Forshaw	40,000
Apr 7	BIRMINGHAM	D 0-0		30,000
Apr 14	Huddersfield Town	D 0-0		17,000
Apr 18	Bolton Wanderers	D 1-1	Forshaw	30,000
Apr 21	HUDDERSFIELD TOWN	D 1-1	Chambers	45,000
Apr 28	Stoke	D 0-0		20,000
May 5	STOKE	W 1-0	Chambers	30,000

FA Cup

Jan 13	ARSENAL	(Rd1)	D 0-0		37,000
Jan 17	Arsenal	(R)	W 4-1	Chambers 2, Johnson, Mackinlay (pen)	40,000
Feb 3	Wolverhampton Wanderers	(Rd2)	W 2-0	Johnson, Forshaw	40,079
Feb 24	SHEFFIELD UNITED	(Rd3)	L 1-2	Chambers	51,859

League & Cup Appearances

PLAYER	LEAGUE	CUP COMPETITION FA CUP	OTHER	TOTAL
Bamber	4			4
Beadles	4			4
Bromilow	41	4		45
Chambers	39	4		43
Forshaw	42	4		46
Gilhespy	10			10
Hopkin	40	4		44
Johnson	37	4		41
Lacey	30	4		34
Longworth	41	4		45
Lucas	1			1
Mackinlay	42	4		46
McNab	39	4		43
Pratt	7			7
Sambrook	2			2
Scott	42	4		46
Shone	1			1
Wadsworth H	3			3
Wadsworth W	37	4		41

Goalscorers

PLAYER	LEAGUE	CUP COMPETITION FA CUP	TOTAL
Chambers	22	3	25
Forshaw	19	1	20
Johnson	14	2	16
Mackinlay	5	1	6
Bromilow	3		3
Gilhespy	2		2
Wadsworth W	2		2
Hopkin	1		1
Lacey	1		1
McNab	1		1

Fact File

A serious fire broke out in the Anfield Road stand during the Bolton Wanderers game on 3 March. It was said to be due to winger Freddie Hopkin scoring a rare goal!

MANAGER: David Ashworth/Matt McQueen from February
CAPTAIN: Don Mackinlay
TOP SCORER: Harry Chambers 25 (22 league)
BIGGEST WIN: 5-1, 6 September 1922, v Sunderland (H) and, 7 October 1922, v Everton (H)
HIGHEST ATTENDANCE: 54,368, 7 October 1922, v Everton (H)
TRANSFERS IN: David Pratt from Bradford City

Final Division One Table

		P	W	D	L	F	A	Pts
1	Liverpool	42	26	8	8	70	31	60
2	Sunderland	42	22	10	10	72	54	54
3	Huddersfield T	42	21	11	10	60	32	53
4	Newcastle United	42	18	12	12	45	37	48
5	Everton	42	20	7	15	63	59	47
6	Aston Villa	42	18	10	14	64	51	46
7	WBA	42	17	11	14	58	49	45
8	Manchester C	42	17	11	14	50	49	45
9	Cardiff C	42	18	7	17	73	59	43
10	Sheffield U	42	16	10	16	68	64	42
11	Arsenal	42	16	10	16	61	62	42
12	Tottenham H	42	17	7	18	50	50	41
13	Bolton W	42	14	12	16	50	58	40
14	Blackburn R	42	14	12	16	47	62	40
15	Burnley	42	16	6	20	58	59	38
16	Preston NE	42	13	11	18	60	64	37
17	Birmingham	42	13	11	18	41	57	37
18	Middlesbrough	42	13	10	19	57	63	36
19	Chelsea	42	9	18	15	45	53	36
20	Nottingham F	42	13	8	21	41	70	34
21	Stoke	42	10	10	22	47	67	30
22	Oldham Ath	42	10	10	22	35	65	30

Season 1923-24

Football League Division One

DATE	OPPONENTS	SCORE	GOALSCORERS	ATTENDANCE
Aug 25	West Bromwich Albion	L 0-2		25,000
Aug 29	BIRMINGHAM	W 6-2	Walsh 2, Forshaw, Chambers 3	16,000
Sep 1	WEST BROMWICH ALBION	D 0-0		40,000
Sep 5	Birmingham	L 1-2	Walsh	25,000
Sep 8	Preston North End	W 1-0	Walsh	20,000
Sep 15	PRESTON NORTH END	W 3-1	Chambers, Walsh 2	35,000
Sep 22	Burnley	L 0-2		18,000
Sep 29	BURNLEY	W 1-0	Forshaw	40,000
Oct 6	Everton	L 0-1		51,000
Oct 13	EVERTON	L 1-2	Walsh	50,000
Oct 20	NOTTINGHAM FOREST	W 4-2	Mackinlay 2 (1 pen), Walsh 2	30,000
Oct 27	Nottingham Forest	W 1-0	Walsh	15,000
Nov 3	HUDDERSFIELD TOWN	D 1-1	Chambers	30,000
Nov 10	Huddersfield Town	L 1-3	Chambers	15,000
Nov 17	Aston Villa	D 0-0		25,000
Nov 24	ASTON VILLA	L 0-1		20,000
Dec 1	Sheffield United	D 1-1	Chambers	20,000
Dec 8	SHEFFIELD UNITED	L 2-3	Chambers, Forshaw	40,000
Dec 15	CARDIFF CITY	L 0-2		35,000
Dec 22	Cardiff City	L 0-2		30,000
Dec 25	NEWCASTLE UNITED	L 0-1		35,000
Dec 26	Newcastle United	L 1-2	Keetley	25,000
Dec 29	WEST HAM UNITED	W 2-0	Walsh 2	30,000
Jan 1	CHELSEA	W 3-1	Shone, Walsh, Keetley	30.000
Jan 5	West Ham United	L 0-1		25,000
Jan 19	Manchester City	W 1-0	Chambers	20,000
Jan 26	MANCHESTER CITY	D 0-0		20,000
Feb 9	BOLTON WANDERERS	W 3-1	Chambers, Forshaw, Mackinlay (pen)	30,000
Feb 16	Sunderland	D 0-0		20,000
Mar 1	Arsenal	L 1-3	Chambers	35,000
Mar 12	Bolton Wanderers	L 1-4	Walsh	10,000
Mar 15	BLACKBURN ROVERS	D 0-0		30,000
Mar 19	SUNDERLAND	W 4-2	Chambers, Mackinlay 2, Shone	30,000
Mar 22	Blackburn Rovers	D 0-0		15,000
Mar 29	TOTTENAHM HOTSPUR	W 1-0	Chambers	20,000
Apr 2	ARSENAL	D 0-0		30,000
Apr 5	Tottenham Hotspur	D 1-1	Shone	22,470
Apr 12	MIDDLESBROUGH	W 3-1	Mackinlay, Walsh 2	20,000
Apr 18	Chelsea	L 1-2	Baker o.g.	38,000
Apr 19	Middlesbrough	D 1-1	Shone	15,000
Apr 26	NOTTS COUNTY	W 1-0	Forshaw	15,000
May 3	Notts County	W 2-1	Cornwall o.g., Shone	8,000

FA Cup

Jan 12	BRADFORD CITY	(Rd1) W 2-1	Chambers 2	25,000
Feb 2	Bolton Wanderers	(Rd2) W 4-1	Walsh 3, Chambers	51,596
Feb 21	Southampton	(Rd3) D 0-0		18,671
Feb 27	SOUTHAMPTON	(R) W 2-0	Chambers, Forshaw	49,000
Mar 8	Newcastle United	(Rd4) L 0-1		56,595

League & Cup Appearances

PLAYER	LEAGUE	CUP COMPETITION FA CUP	TOTAL
Bamber	6		6
Beadles	2		2
Bromilow	27	5	32
Chambers	30	5	35
Forshaw	39	5	44
Gilhespy	5		5
Hopkin	33	5	38
Johnson	2		2
Keetley	9		9
Lacey	8	1	9
Lawson	10	4	14
Longworth	14		14
Lucas	28	5	33
Mackinlay	39	5	44
McDevitt	3		3
McNab	30	4	34
Parry	3		3
Pratt	15		15
Rawlings	11		11
Scott	42	5	47
Shone	15	1	16
Wadsworth H	17		17
Wadsworth W	37	5	42
Walsh	37	5	42

Goalscorers

PLAYER	LEAGUE	CUP COMPETITION FA CUP	TOTAL
Walsh	16	3	19
Chambers	13	4	17
Forshaw	5	1	6
Mackinlay	6		6
Shone	5		5
Keetley	2		2
Opps' o.gs.	2		2

Fact File

Now in his 15th season Don Mackinlay played his 250th league game on 2 April v Arsenal; Ephraim Longworth, now in his 14th season, played his 300th league game on 5 January v West Ham United.

MANAGER: Matt McQueen
CAPTAIN: Don Mackinlay
TOP SCORER: Jimmy Walsh 19 (16 league)
BIGGEST WIN: 6-2, 29 August 1923, v Birmingham (H), Division One
HIGHEST ATTENDANCE: 56,595, 8 March 1924, v Newcastle United (A), FA Cup
TRANSFERS IN: William McDevitt from Belfast United, Archie Rawlings from Preston North End
TRANSFERS OUT: Harry Beadles to Cardiff City, Hugh Wadsworth (younger brother of Walter) to Leicester City

Final Division One Table

		P	W	D	L	F	A	PTS
1	Huddersfield T	42	23	11	8	60	33	57
2	Cardiff C	42	22	13	7	61	34	57
3	Sunderland	42	22	9	11	71	54	53
4	Bolton W	42	18	14	10	68	34	50
5	Sheffield U	42	19	12	11	69	49	50
6	Aston Villa	42	18	13	11	52	37	49
7	Everton	42	18	13	11	62	53	49
8	Blackburn R	42	17	11	14	54	50	45
9	Newcastle United	42	17	10	15	60	54	44
10	Notts Co	42	14	14	14	44	49	42
11	Manchester C	42	15	12	15	54	71	42
12	Liverpool	42	15	11	16	49	48	41
13	West Ham U	42	13	15	14	40	43	41
14	Birmingham	42	13	13	16	41	49	39
15	Tottenham H	42	12	14	16	50	56	38
16	WBA	42	12	14	16	51	62	38
17	Burnley	42	12	12	18	55	60	36
18	Preston NE	42	12	10	20	52	67	34
19	Arsenal	42	12	9	21	40	63	33
20	Nottingham F	42	10	12	20	42	64	32
21	Chelsea	42	9	14	19	31	53	32
22	Middlesbrough	42	7	8	27	37	60	22

Season 1924-25

Football League Division One

DATE	OPPONENTS	SCORE	GOALSCORERS	ATTENDANCE
Aug 30	ASTON VILLA	L 2-4	Mackinlay, Shone	42,000
Sep 6	Arsenal	L 0-2		30,000
Sep 13	MANCHESTER CITY	W 5-3	Mackinlay, Forshaw, Shone 2, Johnson	30,000
Sep 15	Blackburn Rovers	L 1-3	Mackinlay	25,000
Sep 20	Bury	D 0-0		25,000
Sep 27	NOTTINGHAM FOREST	W 3-0	Rawlings 2, Shone	33,000
Oct 4	Everton	W 1-0	Rawlings	53,000
Oct 11	Newcastle United	D 0-0		30,000
Oct 15	BLACKBURN ROVERS	D 0-0		20,000
Oct 18	SHEFFIELD UNITED	W 4-1	Forshaw 4	35,000
Oct 25	SUNDERLAND	W 3-1	Rawlings 2, Chambers	40,000
Nov 8	PRESTON NORTH END	W 3-1	Rawlings, Forshaw 2	20,000
Nov 12	HUDDERSFIELD TOWN	L 2-3	Forshaw, McNab	25,000
Nov 15	Burnley	L 1-2	Forshaw	20,000
Nov 22	LEEDS UNITED	W 1-0	Forshaw	25,000
Nov 29	Birmingham	L 2-5	Chambers, Forshaw	25,000
Dec 6	WEST BROMWICH ALBION	D 1-1	Forshaw	25,000
Dec 13	Tottenham Hotspur	D 1-1	Forshaw	25,604
Dec 15	Cardiff City	W 3-1	Forshaw 2, Shone	25,000
Dec 20	BOLTON WANDERERS	D 0-0		15,000
Dec 25	Notts County	W 2-1	Forshaw 2	10,000
Dec 26	NOTTS COUNTY	W 1-0	Chambers	46,187
Jan 3	ARSENAL	W 2-1	Forshaw, Chambers	24,000
Jan 17	Manchester City	L 0-5		30,000
Jan 21	Aston Villa	W 4-1	Shone, Walsh 2, Chambers	30,000
Jan 24	BURY	W 4-0	Shone 2, Rawlings, Walsh	30,000
Feb 4	Nottingham Forest	W 1-0	McNab	20,000
Feb 7	EVERTON	W 3-1	Shone, Hopkin, Chambers	54,000
Feb 14	NEWCASTLE UNITED	D 1-1	Forshaw	33,000
Feb 28	Sunderland	L 0-3		18,000
Mar 14	Preston North End	L 0-4		12,000
Mar 16	Sheffield United	W 1-0	Shone	30,000
Mar 21	BURNLEY	W 3-0	Baron 2, Shone	25,000
Mar 28	Leeds United	L 1-4	Scott T	25,000
Apr 4	BIRMINGHAM	D 1-1	Baron	28,000
Apr 10	WEST HAM UNITED	W 2-0	Chambers, Shone	30,000
Apr 11	West Bromwich Albion	D 0-0		25,000
Apr 13	West Ham United	W 1-0	Mackinlay	25,000
Apr 18	TOTTENHAM HOTSPUR	W 1-0	Baron	12,000
Apr 25	Bolton Wanderers	L 0-2		20,000
Apr 29	CARDIFF CITY	L 1-2	Baron	20,000
May 2	Huddersfield Town	D 1-1	Wilson T o.g.	16,000

FA Cup

DATE	OPPONENTS	SCORE	GOALSCORERS	ATTENDANCE
Jan 10	LEEDS UNITED	(Rd1) W 3-0	Shone 2, Hopkin	39,000
Jan 31	Bristol City	(Rd2) W 1-0	Rawlings	29,362
Feb 21	BIRMINGHAM	(Rd3) W 2-1	Rawlings, Shone	44,000
Mar 7	Southampton	(Rd4) L 0-1		21,501

League & Cup Appearances

PLAYER	LEAGUE	CUP COMPETITION FA CUP	TOTAL
Baron	9		9
Bromilow	22	2	24
Chalmers	2		2
Chambers	27	4	31
Cockburn	17	1	18
Forshaw	37	3	40
Garner	4		4
Gilhespy	2		2
Hopkin	26	4	30
Johnson	11		11
Jones	4		4
Lawson	2		2
Longworth	22	2	24
Lucas	37	4	41
Mackinlay	28	2	30
McDevitt	1		1
McNab	29	2	31
Parry	1		1
Pratt	26	4	30
Rawlings	40	4	44
Scott E	38	4	42
Scott T	6		6
Shone	42	4	46
Wadsworth	25	3	28
Walsh	4	1	5

Goalscorers

PLAYER	LEAGUE	CUP COMPETITION FA CUP	TOTAL
Forshaw	19		19
Shone	12	3	15
Rawlings	7	2	9
Chambers	7		7
Baron	5		5
Mackinlay	4		4
Walsh	3		3
Hopkin	1	1	2
McNab	2		2
Johnson	1		1
Scott T	1		1
Opps' o.gs.	1		1

Fact File

Walter Wadsworth, 'Big Waddy', played his 200th league game on 29 November 1924 v Birmingham; On 14 March he was sent off along with Jock McNab in the match against Bolton and both were suspended for several weeks.

MANAGER: Matt McQueen

CAPTAIN: Don Mackinlay

TOP SCORER: Dick Forshaw 19 (league)

BIGGEST WIN: 4-0, 24 January 1925, v Bury (H), Division One

HIGHEST ATTENDANCE: 54,000, 7 February 1925, v Everton (H), Division One

TRANSFERS IN: Tom Scott from Darlington, Fred Baron from Mid Rhondda, Bill Cockburn from Stockport County

TRANSFERS OUT: Cyril Gilhespy to Bristol City, Joe Keetley to Wolverhampton Wanderers, W McDevitt to Exeter

Final Division One Table

		P	W	D	L	F	A	Pts
1	Huddersfield T	42	21	16	5	69	28	58
2	WBA	42	23	10	9	58	34	56
3	Bolton W	42	22	11	9	76	34	55
4	Liverpool	42	20	10	12	63	55	50
5	Bury	42	17	15	10	54	51	49
6	Newcastle United	42	16	16	10	61	42	48
7	Sunderland	42	19	10	13	64	51	48
8	Birmingham	42	17	12	13	49	53	46
9	Notts Co	42	16	13	13	42	31	45
10	Manchester C	42	17	9	16	76	68	43
11	Cardiff C	42	16	11	15	56	51	43
12	Tottenham H	42	15	12	15	52	43	42
13	West Ham U	42	15	12	15	62	60	42
14	Sheffield U	42	13	13	16	55	63	39
15	Aston Villa	42	13	13	16	58	71	39
16	Blackburn R	42	11	13	18	53	66	35
17	Everton	42	12	11	19	40	60	35
18	Leeds U	42	11	12	19	46	59	34
19	Burnley	42	11	12	19	46	75	34
20	Arsenal	42	14	5	23	46	58	33
21	Preston NE	42	10	6	26	37	74	26
22	Nottingham F	42	6	12	24	29	65	24

Season 1925-26

Football League Division One

DATE	OPPONENTS	SCORE	GOALSCORERS	ATTENDANCE
Aug 29	Leicester City	L 1-3	Mackinlay	27,000
Sep 2	NOTTS COUNTY	W 2-0	Flint o.g., Forshaw	26,000
Sep 5	WEST HAM UNITED	D 0-0		30,000
Sep 12	Arsenal	D 1-1	Walsh	35,000
Sep 19	MANCHESTER UNITED	W 5-0	Forshaw 3, Chambers, Rawlings	18,000
Sep 26	EVERTON	W 5-1	Forshaw 3, Walsh, Chambers	55,000
Oct 1	Notts County	W 2-1	Bromilow, Walsh	15,000
Oct 3	Burnley	L 1-2	Chambers	15,000
Oct 10	LEEDS UNITED	D 1-1	Baron	27,000
Oct 17	MANCHESTER CITY	W 2-1	Chambers, Forshaw	35,000
Oct 24	Tottenham Hotspur	L 1-3	Forshaw	34,477
Oct 31	SUNDERLAND	D 2-2	Chambers, Forshaw	40,000
Nov 14	WEST BROMWICH ALBION	W 2-0	Oxley 2	30,000
Nov 21	Birmingham	L 0-2		12,000
Nov 25	Huddersfield Town	D 0-0		6,000
Nov 28	BURY	L 0-1		30,000
Dec 5	Blackburn Rovers	D 1-1	Chambers	5,000
Dec 12	CARDIFF CITY	L 0-2		40,000
Dec 19	Sheffield United	L 1-3	Forshaw	20,000
Dec 25	NEWCASTLE UNITED	W 6-3	Chambers 3, Oxley, Forshaw, Pratt	35,000
Dec 26	Newcastle United	L 0-3		50,000
Jan 1	ASTON VILLA	W 3-1	Forshaw 2, Oxley	30,000
Jan 2	LEICESTER CITY	L 0-3		35,000
Jan 16	West Ham United	W 2-1	Mackinlay, Scott T	15,000
Jan 23	ARSENAL	W 3-0	Forshaw 2, Oxley	40,000
Feb 6	Everton	D 3-3	Oxley, Forshaw 2	45,000
Feb 13	BURNLEY	W 3-2	Chambers, Forshaw 2	35,000
Feb 20	Leeds United	D 1-1	Forshaw	40,000
Feb 27	Manchester City	D 1-1	Forshaw	35,000
Mar 6	TOTTENHAM HOTSPUR	D 0-0		25,000
Mar 10	Manchester United	D 3-3	Forshaw, Hodgson 2	30,000
Mar 13	Sunderland	L 2-3	Chambers, Baron	19,944
Mar 20	HUDDERSFIELD TOWN	L 1-2	Forshaw	35,000
Mar 27	West Bromwich Albion	W 3-0	Hodgson, Forshaw 2 (1 pen)	10,500
Apr 2	Bolton Wanderers	W 1-0	Chambers	30,000
Apr 3	BIRMINGHAM	D 2-2	Hodgson, Hunter o.g.	35,000
Apr 5	BOLTON WANDERERS	D 2-2	Chambers, Hopkin	30,000
Apr 6	Aston Villa	L 0-3		15,000
Apr 10	Bury	W 1-0	Chambers	30,000
Apr 17	BLACKBURN ROVERS	D 2-2	Chambers, Forshaw	20,000
Apr 24	Cardiff City	D 2-2	Chambers 2	10,000
May 1	SHEFFIELD UNITED	D 2-2	Reid 2	15,000

FA Cup

Jan 9	Southampton	(Rd3) D 0-0		18,031
Jan 13	SOUTHAMPTON	(R) W 1-0	Forshaw	42,000
Jan 30	Fulham	(Rd4) L 1-3	Forshaw	36,381

League & Cup Appearances

PLAYER	LEAGUE	CUP COMPETITION FA CUP	TOTAL
Baron	10		10
Bromilow	29	3	32
Chambers	42	3	45
Cockburn	37	3	40
Forshaw	32	3	35
Garner	1		1
Hodgson	12		12
Hopkin	33		33
Jackson	12	2	14
Longworth	4	2	6
Lucas	39	1	40
Mackinlay	41	3	44
McMullan	10	3	13
McNab	34	3	37
Oxley	31	3	34
Pratt	15		15
Rawlings	12		12
Reid	1		1
Riley	3		3
Scott E	39	3	42
Scott T	4	1	5
Shears	2		2
Shone	3		3
Wadsworth	4		4
Walsh	12		12

Goalscorers

PLAYER	LEAGUE	CUP COMPETITION FA CUP	TOTAL
Forshaw	27	2	29
Chambers	17		17
Oxley	6		6
Hodgson	4		4
Walsh	3		3
Baron	2		2
Mackinlay	2		2
Reid	2		2
Bromilow	1		1
Hopkin	1		1
Pratt	1		1
Rawlings	1		1
Scott T	1		1
Opps' o.gs.	2		2

Fact File

Following a visit of the touring South Africa team to Anfield, a match which the visitors won 5-2, goalkeeper Arthur Riley and inside forward Gordon Hodgson were signed by the club.

MANAGER: Matt McQueen
CAPTAIN: Don Mackinlay
TOP SCORER: Dick Forshaw 29 (27 league)
BIGGEST WIN: 5-0, 19 September 1925, v Manchester United (H), Division One
HIGHEST ATTENDANCE: 55,000, 26 September 1925, v Everton, (H), Division One
TRANSFERS IN: Arthur Riley and Gordon Hodgson from Transvaal, South Africa, James Jackson from Aberdeen, David McMullan from Belfast Distillery
TRANSFERS OUT: Walter Wadsworth to Bristol City, Archie Rawlings and Ted Parry to Walsall

Final Division One Table

		P	W	D	L	F	A	Pts
1	Huddersfield T	42	23	11	8	92	60	57
2	Arsenal	42	22	8	12	87	63	52
3	Sunderland	42	21	6	15	96	80	48
4	Bury	42	20	7	15	85	77	47
5	Sheffield U	42	19	8	15	102	82	46
6	Aston Villa	42	16	12	14	86	76	44
7	Liverpool	42	14	16	12	70	63	44
8	Bolton W	42	17	10	15	75	76	44
9	Manchester U	42	19	6	17	66	73	44
10	Newcastle United	42	16	10	16	84	75	42
11	Everton	42	12	18	12	72	70	42
12	Blackburn R	42	15	11	16	91	80	41
13	WBA	42	16	8	18	79	78	40
14	Birmingham	42	16	8	18	66	81	40
15	Tottenham H	42	15	9	18	66	79	39
16	Cardiff C	42	16	7	19	61	76	39
17	Leicester C	42	14	10	18	70	80	38
18	West Ham U	42	15	7	20	63	76	37
19	Leeds U	42	14	8	20	64	76	36
20	Burnley	42	13	10	19	85	108	36
21	Manchester C	42	12	11	19	89	100	35
22	Notts Co	42	13	7	22	54	74	33

Season 1926-27

Football League Division One

DATE	OPPONENTS	SCORE	GOALSCORERS	ATTENDANCE
Aug 28	MANCHESTER UNITED	W 4-2	Forshaw 3, Hodgson	40,000
Aug 30	Aston Villa	D 1-1	Forshaw	25,000
Sep 4	Derby County	L 1-2	Edmed	21,526
Sep 8	ASTON VILLA	W 2-1	Forshaw, Chambers	27,000
Sep 11	SHEFFIELD UNITED	W 5-1	Hodgson 3, Forshaw 2 (1 pen)	40,000
Sep 18	Arsenal	L 0-2		35,000
Sep 25	Everton	L 0-1		38,000
Oct 2	LEEDS UNITED	L 2-4	Forshaw, Hodgson	30,000
Oct 9	Newcastle United	L 0-1		30,000
Oct 16	The Wednesday	L 2-3	Reid 2	20,000
Oct 23	LEICESTER CITY	W 1-0	Chambers	35,000
Oct 30	Blackburn Rovers	L 1-2	Chambers	20,000
Nov 6	HUDDERSFIELD TOWN	L 2-3	Forshaw 2	33,000
Nov 13	Sunderland	L 1-2	Forshaw	9,186
Nov 20	WEST BROMWICH ALBION	W 2-1	Hodgson, Chambers	20,000
Nov 27	Bury	W 2-0	Hodgson, Chambers	25,000
Dec 4	BIRMINGHAM	W 2-1	Forshaw 2	35,000
Dec 11	Tottenham Hotspur	W 2-1	Edmed, Chambers	27,839
Dec 18	WEST HAM UNITED	D 0-0		28,000
Dec 25	Burnley	L 0-4		32,000
Dec 27	BURNLEY	D 2-2	Chambers 2	45,000
Dec 28	BOLTON WANDERERS	W 3-2	Hodgson, Chambers 2	20,000
Jan 1	Bolton Wanderers	L 1-2	Edmed	32,223
Jan 15	Manchester United	W 1-0	Forshaw	35,000
Jan 22	DERBY COUNTY	W 3-2	Hodgson 3	25,000
Feb 5	ARSENAL	W 3-0	Chambers, Reid, Cope o.g.	30,000
Feb 7	Sheffield United	W 4-1	Reid 2, Chambers, Scott T	30,000
Feb 12	EVERTON	W 1-0	Chambers	52,677
Feb 23	Leeds United	D 0-0		14,000
Feb 26	NEWCASTLE UNITED	L 1-2	Reid	34,000
Mar 5	THE WEDNESDAY	W 3-0	Chambers 2, Mackinlay	32,000
Mar 12	Leicester City	L 2-3	Reid 2	25,000
Mar 19	BLACKBURN ROVERS	D 2-2	Chambers, Reid	27,000
Mar 26	Huddersfield Town	L 0-1		5,000
Apr 2	SUNDERLAND	L 1-2	Chambers	33,000
Apr 9	West Bromwich Albion	W 1-0	Edmed	12,000
Apr 15	CARDIFF CITY	W 5-0	Reid 2, Edmed, Hodgson, Lucas (pen)	35,037
Apr 16	BURY	D 2-2	Hodgson 2	25,000
Apr 18	Cardiff City	L 0-2		12,000
Apr 23	Birmingham	L 0-3		10,000
Apr 30	TOTTENHAM HOTSPUR	W 1-0	Edmed	20,000
May 7	West Ham United	D 3-3	Devlin, Hodgson 2	25,000

FA Cup

Jan 8	Bournemouth	(Rd3) D 1-1	Hodgson	13,243
Jan 12	BOURNEMOUTH	(R) W 4-1	Hopkin, Chambers 3	36,800
Jan 29	SOUTHPORT	(Rd4) W 3-1	Hodgson, Chambers, Edmed	51,600
Feb 19	Arsenal	(Rd5) L 0-2		43,000

League & Cup Appearances

PLAYER	LEAGUE	CUP COMPETITION FA CUP	TOTAL
Baron	1		1
Bromilow	40	4	44
Chambers	42	4	46
Cockburn	9		9
Devlin	1		1
Done	2		2
Edmed	38	4	42
Forshaw	24	3	27
Hodgson	36	4	40
Hopkin	36	4	40
Jackson	19		19
Longworth	15		15
Lucas	39	4	43
Mackinlay	28	4	32
McMullan	2		2
McNab	29	4	33
Pither	6		6
Pratt	14	4	18
Reid	20	1	21
Riley	10		10
Scott E	32	4	36
Scott T	4		4
Shears	8		8
Walsh	7		7

Goalscorers

PLAYER	LEAGUE	CUP COMPETITION FA CUP	TOTAL
Chambers	17	4	21
Hodgson	16	2	18
Forshaw	14		14
Reid	11		11
Edmed	6	1	7
Devlin	1		1
Hopkin		1	1
Lucas	1		1
Mackinlay	1		1
Scott T	1		1
Opps' o.gs.	1		1

Final Division One Table

		P	W	D	L	F	A	Pts
1	Newcastle United	42	25	6	11	96	58	56
2	Huddersfield T	42	17	17	8	76	60	51
3	Sunderland	42	21	7	14	98	70	49
4	Bolton W	42	19	10	13	84	62	48
5	Burnley	42	19	9	14	91	80	47
6	West Ham U	42	19	8	15	86	70	46
7	Leicester C	42	17	12	13	85	70	46
8	Sheffield U	42	17	10	15	74	86	44
9	Liverpool	42	18	7	17	69	61	43
10	Aston Villa	42	18	7	17	81	83	43
11	Arsenal	42	17	9	16	77	86	43
12	Derby Co	42	17	7	18	86	73	41
13	Tottenham H	42	16	9	17	76	78	41
14	Cardiff C	42	16	9	17	55	65	41
15	Manchester U	42	13	14	15	52	64	40
16	The Wednesday	42	15	9	18	75	92	39
17	Birmingham	42	17	4	21	64	73	38
18	Blackburn R	42	15	8	19	77	96	38
19	Bury	42	12	12	18	68	77	36
20	Everton	42	12	10	20	64	90	34
21	Leeds U	42	11	8	23	69	88	30
22	WBA	42	11	8	23	65	86	30

Fact File

Gordon Hodgson scored the first of his record 17 league hat-tricks against Sheffield United on 11 September 1926.

MANAGER: Matt McQueen
TOP SCORER: Harry Chambers 21 (17 league)
BIGGEST WIN: 5-0, 15 April 1927, v Cardiff City (H), Division One
HIGHEST ATTENDANCE: 52,677, 12 February 1927, v Everton (H), Division One
TRANSFERS IN: William Devlin from Huddersfield Town, George Pither from Merthyr Town
TRANSFERS OUT: Fred Baron to Southend

Season 1927-28

Football League Division One

DATE	OPPONENTS	SCORE	GOALSCORERS	ATTENDANCE
Aug 27	Sheffield United	D 1-1	Devlin	25,000
Aug 31	BURY	W 5-1	Devlin 4, Hodgson	30,000
Sep 3	ASTON VILLA	D 0-0		35,000
Sep 10	Sunderland	L 1-2	Hodgson	29,479
Sep 17	DERBY COUNTY	W 5-2	McNab, Devlin 2, Hodgson, Edmed	35,000
Sep 19	Bury	L 2-5	Crown o.g., Devlin	10,940
Sep 24	West Ham United	L 1-3	Edmed	35,000
Oct 1	PORTSMOUTH	W 8-2	Devlin 4, Hodgson 3, Pither	30,000
Oct 8	Leicester City	D 1-1	Hodgson	30,000
Oct 15	Everton	D 1-1	Edmed	56,000
Oct 22	Bolton Wanderers	L 1-2	Edmed	30,000
Oct 29	BLACKBURN ROVERS	W 4-2	Reid 2, Devlin, Hodgson	28,000
Nov 5	Cardiff City	D 1-1	Devlin	15,000
Nov 12	THE WEDNESDAY	W 5-2	Hodgson 2, Reid 3	35,000
Nov 19	Middlesbrough	D 1-1	Chambers	18,741
Nov 26	HUDDERSFIELD TOWN	W 4-2	Edmed, Bromilow, Hodgson 2	35,000
Dec 3	Newcastle United	D 1-1	Hodgson	40,000
Dec 10	BIRMINGHAM	L 2-3	Hodgson 2	30,000
Dec 17	Tottenham Hotspur	L 1-3	Jackson	28,000
Dec 24	MANCHESTER UNITED	W 2-0	Scott T, Chambers	35,000
Dec 27	ARSENAL	L 0-2		35,000
Dec 31	SHEFFIELD UNITED	W 2-1	Chambers, Reid	30,000
Jan 2	BURNLEY	D 2-2	Edmed, Reid	30,000
Jan 7	Aston Villa	W 4-3	Edmed 2, Reid, Hopkin	45,000
Jan 21	SUNDERLAND	L 2-5	Hopkin, Reid	35,000
Feb 4	WEST HAM UNITED	L 1-3	Edmed (pen)	25,000
Feb 11	Portsmouth	L 0-1		17,000
Feb 15	Derby County	W 3-2	Race, Edmed 2	9,069
Feb 25	EVERTON	D 3-3	Hopkin, Bromilow, Hodgson	56,447
Mar 3	BOLTON WANDERERS	W 4-2	Hodgson, Reid 2, Edmed	30.000
Mar 7	Arsenal	L 3-6	Hodgson 2, Race	40,000
Mar 10	Blackburn Rovers	L 1-2	Edmed (pen)	10,000
Mar 17	CARDIFF CITY	L 1-2	Reid	35,000
Mar 24	The Wednesday	L 0-4		25,000
Mar 31	MIDDLESBROUGH	D 1-1	Hodgson	26,840
Apr 6	Burnley	D 2-2	Walsh, Reid	22,000
Apr 7	Huddersfield Town	W 4-2	Reid, Hodgson, Edmed, Walsh	25,000
Apr 14	NEWCASTLE UNITED	D 0-0		33,000
Apr 21	Birmingham	L 0-2		18,000
Apr 25	LEICESTER CITY	D 1-1	Reid	30,000
Apr 28	TOTTENHAM HOTSPUR	W 2-0	Bromilow, Hodgson	30,000
May 5	Manchester United	L 1-6	Hodgson	31,000

FA Cup

Jan 14	DARLINGTON	(Rd3)	W 1-0	Chambers	28,500
Jan 28	Cardiff City	(Rd4)	L 1-2	Edmed (pen)	20,000

League & Cup Appearances

PLAYER	LEAGUE	CUP COMPETITION FA CUP	TOTAL
Bromilow	42	2	44
Chambers	24	2	26
Clark	2		2
Devlin	18		18
Done	4		4
Edmed	42	2	44
Hodgson	32		32
Hopkin	36	2	38
Jackson	40	2	42
Longworth	1		1
Lucas	28	2	30
McBain	10		10
Mackinlay	40	2	42
McMullan	19	1	20
McNab	7	1	8
Morrison	15		15
Murray	2		2
Pither	6		6
Race	11		11
Reid	25	2	27
Riley	25	2	27
Scott E	17		17
Scott T	3		3
Shears	4		4
Walsh	9	2	11

Goalscorers

PLAYER	LEAGUE	CUP COMPETITION FA CUP	TOTAL
Hodgson	23		23
Edmed	14	1	15
Reid	15		15
Devlin	14		14
Chambers	3	1	4
Bromilow	3		3
Hopkin	3		3
Race	2		2
Walsh	2		2
Jackson	1		1
McNab	1		1
Pither	1		1
Scott T	1		1
Opps' o.gs.	1		1

Fact File

Ephraim Longworth, who began his Liverpool career in 1910-11, played his last game on 21 April. In his 371 league and cup games for Liverpool he never scored a goal.

MANAGER: Matt McQueen. George Patterson from February 1928
TOP SCORER: Gordon Hodgson 23 (league)
BIGGEST WIN: 8-2, 1 October 1927, v Portsmouth (H), Division One
HIGHEST ATTENDANCE: 56,447, 25 February 1928, v Everton (H), Division One
TRANSFERS IN: Jimmy McDougall from Partick Thistle, Tommy Morrison from St Mirren
TRANSFERS OUT: Willie Devlin to Hearts, Cyril Oxley to Southend, Danny Shone to West Ham United, Jimmy Walsh to Hull City, Jock McNab and Willie Cockburn to Queens Park Rangers, Harry Chambers to West Bromwich Albion

Final Division One Table

		P	W	D	L	F	A	PTS
1	Everton	42	20	13	9	102	66	53
2	Huddersfield T	42	22	7	13	91	68	51
3	Leicester C	42	18	12	12	96	72	48
4	Derby Co	42	17	10	15	96	83	44
5	Bury	42	20	4	18	80	80	44
6	Cardiff C	42	17	10	15	70	80	44
7	Bolton W	42	16	11	15	81	66	43
8	Aston Villa	42	17	9	16	78	73	43
9	Newcastle United	42	15	13	14	79	81	43
10	Arsenal	42	13	15	14	82	86	41
11	Birmingham	42	13	15	14	70	75	41
12	Blackburn R	42	16	9	17	66	78	41
13	Sheffield U	42	15	10	17	79	86	40
14	The Wednesday	42	13	13	16	81	78	39
15	Sunderland	42	15	9	18	74	76	39
16	Liverpool	42	13	13	16	84	87	39
17	West Ham U	42	14	11	17	81	88	39
18	Manchester U	42	16	7	19	72	80	39
19	Burnley	42	16	7	19	82	98	39
20	Portsmouth	42	16	7	19	66	90	39
21	Tottenham H	42	15	8	19	74	86	38
22	Middlesbrough	42	11	15	16	81	88	37

Season 1928-29

Football League Division One

DATE	OPPONENTS	SCORE	GOALSCORERS	ATTENDANCE
Aug 25	BURY	W 3-0	Miller 2, Whitehurst	40,000
Sep 1	Aston Villa	L 1-3	McDougall	35,000
Sep 5	SHEFFIELD UNITED	L 1-2	Edmed	30,000
Sep 8	LEICESTER CITY	W 6-3	Edmed, Done, McDougall, Reid, Hodgson 2	25,000
Sep 10	Sheffield United	W 3-1	Edmed 2, Reid	20,000
Sep 15	Manchester United	D 2-2	Hodgson, Edmed	18,000
Sep 22	LEEDS UNITED	D 1-1	McDougall	40,000
Sep 29	Everton	L 0-1		60,000
Oct 6	West Ham United	D 1-1	McDougall	25,000
Oct 13	NEWCASTLE UNITED	W 2-1	Hodgson, McDougall	35,000
Oct 20	HUDDERSFIELD TOWN	L 2-3	Edmed 2	30,000
Oct 27	Arsenal	D 4-4	Edmed, Hodgson 3	50,000
Nov 3	BIRMINGHAM	L 1-2	Clark	35,000
Nov 10	Portsmouth	W 1-0	Salisbury	25,000
Nov 17	BOLTON WANDERERS	W 3-0	Hodgson 2, Edmed	30,000
Nov 24	The Wednesday	L 2-3	McDougall, Bromilow	15,000
Dec 1	DERBY COUNTY	W 3-0	Hodgson, McDougall, Clark	30,000
Dec 8	Sunderland	L 1-2	Done	20,851
Dec 15	BLACKBURN ROVERS	D 1-1	Hodgson	35,000
Dec 22	Manchester City	W 3-2	Hodgson 2, Race	20,000
Dec 25	Burnley	L 2-3	Edmed, Clark	35,000
Dec 26	BURNLEY	W 8-0	Clark 2, Edmed 2, Hodgson 3, Salisbury	45,000
Dec 29	Bury	D 2-2	Hodgson 2	25,000
Jan 5	ASTON VILLA	W 4-0	Edmed 2, Clark, Hodgson	40,000
Jan 19	Leicester City	L 0-2		28,000
Feb 2	Leeds United	D 2-2	McDougall, Whitehurst	15,000
Feb 9	EVERTON	L 1-2	Race	55,000
Feb 13	MANCHESTER UNITED	L 2-3	Hodgson, Done (pen)	12,000
Feb 23	Newcastle United	D 2-2	Edmed, Maitland o.g.	45,000
Mar 9	ARSENAL	L 2-4	Hodgson, Edmed	20,000
Mar 13	WEST HAM UNITED	W 2-1	Lindsay, Davidson	16,000
Mar 16	Birmingham	D 0-0		20,000
Mar 29	CARDIFF CITY	W 2-0	Hodgson 2	30,000
Mar 30	Bolton Wanderers	D 0-0		25,000
Apr 1	Cardiff City	W 2-1	Race, Done (pen)	12,000
Apr 6	THE WEDNESDAY	W 3-2	Race, Clark, Hodgson	30,000
Apr 10	Huddersfield Town	W 3-1	Hodgson 2, Wadsworth o.g.	4,000
Apr 13	Derby County	W 5-2	Race 2, Hodgson, Clark 2	11,516
Apr 17	PORTSMOUTH	D 0-0		25,000
Apr 20	SUNDERLAND	W 5-2	Hodgson 2, Race 3	28,000
Apr 27	Blackburn Rovers	L 1-2	Done (pen)	6,000
May 4	MANCHESTER CITY	D 1-1	Hodgson	25,000

FA Cup

Jan 12	Bristol City	(Rd3) W 2-0	Salisbury, Hodgson	28,500
Jan 26	BOLTON WANDERERS	(Rd4) D 0-0		55,055
Jan 30	Bolton Wanderers	(R) L 2-5*	Lindsay, Hodgson	41,808

*After extra time. Score at 90 mins 2-2.

League & Cup Appearances

PLAYER	LEAGUE	CUP COMPETITION FA CUP	TOTAL
Bromilow	28	2	30
Clark	32	3	35
Davidson	36	3	39
Done	37	3	40
Edmed	39	3	42
Gray	1		1
Hodgson	38	3	41
Hopkin	22		22
Jackson	42	3	45
Lindsay	10	2	12
Lucas	5		5
Mackinlay	2		2
McBain	2		2
McDougall	36	3	39
McFarlane	1		1
Miller	3		3
Morrison	42	3	45
Race	13		13
Reid	5	1	6
Riley	20	3	23
Salisbury	16	1	17
Scott	22		22
Shears	2		2
Whitehurst	8		8

Goalscorers

PLAYER	LEAGUE	CUP COMPETITION FA CUP	TOTAL
Hodgson	30	2	32
Edmed	16		16
Clark	9		9
Race	9		9
McDougall	8		8
Done	5		5
Salisbury	2	1	3
Lindsay	1	1	2
Miller	2		2
Reid	2		2
Whitehurst	2		2
Bromilow	1		1
Davidson	1		1
Opps' o.gs.	2		2

Fact File

Don Mackinlay, club captain during the championship season of 1922-23, moved on after 20 seasons during which he played 434 games (scoring 34 goals) and 140 First World War games.

MANAGER: George Patterson
CAPTAIN: Tom Bromilow
TOP SCORER: Gordon Hodgson 32 (30 league)
BIGGEST WIN: 8-0, 26 December 1928, v Burnley (H), Division One
HIGHEST ATTENDANCE: 60,000, 29 September 1928, v Everton (A), Division One
TRANSFERS IN: William Salisbury from Partick Thistle, Albert Whitehurst from Rochdale, Jimmy McDougall from Partick Thistle, Dave Davidson from Forfar Athletic
TRANSFERS OUT: Don Mackinlay to Prescot Cables, W Salisbury to Bangor (Ireland)

Final Division One Table

		P	W	D	L	F	A	Pts
1	The Wednesday	42	21	10	11	86	62	52
2	Leicester C	42	21	9	12	96	67	51
3	Aston Villa	42	23	4	15	98	81	50
4	Sunderland	42	20	7	15	93	75	47
5	Liverpool	42	17	12	13	90	64	46
6	Derby Co	42	18	10	14	86	71	46
7	Blackburn R	42	17	11	14	72	63	45
8	Manchester C	42	18	9	15	95	86	45
9	Arsenal	42	16	13	13	77	72	45
10	Newcastle United	42	19	6	17	70	72	44
11	Sheffield U	42	15	11	16	86	85	41
12	Manchester U	42	14	13	15	66	76	41
13	Leeds U	42	16	9	17	71	84	41
14	Bolton W	42	14	12	16	73	80	40
15	Birmingham	42	15	10	17	68	77	40
16	Huddersfield T	42	14	11	17	70	61	39
17	West Ham U	42	15	9	18	86	96	39
18	Everton	42	17	4	21	63	75	38
19	Burnley	42	15	8	19	81	103	38
20	Portsmouth	42	15	6	21	56	80	36
21	Bury	42	12	7	23	62	99	31
22	Cardiff C	42	8	13	21	43	59	29

Season 1929-30

Football League Division One

DATE	OPPONENTS	SCORE	GOALSCORERS	ATTENDANCE
Aug 31	Middlesbrough	L 0-5		28,286
Sep 4	HUDDERSFIELD TOWN	W 3-0	Clark, Race, Hodgson	33,000
Sep 7	EVERTON	L 0-3		45,600
Sep 14	WEST HAM UNITED	W 3-1	Edmed 2, Lindsay	25,000
Sep 16	Huddersfield Town	L 0-3		12,000
Sep 21	Manchester United	W 2-1	Smith 2	22,000
Sep 28	GRIMSBY TOWN	W 2-0	Hodgson, Race	28,000
Oct 5	Leicester City	L 1-2	Smith	20,000
Oct 9	BLACKBURN ROVERS	D 1-1	Race	20,000
Oct 12	BIRMINGHAM	D 1-1	Smith	25,000
Oct 19	Derby County	D 2-2	Smith, Hodgson	15,840
Oct 26	MANCHESTER CITY	L 1-6	Smith	25,000
Nov 2	Portsmouth	D 3-3	Hodgson, Davidson, Smith	25,000
Nov 9	BOLTON WANDERERS	W 3-0	Race 3	22,000
Nov 16	Aston Villa	W 3-2	Murray, Mort o.g., Smith	23,000
Nov 23	LEEDS UNITED	W 1-0	Smith	30,000
Nov 30	Sheffield Wednesday	L 1-2	Hodgson	25,000
Dec 7	BURNLEY	L 1-3	Hodgson	35,000
Dec 14	Sunderland	W 3-2	Smith, Hopkin, Hodgson.	21,396
Dec 21	ARSENAL	W 1-0	McPherson	40,000
Dec 25	Sheffield United	L 0-4		30,000
Dec 26	SHEFFIELD UNITED	W 2-0	Smith, McPherson	46,000
Dec 28	MIDDLESBROUGH	W 5-2	Edmed, Smith 2, Hopkin 2	23,982
Jan 4	Everton	D 3-3	Edmed, McPherson, McDougall	55,000
Jan 18	West Ham United	L 1-4	Smith	25,000
Jan 25	MANCHESTER UNITED	W 1-0	Race	35,000
Feb 1	Grimsby Town	L 2-3	Smith 2	15,000
Feb 8	LEICESTER CITY	D 1-1	Hodgson	30,000
Feb 15	Birmingham	L 0-1		20,000
Feb 22	DERBY COUNTY	D 2-2	Hodgson 2	30,000
Mar 1	Manchester City	L 3-4	Smith, McPherson, Hodgson	22,000
Mar 8	PORTSMOUTH	W 2-0	Hodgson 2	25,000
Mar 15	Bolton Wanderers	W 2-0	Smith 2	20,000
Mar 25	ASTON VILLA	W 2-0	Gunson, Smith	35,000
Mar 29	Leeds United	D 1-1	Smith	6,000
Apr 2	Arsenal	W 1-0	McPherson	24,000
Apr 5	SHEFFIELD WEDNESDAY	L 1-3	Hodgson	30,000
Apr 12	Burnley	L 1-4	Smith	12,000
Apr 18	Newcastle United	L 1-3	Smith	35,000
Apr 19	SUNDERLAND	L 0-6		30,000
Apr 21	NEWCASTLE UNITED	D 0-0		20,000
May 3	Blackburn Rovers	L 0-1		15,000

FA Cup

Jan 11	CARDIFF CITY	(Rd3) L 1-2	McPherson	50,141

Fact File

James Jackson was nicknamed 'Parson' because he was studying at Liverpool University to become a minister of the church.

MANAGER: George Patterson
CAPTAIN: James Jackson
TOP SCORER: Jimmy Smith 23 (league)
BIGGEST WIN: 5-2, 28 December 1929, v Middlesbrough (H), Division One
HIGHEST ATTENDANCE: 55,000, 4 January 1930, v Everton (A), Division One
TRANSFERS IN: Tom Bradshaw from Bury, Gordon Gunson and David Wright from Sunderland, Jimmy Smith from Ayr
TRANSFERS OUT: John McFarlane to Halifax Town, David Davidson to Newcastle United, John Lindsay to Swansea Town, Henry Race to Manchester City

League & Cup Appearances

PLAYER	LEAGUE	CUP COMPETITION FA CUP	TOTAL
Barton	12		12
Bradshaw	17		17
Bromilow	9		9
Clark	4		4
Davidson	22	1	23
Done	13		13
Edmed	29	1	30
Gardner	5		5
Gunson	10		10
Hodgson	36	1	37
Hopkin	31	1	32
Jackson	40	1	41
Lindsay	4		4
Lucas	31	1	32
McDougall	34	1	35
McFarlane	1		1
McPherson	25	1	26
Morrison	36	1	37
Murray	2		2
Race	19		19
Riley	34	1	35
Scott A	1		1
Scott E	8		8
Smith	37	1	38
Thompson	1		1
Wright	1		1

Goalscorers

PLAYER	LEAGUE	CUP COMPETITION FA CUP	TOTAL
Smith	23		23
Hodgson	14		14
Race	7		7
McPherson	5	1	6
Edmed	4		4
Hopkin	3		3
Clark	1		1
Davidson	1		1
Gardner	1		1
Lindsay	1		1
McDougall	1		1
Murray	1		1
Opps' o.gs.	1		1

Final Division One Table

		P	W	D	L	F	A	PTS
1	SHEFFIELD W	42	26	8	8	105	57	60
2	DERBY CO	42	21	8	13	90	82	50
3	MANCHESTER C	42	19	9	14	91	81	47
4	ASTON VILLA	42	21	5	16	92	83	47
5	LEEDS U	42	20	6	16	79	63	46
6	BLACKBURN R	42	19	7	16	99	93	45
7	WEST HAM U	42	19	5	18	86	79	43
8	LEICESTER C	42	17	9	16	86	90	43
9	SUNDERLAND	42	18	7	17	76	80	43
10	HUDDERSFIELD T	42	17	9	16	63	69	43
11	BIRMINGHAM	42	16	9	17	67	62	41
12	LIVERPOOL	42	16	9	17	63	79	41
13	PORTSMOUTH	42	15	10	17	66	62	40
14	ARSENAL	42	14	11	17	78	66	39
15	BOLTON W	42	15	9	18	74	74	39
16	MIDDLESBROUGH	42	16	6	20	82	84	38
17	MANCHESTER U	42	15	8	19	67	88	38
18	GRIMSBY T	42	15	7	20	73	89	37
19	NEWCASTLE UNITED	42	15	7	20	71	92	37
20	SHEFFIELD U	42	15	6	21	91	96	36
21	BURNLEY	42	14	8	20	79	97	36
22	EVERTON	42	12	11	19	80	92	35

Season 1930-31

Football League Division One

DATE	OPPONENTS	SCORE	GOALSCORERS	ATTENDANCE
Aug 30	BLACKBURN ROVERS	W 2-1	Smith 2	35,000
Sep 1	West Ham United	L 0-7		28,000
Sep 6	Middlesbrough	D 3-3	Done (pen), Hodgson, Edmed	16,816
Sep 10	BOLTON WANDERERS	W 7-2	McPherson 2, Edmed 2, Smith, Hodgson 2	30,000
Sep 13	HUDDERSFIELD TOWN	L 1-4	Smith	35,000
Sep 20	Aston Villa	L 2-4	Hodgson 2	34,000
Sep 27	CHELSEA	W 3-1	Hodgson 3	30,000
Oct 4	Newcastle United	W 4-0	Smith 2, Hodgson, Edmed	30,000
Oct 11	SHEFFIELD WEDNESDAY	L 1-2	Hodgson	30,000
Oct 18	LEEDS UNITED	W 2-0	Hodgson 2	30,000
Oct 25	Blackpool	W 3-1	Smith 3	15,000
Nov 1	MANCHESTER CITY	L 0-2		25,000
Nov 8	Derby County	D 2-2	Hodgson, McPherson	14,966
Nov 15	LEICESTER CITY	W 3-1	Smith 2, Black o.g.	20,000
Nov 22	Portsmouth	L 0-4		18,000
Nov 29	SHEFFIELD UNITED	W 6-1	Hodgson 3, McPherson 2, Smith	25,000
Dec 6	Sunderland	L 5-6	Hopkin, Hodgson, McRorie, Smith 2	22,616
Dec 13	ARSENAL	D 1-1	Morrison	50,000
Dec 20	Birmingham	L 0-2		18,000
Dec 25	Grimsby Town	D 0-0		20,000
Dec 26	GRIMSBY TOWN	D 1-1	McPherson	30,000
Dec 27	Blackburn Rovers	D 3-3	Hodgson 2, Scott A	20,000
Jan 3	MIDDLESBROUGH	W 3-1	Hodgson 2, Done	21,133
Jan 14	Bolton Wanderers	L 0-2		9,000
Jan 17	Huddersfield Town	L 1-2	McPherson	10,000
Jan 24	ASTON VILLA	D 1-1	Hodgson	30,000
Jan 31	Chelsea	D 2-2	Hodgson, Gunson	40,000
Feb 7	NEWCASTLE UNITED	W 4-2	Wright 3, Barton	30,000
Feb 14	Sheffield Wednesday	W 5-3	Wright, Hodgson 4 (1 pen)	25,000
Feb 21	Leeds United	W 2-1	Wright, Hodgson	15,000
Feb 28	BLACKPOOL	W 5-2	McPherson 2, Hodgson 3 (1 pen)	15,000
Mar 7	Manchester City	D 1-1	Hodgson	18,000
Mar 14	DERBY COUNTY	D 0-0		30,000
Mar 21	Leicester City	L 2-3	Barton 2	15,000
Mar 28	PORTSMOUTH	W 3-1	McDougall, Clark, Wright	20,000
Apr 3	MANCHESTER UNITED	D 1-1	Hodgson	27,000
Apr 4	Sheffield United	L 1-4	Barton	12,000
Apr 6	Manchester United	L 1-4	Scott A	8,000
Apr 11	SUNDERLAND	L 2-4	McPherson, Hodgson (pen)	30,000
Apr 15	BIRMINGHAM	D 0-0		28,000
Apr 18	Arsenal	L 1-3	Roberts o.g.	45,000
May 2	WEST HAM UNITED	W 2-0	Hodgson 2	25,000

FA Cup

Jan 10	BIRMINGHAM	(Rd3) L 0-2		40,500

League & Cup Appearances

PLAYER	LEAGUE	CUP COMPETITION FA CUP	TOTAL
Aitken	1		1
Barkas	4		4
Barton	26		26
Bradshaw	35	1	36
Clark	1		1
Done	14		14
Edmed	12		12
Gunson	8	1	9
Hodgson	40	1	41
Hopkin	36	1	37
Ireland	1		1
Jackson	28	1	29
James	7		7
Lucas	42	1	43
McDougall	40		40
McPherson	42	1	43
McRorie	3		3
Morrison	39	1	40
Riley	27	1	28
Scott A	2	1	3
Scott E	14		14
Smith	21		21
Thompson	4	1	5
Wright	15		15

Goalscorers

PLAYER	LEAGUE	CUP COMPETITION FA CUP	TOTAL
Hodgson	36		36
Smith	14		14
McPherson	10		10
Wright	6		6
Barton	4		4
Edmed	4		4
Done	2		2
Scott A	2		2
Clark	1		1
Gunson	1		1
Hopkin	1		1
McDougall	1		1
McRorie	1		1
Morrison	1		1
Opps' o.gs.	2		2

Fact File

Top scorer, South African Gordon Hodgson, beat the previous league record score of 31 goals in a season set by Sam Raybould and went on to head the list for four more seasons and create club scoring records that lasted until the late 1960s.

MANAGER: George Patterson
CAPTAIN: Tom Morrison
TOP SCORER: Gordon Hodgson 36 (league)
BIGGEST WIN: 7-2, 10 September 1930, v Bolton Wanderers (H), Division One
HIGHEST ATTENDANCE: 50,000, 13 December 1930, v Arsenal (H), Division One
TRANSFERS IN: Daniel McRorie from Morton
TRANSFERS OUT: Fred Hopkin to Darlington, R Clark to Nottingham Forest, Bobby Ireland to St. Johnstone

Final Division One Table

		P	W	D	L	F	A	Pts
1	Arsenal	42	28	10	4	127	59	66
2	Aston Villa	42	25	9	8	128	78	59
3	Sheffield W	42	22	8	12	102	75	52
4	Portsmouth	42	18	13	11	84	67	49
5	Huddersfield T	42	18	12	12	81	65	48
6	Derby Co	42	18	10	14	94	79	46
7	Middlesbrough	42	19	8	15	98	90	46
8	Manchester C	42	18	10	14	75	70	46
9	Liverpool	42	15	12	15	86	85	42
10	Blackburn R	42	17	8	17	83	84	42
11	Sunderland	42	16	9	17	89	85	41
12	Chelsea	42	15	10	17	64	67	40
13	Grimsby T	42	17	5	20	82	87	39
14	Bolton W	42	15	9	18	68	81	39
15	Sheffield U	42	14	10	18	78	84	38
16	Leicester C	42	16	6	20	80	95	38
17	Newcastle United	42	15	6	21	78	87	36
18	West Ham U	42	14	8	20	79	94	36
19	Birmingham	42	13	10	19	55	70	36
20	Blackpool	42	11	10	21	71	125	32
21	Leeds U	42	12	7	23	68	81	31
22	Manchester U	42	7	8	27	53	115	22

Season 1931-32

Football League Division One

DATE	OPPONENTS	SCORE	GOALSCORERS	ATTENDANCE
Aug 29	Newcastle United	W 1-0	Hodgson	36,000
Sep 2	BOLTON WANDERERS	D 2-2	Wright 2	30,000
Sep 5	ASTON VILLA	W 2-0	Wright 2	40,000
Sep 9	Middlesbrough	L 1-4	Wright	15,042
Sep 12	Leicester City	L 1-2	Gunson	15,000
Sep 16	MIDDLESBROUGH	W 7-2	Gunson, Barton 2, Hodgson 2, Smith, Morrison	20,854
Sep 19	EVERTON	L 1-3	Wright	55,000
Sep 26	GRIMSBY TOWN	W 4-0	Hodgson 2, Savage 2	30,000
Oct 3	Chelsea	L 0-2		30,000
Oct 10	WEST HAM UNITED	D 2-2	Gunson, Wright	25,000
Oct 17	West Bromwich Albion	W 2-1	Hodgson, Gunson	30,000
Oct 24	BLACKPOOL	W 3-2	Gunson, Hodgson, Ramsey o.g.	25,000
Oct 31	Sheffield United	L 0-3		20,000
Nov 7	BLACKBURN ROVERS	W 4-2	Barton 2, Gunson, Hodgson	25,000
Nov 14	Sunderland	W 3-1	Wright 2, Hodgson	17,646
Nov 21	MANCHESTER CITY	W 4-3	McPherson, Hodgson, Done 2 (1 pen)	30,000
Nov 28	Arsenal	L 0-6		35,000
Dec 5	BIRMINGHAM	W 4-3	Hodgson, Wright, Gunson, McRorie	25,000
Dec 12	Portsmouth	L 0-2		16,000
Dec 19	DERBY COUNTY	D 1-1	Hodgson	25,000
Dec 25	SHEFFIELD WEDNESDAY	W 3-1	Gunson 2, Barton	35,000
Dec 26	Sheffield Wednesday	D 1-1	McPherson	35,000
Jan 2	NEWCASTLE UNITED	W 4-2	Barton 2, Gunson, Hodgson	28,000
Jan 16	Aston Villa	L 1-6	Barton	25,000
Jan 27	LEICESTER CITY	D 3-3	Hodgson, McRorie, Gunson	30,000
Jan 30	Everton	L 1-2	Wright	50,000
Feb 6	Grimsby Town	L 1-5	Done	17,000
Feb 20	West Ham United	L 0-1		18,000
Mar 2	WEST BROMWICH ALBION	W 4-1	Hodgson 3, Gunson	23,000
Mar 5	Blackpool	D 2-2	Wright, Hodgson	15,000
Mar 12	SHEFFIELD UNITED	W 2-1	Gunson, Hodgson (pen)	30,000
Mar 19	Blackburn Rovers	W 3-1	Hodgson, Gunson 2	10,000
Mar 26	SUNDERLAND	L 1-2	Hodgson	25,000
Mar 28	HUDDERSFIELD TOWN	L 0-3		28,000
Mar 29	Huddersfield Town	L 3-4	Hodgson 2, Wright	12,000
Apr 2	Manchester City	W 1-0	Gunson	20,000
Apr 6	CHELSEA	W 2-1	Hodgson, Hancock	38,000
Apr 9	ARSENAL	W 2-1	Hancock, McRorie	40,000
Apr 16	Birmingham	L 1-3	Gunson (pen)	10,000
Apr 23	PORTSMOUTH	L 1-3	McRorie	20,000
Apr 30	Derby County	W 2-1	Hodgson 2	12,000
May 7	Bolton Wanderers	L 1-8	McRorie	8,000

FA Cup

Jan 9	Everton	(Rd3) W 2-1	Gunson, Hodgson	57,090
Jan 23	Chesterfield	(Rd4) W 4-2	Barton 4	28,393
Feb 13	GRIMSBY TOWN	(Rd5) W 1-0	Gunson	49,479
Feb 27	CHELSEA	(Rd6) L 0-2		57,804

League & Cup Appearances

PLAYER	LEAGUE	CUP COMPETITION FA CUP	TOTAL
Barkas	1		1
Barton	24	4	28
Bradshaw	42	4	46
Bruton	1	1	2
Charlton	3		3
Done	26		26
Gunson	42	4	46
Hancock	9		9
Henderson	5		5
Hodgson	39	4	43
Jackson	17	3	20
Lucas	16	1	17
McDougall	39	4	43
McPherson	28	1	29
McRorie	25	2	27
Morrison	35	4	39
Riley	5		5
Roberts	1		1
Savage	7		7
Scott	37	4	41
Smith	3		3
Steel	22	4	26
Wright	35	4	39

Goalscorers

PLAYER	LEAGUE	CUP COMPETITION FA CUP	TOTAL
Hodgson	26	1	27
Gunson	17	2	19
Wright	13		13
Barton	8	4	12
McRorie	5		5
Done	3		3
Hancock	2		2
McPherson	2		2
Savage	2		2
Morrison	1		1
Smith	1		1
Opps' o.gs.	1		1

Fact File

Harold Barton was the first Liverpool player to score four goals in an FA Cup tie on 23 January against Chesterfield.

MANAGER: George Patterson
CAPTAIN: Tom Bradshaw
TOP SCORER: Gordon Hodgson 27 (26 league)
BIGGEST WIN: 7-2, 16 September 1931, v Middlesbrough (H), Division One
HIGHEST ATTENDANCE: 57,804, 27 February 1932, v Chelsea (H), FA Cup
TRANSFERS IN: Willie Steel from St. Johnstone, Ted Savage from Lincoln City, Alf Hanson from local league football
TRANSFERS OUT: Richard Edmed to Bolton Wanderers, Jimmy Smith to Tunbridge Wells Rangers

Final Division One Table

		P	W	D	L	F	A	Pts
1	Everton	42	26	4	12	116	64	56
2	Arsenal	42	22	10	10	90	48	54
3	Sheffield W	42	22	6	14	96	82	50
4	Huddersfield T	42	19	10	13	80	63	48
5	Aston Villa	42	19	8	15	104	72	46
6	WBA	42	20	6	16	77	55	46
7	Sheffield U	42	20	6	16	80	75	46
8	Portsmouth	42	19	7	16	62	62	45
9	Birmingham	42	18	8	16	78	67	44
10	Liverpool	42	19	6	17	81	93	44
11	Newcastle United	42	18	6	18	80	87	42
12	Chelsea	42	16	8	18	69	73	40
13	Sunderland	42	15	10	17	67	73	40
14	Manchester C	42	13	12	17	83	73	38
15	Derby Co	42	14	10	18	71	75	38
16	Blackburn R	42	16	6	20	89	95	38
17	Bolton W	42	17	4	21	72	80	38
18	Middlesbrough	42	15	8	19	64	89	38
19	Leicester C	42	15	7	20	74	94	37
20	Blackpool	42	12	9	21	65	102	33
21	Grimsby T	42	13	6	23	67	98	32
22	West Ham U	42	12	7	23	62	107	31

Season 1932-33

Football League Division One

DATE	OPPONENTS	SCORE	GOALSCORERS	ATTENDANCE
Aug 27	WOLVERHAMPTON WANDERERS	W 5-1	Hodgson, Wright, Gunson, Crawford 2	45,000
Aug 29	Sheffield United	L 2-6	Gunson, Crawford	25,000
Sep 3	Newcastle United	L 3-4	Hodgson (pen), Crawford, Bradshaw	26,000
Sep 7	SHEFFIELD UNITED	D 2-2	Wright 2	18,000
Sep 10	ASTON VILLA	D 0-0		40,000
Sep 17	Middlesbrough	W 1-0	Gunson	11,371
Sep 24	BOLTON WANDERERS	L 0-1		30,000
Oct 1	Everton	L 1-3	Gunson	46,000
Oct 8	Leicester City	W 2-1	Roberts, Hodgson	15,000
Oct 15	PORTSMOUTH	W 4-3	Wright, Hodgson 3	25,000
Oct 22	ARSENAL	L 2-3	Wright, Hodgson	40,000
Oct 29	Manchester City	D 1-1	McPherson	10,000
Nov 5	LEEDS UNITED	L 0-1		30,000
Nov 12	Blackburn Rovers	D 2-2	Hodgson, Wright.	12,000
Nov 19	DERBY COUNTY	W 6-1	Collins o.g., Hodgson 3, Wright, Roberts	30,000
Nov 26	Blackpool	L 1-4	Wright	12,000
Dec 3	SUNDERLAND	D 3-3	Wright, Barton, Roberts	20,000
Dec 10	Birmingham	L 0-3		12,000
Dec 17	WEST BROMWICH ALBION	W 2-0	Hodgson, Barton	20,000
Dec 24	Sheffield Wednesday	L 0-3		14,000
Dec 26	CHELSEA	W 3-0	Bradshaw, Barton, Gunson	38,000
Dec 27	Chelsea	W 2-0	Bruton, Barton	40,000
Dec 31	Wolverhampton Wanderers	L 1-3	Barton	19,540
Jan 7	NEWCASTLE UNITED	W 3-0	Hodgson 2 (I pen), Wright	25,000
Jan 21	Aston Villa	L 2-5	Hodgson, Roberts	25,000
Feb 1	MIDDLESBROUGH	L 1-3	Hanson	9,973
Feb 4	Bolton Wanderers	D 3-3	Taylor, Barton, Done (pen)	12,000
Feb 11	EVERTON	W 7-4	Barton 3, Hanson, Morrison, Taylor, Roberts	50,000
Feb 18	LEICESTER CITY	L 1-2	Roberts	15,000
Feb 25	Portsmouth	L 1-2	Barton	5,000
Mar 4	Arsenal	W 1-0	Hodgson	47,000
Mar 11	Manchester City	D 1-1	Hodgson (pen)	35,000
Mar 18	Leeds United	L 0-5		10,000
Mar 25	BLACKBURN ROVERS	D 2-2	Hodgson, Barton	20,000
Apr 1	Derby County	D 1-1	Barton	7,200
Apr 8	BLACKPOOL	W 4-3	Hodgson 3, Wright	15,000
Apr 14	HUDDESFIELD TOWN	D 2-2	Barton, Wright	35,000
Apr 15	Sunderland	D 0-0		8,725
Apr 18	Huddersfield Town	L 1-3	Jackson	8,000
Apr 22	BIRMINGHAM	W 1-0	Hodgson	15,000
Apr 29	West Bromwich Albion	L 1-2	Bradshaw	12,000
May 6	SHEFFIELD WEDNESDAY	W 4-1	Wright 2, Hodgson 2	15,000

FA Cup

Jan 14	West Bromwich Albion	(Rd3) L 0-2		29,170

League & Cup Appearances

PLAYER	LEAGUE	CUP COMPETITION FA CUP	TOTAL
Barton	35	1	36
Bradshaw	39	1	40
Bruton	5	1	6
Crawford	8		8
Done	29	1	30
Gunson	21	1	22
Hancock	1		1
Hanson	11		11
Hodgson	37	1	38
Jackson	14		14
James	1		1
Lucas	3		3
McDougall	25	1	26
McPherson	24		24
McRorie	5		5
Morrison	32	1	33
Riley	15		15
Roberts	25		25
Savage	11		11
Scott	27	1	28
Steel	42	1	43
Taylor	22		22
Wright	30	1	31

Goalscorers

PLAYER	LEAGUE	CUP COMPETITION FA CUP	TOTAL
Hodgson	24		24
Wright	14		14
Barton	13		13
Roberts	6		6
Gunson	5		5
Crawford	4		4
Bradshaw	3		3
Hanson	2		2
Taylor	2		2
Bruton	1		1
Done	1		1
Jackson	1		1
McPherson	1		1
Morrison	1		1
Opps' o.gs.	1		1

Final Division One Table

		P	W	D	L	F	A	Pts
1	Arsenal	42	25	8	9	118	61	58
2	Aston Villa	42	23	8	11	92	67	54
3	Sheffield W	42	21	9	12	80	68	51
4	WBA	42	20	9	13	83	70	49
5	Newcastle United	42	22	5	15	71	63	49
6	Huddersfield T	42	18	11	13	66	53	47
7	Derby Co	42	15	14	13	76	69	44
8	Leeds U	42	15	14	13	59	62	44
9	Portsmouth	42	18	7	17	74	76	43
10	Sheffield U	42	17	9	16	74	80	43
11	Everton	42	16	9	17	81	74	41
12	Sunderland	42	15	10	17	63	80	40
13	Birmingham	42	14	11	17	57	57	39
14	Liverpool	42	14	11	17	79	84	39
15	Blackburn R	42	14	10	18	76	102	38
16	Manchester C	42	16	5	21	68	71	37
17	Middlesbrough	42	14	9	19	63	73	37
18	Chelsea	42	14	7	21	63	73	35
19	Leicester C	42	11	13	18	75	89	35
20	Wolverhampton W	42	13	9	20	80	96	35
21	Bolton W	42	12	9	21	78	92	33
22	Blackpool	42	14	5	23	69	85	33

Fact File

Ted Savage, a wing half, represented Great Britain as a sprinter in the 1928 Olympic Games in Amsterdam when he was just 17 years old.

MANAGER: George Patterson

CAPTAIN: Tom Bradshaw

TOP SCORER: Gordon Hodgson 24 (league)

BIGGEST WIN: 7-4, 11 February 1933, v Everton (H); 6-1, 19 November 1932, v Derby County (H), both Division One

HIGHEST ATTENDANCE: 50,000, 11 February 1933, v Everton (H), Division One

TRANSFERS IN: Harold Taylor from Stoke City

TRANSFERS OUT: Tommy Lucas and Edmund Crawford to Clapton Orient

Season 1933-34

Football League Division One

DATE	OPPONENTS	SCORE	GOALSCORERS	ATTENDANCE
Aug 26	Wolverhampton Wanderers	L 2-3	Wright D, Hodgson (pen)	30,000
Aug 30	STOKE CITY	D 1-1	English	40,000
Sep 2	SHEFFIELD UNITED	W 3-2	English, Hodgson 2	35,000
Sep 4	Stoke City	D 1-1	Taylor	28,000
Sep 9	Aston Villa	L 2-4	Hodgson, English	30,000
Sep 16	LEICESTER CITY	L 1-3	Hanson	25,000
Sep 23	Tottenham Hotspur	W 3-0	English 2, Hanson	33,716
Sep 30	EVERTON	W 3-2	Nieuwenhuys, Hanson, English	54,800
Oct 7	CHELSEA	W 3-0	Wright D, Hodgson, English	35,000
Oct 14	Sunderland	L 1-4	English	25,321
Oct 21	Middlesbrough	L 1-4	English	10,899
Oct 28	BLACKBURN ROVERS	W 4-0	Hanson, Nieuwenhuys, Hodgson (pen), Roberts S	20,000
Nov 4	Birmingham	W 2-1	English, Hodgson	15,000
Nov 11	LEEDS UNITED	W 4-3	Done, English 2, Hanson	30,000
Nov 18	Derby County	L 1-3	English	15,733
Nov 25	WEST BROMWICH ALBION	D 1-1	English	35,000
Dec 2	Arsenal	L 1-2	English	38,362
Dec 9	SHEFFIELD WEDNESDAY	L 1-3	Hanson	25,000
Dec 16	Manchester City	L 1-2	Nieuwenhuys	15,000
Dec 23	NEWCASTLE UNITED	L 1-2	Nieuwenhuys	30,000
Dec 25	PORTSMOUTH	D 2-2	Hanson, English	30,000
Dec 26	Portsmouth	L 0-1		23,000
Dec 30	WOLVERHAMPTON WANDERERS	D 1-1	Hanson	30,000
Jan 1	Newcastle United	L 2-9	Taylor, Betton o.g.	18,000
Jan 6	Sheffield United	D 2-2	Roberts S, Hanson	12,000
Jan 20	ASTON VILLA	L 2-3	Roberts S, Done	40,000
Feb 1	Leicester City	L 0-1		15,000
Feb 3	TOTTENHAM HOTSPUR	W 3-1	Hodgson (pen), Nieuwenhuys 2	30,000
Feb 10	Everton	D 0-0		50,000
Feb 21	Chelsea	L 0-2		15,000
Feb 24	SUNDERLAND	D 1-1	Morrison	20,000
Mar 3	MIDDLESBROUGH	W 6-2	Hodgson 3, English 2, Taylor	25,946
Mar 10	Blackburn Rovers	L 1-3	Hodgson	8,000
Mar 17	BIRMINGHAM	W 4-1	Hodgson 4	40,000
Mar 24	Leeds United	L 1-5	Hodgson	13,000
Mar 30	HUDDERSFIELD TOWN	D 2-2	Johnson, Hanson.	35,000
Mar 31	DERBY COUNTY	W 4-2	Nieuwenhuys 2, Johnson, Hodgson	35,000
Apr 3	Huddersfield Town	W 2-0	Hodgson, Nieuwenhuys	26,700
Apr 7	West Bromwich Albion	D 2-2	Wright V, Hodgson	16,000
Apr 14	ARSENAL	L 2-3	Wright V, Hodgson	40,000
Apr 21	Sheffield Wednesday	W 2-1	Hodgson (pen), Hanson	18,000
May 2	MANCHESTER CITY	W 3-2	Hanson, Hodgson 2	16,000

FA Cup

Jan 13	FULHAM	(Rd3)	D 1-1	Hodgson.	45,619
Jan 17	Fulham	(R)	W 3-2*	Hanson, Bradshaw, Roberts S	28,319
Jan 27	Tranmere Rovers**	(Rd4)	W 3-1	English 2, Nieuwenhuys	61,036
Feb 17	BOLTON WANDERERS	(Rd5)	L 0-3		54,912

* After extra time. Score at 90 mins 2-2.

** Tranmere drawn at home but agreed to play at Anfield.

League & Cup Appearances

PLAYER	LEAGUE	CUP COMPETITION FA CUP	TOTAL
Barton	6	1	7
Blenkinsop	9		9
Bradshaw	39	4	43
Bush	2		2
Carr	2		2
Dabbs	1		1
Done	21	4	25
English	28	3	31
Hanson	36	3	39
Hodgson	37	3	40
Johnson	11		11
McDougall	32	4	36
McPherson	9		9
Morrison	33	4	37
Nieuwenhuys	34	4	38
Riley	32		32
Roberts J	1		1
Roberts S	13	2	15
Savage	15		15
Scott E	10	4	14
Steel W	40	3	43
Taylor	19	2	21
Tennant	13	1	14
Wright D	12	2	14
Wright V	7		7

Goalscorers

PLAYER	LEAGUE	CUP COMPETITION FA CUP	TOTAL
Hodgson	24	1	25
English	18	2	20
Hanson	12	1	13
Nieuwenhuys	9	1	10
Roberts S	3	1	4
Taylor	3		3
Done	2		2
Johnson	2		2
Wright D	2		2
Wright V	2		2
Bradshaw		1	1
Morrison	1		1
Opps' o.gs.	1		1

Fact File

Long serving goalkeeper, Elisha Scott returned to Belfast as player/manager of Belfast Celtic. In his 467 league and cup games since 1912-13 he kept 138 clean sheets.

MANAGER: George Patterson
CAPTAIN: Tom Bradshaw
TOP SCORER: Gordon Hodgson 25 (24 league)
BIGGEST WIN: 6-2, 3 March 1934, v Middlesbrough (H), Division One
HIGHEST ATTENDANCE: 61,036, 27 January 1934, v Tranmere Rovers (at Anfield), FA Cup
TRANSFERS IN: Ernie Blenkinsop from Sheffield Wednesday, Ben Dabbs from Birmingham (local league), Sam English from Glasgow Rangers, Tommy Johnson from Everton, John Tennant from Torquay
TRANSFERS OUT: George Gunson to Swindon Town, Dan McRorie to Rochdale

Final Division One Table

		P	W	D	L	F	A	Pts
1	Arsenal	42	25	9	8	75	47	59
2	Huddersfield T	42	23	10	9	90	61	56
3	Tottenham H	42	21	7	14	79	56	49
4	Derby Co	42	17	11	14	68	54	45
5	Manchester C	42	17	11	14	65	72	45
6	Sunderland	42	16	12	14	81	56	44
7	WBA	42	17	10	15	78	70	44
8	Blackburn R	42	18	7	17	74	81	43
9	Leeds U	42	17	8	17	75	66	42
10	Portsmouth	42	15	12	15	52	55	42
11	Sheffield W	42	16	9	17	62	67	41
12	Stoke C	42	15	11	16	58	71	41
13	Aston Villa	42	14	12	16	78	75	40
14	Everton	42	12	16	14	62	63	40
15	Wolverhampton W	42	14	12	16	74	86	40
16	Middlesbrough	42	15	7	19	68	80	39
17	Leicester C	42	14	11	17	59	74	39
18	Liverpool	42	14	10	18	79	87	38
19	Chelsea	42	14	8	20	67	69	36
20	Birmingham	42	12	12	18	54	56	36
21	Newcastle United	42	10	14	18	68	77	34
22	Sheffield U	42	12	7	23	58	101	31

Season 1934-35

Football League Division One

DATE	OPPONENTS	SCORE	GOALSCORERS	ATTENDANCE
Aug 25	BLACKBURN ROVERS	W 2-0	Wright 2	35,000
Aug 29	Manchester City	L 1-3	Hodgson	18,000
Sep 1	Arsenal	L 1-8	Hanson	57,000
Sep 5	MANCHESTER CITY	W 2-1	English, Hodgson	32,000
Sep 8	PORTSMOUTH	L 0-1		30,000
Sep 15	Everton	L 0-1		45,000
Sep 22	Leeds United	W 3-0	Hodgson, Hanson 2	10,900
Sep 29	WEST BROMWICH ALBION	W 3-2	Hanson, English, Hodgson	20,000
Oct 6	Sheffield Wednesday	L 1-4	Hodgson	15,000
Oct 13	BIRMINGHAM	W 5-4	Wright, McDougall, English, Hodgson 2 (1 pen)	20,000
Oct 20	GRIMSBY TOWN	D 1-1	Wright	35,000
Oct 27	Preston North End	D 2-2	Hodgson, Wright	15,000
Nov 3	WOLVERHAMPTON WANDERERS	W 2-1	Wright, Hodgson	20,000
Nov 10	Huddersfield Town	L 0-8		13,000
Nov 17	LEICESTER CITY	W 5-1	Hodgson 3, Wright, Taylor	20,000
Nov 24	Derby County	W 2-1	Wright 2	17,349
Dec 1	ASTON VILLA	W 3-1	Hodgson 2, Johnson	20,000
Dec 8	Chelsea	L 1-4	Wright	30,000
Dec 15	TOTTENHAM HOTSPUR	W 4-1	Hodgson 2, Nieuwenhuys, Wright	20,000
Dec 22	Sunderland	W 3-2	Wright 2, Hanson	24,317
Dec 26	MIDDLESBROUGH	D 2-2	Nieuwenhuys, Roberts	45,936
Dec 29	Blackburn Rovers	W 2-0	Nieuwenhuys, English	15,000
Jan 1	Middlesbrough	L 0-2		19,436
Jan 5	ARSENAL	L 0-2		56,700
Jan 19	Portsmouth	W 2-1	Hodgson, Wright	15,000
Feb 2	LEEDS UNITED	W 4-2	Hodgson 3, Hanson	25,000
Feb 9	West Bromwich Albion	D 1-1	Shaw o.g.	18,000
Feb 20	SHEFFIELD WEDNESDAY	L 1-2	Hanson	16,000
Feb 23	Birmingham	W 3-1	English, Hodgson 2	25,000
Mar 2	Grimsby Town	L 2-3	English, Hodgson	12,000
Mar 9	PRESTON NORTH END	D 0-0		30,000
Mar 16	Wolverhampton Wanderers	L 3-5	Hodgson (pen), Hanson, Wright	20,000
Mar 20	EVERTON	W 2-1	Hodgson 2 (1 pen)	32,000
Mar 23	HUDDERSFIELD TOWN	W 3-2	Johnson 2, Hodgson (pen)	18,000
Mar 30	Leicester City	L 1-3	Johnson	25,000
Apr 6	DERBY COUNTY	L 1-3	Nieuwenhuys	20,000
Apr 13	Aston Villa	L 2-4	Howe, Nieuwenhuys	20,000
Apr 19	STOKE CITY	W 5-0	Wright 2, Carr, Nieuwenhuys, Howe	25,000
Apr 20	CHELSEA	W 6-0	Wright 2, Nieuwenhuys 2, Howe, Carr	15,000
Apr 22	Stoke City	D 1-1	Nieuwenhuys	18,000
Apr 27	Tottenham Hotspur	L 1-5	Nieuwenhuys	16,129
May 4	SUNDERLAND	D 2-2	Johnson, Hanson	20,000

FA Cup

Jan 12	Yeovil & Petters	(Rd3)	W 6-2	Nieuwenhuys, Wright, Hodgson 2, Roberts 2	13,000
Jan 26	Blackburn Rovers	(Rd4)	L 0-1		49,546

League & Cup Appearances

PLAYER	LEAGUE	CUP COMPETITION FA CUP	TOTAL
Blenkinsop	16		16
Bradshaw	31	2	33
Browning	3		3
Carr	8		8
Cooper	23	2	25
Dabbs	2		2
Done	1		1
English	19		19
Hanson	35	2	37
Hodgson	34	2	36
Howe	6		6
Johnson	19		19
Kane	3		3
Low	11		11
McDougall	38	2	40
McPherson	2		2
Morrison	8		8
Nieuwenhuys	29	2	31
Riley	39	2	41
Roberts	11	2	13
Rogers	5		5
Savage	27	2	29
Steel	16		16
Taylor	14		14
Tennant	26	2	28
Wright	36	2	38

Goalscorers

PLAYER	LEAGUE	CUP COMPETITION FA CUP	TOTAL
Hodgson	27	2	29
Wright	19	1	20
Nieuwenhuys	10	1	11
Hanson	9		9
English	6		6
Johnson	5		5
Howe	3		3
Roberts	1	2	3
Carr L	2		2
McDougall	1		1
Taylor	1		1
Opps' o.gs.	1		1

Fact File

Gordon Hodgson scored his 200th league goal on 22 September 1934 in the match against Leeds United. In 377 league and cup appearances he scored a total of 241 goals and still remains in third place in the club's all-time scoring list. He scored his 17th hat-trick on 2 February 1935 also against Leeds United; this remains a club record.

MANAGER: George Patterson
CAPTAIN: Ernie Blenkinsop/Tom Cooper
TOP SCORER: Gordon Hodgson 29 (27 league)
BIGGEST WIN: 6-0, 20 April 1935, v Chelsea (H), Division One
HIGHEST ATTENDANCE: 57,000, 1 September 1934, v Arsenal (A), Division One
TRANSFERS IN: John Browning from Dunoon Athletic, Tom Cooper from Derby County, Fred Howe from Hyde United, Norman Low (amateur) from Newcastle United
TRANSFERS OUT: David Wright to Hull City, Harold Barton to Sheffield United

Final Division One Table

		P	W	D	L	F	A	Pts
1	Arsenal	42	23	12	7	115	46	58
2	Sunderland	42	19	16	7	90	51	54
3	Sheffield W	42	18	13	11	70	64	49
4	Manchester C	42	20	8	14	82	67	48
5	Grimsby T	42	17	11	14	78	60	45
6	Derby Co	42	18	9	15	81	66	45
7	Liverpool	42	19	7	16	85	88	45
8	Everton	42	16	12	14	89	88	44
9	WBA	42	17	10	15	83	83	44
10	Stoke C	42	18	6	18	71	70	42
11	Preston NE	42	15	12	15	62	67	42
12	Chelsea	42	16	9	17	73	82	41
13	Aston Villa	42	14	13	15	74	88	41
14	Portsmouth	42	15	10	17	71	72	40
15	Blackburn R	42	14	11	17	66	78	39
16	Huddersfield T	42	14	10	18	76	71	38
17	Wolverhampton W	42	15	8	19	88	94	38
18	Leeds U	42	13	12	17	75	92	38
19	Birmingham	42	13	10	19	63	81	36
20	Middlesbrough	42	10	14	18	70	90	34
21	Leicester C	42	12	9	21	61	86	33
22	Tottenham H	42	10	10	22	54	93	30**

Season 1935-36

Football League Division One

DATE	OPPONENTS	SCORE	GOALSCORERS	ATTENDANCE
Aug 31	Chelsea	D 2-2	Nieuwenhuys 2	40,000
Sep 4	MANCHESTER CITY	L 0-2		30,000
Sep 7	EVERTON	W 6-0	Howe 4, Hodgson 2	48,000
Sep 11	Manchester City	L 0-6		25,000
Sep 14	GRIMSBY TOWN	W 7-2	Howe 3, Hodgson 2, Carr, Johnson.	25,000
Sep 18	STOKE CITY	W 2-0	Hodgson 2	23,192
Sep 21	Leeds United	L 0-1		12,000
Sep 28	WEST BROMWICH ALBION	W 5-0	Nieuwenhuys, Carr 2, Hodgson, Howe	30,000
Oct 5	Sunderland	L 0-2		30,114
Oct 12	BIRMINGHAM	L 1-2	Nieuwenhuys	30,000
Oct 19	Bolton Wanderers	D 0-0		15,000
Oct 26	HUDDERSFIELD TOWN	W 3-0	Howe 2, Nieuwenhuys	40,000
Nov 2	Middlesbrough	D 2-2	Carr, Hodgson	18,104
Nov 9	ASTON VILLA	W 3-2	Hodgson, Carr (pen), McDougall	40,000
Nov 16	Wolverhampton Wanderers	L 1-3	Carr	20,000
Nov 23	DERBY COUNTY	D 0-0		30,000
Nov 30	Portsmouth	L 1-2	Howe	17,000
Dec 7	PRESTON NORTH END	W 2-1	Glassey, Balmer	25,000
Dec 14	Brentford	W 2-1	Glassey, Wright	20,000
Dec 21	SHEFFIELD WEDNESDAY	W 1-0	Wright	10,000
Dec 25	ARSENAL	L 0-1		47,000
Dec 26	Arsenal	W 2-1	Howe 2	45,000
Dec 28	CHELSEA	L 2-3	Howe, Nieuwenhuys	35,000
Jan 4	Everton	D 0-0		55,000
Jan 18	Grimsby Town	D 0-0		10,000
Feb 1	West Bromwich Albion	L 1-6	Balmer	25,000
Feb 8	SUNDERLAND	L 0-3		35,000
Feb 15	Birmingham	L 0-2		18,000
Feb 22	BOLTON WANDERERS	D 1-1	Balmer	20,000
Feb 29	Aston Villa	L 0-3		12,000
Mar 7	PORTSMOUTH	W 2-0	Wright, Nieuwenhuys	10,000
Mar 14	Huddersfield Town	L 0-1		15,000
Mar 18	LEEDS UNITED	W 2-1	Wright 2	20,000
Mar 21	WOLVERHAMPTON WANDERERS	L 0-2		25,000
Mar 28	Derby County	D 2-2	Howe, Taylor P	16,820
Apr 4	MIDDLESBROUGH	D 2-2	Glassey 2	22,223
Apr 10	Blackburn Rovers	D 2-2	Busby, Howe	20,000
Apr 11	Preston North End	L 1-3	Nieuwenhuys	20,000
Apr 13	BLACKBURN ROVERS	W 4-1	Taylor P, Nieuwenhuys 2, Wright	30,000
Apr 18	BRENTFORD	D 0-0		30,000
Apr 25	Sheffield Wednesday	D 0-0		10,000
May 2	Stoke City	L 1-2	Howe	14,000

FA Cup

Jan 11	SWANSEA TOWN	(Rd3) W 1-0	Wright	33,494
Jan 25	ARSENAL	(Rd4) L 0-2		53,720

League & Cup Appearances

PLAYER	LEAGUE	CUP COMPETITION FA CUP	TOTAL
Balmer	17		17
Blenkinsop	37		37
Bradshaw	41	2	43
Browning	6		6
Busby	11		11
Carr	21	2	23
Collins	6		6
Cooper	26	2	28
Dabbs	13	2	15
Glassey	8		8
Hanson	5		5
Harley	8		8
Hartill	4		4
Hodgson	17		17
Howe	34	2	36
Johnson	6	2	8
Kane	3		3
Low	1		1
McDougall	38	2	40
Nieuwenhuys	39	2	41
Riley	39	2	41
Roberts	6		6
Rogers	2		2
Savage	27	2	29
Shield	1		1
Taylor H	14		14
Taylor P	7		7
Wright	25	2	27

Goalscorers

PLAYER	LEAGUE	CUP COMPETITION FA CUP	TOTAL
Howe	17		17
Nieuwenhuys	10		10
Hodgson	9		9
Wright	6	1	7
Carr	6		6
Glassey	4		4
Balmer	3		3
Taylor P	2		2
Busby	1		1
Johnson	1		1
McDougall	1		1

Fact File

Full back Jim Harley won the Powderhall Sprint, a professional athletics race.

MANAGER: George Patterson

CAPTAIN: Ernie Blenkinsop

TOP SCORER: Fred Howe 17 (league)

BIGGEST WIN: 6-0, 7 September 1935, v Everton (H), 7-2, 14 September 1935, v Grimsby Town (H), both Division One

HIGHEST ATTENDANCE: 55,000, 14 January 1936, v Everton, Division One

TRANSFERS IN: Matt Busby from Manchester City, Jack Balmer from Everton (amateur)

TRANSFERS OUT: Gordon Hodgson to Aston Villa, John Tennant to Bolton Wanderers

Final Division One Table

		P	W	D	L	F	A	Pts
1	Sunderland	42	25	6	11	109	74	56
2	Derby Co	42	18	12	12	61	52	48
3	Huddersfield T	42	18	12	12	59	56	48
4	Stoke C	42	20	7	15	57	57	47
5	Brentford	42	17	12	13	81	60	46
6	Arsenal	42	15	15	12	78	48	45
7	Preston NE	42	18	8	16	67	64	44
8	Chelsea	42	15	13	14	65	72	43
9	Manchester C	42	17	8	17	68	60	42
10	Portsmouth	42	17	8	17	54	67	42
11	Leeds U	42	15	11	16	66	64	41
12	Birmingham	42	15	11	16	61	63	41
13	Bolton W	42	14	13	15	67	76	41
14	Middlesbrough	42	15	10	17	84	70	40
15	Wolverhampton W	42	15	10	17	77	76	40
16	Everton	42	13	13	16	89	89	39
17	Grimsby T	42	17	5	20	65	73	39
18	WBA	42	16	6	20	89	88	38
19	Liverpool	42	13	12	17	60	64	38
20	Sheffield W	42	13	12	17	63	77	38
21	Aston Villa	42	13	9	20	81	110	35
22	Blackburn R	42	12	9	21	55	96	33

Season 1936-37

Football League Division One

DATE	OPPONENTS	SCORE	GOALSCORERS	ATTENDANCE
Aug 29	STOKE CITY	W 2-1	Hanson, Nieuwenhuys	30,000
Sep 2	Portsmouth	L 2-6	Hanson, Nieuwenhuys	18,000
Sep 5	Charlton Athletic	D 1-1	Hanson	31,295
Sep 9	PORTSMOUTH	D 0-0		25,000
Sep 12	GRIMSBY TOWN	W 7-1	Nieuwenhuys, Howe 2, Wright 2, Balmer, Busby	16,000
Sep 16	Chelsea	L 0-2		25,000
Sep 19	Everton	L 0-2		57,587
Sep 26	Leeds United	L 0-2		16,000
Oct 3	BIRMINGHAM	W 2-0	Wright, Taylor P	25,000
Oct 10	Middlesbrough	D 3-3	Howe, Nieuwenhuys, Taylor P	22,858
Oct 17	BOLTON WANDERERS	D 0-0		25,000
Oct 24	Brentford	L 2-5	Balmer, Nieuwenhuys	30,000
Oct 31	ARSENAL	W 2-1	Balmer, Howe	45,000
Nov 7	Preston North End	L 1-3	Nieuwenhuys	15,000
Nov 14	SHEFFIELD WEDNESDAY	D 2-2	Howe 2	20,000
Nov 21	Manchester United	W 5-2	Hanson, Eastham, Howe 3	25,000
Nov 28	DERBY COUNTY	D 3-3	Barker o.g., Nieuwenhuys, Howe	25,000
Dec 5	Wolverhampton Wanderers	L 0-2		17,000
Dec 12	SUNDERLAND	W 4-0	Hanson 2, Nieuwenhuys, Balmer	30,000
Dec 19	Huddersfield Town	L 0-4		14,000
Dec 25	West Bromwich Albion	L 1-3	Howe	30,000
Dec 26	Stoke City	D 1-1	Wright	16,000
Dec 28	WEST BROMWICH ALBION	L 1-2	Hanson	35,000
Jan 2	CHARLTON ATHLETIC	L 1-2	Howe	28,000
Jan 9	Grimsby Town	L 1-2	Nieuwenhuys	12,000
Jan 23	EVERTON	W 3-2	Howe, Taylor P, Balmer	37,632
Jan 30	LEEDS UNITED	W 3-0	Nieuwenhuys 2, Hanson	12,000
Feb 6	Birmingham	L 0-5		20,000
Feb 13	MIDDLESBROUGH	L 0-2		22,459
Feb 24	Bolton Wanderers	W 1-0	Gosling o.g.	18,000
Feb 27	BRENTFORD	D 2-2	Hanson, Balmer	18,000
Mar 10	Arsenal	L 0-1		21,000
Mar 13	PRESTON NORTH END	D 1-1	Hanson (pen)	10,000
Mar 20	Sheffield Wednesday	W 2-1	Balmer, Hanson	18,000
Mar 26	MANCHESTER CITY	L 0-5		32,000
Mar 27	MANCHESTER UNITED	W 2-0	Hanson, Howe	28,000
Mar 29	Manchester City	L 1-5	Howe	25,000
Apr 3	Derby County	L 1-4	Eastham	13,430
Apr 10	WOLVERHAMPTON WANDERERS	W 1-0	Nieuwenhuys	30,000
Apr 17	Sunderland	L 2-4	Nieuwenhuys, Hanson	14,255
Apr 24	HUDDERSFIELD TOWN	D 1-1	Howe	10,000
May 1	CHELSEA	D 1-1	Balmer	12,000

FA Cup

Jan 16	Norwich City (Rd3)	L 0-3		26,800

League & Cup Appearances

PLAYER	LEAGUE	CUP COMPETITION FA CUP	TOTAL
Balmer	33	1	34
Blenkinsop	7		7
Bradshaw	31		31
Browning	3		3
Busby	29	1	30
Bush	9		9
Collins	1		1
Cooper	39	1	40
Dabbs	32		32
Eastham	21	1	22
Glassey	1		1
Hanson	42	1	43
Harley	5	1	6
Hobson	25	1	26
Howe	40	1	41
Kemp	7		7
Low	1		1
McDougall	39	1	40
Nieuwenhuys	40	1	41
Riley	10		10
Roberts	2		2
Rogers	9		9
Savage	8	1	9
Taylor H	1		1
Taylor P	14		14
Wright	13		13

Goalscorers

PLAYER	LEAGUE	CUP COMPETITION FA CUP	TOTAL
Howe	16		16
Hanson	13		13
Nieuwenhuys	13		13
Balmer	8		8
Wright	4		4
Taylor P	3		3
Eastham	2		2
Busby	1		1
Opps' o.gs.	2		2

Fact File

Goalkeeper Dirk Kemp joined the growing number of South Africans at the club. At the time this included Arthur Riley and Berry Nieuwenhuys, although Gordon Hodgson had left the previous season.

MANAGER: George Kay
CAPTAIN: Ernie Blenkinsop/Tom Cooper
TOP SCORER: Fred Howe 16 (league)
BIGGEST WIN: 7-1, 12 September 1936, v Grimsby Town (H), Division One
HIGHEST ATTENDANCE: 57,587, 19 September 1936, v Everton (A), Division One
TRANSFERS IN: Harry Eastham (amateur) from Blackpool, Dirk Kemp from South Africa
TRANSFERS OUT: Vic Wright to Plymouth Argyle, Harry Taylor

Final Division One Table

		P	W	D	L	F	A	Pts
1	Manchester C	42	22	13	7	107	61	57
2	Charlton Ath	42	21	12	9	58	49	54
3	Arsenal	42	18	16	8	80	49	52
4	Derby Co	42	21	7	14	96	90	49
5	Wolverhampton W	42	21	5	16	84	67	47
6	Brentford	42	18	10	14	82	78	46
7	Middlesbrough	42	19	8	15	74	71	46
8	Sunderland	42	19	6	17	89	87	44
9	Portsmouth	42	17	10	15	62	66	44
10	Stoke C	42	15	12	15	72	57	42
11	Birmingham	42	13	15	14	64	60	41
12	Grimsby T	42	17	7	18	86	81	41
13	Chelsea	42	14	13	15	52	55	41
14	Preston NE	42	14	13	15	56	67	41
15	Huddersfield T	42	12	15	15	62	64	39
16	WBA	42	16	6	20	77	98	38
17	Everton	42	14	9	19	81	78	37
18	Liverpool	42	12	11	19	62	84	35
19	Leeds U	42	15	4	23	60	80	34
20	Bolton W	42	10	14	18	43	66	34
21	Manchester U	42	10	12	20	55	78	32
22	Sheffield W	42	9	12	21	53	69	30

Season 1937-38

Football League Division One

DATE	OPPONENTS	SCORE	GOALSCORERS	ATTENDANCE
Aug 28	Chelsea	L 1-6	Harston	42,000
Sep 1	PORTSMOUTH	W 3-2	Harston 2, Nieuwenhuys	20,000
Sep 4	CHARLTON ATHLETIC	L 1-2	Balmer	35,000
Sep 8	Portsmouth	D 1-1	Balmer	17,000
Sep 11	Preston North End	L 1-4	Nieuwenhuys	18,000
Sep 15	STOKE CITY	W 3-0	Nieuwenhuys, Hanson 2 (1 pen)	20,000
Sep 18	GRIMSBY TOWN	W 2-1	Balmer, Nieuwenhuys	30,000
Sep 25	Leeds United	L 0-2		18,000
Oct 2	EVERTON	L 1-2	Nieuwenhuys	45,000
Oct 9	WEST BROMWICH ALBION	L 0-1		25,000
Oct 16	Wolverhampton Wanderers	L 0-2		28,000
Oct 23	LEICESTER CITY	D 1-1	Hanson	20,000
Oct 30	Sunderland	W 3-2	Fagan, Nieuwenhuys, Hanson	25,217
Nov 6	BRENTFORD	L 3-4	Hanson, Fagan, Shafto	35,000
Nov 13	Manchester City	W 3-1	Taylor, Shafto, Fagan	25,000
Nov 20	HUDDERSFIELD TOWN	L 0-1		35,000
Nov 27	Blackpool	W 1-0	Hanson	15,000
Dec 4	DERBY COUNTY	L 3-4	Hanson, Nieuwenhuys 2	20,000
Dec 11	Bolton Wanderers	D 0-0		12,000
Dec 18	ARSENAL	W 2-0	Shafto, Nieuwenhuys	32,000
Dec 27	Birmingham	D 2-2	Taylor, Nieuwenhuys	35,000
Jan 1	CHELSEA	D 2-2	Shafto, Fagan	40,000
Jan 15	Charlton Athletic	L 0-3		23,000
Jan 29	Grimsby Town	D 0-0		8,000
Feb 2	PRESTON NORTH END	D 2-2	Balmer, Fagan (pen)	20,000
Feb 5	LEEDS UNITED	D 1-1	Nieuwenhuys	30,000
Feb 16	Everton	W 3-1	Balmer, Shafto	33,465
Feb 19	West Bromwich Albion	L 1-5	Balmer	18,000
Feb 26	WOLVERHAMPTON WANDERERS	L 0-1		35,000
Mar 5	Leicester City	D 2-2	Hanson 2	15,000
Mar 12	SUNDERLAND	W 4-0	Nieuwenhuys, Balmer 2, Taylor	30,000
Mar 19	Brentford	W 3-1	Balmer, McInnes, Hanson	16,000
Mar 26	MANCHESTER CITY	W 2-0	Balmer, Jones	30,000
Apr 2	Huddersfield Town	W 2-1	Fagan, Balmer	15,000
Apr 6	BIRMINGHAM	W 3-2	Hanson, Taylor, Fagan	15,000
Apr 9	BLACKPOOL	W 4-2	Taylor, Hanson, Nieuwenhuys, Fagan (pen)	30,000
Apr 15	Middlesbrough	D 1-1	Hanson	29,843
Apr 16	Derby County	L 1-4	Hanson	16,384
Apr 18	MIDDLESBROUGH	D 1-1	Balmer	32,010
Apr 23	BOLTON WANDERERS	W 2-1	Balmer, Taylor	25,000
Apr 30	Arsenal	L 0-1		40,000
May 7	Stoke City	L 0-2		25,000

FA Cup

Jan 8	Crystal Palace	(Rd3)	D 0-0		33,000
Jan 12	CRYSTAL PALACE	(R)	W 3-1*	Shafto, Collins o.g., Fagan (pen)	35,919
Jan 22	Sheffield United	(Rd4)	D 1-1	Hanson	50,264
Jan 26	SHEFFIELD UNITED	(R)	W 1-0	Johnson o.g.	48,297
Feb 12	HUDDERSFIELD TOWN	(Rd5)	L 0-1		57,682

*After extra time. Score at 90 mins 1-1.

League & Cup Appearances

PLAYER	LEAGUE	CUP COMPETITION FA CUP	TOTAL
Balmer	30	1	31
Blenkinsop	2		2
Bradshaw	2		2
Browning	5		5
Busby	33	3	36
Bush	24	5	29
Cooper	26	5	31
Dabbs	6		6
Eastham	15	1	16
Fagan	31	5	36
Hanson	37	5	42
Harley	33	5	38
Harston	5		5
Hobson	1		1
Hood	3		3
Howe	9	2	11
Jones	2		2
Kemp	13		13
McDougall	17		17
McInnes	11		11
Nieuwenhuys	40	5	45
Ramsden	14	1	15
Riley	28	5	33
Rogers	24	4	28
Savage	5		5
Shafto	13	3	16
Smith	1		1
Taylor	29	5	34
Van Den Berg	3		3

Goalscorers

PLAYER	LEAGUE	CUP COMPETITION FA CUP	TOTAL
Hanson	14	1	15
Balmer	13		13
Nieuwenhuys	13		13
Fagan	8	1	9
Shafto	6	1	7
Taylor	6		6
Harston	3		3
Jones	1		1
McInnes	1		1
Opps' o.gs.		2	2

Fact File

Jimmy McDougall, distinguished left half and ex-club captain left to player/manage South Liverpool. In his 10-year career, he played in 356 games, scoring 12 goals.

MANAGER: George Kay
CAPTAIN: Tom Cooper
TOP SCORER: Alf Hanson 15 (14 league)
BIGGEST WIN: 4-0, 12 March 1938, v Sunderland (H), Division One
HIGHEST ATTENDANCE: 57,682, 12 February 1938, v Huddersfield Town (H), FA Cup
TRANSFERS IN: Willie Fagan from Preston North End, Jimmy McInnes from Third Lanark, Harman Van Den Berg from Cape Town (South Africa)
TRANSFERS OUT: Jimmy McDougall to South Liverpool, Ernie Blenkinsop to Cardiff City, Bob Savage to Manchester United, Ben Dabbs to Watford

Final Division One Table

		P	W	D	L	F	A	PTS
1	Arsenal	42	21	10	11	77	44	52
2	Wolverhampton W	42	20	11	11	72	49	51
3	Preston NE	42	16	17	9	64	44	49
4	Charlton Ath	42	16	14	12	65	51	46
5	Middlesbrough	42	19	8	15	72	65	46
6	Brentford	42	18	9	15	69	59	45
7	Bolton W	42	15	15	12	64	60	45
8	Sunderland	42	14	16	12	55	57	44
9	Leeds U	42	14	15	13	64	69	43
10	Chelsea	42	14	13	15	65	65	41
11	Liverpool	42	15	11	16	65	71	41
12	Blackpool	42	16	8	18	61	66	40
13	Derby Co	42	15	10	17	66	87	40
14	Everton	42	16	7	19	79	75	39
15	Huddersfield T	42	17	5	20	55	68	39
16	Leicester C	42	14	11	17	54	75	39
17	Stoke C	42	13	12	17	58	59	38
18	Birmingham	42	10	18	14	58	62	38
19	Portsmouth	42	13	12	17	62	68	38
20	Grimsby T	42	13	12	17	51	68	38
21	Manchester C	42	14	8	20	80	77	36
22	WBA	42	14	8	20	74	91	36

Season 1938-39

Football League Division One

DATE	OPPONENTS	SCORE	GOALSCORERS	ATTENDANCE
Aug 27	CHELSEA	W 2-1	Taylor 2	33,933
Sep 3	Preston North End	L 0-1		20,000
Sep 7	MANCHESTER UNITED	W 1-0	Nieuwenhuys	25,070
Sep 10	CHARLTON ATHLETIC	W 1-0	Busby	32,701
Sep 14	MIDDLESBROUGH	W 3-1	Fagan 2, Nieuwenhuys	25,535
Sep 17	Bolton Wanderers	L 1-3	Taylor	25,000
Sep 24	LEEDS UNITED	W 3-0	Fagan, Balmer, Taylor	32,197
Oct 1	Everton	L 1-2	Fagan (pen)	65,076
Oct 8	Leicester City	D 2-2	Nieuwenhuys, Van Den Berg	12,300
Oct 15	ASTON VILLA	W 3-0	Van Den Berg, Balmer, Fagan	41,224
Oct 22	Wolverhampton Wanderers	D 2-2	Taylor, Nieuwenhuys	25,000
Oct 29	HUDDERSFIELD TOWN	D 3-3	Van Den Berg, Fagan (pen), Balmer	33,734
Nov 5	Portsmouth	D 1-1	Nieuwenhuys	24,000
Nov 12	ARSENAL	D 2-2	Nieuwenhuys 2	42,450
Nov 19	Brentford	L 1-2	Nieuwenhuys	22,000
Nov 26	BLACKPOOL	W 1-0	Kinghorn	25,000
Dec 1	Derby County	D 2-2	Taylor, Kinghorn	24,753
Dec 10	GRIMSBY TOWN	D 2-2	Nieuwenhuys, Fagan	26,500
Dec 17	Sunderland	W 3-2	Kinghorn, Bush, Taylor	15,309
Dec 24	Chelsea	L 1-4	Balmer	7,000
Dec 26	Stoke City	L 1-3	Fagan	16,000
Dec 27	STOKE CITY	W 1-0	Fagan	45,814
Dec 31	PRESTON NORTH END	W 4-1	Taylor 2, Fagan (pen), Balmer	40,000
Jan 2	Middlesbrough	L 0-3		25,309
Jan 14	Charlton Athletic	W 3-1	Eastham, Balmer 2	24,000
Jan 25	BOLTON WANDERERS	L 1-2	Fagan	18,000
Jan 28	Leeds United	D 1-1	Balmer	13,600
Feb 4	EVERTON	L 0-3		55,994
Feb 18	Aston Villa	L 0-2		40,000
Feb 25	WOLVERHAMPTON WANDERERS	L 0-2		54,896
Mar 4	LEICESTER CITY	D 1-1	Taylor	20,000
Mar 11	PORTSMOUTH	D 4-4	Fagan, Taylor 2, Nieuwenhuys	18,000
Mar 15	Huddersfield Town	D 1-1	Nieuwenhuys	7,704
Mar 18	Arsenal	L 0-2		35,000
Mar 25	BRENTFORD	W 1-0	Fagan (pen)	18,000
Apr 1	Blackpool	D 1-1	Fagan	17,000
Apr 7	BIRMINGHAM	W 4-0	Nieuwenhuys 2, Balmer 2	30,000
Apr 8	DERBY COUNTY	W 2-1	Taylor 2	26,209
Apr 10	Birmingham	D 0-0		20,000
Apr 15	Grimsby Town	L 1-2	Nieuwenhuys	7,000
Apr 22	SUNDERLAND	D 1-1	Kinghorn	15,000
May 6	Manchester United	L 0-2		14,000

FA Cup

Jan 7	LUTON TOWN	W 3-0	Balmer 2, Paterson	40,431
Jan 21	STOCKPORT COUNTY	W 5-1	Nieuwenhuys 2, Eastham, Balmer 2	39,407
Feb 11	Wolverhampton Wanderers	L 1-4	Fagan (pen)	61,315

League & Cup Appearances

PLAYER	LEAGUE	CUP COMPETITION FA CUP	TOTAL
Balmer	42	3	45
Browning	2		2
Busby	42	3	45
Bush	23	2	25
Cooper	36		36
Eastham	7	2	9
Fagan	39	3	42
Fitzsimmons	1		1
Harley	31	3	34
Kemp	7	3	10
Kinghorn	19		19
Jones	3		3
McInnes	34	3	37
Nieuwenhuys	39	3	42
Paterson	2	1	3
Peters	1		1
Ramsden	10	3	13
Riley	35		35
Rogers	30	1	31
Shafto	4		4
Taylor	39	3	42
Van Den Berg	16		16

Goalscorers

PLAYER	LEAGUE	CUP COMPETITION FA CUP	TOTAL
Nieuwenhuys	14	2	16
Fagan	14	1	15
Balmer	10	4	14
Taylor	14		14
Kinghorn	4		4
Van Den Berg	3		3
Eastham	1	1	2
Busby	1		1
Bush	1		1
Paterson		1	1

Fact File

With war clouds looming, manager George Kay and the entire playing squad enrolled in the 5th Kings Regiment of the territorial army on 5 May 1939.

MANAGER: George Kay

CAPTAIN: Tom Cooper

TOP SCORER: Berry Nieuwenhuys 16 (14 league)

BIGGEST WIN: 4-0, 7 April 1939, v Birmingham (H), Division One; 5-1, 21 January 1939, v Stockport County (H), FA Cup

HIGHEST ATTENDANCE: 65,076, 1 October 1938, v Everton (A), Division One

TRANSFERS IN: W Kinghorn from Queen's Park

MAJOR PRE-WAR SIGNINGS: Bill Jones from junior football, Billy Liddell from Lochgelly Violet, Bob Paisley from Bishop Auckland, Ray Lambert from amateur status to professional

TRANSFERS OUT: Matt Fitzsimmons to Ipswich Town, John Browning

Final Division One Table

		P	W	D	L	F	A	Pts
1	Everton	42	27	5	10	88	52	59
2	Wolverhampton W	42	22	11	9	88	39	55
3	Charlton Ath	42	22	6	14	75	59	50
4	Middlesbrough	42	20	9	13	93	74	49
5	Arsenal	42	19	9	14	55	41	47
6	Derby Co	42	19	8	15	66	55	46
7	Stoke C	42	17	12	13	71	68	46
8	Bolton W	42	15	15	12	67	58	45
9	Preston NE	42	16	12	14	63	59	44
10	Grimsby T	42	16	11	15	61	69	43
11	Liverpool	42	14	14	14	62	63	42
12	Aston Villa	42	15	11	16	71	60	41
13	Leeds U	42	16	9	17	59	67	41
14	Manchester U	42	11	16	15	57	65	38
15	Blackpool	42	12	14	16	56	68	38
16	Sunderland	42	13	12	17	54	67	38
17	Portsmouth	42	12	13	17	47	70	37
18	Brentford	42	14	8	20	53	74	36
19	Huddersfield T	42	12	11	19	58	64	35
20	Chelsea	42	12	9	21	64	80	33
21	Birmingham	42	12	8	22	62	84	32
22	Leicester C	42	9	11	22	48	82	29

FA Cup 1945-46, Season 1946-47

FA Cup 1945-46

DATE	OPPONENTS		SCORE	GOALSCORERS	ATTENDANCE
Jan 5	Chester City	(Rd3/1L)	W 2-0	Liddell, Fagan	12,000
Jan 9	CHESTER CITY	(Rd3/2L)	W 2-1	Fagan 2	11,207
Jan 26	Bolton Wanderers	(Rd4/1L)	L 0-5		39,692
Jan 30	BOLTON WANDERERS	(Rd4/2L)	W 2-0	Balmer, Nieuwenhuys	35,247

Football League Division One 1946-47

DATE	OPPONENTS	SCORE	GOALSCORERS	ATTENDANCE
Aug 31	Sheffield United	W 1-0	Carney	30,000
Sep 4	MIDDLESBROUGH	L 0-1		34,140
Sep 7	CHELSEA	W 7-4	Fagan 2, Jones 2, Liddell 2, Balmer	49,995
Sep 11	Manchester United	L 0-5		50,000
Sep 14	Bolton Wanderers	W 3-1	Nieuwenhuys, Stubbins, Balmer	25,000
Sep 21	EVERTON	D 0-0		49,838
Sep 28	LEEDS UNITED	W 2-0	Balmer, Nieuwenhuys	51,042
Oct 5	Grimsby Town	W 6-1	Stubbins 2, Liddell 2, Balmer, Fagan (pen)	22,000
Oct 9	Middlesbrough	D 2-2	Liddell 2	37,382
Oct 12	CHARLTON ATHLETIC	D 1-1	Done	51,127
Oct 19	Huddersfield Town	W 4-1	Done 3, Balmer	17,000
Oct 26	BRENTFORD	W 1-0	Stubbins	43,894
Nov 2	Blackburn Rovers	D 0-0		23,000
Nov 9	PORTSMOUTH	W 3-0	Balmer 3 (1 pen)	50,000
Nov 16	Derby County	W 4-1	Balmer 4	28,444
Nov 23	ARSENAL	W 4-2	Balmer 3 (1 pen), Stubbins	45,000
Nov 30	Blackpool	L 2-3	Balmer, Done	23,565
Dec 7	WOLVERHAMPTON WANDERERS	L 1-5	Balmer (pen)	52,512
Dec 14	Sunderland	W 4-1	Balmer, Liddell, Nieuwenhuys, Stubbins	33,300
Dec 21	ASTON VILLA	W 4-1	Balmer 2, Stubbins, Nieuwenhuys	35,650
Dec 25	Stoke City	L 1-2	Stubbins	30,420
Dec 26	STOKE CITY	W 2-0	Nieuwenhuys, Stubbins	48,494
Dec 28	SHEFFIELD UNITED	L 1-2	Stubbins	50,961
Jan 4	Chelsea	L 1-3	Balmer	58,375
Jan 18	BOLTON WANDERERS	L 0-3		50,000
Jan 29	Everton	L 0-1		35,000
Feb 1	Leeds United	W 2-1	Stubbins 2	25,000
Feb 12	GRIMSBY TOWN	W 5-0	Done 3, Fagan 2	40,000
Feb 22	HUDDERSFIELD TOWN	W 1-0	Stubbins	35,000
Mar 8	BLACKBURN ROVERS	W 2-1	Done, Stubbins	49,378
Mar 15	Portsmouth	W 2-1	Stubbins 2	30,000
Mar 22	DERBY COUNTY	D 1-1	Taylor	50,848
Apr 4	Preston North End	D 0-0		30,000
Apr 5	BLACKPOOL	L 2-3	Fagan, Done	47,230
Apr 7	PRESTON NORTH END	W 3-0	Stubbins 2, Balmer	47,000
Apr 19	SUNDERLAND	W 1-0	Stubbins	41,589
Apr 26	Aston Villa	W 2-1	Watkinson, Fagan	40,000
May 3	MANCHESTER UNITED	W 1-0	Stubbins	50,000
May 10	Charlton Athletic	W 3-1	Stubbins 3	35,000
May 17	Brentford	D 1-1	Priday	22,000
May 24	Arsenal	W 2-1	Balmer, Priday	48,000
May 31	Wolverhampton Wanderers	W 2-1	Balmer, Stubbins	50,078

FA Cup

DATE	OPPONENTS		SCORE	GOALSCORERS	ATTENDANCE
Jan 11	Walsall	(Rd3)	W 5-2	Foulkes o.g., Done, Liddell, Balmer 2	18,379
Jan 25	GRIMSBY TOWN	(Rd4)	W 2-0	Stubbins, Done	42,265
Feb 8	DERBY COUNTY	(Rd5)	W 1-0	Balmer	44,493
Mar 1	BIRMINGHAM CITY	(Rd6)	W 4-1	Stubbins 3, Balmer	51,911
Mar 29	Burnley	(SF)	D 0-0*		52,570
Apr 12	Burnley**	(R)	L 0-1		72,000

* After extra time. **Played at Maine Road.

Fact File

A pre-season team-blending 10-match tour of USA and Canada with top class food helped the club to its first post-war championship.

MANAGER: George Kay **CAPTAIN:** Willie Fagan

TOP SCORERS: Jack Balmer and Albert Stubbins 28 each (24 league)

BIGGEST WIN: 6-1, 5 October 1946 v Grimsby Town (A), Division One

HIGHEST ATTENDANCE: 72,000, 12 April 1947, v Burnley (Maine Road), FA Cup semi-final replay

TRANSFERS IN: Albert Stubbins from Newcastle United, Ray Minshull from Southport

TRANSFERS OUT: Tom Bush and Berry Nieuwenhuys – retired

League & Cup Appearances

PLAYER	LEAGUE	CUP COMPETITION 1945-46	1946-47	TOTAL
Ashcroft	2			2
Balmer	39	(2)	6	45 (2)
Baron		(3)		(3)
Bush	3	(1)		3 (1)
Carney	2			2
Done	17		6	23
Easdale	2			2
Eastham	19		2	21
Fagan	18	(4)	4	22 (4)
Finney		(2)		(2)
Harley	17	(3)	4	21 (3)
Hobson		(1)		(1)
Hughes	30	(3)	1	31 (3)
Jones	26		6	32
Kaye	1	(1)		1 (1)
Lambert	36	(4)	6	42 (4)
Liddell	34	(2)	6	40 (2)
McLeod	3			3
Minshull	6			6
Nickson		(3)		(3)
Nieuwenhuys	15	(4)		15 (4)
Paisley	33	(4)	6	39 (4)
Palk	6			6
Priday	9	(4)		9 (4)
Ramsden	23	(1)	1	24 (1)
Sidlow	34		6	40
Spicer	10	(1)		10 (1)
Stubbins	36		6	42
Taylor	35	(1)	6	41 (1)
Watkinson	6			6

*Figures in brackets indicate appearances in 1945-46 FA Cup.

Goalscorers

PLAYER	LEAGUE	CUP COMPETITION 1945-46	1946-47	TOTAL
Balmer	24	(1)	4	28 (1)
Stubbins	24		4	28
Done	10		2	12
Liddell	7	(1)	1	8 (1)
Fagan	7	(3)		7 (3)
Nieuwenhuys	5	(1)		5 (1)
Jones	2			2
Priday	2			2
Carney	1			1
Taylor	1			1
Watkinson	1			1
Opps' o.gs.			1	1

*Figures in brackets indicate goals in 1945-46 FA Cup.

Final Division One Table

		P	W	D	L	F	A	Pts
1	Liverpool	42	25	7	10	84	52	57
2	Manchester U	42	22	12	8	95	54	56
3	Wolverhampton W	42	25	6	11	98	56	56
4	Stoke C	42	24	7	11	90	53	55
5	Blackpool	42	22	6	14	71	70	50
6	Sheffield U	42	21	7	14	89	75	49
7	Preston NE	42	18	11	13	76	74	47
8	Aston Villa	42	18	9	15	67	53	45
9	Sunderland	42	18	8	16	65	66	44
10	Everton	42	17	9	16	62	67	43
11	Middlesbrough	42	17	8	17	73	68	42
12	Portsmouth	42	16	9	17	66	60	41
13	Arsenal	42	16	9	17	72	70	41
14	Derby Co	42	18	5	19	73	79	41
15	Chelsea	42	16	7	19	69	84	39
16	Grimsby T	42	13	12	17	61	82	38
17	Blackburn R	42	14	8	20	45	53	36
18	Bolton W	42	13	8	21	57	69	34
19	Charlton Ath	42	11	12	19	57	71	34
20	Huddersfield T	42	13	7	22	53	79	33
21	Brentford	42	9	7	26	45	88	25
22	Leeds U	42	6	6	30	45	90	18

Season 1947-48

Football League Division One

DATE	OPPONENTS	SCORE	GOALSCORERS	ATTENDANCE
Aug 23	PRESTON NORTH END	W 3-1	Liddell, Stubbins 2	49,353
Aug 27	Manchester United	L 0-2		45,000
Aug 30	Stoke City	W 2-0	Liddell 2	30,000
Sep 3	MANCHESTER UNITED	D 2-2	Stubbins, Balmer (pen)	50,000
Sep 6	BURNLEY	D 1-1	Balmer	56,074
Sep 8	Sheffield United	L 1-3	Stubbins	40,000
Sep 13	Portsmouth	L 0-1		32,000
Sep 17	Charlton Athletic	L 0-2		40,000
Sep 20	BOLTON WANDERERS	D 0-0		43,920
Sep 29	Everton	W 3-0	Balmer, Stubbins, Fagan	66,576
Oct 4	Middlesbrough	L 1-3	Balmer	41,140
Oct 11	CHELSEA	W 3-0	Priday, Stubbins, Liddell	51,449
Oct 18	Huddersfield Town	D 1-1	Balmer	27,518
Oct 25	DERBY COUNTY	D 2-2	Priday, Balmer	49,624
Nov 1	Blackpool	L 0-2		25,000
Nov 8	GRIMSBY TOWN	W 3-1	Stubbins, Priday, Baron	36,796
Nov 15	Sunderland	L 1-5	Liddell	37,258
Nov 22	BLACKBURN ROVERS	W 2-1	Balmer, Liddell	35,672
Nov 29	Manchester City	L 0-2		37,464
Dec 6	ASTON VILLA	D 3-3	Spicer, Stubbins, Balmer	37,732
Dec 13	Wolverhampton Wanderers	W 2-1	Stubbins, Balmer	32,000
Dec 20	Preston North End	D 3-3	Jones, Liddell, Stubbins	32,000
Dec 25	ARSENAL	L 1-3	Priday	53,000
Dec 27	Arsenal	W 2-1	Stubbins, Liddell	59,000
Jan 1	CHARLTON ATHLETIC	L 2-3	Stubbins 2	34,533
Jan 3	STOKE CITY	D 0-0		48,665
Jan 17	Burnley	L 0-3		25,000
Jan 31	PORTSMOUTH	L 0-3		23,097
Feb 7	Bolton Wanderers	L 0-3		20,800
Feb 21	MIDDLESBROUGH	L 0-1		36,133
Feb 28	Chelsea	L 1-3	Baron	39,078
Mar 6	HUDDERSFIELD TOWN	W 4-0	Stubbins 4	40,000
Mar 20	BLACKPOOL	W 2-0	Stubbins 2 (1 pen)	48,725
Mar 26	SHEFFIELD UNITED	W 4-0	Fagan 2, Liddell, Stubbins	54,797
Mar 27	Grimsby Town	W 2-0	Balmer, Spicer	18,000
Mar 31	Derby County	W 4-0	Stubbins, Balmer 2, Fagan	16,277
Apr 3	SUNDERLAND	D 0-0		49,687
Apr 10	Blackburn Rovers	W 2-1	Balmer, Stubbins	26,000
Apr 17	MANCHESTER CITY	D 1-1	Fagan	39,348
Apr 21	EVERTON	W 4-0	Stubbins, Liddell, Brierley, Balmer	55,035
Apr 24	Aston Villa	L 1-2	Stubbins	30,000
May 1	WOLVERHAMPTON WANDERERS	W 2-1	Paisley, Balmer	31,773

FA Cup

Jan 10	NOTTINGHAM FOREST	(Rd3)	W 4-1	Priday, Stubbins 2, Liddell	48,569
Jan 24	Manchester United*	(Rd4)	L 0-3		74,721

*Played at Goodison Park due to bomb damage at Old Trafford.

League & Cup Appearances

PLAYER	LEAGUE	CUP COMPETITION FA CUP	TOTAL
Balmer	40	1	41
Baron	6		6
Brierley	10		10
Carney	4		4
Done	4	2	6
Fagan	15		15
Harley	21		21
Hughes	32	2	34
Jones	41	2	43
Lambert	30	2	32
Liddell	37	2	39
McAvoy	1		1
Minshull	13	2	15
Muir	4		4
Paisley	37	2	39
Palk	7		7
Priday	21	2	23
Ramsden	10		10
Shannon	1		1
Sidlow	29		29
Spicer	14	1	15
Stubbins	40	2	42
Taylor	34	2	36
Watkinson	11		11

Goalscorers

PLAYER	LEAGUE	CUP COMPETITION FA CUP	TOTAL
Stubbins	24	2	26
Balmer	15		15
Liddell	10	1	11
Fagan	5		5
Priday	4	1	5
Baron	2		2
Spicer	2		2
Brierley	1		1
Jones	1		1
Paisley	1		1

Fact File

After getting only one point in seven league games in January and February, the season was rescued by winning eight and drawing two of the last 11 games.

MANAGER: George Kay

CAPTAIN: Jack Balmer

TOP SCORER: Albert Stubbins 26 (24 league)

BIGGEST WIN: 4-0, 6 March 1948 v Huddersfield Town (H); 26 March 1948 v Sheffield United (H); 31 March 1948 v Derby County (A); 21 April 1948 v Everton (H), all Division One

HIGHEST ATTENDANCE: 74,721, 24 January 1948, v Manchester United (Goodison Park), FA Cup

TRANSFERS IN: Ken Brierley from Oldham Athletic, Doug McAvoy from Kilmarnock

TRANSFERS OUT: Harry Eastham to Tranmere Rovers, Barney Ramsden to Sunderland

Final Division One Table

		P	W	D	L	F	A	Pts
1	Arsenal	42	23	13	6	81	32	59
2	Manchester U	42	19	14	9	81	48	52
3	Burnley	42	20	12	10	56	43	52
4	Derby Co	42	19	12	11	77	57	50
5	Wolverhampton W	42	19	9	14	83	70	47
6	Aston Villa	42	19	9	14	65	57	47
7	Preston NE	42	20	7	15	67	68	47
8	Portsmouth	42	19	7	16	68	50	45
9	Blackpool	42	17	10	15	57	41	44
10	Manchester C	42	15	12	15	52	47	42
11	Liverpool	42	16	10	16	65	61	42
12	Sheffield U	42	16	10	16	65	70	42
13	Charlton Ath	42	17	6	19	57	66	40
14	Everton	42	17	6	19	52	66	40
15	Stoke C	42	14	10	18	41	55	38
16	Middlesbrough	42	14	9	19	71	73	37
17	Bolton W	42	16	5	21	46	58	37
18	Chelsea	42	14	9	19	53	71	37
19	Huddersfield T	42	12	12	18	51	60	36
20	Sunderland	42	13	10	19	56	67	36
21	Blackburn R	42	11	10	21	54	72	32
22	Grimsby T	42	8	6	28	45	111	22

Season 1948-49

Football League Division One

DATE	OPPONENTS	SCORE	GOALSCORERS	ATTENDANCE
Aug 21	Aston Villa	L 1-2	Balmer	35,000
Aug 25	SHEFFIELD UNITED	D 3-3	Balmer 2, Liddell	37,393
Aug 28	SUNDERLAND	W 4-0	Liddell, Fagan, Watkinson, Balmer	52,253
Aug 30	Sheffield United	W 2-1	Shannon, Liddell	30,000
Sep 4	Wolverhampton Wanderers	D 0-0		40,000
Sep 8	Arsenal	D 1-1	Liddell	46,714
Sep 11	BOLTON WANDERERS	L 0-1		56,561
Sep 15	ARSENAL	L 0-1		46,714
Sep 18	Everton	D 1-1	Fagan	78,599
Sep 25	Blackpool	L 0-1		30,000
Oct 2	DERBY COUNTY	D 0-0		53,776
Oct 9	Chelsea	D 1-1	Payne	42,709
Oct 16	Birmingham City	W 1-0	Done	43,000
Oct 23	MIDDLESBROUGH	W 4-0	Balmer, Stubbins, Liddell (pen), Whitaker o.g.	57,561
Oct 30	Newcastle United	L 0-1		67,362
Nov 6	PORTSMOUTH	W 3-1	Liddell, Balmer, Done	43,665
Nov 13	Manchester City	W 4-2	Payne, Done 2, Taylor	21,659
Nov 20	CHARLTON ATHLETIC	D 1-1	Done	49,377
Nov 27	Stoke City	L 0-3		35,000
Dec 4	BURNLEY	D 1-1	Done	41,001
Dec 11	Preston North End	L 2-3	Done 2	28,000
Dec 18	ASTON VILLA	D 1-1	Done	23,866
Dec 25	Manchester United	D 0-0		47,788
Dec 27	MANCHESTER UNITED	L 0-2		53,273
Jan 1	Sunderland	W 2-0	Hall o.g., Liddell (pen)	43,109
Jan 22	Bolton Wanderers	W 3-0	Balmer, Stubbins, Gillies o.g.	30,000
Feb 5	EVERTON	D 0-0		50,132
Feb 19	BLACKPOOL	D 1-1	Balmer	52,294
Mar 5	Chelsea	L 1-2	Payne	42,746
Mar 12	BIRMINGHAM CITY	W 1-0	Done	43,753
Mar 19	Charlton Athletic	L 1-2	Balmer	30,000
Mar 26	STOKE CITY	W 4-0	Stubbins 2, Done, Balmer	30,797
Apr 2	Portsmouth	L 2-3	Stubbins, Paisley	34,500
Apr 6	WOLVERHAMPTON WANDERERS	D 0-0		35,399
Apr 9	MANCHESTER CITY	L 0-1		31,389
Apr 15	HUDDERSFIELD TOWN	L 0-1		47,319
Apr 16	Middlesbrough	W 1-0	Balmer	32,308
Apr 18	Huddersfield Town	W 4-0	Balmer 2, Baron, Liddell	22,000
Apr 23	NEWCASTLE UNITED	D 1-1	Baron	43,488
Apr 30	Burnley	W 2-0	Balmer, Stubbins	17,693
May 4	Derby County	L 0-3		22,897
May 7	PRESTON NORTH END	L 0-2		31,937

FA Cup

Jan 8	Nottingham Forest	(Rd3) D 2-2*	Fagan, Done	35,000
Jan 15	NOTTINGHAM FOREST	(R) W 4-0	Payne, Balmer 2, Stubbins	52,218
Jan 29	NOTTS COUNTY	(Rd4) W 1-0	Liddell	61,003
Feb 12	Wolverhampton Wanderers	(Rd5) L 1-3	Done	54,983

* After extra time. Score at 90 mins 2-2.

League & Cup Appearances

PLAYER	LEAGUE	CUP COMPETITION FA CUP	TOTAL
Balmer	42	4	46
Baron	6		6
Brierley	13	1	14
Done	24	4	28
Fagan	13	1	14
Hughes	12		12
Jones	38	4	42
Kippax	1		1
Lambert	41	4	45
Liddell	38	4	42
McAvoy	1		1
McLeod	4		4
Minshull	4	1	5
Paisley	36	4	40
Payne	35	3	38
Priday	4		4
Shepherd	41	4	45
Sidlow	38	3	41
Shannon	10		10
Spicer	4		4
Stubbins	15	3	18
Taylor	30	4	34
Watkinson	6		6
Williaams	6		6

Goalscorers

PLAYER	LEAGUE	CUP COMPETITION FA CUP	TOTAL
Balmer	14	2	16
Done	11	2	13
Liddell	8	1	9
Stubbins	6	1	7
Payne	3	1	4
Fagan	2	1	3
Baron	2		2
Paisley	1		1
Shannon	1		1
Taylor	1		1
Watkinson	1		1
Opps' o.gs.	3		3

Fact File

Following another successful tour of USA and Canada (played 11, won 11; goals for 63, against 16), centre half Joe Cadden was signed from New York All Stars.

MANAGER: George Kay
CAPTAIN: Jack Balmer
TOP SCORER: Jack Balmer 16 (14 league)
BIGGEST WIN: 4-0, 28 August 1948, v Sunderland (H); 23 October 1948, v Middlesbrough (H); 25 March 1949, v Stoke City (H); 18 April 1949, v Huddersfield Town (A) – all Division One; 15 January 1949, v Nottingham Forest (H), FA Cup
HIGHEST ATTENDANCE: 78,599, 18 September 1948, v Everton (A), Division One – all-time Goodison Park record attendance
TRANSFERS IN: Joe Cadden from New York All Stars, Roy Saunders from Hull City, Jack Heydon from Everton
TRANSFERS OUT: Jim Harley – retired, Stan Palk to Port Vale

Final Division One Table

		P	W	D	L	F	A	Pts
1	Portsmouth	42	25	8	9	84	42	58
2	Manchester U	42	21	11	10	77	44	53
3	Derby Co	42	22	9	11	74	55	53
4	Newcastle U	42	20	12	10	70	56	52
5	Arsenal	42	18	13	11	74	44	49
6	Wolverhampton W	42	17	12	13	79	66	46
7	Manchester C	42	15	15	12	47	51	45
8	Sunderland	42	13	17	12	49	58	43
9	Charlton Ath	42	15	12	15	63	67	42
10	Aston Villa	42	16	10	16	60	76	42
11	Stoke C	42	16	9	17	66	68	41
12	Liverpool	42	13	14	15	53	43	40
13	Chelsea	42	12	14	16	69	68	38
14	Bolton W	42	14	10	18	59	68	38
15	Burnley	42	12	14	16	43	50	38
16	Blackpool	42	11	16	15	54	67	38
17	Birmingham C	42	11	15	16	36	38	37
18	Everton	42	13	11	18	41	63	37
19	Middlesbrough	42	11	12	19	46	57	34
20	Huddersfield T	42	12	10	20	40	69	34
21	Preston NE	42	11	11	20	62	75	33
22	Sheffield U	42	11	11	20	57	78	33

Season 1949-50

Football League Division One

DATE	OPPONENTS	SCORE	GOALSCORERS	ATTENDANCE
Aug 20	SUNDERLAND	W 4-2	Paisley, Balmer, Baron, Stubbins	49,811
Aug 22	Stoke City	D 0-0		35,000
Aug 27	Everton	D 0-0		70,812
Aug 31	STOKE CITY	D 1-1	Liddell	38,097
Sep 3	Arsenal	W 2-1	Stubbins 2	56,000
Sep 7	MANCHESTER UNITED	D 1-1	Stubbins	51,857
Sep 10	BOLTON WANDERERS	D 1-1	Baron	44,212
Sep 17	Birmingham City	W 3-2	Done, Liddell 2	40,000
Sep 24	DERBY COUNTY	W 3-1	Baron, Fagan, Payne	54,512
Oct 1	West Bromwich Albion	W 1-0	Stubbins	44,219
Oct 8	MIDDLESBROUGH	W 2-0	Payne, Lambert (pen)	49,569
Oct 15	Blackpool	D 0-0		32,000
Oct 22	NEWCASTLE UNITED	D 2-2	Liddell, Baron	48,987
Oct 29	Fulham	W 1-0	Liddell	42,000
Nov 5	MANCHESTER CITY	W 4-0	Liddell 2 (1 pen), Brierley, Baron	50,536
Nov 12	Charlton Athletic	W 3-1	Done, Liddell 2 (1 pen)	38,800
Nov 19	ASTON VILLA	W 2-1	Liddell, Brierley	50,293
Nov 26	Wolverhampton Wanderers	D 1-1	Fagan	55,000
Dec 3	PORTSMOUTH	D 2-2	Done 2	44,851
Dec 10	Huddersfield Town	L 2-3	Fagan, Brierley	25,767
Dec 17	Sunderland	L 2-3	Brierley, Done	46,575
Dec 24	EVERTON	W 3-1	Fagan, Baron 2	50,485
Dec 26	Chelsea	D 1-1	Fagan	55,820
Dec 27	CHELSEA	D 2-2	Fagan 2	58,757
Dec 31	ARSENAL	W 2-0	Liddell, o.g.	55,020
Jan 14	Bolton Wanderers	L 2-3	Liddell, Fagan	41,507
Jan 21	BIRMINGHAM CITY	W 2-0	Payne, Stubbins	37,668
Feb 4	Derby County	D 2-2	Liddell, Stubbins	36,835
Feb 18	WEST BROMWICH ALBION	W 2-1	Stubbins, Brierley	46,634
Feb 25	Middlesbrough	L 1-4	Stubbins	31,804
Mar 8	BLACKPOOL	L 0-1		33,464
Mar 11	Aston Villa	L 0-2		39,035
Mar 15	Manchester United	D 0-0		30,000
Mar 18	WOLVERHAMPTON WANDERERS	L 0-2		41,216
Mar 29	Manchester City	W 2-1	Liddell, Payne	38,000
Apr 1	CHARLTON ATHLETIC	W 1-0	Liddell (pen)	39,721
Apr 7	Burnley	W 2-1	Payne, Liddell	33,035
Apr 8	Newcastle United	L 1-5	Fagan	45,000
Apr 10	BURNLEY	L 0-1		43,716
Apr 15	FULHAM	D 1-1	Fagan	36,274
Apr 22	Portsmouth	L 1-2	Stubbins	47,507
May 3	HUDDERSFIELD TOWN	L 2-3	Fagan, Liddell	35,463

FA Cup

Jan 7	Blackburn Rovers	(Rd3)	D 0-0		52,468
Jan 11	BLACKBURN ROVERS	(R)	W 2-1	Payne, Fagan	52,221
Jan 28	EXETER CITY	(Rd4)	W 3-1	Baron, Fagan, Payne	45,209
Feb 11	Stockport County	(Rd5)	W 2-1	Fagan, Stubbins	27,833
Mar 4	BLACKPOOL	(Rd6)	W 2-1	Fagan, Liddell	53,973
Mar 25	Everton*	(SF)	W 2-0	Paisley, Liddell	72,000
Apr 29	Arsenal**	(F)	L 0-2		98,249

*Played at Maine Road. **Played at Wembley.

League & Cup Appearances

PLAYER	LEAGUE	CUP COMPETITION FA CUP	TOTAL
Balmer	9		9
Baron	38	7	45
Brierley	11		11
Christie	4		4
Done	16		16
Fagan	35	7	42
Hughes	35	6	41
Jones	26	3	29
Lambert	41	7	48
Liddell	41	7	48
Minshull	5		5
Paisley	23	5	28
Payne	31	7	38
Shepherd	6		6
Sidlow	37	7	44
Shields	1		1
Spicer	37	7	44
Stubbins	28	7	35
Taylor	37	7	44
Watkinson	1		1

Goalscorers

PLAYER	LEAGUE	CUP COMPETITION FA CUP	TOTAL
Liddell	17	2	19
Fagan	11	4	15
Stubbins	10	1	11
Baron	7	1	8
Payne	5	2	7
Brierley	5		5
Done	5		5
Paisley	1	1	2
Balmer	1		1
Lambert	1		1
Opps' o.gs.	1		1

Fact File

Liverpool reached the FA Cup final for the second time in the club's history. It was the first of 31 times the club has appeared at Wembley in a major competition comprising 10 FA Cup finals, 7 League Cup finals, 1 European Cup final, and 13 Charity Shield matches.

MANAGER: George Kay
CAPTAIN: Jack Balmer/Phil Taylor
TOP SCORER: Billy Liddell 19 (17 league)
BIGGEST WIN: 4-0, 5 November 1949, v Manchester City (H), Division One
HIGHEST ATTENDANCE: 98,249, 29 April 1950, v Arsenal (Wembley), FA Cup final

Final Division One Table

		P	W	D	L	F	A	Pts
1	Portsmouth	42	22	9	11	74	38	53
2	Wolverhampton W	42	20	13	9	76	49	53
3	Sunderland	42	21	10	11	83	62	52
4	Manchester U	42	18	14	10	69	44	50
5	Newcastle U	42	19	12	11	77	55	50
6	Arsenal	42	19	11	12	79	55	49
7	Blackpool	42	17	15	10	46	35	49
8	Liverpool	42	17	14	11	64	54	48
9	Middlesbrough	42	20	7	15	59	48	47
10	Burnley	42	16	13	13	40	40	45
11	Derby Co	42	17	10	15	69	61	44
12	Aston Villa	42	15	12	15	61	61	42
13	Chelsea	42	12	16	14	58	65	40
14	WBA	42	14	12	16	47	53	40
15	Huddersfield T	42	14	9	19	52	73	37
16	Bolton W	42	10	14	18	45	59	34
17	Fulham	42	10	14	18	41	54	34
18	Everton	42	10	14	18	42	66	34
19	Stoke C	42	11	12	19	45	75	34
20	Charlton Ath	42	13	6	23	53	65	32
21	Manchester C	42	8	13	21	36	68	29
22	Birmingham C	42	7	14	21	31	67	28

Season 1950-51

Football League Division One

DATE	OPPONENTS	SCORE	GOALSCORERS	ATTENDANCE
Aug 19	Wolverhampton Wanderers	L 0-2		50,622
Aug 23	MANCHESTER UNITED	W 2-1	Liddell, Allen o.g.	30,211
Aug 26	SUNDERLAND	W 4-0	Liddell 2, Stubbins 2	52,080
Aug 30	Manchester United	L 0-1		34,835
Sep 2	Aston Villa	D 1-1	Balmer	50,000
Sep 6	TOTTENHAM HOTSPUR	W 2-1	Balmer, Stubbins	39,015
Sep 9	DERBY COUNTY	W 1-0	Done	50,079
Sep 16	Everton	W 3-1	Stubbins, Balmer 2	71,150
Sep 23	Fulham	L 1-2	Liddell	42,000
Sep 30	BOLTON WANDERERS	D 3-3	Payne, Balmer 2	44,534
Oct 7	STOKE CITY	D 0-0		40,239
Oct 14	West Bromwich Albion	D 1-1	Taylor	35,030
Oct 21	MIDDLESBROUGH	D 0-0		47,426
Oct 28	Sheffield Wednesday	L 1-4	Payne	35,000
Nov 4	NEWCASTLE UNITED	L 2-4	Liddell (pen), Payne	48,810
Nov 11	Huddersfield Town	D 2-2	Liddell, Taylor	25,220
Nov 18	ARSENAL	L 1-3	Compton o.g.	44,193
Nov 25	Burnley	D 1-1	Baron	31,990
Dec 2	CHELSEA	W 1-0	Liddell	28,717
Dec 9	Portsmouth	W 3-1	Payne 2, Balmer	29,470
Dec 16	WOLVERHAMPTON WANDERERS	L 1-4	Liddell (pen)	30,959
Dec 23	Sunderland	L 1-2	Balmer	30,150
Dec 25	Blackpool	L 0-3		32,000
Dec 26	BLACKPOOL	W 1-0	Balmer	54,121
Jan 13	Derby County	W 2-1	Haigh, Liddell	21,849
Jan 20	EVERTON	L 0-2		48,688
Jan 27	Charlton Athletic	L 0-1		25,000
Feb 3	FULHAM	W 2-0	Jones, Liddell	38,630
Feb 10	PORTSMOUTH	W 2-1	Jones, Balmer	36,958
Feb 17	Bolton Wanderers	L 1-2	Liddell	35,824
Feb 24	Stoke City	W 3-2	Done, Jones, Liddell	25,000
Mar 3	WEST BROMWICH ALBION	D 1-1	Paisley	33,654
Mar 10	Middlesbrough	D 1-1	Liddell	29,247
Mar 17	SHEFFIELD WEDNESDAY	W 2-1	Liddell 2 (1 pen)	31,413
Mar 23	CHARLTON ATHLETIC	W 1-0	Haigh	31,650
Mar 24	Newcastle United	D 1-1	Done	50,000
Mar 31	HUDDERSFIELD TOWN	L 1-4	Haigh	27,915
Apr 7	Arsenal	W 2-1	Stubbins, Payne	42,000
Apr 14	BURNLEY	W 1-0	Jones	24,118
Apr 21	Chelsea	L 0-1		30,134
Apr 25	ASTON VILLA	D 0-0		23,061
May 5	Tottenham Hotspur	L 1-3	Stubbins	49,072

FA Cup

Jan 6	Norwich City	(Rd3) L 1-3	Balmer	34,641

League & Cup Appearances

PLAYER	LEAGUE	CUP COMPETITION FA CUP	TOTAL
Ashcroft	7		7
Balmer	34	1	35
Baron	7		7
Brierley	5		5
Cadden	4		4
Crossley	24	1	25
Done	24	1	25
Fagan W	4		4
Haigh	8		8
Heydon	13	1	14
Hughes	24		24
Jones	38	1	39
Lambert	34	1	35
Liddell	35	1	36
Paisley	41	1	42
Payne	38	1	39
Shepherd	5		5
Sidlow	11		11
Spicer	42	1	43
Stubbins	23	1	24
Taylor	36		36
Williams	3		3
Woan	2		2

Goalscorers

PLAYER	LEAGUE	CUP COMPETITION FA CUP	TOTAL
Liddell	15		15
Balmer	10	1	11
Payne	6		6
Stubbins	6		6
Jones	4		4
Done	3		3
Haigh	3		3
Taylor	2		2
Heydon	1		1
Paisley	1		1
Opps' o.gs.	2		2

Fact File

The new manager, Don Welsh, had been a wartime guest player, scoring 42 goals in 40 games for the Reds including six in a 12-1 win over Southport in 1944.

MANAGER: George Kay; Don Welsh from March 1951

CAPTAIN: Phil Taylor

TOP SCORER: Billy Liddell 15 (league)

BIGGEST WIN: 4-0, 26 August 1950, v Sunderland (H), Division One

HIGHEST ATTENDANCE: 71,150, 16 September 1950, v Everton (A), Division One

TRANSFERS OUT: Bill Watkinson to Accrington Stanley, Ray Minshull to Southport

Final Division One Table

		P	W	D	L	F	A	PTS
1	Tottenham H	42	25	10	7	82	44	60
2	Manchester U	42	24	8	10	74	40	56
3	Blackpool	42	20	10	12	79	53	50
4	Newcastle U	42	18	13	11	62	53	49
5	Arsenal	42	19	9	14	73	56	47
6	Middlesbrough	42	18	11	13	76	65	47
7	Portsmouth	42	16	15	11	71	68	47
8	Bolton W	42	19	7	16	64	61	45
9	Liverpool	42	16	11	15	53	59	43
10	Burnley	42	14	14	14	48	43	42
11	Derby Co	42	16	8	18	81	75	40
12	Sunderland	42	12	16	14	63	73	40
13	Stoke C	42	13	14	15	50	59	40
14	Wolverhampton W	42	15	8	19	74	61	38
15	Aston Villa	42	12	13	17	66	68	37
16	WBA	42	13	11	18	53	61	37
17	Charlton Ath	42	14	9	19	63	80	37
18	Fulham	42	13	11	18	52	68	37
19	Huddersfield T	42	15	6	21	64	92	36
20	Chelsea	42	12	8	22	53	65	32
21	Sheffield W	42	12	8	22	64	83	32
22	Everton	42	12	8	22	48	86	32

Season 1951-52

Football League Division One

DATE	OPPONENTS	SCORE	GOALSCORERS	ATTENDANCE
Aug 18	PORTSMOUTH	L 0-2		42,270
Aug 21	Burnley	D 0-0		23,162
Aug 25	Chelsea	W 3-1	Baron, Liddell, Stubbins	44,055
Aug 29	BURNLEY	W 3-1	Stubbins, Done, Liddell	32,857
Sep 1	HUDDERSFIELD TOWN	W 2-1	Liddell, Baron	39,818
Sep 5	Arsenal	D 0-0		50,483
Sep 8	Wolverhampton Wanderers	L 1-2	Brierley	50,000
Sep 12	ARSENAL	D 0-0		39,853
Sep 15	SUNDERLAND	D 2-2	Liddell, Baron	37,381
Sep 22	Aston Villa	L 0-2		50,000
Sep 29	DERBY COUNTY	W 2-0	Smith, Williams	40,259
Oct 6	Charlton Athletic	L 0-2		33,000
Oct 13	FULHAM	W 4-0	Smith, Payne 2, Liddell	36,793
Oct 20	Middlesbrough	D 3-3	Liddell, Smith, W. Jones	26,126
Oct 27	WEST BROMWICH ALBION	L 2-5	Payne, Liddell (pen)	34,891
Nov 3	Newcastle United	D 1-1	Payne	50,100
Nov 10	BOLTON WANDERERS	D 1-1	Jackson	49,537
Nov 17	Stoke City	W 2-1	Baron, Payne	24,000
Nov 24	MANCHESTER UNITED	D 0-0		42,378
Dec 1	Tottenham Hotspur	W 3-2	Liddell 3 (1 pen)	51,350
Dec 8	PRESTON NORTH END	D 2-2	Liddell, Hughes	34,722
Dec 15	Portsmouth	W 3-1	Smith, Liddell 2	29,945
Dec 22	CHELSEA	D 1-1	Liddell	26,459
Dec 25	BLACKPOOL	D 1-1	Payne	41,071
Dec 26	Blackpool	L 0-2		27,414
Dec 29	Huddersfield Town	W 2-1	Liddell, Payne	25,500
Jan 5	WOLVERHAMPTON WANDERERS	D 1-1	Taylor	44,768
Jan 19	Sunderland	L 0-3		33,549
Jan 26	ASTON VILLA	L 1-2	Liddell	39,774
Feb 9	Derby County	D 1-1	Done	22,495
Feb 16	CHARLTON ATHLETIC	D 1-1	Done	33,487
Mar 1	Fulham	D 1-1	Payne	37,000
Mar 8	MIDDLESBROUGH	D 1-1	Jones W	41,945
Mar 15	West Bromwich Albion	D 3-3	Liddell, Paisley, Stubbins	27,183
Mar 22	NEWCASTLE UNITED	W 3-0	Smith, Stubbins 2	48,966
Mar 29	Bolton Wanderers	D 1-1	Liddell	14,571
Apr 5	STOKE CITY	W 2-1	Paisley, Baron	19,740
Apr 11	Manchester City	W 2-1	Baron, Payne	35,305
Apr 12	Manchester United	L 0-4		42,970
Apr 14	MANCHESTER CITY	L 1-2	Smith	34,404
Apr 19	TOTTENHAM HOTSPUR	D 1-1	Liddell	36,898
Apr 26	Preston North End	L 0-4		32,000

FA Cup

Jan 12	WORKINGTON TOWN	(Rd3)	W 1-0	Payne	52,581
Feb 2	WOLVERHAMPTON WANDERERS	(Rd4)	W 2-1	Paisley, Done	61,905
Feb 23	Burnley	(Rd5)	L 0-2		52,070

League & Cup Appearances

PLAYER	LEAGUE	CUP COMPETITION FA CUP	TOTAL
Ashcroft	34	1	35
Balmer	2	2	4
Baron	40	1	41
Brierley	11		11
Cadden		1	1
Crossley	8	2	10
Done	10	2	12
Fagan	3		3
Haigh	3		3
Heydon	27	2	29
Hughes	25	1	26
Jackson	15	1	16
Jones M	3		3
Jones W	36	3	39
Lambert	32	3	35
Liddell	40	3	43
Paisley	37	3	40
Parr	16		16
Payne	35	3	38
Shepherd	2		2
Smith	27	1	28
Stubbins	12		12
Taylor	24	2	26
Whitworth	9		9
Williams	11	2	13

Goalscorers

PLAYER	LEAGUE	CUP COMPETITION FA CUP	TOTAL
Liddell	19		19
Payne	9	1	10
Baron	6		6
Smith	6		6
Stubbins	5		5
Done	3	1	4
Paisley	2	1	3
Jones W	2		2
Brierley	1		1
Hughes	1		1
Jackson	1		1
Taylor	1		1
Williams	1		1

Fact File

Signed in 1935, Jackie Balmer retired from football at the end of the season. He played a total of 312 games, scoring 111 goals including a record three hat-tricks (10 goals) in three successive games, the first Football League player to achieve this feat. He played in a further 101 games, scoring 53 goals, during the Second World War.

MANAGER: Don Welsh
CAPTAIN: Phil Taylor
TOP SCORER: Billy Liddell 19 (league)
BIGGEST WIN: 4-0, 13 October 1951, v Fulham (H), Division One
HIGHEST ATTENDANCE: 61,905, 2 February 1952, v Wolverhampton Wanderers (H), FA Cup (a record attendance at Anfield)
TRANSFERS IN: Mervyn Jones from Bangor City
TRANSFERS OUT: Cyril Done to Tranmere Rovers, Cyril Sidlow to New Brighton, Willie Fagan to Weymouth as player/manager, Bill Shepherd to Wigan Athletic

Final Division One Table

		P	W	D	L	F	A	Pts
1	Manchester U	42	23	11	8	95	52	57
2	Tottenham H	42	22	9	11	76	51	53
3	Arsenal	42	21	11	10	80	61	53
4	Portsmouth	42	20	8	14	68	58	48
5	Bolton W	42	19	10	13	65	61	48
6	Aston Villa	42	19	9	14	79	70	47
7	Preston NE	42	17	12	13	74	54	46
8	Newcastle U	42	18	9	15	98	73	45
9	Blackpool	42	18	9	15	64	64	45
10	Charlton Ath	42	17	10	15	68	63	44
11	Liverpool	42	12	19	11	57	61	43
12	Sunderland	42	15	12	15	70	61	42
13	WBA	42	14	13	15	74	77	41
14	Burnley	42	15	10	17	56	63	40
15	Manchester C	42	13	13	16	58	61	39
16	Wolverhampton W	42	12	14	16	73	73	38
17	Derby Co	42	15	7	20	63	80	37
18	Middlesbrough	42	15	6	21	64	88	36
19	Chelsea	42	14	8	20	52	72	36
20	Stoke C	42	12	7	23	49	88	31
21	Huddersfield T	42	10	8	24	49	82	28
22	Fulham	42	8	11	23	58	77	27

Season 1952-53

Football League Division One

DATE	OPPONENTS	SCORE	GOALSCORERS	ATTENDANCE
Aug 23	Preston North End	D 1-1	Smith	38,000
Aug 27	SHEFFIELD WEDNESDAY	W 1-0	Baron	46,614
Aug 30	STOKE CITY	W 3-2	Smith, Baron, Liddell	40,062
Sep 3	Sheffield Wednesday	W 2-0	Baron, Liddell	41,183
Sep 6	Manchester City	W 2-1	Baron, Smith	42,965
Sep 10	TOTTENHAM HOTSPUR	W 2-1	Smith, Liddell (pen)	49,809
Sep 13	PORTSMOUTH	D 1-1	Williams	49,771
Sep 15	Tottenham Hotspur	L 1-3	Williams	37,331
Sep 20	MIDDLESBROUGH	W 4-1	Payne, Smith, Williams, Baron	40,750
Sep 27	West Bromwich Albion	L 0-3		33,774
Oct 4	NEWCASTLE UNITED	W 5-3	Liddell, Smith 2, Baron, Paisley	48,002
Oct 11	Bolton Wanderers	D 2-2	Baron, Payne	35,251
Oct 18	ASTON VILLA	L 0-2		42,573
Oct 25	SUNDERLAND	L 1-3	Liddell	50,555
Nov 1	WOLVERHAMPTON WANDERERS	W 2-1	Payne, Liddell (pen)	46,487
Nov 8	Charlton Athletic	L 2-3	Williams, Brierley	30,000
Nov 15	ARSENAL	L 1-5	Payne	45,010
Nov 22	Derby County	L 2-3	Liddell (pen), Smith	20,758
Nov 29	BLACKPOOL	D 2-2	Payne 2	32,336
Dec 13	MANCHESTER UNITED	L 1-2	Liddell	34,450
Dec 20	PRESTON NORTH END	D 2-2	Liddell, Baron	27,659
Dec 25	Burnley	L 0-2		35,858
Dec 26	BURNLEY	D 1-1	Liddell (pen)	46,589
Jan 3	Stoke City	L 1-3	Baron	25,000
Jan 17	MANCHESTER CITY	L 0-1		41,191
Jan 24	Portsmouth	L 1-3	Paisley	27,045
Feb 7	Middlesbrough	W 3-2	Liddell, Smyth, Taylor	15,445
Feb 14	WEST BROMWICH ALBION	W 3-0	Liddell, Payne, Smyth	24,890
Feb 21	NEWCASTLE United	W 2-1	Smyth, Taylor	35,000
Mar 4	BOLTON WANDERERS	D 0-0		24,999
Mar 7	Aston Villa	L 0-4		30,000
Mar 14	SUNDERLAND	W 2-0	Smyth, A'Court	40,409
Mar 21	Wolverhampton Wanderers	L 0-3		30,000
Mar 23	Chelsea	L 0-3		17,337
Mar 28	CHARLTON ATHLETIC	L 1-2	Payne	23,204
Apr 3	CARDIFF CITY	W 2-1	Jones W, Bimpson	52,079
Apr 4	Arsenal	L 3-5	Bimpson, A'Court, Liddell	40,564
Apr 6	Cardiff City	L 0-4		20,000
Apr 11	DERBY COUNTY	D 1-1	Smyth	34,064
Apr 18	Blackpool	L 1-3	Smyth	22,073
Apr 20	Manchester United	L 1-3	Smyth	20,869
Apr 25	CHELSEA	W 2-0	Jones W, Bimpson	47,699

FA Cup

Jan 10	Gateshead	(Rd3) L 0-1		15,193

League & Cup Appearances

PLAYER	LEAGUE	CUP COMPETITION FA CUP	TOTAL
A'Court	12		12
Anderson	1		1
Ashcroft	24		24
Baron	27	1	28
Bimpson	8		8
Brierley	10		10
Crossley	18	1	19
Gerhardi	6		6
Heydon	23	1	24
Hughes	11		11
Jackson	5		5
Jones M	1	1	2
Jones W	26	1	27
Lambert	36	1	31
Liddell	39	1	40
Maloney	6		6
Moran	11	1	12
Paisley	26		26
Parr	4		4
Payne	33		33
Rowley AA	11		11
Saunders	14	1	15
Smith	27	1	28
Smyth	18		18
Spicer	28		28
Stubbins	5		5
Taylor	21		21
Williams	11	1	12

Goalscorers

PLAYER	LEAGUE	CUP COMPETITION FA CUP	TOTAL
Liddell	13		13
Baron	9		9
Payne	8		8
Smith	8		8
Smyth	7		7
Williams	4		4
Bimpson	3		3
A'Court	2		2
Jones W	2		2
Paisley	2		2
Taylor	2		2
Brierley	1		1

Fact File

Albert Stubbins left Anfield after seven seasons, scoring 83 goals in 178 appearances. He was the record goalscorer in wartime football, netting 231 in 187 games for Newcastle United.

MANAGER: Don Welsh
CAPTAIN: Phil Taylor
TOP SCORER: Billy Liddell 13 (league)
BIGGEST WIN: 4-1, 20 September 1952, v Middlesbrough (H), Division One
HIGHEST ATTENDANCE: 52,079, 3 April 1953, v Cardiff City (H), Division One
TRANSFERS IN: Alan A'Court from Prescot Cables, Louis Bimpson from Burscough, Sammy Smyth from Stoke City
TRANSFERS OUT: Albert Stubbins to Ashington, Jack Heydon to Millwall, Ken Brierley to Oldham Athletic

Final Division One Table

		P	W	D	L	F	A	PTS
1	Arsenal	42	21	12	9	97	64	54
2	Preston NE	42	21	12	9	85	60	54
3	Wolverhampton W	42	19	13	10	86	63	51
4	WBA	42	21	8	13	66	60	50
5	Charlton Ath	42	19	11	12	77	63	49
6	Burnley	42	18	12	12	67	52	48
7	Blackpool	42	19	9	14	71	70	47
8	Manchester U	42	18	10	14	69	72	46
9	Sunderland	42	15	13	14	68	82	43
10	Tottenham H	42	15	11	16	78	69	41
11	Aston Villa	42	14	13	15	63	61	41
12	Cardiff C	42	14	12	16	54	46	40
13	Middlesbrough	42	14	11	17	70	77	39
14	Bolton W	42	15	9	18	61	69	39
15	Portsmouth	42	14	10	18	74	83	38
16	Newcastle U	42	14	9	19	59	70	37
17	Liverpool	42	14	8	20	61	82	36
18	Sheffield W	42	12	11	19	62	72	35
19	Chelsea	42	12	11	19	56	66	35
20	Manchester C	42	14	7	21	72	87	35
21	Stoke C	42	12	10	20	53	66	34
22	Derby Co	42	11	10	21	59	74	32

Season 1953-54

Football League Division One

DATE	OPPONENTS	SCORE	GOALSCORERS	ATTENDANCE
Aug 19	PORTSMOUTH	W 3-1	Jones W 2, Liddell.	39,662
Aug 22	MANCHESTER UNITED	D 4-4	Bimpson 2, Liddell, Jones W	46,725
Aug 26	NEWCASTLE UNITED	D 2-2	Baron 2	47,263
Aug 29	Bolton Wanderers	L 0-2		28,277
Sep 2	Newcastle United	L 0-4		47,000
Sep 5	PRESTON NORTH END	L 1-5	Jones W	46,928
Sep 7	Wolverhampton Wanderers	L 1-2	Jackson	35,701
Sep 12	Tottenham Hotspur	L 1-2	Jones W	47,535
Sep 16	WOLVERHAMPTON WANDERERS	D 1-1	Jones W	29,848
Sep 19	BURNLEY	W 4-0	Bimpson 4	36,643
Sep 26	Charlton Athletic	L 0-6		31,000
Oct 3	SHEFFIELD WEDNESDAY	D 2-2	Paisley, Bimpson	38,647
Oct 10	ASTON VILLA	W 6-1	Liddell, Smyth 2, Paisley, Payne, Blanchflower o.g.	37,759
Oct 17	Huddersfield Town	L 0-2		30,115
Oct 24	SHEFFIELD UNITED	W 3-0	Payne, Smyth 2	37,978
Oct 31	Chelsea	L 2-5	Smyth 2	33,000
Nov 7	MANCHESTER CITY	D 2-2	Bimpson, Baron	30,917
Nov 14	Sunderland	L 2-3	Smyth 2	36,369
Nov 21	ARSENAL	L 1-2	Bimpson	47,814
Nov 28	Cardiff City	L 1-3	Bimpson	15,000
Dec 5	BLACKPOOL	W 5-2	Payne, A'Court 2, Arnell, Smyth	47,320
Dec 12	Portsmouth	L 1-5	Smyth	23,509
Dec 19	Manchester United	L 1-5	Bimpson	26,074
Dec 25	West Bromwich Albion	L 2-5	A'Court, Lambert (pen)	30,390
Dec 26	WEST BROMWICH ALBION	D 0-0		51,167
Jan 2	BOLTON WANDERERS	L 1-2	Evans	44,383
Jan 16	Preston North End	L 1-2	Baron	27,000
Jan 23	TOTTENHAM HOTSPUR	D 2-2	Liddell, Evans	43,592
Feb 6	Burnley	D 1-1	Anderson	23,000
Feb 13	CHARLTON ATHLETIC	L 2-3	Evans, Anderson	47,657
Feb 24	Sheffield Wednesday	D 1-1	Anderson	10,000
Feb 27	Aston Villa	L 1-2	Bimpson	25,000
Mar 6	HUDDERSFIELD TOWN	L 1-3	Evans	46,074
Mar 13	Sheffield United	L 1-3	Liddell (pen)	17,000
Mar 20	CHELSEA	D 1-1	Anderson	36,292
Apr 3	SUNDERLAND	W 4-3	Jackson, Evans, Liddell (pen), Anderson	30,417
Apr 7	Manchester City	W 2-0	Jackson 2	12,593
Apr 10	Arsenal	L 0-3		33,178
Apr 16	Middlesbrough	W 1-0	Smyth	26,882
Apr 17	CARDIFF CITY	L 0-1		41,340
Apr 19	MIDDLESBROUGH	W 4-1	Rowley T, Smyth 2, Liddell	22,174
Apr 24	Blackpool	L 0-3		18,651

FA Cup

Jan 9	Bolton Wanderers	(Rd3) L 0-1		45,341

League & Cup Appearances

PLAYER	LEAGUE	CUP COMPETITION FA CUP	TOTAL
A'Court	16		16
Anderson	13		13
Arnell	3		3
Ashcroft	6		6
Baron	17		17
Bimpson	24		24
Campbell	2		2
Childs	2		2
Crossley	18	1	19
Evans	16	1	17
Hughes	27	1	28
Jackson	27	1	28
Jones H	1		1
Jones W	25	1	26
Lambert	20	1	21
Liddell	36	1	37
Lock	18	1	19
Maloney	6		6
McNulty	12		12
Moran	1		1
Paisley	19		19
Payne	17	1	18
Rowley T*	2		2
Saunders	20		20
Smith	3		3
Smyth	26		26
Spicer	23		23
Taylor	6	1	7
Twentyman	20		20
Underwood	18		18
Wilkinson	18	1	19

Goalscorers

PLAYER	LEAGUE	CUP COMPETITION FA CUP	TOTAL
Smyth	13		13
Bimpson	12		12
Liddell	7		7
Jones W	6		6
Anderson	5		5
Evans	5		5
Baron	4		4
Jackson	4		4
A'Court	3		3
Payne	3		3
Paisley	2		2
Arnell	1		1
Lambert	1		1
Rowley T*	1		1
Opps' o.gs.	1		1

*Rowley AC, known as Tony.

Fact File

An average home crowd of 40,518 saw the Reds slump into the Second Division for the first time in 50 years with a record 23 defeats in a season.

MANAGER: Don Welsh
CAPTAIN: Bill Jones
TOP SCORER: Sammy Smyth 13 (league)
BIGGEST WIN: 6-1, 10 October 1953, v Aston Villa (H), Division One
HIGHEST ATTENDANCE: 51,167, 25 December 1953, v West Bromwich Albion (A), Division One
TRANSFERS IN: Dave Underwood from Watford, Johnny Evans and Frank Lock from Charlton Athletic, Geoff Twentyman from Carlisle, Tom McNulty from Manchester United, Tony Rowley from Stourbridge
TRANSFERS OUT: Jack Smith to Torquay, Kevin Baron to Southend, Russell Crossley to Shrewsbury, Bill Jones to Ellesmere Port, Bob Paisley, Phil Taylor and Eddie Spicer – retired

Final Division One Table

		P	W	D	L	F	A	Pts
1	Wolverhampton W	42	25	7	10	96	56	57
2	WBA	42	22	9	11	86	63	53
3	Huddersfield T	42	20	11	11	78	61	51
4	Manchester U	42	18	12	12	73	58	48
5	Bolton W	42	18	12	12	75	60	48
6	Blackpool	42	19	10	13	80	69	48
7	Burnley	42	21	4	17	78	67	46
8	Chelsea	42	16	12	14	74	68	44
9	Charlton Ath	42	19	6	17	75	77	44
10	Cardiff C	42	18	8	16	51	71	44
11	Preston NE	42	19	5	18	87	58	43
12	Arsenal	42	15	13	14	75	73	43
13	Aston Villa	42	16	9	17	70	68	41
14	Portsmouth	42	14	11	17	81	89	39
15	Newcastle U	42	14	10	18	72	77	38
16	Tottenham H	42	16	5	21	65	76	37
17	Manchester C	42	14	9	19	62	77	37
18	Sunderland	42	14	8	20	81	89	36
19	Sheffield W	42	15	6	21	70	91	36
20	Sheffield U	42	11	11	20	69	90	33
21	Middlesbrough	42	10	10	22	60	91	30
22	Liverpool	42	9	10	23	68	97	28

Season 1954-55

Football League Division Two

DATE	OPPONENTS	SCORE	GOALSCORERS	ATTENDANCE
Aug 21	DONCASTER ROVERS	W 3-2	Rowley T 3	49,741
Aug 23	Plymouth Argyle	L 0-1		25,574
Aug 28	Derby County	L 2-3	Evans, Bimpson	18,774
Sep 1	PLYMOUTH ARGYLE	D 3-3	Evans, Arnell 2	32,777
Sep 4	WEST HAM UNITED	L 1-2	Payne	37,593
Sep 6	Bristol Rovers	L 0-3		25,574
Sep 11	Blackburn Rovers	L 3-4	Evans 2, Liddell	29,200
Sep 15	BRISTOL ROVERS	W 5-3	Evans 5	31,100
Sep 18	FULHAM	W 4-1	Liddell 3 (2 pens), Evans	44,372
Sep 25	Swansea Town	L 2-3	Liddell, Rowley T	25,836
Oct 2	NOTTS COUNTY	W 3-1	Anderson 2, Evans	37,639
Oct 9	ROTHERHAM UNITED	W 3-1	A'Court, Liddell, Evans	45,868
Oct 16	Stoke City	L 0-2		23,569
Oct 23	BURY	D 1-1	Anderson	33,310
Oct 30	Lincoln City	D 3-3	Anderson, Liddell 2	13,800
Nov 6	HULL CITY	W 2-1	Twentyman, Anderson	32,592
Nov 13	Luton Town	L 2-3	Liddell, Evans	15,887
Nov 20	NOTTINGHAM FOREST	W 1-0	Liddell (pen)	33,509
Nov 27	Leeds United	D 2-2	Liddell 2	22,000
Dec 4	MIDDLESBROUGH	W 3-1	Liddell 2 (1 pen), Twentyman	26,749
Dec 11	Birmingham City	L 1-9	Liddell	17,565
Dec 18	Doncaster Rovers	L 1-4	Evans	9,655
Dec 25	IPSWICH TOWN	W 6-2	Liddell 4 (1 pen), Bimpson, Evans	24,073
Dec 27	Ipswich Town	L 0-2		19,481
Jan 1	DERBY COUNTY	W 2-0	Jackson, Liddell	34,327
Jan 22	BLACKBURN ROVERS	W 4-1	Liddell 2 (1 pen), Evans 2	45,543
Feb 5	Fulham	W 2-1	Rowley, Evans	24,000
Feb 12	SWANSEA TOWN	D 1-1	Twentyman	42,249
Mar 3	Notts County	W 3-0	Arnell, A'Court, Rowley	11,000
Mar 5	STOKE CITY	L 2-4	Evans 2	35,655
Mar 12	Bury	W 4-3	Evans 4	16,081
Mar 19	LINCOLN CITY	L 2-4	Liddell 2 (1 pen)	31,805
Mar 26	Hull City	D 2-2	Anderson, Evans	6,000
Apr 2	LUTON TOWN	D 4-4	Evans 2, Anderson, South	30,710
Apr 8	Port Vale	L 3-4	Anderson, Evans, Liddell	25,000
Apr 9	Nottingham Forest	L 1-3	Liddell	15,409
Apr 11	PORT VALE	D 1-1	Jackson	36,285
Apr 16	LEEDS UNITED	D 2-2	Payne, Rowley	34,950
Apr 23	Middlesbrough	W 2-1	Rowley, Liddell	11,737
Apr 26	West Ham United	W 3-0	Evans, Anderson 2	9,000
Apr 30	BIRMINGHAM CITY	D 2-2	Liddell 2 (1 pen)	38,392
May 2	Rotherham United	L 1-6	Liddell	17,000

FA Cup

Jan 8	Lincoln City	(Rd3)	D 1-1	Evans	15,399
Jan 12	LINCOLN CITY	(R)	W 1-0*	Evans	32,179
Jan 29	Everton	(Rd4)	W 4-0	Liddell, A'Court, Evans 2	72,000
Feb 19	HUDDERSFIELD TOWN	(Rd5)	L 0-2		57,115

* After extra time. Score at 90 mins 0-0.

League & Cup Appearances

PLAYER	LEAGUE	CUP COMPETITION FA CUP	TOTAL
A'Court	30	3	33
Anderson	32	3	35
Arnell	7	1	8
Ashcroft	14	1	15
Bimpson	8	1	9
Burkinshaw	1		1
Campbell	12		12
Evans	38	4	42
Hughes	26	3	29
Jackson	23	3	26
Lambert	28	4	32
Liddell	40	4	44
Lock	23		23
McNulty	19		19
Moran	17	4	21
Payne	17	1	18
Rowley T	13		13
Rudham	22	3	25
Saunders	28	4	32
South	6	1	7
Tomley	2		2
Twentyman	35	4	39
Underwood	6		6
Wilkinson	15		15

Note. Antonio Camilio Rowley was generally referred to as Tony to distinguish him from Anthony Arthur Rowley, known as Arthur, who was at the club at the same time.

Goalscorers

PLAYER	LEAGUE	CUP COMPETITION FA CUP	TOTAL
Evans	29	4	33
Liddell	30	1	31
Anderson	10		10
Rowley T	8		8
A'Court	2	1	3
Arnell	3		3
Twentyman	3		3
Bimpson	2		2
Jackson	2		2
Payne	2		2
South	1		1

Fact File

Poor results, including the club's worst defeat of 1-9 away to Birmingham City on 11 December, meant no quick return to the top flight this time.

MANAGER: Don Welsh
CAPTAIN: Laurie Hughes
TOP SCORER: Johnny Evans 33 (29 League)
BIGGEST WIN: 6-2, 25 December 1954, v Ipswich Town (H), Division Two
HIGHEST ATTENDANCE: 72,000, 29 January 1955, v Everton (A), FA Cup
TRANSFERS IN: John Molyneux from Chester City
TRANSFERS OUT: Charlie Ashcroft to Ipswich Town, Arthur Rowley to Wrexham

Final Division Two Table

		P	W	D	L	F	A	PTS
1	BIRMINGHAM C	42	22	10	10	92	47	54
2	LUTON T	42	23	8	11	88	53	54
3	ROTHERHAM U	42	25	4	13	94	64	54
4	LEEDS U	42	23	7	12	70	53	53
5	STOKE C	42	21	10	11	69	46	52
6	BLACKBURN R	42	22	6	14	114	79	50
7	NOTTS CO	42	21	6	15	74	71	48
8	WEST HAM U	42	18	10	14	74	70	46
9	BRISTOL R	42	19	7	16	75	70	45
10	SWANSEA T	42	17	9	16	86	83	43
11	LIVERPOOL	42	16	10	16	92	96	42
12	MIDDLESBROUGH	42	18	6	18	73	82	42
13	BURY	42	15	11	16	77	72	41
14	FULHAM	42	14	11	17	76	79	39
15	NOTTINGHAM F	42	16	7	19	58	62	39
16	LINCOLN C	42	13	10	19	68	79	36
17	PORT VALE	42	12	11	19	48	71	35
18	DONCASTER R	42	14	7	21	58	95	35
19	HULL C	42	12	10	20	44	69	34
20	PLYMOUTH ARG	42	12	7	23	57	82	31
21	IPSWICH T	42	11	6	25	57	92	28
22	DERBY CO	42	7	9	26	53	82	23

Season 1955-56

Football League Division Two

DATE	OPPONENTS	SCORE	GOALSCORERS	ATTENDANCE
Aug 20	Nottingham Forest	W 3-1	A'Court 2, Evans	21,389
Aug 24	SHEFFIELD WEDNESDAY	L 0-3		41,791
Aug 27	HULL CITY	W 3-0	Liddell 2, Arnell	38,928
Aug 31	Sheffield Wednesday	D 1-1	Liddell	30,853
Sep 3	Blackburn Rovers	D 3-3	Arnell 2, Liddell	30,000
Sep 7	BRISTOL ROVERS	L 0-2		38,221
Sep 10	LINCOLN CITY	W 2-1	Arnell 2	39,816
Sep 17	Leicester City	L 1-3	Liddell	21,356
Sep 24	MIDDLESBROUGH	D 1-1	Liddell	35,312
Oct 1	PLYMOUTH ARGYLE	W 4-1	Twentyman 2, A'Court 2	34,397
Oct 8	Bristol City	L 1-2	Rowley	25,279
Oct 15	WEST HAM UNITED	W 3-1	A'Court, Payne, Liddell	32,187
Oct 22	Bury	W 4-1	Arnell 2, Liddell 2	12,296
Oct 29	ROTHERHAM UNITED	W 2-0	Arnell, Liddell	31,810
Nov 5	Swansea Town	L 1-2	Arnell	25,000
Nov 12	NOTTS COUNTY	W 2-1	Liddell, Twentyman	32,654
Nov 19	Leeds United	L 2-4	Liddell (pen), Arnell	22,500
Nov 26	FULHAM	W 7-0	Evans, Arnell, Liddell 2, Twentyman, A'Court, Payne	34,995
Dec 3	Port Vale	D 1-1	Liddell	16,191
Dec 10	BARNSLEY	D 1-1	Evans	20,241
Dec 17	NOTTINGHAM FOREST	W 5-2	Evans, Melia, Liddell 3	29,248
Dec 24	Hull City	W 2-1	Anderson, Evans	19,537
Dec 26	STOKE CITY	D 2-2	Liddell (pen), Evans	49,604
Dec 27	Stoke City	L 2-3	Twentyman, Rowley	29,133
Dec 31	BLACKBURN ROVERS	L 1-2	Anderson	48,071
Jan 21	LEICESTER CITY	W 3-1	Liddell 2 (1 pen), Arnell	39,917
Feb 4	Middlesbrough	W 2-1	Evans, Liddell	12,171
Feb 11	Plymouth Argyle	L 0-4		10,250
Feb 25	West Ham United	L 0-2		18,800
Feb 29	LEEDS UNITED	W 1-0	Evans	21,068
Mar 3	BURY	W 4-2	Evans 2 (1 pen), Liddell, Dickson	35,535
Mar 10	Barnsley	W 5-0	Anderson 2, Liddell 2, Dickson	13,678
Mar 17	SWANSEA TOWN	W 4-1	Liddell, Dickson 2, Anderson	48,217
Mar 24	Notts County	L 1-2	Anderson	14,000
Mar 30	Doncaster Rovers	L 0-1		15,000
Mar 31	BRISTOL CITY	W 2-1	Arnell, Evans (pen)	46,713
Apr 2	DONCASTER ROVERS	L 1-2	Evans	49,659
Apr 7	Fulham	L 1-3	Liddell	15,750
Apr 14	PORT VALE	W 4-1	Rowley 3, Twentyman	29,413
Apr 21	Rotherham United	W 1-0	Rowley	9,031
Apr 28	Bristol Rovers	W 2-1	Evans, Twentyman	24,106
May 2	Lincoln City	L 0-2		11,069

FA Cup

Jan 7	ACCRINGTON STANLEY	(Rd3)	W 2-0	Liddell 2	48,385
Jan 28	SCUNTHORPE UNITED	(Rd4)	D 3-3	Liddell 2, Payne	53,393
Feb 6	Scunthorpe United	(R)	W 2-1	Liddell, Arnell	19,500
Feb 18	Manchester City	(Rd5)	D 0-0		70,640
Feb 22	MANCHESTER CITY	(R)	L 1-2	Arnell	57,528

League & Cup Appearances

PLAYER	LEAGUE	CUP COMPETITION FA CUP	TOTAL
A'Court	40	5	45
Anderson	20		20
Arnell	23	4	27
Bimpson	8	1	9
Dickson	6		6
Evans	31	5	36
Hughes	39	5	44
Jackson	15		15
Lambert	10		10
Liddell	39	5	44
McNulty	1		1
Melia	4		4
Molyneux	32	5	37
Moran	39	5	44
Payne	16	5	21
Perry	1		1
Price	1		1
Rowley	7		7
Rudham	21		21
Saunders	37	5	42
Twentyman	42	5	47
Underwood	21	5	26
White	8		8
Wilkinson	1		1

Goalscorers

PLAYER	LEAGUE	CUP COMPETITION FA CUP	TOTAL
Liddell	27	5	32
Arnell	13	2	15
Evans	13		13
Twentyman	7		7
A'Court	6		6
Anderson	6		6
Rowley	6		6
Dickson	4		4
Payne	2	1	3
Melia	1		1

Fact File

Failure to gain promotion at the second attempt cost manager Don Welsh his job. He was the first Liverpool manager to get the sack.

MANAGER: Don Welsh

CAPTAIN: Billy Liddell

TOP SCORER: Billy Liddell 32 (27 league)

BIGGEST WIN: 7-0, 26 November 1955, v Fulham (H), Division Two

HIGHEST ATTENDANCE: 70,640, 18 February 1956, v Manchester City (A), FA Cup

TRANSFERS IN: Dick White from Scunthorpe United

TRANSFERS OUT: Dave Underwood to Watford, Ray Lambert – retired

Final Division Two Table

		P	W	D	L	F	A	Pts
1	Sheffield W	42	21	13	8	101	62	55
2	Leeds U	42	23	6	13	80	60	52
3	Liverpool	42	21	6	15	85	63	48
4	Blackburn R	42	21	6	15	84	65	48
5	Leicester C	42	21	6	15	94	78	48
6	Bristol R	42	21	6	15	84	70	48
7	Nottingham F	42	19	9	14	68	63	47
8	Lincoln C	42	18	10	14	79	65	46
9	Fulham	42	20	6	16	89	79	46
10	Swansea T	42	20	6	16	83	81	46
11	Bristol C	42	19	7	16	80	64	45
12	Port Vale	42	16	13	13	60	58	45
13	Stoke C	42	20	4	18	71	62	44
14	Middlesbrough	42	16	8	18	76	78	40
15	Bury	42	16	8	18	86	90	40
16	West Ham U	42	14	11	17	74	69	39
17	Doncaster R	42	12	11	19	69	96	35
18	Barnsley	42	11	12	19	47	84	34
19	Rotherham U	42	12	9	21	56	75	33
20	Notts Co	42	11	9	22	55	82	31
21	Plymouth Arg	42	10	8	24	54	87	28
22	Hull C	42	10	6	26	53	97	26

Season 1956-57

Football League Division Two

DATE	OPPONENTS	SCORE	GOALSCORERS	ATTENDANCE
Aug 18	HUDDERSFIELD TOWN	L 2-3	Liddell 2 (1 pen)	49,344
Aug 23	Notts County	D 1-1	Liddell	14,671
Aug 25	Bury	W 2-0	Bimpson, Saunders	17,000
Aug 29	NOTTS COUNTY	D 3-3	Twentyman 2, Arnell	41,095
Sep 1	GRIMSBY TOWN	W 3-2	Bimpson 2, Arnell	43,222
Sep 3	West Ham United	D 1-1	Liddell	25,000
Sep 8	Doncaster Rovers	D 1-1	Liddell	13,580
Sep 15	STOKE CITY	L 0-2		47,119
Sep 22	Middlesbrough	D 1-1	Robinson o.g.	21,912
Sep 29	LEICESTER CITY	W 2-0	Melia, Liddell	41,126
Oct 6	BLACKBURN ROVERS	L 2-3	Anderson, Liddell	41,538
Oct 13	Bristol City	L 1-2	Wheeler	26,042
Oct 20	FULHAM	W 4-3	A'Court, Wheeler, Liddell, Melia	36,735
Oct 27	Barnsley	L 1-4	Melia	13,941
Nov 3	PORT VALE	W 4-1	Liddell, Wheeler 3	32,334
Nov 10	Rotherham United	D 2-2	Bimpson, A'Court	11,524
Nov 17	LINCOLN CITY	W 4-0	Arnell 2, Wheeler 2	29,762
Nov 24	Swansea Town	D 1-1	Arnell	18,000
Dec 1	SHEFFIELD UNITED	W 5-1	Wheeler, Liddell, Melia, A'Court, Arnell	34,159
Dec 8	Nottingham Forest	L 0-1		17,624
Dec 15	Huddersfield Town	W 3-0	Arnell 3	11,577
Dec 22	BURY	W 2-0	Liddell (pen), Melia	18,754
Dec 25	LEYTON ORIENT	W 1-0	A'Court	22,001
Dec 26	Leyton Orient	W 4-0	A'Court, Arnell, Bimpson, Liddell	10,332
Dec 29	Grimsby Town	D 0-0		15,001
Jan 12	DONCASTER ROVERS	W 2-1	Arnell, Twentyman	35,954
Jan 19	Stoke City	L 0-1		31,144
Feb 2	MIDDLESBROUGH	L 1-2	A'Court	38,890
Feb 9	Leicester City	L 2-3	Liddell, Evans	39,622
Feb 16	Blackburn Rovers	W 2-1	Wheeler, Liddell	27,100
Mar 2	Fulham	W 2-1	Evans, Liddell	26,500
Mar 9	BARNSLEY	W 2-1	Wheeler, Liddell	30,672
Mar 16	Port Vale	W 2-1	Rowley 2	14,241
Mar 23	ROTHERHAM UNITED	W 4-1	Liddell, Noble o.g., Rowley, A'Court	33,307
Mar 30	Lincoln City	D 3-3	Jackson 2, Rowley	8,449
Apr 6	SWANSEA TOWN	W 2-0	A'Court 2	34,773
Apr 13	Sheffield United	L 0-3		24,000
Apr 19	BRISTOL ROVERS	W 4-1	Melia, Campbell, Liddell (pen), Rowley	40,776
Apr 20	NOTTINGHAM FOREST	W 3-1	Liddell, A'Court, Rowley	47,621
Apr 22	Bristol Rovers	D 0-0		14,794
Apr 27	WEST HAM UNITED	W 1-0	Liddell (pen)	36,236
May 1	BRISTOL CITY	W 2-1	Rowley, Liddell	15,108

FA Cup

Jan 5	Southend	(Rd3) L 1-2	Wheeler	18,253

League & Cup Appearances

PLAYER	LEAGUE	CUP COMPETITION FA CUP	TOTAL
A'Court	38	1	39
Anderson	7		7
Arnell	14	1	15
Bimpson	21		21
Campbell	6		6
Evans	11		11
Hughes	41	1	42
Jackson	19		19
Liddell	41	1	42
McNulty	2		2
Melia	26	1	27
Molyneux	40	1	41
Moran	42	1	43
Rowley	14		14
Rudham	2		2
Saunders	27	1	28
Twentyman	30	1	31
Wheeler	28	1	29
White	5		5
Wilkinson	8		8
Younger	40	1	41

Goalscorers

PLAYER	LEAGUE	CUP COMPETITION FA CUP	TOTAL
Liddell	21		21
Wheeler	10	1	11
A'Court	10		10
Arnell	10		10
Rowley	7		7
Bimpson	6		6
Melia	6		6
Twentyman	3		3
Evans	2		2
Jackson	2		2
Anderson	1		1
Campbell	1		1
Saunders	1		1
Opps' o.gs.	2		2

Fact File

Billy Liddell played his 400th league game on 22 December v Bury, scoring his 165th league goal with a penalty.

MANAGER: Phil Taylor

CAPTAIN: Billy Liddell

TOP SCORER: Billy Liddell 21 (league)

BIGGEST WIN: 5-1, 1 December 1956, v Sheffield United (H), Division Two

HIGHEST ATTENDANCE: 49,344, 18 August 1956, v Huddersfield Town (H), Division Two

TRANSFERS IN: Tommy Younger from Hibernian, John Wheeler from Bolton Wanderers

Final Division Two Table

		P	W	D	L	F	A	PTS
1	Leicester C	42	25	11	6	109	67	61
2	Nottingham F	42	22	10	10	94	55	54
3	Liverpool	42	21	11	10	82	54	53
4	Blackburn R	42	21	10	11	83	75	52
5	Stoke C	42	20	8	14	83	58	48
6	Middlesbrough	42	19	10	13	84	60	48
7	Sheffield U	42	19	8	15	87	76	46
8	West Ham U	42	19	8	15	59	63	46
9	Bristol R	42	18	9	15	81	67	45
10	Swansea T	42	19	7	16	90	90	45
11	Fulham	42	19	4	19	84	76	42
12	Huddersfield T	42	18	6	18	68	74	42
13	Bristol C	42	16	9	17	74	79	41
14	Doncaster R	42	15	10	17	77	77	40
15	Leyton Orient	42	15	10	17	66	84	40
16	Grimsby T	42	17	5	20	61	62	39
17	Rotherham U	42	13	11	18	74	75	37
18	Lincoln C	42	14	6	22	54	80	34
19	Barnsley	42	12	10	20	59	89	34
20	Notts Co	42	9	12	21	58	86	30
21	Bury	42	8	9	25	60	96	25
22	Port Vale	42	8	6	28	57	101	22

Season 1957-58

Football League Division Two

DATE	OPPONENTS	SCORE	GOALSCORERS	ATTENDANCE
Aug 24	Bristol City	W 2-1	Rowley 2	28,191
Aug 28	HUDDERSFIELD TOWN	D 1-1	A'Court	41,447
Aug 31	CARDIFF CITY	W 3-0	Melia, Liddell, Malloy o.g.	45,698
Sep 4	Huddersfield Town	L 1-2	Rowley	16,614
Sep 7	Fulham	D 2-2	Liddell, A'Court	33,000
Sep 14	Middlesbrough	D 2-2	Melia, Rowley	30,645
Sep 19	Rotherham United	D 2-2	Arnell, Melia	10,359
Sep 21	LEYTON ORIENT	W 3-0	Wheeler, Rowley, Jackson	36,077
Sep 23	Stoke City	W 2-1	Bimpson, Rowley	23,231
Sep 28	Charlton Athletic	L 1-5	Rowley	25,403
Oct 5	DONCASTER ROVERS	W 5-0	Rowley 2, Melia 2, Bimpson	33,701
Oct 12	SWANSEA	W 4-0	Rowley 2, Melia, Campbell	37,204
Oct 19	Derby County	L 1-2	Rowley	22,631
Oct 26	BRISTOL Rovers	W 2-0	Liddell, A'Court	36,686
Nov 2	Lincoln City	W 1-0	Wheeler	9,983
Nov 9	NOTTS COUNTY	W 4-0	Melia, A'Court, Liddell, Rowley	39,735
Nov 16	Ipswich Town	L 1-3	Wheeler	20,452
Nov 23	BLACKBURN ROVERS	W 2-0	Liddell 2	55,232
Nov 27	ROTHERHAM UNITED	W 2-0	Wheeler, Liddell	37,518
Nov 30	Sheffield United	D 1-1	Liddell	20,122
Dec 7	WEST HAM UNITED	D 1-1	Liddell	34,030
Dec 14	Barnsley	L 1-2	Jackson	15,205
Dec 21	BRISTOL CITY	W 4-3	Rowley 2, McNamara, A'Court	38,051
Dec 25	Grimsby Town	L 1-3	Rowley	17,705
Dec 26	GRIMSBY TOWN	W 3-2	Liddell 2 (1 pen), McNamara	47,766
Dec 28	Cardiff City	L 1-6	Wheeler	32,000
Jan 11	FULHAM	W 2-1	McNamara, Bimpson	51,701
Jan 18	MIDDLESBROUGH	L 0-2		39,246
Feb 1	Leyton Orient	L 0-1		18,568
Feb 8	CHARLTON ATHLETIC	W 3-1	Twentyman, Liddell, Murdoch	38,528
Feb 19	Doncaster Rovers	D 1-1	Liddell	6,093
Feb 22	Blackburn Rovers	D 3-3	Liddell 3	41,700
Mar 5	DERBY COUNTY	W 2-0	Liddell, Murdoch	30,832
Mar 8	Bristol Rovers	L 1-3	Murdoch	19,299
Mar 15	LINCOLN CITY	W 1-0	Liddell	31,403
Mar 22	Notts County	W 2-0	Melia, Bimpson	13,040
Mar 29	IPSWICH TOWN	W 3-1	Melia, Harrower, A'Court	24,026
Apr 5	Swansea Town	W 2-0	Melia, Murdoch	13,500
Apr 7	STOKE CITY	W 3-0	Murdoch, Liddell 2 (1 pen)	39,446
Apr 12	SHEFFIELD UNITED	W 1-0	Liddell	43,222
Apr 19	West Ham United	D 1-1	Liddell	37,750
Apr 26	BARNSLEY	D 1-1	Harrower	26,440

FA Cup

Jan 4	SOUTHEND UNITED	(Rd3)	D 1-1	Smith o.g.	43,454
Jan 8	Southend United	(R)	W 3-2	Molyneux, White, Rowley	20,000
Jan 25	NORTHAMPTON TOWN	(Rd4)	W 3-1	Liddell, Collins o.g., Bimpson	56,939
Feb 15	Scunthorpe United	(Rd5)	W 1-0	Murdoch	23,000
Mar 1	Blackburn Rovers	(Rd6)	L 1-2	Murdoch	51,000

League & Cup Appearances

PLAYER	LEAGUE	CUP COMPETITION FA CUP	TOTAL
A'Court	39	5	44
Arnell	8		8
Bimpson	7	3	10
Byrne	1		1
Campbell	27	1	28
Evans	1		1
Harrower	12	2	14
Hughes	1		1
Jackson	22	2	24
Liddell	35	5	40
McNamara	9	1	10
McNulty	2		2
Melia	34	2	36
Molyneux	40	5	45
Moran	41	5	46
Morrissey	2		2
Murdoch	15	2	17
Rowley	24	3	27
Rudham	3		3
Saunders	4	1	5
Twentyman	7	3	10
Wheeler	38	5	43
White	41	5	46
Wilkinson	10		10
Younger	39	5	44

Goalscorers

PLAYER	LEAGUE	CUP COMPETITION FA CUP	TOTAL
Liddell	22	1	23
Rowley	16	1	17
Melia	10		10
Murdoch	5	2	7
A'Court	6		6
Bimpson	4	1	5
Wheeler	5		5
McNamara	3		3
Harrower	2		2
Jackson	2		2
Arnell	1		1
Campbell	1		1
Molyneux		1	1
Twentyman	1		1
White		1	1
Opps' o.gs.	1	2	3

Fact File

With Billy Liddell, club captain, becoming top scorer for the 4th consecutive season, the team was known as 'Liddellpool'.

MANAGER: Phil Taylor

CAPTAIN: Billy Liddell

TOP SCORER: Billy Liddell 23 (22 league)

BIGGEST WIN: 5-0, 5 October 1957, v Doncaster Rovers (H), Division Two

HIGHEST ATTENDANCE: 56,939, 25 January 1958, v Northampton Town (H), FA Cup

TRANSFERS IN: Jimmy Harrower from Hibernian, Tony McNamara from Everton

TRANSFERS OUT: Brian Jackson to Port Vale, Tony Rowley to Crewe Alexandra, John Evans to Colchester, Tom McNulty to Hyde United

Final Division Two Table

		P	W	D	L	F	A	Pts
1	West Ham U	42	23	11	8	101	54	57
2	Blackburn R	42	22	12	8	93	57	56
3	Charlton Ath	42	24	7	11	107	69	55
4	Liverpool	42	22	10	10	79	54	54
5	Fulham	42	20	12	10	97	59	52
6	Sheffield U	42	21	10	11	75	50	52
7	Middlesbrough	42	19	7	16	83	74	45
8	Ipswich T	42	16	12	14	68	69	44
9	Huddersfield T	42	14	16	12	63	66	44
10	Bristol R	42	17	8	17	85	80	42
11	Stoke C	42	18	6	18	75	73	42
12	Leyton O	42	18	5	19	77	79	41
13	Grimsby T	42	17	6	19	86	83	40
14	Barnsley	42	14	12	16	70	74	40
15	Cardiff C	42	14	9	19	63	77	37
16	Derby C	42	14	8	20	60	81	36
17	Bristol C	42	13	9	20	63	88	35
18	Rotherham U	42	14	5	23	65	101	33
19	Swansea T	42	11	9	22	72	99	31
20	Lincoln C	42	11	9	22	55	82	31
21	Notts C	42	12	6	24	44	80	30
22	Doncaster R	42	8	11	23	56	88	27

Season 1958-59

Football League Division Two

DATE	OPPONENTS	SCORE	GOALSCORERS	ATTENDANCE
Aug 23	GRIMSBY TOWN	D 3-3	Melia, Liddell 2 (1 pen)	47,502
Aug 30	Sunderland	L 1-2	Liddell	36,168
Sep 3	BRIGHTON & HOVE ALBION	W 5-0	Arnell 2, Harrower, Banks, Molyneux	39,520
Sep 6	Middlesbrough	L 1-2	Harrower	34,714
Sep 10	SHEFFIELD UNITED	W 2-1	Liddell, Twentyman.	44,232
Sep 13	CHARLTON ATHLETIC	W 3-0	Liddell 2 (1 pen), A'Court	43,329
Sep 15	Sheffield United	L 0-2		14,727
Sep 20	Bristol City	W 3-1	Liddell 2, Campbell	26,896
Sep 24	Brighton & Hove Albion	D 2-2	Liddell, Morris	21,323
Sep 27	CARDIFF CITY	L 1-2	Banks	41,866
Oct 4	Huddersfield Town	L 0-5		15,934
Oct 11	LINCOLN CITY	W 3-2	Harrower, Morris 2	31,344
Oct 18	Fulham	W 1-0	Bimpson	32,200
Oct 25	SHEFFIELD WEDNESDAY	W 3-2	Martin o.g., Morris (pen), Harrower	39,912
Nov 1	Stoke City	W 2-0	Bimpson, Melia	26,919
Nov 8	LEYTON ORIENT	W 3-0	Twentyman, Bimpson, Melia	34,920
Nov 15	Derby County	L 2-3	Mays o.g., Bimpson	16,907
Nov 22	BRISTOL ROVERS	W 2-1	Twentyman, Melia	39,365
Nov 29	Ipswich Town	L 0-2		15,637
Dec 6	SWANSEA TOWN	W 4-0	Bimpson, Morris, Harrower, A'Court	27,561
Dec 13	Scunthorpe United	W 2-1	Melia, A'Court	11,194
Dec 20	Grimsby Town	W 3-2	Morris, Bimpson, A'Court	10,004
Dec 26	Rotherham United	W 1-0	Melia	12,960
Dec 27	ROTHERHAM UNITED	W 4-0	Morris, Bimpson 2, Harrower	44,729
Jan 3	SUNDERLAND	W 3-1	Wheeler, Bimpson, Morris	36,953
Jan 31	Charlton Athletic	W 3-2	Twentyman, Morris, Melia	17,566
Feb 7	BRISTOL CITY	W 3-2	Arnell 2, Melia	34,091
Feb 14	Cardiff City	L 0-3		25,000
Feb 21	HUDDERSFIELD TOWN	D 2-2	Melia, Morris	28,860
Feb 28	Leyton Orient	W 3-1	Melia, Morris, A'Court	14,064
Mar 7	FULHAM	D 0-0		43,926
Mar 20	STOKE CITY	L 3-4	Melia 2, Bimpson	35,507
Mar 27	BARNSLEY	W 3-2	Melia, Liddell 2	52,546
Mar 28	Lincoln City	L 1-2	Bimpson	11,012
Mar 30	Barnsley	W 2-0	Melia 2	7,517
Apr 4	DERBY COUNTY	W 3-0	Liddell, Melia 2	38,879
Apr 8	MIDDLESBROUGH	L 1-2	Melia	36,288
Apr 11	Bristol Rovers	L 0-3		14,810
Apr 14	Sheffield Wednesday	L 0-1		28,264
Apr 18	IPSWICH TOWN	W 3-1	Melia, Liddell, A'Court	16,415
Apr 22	SCUNTHORPE UNITED	W 3-0	Arnell, Liddell, Morris	11,976
Apr 25	Swansea Town	D 3-3	A'Court, Melia 2	8,000

FA Cup

Jan 15	Worcester City	(Rd3) L 1-2	Twentyman (pen)	15,011

League & Cup Appearances

PLAYER	LEAGUE	CUP COMPETITION FA CUP	TOTAL
A'Court	39	1	40
Arnell	12		12
Banks	3		3
Bimpson	15	1	16
Byrne	1		1
Campbell	10		10
Harrower	37	1	38
Liddell	19		19
Melia	39	1	40
Molyneux	37	1	38
Moran	40	1	41
Morris	40	1	41
Morrissey	2		2
Murdoch	2		2
Rudham	1		1
Saunders	4		4
Twentyman	25	1	26
Wheeler	41	1	42
White	42	1	43
Wilkinson	12		12
Younger	41	1	42

Goalscorers

PLAYER	LEAGUE	CUP COMPETITION FA CUP	TOTAL
Melia	21		21
Liddell	14		14
Morris	12		12
Bimpson	11		11
A'Court	7		7
Harrower	6		6
Arnell	5		5
Twentyman	4	1	5
Banks	2		2
Campbell	1		1
Molyneux	1		1
Wheeler	1		1
Opps' o.gs.	2		2

Fact File

Three consecutive defeats in April cost the club promotion and led to the lowest post-war league attendance at Anfield, 11,976 v Scunthorpe United on 22 April 1959.

MANAGER: Phil Taylor

CAPTAIN: Johnny Wheeler

TOP SCORER: Jimmy Melia 21 (league)

BIGGEST WIN: 5-0, 3 September 1958, v Brighton & Hove Albion (H), Division Two

HIGHEST ATTENDANCE: 52,546, 27 March 1959, v Barnsley (H), Division Two

TRANSFERS IN: Fred Morris from Mansfield Town

TRANSFERS OUT: Roy Saunders to Swansea Town

Final Division Two Table

		P	W	D	L	F	A	PTS
1	Sheffield W	42	28	6	8	106	48	62
2	Fulham	42	27	6	9	96	61	60
3	Sheffield U	42	23	7	12	82	48	53
4	Liverpool	42	24	5	13	87	62	53
5	Stoke C	42	21	7	14	72	58	49
6	Bristol R	42	18	12	12	80	64	48
7	Derby C	42	20	8	14	74	71	48
8	Charlton Ath	42	18	7	17	92	90	43
9	Cardiff C	42	18	7	17	65	65	43
10	Bristol C	42	17	7	18	74	70	41
11	Swansea T	42	16	9	17	79	81	41
12	Brighton & HA	42	15	11	16	74	90	41
13	Middlesbrough	42	15	10	17	87	71	40
14	Huddersfield T	42	16	8	18	62	55	40
15	Sunderland	42	16	8	18	64	75	40
16	Ipswich T	42	17	6	19	62	77	40
17	Leyton O	42	14	8	20	71	78	36
18	Scunthorpe U	42	12	9	21	55	84	33
19	Lincoln C	42	11	7	24	63	93	29
20	Rotherham U	42	10	9	23	42	82	29
21	Grimsby T	42	9	10	23	62	90	28
22	Barnsley	42	10	7	25	55	91	27

Season 1959-60

Football League Division Two

DATE	OPPONENTS	SCORE	GOALSCORERS	ATTENDANCE
Aug 22	Cardiff City	L 2-3	Malloy o.g. 2	34,000
Aug 26	BRISTOL CITY	W 4-2	Liddell 2, Melia (pen), A'Court	33,071
Aug 29	HULL CITY	W 5-3	Harrower, Melia, Moran, A'Court, Liddell	35,520
Sep 1	Bristol City	L 0-1		22,528
Sep 5	Sheffield United	L 1-2	Morrissey	25,073
Sep 9	SCUNTHORPE UNITED	W 2-0	Melia, Hunt	31,713
Sep 12	MIDDLESBROUGH	L 1-2	Liddell	39,000
Sep 17	Scunthorpe United	D 1-1	Melia	18,851
Sep 19	Derby County	W 2-1	A'Court, Hunt	11,822
Sep 26	PLYMOUTH ARGYLE	W 4-1	Melia, A'Court, Hunt, Moran	29,278
Oct 3	Swansea Town	L 4-5	Kennedy o.g., Melia (pen), Hunt, Moran	16,500
Oct 10	BRIGHTON & HOVE ALBION	D 2-2	A'Court, Melia	30,366
Oct 17	Stoke City	D 1-1	Harrower	17,000
Oct 24	PORTSMOUTH	D 1-1	Moran	21.075
Oct 31	Sunderland	D 1-1	Hunt	30,208
Nov 7	ASTON VILLA	W 2-1	Hickson 2	49,981
Nov 14	Lincoln City	L 2-4	Hickson, Hunt	10,801
Nov 21	LEYTON ORIENT	W 4-3	Morris 2, Melia, Hickson	34,321
Nov 28	Huddersfield Town	L 0-1		16,185
Dec 5	IPSWICH TOWN	W 3-1	Hunt 2, Hickson	24,843
Dec 12	Bristol Rovers	W 2-0	Melia 2	15,615
Dec 19	CARDIFF CITY	L 0-4		27,291
Dec 26	Charlton Athletic	L 0-3		15,491
Dec 28	CHARLTON ATHLETIC	W 2-0	A'Court, Hunt	25,658
Jan 2	Hull City	W 1-0	Melia	18,681
Jan 16	SHEFFIELD UNITED	W 3-0	Melia, Hunt 2	33,297
Jan 23	Middlesbrough	D 3-3	Thompson o.g., Hickson, Hunt	28,800
Feb 13	Plymouth Argyle	D 1-1	Hickson	16,996
Feb 20	SWANSEA TOWN	W 4-1	Hickson 2, Hunt 2	31,663
Feb 27	Brighton & Hove Albion	W 2-1	Hickson 2	21,118
Mar 5	STOKE CITY	W 5-1	Hunt, Harrower 2, Liddell, Hickson	35,101
Mar 12	Portsmouth	L 1-2	Harrower	14,622
Mar 19	HUDDERSFIELD TOWN	D 2-2	Hickson, Wheeler	30,009
Mar 30	Aston Villa	D 4-4	Hunt, Hickson 2, Molyneux	27,000
Apr 2	LINCOLN CITY	L 1-3	Moran (pen)	24,081
Apr 6	DERBY COUNTY	W 4-1	Hunt, A'Court, Wheeler, Hickson	19,411
Apr 9	Leyton Orient	L 0-2		13,007
Apr 16	BRISTOL ROVERS	W 4-0	Melia, A'Court, Campbell, Hunt	27,317
Apr 18	ROTHERHAM UNITED	W 3-0	Hunt, Hickson 2	26,776
Apr 19	Rotherham United	D 2-2	Hickson, Hunt	10,123
Apr 23	Ipswich Town	W 1-0	Hickson	12,048
Apr 30	SUNDERLAND	W 3-0	Hickson, Hunt, Melia	25,916

FA Cup

Jan 9	LEYTON ORIENT	(Rd3)	W 2-1	Hunt 2	40,343
Jan 30	MANCHESTER UNITED	(Rd4)	L 1-3	Wheeler	56,736

Fact File

Bill Shankly officially took up his appointment on 14 December 1959 and led the club to a Second Division championship, three First Division championships, two FA Cups and the club's first European trophy, the UEFA Cup. He was awarded the Manager of the Year trophy in 1973 and set the foundations for continuing success.

MANAGER: Phil Taylor until November, Bill Shankly
CAPTAIN: Ronnie Moran
TOP SCORER: Roger Hunt 23 (21 league)
BIGGEST WIN: 5-1, 5 March 1960, v Stoke City (H), Division Two
HIGHEST ATTENDANCE: 56,736, 30 January 1960, v Manchester United (H), FA Cup
TRANSFERS IN: Bert Slater* from Falkirk, Dave Hickson from Everton, Tommy Leishman from St. Mirren
TRANSFERS OUT: Tommy Younger to Falkirk (*in exchange for Slater), Bobby Murdoch to Barrow, Louis Bimpson to Blackburn Rovers, Geoff Twentyman to Ballymena United

League & Cup Appearances

PLAYER	LEAGUE	CUP COMPETITION FA CUP	TOTAL
A'Court	42	2	44
Arnell	1		1
Bimpson	5		5
Blore	1		1
Byrne	5		5
Callaghan	4		4
Campbell	13		13
Carlin	1		1
Harrower	26	2	28
Hickson	27	2	29
Hunt	36	2	38
Jones	1		1
Leishman	15	2	17
Liddell	17		17
Melia	34	2	36
Molyneux	38	2	40
Moran	42	2	44
Morris	7		7
Morrissey	9		9
Nicholson	1		1
Rudham	14		14
Slater	28	2	30
Twentyman	11		11
Wheeler	29	2	31
White	41	2	43
Wilkinson	14		14

Goalscorers

PLAYER	LEAGUE	CUP COMPETITION FA CUP	TOTAL
Hunt	21	2	23
Hickson	21		21
Melia	14		14
A'Court	8		8
Harrower	5		5
Liddell	5		5
Moran	5		5
Wheeler	2	1	3
Morris	2		2
Campbell	1		1
Molyneux	1		1
Morrissey	1		1
Opps' o.gs.	4		4

Final Division Two Table

		P	W	D	L	F	A	Pts
1	Aston Villa	42	25	9	8	89	43	59
2	Cardiff C	42	23	12	7	90	62	58
3	Liverpool	42	20	10	12	90	66	50
4	Sheffield U	42	19	12	11	68	51	50
5	Middlesbrough	42	19	10	13	90	64	48
6	Huddersfield T	42	19	9	14	73	52	47
7	Charlton Ath	42	17	13	12	90	87	47
8	Rotherham U	42	17	13	12	61	60	47
9	Bristol R	42	18	11	13	72	78	47
10	Leyton O	42	15	14	13	76	61	44
11	Ipswich T	42	19	6	17	78	68	44
12	Swansea T	42	15	10	17	82	84	40
13	Lincoln City	42	16	7	19	75	78	39
14	Brighton & HA	42	13	12	17	67	76	38
15	Scunthorpe U	42	13	10	19	57	71	36
16	Sunderland	42	12	12	18	52	65	36
17	Stoke C	42	14	7	21	66	83	35
18	Derby C	42	14	7	21	61	77	35
19	Plymouth Arg	42	13	9	20	61	89	35
20	Portsmouth	42	10	12	20	59	77	32
21	Hull C	42	10	10	22	48	76	30
22	Bristol C	42	11	5	26	60	97	27

Season 1960-61

Football League Division Two

DATE	OPPONENTS	SCORE	GOALSCORERS	ATTENDANCE
Aug 20	LEEDS UNITED	W 2-0	Lewis, Hickson	43,041
Aug 24	Southampton	L 1-4	Leishman	24,823
Aug 27	Middlesbrough	D 1-1	Lewis	21,236
Aug 31	SOUTHAMPTON	L 0-1		37,604
Sep 3	BRIGHTON & HOVE ALBION	W 2-0	Harrower 2	24,390
Sep 7	LUTON TOWN	D 2-2	Hickson, Moran (pen)	27,339
Sep 10	Ipswich Town	L 0-1		13,502
Sep 14	Luton Town	L 1-2	Moran (pen)	10,055
Sep 17	SCUNTHORPE UNITED	W 3-2	Harrower, Leishman, Hunt	23,797
Sep 24	Leyton Orient	W 3-1	Hickson, A'Court, Morrissey	10,921
Oct 1	DERBY COUNTY	W 1-0	Wheeler	24,695
Oct 8	Lincoln City	W 2-1	Hunt 2	6,656
Oct 15	PORTSMOUTH	D 3-3	Hickson 2, Hunt	26,302
Oct 22	Huddersfield Town	W 4-2	Lewis, Hunt, A'Court, Hickson	15,719
Oct 29	SUNDERLAND	D 1-1	Harrower (pen)	30,612
Nov 5	Plymouth Argyle	W 4-0	A'Court, Hickson, Hunt 2	17,641
Nov 12	NORWICH CITY	W 2-1	Hunt, Harrower	32,473
Nov 19	Charlton Athletic	W 3-1	Lawrie o.g., Hunt, Wheeler	13,439
Nov 26	SHEFFIELD UNITED	W 4-2	Harrower 3, Hickson	39,999
Dec 10	SWANSEA TOWN	W 4-0	Lewis 2, A'Court, Hickson	25,739
Dec 17	Leeds United	D 2-2	Lewis, Leishman	11,900
Dec 26	ROTHERHAM UNITED	W 2-1	Hunt, Lewis	39,426
Dec 27	Rotherham United	L 0-1		17,815
Dec 31	MIDDLESBROUGH	L 3-4	A'Court, Lewis 2	34,645
Jan 14	Brighton & Hove Albion	L 1-3	A'Court	17,495
Jan 21	IPSWICH TOWN	D 1-1	Lewis	33,401
Feb 4	Scunthorpe United	W 3-2	Lewis, Melia, Leishman	7,970
Feb 11	LEYTON ORIENT	W 5-0	Hickson 3, Morrissey, Lewis	22,131
Feb 18	Derby County	W 4-1	Hickson, Melia 2, Lewis	16,301
Feb 25	LINCOLN CITY	W 2-0	Morrissey, Lewis	24,759
Mar 4	Portsmouth	D 2-2	Banks, Morrissey	14,301
Mar 11	HUDDERSFIELD TOWN	W 3-1	Banks 2, Lewis	29,733
Mar 18	Swansea Town	L 0-2		13,181
Mar 24	PLYMOUTH ARGYLE	D 1-1	Banks	25,250
Mar 31	BRISTOL ROVERS	W 3-0	Hunt, Wheeler, Hickson	36,538
Apr 1	Sheffield United	D 1-1	Morrissey	28,853
Apr 4	Bristol Rovers	L 3-4	Lewis 3 (1 pen)	16,522
Apr 8	CHARLTON ATHLETIC	W 2-1	Hunt 2	26,390
Apr 15	Norwich City	L 1-2	Hickson	21,204
Apr 22	STOKE CITY	W 3-0	Hunt 2, Hickson, Lewis	13,389
Apr 29	Sunderland	D 1-1	Hunt	30,040
May 3	Stoke City	L 1-3	A'Court	4,463

FA Cup

Jan 7	COVENTRY CITY	(Rd3)	W 3-2	Hunt, Lewis, Harrower	50,909
Jan 28	SUNDERLAND	(Rd4)	L 0-2		46,185

League Cup

Oct 19	LUTON TOWN	(Rd2)	D 1-1	Leishman	10,502
Oct 24	Luton Town	(R)	W 5-2	Lewis 2, Hickson, Hunt 2	6,125
Nov 16	SOUTHAMPTON	(Rd3)	L 1-2	Hunt	14,036

League & Cup Appearances

PLAYER	LEAGUE	CUP COMPETITION FA CUP	LC	TOTAL
A'Court	33	2	2	37
Arnell	1			1
Banks	5			5
Byrne	33	2	3	38
Callaghan	3		2	5
Campbell	1		1	2
Harrower	21	1	3	25
Hickson	33	2	3	38
Hunt	32	1	3	36
Leishman	40	2	2	44
Lewis	32	2	2	36
Liddell	1			1
Melia	26	1		27
Milne	16	1		17
Molyneux	39	2	3	44
Moran	12			12
Morrissey	23	1		24
Slater	42	2	3	47
Wheeler	27	1	3	31
White	42	2	3	47

Goalscorers

PLAYER	LEAGUE	CUP COMPETITION FA CUP	LC	TOTAL
Lewis	19		2	21
Hunt	15	1	3	19
Hickson	16	1	1	18
Harrower	8	1		9
A'Court	7			7
Leishman	4		1	5
Morrissey	5			5
Banks	4			4
Melia	3			3
Wheeler	3			3
Moran	2			2
Opps' o.gs.	1			1

Fact File

The Shankly team building began with two successive club-record signings: Lewis for £13,000 and Milne for £16,000. The great Billy Liddell retired from playing having scored 229 goals in 534 appearances.

MANAGER: Bill Shankly

CAPTAIN: Dick White

TOP SCORER: Kevin Lewis 21 (19 league)

BIGGEST WIN: 5-0, 11 February 1961, v Leyton Orient (H), Division Two

HIGHEST ATTENDANCE: 50,909, 7 January 1961 v Coventry City (H), FA Cup

TRANSFERS IN: Kevin Lewis from Sheffield United, Gordon Milne from Preston North End

TRANSFERS OUT: Doug Rudham to Johannesburg Ramblers, Jimmy Harrower to Newcastle, Billy Liddell – retired

Final Division Two Table

		P	W	D	L	F	A	Pts
1	Ipswich T	42	26	7	9	100	55	59
2	Sheffield U	42	26	6	10	81	51	58
3	Liverpool	42	21	10	11	82	59	52
4	Norwich C	42	20	9	13	69	53	49
5	Middlesbrough	42	18	12	12	83	74	48
6	Sunderland	42	17	13	12	85	70	47
7	Swansea T	42	18	11	13	77	73	47
8	Southampton	42	18	8	16	84	81	44
9	Scunthorpe U	42	14	15	13	69	64	43
10	Charlton Ath	42	16	11	15	97	91	43
11	Plymouth Arg	42	17	8	17	81	82	42
12	Derby C	42	15	10	17	80	80	40
13	Luton T	42	15	9	18	71	77	39
14	Leeds U	42	14	10	18	75	83	38
15	Rotherham U	42	12	13	17	65	64	37
16	Brighton & HA	42	14	9	19	61	75	37
17	Bristol R	42	15	7	20	73	92	37
18	Stoke C	42	12	12	18	42	59	36
19	Leyton O	42	14	8	20	55	78	36
20	Huddersfield T	42	13	9	20	62	71	35
21	Portsmouth	42	11	11	20	64	91	33
22	Lincoln City	42	8	8	26	48	95	24

Season 1961-62

Football League Division Two

DATE	OPPONENTS	SCORE	GOALSCORERS	ATTENDANCE
Aug 19	Bristol Rovers	W 2-0	Lewis, Mills o.g.	19,438
Aug 23	SUNDERLAND	W 3-0	Hunt 2, Lewis	48,963
Aug 26	LEEDS UNITED	W 5-0	Hunt 3, Lewis (pen), Melia	42,950
Aug 30	Sunderland	W 4-1	Hunt 2, St John 2	47,261
Sep 2	Norwich City	W 2-1	Hunt 2	28,049
Sep 9	SCUNTHORPE UNITED	W 2-1	Hemstead o.g., A'Court	46,837
Sep 16	Brighton & Hove Albion	D 0-0		18,764
Sep 20	Newcastle United	W 2-1	Milne, Heslop o.g.	38,180
Sep 23	BURY	W 5-0	Melia 2, St John, Hunt, Lewis	46,609
Sep 30	Charlton Athletic	W 4-0	Hunt 2, Lewis, St John	14,236
Oct 4	NEWCASTLE UNITED	W 2-0	Lewis, Hunt	52,419
Oct 7	Middlesbrough	L 0-2		24,123
Oct 14	WALSALL	W 6-1	Lewis, Melia, Hunt 3, St John	42,229
Oct 21	Derby County	L 0-2		27,355
Oct 28	LEYTON ORIENT	D 3-3	Hunt 2, Leishman	36,612
Nov 4	Preston North End	W 3-1	Milne, Callaghan, St John	29,243
Nov 11	LUTON TOWN	D 1-1	Lewis	34,924
Nov 18	Huddersfield Town	W 2-1	Melia, Hunt	23,086
Nov 25	SWANSEA TOWN	W 5-0	Melia 2, Hunt 3	35.725
Dec 2	Southampton	L 0-2		21,445
Dec 9	PLYMOUTH ARGYLE	W 2-1	A'Court, St John	32,543
Dec 16	BRISTOL ROVERS	W 2-0	St John, Hunt	29,957
Dec 23	Leeds United	L 0-1		17,214
Dec 26	Rotherham United	L 0-1		13,577
Jan 13	NORWICH CITY	W 5-4	Melia 2, Hunt 2, A'Court	35,576
Jan 20	Scunthorpe United	D 1-1	St John	11,200
Feb 3	BRIGHTON & HOVE ALBION	W 3-1	Byrne, Hunt, St John	36,414
Feb 10	Bury	W 3-0	Hunt 3	21,872
Feb 24	MIDDLESBROUGH	W 5-1	St John 2, Hunt 3	37,629
Mar 3	Walsall	D 1-1	A'Court	13,660
Mar 10	DERBY COUNTY	W 4-1	Hunt 2, Melia 2	38,152
Mar 17	Leyton Orient	D 2-2	A'Court 2	25,880
Mar 24	PRESTON NORTH END	W 4-1	Melia, St John, Hunt 2	39,701
Mar 28	ROTHERHAM UNITED	W 4-1	Hunt, St John 3	32,827
Mar 31	Luton Town	L 0-1		9,086
Apr 7	HUDDERSFIELD TOWN	D 1-1	Hunt.	38,022
Apr 21	SOUTHAMPTON	W 2-0	Lewis 2	40,410
Apr 23	STOKE CITY	W 2-1	Moran (pen), Melia	41,005
Apr 24	Stoke City	D 0-0		15,472
Apr 28	Plymouth Argyle	W 3-2	A'Court, St John, Hunt	13,427
Apr 30	CHARLTON ATHLETIC	W 2-1	Hunt, A'Court	34,327
May 4	Swansea Town	L 2-4	St John, Hunt	15,000

FA Cup

Jan 6	CHELSEA	(Rd3)	W 4-3	St John 2, Hunt, A'Court	48,455
Jan 27	Oldham Athletic	(Rd4)	W 2-1	St John 2	42,000
Feb 17	PRESTON NORTH END	(Rd5)	D 0-0		54,967
Feb 20	Preston North End	(R)	D 0-0*		37,831
Feb 26	Preston North End†	(2nd R)	L 0-1		43,944

*After extra time. †Played at Old Trafford.

League & Cup Appearances

PLAYER	LEAGUE	CUP COMPETITION FA CUP	TOTAL
A'Court	42	5	47
Arrowsmith	1		1
Byrne	42	5	47
Callaghan	23	5	28
Furnall	13		13
Hunt	41	5	46
Leishman	41	5	46
Lewis	21		21
Melia	42	5	47
Milne	42	5	47
Molyneux	3	1	4
Moran	16	3	19
Slater	29	5	34
St John	40	5	45
Wheeler	1		1
White	24	1	25
Yeats	41	5	46

Goalscorers

PLAYER	LEAGUE	CUP COMPETITION FA CUP	TOTAL
Hunt	41	1	42
St John	18	4	22
Melia	13		13
Lewis	10		10
A'Court	8	1	9
Milne	2		2
Byrne	1		1
Callaghan	1		1
Leishman	1		1
Moran	1		1
Opps' o.gs.	3		3

Fact File

Roger Hunt's record 41 league goals in a season surpassed Gordon Hodgson's record of 36 goals in 1930-31.

MANAGER: Bill Shankly

CAPTAIN: Dick White, Ron Yeats from December

TOP SCORER: Roger Hunt 42 (41 league)

BIGGEST WIN: 6-1, 14 October 1961, v Walsall (H), Division Two

HIGHEST ATTENDANCE: 54,967, 17 February 1962, v Preston North End (H), FA Cup

TRANSFERS IN: Ian St John from Motherwell, Ron Yeats from Dundee United, Jim Furnell from Burnley

TRANSFERS OUT: Bert Slater to Dundee, Dick White to Doncaster Rovers, John Molyneux to Chester City

Final Division Two Table

		P	W	D	L	F	A	Pts
1	Liverpool	42	27	8	7	99	43	62
2	Leyton O	42	22	10	10	69	40	54
3	Sunderland	42	22	9	11	85	50	53
4	Scunthorpe U	42	21	7	14	86	71	49
5	Plymouth Arg	42	19	8	15	75	75	46
6	Southampton	42	18	9	15	77	62	45
7	Huddersfield T	42	16	12	14	67	59	44
8	Stoke City	42	17	8	17	55	57	42
9	Rotherham U	42	16	9	17	70	76	41
10	Preston NE	42	15	10	17	55	57	40
11	Newcastle U	42	15.	9	18	64	58	39
12	Middlesbrough	42	16	7	19	76	72	39
13	Luton T	42	17	5	20	69	71	39
14	Walsall	42	14	11	17	70	75	39
15	Charlton Ath	42	15	9	18	69	75	39
16	Derby C	42	14	11	17	68	75	39
17	Norwich C	42	14	11	17	61	70	39
18	Bury	42	17	5	20	52	76	39
19	Leeds U	42	12	12	18	50	61	36
20	Swansea T	42	12	12	18	61	83	36
21	Bristol R	42	13	7	22	53	81	33
22	Brighton & HA	42	10	11	21	42	86	31

Season 1962-63

Football League Division One

DATE	OPPONENTS	SCORE	GOALSCORERS	ATTENDANCE
Aug 18	BLACKPOOL	L 1-2	Lewis	51,207
Aug 22	Manchester City	D 2-2	Moran (pen), Hunt	33,165
Aug 26	Blackburn Rovers	L 0-1		21,700
Aug 29	MANCHESTER CITY	W 4-1	St John, Hunt 2, A'Court	46,073
Sep 1	SHEFFIELD UNITED	W 2-0	Callaghan, St John	47,742
Sep 3	West Ham United	L 0-1		22,262
Sep 8	Nottingham Forest	L 1-3	Leishman	24,126
Sep 12	WEST HAM UNITED	W 2-1	St John 2	39,261
Sep 15	IPSWICH TOWN	D 1-1	Hunt	40,121
Sep 22	Everton	D 2-2	Lewis, Hunt	73,000
Sep 29	Wolverhampton Wanderers	L 2-3	Melia 2	34,368
Oct 6	BOLTON WANDERERS	W 1-0	Hunt	41,155
Oct 13	Leicester City	L 0-3		24,137
Oct 27	West Bromwich Albion	L 0-1		17,850
Nov 3	BURNLEY	L 1-2	St John	43,870
Nov 10	Manchester United	D 3-3	St John, Melia, Moran	43,810
Nov 14	ARSENAL	W 2-1	Hunt, Moran (pen)	38,452
Nov 17	LEYTON ORIENT	W 5-0	Hunt 3, Stevenson, St John	30,009
Nov 24	Birmingham City	W 2-0	Hunt 2	27,050
Dec 1	FULHAM	W 2-1	Hunt, A'Court	38,267
Dec 8	Sheffield Wednesday	W 2-0	Lewis, Hunt	15,939
Dec 15	Blackpool	W 2-1	St John, Hunt	16,271
Dec 22	BLACKBURN ROVERS	W 3-1	Lewis, St John, Moran	35,371
Feb 13	ASTON VILLA	W 4-0	Hunt 2, St John 2	46,374
Feb 16	WOLVERHAMPTON WANDERERS	W 4-1	Lewis 2, St John 2	53,517
Mar 2	LEICESTER CITY	L 0-2		54,842
Mar 5	Ipswich Town	D 2-2	Lewis, St John	14,059
Mar 9	Arsenal	D 2-2	Lewis, Hunt	30,496
Mar 20	WEST BROMWICH ALBION	D 2-2	Hunt, Moran (pen)	43,977
Mar 23	Burnley	W 3-1	St John, Hunt, Lewis	28,500
Apr 8	EVERTON	D 0-0		56,060
Apr 12	TOTTENHAM HOTSPUR	W 5-2	Stevenson, Melia 2, St John, Lewis	54,463
Apr 13	MANCHESTER UNITED	W 1-0	St John	51,529
Apr 15	Tottenham Hotspur	L 2-7	Hunt 2	53,727
Apr 18	NOTTINGHAM FOREST	L 0-2		36,599
Apr 20	Fulham	D 0-0		18,894
Apr 29	SHEFFIELD WEDNESDAY	L 0-2		29,144
May 2	Leyton Orient	L 1-2	St John	8,273
May 8	BIRMINGHAM CITY	W 5-1	Wallace, St John, Callaghan, Hunt 2	23,684
May 11	Sheffield United	D 0-0		18,494
May 13	Bolton Wanderers	L 0-1		15,739
May 18	Aston Villa	L 0-2		18,000

FA Cup

Jan 9	Wrexham	(Rd3)	W 3-0	Hunt, Lewis, Melia	29,992
Jan 26	Burnley	(Rd4)	D 1-1	Lewis	49,885
Feb 21	BURNLEY	(R)	W 2-1*	St John, Moran (pen)	57,906
Mar 16	Arsenal	(Rd5)	W 2-1	Melia, Moran (pen)	55,245
Mar 30	WEST HAM UNITED	(Rd6)	W 1-0	Hunt	49,036
Apr 27	Leicester City**	(SF)	L 0-1		65,000

* After extra time. Score at 90 mins 1-1.
** Played at Hillsborough.

League & Cup Appearances

PLAYER	LEAGUE	CUP COMPETITION FA CUP	TOTAL
A'Court	23		23
Arrowsmith	3		3
Byrne	38	6	44
Callaghan	37	6	43
Ferns	5		5
Furnell	13		13
Hunt	42	6	48
Jones	4		4
Lawler	6	1	7
Lawrence	29	6	35
Leishman	11		11
Lewis	19	6	25
Melia	39	5	44
Milne	41	6	47
Moran	33	6	39
Smith	1		1
Stevenson	28	6	34
St John	40	6	46
Thomson	5		5
Wallace	7		7
Yeats	38	6	44

Goalscorers

PLAYER	LEAGUE	CUP COMPETITION FA CUP	TOTAL
Hunt	24	2	26
St John	19	1	20
Lewis	10	2	12
Melia	5	2	7
Moran	5	2	7
A'Court	2		2
Callaghan	2		2
Stevenson	2		2
Leishman	1		1
Wallace	1		1

Fact File

On 8 May 1963, Roger Hunt scored his 100th league goal in his 148th league game for the club.

MANAGER: Bill Shankly
CAPTAIN: Ron Yeats
TOP SCORER: Roger Hunt 26 (24 league)
BIGGEST WIN: 5-0, 17 November 1962 v Leyton Orient (H), Division One
HIGHEST ATTENDANCE: 73,000, 22 September 1962 v Everton (A), Division One
TRANSFERS IN: Willie Stevenson from Glasgow Rangers, Bobby Thomson from Partick Thistle
TRANSFERS OUT: Tommy Leishman to Hibernian, Kevin Lewis to Huddersfield Town

Final Division One Table

		P	W	D	L	F	A	PTS
1	Everton	42	25	11	6	84	42	61
2	Tottenham H	42	23	9	10	111	62	55
3	Burnley	42	22	10	10	78	57	54
4	Leicester C	42	20	12	10	79	53	52
5	Wolverhampton W	42	20	10	12	93	65	50
6	Sheffield W	42	19	10	13	77	63	48
7	Arsenal	42	18	10	14	86	77	46
8	Liverpool	42	17	10	15	71	59	44
9	Nottingham F	42	17	10	15	67	69	44
10	Sheffield U	42	16	12	14	58	60	44
11	Blackburn R	42	15	12	15	79	71	42
12	West Ham U	42	14	12	16	73	69	40
13	Blackpool	42	13	14	15	58	64	40
14	WBA	42	16	7	19	71	79	39
15	Aston Villa	42	15	8	19	62	68	38
16	Fulham	42	14	10	18	50	71	38
17	Ipswich T	42	12	11	19	59	78	35
18	Bolton W	42	15	5	22	55	75	35
19	Manchester U	42	12	10	20	67	81	34
20	Birmingham C	42	10	13	19	63	90	33
21	Manchester C	42	10	11	21	58	102	31
22	Leyton Orient	42	6	9	27	37	81	21

Season 1963-64

Football League Division One

DATE	OPPONENTS	SCORE	GOALSCORERS	ATTENDANCE
Aug 24	Blackburn Rovers	W 2-1	Moran (pen), Callaghan	34,390
Aug 28	NOTTINGHAM FOREST	L 1-2	McKinlay o.g.	49,829
Aug 31	BLACKPOOL	L 1-2	Melia	42,767
Sep 3	Nottingham Forest	D 0-0		21,788
Sep 7	Chelsea	W 3-1	St John 2, Hunt	38,202
Sep 9	Wolverhampton Wanderers	W 3-1	Hunt 2, Melia	25,000
Sep 14	WEST HAM UNITED	L 1-2	Hunt	45,497
Sep 16	WOLVERHAMPTON WANDERERS	W 6-0	Arrowsmith, Thompson, Callaghan, Hunt 2, Milne	44,050
Sep 21	Sheffield United	L 0-3		24,932
Sep 28	EVERTON	W 2-1	Callaghan 2	51,973
Oct 5	ASTON VILLA	W 5-2	St John, Callaghan, Thompson, Hunt 2	39,106
Oct 9	SHEFFIELD WEDNESDAY	W 3-1	St John 2, Melia	46,107
Oct 19	WEST BROMWICH ALBION	W 1-0	Milne	43,099
Oct 26	Ipswich Town	W 2-1	Melia, Hunt	16,356
Nov 2	LEICESTER CITY	L 0-1		47,438
Nov 9	Bolton Wanderers	W 2-1	Hunt, Callaghan	23,824
Nov 16	FULHAM	W 2-0	St John, Hunt	38,478
Nov 23	Manchester United	W 1-0	Yeats	54,654
Nov 30	BURNLEY	W 2-0	St John, Hunt (pen)	42,968
Dec 7	Arsenal	D 1-1	Callaghan	40,551
Dec 14	BLACKBURN ROVERS	L 1-2	Hunt	45,182
Dec 21	Blackpool	W 1-0	St John	13,254
Dec 26	STOKE CITY	W 6-1	St John, Hunt 4, Arrowsmith	49,942
Jan 11	CHELSEA	W 2-1	Hunt, Arrowsmith	45,848
Jan 18	West Ham United	L 0-1		25,546
Feb 1	SHEFFIELD UNITED	W 6-1	Hunt 2, Thompson, St John 3	43,309
Feb 8	Everton	L 1-3	St John	66,515
Feb 19	Aston Villa	D 2-2	Hunt, Arrowsmith	13,769
Feb 22	BIRMINGHAM CITY	W 2-1	Moran, St John	41,823
Mar 4	Sheffield Wednesday	D 2-2	St John, Stevenson	23,703
Mar 7	IPSWICH TOWN	W 6-0	St John, Hunt 2, Arrowsmith 2, Thompson	35,575
Mar 14	Fulham	L 0-1		14,022
Mar 20	BOLTON WANDERERS	W 2-0	Arrowsmith, St John	38,583
Mar 27	Tottenham Hotspur	W 3-1	Hunt 3	56,952
Mar 28	Leicester City	W 2-0	Hunt, Arrowsmith	31,209
Mar 30	TOTTENHAM HOTSPUR	W 3-1	St John 2, Arrowsmith	52,904
Apr 4	MANCHESTER UNITED	W 3-0	Callaghan, Arrowsmith 2	52,559
Apr 14	Burnley	W 3-0	Arrowsmith 2, St John	34,900
Apr 18	ARSENAL	W 5-0	St John, Arrowsmith, Thompson 2, Hunt	48,623
Apr 22	Birmingham City	L 1-3	Hunt	22,623
Apr 25	West Bromwich Albion	D 2-2	Hunt 2	19,279
Apr 29	Stoke City	L 1-3	Arrowsmith	32,149

FA Cup

Jan 4	DERBY COUNTY	(Rd3)	W 5-0	Arrowsmith 4, Hunt	46,460
Jan 25	PORT VALE	(Rd4)	D 0-0		52,327
Jan 27	Port Vale	(R)	W 2-1*	Hunt, Thompson	42,179
Feb 15	Arsenal	(Rd5)	W 1-0	St John	61,295
Feb 29	SWANSEA TOWN	(Rd6)	L 1-2	Thompson	52,608

*After extra time. Score at 90 mins 1-1.

Fact File

945,660 spectators (average 45,031) saw the Reds score 60 goals at Anfield, the most scored in a championship-winning season. Six goals were scored in four games and five goals were scored in two games, the last one at home to Arsenal – a result that clinched the title.

MANAGER: Bill Shankly
CAPTAIN: Ron Yeats
TOP SCORER: Roger Hunt 33 (31 league)
BIGGEST WIN: 6-0, 16 September 1963, v Wolverhampton Wanderers (H); 6-0, 7 March 1964 v Ipswich Town (H), both Division One
HIGHEST ATTENDANCE: 66,515, 8 February 1964, v Everton (A), Division One
TRANSFERS IN: Peter Thompson from Preston North End
TRANSFERS OUT: Jim Furnell to Arsenal

League & Cup Appearances

PLAYER	LEAGUE	CUP COMPETITION FA CUP	TOTAL
Arrowsmith	20	4	24
Byrne	35	4	39
Callaghan	42	5	47
Ferns	18	1	19
Furnell	2		2
Hunt	41	5	46
Lawler	6		6
Lawrence	40	5	45
Melia	24	1	25
Milne	42	5	47
Moran	35	4	39
Stevenson	38	5	43
St John	40	5	45
Thompson	42	5	47
Thomson	2	1	3
Wallace	1		1
Yeats	36	5	41

Goalscorers

PLAYER	LEAGUE	CUP COMPETITION FA CUP	TOTAL
Hunt	31	2	33
St John	21	1	22
Arrowsmith	15	4	19
Callaghan	8		8
Thompson	6	2	8
Melia	4		4
Milne	2		2
Moran	2		2
Stevenson	1		1
Yeats	1		1
Opps' o.gs.	1		1

Final Division One Table

	P	W	D	L	F	A	Pts
1 Liverpool	42	26	5	11	92	45	57
2 Manchester U	42	23	7	12	90	62	53
3 Everton	42	21	10	11	84	64	52
4 Tottenham H	42	22	7	13	97	81	51
5 Chelsea	42	20	10	12	72	56	50
6 Sheffield W	42	19	11	12	84	67	49
7 Blackburn R	42	18	10	14	89	65	46
8 Arsenal	42	17	11	14	90	82	45
9 Burnley	42	17	10	15	71	64	44
10 WBA	42	16	11	15	70	61	43
11 Leicester C	42	16	11	15	61	58	43
12 Sheffield U	42	16	11	15	61	64	43
13 Nottingham F	42	16	9	17	64	68	41
14 West Ham U	42	14	12	16	69	74	40
15 Fulham	42	13	13	16	58	65	39
16 Wolverhampton W	42	12	15	15	70	80	39
17 Stoke C	42	14	10	18	77	78	38
18 Blackpool	42	13	9	20	52	73	35
19 Aston Villa	42	11	12	19	62	71	34
20 Birmingham C	42	11	7	24	54	92	29
21 Bolton W	42	10	8	24	48	80	28
22 Ipswich T	42	9	7	26	56	121	25

Season 1964-65

Football League Division One

DATE	OPPONENTS	SCORE	GOALSCORERS	ATTENDANCE
Aug 22	ARSENAL	W 3-2	Hunt, Wallace 2	47,620
Aug 26	Leeds United	L 2-4	Hunt, Milne	36,200
Aug 29	Blackburn Rovers	L 2-3	Ferns, Smith	26,865
Sep 2	LEEDS UNITED	W 2-1	Thompson, Smith	52,548
Sep 5	BLACKPOOL	D 2-2	Thompson, Hunt	45,464
Sep 9	Leicester City	L 0-2		27,114
Sep 12	Sheffield Wednesday	L 0-1		22,701
Sep 19	EVERTON	L 0-4		52,619
Sep 26	ASTON VILLA	W 5-1	Graham 3, Callaghan, Hunt	38,940
Oct 7	SHEFFIELD UNITED	W 3-1	Hunt 2, Graham	37,745
Oct 10	Birmingham City	D 0-0		19,850
Oct 13	LEICESTER CITY	L 0-1		42,558
Oct 17	WEST HAM UNITED	D 2-2	St John, Hunt	36,029
Oct 24	West Bromwich Albion	L 0-3		17,500
Oct 31	MANCHESTER UNITED	L 0-2		52,402
Nov 7	Fulham	D 1-1	Callaghan.	18,367
Nov 14	NOTTINGHAM FOREST	W 2-0	Thompson, Hunt	40,498
Nov 21	Stoke City	D 1-1	Hunt	28,816
Nov 28	TOTTENHAM HOTSPUR	D 1-1	Hunt	41,198
Dec 5	Burnley	W 5-1	Hunt 3, Strong, Lawler	12,490
Dec 12	Arsenal	D 0-0		26,171
Dec 19	BLACKBURN ROVERS	W 3-2	Smith, Hunt 2	33,316
Dec 26	Sunderland	W 3-2	Milne, Stevenson 2	49,902
Dec 28	SUNDERLAND	D 0-0		43,528
Jan 2	Blackpool	W 3-2	Hunt 2, St John	21,863
Jan 16	SHEFFIELD WEDNESDAY	W 4-2	Hunt 2, Milne, St John	42,422
Feb 6	Aston Villa	W 1-0	Hunt	24,396
Feb 13	WOLVERHAMPTON WANDERERS	W 2-1	Hunt, Lawler	40,803
Feb 24	BIRMINGHAM CITY	W 4-3	Callaghan 2, Hunt, Thompson	39,253
Feb 27	West Ham United	L 1-2	Hunt	25,780
Mar 13	Sheffield United	L 0-3		19,034
Mar 20	FULHAM	W 3-2	Callaghan 2, Milne	28,465
Apr 1	Nottingham Forest	D 2-2	Thompson, Hunt	23,926
Apr 3	STOKE CITY	W 3-2	Milne, St John, Hunt	40,315
Apr 6	WEST BROMWICH ALBION	L 0-3		34,152
Apr 9	Tottenham Hotspur	L 0-3		27,057
Apr 12	Everton	L 1-2	Stevenson (pen)	62,720
Apr 16	Chelsea	L 0-4		62,587
Apr 17	BURNLEY	D 1-1	Smith	30,004
Apr 19	CHELSEA	W 2-0	Chisnall, Strong	41,847
Apr 24	Manchester United	L 0-3		55,772
Apr 26	Wolverhampton Wanderers	W 3-1	Strong, Sealey, Arrowsmith	13,839

FA Cup

Jan 9	West Bromwich Albion	(Rd3)	W 2-1	Hunt, St John	28,360
Jan 30	STOCKPORT COUNTY	(Rd4)	D 1-1	Milne	51,587
Feb 3	Stockport County	(R)	W 2-0	Hunt 2	24,080
Feb 20	Bolton Wanderers	(Rd5)	W 1-0	Callaghan	52,207
Mar 6	Leicester City	(Rd6)	D 0-0		39,356
Mar 10	LEICESTER CITY	(R)	W 1-0	Hunt	53,324
Mar 27	Chelsea*	(SF)	W 2-0	Thompson, Stevenson (pen)	67,686
May 1	Leeds United†	(F)	W 2-1**	Hunt, St John	100,000

*Played at Villa Park. **After extra time. Score at 90 mins 0-0. †Played at Wembley.

European Cup

Aug 17	Reykjavik	(Rd1/1L)	W 5-0	Wallace 2, Hunt 2, Chisnall	10,000
Sep 14	REYKJAVIK	(Rd1/2L)	W 6-1	Byrne, St John 2, Hunt, Graham, Stevenson	32,597
Nov 25	ANDERLECHT	(Rd2/1L)	W 3-0	St John, Hunt, Yeats	44,516
Dec 16	Anderlecht	(Rd2/2L)	W 1-0	Hunt	60,000
Feb 10	FC Cologne	(Rd3/1L)	D 0-0		40,000
Mar 17	FC COLOGNE	(Rd3/2L)	D 0-0		48,432
Mar 24	FC Cologne	(R)	D 2-2*	St John, Hunt	45,000
May 4	INTER MILAN	(SF/1L)	W 3-1	Hunt, Callaghan, St John	54,082
May 12	Inter Milan	(SF/2L)	L 0-3		90,000

*Liverpool won on toss of plastic red/white disc.

Charity Shield

Aug 15	WEST HAM UNITED	D 2-2*	Wallace, Byrne	38,858

*Trophy shared.

MANAGER: Bill Shankly **CAPTAIN:** Ron Yeats
TOP SCORER: Roger Hunt, 37 (25 league)
BIGGEST WIN: 6-1, 14 September 1964, v Reykjavik (H), European Cup
HIGHEST ATTENDANCE: 100,000, 1 May 1965 v Leeds United (Wembley), FA Cup final
TRANSFERS IN: Phil Chisnall from Manchester United, Geoff Strong from Arsenal **TRANSFERS OUT:** Alan A'Court to Tranmere Rovers

League & Cup Appearances

PLAYER	LEAGUE	CUP COMPETITION		OTHER	TOTAL
		FA CUP	EC		
A'Court			1		1
Arrowsmith	7	1		1	9
Byrne	40	8	7	1	56
Callaghan	37	8	9	1	55
Chisnall	6		1	0 (1)	7 (1)
Ferns	4				4
Graham	14		1		15
Hignett	1				1
Hunt	40	8	9	1	58
Lawler	33	8	7		48
Lawrence	41	8	9	1	59
Lowry	1				1
Milne	34	6	7	1	48
Molyneux	1				1
Moran	13		4	1	18
Sealey	1				1
Smith	25	8	7		40
Stevenson	39	8	9	1	57
St John	37	8	8		53
Strong	13	1	2		16
Thompson	38	8	8	1	55
Wallace	12		1	1	14
Yeats	35	8	9	1	53

Goalscorers

PLAYER	LEAGUE	CUP COMPETITION		OTHER	TOTAL
		FA CUP	EC		
Hunt	25	5	7		37
Thompson	5	1	5		11
Callaghan	6	1	1		8
St John	4	2	1		7
Milne	5	1			6
Stevenson	3	1	1		5
Wallace	2		2	1	5
Graham	4				4
Smith	4				4
Strong	3				3
Byrne			1	1	2
Chisnall	1		1		2
Lawler	2				2
Arrowsmith	1				1
Ferns	1				1
Sealey	1				1
Yeats			1		1

Fact File

Liverpool won the FA Cup for the first time in the club's history. The final was their 107th cup tie in 63 seasons of trying.

Final Division One Table

		P	W	D	L	F	A	PTS
1	MANCHESTER U	42	26	9	7	89	39	61
2	LEEDS U	42	26	9	7	83	52	61
3	CHELSEA	42	24	8	10	89	54	56
4	EVERTON	42	17	15	10	69	60	49
5	NOTTINGHAM F	42	17	13	12	71	67	47
6	TOTTENHAM H	42	19	7	16	87	71	45
7	LIVERPOOL	42	17	10	15	67	73	44
8	SHEFFIELD W	42	16	11	15	57	55	43
9	WEST HAM U	42	19	4	19	82	71	42
10	BLACKBURN R	42	16	10	16	83	79	42
11	STOKE C	42	16	10	16	67	66	42
12	BURNLEY	42	16	10	16	70	70	42
13	ARSENAL	42	17	7	18	69	75	41
14	WBA	42	13	13	16	70	65	39
15	SUNDERLAND	42	14	9	19	64	74	37
16	ASTON VILLA	42	16	5	21	57	82	37
17	BLACKPOOL	42	12	11	19	67	78	35
18	LEICESTER C	42	11	13	18	69	85	35
19	SHEFFIELD U	42	12	11	19	50	64	35
20	FULHAM	42	11	12	19	60	78	34
21	WOLVERHAMPTON W	42	13	4	25	59	89	30
22	BIRMINGHAM C	42	8	11	23	64	96	27

Season 1965-66

Football League Division One

DATE	OPPONENTS	SCORE	GOALSCORERS	ATTENDANCE
Aug 21	Leicester City	W 3-1	Hunt 2, Strong	29,698
Aug 25	SHEFFIELD UNITED	L 0-1		47,259
Sep 1	Sheffield United	D 0-0		20,798
Sep 4	Blackpool	W 3-2	Hunt 2, Callaghan	25,616
Sep 6	West Ham United	W 5-1	Milne, Callaghan, Hunt 3	32,144
Sep 11	FULHAM	W 2-1	Lawler, Hunt	46,382
Sep 15	WEST HAM UNITED	D 1-1	Strong	44,397
Sep 18	Tottenham Hotspur	L 1-2	Strong	46,770
Sep 25	EVERTON	W 5-0	Smith, Hunt 2, Stevenson, St John	53,557
Oct 2	ASTON VILLA	W 3-1	Thompson 2, St John	43,859
Oct 9	Manchester United	L 0-2		58,161
Oct 16	NEWCASTLE UNITED	W 2-0	Hunt, Callaghan	47,984
Oct 23	West Bromwich Albion	L 0-3		30,000
Oct 30	NOTTINGHAM FOREST	W 4-0	Stevenson (pen), Hunt 2, St John	38,420
Nov 6	Sheffield Wednesday	W 2-0	Hunt, Thompson	24,456
Nov 13	NORTHAMPTON TOWN	W 5-0	St John, Stevenson (pen), Hunt, Callaghan, Thompson	41,904
Nov 17	BLACKBURN ROVERS	W 5-2	Stevenson (pen), St John 2, Hunt, Smith	36,450
Nov 20	Stoke City	D 0-0		28,622
Nov 27	BURNLEY	W 2-1	Hunt, Milne	50,282
Dec 4	Chelsea	W 1-0	Hunt	36,839
Dec 11	ARSENAL	W 4-2	Thompson, Strong, St John, Hunt	43,727
Dec 18	Newcastle United	D 0-0		42,910
Dec 27	LEEDS UNITED	L 0-1		53,430
Dec 28	Leeds United	W 1-0	Milne	49,192
Jan 1	MANCHESTER UNITED	W 2-1	Smith, Milne	53,970
Jan 8	Arsenal	W 1-0	Yeats	43,917
Jan 15	WEST BROMWICH ALBION	D 2-2	Milne, Byrne	46,687
Jan 29	LEICESTER CITY	W 1-0	Lawler	45,409
Feb 5	Blackburn Rovers	W 4-1	Lawler, Hunt, St John 2	30,414
Feb 12	SUNDERLAND	W 4-0	Hunt 3, Yeats	43,859
Feb 19	BLACKPOOL	W 4-1	Hunt 2, Arrowsmith, Milne	45,046
Feb 26	Fulham	L 0-2		31,626
Mar 12	TOTTENHAM HOTSPUR	W 1-0	Clayton o.g.	50,760
Mar 19	Everton	D 0-0		62,537
Mar 26	Aston Villa	W 3-0	Hunt 2, Callaghan	23,625
Apr 6	SHEFFIELD WEDNESDAY	W 1-0	Stevenson	44,792
Apr 9	Northampton Town	D 0-0		20,029
Apr 11	Sunderland	D 2-2	Lawler 2	38,355
Apr 16	STOKE CITY	W 2-0	Strong, St John	41,106
Apr 23	Burnley	L 0-2		36,741
Apr 30	CHELSEA	W 2-1	Hunt 2	53,754
May 10	Nottingham Forest	D 1-1	Milne	22,105

FA Cup

Jan 22	CHELSEA	(Rd3)	L 1-2	Hunt	54,097

European Cup-Winners' Cup

Sep 29	Juventus	(Prelim Rd/1L)	L 0-1		12,000
Oct 13	JUVENTUS	(Prelim Rd/2L)	W 2-0	Lawler, Strong	51,055
Dec 1	STANDARD LIEGE	(Rd1/1L)	W 3-1	Lawler 2, Thompson	46,112
Dec 15	Standard Liege	(Rd1/2L)	W 2-1	Hunt, St John	35,000
Mar 1	Honved	(Rd2/1L)	D 0-0		20,000
Mar 8	HONVED	(Rd2/2L)	W 2-0	Lawler, St John	54,631
Apr 14	Celtic	(SF/1L)	L 0-1		80,000
Apr 19	CELTIC	(SF/2L)	W 2-0	Smith, Strong	54,208
May 5	Borussia Dortmund	(F)	L 1-2*	Hunt	41,657

* After extra time. Score at 90 mins 1-1. Played at Hampden Park.

Charity Shield

Aug 14	Manchester United	D 2-2**	Yeats, Stevenson	48,502

**Trophy shared. Played at Wembley.

MANAGER: Bill Shankly **CAPTAIN:** Ron Yeats

TOP SCORER: Roger Hunt 32 (29 league)

BIGGEST WIN: 5-0, 25 September 1965, v Everton (H), and 13 November 1965, v Northampton Town (H); both Division One

HIGHEST ATTENDANCE: 80,000, 14 April 1966, v Celtic (A), European Cup-Winners' Cup semi-final

TRANSFERS IN: Ian Ross from Glasgow junior side, John Ogston from Aberdeen

TRANSFERS OUT: Bobby Thomson to Luton Town, Phil Ferns to Bournemouth

League & Cup Appearances

PLAYER	LEAGUE	CUP COMPETITION		OTHER	TOTAL
		FA CUP	ECWC		
Arrowsmith	3 (2)		1		4 (2)
Byrne	42	1	9	1	53
Callaghan	42	1	9	1	53
Chisnall			1		1
Graham	1				1
Hunt	37	1	7	1	46
Lawler	40	1	8	1	50
Lawrence	42	1	9	1	53
Milne	28	1	6	1	36
Stevenson	41	1	9	1	52
St John	41	1	9	1	52
Smith	42	1	9	1	53
Strong	21 (1)		4	1	26 (1)
Thompson	40	1	9		50
Yeats	42	1	9	1	53

Goalscorers

PLAYER	LEAGUE	CUP COMPETITION		OTHER	TOTAL
		FA CUP	ECWC		
Hunt	29	1	2		32
St John	10		2		12
Lawler	5		4		9
Milne	7				7
Strong	5		2		7
Stevenson	5			1	6
Thompson	5		1		6
Callaghan	5				5
Smith	3		1		4
Yeats	2			1	3
Arrowsmith	1				1
Byrne	1				1
Opps' o.gs.	1				1

Fact File

Only 14 players were used during this championship-winning season; 12 of the 13 outfield players scored goals. The only outfield player not to score was Bobby Graham who made only one appearance.

Final Division One Table

		P	W	D	L	F	A	Pts
1	Liverpool	42	26	9	7	79	34	61
2	Leeds U	42	23	9	10	79	38	55
3	Burnley	42	24	7	11	79	47	55
4	Manchester U	42	18	15	9	84	59	51
5	Chelsea	42	22	7	13	65	53	51
6	WBA	42	19	12	11	91	69	50
7	Leicester C	42	21	7	14	80	65	49
8	Tottenham H	42	16	12	14	75	66	44
9	Sheffield U	42	16	11	15	56	59	43
10	Stoke C	42	15	12	15	65	64	42
11	Everton	42	15	11	16	56	62	41
12	West Ham U	42	15	9	18	70	83	39
13	Blackpool	42	14	9	19	55	65	37
14	Arsenal	42	12	13	17	62	75	37
15	Newcastle U	42	14	9	19	50	63	37
16	Aston Villa	42	15	6	21	69	80	36
17	Sheffield W	42	14	8	20	56	66	36
18	Nottingham F	42	14	8	20	56	72	36
19	Sunderland	42	14	8	20	51	72	36
20	Fulham	42	14	7	21	67	85	35
21	Northampton T	42	10	13	19	55	92	33
22	Blackburn R	42	8	4	30	57	88	20

Season 1966-67

Football League Division One

DATE	OPPONENTS	SCORE	GOALSCORERS	ATTENDANCE
Aug 20	LEICESTER CITY	W 3-2	Hunt, Strong, Stevenson (pen)	49,076
Aug 24	Manchester City	L 1-2	Strong	50,923
Aug 27	Everton	L 1-3	Smith	64,318
Aug 30	MANCHESTER CITY	W 3-2	Hunt 2, Strong	51,645
Sep 3	West Ham United	D 1-1	Strong	33,000
Sep 5	Blackpool	W 2-1	Hunt, Thompson	24,375
Sep 10	SHEFFIELD WEDNESDAY	D 1-1	Strong	48,717
Sep 17	Southampton	W 2-1	St John, Callaghan	28,287
Sep 24	SUNDERLAND	D 2-2	Yeats, Hunt	45,706
Oct 1	Aston Villa	W 3-2	St John, Callaghan, Graham	24,909
Oct 8	FULHAM	D 2-2	Strong, St John	44,024
Oct 15	Nottingham Forest	D 1-1	Hunt	32,887
Oct 29	Stoke City	L 0-2		37,933
Nov 5	NOTTINGHAM FOREST	W 4-0	Strong, Hunt 2, Thompson	40,624
Nov 9	BURNLEY	W 2-0	Lawler, Thompson	50,124
Nov 12	Newcastle United	W 2-0	St John, Hunt	36,910
Nov 19	LEEDS UNITED	W 5-0	Lawler, Thompson, Strong 2, St John	51,014
Nov 26	West Bromwich Albion	L 1-2	Strong	25,900
Dec 3	SHEFFIELD UNITED	W 1-0	St John	42,762
Dec 10	Manchester United	D 2-2	St John 2	62,500
Dec 24	Chelsea	W 2-1	Hinton o.g., Strong	36,921
Dec 26	CHELSEA	W 2-1	Stevenson, Hunt	51,920
Dec 31	EVERTON	D 0-0		53,744
Jan 7	WEST HAM UNITED	W 2-0	Thompson 2	48,518
Jan 14	Sheffield Wednesday	W 1-0	Thompson	43,951
Jan 18	Leicester City	L 1-2	Rodrigues o.g.	32,049
Jan 21	SOUTHAMPTON	W 2-1	Lawler, Arrowsmith	47,545
Feb 4	Sunderland	D 2-2	Yeats, Thompson	45,301
Feb 11	ASTON VILLA	W 1-0	Milne	45,747
Feb 25	Fulham	D 2-2	St John, Strong	37,481
Mar 4	STOKE CITY	W 2-1	Lawler, Hunt	48,891
Mar 18	Burnley	L 0-1		29,388
Mar 25	MANCHESTER UNITED	D 0-0		53,813
Mar 27	ARSENAL	D 0-0		46,168
Mar 28	Arsenal	D 1-1	Arrowsmith	35,795
Apr 1	Tottenham Hotspur	L 1-2	Thompson	53,135
Apr 7	NEWCASTLE UNITED	W 3-1	Hunt 2, Callaghan	44,824
Apr 22	WEST BROMWICH ALBION	L 0-1		39,883
Apr 28	Sheffield United	W 1-0	Hunt	19,110
May 3	Leeds United	L 1-2	Stevenson (pen)	36,597
May 6	TOTTENHAM HOTSPUR	D 0-0		40,845
May 13	BLACKPOOL	L 1-3	Thompson	28,773

FA Cup

Jan 28	Watford	(Rd3) D 0-0		33,000
Feb 1	WATFORD	(R) W 3-1	St John, Hunt, Lawler	54,451
Feb 18	ASTON VILLA	(Rd4) W 1-0	St John	52,447
Mar 11	Everton	(Rd5) L 0-1		64,851*

*A further 40,149 watched on closed-circuit TV at Anfield – total 105,000.

European Cup

Sep 28	PETROLUL PLOESTI	(Prelim Rd/1L) W 2-0	St John, Callaghan	44,463
Oct 12	Petrolul Ploesti	(Prelim Rd/2L) L 1-3	Hunt	20,000
Oct 19	Petrolul Ploesti**	(R) W 2-0	St John, Thompson	15,000
Dec 7	Ajax	(Rd1/1L) L 1-5	Lawler	65,000
Dec 14	AJAX	(Rd1/2L) D 2-2	Hunt 2	53,846

**Played in Brussels.

Charity Shield

Aug 13	Everton†	W 1-0	Hunt	63,329

†Played at Goodison Park.

MANAGER: Bill Shankly
CAPTAIN: Ron Yeats
TOP SCORER: Roger Hunt 19 (14 league)
BIGGEST WIN: 5-0, 19 November 1966, v Leeds United (H), Division One
HIGHEST ATTENDANCE: 65,000, 7 December 1966, v Ajax (A), European Cup; 64,851; (40,149 watched on closed circuit TV at Anfield, 11 March 1967, v Everton (A), FA Cup)
TRANSFERS IN: Emlyn Hughes from Blackpool
TRANSFERS OUT: Gordon Milne to Blackpool

League & Cup Appearances

PLAYER	LEAGUE	CUP COMPETITION FA CUP	EC	OTHER	TOTAL
Arrowsmith	6 (3)				6 (3)
Byrne	9	2		1	12
Callaghan	40	4	5	1	50
Graham	3		2		5
Hughes	10				10
Hunt	39	3	5	1	48
Lawler	42	4	5	1	52
Lawrence	41	4	5	1	51
Milne	31 (2)	4	3		38 (2)
Ogston	1				1
Ross	0 (1)				0 (1)
Smith	42	4	5	1	52
Stevenson	41	4	5	1	51
St John	39	4	5	1	49
Strong	36	3	5	1	45
Thompson	42	4	5	1	52
Wilson	0 (1)				0 (1)
Yeats	40	4	5	1	50

Goalscorers

PLAYER	LEAGUE	CUP COMPETITION FA CUP	EC	OTHER	TOTAL
Hunt	14	1	3	1	19
St John	9	2	2		13
Strong	12				12
Thompson	10		1		11
Lawler	4	1	1		6
Callaghan	3		1		4
Stevenson	3				3
Arrowsmith	2				2
Yeats	2				2
Graham	1				1
Milne	1				1
Smith	1				1
Opps' o.gs.	2				2

Fact File

Upon signing Emlyn Hughes, Shankly told him that he was the future England captain. This came true and Emlyn gained 59 England caps, more than any other Liverpool player.

Final Division One Table

	P	W	D	L	F	A	Pts
1 Manchester U	42	24	12	6	84	45	60
2 Nottingham F	42	23	10	9	64	41	56
3 Tottenham H	42	24	8	10	71	48	56
4 Leeds U	42	22	11	9	62	42	55
5 Liverpool	42	19	13	10	64	47	51
6 Everton	42	19	10	13	65	46	48
7 Arsenal	42	16	14	12	58	47	46
8 Leicester C	42	18	8	16	78	71	44
9 Chelsea	42	15	14	13	67	62	44
10 Sheffield U	42	16	10	16	52	59	42
11 Sheffield W	42	14	13	15	56	47	41
12 Stoke C	42	17	7	18	63	58	41
13 WBA	42	16	7	19	77	73	39
14 Burnley	42	15	9	18	66	76	39
15 Manchester C	42	12	15	15	43	52	39
16 West Ham U	42	14	8	20	80	84	36
17 Sunderland	42	14	8	20	58	72	36
18 Fulham	42	11	12	19	71	83	34
19 Southampton	42	14	6	22	74	92	34
20 Newcastle U	42	12	9	21	39	81	33
21 Aston Villa	42	11	7	24	54	85	29
22 Blackpool	42	6	9	27	41	76	21

Season 1967-68

Football League Division One

DATE	OPPONENTS	SCORE	GOALSCORERS	ATTENDANCE
Aug 19	Manchester City	D 0-0		49,343
Aug 22	ARSENAL	W 2-0	Hunt 2	52,033
Aug 26	NEWCASTLE UNITED	W 6-0	Hateley 3, Hughes, Hunt 2	51,829
Aug 28	Arsenal	L 0-2		33,420
Sep 2	West Bromwich Albion	W 2-0	Hateley, Hunt	32,737
Sep 5	Nottingham Forest	W 1-0	Hughes	39,352
Sep 9	CHELSEA	W 3-1	Smith (pen), Hateley 2	53,839
Sep 16	Southampton	L 0-1		29,512
Sep 23	EVERTON	W 1-0	Hunt	54,189
Sep 30	STOKE CITY	W 2-1	Thompson, Smith (pen)	50,220
Oct 7	Leicester City	L 1-2	St John	25,609
Oct 14	WEST HAM UNITED	W 3-1	St John 2, Smith	46,951
Oct 24	Burnley	D 1-1	Lawler	29,855
Oct 28	SHEFFIELD WEDNESDAY	W 1-0	Lawler	50,399
Nov 4	Tottenham Hotspur	D 1-1	Hunt	47,682
Nov 11	MANCHESTER UNITED	L 1-2	Hunt	54,515
Nov 18	Sunderland	D 1-1	Irwin o.g.	29,993
Nov 25	WOLVERHAMPTON WANDERERS	W 2-1	Hateley, Stevenson (pen)	43,885
Dec 2	Fulham	D 1-1	Hateley	29,330
Dec 9	LEEDS UNITED	W 2-0	Hunt, Sprake o.g.	39,676
Dec 16	MANCHESTER CITY	D 1-1	Hunt	53,268
Dec 23	Newcastle United	D 1-1	St John	46,190
Dec 26	Coventry City	D 1-1	Hunt	42,209
Dec 30	COVENTRY CITY	W 1-0	Callaghan	48,866
Jan 6	WEST BROMWICH ALBION	W 4-1	Strong, Hunt 3	51,092
Jan 20	SOUTHAMPTON	W 2-0	Strong, Yeats	44,906
Feb 3	Everton	L 0-1		64,482
Feb 12	Chelsea	L 1-3	Thompson	40,670
Feb 24	LEICESTER CITY	W 3-1	Callaghan, Strong, Hateley	41,451
Mar 2	Wolverhampton Wanderers	D 1-1	Hunt	33,207
Mar 16	BURNLEY	W 3-2	Hateley 2, Strong	41,114
Mar 23	Sheffield Wednesday	W 2-1	Hunt, Arrowsmith	32,177
Apr 6	Manchester United	W 2-1	Yeats, Hunt	63,050
Apr 12	SHEFFIELD UNITED	L 1-2	Hunt	50,422
Apr 13	SUNDERLAND	W 2-1	Hunt 2	40,350
Apr 15	Sheffield United	D 1-1	Strong (pen)	22,743
Apr 20	West Ham United	L 0-1		33,060
Apr 27	FULHAM	W 4-1	Callaghan, Hunt 2, Hateley	32,307
Apr 29	TOTTENHAM HOTSPUR	D 1-1	Hateley	41,688
May 4	Leeds United	W 2-1	Lawler, Graham	44,553
May 11	NOTTINGHAM FOREST	W 6-1	Hateley 3, St John, Hunt 2	38,850
May 15	Stoke City	L 1-2	Hunt	27,693

FA Cup

Jan 27	Bournemouth	(Rd3)	D 0-0		24,388
Jan 30	BOURNEMOUTH	(R)	W 4-1	Hateley, Thompson, Hunt, Lawler	54,075
Feb 17	Walsall	(Rd4)	D 0-0		21,066
Feb 19	WALSALL	(R)	W 5-2	Hateley 4, Strong	39,113
Mar 9	Tottenham Hotspur	(Rd5)	D 1-1	Hateley	54,005
Mar 12	TOTTENHAM HOTSPUR	(R)	W 2-1	Hunt, Smith (pen)	53,658
Mar 30	West Bromwich Albion	(Rd6)	D 0-0		53,062
Apr 8	WEST BROMWICH ALBION	(R)	D 1-1*	Hateley	54,273
Apr 18	West Bromwich Albion**	(2nd R)	L 1-2	Hateley	56,000

*After extra time. Score at 90 mins 1-1. **Played at Maine Road.

League Cup

Sep 13	BOLTON WANDERERS	D 1-1	Thompson	45,957
Sep 27	Bolton Wanderers	L 2-3	Smith (pen), Callaghan	31,500

Inter-Cities' Fairs Cup

Sep 19	Malmo	(Rd1/1L)	W 2-0	Hateley 2	14,314
Oct 4	MALMO	(Rd1/2L)	W 2-1	Yeats, Hunt	39,795
Nov 7	TSV MÜNCHEN 1860	(Rd2/1L)	W 8-0	St John, Hateley, Smith (pen), Hunt 2, Thompson, Callaghan 2	44,812
Nov 14	TSV München 1860	(Rd2/2L)	L 1-2	Callaghan	10,000
Nov 28	Ferencvaros	(Rd3/1L)	L 0-1		30,000
Jan 9	FERENCVAROS	(Rd3/2L)	L 0-1		46,892

MANAGER: Bill Shankly **CAPTAIN:** Ron Yeats

TOP SCORER: Roger Hunt 30 (25 league)

BIGGEST WIN: 8-0, 7 November 1967, v TSV München 1860 (H), Inter-Cities' Fairs Cup

HIGHEST ATTENDANCE: 64,482, 3 February 1968, v Everton (A), Division One

TRANSFERS IN: Tony Hateley from Chelsea, Ray Clemence from Scunthorpe United **TRANSFERS OUT:** Willie Stevenson to Stoke City

League & Cup Appearances

PLAYER	LEAGUE	CUP COMPETITION			TOTAL
		FA CUP	LC	ICFC	
Arrowsmith	2 (1)	1			3 (1)
Byrne	27	1	2	6	36
Callaghan	41	9	2	6	58
Graham	3 (2)	0 (1)			3 (3)
Hateley	38	7	2	5	52
Hughes	39	9	2	6	56
Hunt	40	9	2	6	57
Lawler	42	9	2	6	59
Lawrence	42	9	2	6	59
Livermore	0 (1)				0 (1)
Ross	4	2			6
Smith	36	7	2	6	51
Stevenson	1			2 (1)	3 (1)
St John	41	9	2	4	56
Strong	18 (1)	9		1	28 (1)
Thompson	41	9	2	6	58
Wall	9				9
Yeats	38	9	2	6	55

Goalscorers

PLAYER	LEAGUE	CUP COMPETITION			TOTAL
		FA CUP	LC	ICFC	
Hunt	25	2		3	30
Hateley	16	8		3	27
Callaghan	3		1	3	7
Smith	3	1	1	1	6
St John	5			1	6
Strong	5	1			6
Thompson	2	1	1	1	5
Lawler	3	1			4
Yeats	2			1	3
Hughes	2				2
Arrowsmith	1				1
Graham	1				1
Stevenson	1				1
Opps' o.gs.	2				2

Fact File

Roger Hunt began the season on 200 league goals. By the end he had added 25 more, including his 12th and last hat-trick for the club on 6 January, v West Bromwich Albion. Hunt had topped the scoring charts for seven consecutive seasons.

Final Division One Table

		P	W	D	L	F	A	PTS
1	MANCHESTER C	42	26	6	10	86	43	58
2	MANCHESTER U	42	24	8	10	89	55	56
3	LIVERPOOL	42	22	11	9	71	40	55
4	LEEDS U	42	22	9	11	71	41	53
5	EVERTON	42	23	6	13	67	40	52
6	CHELSEA	42	18	12	12	62	68	48
7	TOTTENHAM H	42	19	9	14	70	59	47
8	WBA	42	17	12	13	75	62	46
9	ARSENAL	42	17	10	15	60	56	44
10	NEWCASTLE U	42	13	15	14	54	67	41
11	NOTTINGHAM F	42	14	11	17	52	64	39
12	WEST HAM U	42	14	10	18	73	69	38
13	LEICESTER C	42	13	12	17	64	69	38
14	BURNLEY	42	14	10	18	64	71	38
15	SUNDERLAND	42	13	11	18	51	61	37
16	SOUTHAMPTON	42	13	11	18	66	83	37
17	WOLVERHAMPTON W	42	14	8	20	66	75	36
18	STOKE C	42	14	7	21	50	73	35
19	SHEFFIELD W	42	11	12	19	51	63	34
20	COVENTRY C	42	9	15	18	51	71	33
21	SHEFFIELD U	42	11	10	21	49	70	32
22	FULHAM	42	10	7	25	56	98	27

Season 1968-69

Football League Division One

DATE	OPPONENTS	SCORE	GOALSCORERS	ATTENDANCE
Aug 10	MANCHESTER CITY	W 2-1	Graham, Thompson	51,236
Aug 14	Southampton	L 0-2		24,453
Aug 17	Arsenal	D 1-1	Hunt	43,535
Aug 20	STOKE CITY	W 2-1	Callaghan, Allen o.g.	46,674
Aug 24	SUNDERLAND	W 4-1	Smith, Lawler, Callaghan, Hateley	46,547
Aug 27	Everton	D 0-0		63,898
Aug 31	Leeds United	L 0-1		38,929
Sep 7	QUEENS PARK RANGERS	W 2-0	Yeats, Graham	46,025
Sep 14	Ipswich Town	W 2-0	Graham, St John	24,514
Sep 21	LEICESTER CITY	W 4-0	Yeats, Smith (pen), Evans, Callaghan	48,375
Sep 28	Wolverhampton Wanderers	W 6-0	Hunt 2, Thompson 2, Evans 2	39,310
Oct 5	Burnley	W 4-0	Hunt 2, Thompson, Strong	26,238
Oct 8	EVERTON	D 1-1	Smith	54,496
Oct 12	MANCHESTER UNITED	W 2-0	St John, Evans	53,392
Oct 19	Tottenham Hotspur	L 1-2	Hunt	44,122
Oct 26	NEWCASTLE UNITED	W 2-1	Evans, Thompson	45,223
Nov 2	West Bromwich Albion	D 0-0		34,600
Nov 9	CHELSEA	W 2-1	Callaghan, Smith (pen)	47,248
Nov 16	Sheffield Wednesday	W 2-1	Lawler, Callaghan	31,245
Nov 23	COVENTRY CITY	W 2-0	Strong, Callaghan	44,820
Nov 30	Nottingham Forest	W 1-0	Hunt	25,175
Dec 3	SOUTHAMPTON	W 1-0	Callaghan	45,527
Dec 7	WEST HAM UNITED	W 2-0	Hughes, Thompson	48,632
Dec 14	Manchester United	L 0-1		59,000
Dec 21	TOTTENHAM HOTSPUR	W 1-0	Hughes	43,843
Dec 26	BURNLEY	D 1-1	Lawler	52,515
Jan 11	WEST BROMWICH ALBION	W 1-0	Thompson	47,587
Jan 18	Chelsea	W 2-1	Hunt, Evans	51,872
Feb 1	SHEFFIELD WEDNESDAY	W 1-0	Hunt	45,406
Feb 15	NOTTINGHAM FOREST	L 0-2		42,359
Feb 22	West Ham United	D 1-1	Hunt	36,498
Mar 15	Sunderland	W 2-0	St John, Evans	17,855
Mar 29	Queens Park Rangers	W 2-1	Smith (pen), Hunt	16,792
Mar 31	ARSENAL	D 1-1	Smith (pen)	44,843
Apr 5	WOLVERHAMPTON WANDERERS	W 1-0	Hunt	45,399
Apr 7	Stoke City	D 0-0		27,389
Apr 12	Leicester City	W 2-1	Hughes, Callaghan	28,671
Apr 19	IPSWICH TOWN	W 4-0	Thompson, Graham 2, St John	40,449
Apr 22	Coventry City	D 0-0		35,106
Apr 28	LEEDS UNITED	D 0-0		53,750
May 12	Manchester City	L 0-1		28,309
May 17	Newcastle United	D 1-1	Hunt	34,910

FA Cup

Jan 4	DONCASTER ROVERS	(Rd3)	W 2-0	Hunt, Callaghan	48,330
Jan 25	BURNLEY	(Rd4)	W 2-1	Smith (pen), Hughes	53,677
Mar 1	Leicester City	(Rd5)	D 0-0		42,002
Mar 3	LEICESTER CITY	(R)	L 0-1		54,666

League Cup

Sep 4	SHEFFIELD UNITED	(Rd2)	W 4-0	Hunt, Lawler, Callaghan, Thompson	32,358
Sep 25	SWANSEA TOWN	(Rd3)	W 2-0	Lawler, Hunt	31,051
Oct 15	Arsenal	(Rd4)	L 1-2	Lawler	39,299

Inter-Cities' Fairs Cup

Sep 18	Athletic Bilbao	(Rd1/1L)	L 1-2	Hunt	35,000
Oct 2	ATHLETIC BILBAO	(Rd1/2L)	W 2-1*	Lawler, Hughes	49,567

*After extra time. Liverpool lost on toss of coin.

MANAGER: Bill Shankly

CAPTAIN: Ron Yeats

TOP SCORER: Roger Hunt 17 (13 league)

BIGGEST WIN: 6-0, 28 September 1968, v Wolverhampton Wanderers (A), Division One

HIGHEST ATTENDANCE: 63,898, 27 August 1968, v Everton (A), Division One

TRANSFERS IN: Alun Evans from Wolverhampton Wanderers, Alec Lindsay from Bury

TRANSFERS OUT: Tony Hateley to Coventry City, Alf Arrowsmith to Bury

League & Cup Appearances

PLAYER	LEAGUE	CUP COMPETITION			TOTAL
		FA CUP	LC	ICFC	
Byrne	2 (1)				2 (1)
Callaghan	42	4	3	2	51
Clemence			1		1
Evans	33	4	1	1	39
Graham	11 (2)	0 (1)	1	1	13 (3)
Hall	0 (2)				0 (2)
Hateley	4				4
Hughes	40	4	3	2	49
Hunt	38	4	3	2	47
Lawler	42	4	3	2	51
Lawrence	42	4	2	2	50
Ross	3			0 (1)	3 (1)
Smith	42	4	3	2	51
St John	41	4	3	2	50
Strong	28 (3)	4	2	0 (1)	34 (4)
Thompson	42	4	3	2	51
Wall	13		2	2	17
Yeats	39	4	3	2	48

Goalscorers

PLAYER	LEAGUE	CUP COMPETITION			TOTAL
		FA CUP	LC	ICFC	
Hunt	13	1	2	1	17
Callaghan	8	1	1		10
Thompson	8		1		9
Evans	7				7
Lawler	3		3	1	7
Smith	6	1			7
Graham	5				5
Hughes	3	1		1	5
St John	4				4
Strong	2				2
Yeats	2				2
Hateley	1				1
Opps' o.gs.	1				1

Fact File

Roger Hunt createc a new club record of 234 league goals on 1 February 1969, overtaking Gordon Hodgson's 1935 record. Hunt went on to set a new record of 245 league goals and 286 in all competitions.

Final Division One Table

		P	W	D	L	F	A	Pts
1	Leeds U	42	27	13	2	66	26	67
2	Liverpool	42	25	11	6	63	24	61
3	Everton	42	21	15	6	77	36	57
4	Arsenal	42	22	12	8	56	27	56
5	Chelsea	42	20	10	12	73	53	50
6	Tottenham H	42	14	17	11	61	51	45
7	Southampton	42	16	13	13	57	48	45
8	West Ham U	42	13	18	11	66	50	44
9	Newcastle U	42	15	14	13	61	55	44
10	WBA	42	16	11	15	64	67	43
11	Manchester U	42	15	12	15	57	53	42
12	Ipswich T	42	15	11	16	59	60	41
13	Manchester C	42	15	10	17	64	55	40
14	Burnley	42	15	9	18	55	82	39
15	Sheffield W	42	10	16	16	41	54	36
16	Wolverhampton W	42	10	15	17	41	58	35
17	Sunderland	42	11	12	19	43	67	34
18	Nottingham F	42	10	13	19	45	57	33
19	Stoke C	42	9	15	18	40	63	33
20	Coventry C	42	10	11	21	46	64	31
21	Leicester C	42	9	12	21	39	68	30
22	QPR	42	4	10	28	39	95	18

Season 1969-70

Football League Division One

DATE	OPPONENTS	SCORE	GOALSCORERS	ATTENDANCE
Aug 9	CHELSEA	W 4-1	Lawler, St John 2, Strong	48,383
Aug 12	MANCHESTER CITY	W 3-2	St John 2, Hunt	51,959
Aug 16	Tottenham Hotspur	W 2-0	Hughes, Lawler	50,474
Aug 20	Manchester City	W 2-0	Graham 2	47,888
Aug 23	BURNLEY	D 3-3	Smith 2 (1 pen), Graham	51,113
Aug 27	Crystal Palace	W 3-1	Hughes, Hunt, Thompson	36,369
Aug 30	Sheffield Wednesday	D 1-1	Lawler	33,600
Sep 6	COVENTRY CITY	W 2-1	St John, Strong	48,337
Sep 9	SUNDERLAND	W 2-0	Strong, Smith	46,370
Sep 13	Manchester United	L 0-1		59,387
Sep 20	STOKE CITY	W 3-1	Hunt, Hughes, Callaghan	45,745
Sep 27	West Bromwich Albion	D 2-2	Graham, Hunt	34,343
Oct 4	NOTTINGHAM FOREST	D 1-1	Chapman o.g.	44,859
Oct 7	TOTTENHAM HOTSPUR	D 0-0		46,518
Oct 11	Newcastle United	L 0-1		43,830
Oct 18	Ipswich Town	D 2-2	Graham, Lindsay	23,263
Oct 25	SOUTHAMPTON	W 4-1	Hughes, Hunt 2, Byrne o.g.	41,611
Nov 1	Derby County	L 0-4		40,993
Nov 8	WOLVERHAMPTON WANDERERS	D 0-0		39,114
Nov 15	WEST HAM UNITED	W 2-0	Lawler, Graham	39,668
Nov 22	Leeds United	D 1-1	Yeats	43,293
Nov 29	ARSENAL	L 0-1		40,295
Dec 6	Everton	W 3-0	Hughes, Brown o.g., Graham	57,026
Dec 13	MANCHESTER UNITED	L 1-4	Hughes	47,682
Dec 26	Burnley	W 5-1	Ross, Graham, Lawler, Thompson, Callaghan	22,944
Jan 10	Stoke City	W 2-0	Graham, Thompson	30,038
Jan 17	WEST BROMWICH ALBION	D 1-1	Lawler	43,526
Jan 31	Nottingham Forest	L 0-1		30,838
Feb 16	NEWCASTLE UNITED	D 0-0		38,218
Feb 28	DERBY COUNTY	L 0-2		43,594
Mar 3	Coventry City	W 3-2	Hughes, Evans 2	29,497
Mar 7	LEEDS UNITED	D 0-0		51,435
Mar 11	Southampton	W 1-0	Evans	23,239
Mar 14	Arsenal	L 1-2	Yeats	32,333
Mar 16	SHEFFIELD WEDNESDAY	W 3-0	Lawler, Yeats, Graham	31,931
Mar 21	EVERTON	L 0-2		54,496
Mar 24	IPSWICH TOWN	W 2-0	Callaghan, Smith (pen)	29,548
Mar 28	West Ham United	L 0-1		38,239
Mar 30	Wolverhampton Wanderers	W 1-0	Lawler	32,754
Apr 3	CRYSTAL PALACE	W 3-0	Graham 2, Lawler	30,999
Apr 15	Sunderland	W 1-0	Lawler	33,007
Apr 18	Chelsea	L 1-2	Graham	36,521

FA Cup

Jan 7	Coventry City	(Rd3)	D 1-1	Graham	33,688
Jan 12	COVENTRY CITY	(R)	W 3-0	Ross, Thompson, Graham	51,261
Jan 24	WREXHAM	(Rd4)	W 3-1	Graham 2, St John	54,096
Feb 7	LEICESTER CITY	(Rd5)	D 0-0		53,785
Feb 11	Leicester City	(R)	W 2-0	Evans 2	42,100
Feb 21	Watford	(Rd6)	L 0-1		34,047

League Cup

Sep 3	Watford	(Rd2)	W 2-1	Slater o.g., St John	21,149
Sep 24	Manchester City	(Rd3)	L 2-3	Evans, Graham	28,019

Inter-Cities' Fairs Cup

Sep 18	DUNDALK	(Rd1/1L)	W10-0	Evans 2, Lawler, Smith 2, Graham 2, Lindsay, Thompson, Callaghan	32,562
Sep 30	Dundalk	(Rd1/2L)	W 4-0	Thompson 2, Graham, Callaghan	6,000
Nov 12	Vitoria Setubal	(Rd2/1L)	L 0-1		16,000
Nov 26	VITORIA SETUBAL	(Rd2/2L)	W 3-2*	Smith (pen), Evans, Hunt	41,633

*Liverpool lost on away goals rule.

MANAGER: Bill Shankly
CAPTAIN: Ron Yeats, Tommy Smith from 28 February
TOP SCORER: Bobby Graham 21 (13 league)
BIGGEST WIN: 10-0, 18 September 1969, v Dundalk (H), Inter-Cities' Fairs Cup
HIGHEST ATTENDANCE: 59,387, 13 September 1969, v Manchester United (A), Division One
TRANSFERS IN: Larry Lloyd from Bristol Rovers
TRANSFERS OUT: Roger Hunt to Bolton Wanderers, Peter Wall to Crystal Palace

League & Cup Appearances

PLAYER	LEAGUE	CUP COMPETITION			TOTAL
		FA CUP	LC	ICFC	
Boersma	4		0 (1)	1	5 (1)
Callaghan	41	6	2	3 (1)	52 (1)
Clemence	14	1		2	17
Evans	17 (2)	1 (1)	1	2 (1)	21 (4)
Evans	3				3
Graham	42	6	2	4	54
Hall	0 (1)				0 (1)
Hughes	41	6	2	4	53
Hunt	15 (3)		2	0 (2)	17 (5)
Lawler	42	6	2	4	54
Lawrence	28	5	2	2	37
Lindsay	4 (2)			1	5 (2)
Livermore	13 (1)				13 (1)
Lloyd	8			1	9
McLaughlin	1				1
Peplow	2			1	3
Ross	7	4 (1)		1	12 (1)
Smith	36	3	2	4	45
St John	25 (1)	6	1	2 (1)	34 (2)
Strong	34	6	2	4	46
Thompson	39	4	2	4	49
Wall	9	6		1	16
Yeats	37	6	2	3	48

Goalscorers

PLAYER	LEAGUE	CUP COMPETITION			TOTAL
		FA CUP	LC	ICFC	
Graham	13	4	1	3	21
Lawler	10			1	11
Evans	3	2	1	3	9
Hughes	7				7
Hunt	6			1	7
St John	5	1	1		7
Smith	4			3	7
Thompson	3	1		3	7
Callaghan	3			2	5
Strong	3				3
Yeats	3				3
Lindsay	1			1	2
Ross	1	1			2
Opps' o.gs.	3		1		4

Fact File

Liverpool achieved their record aggregate European win – 14-0 v Dundalk – in the first round of Inter-Cities' Fairs Cup.

Final Division One Table

		P	W	D	L	F	A	Pts
1	Everton	42	29	8	5	72	34	66
2	Leeds U	42	21	15	6	84	49	57
3	Chelsea	42	21	13	8	70	50	55
4	Derby Co	42	22	9	11	64	37	53
5	Liverpool	42	20	11	11	65	42	51
6	Coventry C	42	19	11	12	58	48	49
7	Newcastle U	42	17	13	12	57	35	47
8	Manchester U	42	14	17	11	66	61	45
9	Stoke C	42	15	15	12	56	52	45
10	Manchester C	42	16	11	15	55	48	43
11	Tottenham H	42	17	9	16	54	55	43
12	Arsenal	42	12	18	12	51	49	42
13	Wolverhampton W	42	12	16	14	55	57	40
14	Burnley	42	12	15	15	56	61	39
15	Nottingham F	42	10	18	14	50	71	38
16	WBA	42	14	9	19	58	66	37
17	West Ham U	42	12	12	18	51	60	36
18	Ipswich T	42	10	11	21	40	63	31
19	Southampton	42	6	17	19	46	67	29
20	Crystal Palace	42	6	15	21	34	68	27
21	Sunderland	42	6	14	22	30	68	26
22	Sheffield W	42	8	9	25	40	71	25

Season 1970-71

Football League Division One

DATE	OPPONENTS	SCORE	GOALSCORERS	ATTENDANCE
Aug 15	Burnley	W 2-1	Evans A, Hughes	26,702
Aug 17	Blackpool	D 0-0		28,818
Aug 22	HUDDERSFIELD TOWN	W 4-0	McLaughlin 2, Evans A 2	52,628
Aug 25	CRYSTAL PALACE	D 1-1	Graham	47,612
Aug 29	West Bromwich Albion	D 1-1	Evans A	31,624
Sep 5	MANCHESTER UNITED	D 1-1	Evans A	52,541
Sep 12	Newcastle United	D 0-0		35,501
Sep 19	NOTTINGHAM FOREST	W 3-0	Graham, Thompson, Evans A	40,676
Sep 26	Southampton	L 0-1		26,155
Oct 3	CHELSEA	W 1-0	Evans A	46,196
Oct 10	Tottenham Hotspur	L 0-1		44,457
Oct 17	BURNLEY	W 2-0	Yeats, Heighway	40,804
Oct 24	Ipswich Town	L 0-1		22,577
Oct 31	WOLVERHAMPTON WANDERERS	W 2-0	Smith (pen), Evans A	45,391
Nov 7	Derby County	D 0-0		33,004
Nov 14	COVENTRY CITY	D 0-0		40,303
Nov 21	EVERTON	W 3-2	Heighway, Toshack, Lawler	53,777
Nov 28	Arsenal	L 0-2		45,097
Dec 5	LEEDS UNITED	D 1-1	Toshack	51,357
Dec 12	West Ham United	W 2-1	Whitham, Boersma	27,459
Dec 19	Huddersfield Town	D 0-0		25,033
Dec 26	STOKE CITY	D 0-0		47,103
Jan 9	BLACKPOOL	D 2-2	Heighway, Craven o.g.	42,939
Jan 12	MANCHESTER CITY	D 0-0		45,985
Jan 16	Crystal Palace	L 0-1		28,253
Jan 30	ARSENAL	W 2-0	Toshack, Smith	43,847
Feb 6	Leeds United	W 1-0	Toshack	48,425
Feb 16	WEST HAM UNITED	W 1-0	Toshack	38,032
Feb 20	Everton	D 0-0		56,846
Feb 27	Wolverhampton Wanderers	L 0-1		32,290
Mar 13	Coventry City	L 0-1		27,687
Mar 20	DERBY COUNTY	W 2-0	Mackay o.g., Lawler	40,990
Mar 29	IPSWICH TOWN	W 2-1	Evans A, Graham	42,017
Apr 2	WEST BROMWICH ALBION	D 1-1	Evans A	43,580
Apr 6	NEWCASTLE UNITED	D 1-1	Lawler	44,289
Apr 10	Stoke City	W 1-0	Thompson	28,810
Apr 12	Chelsea	L 0-1		38,705
Apr 17	TOTTENHAM HOTSPUR	D 0-0		49,363
Apr 19	Manchester United	W 2-0	Heighway, Edwards o.g.	44,004
Apr 24	Nottingham Forest	W 1-0	Hall	20,678
Apr 26	Manchester City	D 2-2	Graham 2	17,975
May 1	SOUTHAMPTON	W 1-0	Hughes	38,427

FA Cup

Jan 2	ALDERSHOT	(Rd3)	W 1-0	McLaughlin	45,500
Jan 23	SWANSEA CITY	(Rd4)	W 3-0	Toshack, St John, Lawler	47,229
Feb 13	SOUTHAMPTON	(Rd5)	W 1-0	Lawler	50,226
Mar 6	TOTTENHAM HOTSPUR	(Rd6)	D 0-0		54,731
Mar 16	Tottenham Hotspur	(R)	W 1-0	Heighway	56,283
Mar 27	Everton*	(SF)	W 2-1	Evans A, Hall	62,144
May 8	Arsenal	(F)	L 1-2**	Heighway	100,000

*Played at Old Trafford.

**After extra time. Score at 90 mins, 0-0. Played at Wembley.

League Cup

Sep 8	Mansfield Town	(Rd2)	D 0-0		12,532
Sep 22	MANSFIELD TOWN	(R)	W 3-2†	Hughes, Smith, Evans A	31,087
Oct 6	Swindon Town		L 0-2		23,992

†After extra time. Score at 90 mins 2-2.

Inter-Cities' Fairs Cup

Sep 15	FERENCVAROS	(Rd1/1L)	W 1-0	Graham	37,531
Sep 29	Ferencvaros	(Rd1/2L)	D 1-1	Hughes	25,000
Oct 21	DINAMO BUCHAREST	(Rd2/1L)	W 3-0	Lindsay, Lawler, Hughes	36,525
Nov 4	Dinamo Bucharest	(Rd2/2L)	D 1-1	Boersma	45,000
Dec 9	Hibernian	(Rd3/1L)	W 1-0	Toshack	30,296
Dec 22	HIBERNIAN	(Rd3/2L)	W 2-0	Heighway, Boersma	37,815
Mar 10	BAYERN MUNICH	(Rd4/1L)	W 3-0	Evans A 3	45,616
Mar 24	Bayern Munich	(Rd4/2L)	D 1-1	Ross	23,000
Apr 14	LEEDS UNITED	(SF/1L)	L 0-1		52,577
Apr 28	Leeds United	(SF/2L)	D 0-0		40,462

Fact File

Ian St John, Shankly's record signing in 1961, left after 10 years. He scored 118 goals in 425 competitive games and will always be remembered for scoring the winning goal in the FA Cup final in 1965 to bring the trophy to Anfield for the first time ever.

League & Cup Appearances

PLAYER	LEAGUE	CUP COMPETITION			TOTAL
		FA CUP	LC	ICFC	
Arnold	1 (1)				1 (1)
Boersma	13 (2)	3		2 (1)	18 (3)
Callaghan	21 (2)	4 (1)	1	5	31 (3)
Clemence	41	7	3	10	61
Evans A	21	3 (1)	3	6	33 (1)
Evans R	4		1	1	6
Fagan	1		0 (1)		1 (1)
Graham	13 (1)		2	2 (2)	17 (3)
Hall	32 (3)	7	3	8	50 (3)
Heighway	29 (4)	7	2	7	45 (4)
Hughes	39	7	3	10	59
Lawler	41	7	3	10	61
Lawrence	1				1
Lindsay	21	4	2	8	35
Livermore	0 (1)		1		1 (1)
Lloyd	40	7	3	10	60
McLaughlin	33	4	1	7	45
Ross	8 (4)			1 (1)	9 (5)
Smith	41	7	3	10	61
St John	0 (1)	0 (1)		0 (1)	0 (3)
Thompson	24 (4)	1 (1)	1	6 (2)	32 (7)
Toshack	21	7		5	33
Whitham	6		1 (1)		7 (1)
Yeats	11 (1)	2		2	15 (1)

Goalscorers

PLAYER	LEAGUE	CUP COMPETITION			TOTAL
		FA CUP	LC	ICFC	
Evans A	10	1	1	3	15
Heighway	4	2		1	7
Toshack	5	1		1	7
Graham	5			1	6
Lawler	3	2		1	6
Hughes	2		1	2	5
Boersma	1			2	3
McLaughlin	2	1			3
Smith	2		1		3
Hall	1	1			2
Thompson	2				2
Lindsay				1	1
Ross				1	1
St John		1			1
Whitham	1				1
Yeats	1				1
Opps' o.gs.	3				3

MANAGER: Bill Shankly

CAPTAIN: Tommy Smith

TRANSFERS IN: Jack Whitham from Sheffield Wednesday, John Toshack from Cardiff City

TRANSFERS OUT: Geoff Strong to Coventry City, St John to Coventry City

Final Division One Table

		P	W	D	L	F	A	PTS
1	ARSENAL	42	29	7	6	71	29	65
2	LEEDS U	42	27	10	5	72	30	64
3	TOTTENHAM H	42	19	14	9	54	33	52
4	WOLVERHAMPTON W	42	22	8	12	64	54	52
5	LIVERPOOL	42	17	17	8	42	24	51
6	CHELSEA	42	18	15	9	52	42	51
7	SOUTHAMPTON	42	17	12	13	56	44	46
8	MANCHESTER U	42	16	11	15	65	66	43
9	DERBY CO	42	16	10	16	56	54	42
10	COVENTRY C	42	16	10	16	37	38	42
11	MANCHESTER C	42	12	17	13	47	42	41
12	NEWCASTLE U	42	14	13	15	44	46	41
13	STOKE C	42	12	13	17	44	48	37
14	EVERTON	42	12	13	17	54	60	37
15	HUDDERSFIELD T	42	11	14	17	40	49	36
16	NOTTINGHAM F	42	14	8	20	42	61	36
17	WBA	42	10	15	17	58	75	35
18	CRYSTAL PALACE	42	12	11	19	39	57	35
19	IPSWICH T	42	12	10	20	42	48	34
20	WEST HAM U	42	10	14	18	47	60	34
21	BURNLEY	42	7	13	22	29	63	27
22	BLACKPOOL	42	4	15	23	34	66	23

Season 1971-72

Football League Division One

DATE	OPPONENTS	SCORE	GOALSCORERS	ATTENDANCE
Aug 14	NOTTINGHAM FOREST	W 3-1	Keegan, Smith, Hughes	51,427
Aug 17	WOLVERHAMPTON WANDERERS	W 3-2	Toshack, Heighway, Smith (pen)	51,869
Aug 21	Newcastle United	L 2-3	Hughes, Keegan	39,720
Aug 24	Crystal Palace	W 1-0	Toshack	29,489
Aug 28	LEICESTER CITY	W 3-2	Heighway, Keegan, Toshack	50,970
Sep 1	Manchester City	L 0-1		45,144
Sep 4	Tottenham Hotspur	L 0-2		50,124
Sep 11	SOUTHAMPTON	W 1-0	Toshack	45,878
Sep 18	Leeds United	L 0-1		41,381
Sep 25	MANCHESTER UNITED	D 2-2	Graham, Hall	55,634
Oct 2	Stoke City	D 0-0		28,698
Oct 9	CHELSEA	D 0-0		48,464
Oct 16	Nottingham Forest	W 3-2	Hughes, Heighway, Smith (pen)	20,945
Oct 23	HUDDERSFIELD TOWN	W 2-0	Smith (pen), Evans	41,627
Oct 30	Sheffield United	D 1-1	Keegan	39,023
Nov 6	ARSENAL	W 3-2	Hughes, Callaghan, Ross	46,929
Nov 13	Everton	L 0-1		56,563
Nov 20	Coventry City	W 2-0	Whitham 2	25,325
Nov 27	WEST HAM UNITED	W 1-0	Hughes	43,399
Dec 4	Ipswich Town	D 0-0		21,359
Dec 11	DERBY COUNTY	W 3-2	Whitham 3	44,601
Dec 18	TOTTENHAM HOTSPUR	D 0-0		43,409
Dec 27	West Bromwich Albion	L 0-1		43,804
Jan 1	LEEDS UNITED	L 0-2		53,847
Jan 8	Leicester City	L 0-1		26,421
Jan 22	Wolverhampton Wanderers	D 0-0		33,692
Jan 29	CRYSTAL PALACE	W 4-1	Lawler 2, Callaghan, Keegan	39,538
Feb 12	Huddersfield Town	W 1-0	Whitham	18,702
Feb 19	SHEFFIELD UNITED	W 2-0	Toshack 2	42,005
Feb 26	MANCHESTER CITY	W 3-0	Lloyd, Keegan, Graham	50,074
Mar 4	EVERTON	W 4-0	Wright o.g., McLaughlin o.g., Lawler, Hughes	53,922
Mar 11	Chelsea	D 0-0		38,691
Mar 18	NEWCASTLE UNITED	W 5-0	Lawler, Keegan, Toshack, Hughes, Heighway	43,899
Mar 25	Southampton	W 1-0	Toshack	21,680
Mar 28	STOKE CITY	W 2-1	Burrows o.g., Keegan	42,489
Apr 1	WEST BROMWICH ALBION	W 2-0	Smith (pen), Lawler	46,564
Apr 3	Manchester United	W 3-0	Lawler, Toshack, Hughes	54,000
Apr 8	COVENTRY CITY	W 3-1	Keegan, Smith (pen), Toshack	50,628
Apr 15	West Ham United	W 2-0	Toshack, Heighway	32,660
Apr 22	IPSWICH TOWN	W 2-0	Toshack 2	54,316
May 1	Derby County	L 0-1		39,420
May 8	Arsenal	D 0-0		39,285

FA Cup

Jan 15	Oxford United	(Rd3)	W 3-0	Keegan 2, Lindsay	18,000
Feb 5	LEEDS UNITED	(Rd4)	D 0-0		56,300
Feb 9	Leeds United	(R)	L 0-2		45,821

League Cup

Sep 7	HULL CITY	(Rd2)	W 3-0	Lawler, Heighway, Hall (pen)	31,612
Oct 5	SOUTHAMPTON	(Rd3)	W 1-0	Heighway	28,964
Oct 27	West Ham United	(Rd4)	L 1-2	Graham	40,878

European Cup-Winners' Cup

Sep 15	Servette Geneva	(Rd1/1L)	L 1-2	Lawler	16,000
Sep 29	SERVETTE GENEVA	(Rd1/2L)	W 2-0	Hughes, Heighway	38,591
Oct 20	BAYERN MUNICH	(Rd2/1L)	D 0-0		42,949
Nov 3	Bayern Munich	(Rd2/2L)	L 1-3	Evans	40,000

Charity Shield

Aug 7	Leicester City	L 0-1*	25,014

*Played at Leicester.

MANAGER: Bill Shankly

CAPTAIN: Tommy Smith

TOP SCORER: John Toshack 13 (league)

BIGGEST WIN: 5-0, 18 March 1972, v Newcastle United (H), Division One

HIGHEST ATTENDANCE: 56,563, 13 November 1971, v Everton (A), Division One

TRANSFERS IN: Kevin Keegan from Scunthorpe United

TRANSFERS OUT: Ron Yeats to Tranmere Rovers, Tommy Lawrence to Tranmere Rovers

League & Cup Appearances

PLAYER	LEAGUE	CUP COMPETITION			OTHER	TOTAL
		FA CUP	LC	ECWC		
Boersma	3 (3)	0 (1)				3 (4)
Callaghan	41	3	3	4	1	52
Clemence	42	3	3	4	1	53
Evans	6	1	2	2 (1)	1	12 (1)
Graham	10 (1)	1 (1)	2 (1)	3	1	17 (3)
Hall	24 (2)	1	2	3	1	31 (2)
Heighway	40	2	3	4	1	50
Hughes	42	3	3	4	1	53
Keegan	35	3	1	3		42
Lawler	42	3	3	4	1	53
Lindsay	38	3	1	2	1	45
Lloyd	33	2	3	4	1	43
McLaughlin	3 (2)		1			4 (2)
Ross	20 (1)	3	3	3 (1)		29 (2)
Smith	37	3	1	3	1	45
Thompson Peter	9 (1)	1	1	0 (2)		11 (3)
Thompson Phil	0 (1)					0 (1)
Toshack	28 (1)	1	1	1 (1)		31 (2)
Whitham	9					9

Goalscorers

PLAYER	LEAGUE	CUP COMPETITION			TOTAL
		FA CUP	LC	ECWC	
Toshack	13				13
Keegan	9	2			11
Hughes	8			1	9
Heighway	5		2	1	8
Lawler	6		1	1	8
Smith	6				6
Whitham	6				6
Graham	2		1		3
Callaghan	2				2
Evans	1			1	2
Hall	1		1		2
Lindsay		1			1
Lloyd	1				1
Ross	1				1
Opps' o.gs.	3				3

Fact File

Kevin Keegan's signing as a virtual 'unknown' from a lower division side proved to be a catalyst as he went on to win seven major trophies in his six seasons at Anfield.

Final Division One Table

		P	W	D	L	F	A	Pts
1	Derby Co	42	24	10	8	69	33	58
2	Leeds U	42	24	9	9	73	31	57
3	Liverpool	42	24	9	9	64	30	57
4	Manchester C	42	23	11	8	77	45	57
5	Arsenal	42	22	8	12	58	40	52
6	Tottenham H	42	19	13	10	63	42	51
7	Chelsea	42	18	12	12	58	49	48
8	Manchester U	42	19	10	13	69	61	48
9	Wolverhampton W	42	18	11	13	65	57	47
10	Sheffield U	42	17	12	13	61	60	46
11	Newcastle U	42	15	11	16	49	52	41
12	Leicester C	42	13	13	16	41	46	39
13	Ipswich T	42	11	16	15	39	53	38
14	West Ham U	42	12	12	18	47	51	36
15	Everton	42	9	18	15	37	48	36
16	WBA	42	12	11	19	42	54	35
17	Stoke C	42	10	15	17	39	56	35
18	Coventry C	42	9	15	18	44	67	33
19	Southampton	42	12	7	23	52	80	31
20	Crystal Palace	42	8	13	21	39	65	29
21	Nottingham F	42	8	9	25	47	81	25
22	Huddersfield T	42	6	13	23	27	59	25

Season 1972-73

Football League Division One

DATE	OPPONENTS	SCORE	GOALSCORERS	ATTENDANCE
Aug 12	MANCHESTER CITY	W 2-0	Hall, Callaghan	55,383
Aug 15	MANCHESTER UNITED	W 2-0	Toshack, Heighway	54,779
Aug 19	Crystal Palace	D 1-1	Hughes	30,054
Aug 23	Chelsea	W 2-1	Toshack, Callaghan	35,375
Aug 26	WEST HAM UNITED	W 3-2	Toshack, Ferguson o.g., Hughes	50,491
Aug 30	Leicester City	L 2-3	Toshack 2	28,694
Sep 2	Derby County	L 1-2	Toshack	32,524
Sep 9	WOLVERHAMPTON WANDERERS	W 4-2	Hughes, Cormack, Smith (pen), Keegan	43,386
Sep 16	Arsenal	D 0-0		47,597
Sep 23	SHEFFIELD UNITED	W 5-0	Boersma, Lindsay, Heighway, Cormack, Keegan (pen)	42,940
Sep 30	Leeds United	W 2-1	Lloyd, Boersma	46,468
Oct 7	EVERTON	W 1-0	Cormack	55,975
Oct 14	Southampton	D 1-1	Lawler	24,100
Oct 21	STOKE CITY	W 2-1	Hughes, Callaghan	45,604
Oct 28	Norwich City	D 1-1	Cormack	36,625
Nov 4	CHELSEA	W 3-1	Toshack 2, Keegan	48,932
Nov 11	Manchester United	L 0-2		53,944
Nov 18	NEWCASTLE UNITED	W 3-2	Cormack, Lindsay, Toshack	46,153
Nov 25	Tottenham Hotspur	W 2-1	Heighway, Keegan	45,399
Dec 2	BIRMINGHAM CITY	W 4-3	Lindsay 2, Cormack, Toshack	45,407
Dec 9	West Bromwich Albion	D 1-1	Boersma	27,213
Dec 16	Ipswich Town	D 1-1	Heighway	25,693
Dec 23	COVENTRY CITY	W 2-0	Toshack 2	41,550
Dec 26	Sheffield United	W 3-0	Boersma, Lawler, Heighway	34,040
Dec 30	CRYSTAL PALACE	W 1-0	Cormack	50,862
Jan 6	West Ham United	W 1-0	Keegan	34,480
Jan 20	DERBY COUNTY	D 1-1	Toshack	45,996
Jan 27	Wolverhampton Wanderers	L 1-2	Keegan	32,957
Feb 10	ARSENAL	L 0-2		49,898
Feb 17	Manchester City	D 1-1	Boersma	40,528
Feb 24	IPSWICH TOWN	W 2-1	Heighway, Keegan	43,875
Mar 3	Everton	W 2-0	Hughes 2	54,269
Mar 10	SOUTHAMPTON	W 3-2	Lloyd, Keegan 2	41,674
Mar 17	Stoke City	W 1-0	Mahoney o.g.	33,540
Mar 24	NORWICH CITY	W 3-1	Lawler, Hughes, Hall	42,995
Mar 31	TOTTENHAM HOTSPUR	D 1-1	Keegan	48,477
Apr 7	Birmingham City	L 1-2	Smith	48,114
Apr 14	WEST BROMWICH ALBION	W 1-0	Keegan (pen)	43,853
Apr 17	Coventry City	W 2-1	Boersma 2	27,280
Apr 21	Newcastle United	L 1-2	Keegan	37,240
Apr 23	LEEDS UNITED	W 2-0	Cormack, Keegan	55,738
Apr 28	LEICESTER CITY	D 0-0		56,202

FA Cup

Jan 13	Burnley	(Rd3)	D 0-0		35,730
Jan 16	BURNLEY	(R)	W 3-0	Toshack 2, Cormack	56,124
Feb 3	MANCHESTER CITY	(Rd4)	D 0-0		56,296
Feb 7	Manchester City	(R)	L 0-2		49,572

League Cup

Sep 5	Carlisle United	(Rd2)	D 1-1	Keegan	16,257
Sep 19	CARLISLE UNITED	(R)	W 5-1	Keegan, Boersma 2, Lawler, Heighway	22,128
Oct 3	West Bromwich Albion	(Rd3)	D 1-1	Heighway	17,756
Oct 10	WEST BROMWICH ALBION	(R)	W 2-1*	Hughes, Keegan	26,461
Oct 31	LEEDS UNITED	(Rd4)	D 2-2	Keegan, Toshack	44,609
Nov 22	Leeds United	(R)	W 1-0	Keegan	34,856
Dec 4	TOTTENHAM HOTSPUR	(Rd5)	D 1-1	Hughes	48,677
Dec 6	Tottenham Hotspur	(R)	L 1-3	Callaghan	34,565

*After extra time. Score at 90 mins 1-1.

UEFA Cup

Sep 12	EINTRACHT FRANKFURT	(Rd1/1L)	W 2-0	Keegan, Hughes	33,380
Sep 26	Eintracht Frankfurt	(Rd1/2L)	D 0-0		20,000
Oct 24	AEK ATHENS	(Rd2/1L)	W 3-0	Boersma, Cormack, Smith (pen)	31,906
Nov 7	AEK Athens	(Rd2/2L)	W 3-1	Hughes 2, Boersma	25,000
Nov 29	Dynamo Berlin	(Rd3/1L)	D 0-0		19,000
Dec 13	DYNAMO BERLIN	(Rd3/2L)	W 3-1	Boersma, Heighway, Toshack	34,140
Mar 7	DYNAMO DRESDEN	(Rd4/1L)	W 2-0	Hall, Boersma	33,270
Mar 21	Dynamo Dresden	(Rd4/2L)	W 1-0	Keegan	35,000
Apr 10	TOTTENHAM HOTSPUR	(SF/1L)	W 1-0	Lindsay	42,174
Apr 25	Tottenham Hotspur	(SF/2L)	L 1-2**	Heighway	46,919
May 10	BORUSSIA MÖNCHENGLADBACH	(F/1L)	W 3-0	Keegan 2, Lloyd	41,169
May 23	Borussia Mönchengladbach	(F/2L)	L 0-2	(aggregate win)	35,000

**Aggregate 2-2. Liverpool won on away goals rule.

League & Cup Appearances

PLAYER	LEAGUE	CUP COMPETITION			TOTAL
		FA CUP	LC	UEFA	
Boersma	19	0 (1)	2 (1)	5 (3)	26 (5)
Callaghan	42	4	8	12	66
Clemence	41	4	7	12	64
Cormack	30	4	8	10	52
Hall	17 (4)		1 (1)	4 (4)	22 (9)
Heighway	38	4	8	12	62
Hughes	41	4	8	12	65
Keegan	41	4	8	11	64
Lane	1		1		2
Lawler	42	4	8	12	66
Lindsay	37	4	7	11	59
Lloyd	42	4	8	12	66
Smith	33	2	4	10	49
Storton	4		4	1 (1)	9 (1)
Thompson	12 (2)	2	0 (1)	2 (1)	16 (4)
Toshack	22	4	6	6 (2)	38 (2)
Whitham				0 (1)	0 (1)

Goalscorers

PLAYER	LEAGUE	CUP COMPETITION			TOTAL
		FA CUP	LC	UEFA	
Keegan	13		5	4	22
Toshack	13	2	1	1	17
Boersma	7		2	4	13
Hughes	7		2	3	12
Cormack	8	1		1	10
Heighway	6		2	2	10
Lindsay	4			1	5
Callaghan	3		1		4
Lawler	3		1		4
Hall	2			1	3
Lloyd	2			1	3
Smith	2			1	3
Opps' o.gs.	2				2

Fact File

For the first time two major trophies were won by the club in one season: the League Division One championship and the UEFA Cup.

MANAGER: Bill Shankly
CAPTAIN: Tommy Smith
TOP SCORER: Kevin Keegan, 22 (13 league)
TRANSFERS IN: Peter Cormack from Nottingham Forest

Final Division One Table

		P	W	D	L	F	A	Pts
1	Liverpool	42	25	10	7	72	42	60
2	Arsenal	42	23	11	8	57	43	57
3	Leeds U	42	21	11	10	71	45	53
4	Ipswich T	42	17	14	11	55	45	48
5	Wolverhampton W	42	18	11	13	66	54	47
6	West Ham U	42	17	12	13	67	53	46
7	Derby Co	42	19	8	15	56	54	46
8	Tottenham H	42	16	13	13	58	48	45
9	Newcastle U	42	16	13	13	60	51	45
10	Birmingham C	42	15	12	15	53	54	42
11	Manchester C	42	15	11	16	57	60	41
12	Chelsea	42	13	14	15	49	51	40
13	Southampton	42	11	18	13	47	52	40
14	Sheffield U	42	15	10	17	51	59	40
15	Stoke C	42	14	10	18	61	56	38
16	Leicester C	42	10	17	15	40	46	37
17	Everton	42	13	11	18	41	49	37
18	Manchester U	42	12	13	17	44	60	37
19	Coventry C	42	13	9	20	40	55	35
20	Norwich C	42	11	10	21	36	63	32
21	Crystal Palace	42	9	12	21	41	58	30
22	WBA	42	9	10	23	38	62	28

Season 1973-74

Football League Division One

DATE	OPPONENTS	SCORE	GOALSCORERS	ATTENDANCE
Aug 25	STOKE CITY	W 1-0	Heighway	52,935
Aug 28	Coventry City	L 0-1		29,305
Sep 1	Leicester City	D 1-1	Toshack	29,347
Sep 4	DERBY COUNTY	W 2-0	Thompson, Keegan (pen)	45,237
Sep 8	CHELSEA	W 1-0	Keegan	47,016
Sep 12	Derby County	L 1-3	Boersma	32,867
Sep 15	Birmingham City	D 1-1	Hall	35,719
Sep 22	TOTTENHAM HOTSPUR	W 3-2	Lawler 2, Lindsay (pen)	42,901
Sep 29	Manchester United	D 0-0		53,882
Oct 6	NEWCASTLE UNITED	W 2-1	Cormack, Lindsay (pen)	45,612
Oct 13	Southampton	L 0-1		22,018
Oct 20	Leeds United	L 0-1		44,811
Oct 27	SHEFFIELD WEDNESDAY	W 1-0	Keegan	40,641
Nov 3	Arsenal	W 2-0	Hughes, Toshack	39,837
Nov 10	WOLVERHAMPTON WANDERERS	W 1-0	Heighway	38,088
Nov 17	IPSWICH TOWN	W 4-2	Keegan 3 (1 pen), Cormack	37,420
Nov 24	Queens Park Rangers	D 2-2	Lloyd, Toshack	26,254
Dec 1	WEST HAM UNITED	W 1-0	Cormack	34,857
Dec 8	Everton	W 1-0	Waddle	56,098
Dec 15	Norwich City	D 1-1	Cormack	20,628
Dec 22	MANCHESTER UNITED	W 2-0	Keegan (pen), Heighway	40,420
Dec 26	Burnley	L 1-2	Cormack	24,404
Dec 29	Chelsea	W 1-0	Cormack	32,901
Jan 1	LEICESTER CITY	D 1-1	Cormack	39,110
Jan 12	BIRMINGHAM CITY	W 3-2	Keegan 2, Thompson	39,094
Jan 19	Stoke City	D 1-1	Smith	32,789
Feb 2	NORWICH CITY	W 1-0	Cormack	31,742
Feb 5	COVENTRY CITY	W 2-1	Lindsay (pen), Keegan	21,656
Feb 23	Newcastle United	D 0-0		41,727
Feb 26	SOUTHAMPTON	W 1-0	Boersma	27,015
Mar 2	BURNLEY	W 1-0	Toshack	42,562
Mar 16	LEEDS UNITED	W 1-0	Heighway	56,003
Mar 23	Wolverhampton Wanderers	W 1-0	Hall	35,867
Apr 6	QUEENS PARK RANGERS	W 2-1	Lindsay (pen), Mancini o.g.	54,027
Apr 8	Sheffield United	L 0-1		31,809
Apr 12	Manchester City	D 1-1	Cormack	43,284
Apr 13	Ipswich Town	D 1-1	Hughes	33,285
Apr 16	MANCHESTER CITY	W 4-0	Hall 2, Boersma, Keegan	50,781
Apr 20	EVERTON	D 0-0		55,858
Apr 24	ARSENAL	L 0-1		47,997
Apr 27	West Ham United	D 2-2		36,160
May 8	Tottenham Hotspur	D 1-1	Heighway	24,178

FA Cup

Jan 5	DONCASTER ROVERS	(Rd3)	D 2-2	Keegan 2	31,483
Jan 8	Doncaster Rovers	(R)	W 2-0	Heighway, Cormack	22,499
Jan 26	CARLISLE UNITED	(Rd4)	D 0-0		47,211
Jan 29	Carlisle United	(R)	W 2-0	Boersma, Toshack	21,262
Feb 16	IPSWICH TOWN	(Rd5)	W 2-0	Hall, Keegan	45,340
Mar 9	Bristol City	(Rd6)	W 1-0	Toshack	37,671
Mar 30	Leicester City*	(SF)	D 0-0		60,000
Apr 3	Leicester City**	(R)	W 3-1	Hall, Keegan, Toshack	55,619
May 4	Newcastle United†	(F)	W 3-0	Keegan 2, Heighway	100,000

*Played at Old Trafford. **Played at Villa Park. †Played at Wembley.

League Cup

Oct 8	West Ham United	(Rd2)	D 2-2	Cormack, Heighway	25,823
Oct 29	WEST HAM UNITED	(R)	W 1-0	Toshack	26,002
Nov 21	Sunderland	(Rd3)	W 2-0	Keegan, Toshack	36,208
Nov 27	Hull City	(Rd4)	D 0-0		19,748
Dec 4	HULL CITY	(R)	W 3-1	Callaghan 3	17,120
Dec 19	Wolverhampton Wanderers	(Rd5)	L 0-1		15,242

European Cup

Sep 19	Jeunesse D'Esch	(Rd1/1L)	D 1-1	Hall	5,000
Oct 3	JEUNESSE D'ESCH	(Rd1/2L)	W 2-0	Mond o.g., Toshack	28,714
Oct 24	RED STAR BELGRADE	(Rd2/2L)	L 1-2	Lawler	40,000
Nov 6	Red Star Belgrade	(Rd2/2L)	L 1-2	Lawler	41,774

MANAGER: Bill Shankly
CAPTAIN: Emlyn Hughes
TOP SCORER: Kevin Keegan 19 (12 league)
BIGGEST WIN: 4-0, 16 April 1974, v Manchester City (H), Division One
HIGHEST ATTENDANCE: 100,000, 4 May 1974, v Newcastle United , FA Cup final, played at Wembley
TRANSFERS IN: Alan Waddle from Halifax Town
TRANSFERS OUT: Peter Thompson to Bolton Wanderers

League & Cup Appearances

PLAYER	LEAGUE	CUP COMPETITION FA CUP	LC	EC	TOTAL
Boersma	13 (2)	4 (1)		1 (1)	18 (4)
Brownbill	1				1
Callaghan	42	9	6	4	61
Clemence	42	9	6	4	61
Cormack	40 (2)	8	6	1	55 (2)
Evans	2				2
Hall	20 (2)	7 (1)	1	2 (1)	30 (4)
Heighway	35 (1)	6	6	4	51 (1)
Hughes	42	9	6	4	61
Keegan	42	9	6	4	61
Lawler	18		3	4	25
Lindsay	36	9	6	3	54
Lloyd	27	3	6	4	40
McLaughlin	1			1	2
Ryands		1			1
Smith	34	7	5	3	49
Storton	1	1			2
Thompson Ph	35	9	4	2 (1)	50 (1)
Thompson M	1				1
Toshack	19	6	2	3	30
Waddle	11	2	3		16

Goalscorers

PLAYER	LEAGUE	CUP COMPETITION FA CUP	LC	EC	TOTAL
Keegan	12	6	1		19
Cormack	9	1	1		11
Toshack	5	3	2	1	11
Heighway	5	2	1		8
Hall	4	2		1	7
Boersma	3	1			4
Lawler	2			2	4
Lindsay	4				4
Callaghan			3		3
Hughes	2				2
Thompson Ph	2				2
Lloyd	1				1
Smith	1				1
Waddle	1				1
Opps' o.gs.	1			1	2

Fact File

Liverpool won the FA Cup for the second time.
Bill Shankly sensationally resigned.

Final Division One Table

		P	W	D	L	F	A	Pts
1	Leeds U	42	24	14	4	66	31	62
2	Liverpool	42	22	13	7	52	31	57
3	Derby Co	42	17	14	11	52	42	48
4	Ipswich T	42	18	11	13	67	58	47
5	Stoke C	42	15	16	11	54	42	46
6	Burnley	42	16	14	12	56	53	46
7	Everton	42	16	12	14	50	48	44
8	QPR	42	13	17	12	56	52	43
9	Leicester C	42	13	16	13	51	41	42
10	Arsenal	42	14	14	14	49	51	42
11	Tottenham H	42	14	14	14	45	50	42
12	Wolverhampton W	42	13	15	14	49	49	41
13	Sheffield U	42	14	12	16	44	49	40
14	Manchester C	42	14	12	16	39	46	40
15	Newcastle U	42	13	12	17	49	48	38
16	Coventry C	42	14	10	18	43	54	38
17	Chelsea	42	12	13	17	56	60	37
18	West Ham U	42	11	15	16	55	60	37
19	Birmingham C	42	12	13	17	52	64	37
20	Southampton	42	11	14	17	47	68	36
21	Manchester U	42	10	12	20	38	48	32
22	Norwich C	42	7	15	20	37	62	29

Season 1974-75

Football League Division One

DATE	OPPONENTS	SCORE	GOALSCORERS	ATTENDANCE
Aug 17	Luton Town	W 2-1	Smith, Heighway	21,062
Aug 20	Wolverhampton Wanderers	D 0-0		33,499
Aug 24	LEICESTER CITY	W 2-1	Lindsay 2 (2 pen)	49,398
Aug 27	WOLVERHAMPTON WANDERERS	W 2-0	Heighway, Toshack	42,449
Aug 31	Chelsea	W 3-0	Kennedy, Boersma 2	39,461
Sep 7	TOTTENHAM HOTSPUR	W 5-2	Boersma 3, Hughes, Kennedy	47,538
Sep 14	Manchester City	L 0-2		45,194
Sep 21	STOKE CITY	W 3-0	Ritchie o.g., Boersma, Heighway	51,423
Sep 24	BURNLEY	L 0-1		44,639
Sep 28	Sheffield United	L 0-1		29,443
Oct 5	Carlisle United	W 1-0	Kennedy	20,844
Oct 12	MIDDLESBROUGH	W 2-0	Callaghan, Keegan (pen)	52,590
Oct 19	Queens Park Rangers	W 1-0	Hall	27,392
Oct 26	LEEDS UNITED	W 1-0	Heighway	54,996
Nov 2	Ipswich Town	L 0-1		30,564
Nov 9	ARSENAL	L 1-3	Kennedy	43,850
Nov 16	Everton	D 0-0		56,797
Nov 23	WEST HAM UNITED	D 1-1	Smith	46,348
Nov 30	Coventry City	D 1-1	Keegan	23,089
Dec 7	DERBY COUNTY	D 2-2	Kennedy, Heighway	41,058
Dec 14	LUTON TOWN	W 2-0	Toshack, Heighway	35,151
Dec 21	Birmingham City	L 1-3	Toshack	23,608
Dec 26	MANCHESTER CITY	W 4-1	Hall 2, Toshack, Heighway	46,062
Jan 11	Derby County	L 0-2		33,463
Jan 18	COVENTRY CITY	W 2-1	Heighway, Keegan	43,668
Feb 1	Arsenal	L 0-2		43,028
Feb 8	IPSWICH TOWN	W 5-2	Hall, Toshack 2, Lindsay, Cormack	47,421
Feb 12	Newcastle United	L 1-4	Hall	38,115
Feb 19	West Ham United	D 0-0		40,256
Feb 22	EVERTON	D 0-0		55,853
Mar 1	CHELSEA	D 2-2	Heighway, Cormack	42,762
Mar 8	Burnley	D 1-1	McDermott	31,812
Mar 15	SHEFFIELD UNITED	D 0-0		40,862
Mar 19	Leicester City	D 1-1	Toshack	28,012
Mar 22	Tottenham Hotspur	W 2-0	Keegan, Cormack	34,331
Mar 25	NEWCASTLE UNITED	W 4-0	Keegan, Toshack 2, McDermott	41,147
Mar 29	BIRMINGHAM CITY	W 1-0	Keegan (pen)	49,454
Mar 31	Stoke City	L 0-2		45,954
Apr 5	Leeds United	W 2-0	Keegan 2	34,971
Apr 12	CARLISLE UNITED	W 2-0	Toshack, Keegan	46,073
Apr 19	Middlesbrough	L 0-1		33,982
Apr 26	QUEENS PARK RANGERS	W 3-1	Toshack 2, Keegan (pen)	42,546

FA Cup

Jan 4	STOKE CITY	(Rd3)	W 2-0	Heighway, Keegan	48,723
Jan 25	Ipswich Town	(Rd4)	L 0-1		34,708

League Cup

Sep 10	BRENTFORD	(Rd2)	W 2-1	Kennedy, Boersma	21,413
Oct 8	Bristol City	(Rd3)	D 0-0		25,573
Oct 16	BRISTOL CITY	(R)	W 4-0	Heighway 2, Kennedy 2	23,694
Nov 12	MIDDLESBROUGH	(Rd4)	L 0-1		24,906

European Cup-Winners' Cup

Sep 17	STROMSGODSET DRAMMEN	(Rd1/1L)	W11-0	Lindsay (pen), Boersma 2, Thompson 2, Heighway, Cormack, Hughes, Smith, Callaghan, Kennedy	24,743
Oct 1	Stromsgodset Drammen	(Rd1/2L)	W 1-0	Kennedy	17,000
Oct 23	FERENCVAROS	(Rd2/1L)	D 1-1	Keegan	35,027
Nov 5	Ferencvaros	(Rd2/2L)	D 0-0*		30,000

*Liverpool lost on away goals rule.

Charity Shield

Aug 10	Leeds United	D 1-1**	Boersma	67,000

**Played at Wembley. Liverpool won trophy 6-5 on penalties. Scorers: Lindsay, Hughes, Hall, Smith, Cormack, Callaghan.

MANAGER: Bob Paisley

CAPTAIN: Emlyn Hughes

TOP SCORER: Steve Heighway 13 (9 league)

TRANSFERS IN: Ray Kennedy from Arsenal, Terry McDermott from Newcastle United, Phil Neal from Northampton Town

TRANSFERS OUT: Larry Lloyd to Coventry City

League & Cup Appearances

PLAYER	LEAGUE	CUP COMPETITION			OTHER	TOTAL
		FA CUP	LC	ECWC		
Boersma	20 (1)		3	4	1	28 (1)
Callaghan	41	2	3	4	1	51
Case	1					1
Clemence	42	2	4	4	1	53
Cormack	33 (3)	2	3	1 (2)	1	40 (5)
Hall	35	2	3	4	1	45
Heighway	32 (3)	2	4	4	1	43 (3)
Hughes	42	2	4	4	1	53
Keegan	33	2	3	3	1	42
Kennedy	23 (2)		4	4		31 (2)
Lawler	10		3	3		16
Lindsay	25	2	4	4	1	36
McDermott	14 (1)					14 (1)
McLaughlin			1			1
Neal	23	2				25
Smith	36		4	4	1	45
Thompson P	32	2	1	1	1	37
Toshack	20 (1)	2		0 (2)		22 (3)
Waddle	0 (5)					0 (5)

Goalscorers

PLAYER	LEAGUE	CUP COMPETITION			OTHER	TOTAL
		FA CUP	LC	ECWC		
Heighway	9	1	2	1		13
Keegan	10	1		1		12
Toshack	12					12
Boersma	6		1	2	1	10
Kennedy	5		3	2		10
Hall	5				(1)	5 (1)
Cormack	3			1	(1)	4 (1)
Lindsay	3			1	(1)	4 (1)
Smith	2			1	(1)	3 (1)
Callaghan	1			1	(1)	2 (1)
Hughes	1			1		2
McDermott	2					2
Thompson P				2		2
Hughes					(1)	(1)
Opps' o.gs.	1					1

Penalty shoot-out goals in brackets.

Fact File

Bill Shankly's last official duty was to lead out the team for the Charity Shield at Wembley. He saw Keegan and Bremner of Leeds sent off for fighting. Keegan was subsequently banned from playing until October.

Final Division One Table

		P	W	D	L	F	A	PTS
1	Derby Co	42	21	11	10	67	49	53
2	Liverpool	42	20	11	11	60	39	51
3	Ipswich T	42	23	5	14	66	44	51
4	Everton	42	16	18	8	56	42	50
5	Stoke C	42	17	15	10	64	48	49
6	Sheffield U	42	18	13	11	58	51	49
7	Middlesbrough	42	18	12	12	54	40	48
8	Manchester C	42	18	10	14	54	54	46
9	Leeds U	42	16	13	13	57	49	45
10	Burnley	42	17	11	14	68	67	45
11	QPR	42	16	10	16	54	54	42
12	Wolverhampton W	42	14	11	17	57	54	39
13	West Ham U	42	13	13	16	58	59	39
14	Coventry C	42	12	15	15	51	62	39
15	Newcastle U	42	15	9	18	59	72	39
16	Arsenal	42	13	11	18	47	49	37
17	Birmingham C	42	14	9	19	53	61	37
18	Leicester C	42	12	12	18	46	60	36
19	Tottenham H	42	13	8	21	52	63	34
20	Luton T	42	11	11	20	47	65	33
21	Chelsea	42	9	15	18	42	72	33
22	Carlisle U	42	12	5	25	43	59	29

Season 1975-76

Football League Division One

DATE	OPPONENTS	SCORE	GOALSCORERS	ATTENDANCE
Aug 16	Queens Park Rangers	L 0-2		27,113
Aug 19	WEST HAM UNITED	D 2-2	Callaghan, Toshack	40,564
Aug 23	TOTTENHAM HOTSPUR	W 3-2	Keegan (pen), Case, Heighway	42,729
Aug 26	Leeds United	W 3-0	Kennedy, Callaghan 2	36,186
Aug 30	Leicester City	D 1-1	Keegan	25,008
Sep 6	SHEFFIELD UNITED	W 1-0	Kennedy	37,340
Sep 13	Ipswich Town	L 0-2		28,132
Sep 20	ASTON VILLA	W 3-0	Toshack, Keegan, Case	42,779
Sep 27	Everton	D 0-0		55,570
Oct 4	WOLVERHAMPTON WANDERERS	W 2-0	Hall, Case	36,391
Oct 11	BIRMINGHAM CITY	W 3-1	Toshack 3	36,532
Oct 18	Coventry City	D 0-0		20,695
Oct 25	DERBY COUNTY	D 1-1	Toshack	46,324
Nov 1	Middlesbrough	W 1-0	McDermott	30,952
Nov 8	MANCHESTER UNITED	W 3-1	Heighway, Toshack, Keegan	49,136
Nov 15	Newcastle United	W 2-1	Hall, Kennedy	39,686
Nov 22	COVENTRY CITY	D 1-1	Toshack	36,929
Nov 29	NORWICH CITY	L 1-3	Hughes	34,780
Dec 2	ARSENAL	D 2-2	Neal 2 (2 pen)	27,447
Dec 6	Burnley	D 0-0		18,426
Dec 13	Tottenham Hotspur	W 4-0	Keegan, Case, Neal, Heighway	29,891
Dec 20	QUEENS PARK RANGERS	W 2-0	Toshack, Neal (pen)	39,182
Dec 26	Stoke City	D 1-1	Toshack	32,092
Dec 27	MANCHESTER CITY	W 1-0	Cormack	53,386
Jan 10	IPSWICH TOWN	D 3-3	Keegan 2, Case	40,547
Jan 17	Sheffield United	D 0-0		31,255
Jan 31	West Ham United	W 4-0	Toshack 3, Keegan	26,741
Feb 7	LEEDS UNITED	W 2-0	Keegan, Toshack	54,525
Feb 18	Manchester United	D 0-0		59,709
Feb 21	NEWCASTLE UNITED	W 2-0	Keegan, Case	43,404
Feb 24	Arsenal	L 0-1		36,127
Feb 28	Derby County	D 1-1	Kennedy	32,800
Mar 6	MIDDLESBROUGH	L 0-2		41,391
Mar 13	Birmingham City	W 1-0	Neal (pen)	31,797
Mar 20	Norwich City	W 1-0	Fairclough	29,038
Mar 27	BURNLEY	W 2-0	Fairclough 2	36,708
Apr 3	EVERTON	W 1-0	Fairclough	54,632
Apr 6	LEICESTER CITY	W 1-0	Keegan	35,290
Apr 10	Aston Villa	D 0-0		44,250
Apr 17	STOKE CITY	W 5-3	Neal (pen), Toshack, Kennedy, Hughes, Fairclough	44,069
Apr 19	Manchester City	W 3-0	Heighway, Fairclough 2	50,439
May 4	Wolverhampton Wanderers	W 3-1	Keegan, Toshack, Kennedy	48,900*

*Unofficial figures estimate nearer 60,000.

FA Cup

Jan 3	West Ham United	(Rd3)	W 2-0	Keegan, Toshack	32,363
Jan 24	Derby County	(Rd4)	L 0-1		38,200

League Cup

Sep 10	York City	(Rd2)	W 1-0	Lindsay (pen)	9,421
Oct 7	BURNLEY	(Rd3)	D 1-1	Case	24,607
Oct 14	Burnley	(R)	L 0-1		20,022

UEFA Cup

Sep 17	Hibernian	(Rd1/1L)	L 0-1		19,219
Sep 30	HIBERNIAN	(Rd1/2L)	W 3-1	Toshack 3	29,963
Oct 22	Real Sociedad	(Rd2/1L)	W 3-1	Heighway, Callaghan, Thompson P	20,000
Nov 4	REAL SOCIEDAD	(Rd2/2L)	W 6-0	Toshack, Kennedy 2, Fairclough, Heighway, Neal	23,796
Nov 26	Slask Wroclaw	(Rd3/1L)	W 2-1	Kennedy, Toshack	46,000
Dec 10	SLASK WROCLAW	(Rd3/2L)	W 3-0	Case 3	17,886
Mar 3	Dynamo Dresden	(Rd4/1L)	D 0-0		33,000
Mar 17	DYNAMO DRESDEN	(Rd4/2L)	W 2-1	Case, Keegan	39,300
Mar 30	Barcelona	(SF/1L)	W 1-0	Toshack	70,000
Apr 14	BARCELONA	(SF/2L)	D 1-1	Thompson P	55,104
Apr 28	FC BRUGES	(F/1L)	W 3-2	Kennedy, Case, Keegan (pen)	49,981
May 19	FC Bruges	(F/2L)	D 1-1	Keegan	33,000

MANAGER: Bob Paisley **CAPTAIN:** Emlyn Hughes

TOP SCORER: John Toshack 23 (16 league)

BIGGEST WIN: 6-0, 4 November 1975, v Real Sociedad (H), UEFA Cup

HIGHEST ATTENDANCE: 70,000, 30 March 1976, v Barcelona (A), UEFA Cup

TRANSFERS IN: Joey Jones from Wrexham

TRANSFERS OUT: Chris Lawler to Portsmouth

League & Cup Appearances

PLAYER	LEAGUE	CUP COMPETITION FA CUP	LC	UEFA	TOTAL
Boersma	1 (2)		0 (1)	0 (1)	1 (4)
Callaghan	40	2	3	12	57
Case	27	2	1	7 (2)	37 (2)
Clemence	42	2	3	12	59
Cormack	16 (1)		3	3 (1)	22 (2)
Fairclough	5 (9)			2 (3)	7 (12)
Hall	12 (1)	0 (1)	2	6 (3)	20 (5)
Heighway	39	2	2	11	54
Hughes	41	2	3	11	57
Jones	13			1	14
Keegan	41	2	3	11	57
Kennedy	29 (1)	2	1	10	42 (1)
Kettle	1			1	2
Lawler				1	1
Lindsay	6		3	2	11
McDermott	7 (2)		1		8 (2)
Neal	42	2	3	12	59
Smith	24	2		9	35
Thompson M				0 (1)	0 (1)
Thompson P	41	2	3	11	57
Toshack	35	2	2	10 (1)	49 (1)

Goalscorers

PLAYER	LEAGUE	CUP COMPETITION FA CUP	LC	UEFA	TOTAL
Toshack	16	1		6	23
Keegan	12	1		3	16
Case	6		1	5	12
Kennedy	6			4	10
Fairclough	7			1	8
Neal	6			1	7
Heighway	4			2	6
Callaghan	3			1	4
Hall	2				2
Hughes	2				2
Thompson P				2	2
Cormack	1				1
Lindsay			1		1
McDermott	1				1

Fact File

Two trophies brought the Manager of Year award to Bob Paisley, European Team of the Year award, Kevin Keegan the Football Writers' Footballer of the Year award and Ian Callaghan an MBE.

Final Division One Table

		P	W	D	L	F	A	Pts
1	Liverpool	42	23	14	5	66	31	60
2	QPR	42	24	11	7	67	33	59
3	Manchester U	42	23	10	10	68	42	56
4	Derby Co	42	21	11	10	75	58	53
5	Leeds U	42	21	9	12	65	46	51
6	Ipswich T	42	16	14	12	54	48	46
7	Leicester C	42	13	19	10	48	51	45
8	Manchester C	42	16	12	15	64	46	43
9	Tottenham H	42	14	15	13	63	63	43
10	Norwich C	42	16	10	16	58	58	42
11	Everton	42	15	12	15	60	66	42
12	Stoke C	42	15	11	16	48	50	41
13	Middlesbrough	42	15	10	17	46	45	40
14	Coventry C	42	13	14	15	47	57	40
15	Newcastle U	42	15	9	18	71	62	39
16	Aston Villa	42	11	17	14	51	59	39
17	Arsenal	42	13	10	19	47	53	36
18	West Ham U	42	13	10	19	48	71	36
19	Birmingham C	42	13	7	22	57	75	33
20	Wolverhampton W	42	10	10	22	51	68	30
21	Burnley	42	9	10	23	43	66	28
22	Sheffield U	42	6	10	26	33	82	22

Season 1976-77

Football League Division One

DATE	OPPONENTS	SCORE	GOALSCORERS	ATTENDANCE
Aug 21	NORWICH CITY	W 1-0	Heighway	49,753
Aug 25	West Bromwich Albion	W 1-0	Toshack	30,334
Aug 28	Birmingham City	L 1-2	Johnson	33,228
Sep 4	COVENTRY CITY	W 3-1	Keegan, Johnson, Toshack	40,371
Sep 11	Derby County	W 3-2	Kennedy, Toshack, Keegan	26,833
Sep 18	TOTTENHAM HOTSPUR	W 2-0	Johnson, Heighway	47,421
Sep 25	Newcastle United	L 0-1		33,204
Oct 2	MIDDLESBROUGH	D 0-0		45,107
Oct 16	EVERTON	W 3-1	Heighway, Neal (pen), Toshack	55,141
Oct 23	Leeds United	D 1-1	Kennedy	44,696
Oct 27	Leicester City	W 1-0	Toshack	29,384
Oct 30	ASTON VILLA	W 3-0	Callaghan, McDermott, Keegan	51,751
Nov 6	Sunderland	W 1-0	Fairclough	39,956
Nov 9	LEICESTER CITY	W 5-1	Heighway, Toshack, Neal (pen), Jones, Keegan (pen)	39,851
Nov 20	Arsenal	D 1-1	Kennedy	45,016
Nov 27	BRISTOL CITY	W 2-1	Keegan, Jones	44,323
Dec 4	Ipswich Town	L 0-1		35,082
Dec 11	QUEENS PARK RANGERS	W 3-1	Toshack, Keegan, Kennedy	37,154
Dec 15	Aston Villa	L 1-5	Kennedy	42,851
Dec 18	West Ham United	L 0-2		24,175
Dec 27	STOKE CITY	W 4-0	Thompson, Neal (pen), Keegan, Johnson	50,371
Dec 29	Manchester City	D 1-1	Watson o.g.	50,020
Jan 1	SUNDERLAND	W 2-0	Kennedy, Thompson	44,687
Jan 15	WEST BROMWICH ALBION	D 1-1	Fairclough	39,195
Jan 22	Norwich City	L 1-2	Neal (pen)	25,913
Feb 5	BIRMINGHAM CITY	W 4-1	Neal (pen), Toshack 2, Heighway	41,072
Feb 16	Manchester United	D 0-0		57,487
Feb 19	DERBY COUNTY	W 3-1	Toshack, Jones, Keegan	44,202
Mar 5	NEWCASTLE UNITED	W 1-0	Heighway	45,553
Mar 9	Tottenham Hotspur	L 0-1		32,098
Mar 12	Middlesbrough	W 1-0	Hughes	29,166
Mar 22	Everton	D 0-0		56,562
Apr 2	LEEDS UNITED	W 3-1	Neal (pen), Fairclough, Heighway	48,791
Apr 9	MANCHESTER CITY	W 2-1	Keegan, Heighway	55,283
Apr 11	Stoke City	D 0-0		29,905
Apr 16	ARSENAL	W 2-0	Neal, Keegan	48,174
Apr 30	IPSWICH TOWN	W 2-1	Kennedy, Keegan	56,044
May 3	MANCHESTER UNITED	W 1-0	Keegan	53,046
May 7	Queens Park Rangers	D 1-1	Case	29,382
May 10	Coventry City	D 0-0		38,032
May 14	WEST HAM UNITED	D 0-0		55,675
May 16	Bristol City	L 1-2	Johnson	38,688

FA Cup

Jan 8	CRYSTAL PALACE	(Rd3) D 0-0		44,730
Jan 11	Crystal Palace	(R) W 3-2	Keegan, Heighway 2	42,644
Jan 29	CARLISLE UNITED	(Rd4) W 3-0	Keegan, Toshack, Heighway	45,358
Feb 26	OLDHAM ATHLETIC	(Rd5) W 3-1	Keegan, Case, Neal (pen)	52,455
Mar 19	MIDDLESBROUGH	(Rd6) W 2-0	Fairclough, Keegan	55,881
Apr 23	Everton*	(SF) D 2-2	McDermott, Case	52,637
Apr 27	Everton*	(R) W 3-0	Neal (pen), Case, Kennedy	52,579
May 21	Manchester United**	(F) L 1-2	Case	100,000

*Played at Maine Road. **Played at Wembley.

League Cup

Aug 31	WEST BROMWICH ALBION	(Rd2) D 1-1	Callaghan	23,378
Sep 6	West Bromwich Albion	(R) L 0-1		22,662

European Cup

Sep 14	CRUSADERS	(Rd1/1L) W 2-0	Neal (pen), Toshack	22,442
Sep 28	Crusaders	(Rd1/2L) W 5-0	Keegan, Johnson 2, McDermott, Heighway	10,500
Oct 20	Trabzonspor	(Rd2/1L) L 0-1		25,000
Nov 3	TRABZONSPOR	(Rd2/2L) W 3-0	Heighway, Johnson, Keegan	42,275
Mar 2	St Etienne	(Rd3/1L) L 0-1		38,000
Mar 16	ST ETIENNE	(Rd3/2L) W 3-1	Keegan, Kennedy, Fairclough	55,043
Apr 6	FC Zurich	(SF/1L) W 3-1	Neal 2 (1 pen), Heighway	30,500
Apr 20	FC ZURICH	(SF/2L) W 3-0	Case 2, Keegan	50,611
May 25	Borussia Mönchengladbach†	(F) W 3-1	McDermott, Smith, Neal (pen)	57,000

†Played in Rome.

Charity Shield

Aug 14	Southampton††	W 1-0	Toshack	76,500

††Played at Wembley.

League & Cup Appearances

PLAYER	LEAGUE	CUP COMPETITION			OTHER	TOTAL
		FA CUP	LC	EC		
Callaghan	32 (1)	4 (1)	2	7	1	46 (2)
Case	24 (3)	7	1	6	1	39 (3)
Clemence	42	8	2	9	1	62
Fairclough	12 (8)	4 (1)	0 (2)	1 (2)		17 (13)
Heighway	39	7	2	9	1	58
Hughes	42	8	2	9	1	62
Johnson	19 (7)	3 (1)	2	4 (2)		28 (10)
Jones	39	8	2	9	1	59
Keegan	38	8	2	8	1	57
Kennedy	41	8	2	9	1	61
Kettle	2					2
Lindsay	1					1
McDermott	25 (1)	5		6 (1)		36 (2)
Neal	42	8	2	8	1	61
Smith	16	4		7		27
Thompson	26	4	2	3	1	36
Toshack	22	2	1	4	1	30
Waddle				0 (1)		0 (1)

Goalscorers

PLAYER	LEAGUE	CUP COMPETITION			OTHER	TOTAL
		FA CUP	LC	EC		
Keegan	12	4		4		20
Heighway	8	3		3		14
Neal	7	2		4		13
Toshack	10	1		1	1	13
Kennedy	7	1		1		9
Johnson	5			3		8
Case	1	4		2		7
Fairclough	3	1		1		5
McDermott	1	1		2		4
Jones	3					3
Callaghan	1		1			2
Thompson	2					2
Hughes	1					1
Smith				1		1
Opps' o.gs.	1					1

MANAGER: Bob Paisley **CAPTAIN:** Emlyn Hughes
TOP SCORER: Kevin Keegan 20 (12 league)
TRANSFERS IN: David Johnson from Ipswich Town
TRANSFERS OUT: Brian Hall to Plymouth Argyle, Kevin Keegan to Hamburg

Fact File

Bob Paisley was awarded an OBE for services to football and Manager of the Year for his second double of League championship and European Cup.

Final Division One Table

		P	W	D	L	F	A	Pts
1	Liverpool	42	23	11	8	62	33	57
2	Manchester C	42	21	14	7	60	34	56
3	Ipswich T	42	22	8	12	66	39	56
4	Aston Villa	42	22	7	13	76	50	51
5	Newcastle U	42	18	13	11	64	49	49
6	Manchester U	42	18	11	13	71	62	47
7	WBA	42	16	13	13	62	56	45
8	Arsenal	42	16	11	15	64	59	43
9	Everton	42	14	14	14	62	64	42
10	Leeds U	42	15	12	15	48	51	42
11	Leicester C	42	12	18	12	47	60	42
12	Middlesbrough	42	14	13	15	40	45	41
13	Birmingham C	42	13	12	17	63	61	38
14	QPR	42	13	12	17	47	52	38
15	Derby Co	42	9	19	14	50	55	37
16	Norwich C	42	14	9	19	47	64	37
17	West Ham U	42	11	14	17	46	65	36
18	Bristol C	42	11	13	18	38	48	35
19	Coventry C	42	10	15	17	48	59	35
20	Sunderland	42	11	12	19	46	54	34
21	Stoke C	42	10	14	18	28	51	34
22	Tottenham H	42	12	9	21	48	72	33

Season 1977-78

Football League Division One

DATE	OPPONENTS	SCORE	GOALSCORERS	ATTENDANCE
Aug 20	Middlesbrough	D 1-1	Dalglish	30,805
Aug 23	NEWCASTLE UNITED	W 2-0	Dalglish, McDermott	48,267
Aug 27	WEST BROMWICH ALBION	W 3-0	Dalglish, Heighway, Case	48,525
Sep 3	Birmingham City	W 1-0	Kennedy	28,239
Sep 10	COVENTRY CITY	W 2-0	Fairclough, Dalglish	45,574
Sep 17	Ipswich Town	D 1-1	Dalglish	29,658
Sep 24	DERBY COUNTY	W 1-0	McDermott	48,359
Oct 1	Manchester United	L 0-2		55,109
Oct 4	Arsenal	D 0-0		47,110
Oct 8	CHELSEA	W 2-0	Dalglish, Fairclough	40,499
Oct 15	Leeds United	W 2-1	Case 2	45,500
Oct 22	EVERTON	D 0-0		51,668
Oct 29	Manchester City	L 1-3	Fairclough	49,207
Nov 5	ASTON VILLA	L 1-2	Carrodus o.g.	50,436
Nov 12	Queens Park Rangers	L 0-2		25,625
Nov 19	BRISTOL CITY	D 1-1	Dalglish	41,053
Nov 26	Leicester City	W 4-0	Fairclough, Heighway, Dalglish, McDermott	26,051
Dec 3	WEST HAM UNITED	W 2-0	Dalglish, Fairclough	39,659
Dec 10	Norwich City	L 1-2	Thompson	24,983
Dec 17	QUEENS PARK RANGERS	W 1-0	Neal (pen)	38,249
Dec 26	Nottingham Forest	D 1-1	Heighway	47,218
Dec 27	WOLVERHAMPTON WANDERERS	W 1-0	Neal (pen)	50,294
Dec 31	Newcastle United	W 2-0	Thompson, Dalglish	36,456
Jan 2	MIDDLESBROUGH	W 2-0	Johnson, Heighway	49,305
Jan 14	West Bromwich Albion	W 1-0	Johnson	35,809
Jan 21	BIRMINGHAM CITY	L 2-3	Thompson, Kennedy R	48,401
Feb 4	Coventry City	L 0-1		28,965
Feb 25	MANCHESTER UNITED	W 3-1	Souness, Kennedy R, Case	49,590
Mar 4	Chelsea	L 1-3	Neal (pen)	35,550
Mar 8	Derby County	L 2-4	Fairclough, Dalglish	23,413
Mar 11	LEEDS UNITED	W 1-0	Dalglish	48,233
Mar 25	Wolverhampton Wanderers	W 3-1	Case, Dalglish 2	27,531
Apr 1	Aston Villa	W 3-0	Dalglish 2, Kennedy	40,190
Apr 5	Everton	W 1-0	Johnson	52,759
Apr 8	LEICESTER CITY	W 3-2	Smith 2, Lee	42,979
Apr 15	Bristol City	D 1-1	Heighway	31,471
Apr 18	IPSWICH TOWN	D 2-2	Dalglish, Souness	40,044
Apr 22	NORWICH CITY	W 3-0	Ryan o.g., Fairclough 2	44,857
Apr 25	ARSENAL	W 1-0	Fairclough	38,318
Apr 29	West Ham United	W 2-0	McDermott, Fairclough	37,448
May 1	MANCHESTER CITY	W 4-0	Dalglish 3, Neal (pen)	44,528
May 4	NOTTINGHAM FOREST	D 0-0		50,021

FA Cup

Jan 7	Chelsea	(Rd3)	L 2-4	Johnson, Dalglish	45,449

League Cup

Aug 30	CHELSEA	(Rd2)	W 2-0	Dalglish, Case	33,170
Oct 26	DERBY COUNTY	(Rd3)	W 2-0	Fairclough 2	30,400
Nov 29	COVENTRY CITY	(Rd4)	D 2-2	Fairclough, Neal (pen)	33,817
Dec 20	Coventry City	(R)	W 2-0	Case, Dalglish	36,105
Jan 17	Wrexham	(Rd5)	W 3-1	Dalglish 3	25,641
Feb 7	ARSENAL	(SF/1L)	W 2-1	Dalglish, Kennedy	44,764
Feb 14	Arsenal	(SF/2L)	D 0-0		49,561
Mar 18	Nottingham Forest	(F)	D 0-0*		100,000
Mar 22	Nottingham Forest**	(R)	L 0-1		54,375

*After extra time. Played at Wembley. **Played at Old Trafford.

European Cup

Oct 19	DYNAMO DRESDEN	(Rd2/1L)	W 5-1	Hansen, Case 2, Neal (pen), Kennedy	39,835
Nov 2	Dynamo Dresden	(Rd2/2L)	L 1-2	Heighway	33,000
Mar 1	Benfica	(Rd3/1L)	W 2-1	Case, Hughes	70,000
Mar 15	BENFICA	(Rd3/2L)	W 4-1	Callaghan, Dalglish, McDermott, Neal	48,364
Mar 29	Borussia Mönchengladbach	(SF/1L)	L 1-2	Johnson	66,000
Apr 12	BORUSSIA MÖNCHENGLADBACH	(SF/2L)	W 3-0	Kennedy, Dalglish, Case	51,500
May 10	FC Bruges†	(F)	W 1-0	Dalglish	92,000

†Played at Wembley.

European Super Cup

Nov 22	SV Hamburg	D 1-1	Fairclough	16,000
Dec 6	SV HAMBURG	W 6-0††	Thompson, McDermott 3, Fairclough, Dalglish	34,931

††Trophy won 7-1 on aggregate.

Charity Shield

Aug 13	Manchester United#	D 0-0		82,000

#Played at Wembley. Trophy shared.

League & Cup Appearances

PLAYER	LEAGUE	CUP COMPETITION FA CUP	LC	EC	OTHER	TOTAL
Callaghan	25 (1)	1	7	5	2	40 (1)
Case	30 (3)		8	7	3	48 (3)
Clemence	40	1	9	7	3	60
Dalglish	42	1	9	7	3	62
Fairclough	26 (3)	1	3 (4)	1 (1)	3	34 (8)
Hansen	18	0 (1)	3	3 (1)		24 (2)
Heighway	28	1	8	6 (1)	2	45 (1)
Hughes	39	1	9	7	3	59
Johnson	7 (5)	1	1	0 (1)	0 (2)	9 (8)
Jones	20	1	2	2	2	27
Kennedy	41	1	9	7	3	61
Kewley	0 (1)					0 (1)
Lee	0 (2)					0 (2)
McDermott	36 (1)		8	6	2	52 (1)
Neal	42	1	9	7	3	62
Ogrizovic	2					2
Smith	22		6	4	1 (1)	33 (1)
Souness	15			2 (1)		17 (1)
Thompson	27	1	7	5	3	43
Toshack	2 (1)		1	1		4 (1)

Goalscorers

PLAYER	LEAGUE	CUP COMPETITION FA CUP	LC	EC	OTHER	TOTAL
Dalglish	20	1	6	3	1	31
Fairclough	10		3		2	15
Case	5		2	4		11
McDermott	4	1		1	3	8
Kennedy	4		1	2		7
Neal	4		1	2		7
Heighway	5			1		6
Johnson	3	1		1		5
Thompson	3				1	4
Smith	2					2
Souness	2					2
Callaghan				1		1
Hansen				1		1
Hughes				1		1
Lee	1					1
Opps' o.gs.	2					2

Fact File

Liverpool became the first English club to retain the European Cup.

MANAGER: Bob Paisley **CAPTAIN:** Emlyn Hughes
TOP SCORER: Kenny Dalglish 31 (20 league)
TRANSFERS IN: Kenny Dalglish from Glasgow Celtic, Alan Hansen from Partick Thistle, Graeme Souness from Middlesbrough **TRANSFERS OUT:** Alec Lindsay to Stoke City, John Toshack to Swansea City

Final Division One Table

		P	W	D	L	F	A	Pts
1	Nottingham F	42	25	14	3	69	24	64
2	Liverpool	42	24	9	9	65	34	57
3	Everton	42	22	11	9	76	45	55
4	Manchester C	42	20	12	10	74	51	52
5	Arsenal	42	21	10	11	60	37	52
6	WBA	42	18	14	10	62	53	50
7	Coventry C	42	18	12	12	75	62	48
8	Aston Villa	42	18	10	14	57	42	46
9	Leeds U	42	18	10	14	63	53	46
10	Manchester U	42	16	10	16	67	63	42
11	Birmingham C	42	16	9	17	55	60	41
12	Derby Co	42	14	13	15	54	59	41
13	Norwich C	42	11	18	13	52	66	40
14	Middlesbrough	42	12	15	15	42	54	39
15	Wolverhampton W	42	12	12	18	51	64	36
16	Chelsea	42	11	14	17	46	69	36
17	Bristol C	42	11	13	18	49	53	35
18	Ipswich T	42	11	13	18	47	61	35
19	QPR	42	9	15	18	47	64	33
20	West Ham U	42	12	8	22	52	69	32
21	Newcastle U	42	6	10	26	42	78	22
22	Leicester C	42	5	12	25	26	70	22

Season 1978-79

Football League Division One

DATE	OPPONENTS	SCORE	GOALSCORERS	ATTENDANCE
Aug 19	QUEENS PARK RANGERS	W 2-1	Dalglish, Heighway	50,793
Aug 22	Ipswich Town	W 3-0	Souness, Dalglish 2	28,114
Aug 26	Manchester City	W 4-1	Souness 2, Kennedy R, Dalglish	46,710
Sep 2	TOTTENHAM HOTSPUR	W 7-0	Dalglish 2, Kennedy R, Johnson 2, Neal (pen), McDermott	50,705
Sep 9	Birmingham City	W 3-0	Souness 2, Kennedy A	31,740
Sep 16	COVENTRY CITY	W 1-0	Souness	51,130
Sep 23	West Bromwich Albion	D 1-1	Dalglish	33,834
Sep 30	BOLTON WANDERERS	W 3-0	Case 3	47,099
Oct 7	Norwich City	W 4-1	Heighway 2, Johnson, Case	25,632
Oct 14	DERBY COUNTY	W 5-0	Johnson, Kennedy R 2, Dalglish 2	47,475
Oct 21	CHELSEA	W 2-0	Johnson, Dalglish	45,775
Oct 28	Everton	L 0-1		53,131
Nov 4	LEEDS UNITED	D 1-1	McDermott (pen)	51,657
Nov 11	Queens Park Rangers	W 3-1	Heighway, Kennedy R, Johnson	26,626
Nov 18	MANCHESTER CITY	W 1-0	Neal (pen)	47,765
Nov 22	Tottenham Hotspur	D 0-0		50,393
Nov 25	MIDDLESBROUGH	W 2-0	McDermott, Souness	39,812
Dec 2	Arsenal	L 0-1		51,902
Dec 9	NOTTINGHAM FOREST	W 2-0	McDermott 2 (1 pen)	51,469
Dec 16	Bristol City	L 0-1		28,722
Dec 26	Manchester United	W 3-0	Kennedy R, Case, Fairclough	54,940
Feb 3	WEST BROMWICH ALBION	W 2-1	Dalglish, Fairclough	52,211
Feb 13	BIRMINGHAM CITY	W 1-0	Souness	35,207
Feb 21	NORWICH CITY	W 6-0	Dalglish 2, Johnson 2, Kennedy A, Kennedy R	35,754
Feb 24	Derby County	W 2-0	Dalglish, Kennedy R	27,859
Mar 3	Chelsea	D 0-0		40,594
Mar 6	Coventry City	D 0-0		26,629
Mar 13	EVERTON	D 1-1	Dalglish	52,352
Mar 20	WOLVERHAMPTON WANDERERS	W 2-0	McDermott, Johnson	39,695
Mar 24	IPSWICH TOWN	W 2-0	Dalglish, Johnson	43,343
Apr 7	ARSENAL	W 3-0	Case, Dalglish, McDermott	47,297
Apr 10	Wolverhampton Wanderers	W 1-0	Hansen	30,857
Apr 14	MANCHESTER UNITED	W 2-0	Dalglish, Neal	46,608
Apr 16	Aston Villa	L 1-3	Johnson	44,029
Apr 21	BRISTOL CITY	W 1-0	Dalglish	43,191
Apr 24	Southampton	D 1-1	Johnson	23,184
Apr 28	Nottingham Forest	D 0-0		41,598
May 1	Bolton Wanderers	W 4-1	Johnson, Kennedy R 2, Dalglish	35,200
May 5	SOUTHAMPTON	W 2-0	Neal 2	46,687
May 8	ASTON VILLA	W 3-0	Kennedy A, Dalglish, McDermott	50,576
May 11	Middlesbrough	W 1-0	Johnson	32,244
May 17	Leeds United	W 3-0	Johnson 2, Case	41,324

FA Cup

Jan 10	Southend	(Rd3)	D 0-0		31,033
Jan 17	SOUTHEND	(R)	W 3-0	Case, Dalglish, Kennedy R	37,797
Jan 30	BLACKBURN ROVERS	(Rd4)	W 1-0	Dalglish	43,432
Feb 28	BURNLEY	(Rd5)	W 3-0	Johnson 2, Souness	47,161
Mar 10	Ipswich Town	(Rd6)	W 1-0	Dalglish	31,322
Mar 31	Manchester United*	(SF)	D 2-2	Dalglish, Hansen	52,584
Apr 4	Manchester United**	(R)	L 0-1		53,069

*Played at Maine Road. **Played at Goodison Park.

League Cup

Aug 28	Sheffield United	(Rd2)	L 0-1		35,753

European Cup

Sep 13	Nottingham Forest	(Rd1/1L)	L 0-2		38,316
Sep 27	NOTTINGHAM FOREST	(Rd1/2L)	D 0-0		51,679

European Super Cup

Dec 4	Anderlecht	L 1-3	Case	35,000
Dec 19	ANDERLECHT	W 2-1†	Hughes, Fairclough	23,598

†Lost on 3-4 aggregate.

Fact File

The 11th championship win brought a £50,000 prize from Sun/Coral for scoring more than 84 league goals.

League & Cup Appearances

PLAYER	LEAGUE	CUP COMPETITION FA CUP	LC	EC	OTHER	TOTAL
Case	37	5 (1)	1	2	2	47 (1)
Clemence	42	7	1	2	1	53
Dalglish	42	7	1	2	2	54
Fairclough	3 (1)	3	0 (1)	0 (1)	1	7 (3)
Hansen	34	6			2	42
Heighway	26 (2)	2 (3)	1	2	0 (1)	31 (6)
Hughes	16	7	1	2	2	28
Johnson	26 (4)	4		0 (2)	1	31 (6)
Kennedy A	37	2	1	2	1	43
Kennedy R	42	7	1	2	2	54
Lee	1 (1)					1 (1)
McDermott	34 (3)	7	1	2	2	46 (3)
Neal	42	7	1	2	2	54
Ogrizovic					1	1
Souness	41	7	1	2	2	53
Thompson	39	6	1	2	1	49

Goalscorers

PLAYER	LEAGUE	CUP COMPETITION FA CUP	LC	EC	OTHER	TOTAL
Dalglish	21	4				25
Johnson	16	2				18
Kennedy R	10	1				11
Case	7	1			1	9
Souness	8	1				9
McDermott	8					8
Neal	5					5
Heighway	4					4
Fairclough	2				1	3
Kennedy A	3					3
Hansen	1	1				2
Hughes					1	1

MANAGER: Bob Paisley

CAPTAIN: Emlyn Hughes/Phil Thompson

TOP SCORER: Kenny Dalglish 25 (21 league)

BIGGEST WIN: 7-0 2 September 1978, v Tottenham Hotspur (H), Division One

HIGHEST ATTENDANCE: 54,940, 26 December 1978, v Manchester United (A), Division One

TRANSFERS IN: Alan Kennedy from Newcastle United

TRANSFERS OUT: Tommy Smith to Swansea City, Joey Jones to Wrexham

Final Division One Table

		P	W	D	L	F	A	Pts
1	Liverpool	42	30	8	4	85	16	68
2	Nottingham F	42	21	18	3	61	26	60
3	WBA	42	24	11	7	72	35	59
4	Everton	42	17	17	8	52	40	51
5	Leeds U	42	18	14	10	70	52	50
6	Ipswich T	42	20	9	13	63	49	49
7	Arsenal	42	17	14	11	61	48	48
8	Aston Villa	42	15	16	11	59	49	46
9	Manchester U	42	15	15	12	60	63	45
10	Coventry C	42	14	16	12	58	68	44
11	Tottenham H	42	13	15	14	48	61	41
12	Middlesbrough	42	15	10	17	57	50	40
13	Bristol C	42	15	10	17	47	51	40
14	Southampton	42	12	16	14	47	53	40
15	Manchester C	42	13	13	16	58	56	39
16	Norwich C	42	7	23	12	51	57	37
17	Bolton W	42	12	11	19	54	75	35
18	Wolverhampton W	42	13	8	21	44	68	34
19	Derby Co	42	10	11	21	44	71	31
20	QPR	42	6	13	23	45	73	25
21	Birmingham C	42	6	10	26	37	64	22
22	Chelsea	42	5	10	27	44	92	20

Season 1979-80

Football League Division One

DATE	OPPONENTS	SCORE	GOALSCORERS	ATTENDANCE
Aug 21	BOLTON WANDERERS	D 0-0		45,900
Aug 25	WEST BROMWICH ALBION	W 3-1	Johnson 2, McDermott	48,021
Sep 1	Southampton	L 2-3	Johnson, Irwin	21,402
Sep 8	COVENTRY CITY	W 4-0	Johnson 2, Case, Dalglish	39.926
Sep 15	Leeds United	D 1-1	McDermott	39,779
Sep 22	NORWICH CITY	D 0-0		44,120
Sep 29	Nottingham Forest	L 0-1		28,262
Oct 6	BRISTOL CITY	W 4-0	Johnson, Dalglish, Kennedy R, McDermott	38,213
Oct 9	Bolton Wanderers	D 1-1	Dalglish	25,571
Oct 13	Ipswich Town	W 2-1	Hunter o.g., Johnson	25,310
Oct 20	EVERTON	D 2-2	Lyons o.g., Kennedy R	52,201
Oct 27	Manchester City	W 4-0	Johnson, Dalglish 2, Kennedy R	48,128
Nov 3	WOLVERHAMPTON WANDERERS	W 3-0	Dalglish 2, Kennedy R	49,541
Nov 10	Brighton & Hove Albion	W 4-1	Kennedy R, Dalglish 2, Johnson	29,682
Nov 17	TOTTENHAM HOTSPUR	W 2-1	McDermott 2	51,092
Nov 24	Arsenal	D 0-0		55,561
Dec 1	MIDDLESBROUGH	W 4-0	McDermott, Hansen, Johnson, Kennedy R	39,885
Dec 8	Aston Villa	W 3-1	Kennedy R, Hansen, McDermott	41,160
Dec 15	CRYSTAL PALACE	W 3-0	Case, Dalglish, McDermott	42,898
Dec 22	Derby County	W 3-1	Davies o.g., McDermott (pen), Johnson	24,945
Dec 26	MANCHESTER UNITED	W 2-0	Hansen, Johnson	51,073
Dec 29	West Bromwich Albion	W 2-0	Johnson 2	34,915
Jan 12	SOUTHAMPTON	D 1-1	McDermott (pen)	44,655
Jan 19	Coventry City	L 0-1		31,578
Feb 9	Norwich City	W 5-3	Fairclough 3, Dalglish, Case	25,624
Feb 19	NOTTINGHAM FOREST	W 2-0	McDermott, Kennedy R	45,093
Feb 23	IPSWICH TOWN	D 1-1	Fairclough	47,566
Feb 26	Wolverhampton Wanderers	L 0-1		36,693
Mar 1	Everton	W 2-1	Johnson, Neal (pen)	53,013
Mar 11	MANCHESTER CITY	W 2-0	Caton o.g., Souness	40,443
Mar 15	Bristol City	W 3-1	Kennedy R, Dalglish 2	27,187
Mar 19	LEEDS UNITED	W 3-0	Johnson 2, Kennedy A	37,008
Mar 22	BRIGHTON & HOVE ALBION	W 1-0	Hansen	42,747
Mar 29	Tottenham Hotspur	L 0-2		32,114
Apr 1	STOKE CITY	W 1-0	Dalglish	36,415
Apr 5	Manchester United	L 1-2	Dalglish	57,342
Apr 8	DERBY COUNTY	W 3-0	Irwin, Johnson, Osgood o.g.	40,932
Apr 19	ARSENAL	D 1-1	Dalglish	46,878
Apr 23	Stoke City	W 2-0	Johnson, Fairclough	32,000
Apr 26	Crystal Palace	D 0-0		45,583
May 3	ASTON VILLA	W 4-1	Johnson 2, Cohen, Blake o.g.	51,541
May 6	Middlesbrough	L 0-1		24,458

FA Cup

Jan 5	GRIMSBY TOWN	(Rd3)	W 5-0	Souness, Johnson 3, Case	49,706
Jan 26	Nottingham Forest	(Rd4)	W 2-0	Dalglish, McDermott (pen)	33,277
Feb 16	BURY	(Rd5)	W 2-0	Fairclough 2	43,769
Mar 8	Tottenham Hotspur	(Rd6)	W 1-0	McDermott	48,033
Apr 12	Arsenal*	(SF)	D 0-0		50,174
Apr 16	Arsenal**	(R)	D 1-1	Fairclough	40,679
Apr 28	Arsenal**	(2nd R)	D 1-1	Dalglish	42,975
May 1	Arsenal†	(3rd R)	L 0-1		35,335

*Played at Hillsborough.
**Played at Villa Park. After extra time. Both games 1-1 at 90 mins.
†Played at Coventry.

League Cup

Aug 29	Tranmere Rovers	(Rd2)	D 0-0		16,759
Sep 4	TRANMERE ROVERS	(R)	W 4-0	Thompson, Dalglish 2, Fairclough	24,785
Sep 25	CHESTERFIELD	(Rd3)	W 3-1	Fairclough, Dalglish, McDermott	20,960
Oct 30	EXETER CITY	(Rd4)	W 2-0	Fairclough 2	21,019
Dec 5	Norwich City	(Rd5)	W 3-1	Johnson 2, Dalglish	23,000
Jan 22	Nottingham Forest	(SF/1L)	L 0-1		32,234
Feb 12	NOTTINGHAM FOREST	(SF/2L)	D 1-1	Fairclough	50,880

European Cup

Sep 19	DYNAMO TBILISI	(Rd1/1L)	W 2-1	Johnson, Case	35,270
Oct 3	Dynamo Tbilisi	(Rd1/2L)	L 0-3		80,000

Charity Shield

Aug 11	Arsenal	W 3-1*	McDermott 2, Dalglish	92,000

*Played at Wembley.

League & Cup Appearances

PLAYER	LEAGUE	CUP COMPETITION FA CUP	LC	EC	OTHER	TOTAL
Case	37	5	7	2	1	52
Clemence	41	8	7	2	1	59
Cohen	3 (1)	1				4 (1)
Dalglish	42	8	7	2	1	60
Fairclough	9 (5)	1 (4)	1 (4)	1 (1)		12 (14)
Hansen	38	8	5	1	1	53
Heighway	2 (7)		1	0 (1)		3 (8)
Irwin	7 (1)	2	2	2		13 (1)
Johnson	37	8	6	2	1	54
Kennedy A	37	5	7	1	1	51
Kennedy R	40	8	6	1	1	56
Lee	6 (1)	4				10 (1)
McDermott	37	6	7	2	1	53
Neal	42	8	7	2	1	60
Ogrizovic	1					1
Souness	41	8	7	2	1	59
Thompson	42	8	7	2	1	60

Goalscorers

PLAYER	LEAGUE	CUP COMPETITION FA CUP	LC	EC	OTHER	TOTAL
Johnson	21	3	2	1		27
Dalglish	16	2	4		1	23
McDermott	11	2	1		2	16
Fairclough	5	3	5			13
Kennedy R	9					9
Case	3	1		1		5
Hansen	4					4
Irwin	2					2
Souness	1	1				2
Cohen	1					1
Kennedy A	1					1
Neal	1					1
Thompson			1			1
Opps' o.gs.	6					6

Fact File

This was Liverpool's 12th championship; they were unbeaten at Anfield for the second successive season, clinching the title both times by beating Aston Villa.

MANAGER: Bob Paisley **CAPTAIN:** Phil Thompson
TOP SCORER: David Johnson 27 (21 league)
TRANSFERS IN: Ronnie Whelan from Home Farm, Ireland, Ian Rush from Chester City, Avi Cohen from Macabbi, Tel Aviv **TRANSFERS OUT:** Emlyn Hughes to Wolverhampton Wanderers

Final Division One Table

	P	W	D	L	F	A	PTS
1 LIVERPOOL	42	25	10	7	81	30	60
2 MANCHESTER U	42	24	10	8	65	35	58
3 IPSWICH T	42	22	9	11	68	39	53
4 ARSENAL	42	18	16	8	52	36	52
5 NOTTINGHAM F	42	20	8	14	63	43	48
6 WOLVERHAMPTON W	42	19	9	14	58	47	47
7 ASTON VILLA	42	16	14	12	51	50	46
8 SOUTHAMPTON	42	18	9	15	65	53	45
9 MIDDLESBROUGH	42	16	12	14	50	44	44
10 WBA	42	11	19	12	54	50	41
11 LEEDS U	42	13	14	15	46	50	40
12 NORWICH C	42	13	14	15	58	66	40
13 CRYSTAL PALACE	42	12	16	14	41	50	40
14 TOTTENHAM H	42	15	10	17	52	62	40
15 COVENTRY C	42	16	7	19	56	66	39
16 BRIGHTON & HA	42	11	15	16	47	57	37
17 MANCHESTER C	42	12	13	17	43	66	37
18 STOKE C	42	13	10	19	44	58	36
19 EVERTON	42	9	17	16	43	51	35
20 BRISTOL C	42	9	13	20	37	66	31
21 DERBY CO	42	11	8	23	47	67	30
22 BOLTON W	42	5	15	22	38	73	25

Season 1980-81

Football League Division One

DATE	OPPONENTS	SCORE	GOALSCORERS	ATTENDANCE
Aug 16	CRYSTAL PALACE	W 3-0	Dalglish, Kennedy R, Kennedy A	42,777
Aug 19	Coventry City	D 0-0		22,807
Aug 23	Leicester City	L 0-2		28,455
Aug 30	NORWICH CITY	W 4-1	Hansen, McDermott, Kennedy A, Johnson	35,315
Sep 6	Birmingham City	D 1-1	Dalglish	27,042
Sep 13	WEST BROMWICH ALBION	W 4-0	McDermott (pen), Souness, Fairclough 2	36,792
Sep 20	Southampton	D 2-2	Souness, Fairclough	24,085
Sep 27	BRIGHTON & HOVE ALBION	W 4-1	Souness 2, McDermott (pen), Fairclough	35,836
Oct 4	Manchester City	W 3-0	Dalglish, Souness, Lee	41,022
Oct 7	MIDDLESBROUGH	W 4-2	McDermott 2 (1 pen), Kennedy R, Dalglish	28,204
Oct 11	IPSWICH TOWN	D 1-1	McDermott (pen)	48,084
Oct 18	Everton	D 2-2	Lee, Dalglish	52,565
Oct 25	ARSENAL	D 1-1	Souness	40,310
Nov 1	Stoke City	D 2-2	Johnson, Dalglish	22,864
Nov 8	NOTTINGHAM FOREST	D 0-0		43,143
Nov 11	COVENTRY CITY	W 2-1	Johnson 2	26,744
Nov 15	Crystal Palace	D 2-2	Kennedy R, McDermott	31,154
Nov 22	ASTON VILLA	W 2-1	Dalglish 2	48,114
Nov 25	Wolverhampton Wanderers	L 1-4	Neal	25,497
Nov 29	Sunderland	W 4-2	Johnson, McDermott, Lee 2	32,340
Dec 6	TOTTENHAM HOTSPUR	W 2-1	Johnson, Kennedy R	39,545
Dec 13	Ipswich Town	D 1-1	Case	32,274
Dec 20	WOLVERHAMPTON WANDERERS	W 1-0	Kennedy R	33,563
Dec 26	Manchester United	D 0-0		57,073
Dec 27	LEEDS UNITED	D 0-0		44,086
Jan 10	Aston Villa	L 0-2		47,960
Jan 17	Norwich City	W 1-0	McDermott	23,829
Jan 31	LEICESTER CITY	L 1-2	Young o.g.	35,154
Feb 7	West Bromwich Albion	L 0-2		27,905
Feb 14	BIRMINGHAM CITY	D 2-2	Johnson, Neal	32,199
Feb 21	Brighton & Hove Albion	D 2-2	Johnson, McDermott	23,275
Feb 28	SOUTHAMPTON	W 2-0	Kennedy R, McDermott	41,575
Mar 21	EVERTON	W 1-0	Bailey o.g.	49,743
Mar 28	Arsenal	L 0-1		47,058
Apr 3	STOKE CITY	W 3-0	Whelan, McDermott 2	33,308
Apr 11	Nottingham Forest	D 0-0		27,363
Apr 14	MANCHESTER UNITED	L 0-1		31,276
Apr 18	Leeds United	D 0-0		39,206
Apr 25	Tottenham Hotspur	D 1-1	Gayle	35,334
May 2	SUNDERLAND	L 0-1		40,337
May 5	Middlesbrough	W 2-1	Kennedy R, Irwin	19,102
May 19	MANCHESTER CITY	W 1-0	Kennedy R	24,462

FA Cup

Jan 3	ALTRINCHAM	(Rd3) W 4-1	McDermott, Dalglish 2, Kennedy R	37,170
Jan 24	Everton	(Rd4) L 1-2	Case	53,804

League Cup

Aug 27	Bradford City	(Rd2/1L) L 0-1		16,232
Sep 2	BRADFORD CITY	(Rd2/2L) W 4-0	Dalglish 2, Kennedy R, Johnson	21,017
Sep 23	SWINDON TOWN	(Rd3) W 5-0	Lee 2, Dalglish, Cockerill o.g., Fairclough	16,566
Oct 28	PORTSMOUTH	(Rd4) W 4-1	Dalglish, Johnson 2, Souness	32,021
Dec 5	BIRMINGHAM CITY	(Rd5) W 3-1	Dalglish, McDermott, Johnson	30,236
Jan 14	Manchester City	(SF/1L) W 1-0	Kennedy R	48,045
Feb 10	MANCHESTER CITY	(SF/2L) D 1-1	Dalglish	46,711
Mar 14	West Ham United	(F) D 1-1*	Kennedy A	100,000
Apr 1	West Ham United**	(R) W 2-1	Dalglish, Hansen	36,693

*After extra time. Score at 90 mins 0-0. Played at Wembley. **Played at Villa Park.

European Cup

Sep 17	Oulu Palloseura	(Rd1/1L) D 1-1	McDermott	14,000
Oct 1	OULU PALLOSEURA	(Rd1/2L) W10-1	Souness 3 (1 pen), Lee, McDermott 3, Kennedy R, Fairclough 2	21,013
Oct 22	Aberdeen	(Rd2/1L) W 1-0	McDermott	24,000
Nov 5	ABERDEEN	(Rd2/2L) W 4-0	Miller o.g., Neal, Dalglish, Hansen	36,182
Mar 4	CSKA SOFIA	(Rd3/1L) W 5-1	Souness 3, Lee, McDermott	37,255
Mar 18	CSKA Sofia	(Rd3/2L) W 1-0	Johnson	65,000
Apr 8	BAYERN MUNICH	SF/1L) D 0-0		44,543
Apr 22	Bayern Munich	(SF/2L) D 1-1†	Kennedy R	77,600
May 27	Real Madrid††	(F) W 1-0	Kennedy A	48,360

†Won on away goal rule. ††Played in Paris.

Charity Shield

Aug 9	West Ham United#	W 1-0	McDermott	90,000

#Played at Wembley.

League & Cup Appearances

PLAYER	LEAGUE	CUP COMPETITION FA CUP	LC	EC	OTHER	TOTAL
Case	14 (10)	1 (1)	3 (1)	2 (3)	1	21 (15)
Clemence	41	2	9	9	1	62
Cohen	13 (1)	1	1	2 (1)		17 (2)
Dalglish	34	2	8	9	1	54
Fairclough	6 (3)	1	3 (1)	2		12 (4)
Gayle	3 (1)			0 (1)		3 (2)
Hansen	36		8	9	1	54
Heighway	4 (2)		1	1 (2)		6 (4)
Irwin	19 (2)	2	4	2 (1)		27 (3)
Kennedy A	19	1	7	6	1	34
Kennedy R	41	2	9	9	1	62
Johnson	29	1	5	5	1	41
Lee	37	2	7	9		55
McDermott	40	2	9	8	1	60
Money	12 (2)	1	1	1		15 (2)
Neal	42	2	9	9	1	63
Ogrizovic	1					1
Rush	7		1	1		9
Russell	0 (1)					0 (1)
Sheedy	1					1
Souness	37	1	8	8	1	55
Thompson	25	1	6	7	1	40
Whelan	1					1

Goalscorers

PLAYER	LEAGUE	CUP COMPETITION FA CUP	LC	EC	OTHER	TOTAL
McDermott	13	1	1	6	1	22
Dalglish	8	2	7	1		18
Johnson	8		4	1		13
Kennedy R	8	1	2	2		13
Souness	6		1	6		13
Lee	4		2	2		8
Fairclough	4		1	2		7
Kennedy A	2		1	1		4
Hansen	1		1	1		3
Neal	2			1		3
Case	1	1				2
Gayle	1					1
Irwin	1					1
Whelan	1					1
Opps' o.gs.	2		1	1		4

Fact File

Liverpool won their third European Cup and their first League Cup to go with the Charity Shield.

MANAGER: Bob Paisley **CAPTAIN:** Phil Thompson **TRANSFERS IN:** Richard Money from Fulham, Craig Johnston from Middlesbrough, Bruce Grobbelaar from Crewe Alexandra **TRANSFERS OUT:** Steve Heighway to Minnesota Kicks (USA)

Final Division One Table

		P	W	D	L	F	A	PTS
1	Aston Villa	42	26	8	8	72	40	60
2	Ipswich T	42	23	10	9	77	43	56
3	Arsenal	42	19	15	8	61	45	53
4	WBA	42	20	12	10	60	42	52
5	Liverpool	42	17	17	8	62	46	51
6	Southampton	42	20	10	12	76	56	50
7	Nottingham F	42	19	12	11	62	44	50
8	Manchester U	42	15	18	9	51	36	48
9	Leeds U	42	17	10	15	39	47	44
10	Tottenham H	42	14	15	13	70	68	43
11	Stoke C	42	12	18	12	51	60	42
12	Manchester C	42	14	11	17	56	59	39
13	Birmingham C	42	13	12	17	50	61	38
14	Middlesbrough	42	16	5	21	53	61	37
15	Everton	42	13	10	19	55	58	36
16	Coventry C	42	13	10	19	48	68	36
17	Sunderland	42	14	7	21	52	53	35
18	Wolverhampton W	42	13	9	20	43	55	3
19	Brighton & HA	42	14	7	21	54	67	35
20	Norwich C	42	13	7	22	49	73	33
21	Leicester C	42	13	6	23	40	67	32
22	Crystal Palace	42	6	7	29	47	83	19

Season 1981-82

Football League Division One

DATE	OPPONENTS	SCORE	GOALSCORERS	ATTENDANCE
Aug 29	Wolverhampton Wanderers	L 0-1		28,001
Sep 1	MIDDLESBROUGH	D 1-1	Neal (pen)	31,963
Sep 5	ARSENAL	W 2-0	McDermott, Johnson	35,269
Sep 12	Ipswich Town	L 0-2		26,703
Sep 19	ASTON VILLA	D 0-0		37,474
Sep 22	Coventry City	W 2-1	Kennedy A, McDermott (pen)	16,731
Sep 26	West Ham United	D 1-1	Johnson	30,802
Oct 3	SWANSEA CITY	D 2-2	McDermott 2 (2 pens)	48,645
Oct 10	LEEDS UNITED	W 3-0	Rush 2, Cherry o.g.	35,840
Oct 17	Brighton & Hove Albion	D 3-3	Dalglish, Kennedy R, McDermott	26,321
Oct 24	MANCHESTER UNITED	L 1-2	McDermott (pen)	41,438
Oct 31	Sunderland	W 2-0	Souness, McDermott	27,854
Nov 7	EVERTON	W 3-1	Dalglish 2, Rush	48,861
Nov 21	West Bromwich Albion	D 1-1	Dalglish	20,871
Nov 28	SOUTHAMPTON	L 0-1		37,189
Dec 5	Nottingham Forest	W 2-0	Lawrenson, Kennedy R	24,521
Dec 26	MANCHESTER CITY	L 1-3	Whelan	37,929
Jan 5	WEST HAM UNITED	W 3-0	McDermott, Whelan, Dalglish	28,427
Jan 16	WOLVERHAMPTON WANDERERS	W 2-1	Whelan, Dalglish	26,438
Jan 26	Notts County	W 4-0	Whelan, Rush 3	14,407
Jan 30	Aston Villa	W 3-0	Rush, McDermott 2	35,947
Feb 6	IPSWICH TOWN	W 4-0	McDermott, Rush, Dalglish, Whelan	41,316
Feb 16	Swansea City	L 0-2		22,604
Feb 20	COVENTRY CITY	W 4-0	Souness, Lee, Rush, McDermott (pen)	28,286
Feb 27	Leeds United	W 2-0	Souness, Rush	33,689
Mar 6	BRIGHTON & HOVE ALBION	L 0-1		28,574
Mar 9	Stoke City	W 5-1	McDermott, Dalglish, Souness, Lee, Whelan	16,758
Mar 20	SUNDERLAND	W 1-0	Rush	30,344
Mar 27	Everton	W 3-1	Whelan, Souness, Johnson	51,847
Mar 30	BIRMINGHAM CITY	W 3-1	Rush 2, McDermott	24,224
Apr 2	NOTTS COUNTY	W 1-0	Dalglish	30,126
Apr 7	Manchester United	W 1-0	Johnston	50,969
Apr 10	Manchester City	W 5-0	Lee, Neal (pen), Johnston, Kennedy A, Rush	40,112
Apr 13	STOKE CITY	W 2-0	Kennedy A, Johnston	30,419
Apr 17	WEST BROMWICH ALBION	W 1-0	Dalglish	34,286
Apr 24	Southampton	W 3-2	Rush, Whelan 2	24,704
May 1	NOTTINGHAM FOREST	W 2-0	Johnston 2	34,321
May 3	Tottenham Hotspur	D 2-2	Dalglish 2	38,091
May 8	Birmingham City	W 1-0	Rush	26,381
May 11	Arsenal	D 1-1	Rush	30,932
May 15	TOTTENHAM HOTSPUR	W 3-1	Lawrenson, Dalglish, Whelan	48,122
May 18	Middlesbrough	D 0-0		17,431

FA Cup

Jan 2	Swansea City	(Rd3)	W 4-0	Hansen, Rush 2, Lawrenson	24,179
Jan 23	Sunderland	(Rd4)	W 3-0	Dalglish 2, Rush.	28,582
Feb 13	Chelsea	(Rd5)	L 0-2		41,422

League Cup (Milk Cup)

Oct 7	EXETER CITY	(Rd2/1L)	W 5-0	Rush 2, McDermott, Dalglish, Whelan	11,478
Oct 28	Exeter City	(Rd2/2L)	W 6-0	Rush 2, Dalglish, Neal, Sheedy, Marker o.g.	11,740
Nov 10	MIDDLESBROUGH	(Rd3)	W 4-1	Sheedy, Rush, Johnson 2	16,145
Dec 1	Arsenal	(Rd4)	D 0-0		37,917
Dec 8	ARSENAL	(R)	W 3-0*	Johnston, McDermott, Dalglish	21,375
Jan 12	BARNSLEY	(Rd5)	D 0-0		33,707
Jan 19	Barnsley	(R)	W 3-1	Souness, Johnson, Dalglish	29,639
Feb 2	Ipswich Town	(SF/1L)	W 2-0	McDermott, Rush	26,690
Feb 9	IPSWICH TOWN	(SF/2L)	D 2-2	Rush, Dalglish	34,933
Mar 13	Tottenham Hotspur	(F)	W 3-1**	Whelan 2, Rush	100,000

*After extra time. Score at 90 mins 0-0.
**After extra time. Score at 90 mins 1-1. Played at Wembley.

European Cup

Sep 16	Oulu Palloseura	(Rd1/1L)	W 1-0	Dalglish	8,400
Sep 30	OULU PALLOSEURA	(Rd1/2L)	W 7-0	Dalglish, Rush, McDermott 2, Kennedy R, Johnson, Lawrenson	20,789
Oct 21	AZ 67 Alkmaar	(Rd2/1L)	D 2-2	Johnson, Lee	15,000
Nov 4	AZ 67 ALKMAAR	(Rd2/2L)	W 3-2	McDermott (pen), Rush, Hansen	29,703
Mar 3	CSKA SOFIA	(Rd3/1L)	W 1-0	Whelan	27,388
Mar 17	CSKA Sofia	(Rd3/2L)	L 0-2†		60,000

†After extra time. Score at 90 mins 0-1.

World Club Championship

Dec 13	Flamengo††	L 0-3		62,000

††Played in Tokyo.

League & Cup Appearances

PLAYER	LEAGUE	CUP COMPETITION FA CUP	LC	EC	OTHER	TOTAL
Dalglish	42	3	10	6	1	62
Grobbelaar	42	3	10	6	1	62
Hansen	35	3	8	5	1	52
Johnson	10 (5)	0 (1)	1 (4)	3 (1)	0 (1)	14 (12)
Johnston	13 (5)	0 (1)	0 (2)	0 (1)	1	14 (9)
Kennedy A	32 (2)	3	6	4		45 (2)
Kennedy R	15		3	4	1	23
Lawrenson	37 (2)	3	10	5 (1)	1	56 (3)
Lee	35	2	6	5	1	49
McDermott	28 (1)	3	10	5	1	47 (1)
Neal	42	3	10	6	1	62
Rush	32	3	10	3 (1)		48 (1)
Sheedy	0 (2)		2			2 (2)
Souness	34 (1)	3	9	6	1	53
Thompson	34	1	7	5	1	48
Whelan	31 (1)	3	8	3 (1)		45 (2)

Goalscorers

PLAYER	LEAGUE	CUP COMPETITION FA CUP	LC	EC	OTHER	TOTAL
Rush	17	3	8	2		30
Dalglish	13	2	5	2		22
McDermott	14		3	3		20
Whelan	10		3	1		14
Johnson	2		3	2		7
Johnston	6		1			7
Souness	5		1			6
Lawrenson	2	1		1		4
Lee	3			1		4
Kennedy A	3					3
Kennedy R	2			1		3
Neal	2		1			3
Hansen		1		1		2
Sheedy			2			2
Opps' o.gs.	1		1			2

Fact File

The Dalglish and Rush partnership scores 52 of a total of 129 goals to bring the 13th championship and the League Cup to Anfield for the second year in succession.

MANAGER: Bob Paisley **CAPTAIN:** Phil Thompson/ Graeme Souness from January
TOP SCORER: Ian Rush 30 (17 league)
TRANSFERS IN: Mark Lawrenson from Brighton & HA, Steve Nicol from Ayr United **TRANSFERS OUT:** Ray Clemence to Tottenham Hotspur, Avi Cohen to Macabbi, Tel Aviv, Ray Kennedy to Swansea City

Final Division One Table

		P	W	D	L	F	A	Pts
1	Liverpool	42	26	9	7	80	32	87
2	Ipswich T	42	26	5	11	75	53	83
3	Manchester U	42	22	12	8	59	29	78
4	Tottenham H	42	20	11	11	67	48	71
5	Arsenal	42	20	11	11	48	37	71
6	Swansea C	42	21	6	15	58	51	69
7	Southampton	42	19	9	14	72	67	66
8	Everton	42	17	13	12	56	50	64
9	West Ham U	42	14	16	12	66	57	58
10	Manchester C	42	15	13	14	49	50	58
11	Aston Villa	42	15	12	15	55	53	57
12	Nottingham F	42	15	12	15	42	48	57
13	Brighton & HA	42	13	13	16	43	52	52
14	Coventry C	42	13	11	18	56	62	50
15	Notts Co	42	13	8	21	61	69	47
16	Birmingham C	42	10	14	18	53	61	44
17	WBA	42	11	11	20	46	57	44
18	Stoke C	42	12	8	22	44	63	44
19	Sunderland	42	11	11	20	38	58	44
20	Leeds U	42	10	12	20	39	61	42
21	Wolverhampton W	42	10	10	22	32	63	40
22	Middlesbrough	42	8	15	19	34	52	39

Season 1982-83

Football League Division One

DATE	OPPONENTS	SCORE	GOALSCORERS	ATTENDANCE
Aug 28	WEST BROMWICH ALBION	W 2-0	Lee, Neal (pen)	35,652
Aug 31	Birmingham City	D 0-0		20,176
Sep 4	Arsenal	W 2-0	Hodgson, Neal	36,429
Sep 7	NOTTINGHAM FOREST	W 4-3	Hodgson 2, Souness, Rush	27,145
Sep 11	LUTON TOWN	D 3-3	Souness, Rush, Johnston	33,694
Sep 18	Swansea City	W 3-0	Rush 2, Johnston	20,322
Sep 25	SOUTHAMPTON	W 5-0	Whelan 2, Souness, Lawrenson 2	32,996
Oct 2	Ipswich Town	L 0-1		24,342
Oct 9	West Ham United	L 1-3	Souness	32,500
Oct 16	MANCHESTER UNITED	D 0-0		40,853
Oct 23	Stoke City	D 1-1	Lawrenson	29,411
Oct 30	BRIGHTON & HOVE ALBION	W 3-1	Lawrenson, Dalglish 2	27,929
Nov 6	Everton	W 5-0	Rush 4, Lawrenson	52,741
Nov 13	COVENTRY CITY	W 4-0	Dalglish, Rush 3	27,870
Nov 20	Notts County	W 2-1	Johnston, Dalglish	16,914
Nov 27	TOTTENHAM HOTSPUR	W 3-0	Neal (pen), Dalglish 2	40,691
Dec 4	Norwich City	L 0-1		22,909
Dec 11	WATFORD	W 3-1	Rush, Neal 2 (2 pens)	36,690
Dec 18	Aston Villa	W 4-2	Hodgson, Dalglish, Kennedy A, Rush	34,568
Dec 27	MANCHESTER CITY	W 5-2	Dalglish 3, Neal, Rush	44,664
Dec 28	Sunderland	D 0-0		35,041
Jan 1	NOTTS COUNTY	W 5-1	Rush 3, Dalglish 2	33,643
Jan 3	ARSENAL	W 3-1	Rush, Souness, Dalglish	37,713
Jan 15	West Bromwich Albion	W 1-0	Rush	24,560
Jan 22	BIRMINGHAM CITY	W 1-0	Neal	30,986
Feb 5	Luton Town	W 3-1	Rush, Kennedy A, Souness	18,434
Feb 12	IPSWICH TOWN	W 1-0	Dalglish	34,976
Feb 26	Manchester United	D 1-1	Dalglish	57,397
Mar 5	STOKE CITY	W 5-1	Dalglish 2, Neal, Johnston, Souness	30,020
Mar 12	WEST HAM UNITED	W 3-0	Pike o.g., Lee, Rush	28,511
Mar 19	EVERTON	D 0-0		44,737
Mar 22	Brighton & Hove Albion	D 2-2	Rush 2	25,030
Apr 2	SUNDERLAND	W 1-0	Souness	35,821
Apr 4	Manchester City	W 4-0	Souness, Fairclough 2, Kennedy A	35,647
Apr 9	SWANSEA CITY	W 3-0	Rush, Lee, Fairclough	30,010
Apr 12	Coventry City	D 0-0		14,821
Apr 16	Southampton	L 2-3	Dalglish, Johnston	25,578
Apr 23	NORWICH CITY	L 0-2		37,022
Apr 30	Tottenham Hotspur	L 0-2		44,907
May 2	Nottingham Forest	L 0-1		25,107
May 7	ASTON VILLA	D 1-1	Johnston	39,939
May 14	Watford	L 1-2	Johnston	27,173

FA Cup

Jan 8	Blackburn Rovers	(Rd3)	W 2-1	Hodgson, Rush	21,967
Jan 29	STOKE CITY	(Rd4)	W 2-0	Dalglish, Rush	36,666
Feb 20	BRIGHTON & HOVE ALBION	(Rd5)	L 1-2	Johnston	44,868

League Cup (Milk Cup)

Oct 5	Ipswich Town	(Rd2/1L)	W 2-1	Rush 2	19,328
Oct 26	IPSWICH TOWN	(Rd2/2L)	W 2-0	Whelan, Lawrenson	17,698
Nov 11	ROTHERHAM UNITED	(Rd3)	W 1-0	Johnston	20,412
Nov 30	NORWICH CITY	(Rd4)	W 2-0	Lawrenson, Fairclough	13,235
Jan 18	WEST HAM UNITED	(Rd5)	W 2-1	Hodgson, Souness	23,953
Feb 8	BURNLEY	(SF/1L)	W 3-0	Souness, Neal (pen), Hodgson	33,520
Feb 15	Burnley	(SF/2L)	L 0-1		20,000
Mar 26	Manchester United		W 2-1*	Kennedy A, Whelan	100,000

*After extra time. Score at 90 mins 1-1. Played at Wembley.

European Cup

Sep 14	Dundalk	(Rd1/1L)	W 4-1	Whelan 2, Rush, Hodgson	16,500
Sep 28	DUNDALK	(Rd1/2L)	W 1-0	Whelan	12,021
Oct 19	JK Helsinki	(Rd2/1L)	L 0-1		5,722
Nov 2	JK HELSINKI	(Rd2/2L)	W 5-0	Dalglish, Johnston, Neal, Kennedy A 2	16,434
Mar 2	Widzew Lodz	(Rd3/1L)	L 0-2		45,531
Mar 16	WIDZEW LODZ	(Rd3/2L)	W 3-2	Neal (pen), Rush, Hodgson	44,494

Charity Shield

Aug 21	Tottenham Hotspur	W 1-0	Rush	82,500

Fact File

Liverpool won their third successive League Cup to add to their 14th championship win and the Charity Shield.

League & Cup Appearances

PLAYER	LEAGUE	CUP COMPETITION			OTHER	TOTAL
		FA CUP	LC	EC		
Dalglish	42	3	7	5	1	58
Fairclough	3 (5)		0 (2)	0 (1)		3 (8)
Grobbelaar	42	3	8	6	1	60
Hansen	34	3	8	6	1	52
Hodgson	20 (3)	3	4 (1)	3 (2)	0 (1)	30 (7)
Johnston	30 (3)	2 (1)	6	4		42 (4)
Kennedy A	42	3	8	6	1	60
Lawrenson	40	3	8	3	1	55
Lee	40	3	8	6	1	58
McDermott	0 (2)			1		1 (2)
Neal	42	3	8	6	1	60
Nicol	2 (2)					2 (2)
Rush	34	3	8	5	1	51
Souness	41	3	8	6	1	59
Thompson	24		4	4 (1)	1	33 (1)
Whelan	26 (2)	1	3 (3)	5	1	36 (5)

Goalscorers

PLAYER	LEAGUE	CUP COMPETITION			OTHER	TOTAL
		FA CUP	LC	EC		
Rush	24	2	2	2	1	31
Dalglish	18	1		1		20
Neal	8		1	2		11
Souness	9		2			11
Johnston	7	1	1	1		10
Hodgson	4	1	2	2		9
Lawrenson	5		2			7
Whelan	2		2	3		7
Kennedy A	3		1	2		6
Fairclough	3		1			4
Lee	3					3
Opps' o.gs.	1					1

MANAGER: Bob Paisley

CAPTAIN: Graeme Souness

TOP SCORER: Ian Rush 31 (24 league)

BIGGEST WIN: 5-0, 25 September 1982, v Southampton (H); 6 November 1982, v Everton (A), both Division One; 2 November 1982, v JK Helsinki (H), European Cup

HIGHEST ATTENDANCE: 100,000, 26 March 1983 v Manchester United, Milk Cup final at Wembley

TRANSFERS IN: David Hodgson from Middlesbrough

TRANSFERS OUT: David Johnson to Everton, Terry McDermott to Newcastle United

Final Division One Table

	P	W	D	L	F	A	Pts
1 Liverpool	42	24	10	8	87	37	82
2 Watford	42	22	5	15	74	57	71
3 Manchester U	42	19	13	8	56	38	70
4 Tottenham H	42	20	9	13	65	50	69
5 Nottingham F	42	20	9	13	62	50	69
6 Aston Villa	42	21	5	16	62	50	68
7 Everton	42	18	10	14	66	48	64
8 West Ham U	42	20	4	18	68	62	64
9 Ipswich T	42	15	13	14	64	50	58
10 Arsenal	42	16	10	16	58	56	58
11 WBA	42	15	12	15	51	49	57
12 Southampton	42	15	12	15	54	58	57
13 Stoke C	42	16	9	17	53	64	57
14 Norwich C	42	14	12	16	52	58	54
15 Notts Co	42	15	7	20	55	71	52
16 Sunderland	42	12	14	16	48	61	50
17 Birmingham C	42	12	15	16	40	55	50
18 Luton T	42	12	13	17	65	84	49
19 Coventry C	42	13	9	20	48	59	48
20 Manchester C	42	13	8	21	47	70	47
21 Swansea C	42	10	11	21	51	69	41
22 Brighton & HA	42	9	13	20	38	68	40

Season 1983-84

Football League Division One

DATE	OPPONENTS	SCORE	GOALSCORERS	ATTENDANCE
Aug 27	Wolverhampton Wanderers	D 1-1	Rush	26,249
Aug 31	Norwich City	W 1-0	Souness	23,859
Sep 3	NOTTINGHAM FOREST	W 1-0	Rush	31,376
Sep 6	SOUTHAMPTON	D 1-1	Rush	26,331
Sep 10	Arsenal	W 2-0	Johnston, Dalglish	47,896
Sep 17	ASTON VILLA	W 2-1	Dalglish, Rush	34,246
Sep 24	Manchester United	L 0-1		56,121
Oct 1	SUNDERLAND	L 0-1		29,534
Oct 15	West Ham United	W 3-1	Robinson 3	32,555
Oct 22	Queens Park Rangers	W 1-0	Nicol	27,140
Oct 29	LUTON TOWN	W 6-0	Rush 5, Dalglish	31,940
Nov 6	EVERTON	W 3-0	Rush, Robinson, Nicol	40,875
Nov 12	Tottenham Hotspur	D 2-2	Robinson, Rush	45,032
Nov 19	STOKE CITY	W 1-0	Rush	26,529
Nov 26	Ipswich Town	D 1-1	Dalglish	23,826
Dec 3	BIRMINGHAM CITY	W 1-0	Rush	24,791
Dec 10	Coventry City	L 0-4		20,586
Dec 17	NOTTS COUNTY	W 5-0	Nicol, Souness 2 (1 pen), Hunt o.g., Rush	22,436
Dec 26	West Bromwich Albion	W 2-1	Nicol, Souness	25,139
Dec 27	LEICESTER CITY	D 2-2	Lee, Rush	33,664
Dec 31	Nottingham Forest	W 1-0	Rush	29,692
Jan 2	MANCHESTER UNITED	D 1-1	Johnston	45,122
Jan 14	WOLVERHAMPTON WANDERERS	L 0-1		23,325
Jan 20	Aston Villa	W 3-1	Rush 3	19,566
Feb 1	WATFORD	W 3-0	Rush, Nicol, Whelan	20,746
Feb 4	Sunderland	D 0-0		25,646
Feb 11	ARSENAL	W 2-1	Kennedy, Neal	34,642
Feb 18	Luton Town	D 0-0		14,877
Feb 25	QUEENS PARK RANGERS	W 2-0	Rush, Robinson	32,206
Mar 3	Everton	D 1-1	Rush	51,245
Mar 10	TOTTENHAM HOTSPUR	W 3-1	Dalglish, Whelan, Lee	36,718
Mar 16	Southampton	L 0-2		19,698
Mar 31	Watford	W 2-0	Wark, Rush	21,293
Apr 7	WEST HAM UNITED	W 6-0	Rush 2, Dalglish, Whelan, Souness 2	38,359
Apr 14	Stoke City	L 0-2		24,372
Apr 18	Leicester City	D 3-3	Whelan, Rush, Wark	26,553
Apr 21	WEST BROMWICH ALBION	W 3-0	McNaught o.g., Souness, Dalglish	35,320
Apr 28	IPSWICH TOWN	D 2-2	Kennedy, Rush	32,069
May 5	Birmingham City	D 0-0		18,809
May 7	COVENTRY CITY	W 5-0	Rush 4 (1 pen), Hansen	33,393
May 12	Notts County	D 0-0		18,745
May 15	NORWICH CITY	D 1-1	Rush	38,837

FA Cup

Jan 6	NEWCASTLE UNITED	(Rd3)	W 4-0	Robinson, Rush 2, Johnston	33,566
Jan 29	Brighton & Hove Albion	(Rd4)	L 0-2		19,057

League Cup (Milk Cup)

Oct 5	Brentford	(Rd2/1L)	W 4-1	Rush 2, Robinson, Souness	17,859
Oct 25	BRENTFORD	(Rd2/2L)	W 4-0	Souness (pen), Hodgson, Dalglish, Robinson	9,902
Nov 8	Fulham	(Rd3)	D 1-1	Rush	20,142
Nov 22	FULHAM	(R)	D 1-1*	Dalglish	15,783
Nov 29	Fulham	(2nd R)	W 1-0**	Souness	20,905
Dec 20	Birmingham City	(Rd4)	D 1-1	Souness	17,405
Dec 22	BIRMINGHAM CITY	(R)	W 3-0	Nicol, Rush 2 (1 pen)	11,638
Jan 17	Sheffield Wednesday	(Rd5)	D 2-2	Nicol, Neal (pen)	49,357
Jan 25	SHEFFIELD WEDNESDAY	(R)	W 3-0	Rush 2, Robinson	40,485
Feb 7	WALSALL	(SF/1L)	D 2-2	Whelan 2	31,073
Feb 14	Walsall	(SF/2L)	W 2-0	Rush, Whelan	19,591
Mar 25	Everton	(F)	D 0-0†		100,000
Mar 28	Everton††	(R)	W 1-0	Souness	52,089

*After extra time. Score at 90 mins 1-1. **After extra time. Score at 90 mins 0-0.
†After extra time. Played at Wembley. ††Played at Maine Road.

European Cup

Sep 14	BK Odense	(Rd1/1L)	W 1-0	Dalglish	30,000
Sep 28	BK ODENSE	(Rd1/2L)	W 5-0	Robinson 2, Dalglish 2, Clausen o.g.	14,985
Oct 19	ATHLETIC BILBAO	(Rd2/1L)	D 0-0		33,063
Nov 2	Athletic Bilbao	(Rd2/2L)	W 1-0	Rush	47,500
Mar 7	BENFICA	(Rd3/1L)	W 1-0	Rush	39,096
Mar 21	Benfica	(Rd3/2L)	W 4-1	Whelan 2, Johnston, Rush	70,000
Apr 11	DINAMO BUCHAREST	(SF/1L)	W 1-0	Lee	36,941
Apr 25	Dinamo Bucharest	(SF/2L)	W 2-1	Rush 2	60,000
May 30	AS Roma	(F)	D 1-1#	Neal	69,693

#After extra time. Liverpool won cup 4-2 on penalties.
Scorers: Neal, Souness, Rush, Kennedy. Played in Rome.

Charity Shield

Aug 20	Manchester United§	L 0-2		92,000

§Played at Wembley.

League & Cup Appearances

PLAYER	LEAGUE	CUP COMPETITION			OTHER	TOTAL
		FA CUP	LC	EC		
Dalglish	33		8	8 (1)	1	50 (1)
Gillespie			1			1
Grobbelaar	42	2	13	9	1	67
Hansen	42	2	13	9	1	67
Hodgson	1 (4)		2 (2)	0 (2)	0 (1)	3 (9)
Johnston	28 (1)	2	11 (1)	8	0 (1)	49 (3)
Kennedy	42	2	13	9	1	67
Lawrenson	42	2	12	9	1	66
Lee	42	2	13	9	1	67
Neal	41	2	12	8	1	64
Nicol	19 (4)	2	9	2 (2)		32 (6)
Robinson	23 (1)	2	8 (1)	5 (1)	1	39 (3)
Rush	41	2	12	9	1	65
Souness	37	2	12	9	1	61
Thompson					1	1
Wark	9					9
Whelan	20 (3)	0 (1)	4 (1)	5		29 (5)

Goalscorers

PLAYER	LEAGUE	CUP COMPETITION			OTHER	TOTAL
		FA CUP	LC	EC		
Rush	32	2	8	5 (1)		47 (1)
Dalglish	7		2	3		12
Robinson	6	1	3	2		12
Souness	7		5	(1)		12 (1)
Whelan	4		3	2		9
Nicol	5		2			7
Johnston	2	1		1		4
Lee	2			1		3
Neal	1		1	1 (1)		3 (1)
Kennedy	2			(1)		2 (1)
Wark	2					2
Hansen	1					1
Hodgson			1			1
Opps' o.gs.	2			1		3

Penalty shoot-out goals in brackets.

MANAGER: Joe Fagan **CAPTAIN:** Graeme Souness
TRANSFERS IN: John Wark from Ipswich Town, Jim Beglin from Shamrock Rovers, Gary Gillespie from Coventry City **TRANSFERS OUT:** David Fairclough to Lucerne FC

Fact File

In his first managerial season, Joe Fagan led his side to three major trophies: the European Cup for the fourth time; the League Cup a record fourth time in succession and the League championship (the third in succession) for the 15th time.

Final Division One Table

		P	W	D	L	F	A	Pts
1	Liverpool	42	22	14	6	73	32	80
2	Southampton	42	22	11	9	66	38	77
3	Nottingham F	42	22	8	12	76	45	74
4	Manchester U	42	20	14	8	71	41	74
5	QPR	42	22	7	13	67	37	73
6	Arsenal	42	19	9	15	74	60	63
7	Everton	42	16	14	12	44	42	62
8	Tottenham H	42	17	10	15	64	65	61
9	West Ham U	42	17	9	16	60	55	60
10	Aston Villa	42	17	9	16	59	61	60
11	Watford	42	16	9	17	68	77	57
12	Ipswich T	42	15	8	19	55	57	53
13	Sunderland	42	13	13	16	42	53	52
14	Norwich C	42	12	15	15	48	49	51
15	Leicester C	42	13	12	17	65	68	51
16	Luton T	42	14	9	19	53	66	51
17	WBA	42	14	9	19	48	62	51
18	Stoke C	42	13	11	18	44	63	50
19	Coventry C	42	13	11	18	57	77	50
20	Birmingham C	42	12	12	18	39	50	48
21	Notts Co	42	10	11	21	50	72	41
22	Wolverhampton W	42	6	11	25	27	80	29

Season 1984-85

Football League Division One

DATE	OPPONENTS	SCORE	GOALSCORERS	ATTENDANCE
Aug 25	Norwich City	D 3-3	Bruce o.g., Dalglish, Neal (pen)	22,005
Aug 27	WEST HAM UNITED	W 3-0	Walsh, Wark 2	32,633
Sep 1	QUEENS PARK RANGERS	D 1-1	Whelan	33,982
Sep 4	Luton Town	W 2-1	Neal (pen), Dalglish	14,127
Sep 8	Arsenal	L 1-3	Kennedy	50,006
Sep 15	SUNDERLAND	D 1-1	Walsh	34,044
Sep 22	Manchester United	D 1-1	Walsh	56,638
Sep 29	SHEFFIELD WEDNESDAY	L 0-2		40,196
Oct 6	WEST BROMWICH ALBION	D 0-0		29,346
Oct 12	Tottenham Hotspur	L 0-1		28,599
Oct 20	EVERTON	L 0-1		45,545
Oct 28	Nottingham Forest	W 2-0	Whelan, Rush	19,838
Nov 3	Stoke City	W 1-0	Whelan	20,611
Nov 10	SOUTHAMPTON	D 1-1	Rush	36,382
Nov 18	Newcastle United	W 2-0	Nicol, Wark	28,003
Nov 24	IPSWICH TOWN	W 2-0	Wark 2	34,918
Dec 1	Chelsea	L 1-3	Molby	40,972
Dec 4	COVENTRY CITY	W 3-1	Wark 2, Rush (pen)	27,237
Dec 15	Aston Villa	D 0-0		24,007
Dec 21	Queens Park Rangers	W 2-0	Wark, Rush	11,007
Dec 26	LEICESTER CITY	L 1-2	Neal (pen)	38,419
Dec 29	LUTON TOWN	W 1-0	Wark	35,403
Jan 1	Watford	D 1-1	Rush	27,073
Jan 19	NORWICH CITY	W 4-0	Wark, Rush 2, Dalglish	30,627
Feb 2	Sheffield Wednesday	D 1-1	Lawrenson	48,246
Feb 12	ARSENAL	W 3-0	Rush, Neal, Whelan	28,645
Feb 23	STOKE CITY	W 2-0	Nicol, Dalglish	31,368
Mar 2	NOTTINGHAM FOREST	W 1-0	Wark (pen)	35,696
Mar 16	TOTTENHAM HOTSPUR	L 0-1		43,852
Mar 23	West Bromwich Albion	W 5-0	Nicol, Dalglish, Wark 3	20,500
Mar 31	MANCHESTER UNITED	L 0-1		34,886
Apr 3	Sunderland	W 3-0	Rush 2, Wark	24,096
Apr 6	Leicester City	W 1-0	Whelan	22,942
Apr 20	NEWCASTLE UNITED	W 3-1	Wark, Gillespie, Walsh	34,733
Apr 27	Ipswich Town	D 0-0		24,484
May 4	CHELSEA	W 4-3	Whelan, Nicol 2, Rush	33,733
May 6	Coventry City	W 2-0	Walsh 2	18,951
May 11	ASTON VILLA	W 2-1	Whelan, Rush	33,001
May 14	Southampton	D 1-1	Wark	23,001
May 17	WATFORD	W 4-3	Rush 2, Dalglish, Wark (pen)	29,130
May 20	West Ham United	W 3-0	Walsh 2, Beglin	22,408
May 23	Everton	L 0-1		51,045

FA Cup

Jan 5	ASTON VILLA	(Rd3)	W 3-0	Rush 2, Wark	36,877
Jan 27	TOTTENHAM HOTSPUR	(Rd4)	W 1-0	Rush	27,905
Feb 16	York City	(Rd5)	D 1-1	Rush	13,485
Feb 20	YORK CITY	(R)	W 7-0	Whelan 2, Wark 3, Neal, Walsh	43,010
Mar 10	Barnsley	(Rd6)	W 4-0	Rush 3, Whelan	19,838
Apr 13	Manchester United	(SF)	D 2-2*	Whelan, Walsh.	51,690
Apr 17	Manchester United**	(R)	L 1-2	McGrath o.g.	45,775

*After extra time. Score at 90 mins 1-1. Played at Goodison Park. **Played at Maine Road.

League Cup (Milk Cup)

Sep 24	Stockport County	(Rd2)	D 0-0		11,169
Oct 9	STOCKPORT COUNTY	(R)	W 2-0†	Robinson, Whelan	13,422
Oct 31	Tottenham Hotspur	(Rd3)	L 0-1		38,690

†After extra time.

European Cup

Sep 19	Lech Poznan	(Rd1/1L)	W 1-0	Wark	35,000
Oct 3	LECH POZNAN	(Rd1/2L)	W 4-0	Wark 3, Walsh	22,143
Oct 24	BENFICA	(Rd2/1L)	W 3-1	Rush 3	27,733
Nov 7	Benfica	(Rd2/2L)	L 0-1		50,000
Mar 6	Austria Vienna	(Rd3/1L)	D 1-1	Nicol	21,000
Mar 20	AUSTRIA VIENNA	(Rd3/2L)	W 4-1	Walsh 2, Nicol, Obermayer o.g.	32,761
Apr 10	PANATHINAIKOS	(SF/1L)	W 4-0	Wark, Rush 2, Beglin	39,488
Apr 24	Panathinaikos	(SF/2L)	W 1-0	Lawrenson	60,000
May 29	Juventus††	(F)	L 0-1		60,000

††Played in Brussels.

World Club Championship

Dec 9	Independiente#	L 0-1	62,000

#Played in Tokyo.

European Super Cup

Jan 16	Juventus##	L 0-2	60,000

##Played in Turin.

Charity Shield

Aug 18	Everton§	L 0-1	100,000

§Played at Wembley.

League & Cup Appearances

PLAYER	LEAGUE	CUP COMPETITION			OTHER	TOTAL
		FA CUP	LC	EC		
Beglin	10	2		3		15
Dalglish	36	7	1	7	2	53
Gillespie	10 (2)	3 (1)	3	2 (1)	1 (1)	19 (5)
Grobbelaar	42	7	3	9	3	64
Hansen	41	7	2	9	3	62
Johnston	11		1	1 (3)	1	14 (3)
Kennedy	32	5	3	6	3	49
Lawrenson	33	4	2	9	2	50
Lee	16 (1)	1	2	4	1	24 (1)
MacDonald	13	7		3	1	24
Molby	19 (3)		0 (1)		1	20 (4)
Neal	42	7	3	9	3	64
Nicol	29 (2)	6	2	6	3	46 (2)
Robinson	3 (3)		3	1		7 (3)
Rush	28	6	1	6	3	44
Walsh	22 (4)	1 (2)	2	6	1 (1)	32 (7)
Wark	40	7	2 (1)	9	3	61 (1)
Whelan	35 (2)	7	3	9	2 (1)	56 (3)

Goalscorers

PLAYER	LEAGUE	CUP COMPETITION			OTHER	TOTAL
		FA CUP	LC	EC		
Wark	18	4		5		27
Rush	14	7		5		26
Walsh	8	2		3		13
Whelan	7	4	1			12
Nicol	5			2		7
Dalglish	6					6
Neal	4	1				5
Beglin	1			1		2
Lawrenson	1			1		2
Gillespie	1					1
Kennedy	1					1
Molby	1					1
Robinson			1			1
Opps' o.gs.	1	1		1		3

MANAGER: Joe Fagan **CAPTAIN:** Phil Neal
TRANSFERS IN: Paul Walsh from Luton Town, Jan Molby from Ajax **TRANSFERS OUT:** Phil Thompson to Sheffield United

Fact File

Liverpool's fifth European Cup final against Juventus in the Heysel Stadium in Brussels was a disaster with 39 people losing their lives. This led to a general ban for English clubs in Europe and a 6-year ban for Liverpool.

Final Division One Table

		P	W	D	L	F	A	Pts
1	Everton	42	28	6	8	88	43	90
2	Liverpool	42	22	11	9	68	35	77
3	Tottenham H	42	23	8	11	78	51	77
4	Manchester U	42	22	10	10	77	47	76
5	Southampton	42	19	11	12	56	47	68
6	Chelsea	42	18	12	12	63	48	66
7	Arsenal	42	19	9	14	61	49	66
8	Sheffield W	42	17	14	11	58	45	65
9	Nottingham F	42	19	7	16	56	48	64
10	Aston Villa	42	15	11	16	60	60	56
11	Watford	42	14	13	15	81	71	55
12	WBA	42	16	7	19	58	62	55
13	Luton T	42	15	9	18	57	61	54
14	Newcastle U	42	13	13	16	55	70	52
15	Leicester C	42	15	6	21	65	73	51
16	West Ham U	42	13	12	17	51	68	51
17	Ipswich T	42	13	11	18	46	57	50
18	Coventry C	42	15	5	22	47	64	50
19	QPR	42	13	11	18	53	72	50
20	Norwich C	42	13	10	19	46	64	49
21	Sunderland	42	10	10	22	40	62	40
22	Stoke C	42	3	8	31	24	91	17

Season 1985-86

Football League Division One

DATE	OPPONENTS	SCORE	GOALSCORERS	ATTENDANCE
Aug 17	ARSENAL	W 2-0	Whelan, Nicol	38,261
Aug 21	Aston Villa	D 2-2	Rush, Molby	20,197
Aug 24	Newcastle United	L 0-1		29,670
Aug 26	IPSWICH TOWN	W 5-0	Nicol, Rush 2, Molby, Johnston	29,383
Aug 31	West Ham United	D 2-2	Johnston, Whelan	19,726
Sep 3	NOTTINGHAM FOREST	W 2-0	Whelan 2	27,135
Sep 7	WATFORD	W 3-1	Neal (pen), Johnston, Rush	31,395
Sep 14	Oxford United	D 2-2	Rush, Johnston	11,474
Sep 21	Everton	W 3-2	Dalglish, Rush, McMahon	51,509
Sep 28	TOTTENHAM HOTSPUR	W 4-1	Lawrenson, Rush, Molby 2 (2 pens)	41,521
Oct 5	Queens Park Rangers	L 1-2	Walsh	24,621
Oct 12	SOUTHAMPTON	W 1-0	McMahon	31,070
Oct 19	Manchester United	D 1-1	Johnston	54,492
Oct 26	LUTON TOWN	W 3-2	Walsh 2, Molby	31,488
Nov 2	LEICESTER CITY	W 1-0	Rush	31,718
Nov 9	Coventry City	W 3-0	Beglin, Walsh, Rush	16,947
Nov 16	WEST BROMWICH ALBION	W 4-1	Nicol, Molby, Lawrenson, Walsh	28,407
Nov 23	Birmingham City	W 2-0	Rush, Walsh	15,062
Nov 30	CHELSEA	D 1-1	Molby (pen)	38,482
Dec 7	ASTON VILLA	W 3-0	Molby, Walsh, Johnston	29,418
Dec 14	Arsenal	L 0-2		35,048
Dec 21	NEWCASTLE UNITED	D 1-1	Nicol	30,746
Dec 26	Manchester City	L 0-1		35,584
Dec 28	Nottingham Forest	D 1-1	MacDonald	27,141
Jan 1	SHEFFIELD WEDNESDAY	D 2-2	Rush, Walsh	38,946
Jan 12	Watford	W 3-2	Walsh 2, Rush	16,967
Jan 18	WEST HAM UNITED	W 3-1	Molby (pen), Rush, Walsh	41,056
Feb 1	Ipswich Town	L 1-2	Whelan	20,551
Feb 9	MANCHESTER UNITED	D 1-1	Wark	35,064
Feb 22	EVERTON	L 0-2		45,445
Mar 2	Tottenham Hotspur	W 2-1	Molby, Rush	16,436
Mar 8	QUEENS PARK RANGERS	W 4-1	McMahon 2, Rush, Wark	26,219
Mar 15	Southampton	W 2-1	Wark, Rush	19,784
Mar 22	OXFORD UNITED	W 6-0	Rush 2, Lawrenson, Whelan, Molby 2 (1 pen)	37,861
Mar 29	Sheffield Wednesday	D 0-0		37,946
Mar 31	MANCHESTER CITY	W 2-0	McMahon 2	43,316
Apr 12	COVENTRY CITY	W 5-0	Whelan 3, Molby, Rush	42,729
Apr 16	Luton Town	W 1-0	Johnston	15,390
Apr 19	West Bromwich Albion	W 2-1	Dalglish, Rush	22,010
Apr 26	BIRMINGHAM CITY	W 5-0	Rush, Gillespie 3 (1 pen), Molby (pen)	42,021
Apr 30	Leicester City	W 2-0	Rush, Whelan	25,799
May 3	Chelsea	W 1-0	Dalglish	43,900

FA Cup

Jan 4	NORWICH CITY	(Rd3) W 5-0	MacDonald, Walsh, McMahon, Whelan, Wark	29,082
Jan 26	Chelsea	(Rd4) W 2-1	Rush, Lawrenson	33,625
Feb 15	York City	(Rd5) D 1-1	Molby (pen)	12,443
Feb 18	YORK CITY*	(R) W 3-1	Wark, Molby, Dalglish	29,362
Mar 11	WATFORD	(Rd6) D 0-0		36,775
Mar 17	Watford*	(R) W 2-1	Molby (pen), Rush	28,097
Apr 5	Southampton*†	(SF) W 2-0	Rush 2	44,605
May 10	Everton**	(F) W 3-1	Rush 2, Johnston	98,000

*After extra time. †Played at White Hart Lane. **After extra time. Played at Wembley.

League Cup (Milk Cup)

Sep 24	OLDHAM ATHLETIC	(Rd2/1L) W 3-0	McMahon 2, Rush	16,150
Oct 9	Oldham Athletic	(Rd2/2L) W 5-2	Whelan 2, Wark, Rush, MacDonald	7,719
Oct 29	BRIGHTON & HOVE ALBION	(Rd3) W 4-0	Walsh 3, Dalglish	15,291
Nov 26	MANCHESTER UNITED	(Rd4) W 2-1	Molby 2 (1 pen)	41,291
Jan 21	IPSWICH TOWN	(Rd5) W 3-0	Walsh, Whelan, Rush	19,762
Feb 12	Queens Park Rangers	(SF/1L) L 0-1		15,051
Mar 5	QUEENS PARK RANGERS	(SF/2L) D 2-2	McMahon, Johnston	23,863

Screen Sport Super Cup

Sep 17	SOUTHAMPTON	W 2-1	Molby, Dalglish	16,189
Oct 22	Southampton	D 1-1	Walsh	10,503
Dec 3	TOTTENHAM HOTSPUR	W 2-0	MacDonald, Walsh	14,855
Jan 14	Tottenham Hotspur	W 3-0	Rush 2, Lawrenson	10,078
Feb 5	Norwich City	D 1-1	Dalglish	15,330
May 6	NORWICH CITY	W 3-1	MacDonald, Molby (pen), Johnston	26,696

Note: final ties held over until 1986-87. Statistics included this season for convenience.

Sep 16	EVERTON	W 3-1	Rush 2, McMahon	20,660
Sep 30	Everton	W 4-1	Rush 3, Nicol	26,068

League & Cup Appearances

PLAYER	LEAGUE	CUP COMPETITION		OTHER	TOTAL
		FA CUP	LC		
Beglin	34	7	7	7	55
Dalglish	17 (4)	6	2	3	28 (4)
Gillespie	14	5	2	4 (1)	25 (1)
Grobbelaar	42	8	7	7	64
Hansen	41	8	7	5	61
Hooper				1	1
Johnston	38 (3)	6 (2)	7	5	56 (5)
Kennedy	8				8
Lawrenson	36 (2)	7	7	8	58 (2)
Lee	13 (2)	3	3	5	24 (2)
MacDonald	10 (7)	2	0 (2)	4 (1)	16 (10)
McMahon	23	4	5	6	38
Molby	39	8	5	6 (2)	58 (2)
Neal	11 (2)		2	1	14 (2)
Nicol	33 (1)	4	3	8	48 (1)
Rush	40	8	6	4	58
Seagraves		1	1		2
Venison				1 (1)	1 (1)
Walsh	17 (3)	2	4	6 (1)	29 (4)
Wark	7 (2)	2 (2)	2 (1)	1 (2)	12 (7)
Whelan	39	7	7	6	59

Goalscorers

PLAYER	LEAGUE	CUP COMPETITION		OTHER	TOTAL
		FA CUP	LC		
Rush	22	6	3	7	38
Molby	14	3	2	2	21
Walsh.	11	1	4	2	18
Whelan	10	1	3		14
McMahon	6	1	3	1	11
Johnston	7	1	1	1	10
Dalglish	3	1	1	2	7
Wark	3	2	1		6
Lawrenson	3	1		1	5
MacDonald	1	1	1	2	5
Nicol	4			1	5
Gillespie	3				3
Beglin	1				1
Neal	1				1

PLAYER/MANAGER: Kenny Dalglish
CAPTAIN: Phil Neal/Alan Hansen
TRANSFERS IN: Steve McMahon from Aston Villa
TRANSFERS OUT: Alan Kennedy to Sunderland, Phil Neal to Bolton Wanderers

Fact File

Ian Rush scored his 100th league goal on 18 January v West Ham United, while Kenny Dalglish became the first player/manager to win the classic League and FA Cup double.

Final Division One Table

	P	W	D	L	F	A	Pts
1 Liverpool	42	26	10	6	89	37	88
2 Everton	42	26	8	8	87	41	86
3 West Ham U	42	26	6	10	74	40	84
4 Manchester U	42	22	10	10	70	36	76
5 Sheffield W	42	21	10	11	63	54	73
6 Chelsea	42	20	11	11	57	56	71
7 Arsenal	42	20	9	13	49	47	69
8 Nottingham F	42	19	11	12	69	53	68
9 Luton T	42	18	12	12	61	44	66
10 Tottenham H	42	19	8	15	74	52	65
11 Newcastle U	42	17	12	13	67	72	63
12 Watford	42	16	11	15	69	62	59
13 QPR	42	15	7	20	53	64	52
14 Southampton	42	12	10	20	51	62	46
15 Manchester C	42	11	12	19	43	57	45
16 Aston Villa	42	10	14	18	51	67	44
17 Coventry C	42	11	10	21	48	71	43
18 Oxford U	42	10	12	20	62	80	42
19 Leicester C	42	10	12	20	54	76	42
20 Ipswich T	42	11	8	23	32	55	41
21 Birmingham C	42	8	5	29	30	73	29
22 WBA	42	4	12	26	35	89	24

Season 1986-87

Football League Division One

DATE	OPPONENTS	SCORE	GOALSCORERS	ATTENDANCE
Aug 23	Newcastle United	W 2-0	Rush 2	33,306
Aug 25	MANCHESTER CITY	D 0-0		39,989
Aug 30	ARSENAL	W 2-1	Molby (pen), Rush	38,637
Sep 3	Leicester City	L 1-2	Dalglish	16,344
Sep 6	West Ham United	W 5-2	Whelan, Johnston, Dalglish 2, Rush	29,807
Sep 13	CHARLTON ATHLETIC	W 2-0	Molby (pen), Rush	37,413
Sep 20	Southampton	L 1-2	McMahon	20,452
Sep 27	ASTON VILLA	D 3-3	Wark 2 (1 pen), McMahon	38,298
Oct 4	Wimbledon	W 3-1	Molby, Rush 2	15,978
Oct 11	TOTTENHAM HOTSPUR	L 0-1		43,139
Oct 18	OXFORD UNITED	W 4-0	Rush 2, Dalglish, Molby (pen)	34,512
Oct 25	Luton Town	L 1-4	Molby (pen)	13,140
Nov 1	NORWICH CITY	W 6-2	Nicol, Walsh 3, Rush 2	36,915
Nov 8	Queens Park Rangers	W 3-1	Rush, Nicol, Johnston	24,045
Nov 16	SHEFFIELD WEDNESDAY	D 1-1	Rush	28,020
Nov 23	Everton	D 0-0		48,247
Nov 29	COVENTRY CITY	W 2-0	Molby (pen), Wark	31,614
Dec 6	Watford	L 0-2		23,954
Dec 14	CHELSEA	W 3-0	Whelan, Rush, Nicol	25,856
Dec 20	Charlton Athletic	D 0-0		16,564
Dec 26	MANCHESTER UNITED	L 0-1		40,663
Dec 27	Sheffield Wednesday	W 1-0	Rush	40,959
Jan 1	Nottingham Forest	D 1-1	Rush	32,854
Jan 3	WEST HAM UNITED	W 1-0	McMahon	41,286
Jan 17	Manchester City	W 1-0	Rush	35,336
Jan 24	NEWCASTLE UNITED	W 2-0	Walsh, Rush	38,054
Feb 14	LEICESTER CITY	W 4-3	Walsh, Rush 3	34,259
Feb 21	Aston Villa	D 2-2	Johnston, Walsh	32,093
Feb 28	SOUTHAMPTON	W 1-0	Aldridge	33,133
Mar 7	LUTON TOWN	W 2-0	Molby (pen), Donaghy o.g.	32,433
Mar 10	Arsenal	W 1-0	Rush	47,777
Mar 14	Oxford United	W 3-1	Wark 2, Rush	14,211
Mar 18	QUEENS PARK RANGERS	W 2-1	Rush 2	28,988
Mar 22	Tottenham Hotspur	L 0-1		32,763
Mar 28	WIMBLEDON	L 1-2	Dalglish	36,409
Apr 11	Norwich City	L 1-2	Rush	22,879
Apr 18	NOTTINGHAM FOREST	W 3-0	Dalglish, Whelan, Ablett	37,359
Apr 20	Manchester United	L 0-1		54,103
Apr 25	EVERTON	W 3-1	McMahon, Rush 2	44,827
May 2	Coventry City	L 0-1		26,209
May 4	WATFORD	W 1-0	Rush	40,150
May 9	Chelsea	D 3-3	Rush, McMahon, Aldridge	29,245

FA Cup

Jan 11	Luton Town	(Rd3) D 0-0		11,085
Jan 26	LUTON TOWN	(R) D 0-0*		34,822
Jan 28	Luton Town	(2nd R) L 0-3		14,687

*After extra time.

League Cup (Littlewoods Cup)

Sep 23	FULHAM	(Rd2/1L) W10-0	Rush 2, Wark 2, Whelan, McMahon 4, Nicol	13,498
Oct 7	Fulham	(Rd2/2L) W 3-2	McMahon, Parker o.g., Molby (pen)	7,864
Oct 29	LEICESTER CITY	(Rd3) W 4-1	McMahon 3, Dalglish	20,248
Nov 19	Coventry City	(Rd4) D 0-0		26,385
Nov 26	COVENTRY CITY	(R) W 3-1	Molby 3 (all pens)	19,179
Jan 21	Everton	(Rd5) W 1-0	Rush	53,325
Feb 11	Southampton	(SF/1L) D 0-0		22,818
Feb 25	SOUTHAMPTON	(SF/2L) W 3-0	Whelan, Dalglish, Molby	38,481
Apr 3	Arsenal**	(F) L 1-2	Rush	96,000

**Played at Wembley.

Charity Shield

Aug 16	Everton†	D 1-1	Rush	88,231

†Played at Wembley.

PLAYER/MANAGER: Kenny Dalglish **CAPTAIN:** Alan Hansen

TOP SCORER: Ian Rush 35 (30 league)

BIGGEST WIN: 10-0, 23 September 1986, v Fulham (H), League Cup

HIGHEST ATTENDANCE: 96,000, 3 April 1987 (Wembley), League Cup Final

TRANSFERS IN: Nigel Spackman from Chelsea, John Aldridge from Oxford United

TRANSFERS OUT: Ian Rush to Juventus, Sammy Lee to Queens Park Rangers

League & Cup Appearances

PLAYER	LEAGUE	CUP COMPETITION		OTHER	TOTAL
		FA CUP	LC		
Ablett	5	0 (1)			5 (1)
Aldridge	2 (8)				2 (8)
Beglin	20	1	6	1	28
Dalglish	12 (6)		4 (1)	0 (1)	16 (8)
Durnin			1		1
Gillespie	37	3	9		49
Grobbelaar	31	3	9	1	44
Hansen	39	3	9	1	52
Hooper	11			0 (1)	11 (1)
Irvine	0 (2)	0 (1)	0 (1)		0 (4)
Johnston	27 (1)	3	5	1	36 (1)
Lawrenson	35	3	8	1	47
MacDonald	3 (3)			1	4 (3)
McMahon	37	1	9	1	48
Molby	34	3	7	1	45
Mooney			0 (1)		0 (1)
Nicol	14		5		19
Rush	42	3	9	1	55
Spackman	12		1 (1)		13 (1)
Venison	31 (2)	2	4 (2)	1	38 (4)
Walsh	23	3	4 (1)		30 (1)
Wark	8 (3)	2	1 (2)		11 (5)
Whelan	39	3	8	1	51

Goalscorers

PLAYER	LEAGUE	CUP COMPETITION		OTHER	TOTAL
		FA CUP	LC		
Rush	30		4	1	35
McMahon	5		8		13
Molby	7		5		12
Dalglish	6		2		8
Wark	5		2		7
Walsh	6				6
Whelan	3		2		5
Nicol	3		1		4
Johnston	3				3
Aldridge	2				2
Ablett	1				1
Opps' o.gs.	1		1		2

Fact File

Jan Molby's hat-trick of penalties in the 3-1 win over Coventry City on 26 November 1986 contributed towards his club record of 42 penalty goals out of a total of 60.

Final Division One Table

		P	W	D	L	F	A	Pts
1	Everton	42	26	8	8	76	31	86
2	Liverpool	42	23	8	11	72	42	77
3	Tottenham H	42	21	8	13	68	43	71
4	Arsenal	42	20	10	12	58	35	70
5	Norwich City	42	17	17	8	53	51	68
6	Wimbledon	42	19	9	14	57	50	66
7	Luton Town	42	18	12	12	47	45	66
8	Nottingham F	42	18	11	13	64	51	65
9	Watford	42	18	9	15	67	54	63
10	Coventry C	42	17	12	13	50	45	63
11	Manchester U	42	14	14	14	52	45	56
12	Southampton	42	14	10	18	69	68	52
13	Sheffield W	42	13	13	16	58	59	52
14	Chelsea	42	13	13	16	53	64	52
15	West Ham U	42	14	10	18	52	67	52
16	QPR	42	13	11	18	48	64	50
17	Newcastle U	42	12	11	19	47	65	47
18	Oxford U	42	11	13	18	44	69	46
19	Charlton Ath	42	11	11	20	45	55	44
20	Leicester C	42	11	9	22	54	76	42
21	Manchester C	42	8	15	19	36	57	39
22	Aston Villa	42	8	12	22	45	79	36

Season 1987-88

Football League Division One

DATE	OPPONENTS	SCORE	GOALSCORERS	ATTENDANCE
Aug 15	Arsenal	W 2-1	Aldridge, Nicol	54,703
Aug 29	Coventry City	W 4-1	Nicol 2, Aldridge (pen), Beardsley	27,637
Sep 5	West Ham United	D 1-1	Aldridge (pen)	29,865
Sep 12	OXFORD UNITED	W 2-0	Aldridge, Barnes	42,266
Sep 15	CHARLTON ATHLETIC	W 3-2	Aldridge (pen), Hansen, McMahon	36,637
Sep 20	Newcastle United	W 4-1	Nicol 3, Aldridge	24,141
Sep 29	DERBY COUNTY	W 4-0	Beardsley, Aldridge 3 (2 pens)	43,405
Oct 3	PORTSMOUTH	W 4-0	Beardsley, McMahon, Aldridge (pen), Whelan	44,366
Oct 17	QUEENS PARK RANGERS	W 4-0	Johnston, Aldridge (pen), Barnes 2	43,735
Oct 24	Luton Town	W 1-0	Gillespie	12,452
Nov 1	EVERTON	W 2-0	McMahon, Beardsley	44,260
Nov 4	Wimbledon	D 1-1	Houghton	13,544
Nov 15	Manchester United	D 1-1	Aldridge	47,106
Nov 21	NORWICH CITY	D 0-0		37,446
Nov 24	WATFORD	W 4-0	McMahon, Houghton, Aldridge, Barnes	32,396
Nov 28	Tottenham Hotspur	W 2-0	McMahon, Johnston	47,362
Dec 6	CHELSEA	W 2-1	Aldridge (pen), McMahon	31,211
Dec 12	Southampton	D 2-2	Barnes 2	19,507
Dec 19	SHEFFIELD WEDNESDAY	W 1-0	Gillespie	35,383
Dec 26	Oxford United	W 3-0	Aldridge, Barnes, McMahon	13,680
Dec 28	NEWCASTLE UNITED	W 4-0	McMahon, Aldridge 2 (1 pen), Houghton	44,637
Jan 1	COVENTRY CITY	W 4-0	Beardsley 2, Aldridge, Houghton	38,790
Jan 16	ARSENAL	W 2-0	Aldridge, Beardsley	44,294
Jan 23	Charlton Athletic	W 2-0	Beardsley, Barnes	28,095
Feb 6	WEST HAM UNITED	D 0-0		42,049
Feb 13	Watford	W 4-1	Beardsley 2, Aldridge, Barnes	23,838
Feb 27	Portsmouth	W 2-0	Barnes 2	28,117
Mar 5	Queens Park Rangers	W 1-0	Barnes	23,171
Mar 16	Derby County	D 1-1	Johnston	26,356
Mar 20	Everton	L 0-1		44,162
Mar 26	WIMBLEDON	W 2-1	Aldridge, Barnes	36,464
Apr 2	Nottingham Forest	L 1-2	Aldridge (pen)	29,188
Apr 4	MANCHESTER UNITED	D 3-3	Beardsley, Gillespie, McMahon	43,497
Apr 13	NOTTINGHAM FOREST	W 5-0	Houghton, Aldridge 2, Gillespie, Beardsley	39,535
Apr 20	Norwich City	D 0-0		22,509
Apr 23	TOTTENHAM HOTSPUR	W 1-0	Beardsley	44,798
Apr 30	Chelsea	D 1-1	Barnes	35,625
May 2	SOUTHAMPTON	D 1-1	Aldridge	37,610
May 7	Sheffield Wednesday	W 5-1	Johnston 2, Barnes, Beardsley 2	35,893
May 9	LUTON TOWN	D 1-1	Aldridge	30,736

FA Cup

Jan 9	Stoke City	(Rd3)	D 0-0		31,979
Jan 12	STOKE CITY	(R)	W 1-0	Beardsley	39,147
Jan 31	Aston Villa	(Rd4)	W 2-0	Barnes, Beardsley	46,324
Feb 21	Everton	(Rd5)	W 1-0	Houghton	48,270
Mar 13	Manchester City	(Rd6)	W 4-0	Houghton, Beardsley (pen), Johnston, Barnes	44,077
Apr 9	Nottingham Forest*	(SF)	W 2-1	Aldridge 2 (1 pen)	51,627
May 14	Wimbledon**	(F)	L 0-1		98,203

*Played at Hillsborough, Sheffield. **Played at Wembley.

League Cup (Littlewoods Cup)

Sep 23	Blackburn Rovers	(Rd2/1L)	D 1-1	Nicol	13,924
Oct 6	BLACKBURN ROVERS	(Rd2/2L)	W 1-0	Aldridge	28,994
Oct 28	EVERTON	(Rd3)	L 0-1		44,071

PLAYER/MANAGER: Kenny Dalglish
CAPTAIN: Alan Hansen
TOP SCORER: John Aldridge 29 (26 league)
BIGGEST WIN: 5-0, 13 April 1988, v Nottingham Forest (H), Division One
HIGGEST ATTENDANCE: 98,203, 14 May 1988, v Wimbledon (Wembley), FA Cup final
TRANSFERS IN: John Barnes from Watford, Peter Beardsley from Newcastle United, Ray Houghton from Oxford United
TRANSFERS OUT: Paul Walsh to Tottenham Hotspur, John Wark to Ipswich Town, Mark Lawrenson and Craig Johnston – retired

League & Cup Appearances

PLAYER	LEAGUE	CUP COMPETITION		TOTAL
		FA CUP	LC	
Ablett	15 (2)	5		20 (2)
Aldridge	36	6	3	45
Barnes	38	7	3	48
Beardsley	36 (2)	7	3	46 (2)
Dalglish	0 (2)			0 (2)
Gillespie	35	5	2	42
Grobbelaar	38	5	3	46
Hansen	39	7	3	49
Hooper	2	2		4
Houghton	26 (2)	7		33 (2)
Johnston	18 (12)	1 (2)	2	21 (14)
Lawrenson	10 (4)	2	2 (1)	14 (5)
MacDonald	0 (1)			0 (1)
McMahon	40	7	2	49
Molby	1 (6)	0 (1)		1 (7)
Nicol	40	7	3	50
Spackman	19 (8)	5	1	25 (8)
Venison	18	2	2	22
Walsh	1 (7)		0 (1)	1 (8)
Wark	0 (1)		1	1 (1)
Watson	2			2
Whelan	26 (2)	2	3	31 (2)

Goalscorers

PLAYER	LEAGUE	CUP COMPETITION		TOTAL
		FA CUP	LC	
Aldridge	26	2	1	29
Beardsley	15	3		18
Barnes	15	2		17
McMahon	9			9
Houghton	5	2		7
Nicol	6		1	7
Johnston	5	1		6
Gillespie	4			4
Hansen	1			1
Whelan	1			1

Fact File

Liverpool equalled the record set by Leeds United of 27 unbeaten games from the start of the season losing for the first time to Everton away on 20 March. The team went on to secure their 17th league championship by 9 points.

Final Division One Table

	P	W	D	L	F	A	Pts
1 Liverpool	40	26	12	2	87	24	90
2 Manchester U	40	23	12	5	71	38	81
3 Nottingham F	40	20	13	7	67	39	73
4 Everton	40	19	13	8	53	27	70
5 QPR	40	19	10	11	48	38	67
6 Arsenal	40	18	12	10	58	39	66
7 Wimbledon	40	14	15	11	58	47	57
8 Newcastle U	40	14	14	12	55	53	56
9 Luton T	40	14	11	15	57	58	53
10 Coventry C	40	13	14	13	46	53	53
11 Sheffield W	40	15	8	17	52	66	53
12 Southampton	40	12	14	14	49	53	50
13 Tottenham H	40	12	11	17	38	48	47
14 Norwich C	40	12	9	19	40	52	45
15 Derby Co	40	10	13	17	35	45	43
16 West Ham U	40	9	15	16	40	52	42
17 Charlton Ath	40	9	15	16	38	52	42
18 Chelsea	40	9	15	16	50	68	42
19 Portsmouth	40	7	14	19	36	66	35
20 Watford	40	7	11	22	27	51	32
21 Oxford U	40	6	13	21	44	80	31

Season 1988-89

Football League Division One

DATE	OPPONENTS	SCORE	GOALSCORERS	ATTENDANCE
Aug 27	Charlton Athletic	W 3-0	Aldridge 3	21,389
Sep 3	MANCHESTER UNITED	W 1-0	Molby (pen)	42,026
Sep 10	Aston Villa	D 1-1	Houghton	41,409
Sep 17	TOTTENHAM HOTSPUR	D 1-1	Beardsley	40,929
Sep 24	Southampton	W 3-1	Aldridge, Beardsley, Molby (pen)	21,046
Oct 1	NEWCASTLE UNITED	L 1-2	Gillespie	39,139
Oct 8	Luton Town	L 0-1		12,117
Oct 22	COVENTRY CITY	D 0-0		38,742
Oct 26	Nottingham Forest	L 1-2	Rush	29,755
Oct 29	West Ham United	W 2-0	Rush, Beardsley	30,198
Nov 5	MIDDLESBROUGH	W 3-0	Rush, Aldridge, Beardsley	39,489
Nov 12	MILLWALL	D 1-1	Nicol	41,966
Nov 19	Queens Park Rangers	W 1-0	Aldridge	20,063
Nov 26	WIMBLEDON	D 1-1	Houghton	36,188
Dec 4	Arsenal	D 1-1	Barnes	31,863
Dec 11	EVERTON	D 1-1	Houghton	42,372
Dec 17	NORWICH CITY	L 0-1		34,325
Dec 26	Derby County	W 1-0	Rush	25,213
Jan 1	Manchester United	L 1-3	Barnes	44,745
Jan 3	ASTON VILLA	W 1-0	Whelan	39,014
Jan 14	Sheffield Wednesday	D 2-2	Nicol, Aldridge	31,524
Jan 21	SOUTHAMPTON	W 2-0	Aldridge, Rush	35,565
Feb 4	Newcastle United	D 2-2	Rush, Aldridge	30,966
Mar 1	CHARLTON ATHLETIC	W 2-0	Beardsley, Aldridge (pen)	30,283
Mar 11	Middlesbrough	W 4-0	Beardsley, Houghton, Aldridge, McMahon	25,197
Mar 14	LUTON TOWN	W 5-0	Aldridge 3 (1 pen), Beardsley, McMahon	31,447
Mar 22	Coventry City	W 3-1	Barnes, Aldridge, Whelan	23,807
Mar 26	Tottenham Hotspur	W 2-1	Aldridge (pen), Beardsley	30,012
Mar 29	DERBY COUNTY	W 1-0	Barnes	42,518
Apr 1	Norwich City	W 1-0	Whelan	26,338
Apr 8	SHEFFIELD WEDNESDAY	W 5-1	McMahon, Beardsley 2, Houghton, Barnes	39,672
Apr 11	Millwall	W 2-1	Barnes, Aldridge	22,130
May 3	Everton	D 0-0		45,994
May 10	NOTTINGHAM FOREST	W 1-0	Aldridge (pen)	39,793
May 13	Wimbledon	W 2-1	Aldridge, Barnes	14,730
May 16	QUEENS PARK RANGERS	W 2-0	Aldridge, Whelan	38,368
May 23	WEST HAM UNITED	W 5-1	Aldridge, Houghton 2, Rush, Barnes	41,855
May 26	ARSENAL	L 0-2		41,718

FA Cup

Jan 7	Carlisle	(Rd3)	W 3-0	Barnes, McMahon 2	18,556
Jan 29	Millwall	(Rd4)	W 2-0	Aldridge, Rush	23,615
Feb 18	Hull City	(Rd5)	W 3-2	Barnes, Aldridge 2	20,058
Mar 18	BRENTFORD	(Rd6)	W 4-0	McMahon, Barnes, Beardsley 2	42,376
Apr 15	Nottingham Forest*	(SF)	0-0		53,000
May 7	Nottingham Forest**	(SF)	W 3-1	Aldridge 2, Laws o.g.	38,000
May 20	Everton†	(F)	W 3-2	Aldridge, Rush 2	82,800

*Semi-final played at Hillsborough, match abandoned after 6 minutes.
**Played at Old Trafford. †Played at Wembley.

League Cup (Littlewoods Cup)

Sep 28	WALSALL	(Rd2/1L)	W 1-0	Gillespie	18,084
Oct 12	Walsall	(Rd2/2L)	W 3-1	Barnes, Rush, Molby (pen)	12,015
Nov 2	ARSENAL	(Rd3)	D 1-1	Barnes	31,951
Nov 9	Arsenal	(R)	D 0-0		54,029
Nov 23	Arsenal††	(2nd R)	W 2-1	McMahon, Aldridge	21,708
Nov 30	West Ham United	(Rd4)	L 1-4	Aldridge (pen)	26,971

††Played at Villa Park.

Charity Shield

Aug 20	Wimbledon#	W 2-1	Aldridge 2	54,887

#Played at Wembley.

Mercantile Credit Trophy (Football League Centenary)

Aug 29	NOTTINGHAM FOREST	(QF)	W 4-1	Venison, Molby (pen), Houghton, Barnes	20,141
Sep 20	Arsenal	(SF)	L 1-2	Staunton	29,135

Fact File

15 April 1989 – LEST WE FORGET

League & Cup Appearances

PLAYER	LEAGUE	CUP COMPETITION FA CUP	LC	OTHER	TOTAL
Ablett	34 (1)	6	6	2	48 (1)
Aldridge	31 (4)	6	4 (1)	1	42 (5)
Barnes	33	6	3	2	44
Beardsley	33 (4)	5	6	3	47 (4)
Burrows	16 (5)	3			19 (5)
Dalglish			0 (1)	0 (1)	0 (2)
Durnin			0 (1)	1	1 (1)
Gillespie	15	2	1	3	21
Grobbelaar	21	5		2	28
Hansen	6	2			8
Hooper	17	1	6	1	25
Houghton	38	5	6	3	52
MacDonald	3		1 (1)	1	5 (1)
Marsh	0 (1)				0 (1)
McMahon	28 (1)	6	3	2	39 (1)
Molby	12 (1)	3	2	1	18 (1)
Nicol	38	6	6	2	52
Rush	16 (8)	1 (1)	4	2	23 (9)
Spackman	8 (4)		4		12 (4)
Staunton	17 (4)	3	4	1	25 (4)
Venison	14 (1)	0 (1)	4	2	20 (2)
Watson	1 (1)	1 (1)	0 (1)	1	3 (3)
Whelan	37	5	6	3	51

Goalscorers

PLAYER	LEAGUE	CUP COMPETITION FA CUP	LC	OTHER	TOTAL
Aldridge	21	6	2	2	31
Barnes	8	3	2	1	14
Beardsley	10	2			12
Rush	7	3	1		11
Houghton	7			1	8
McMahon	3	3	1		7
Whelan	4				4
Molby	2		1	1	4
Gillespie	1		1		2
Nicol	2				2
Staunton				1	1
Venison				1	1
Opps' o.gs.		1			1

PLAYER/MANAGER: Kenny Dalglish
CAPTAIN: Ronnie Whelan
TOP SCORER: John Aldridge 31 (21 league)
TRANSFERS IN: Ian Rush from Juventus, David Burrows from West Bromwich Albion
TRANSFERS OUT: Nigel Spackman to Queens Park Rangers

Final Division One Table

		P	W	D	L	F	A	Pts
1	Arsenal	38	22	10	6	73	36	76
2	Liverpool	38	22	10	6	65	28	76
3	Nottingham F	38	17	13	8	64	43	64
4	Norwich C	38	17	11	10	48	45	62
5	Derby Co	38	17	7	14	40	38	58
6	Tottenham H	38	15	12	11	60	46	57
7	Coventry C	38	14	13	11	47	42	55
8	Everton	38	14	12	12	50	45	54
9	QPR	38	14	11	13	43	37	53
10	Millwall	38	14	11	13	47	52	53
11	Manchester U	38	13	12	13	45	35	51
12	Wimbledon	38	14	9	15	50	46	51
13	Southampton	38	10	15	13	52	66	45
14	Charlton Ath	38	10	12	16	44	58	42
15	Sheffield W	38	10	12	16	34	51	42
16	Luton T	38	10	11	17	42	52	41
17	Aston Villa	38	9	13	16	45	56	40
18	Middlesbrough	38	9	12	17	44	61	39
19	West Ham U	38	10	8	20	37	62	38
20	Newcastle U	38	7	10	21	32	63	31

Season 1989-90

Football League Division One

DATE	OPPONENTS	SCORE	GOALSCORERS	ATTENDANCE
Aug 19	MANCHESTER CITY	W 3-1	Barnes (pen), Beardsley, Nicol	37,628
Aug 23	Aston Villa	D 1-1	Barnes	35,796
Aug 26	Luton Town	D 0-0		11,124
Sep 9	Derby County	W 3-0	Rush, Barnes (pen), Beardsley	20,034
Sep 12	CRYSTAL PALACE	W 9-0	Nicol 2, McMahon, Rush, Gillespie, Beardsley, Aldridge (pen), Barnes, Hysen	35,779
Sep 16	NORWICH CITY	D 0-0		36,885
Sep 23	Everton	W 3-1	Barnes, Rush 2	42,453
Oct 14	Wimbledon	W 2-1	Beardsley, Whelan	13,510
Oct 21	Southampton	L 1-4	Beardsley (pen)	20,501
Oct 29	TOTTENHAM HOTSPUR	W 1-0	Barnes	36,550
Nov 4	COVENTRY CITY	L 0-1		36,433
Nov 11	Queens Park Rangers	L 2-3	Barnes 2 (1 pen)	18,304
Nov 19	Millwall	W 2-1	Barnes, Rush	13,547
Nov 26	ARSENAL	W 2-1	McMahon, Barnes	35,983
Nov 29	Sheffield Wednesday	L 0-2		32,732
Dec 2	Manchester City	W 4-1	Rush 2, Beardsley, McMahon	31,641
Dec 9	ASTON VILLA	D 1-1	Beardsley	37,435
Dec 16	Chelsea	W 5-2	Beardsley, Rush 2, Houghton, McMahon	31,005
Dec 23	MANCHESTER UNITED	D 0-0		37,426
Dec 26	SHEFFIELD WEDNESDAY	W 2-1	Molby, Rush	37,488
Dec 30	CHARLTON ATHLETIC	W 1-0	Barnes	36,678
Jan 1	Nottingham Forest	D 2-2	Rush 2	24,518
Jan 13	LUTON TOWN	D 2-2	Barnes, Nicol	35,312
Jan 20	Crystal Palace	W 2-0	Rush, Beardsley	29,807
Feb 3	EVERTON	W 2-1	Barnes, Beardsley (pen)	38,730
Feb 10	Norwich City	D 0-0		20,210
Mar 3	MILLWALL	W 1-0	Gillespie	36,427
Mar 18	Manchester United	W 2-1	Barnes 2 (1 pen)	46,629
Mar 21	Tottenham Hotspur	L 0-1		25,656
Mar 31	SOUTHAMPTON	W 3-2	Barnes, Osman o.g., Rush	37,027
Apr 3	WIMBLEDON	W 2-1	Rush, Gillespie	33,319
Apr 11	Charlton Athletic	W 4-0	Rosenthal 3, Barnes	13,982
Apr 14	NOTTINGHAM FOREST	D 2-2	Rosenthal, McMahon	37,265
Apr 18	Arsenal	D 1-1	Barnes	33,395
Apr 21	CHELSEA	W 4-1	Rosenthal, Nicol 2, Rush	38,481
Apr 28	QUEENS PARK RANGERS	W 2-1	Rush, Barnes (pen)	37,758
May 1	DERBY COUNTY	W 1-0	Gillespie	38,038
May 5	Coventry City	W 6-1	Rush, Barnes 3, Rosenthal 2	23,204

FA Cup

Jan 6	Swansea City	(Rd3)	D 0-0		16,098
Jan 9	SWANSEA CITY	(R)	W 8-0	Barnes 2, Whelan, Rush 3, Beardsley, Nicol	29,194
Jan 28	Norwich City	(Rd4)	D 0-0		23,152
Jan 31	NORWICH CITY	(R)	W 3-1	Nicol, Barnes, Beardsley (pen)	29,339
Feb 17	SOUTHAMPTON	(Rd5)	W 3-0	Rush, Beardsley, Nicol	35,961
Mar 11	Queens Park Rangers	(Rd6)	D 2-2	Barnes, Rush	21,057
Mar 14	QUEENS PARK RANGERS	(R)	W 1-0	Beardsley	38,090
Apr 8	Crystal Palace	(SF)	L 3-4*	Rush, McMahon, Barnes (pen)	38,389

*After extra time. Score at 90 mins 3-3. Played at Villa Park.

League Cup (Littlewoods Cup)

Sep 19	WIGAN ATHLETIC	(Rd2/1L)	W 5-2	Hysen, Rush 2, Beardsley, Barnes	19,231
Oct 4	Wigan Athletic**	(Rd2/2L)	W 3-0	Staunton 3	17,954
Oct 25	Arsenal	(Rd3)	L 0-1		40,814

**Wigan opted to play at Anfield.

Charity Shield

Aug 12	Arsenal†	W 1-0	Beardsley	63,149

†Played at Wembley.

PLAYER/MANAGER: Kenny Dalglish **CAPTAIN:** Alan Hansen

TOP SCORER: John Barnes 28 (22 league)

BIGGEST WIN: 9-0, 12 September 1989, v Crystal Palace (H), Division One

HIGHEST ATTENDANCE: 63,149, 12 August 1989, v Arsenal, Charity Shield, Wembley

TRANSFERS IN: Glenn Hysen from Fiorentina, Ronnie Rosenthal from Standard Liege

TRANSFERS OUT: John Aldridge to Real Sociedad

League & Cup Appearances

PLAYER	LEAGUE	CUP COMPETITION		OTHER	TOTAL
		FA CUP	LC		
Ablett	13 (2)		1		14 (2)
Aldridge	0 (2)				0 (2)
Barnes	34	8	2	1	45
Beardsley	27 (2)	8	2 (1)	1	38 (3)
Burrows	23 (3)	2 (1)	3	1	29 (4)
Dalglish	0 (1)				0 (1)
Gillespie	11 (2)	1 (1)	1		13 (3)
Grobbelaar	38	8	3	1	50
Hansen	31	8	2	1	42
Houghton	16 (3)	3 (1)	2		21 (4)
Hysen	35	8	2	1	46
Marsh	0 (2)				0 (2)
McMahon	37 (1)	8	2	1	48 (1)
Molby	12 (5)		2 (1)		14 (6)
Nicol	21 (2)	7	2	1	31 (2)
Rosenthal	5 (3)				5 (3)
Rush	36	8	3	1	48
Staunton	18 (2)	4 (2)	0 (2)		22 (6)
Tanner	2 (2)				2 (2)
Venison	25	7 (1)	2 (1)	1	35 (2)
Watson			1		1
Whelan	34	8	3	1	46

Goalscorers

PLAYER	LEAGUE	CUP COMPETITION		OTHER	TOTAL
		FA CUP	LC		
Barnes	22	5	1		28
Rush	18	6	2		26
Beardsley	10	4	1	1	16
Nicol	6	3			9
Rosenthal	7				7
McMahon	5	1			6
Gillespie	4				4
Staunton			3		3
Hysen	1		1		2
Whelan	1	1			2
Aldridge	1				1
Houghton	1				1
Molby	1				1
Opps' o.gs.	1				1

Fact File

Liverpool win a record 18th League championship. The 9-0 win against Crystal Palace on 12 September saw eight outfield players scoring goals – this was a record in English football.

Final Division One Table

	P	W	D	L	F	A	PTS
1 Liverpool	38	23	10	5	78	37	79
2 Aston Villa	38	21	7	10	57	38	70
3 Tottenham H	38	19	6	13	59	47	63
4 Arsenal	38	18	8	12	54	38	62
5 Chelsea	38	16	12	10	58	50	60
6 Everton	38	17	8	13	57	46	59
7 Southampton	38	15	10	13	71	63	55
8 Wimbledon	38	13	16	9	47	40	55
9 Nottingham F	38	15	9	14	55	47	54
10 Norwich City	38	13	14	11	44	42	53
11 QPR	38	13	11	14	45	44	50
12 Coventry City	38	14	7	17	39	59	49
13 Manchester U	38	13	9	16	46	47	48
14 Manchester C	38	12	12	14	43	52	48
15 Crystal P	38	13	9	16	42	66	48
16 Derby C	38	13	7	18	43	40	46
17 Luton T	38	10	13	15	43	57	43
18 Sheffield W	38	11	10	17	35	51	43
19 Charlton Ath	38	7	9	22	31	57	30
20 Millwall	38	5	11	22	39	65	26

Season 1990-91

Football League Division One

DATE	OPPONENTS	SCORE	GOALSCORERS	ATTENDANCE
Aug 25	Sheffield United	W 3-1	Barnes, Houghton, Rush	27,009
Aug 28	NOTTINGHAM FOREST	W 2-0	Rush, Beardsley	33,633
Sep 1	ASTON VILLA	W 2-1	Beardsley, Barnes	38,061
Sep 8	Wimbledon	W 2-1	Barnes, Whelan	12,364
Sep 16	MANCHESTER UNITED	W 4-0	Beardsley 3, Barnes	35,726
Sep 22	Everton	W 3-2	Beardsley 2, Barnes (pen)	39,847
Sep 29	Sunderland	W 1-0	Houghton	31,107
Oct 6	DERBY COUNTY	W 2-0	Houghton, Beardsley	37,036
Oct 20	Norwich City	D 1-1	Gillespie	21,275
Oct 27	CHELSEA	W 2-0	Rush, Nicol	38,463
Nov 4	Tottenham Hotspur	W 3-1	Rush 2, Beardsley	35,033
Nov 10	LUTON TOWN	W 4-0	Rush 2, Molby (pen), Beardsley	35,207
Nov 17	Coventry City	W 1-0	Beardsley	22,571
Nov 24	MANCHESTER CITY	D 2-2	Rush, Rosenthal	37,849
Dec 2	Arsenal	L 0-3		40,419
Dec 15	SHEFFIELD UNITED	W 2-0	Barnes, Rush	33,516
Dec 22	SOUTHAMPTON	W 3-2	Rosenthal 2, Houghton	31,894
Dec 26	Queens Park Rangers	D 1-1	Barnes	17,848
Dec 30	Crystal Palace	L 0-1		26,280
Jan 1	LEEDS UNITED	W 3-0	Barnes, Rosenthal, Rush	36,975
Jan 12	Aston Villa	D 0-0		40,026
Jan 19	WIMBLEDON	D 1-1	Barnes	35,030
Feb 3	Manchester United	D 1-1	Speedie	43,690
Feb 9	EVERTON	W 3-1	Molby, Speedie 2	38,129
Feb 23	Luton Town	L 1-3	Molby (pen)	12,032
Mar 3	ARSENAL	L 0-1		37,221
Mar 9	Manchester City	W 3-0	Molby 2 (both pens), Barnes	35,150
Mar 16	SUNDERLAND	W 2-1	Rush, Owers o.g.	37,582
Mar 23	Derby County	W 7-1	Molby (pen), Barnes 2, Rush, Nicol 2, Houghton	20,531
Mar 30	QUEENS PARK RANGERS	L 1-3	Molby (pen)	37,251
Apr 1	Southampton	L 0-1		20,255
Apr 9	COVENTRY CITY	D 1-1	Rush	31,063
Apr 13	Leeds United	W 5-4	Houghton, Molby (pen), Speedie, Barnes 2	31,460
Apr 20	NORWICH CITY	W 3-0	Barnes, Houghton, Rush	37,065
Apr 23	CRYSTAL PALACE	W 3-0	Rush, Barnes, McGoldrick o.g.	36,767
May 4	Chelsea	L 2-4	Speedie, Rosenthal	32,266
May 6	Nottingham Forest	L 1-2	Molby (pen)	26,151
May 11	TOTTENHAM HOTSPUR	W 2-0	Rush, Speedie	36,192

FA Cup

Jan 5	Blackburn Rovers	(Rd3) D 1-1	Atkins o.g.	18,524
Jan 8	BLACKBURN ROVERS	(R) W 3-0	Houghton, Rush, Staunton	34,175
Jan 26	BRIGHTON & HOVE ALBION	(Rd4) D 2-2	Rush 2	32,670
Jan 30	Brighton & Hove Albion	(R) W 3-2*	McMahon 2, Rush	14,392
Feb 17	EVERTON	(Rd5) D 0-0		38,323
Feb 20	Everton	(R) D 4-4**	Beardsley 2, Rush, Barnes	37,766
Feb 27	Everton	(2nd R) L 0-1		40,201

*After extra time. Score at 90 mins 1-1. **After extra time. Score at 90 mins 3-3.

League Cup (Rumbelows Cup)

Sep 25	CREWE ALEXANDRA	(Rd2/1L) W 5-1	McMahon, Gillespie, Houghton, Rush 2	17,228
Oct 9	Crewe Alexandra	(Rd2/2L) W 4-1	Rush 3, Staunton	7,200
Oct 31	Manchester United	(Rd3) L 1-3	Houghton	42,033

Charity Shield

Aug 18	Manchester United†	D 1-1	Barnes	66,558

†Played at Wembley.

MANAGER: Kenny Dalglish (resigned in February), Graeme Souness
CAPTAIN: Ronnie Whelan/Steve Nicol
TOP SCORER: Ian Rush 26 (16 league)
BIGGEST WIN: 7-1, 23 March 1991, v Derby County (A), Division One
HIGHEST ATTENDANCE: 66,558, 18 August 1990, v Manchester United (Wembley), Charity Shield
TRANSFERS IN: David Speedie from Coventry City, Jimmy Carter from Millwall
TRANSFERS OUT: Peter Beardsley to Everton, Steve Staunton to Aston Villa, Alan Hansen – retired

League & Cup Appearances

PLAYER	LEAGUE	CUP COMPETITION		OTHER	TOTAL
		FA CUP	LC		
Ablett	23	5 (1)	1	1	30 (1)
Barnes	35	7	2	1	45
Beardsley	24 (3)	2 (3)	2	1	29 (6)
Burrows	34 (1)	5	3	1	43 (1)
Carter	2 (3)	2			4 (3)
Gillespie	30	2	3		35
Grobbelaar	31	7	3	1	42
Hooper	7				7
Houghton	31 (1)	3	3	1	38 (1)
Hysen	32	5	2	1	40
Marsh	1 (1)		1		2 (1)
McMahon	22	4	2	1	29
McManaman	0 (2)	0 (1)			0 (3)
Molby	22 (3)	5 (2)	1 (1)		28 (6)
Nicol	35	7	2		44
Rosenthal	4 (12)	3	0 (3)	0 (1)	7 (16)
Rush	37	7	3	1	48
Speedie	8 (4)	1 (1)			9 (5)
Staunton	20 (4)	7	2		29 (4)
Venison	6	4 (1)	2	1	13 (1)
Whelan	14	1	1	1	17

Goalscorers

PLAYER	LEAGUE	CUP COMPETITION		OTHER	TOTAL
		FA CUP	LC		
Rush	16	5	5		26
Barnes	16	1		1	18
Beardsley	11	2			13
Houghton	7	1	2		10
Molby	9				9
Speedie	6				6
Rosenthal	5				5
McMahon		2	1		3
Nicol	3				3
Gillespie	1		1		2
Staunton		1	1		2
Whelan	1				1
Opps' o.gs.	2	1			3

Fact File

Alan Hansen retired in March after 13 seasons. He scored 14 goals in his 620 games and is second only to Phil Neal (20) in winning 19 medals comprising 8 league championships, two FA Cups, three League Cups, three European Cups and three runners-up medals.

Final Division One Table

		P	W	D	L	F	A	Pts
1	Arsenal	38	24	13	1	74	18	83
2	Liverpool	38	23	7	8	77	40	76
3	Crystal Palace	38	20	9	9	50	41	69
4	Leeds U	38	19	7	12	65	47	64
5	Manchester C	38	17	11	10	64	53	62
6	Manchester U	38	16	12	10	58	45	59
7	Wimbledon	38	14	14	10	53	46	56
8	Nottingham F	38	14	12	12	65	50	54
9	Everton	38	13	12	13	50	46	51
10	Tottenham H	38	11	16	11	51	50	49
11	Chelsea	38	13	10	15	58	69	49
12	QPR	38	12	10	16	44	53	46
13	Sheffield U	38	13	7	18	36	55	46
14	Southampton	38	12	9	17	58	69	45
15	Norwich C	38	13	6	19	41	64	45
16	Coventry C	38	11	11	16	42	49	44
17	Aston Villa	38	9	14	15	46	58	41
18	Luton T	38	10	7	21	42	61	37
19	Sunderland	38	8	10	20	38	60	34
20	Derby Co	38	5	9	24	37	75	24

Arsenal had two points deducted; Manchester United had one point deducted for disciplinary reasons.

Season 1991-92

Football League Division One

DATE	OPPONENTS	SCORE	GOALSCORERS	ATTENDANCE
Aug 17	OLDHAM ATHLETIC	W 2-1	Houghton, Barnes	38,841
Aug 21	Manchester City	L 1-2	McManaman	37,322
Aug 24	Luton Town	D 0-0		11,132
Aug 27	QUEENS PARK RANGERS	W 1-0	Saunders	32,700
Aug 31	EVERTON	W 3-1	Burrows, Saunders, Houghton	39,072
Sep 7	Notts County	W 2-1	Rosenthal, Walters (pen)	16,051
Sep 14	ASTON VILLA	D 1-1	Walters (pen)	38,400
Sep 21	Leeds United	L 0-1		32,917
Sep 28	SHEFFIELD WEDNESDAY	D 1-1	Houghton	37,071
Oct 6	Manchester United	D 0-0		44,997
Oct 19	Chelsea	D 2-2	McManaman, Rush	30,230
Oct 26	COVENTRY CITY	W 1-0	Houghton	33,339
Nov 2	CRYSTAL PALACE	L 1-2	Hysen	34,231
Nov 17	West Ham United	D 0-0		23,569
Nov 23	Wimbledon	D 0-0		13,373
Nov 30	NORWICH CITY	W 2-1	Molby, Houghton	34,881
Dec 7	Southampton	D 1-1	Redknapp	19,503
Dec 14	NOTTINGHAM FOREST	W 2-0	McMahon, Molby	35,285
Dec 18	Tottenham Hotspur	W 2-1	Saunders, Houghton	27,434
Dec 21	MANCHESTER CITY	D 2-2	Saunders, Nicol	36,743
Dec 26	Queens Park Rangers	D 0-0		21,693
Dec 28	Everton	D 1-1	Tanner	37,681
Jan 1	SHEFFIELD UNITED	W 2-1	Houghton, Saunders	35,993
Jan 11	LUTON TOWN	W 2-1	McManaman, Saunders	35,095
Jan 18	Oldham Athletic	W 3-2	McManaman, Saunders, Thomas	18,952
Jan 29	ARSENAL	W 2-0	Molby (pen), Houghton	33,753
Feb 1	CHELSEA	L 1-2	Rosenthal	38,681
Feb 8	Coventry City	D 0-0		21,540
Feb 22	Norwich City	L 0-3		20,411
Feb 29	SOUTHAMPTON	D 0-0		34,449
Mar 11	WEST HAM UNITED	W 1-0	Saunders	30,821
Mar 14	Crystal Palace	L 0-1		23,680
Mar 21	TOTTENHAM HOTSPUR	W 2-1	Saunders 2	36,968
Mar 28	Sheffield United	L 0-2		26,943
Mar 31	NOTTS COUNTY	W 4-0	Thomas, McManaman, Rush, Venison	25,457
Apr 8	WIMBLEDON	L 2-3	Thomas, Rosenthal	26,134
Apr 11	Aston Villa	L 0-1		35,755
Apr 18	LEEDS UNITED	D 0-0		37,186
Apr 20	Arsenal	L 0-4		38,517
Apr 22	Nottingham Forest	D 1-1	Rush	23,787
Apr 26	MANCHESTER UNITED	W 2-0	Rush, Walters	38,669
May 2	Sheffield Wednesday	D 0-0		34,861

FA Cup

Jan 6	Crewe Alexandra	(Rd3)	W 4-0	McMahon, Barnes 3 (1 pen)	7,400
Feb 5	Bristol Rovers	(Rd4)	D 1-1	Saunders	9,464
Feb 11	BRISTOL ROVERS	(R)	W 2-1	McManaman, Saunders	30,142
Feb 16	Ipswich Town	(Rd5)	D 0-0		26,140
Feb 26	IPSWICH TOWN	(R)	W 3-2*	Houghton, Molby, McManaman	27,335
Mar 8	ASTON VILLA	(Rd6)	W 1-0	Thomas	29,109
Apr 5	Portsmouth	(SF)	D 1-1**	Whelan	41,869
Apr 13	Portsmouth	(R)	D 0-0†		40,077
May 9	Sunderland††	(F)	W 2-0	Thomas, Rush	79,544

*After extra time. Score at 90 mins 1-1.
**After extra time. Score at 90 mins 0-0. Played at Highbury.
†After extra time. Liverpool win 3-1 on penalties. Scorers: Barnes, Rush, Saunders.
††Played at Wembley.

Rumbelows Cup

Sep 25	STOKE CITY	(Rd2/1L)	D 2-2	Rush 2	18,389
Oct 9	Stoke City	(Rd2/2L)	W 3-2	McManaman, Saunders, Walters	22,335
Oct 29	PORT VALE	(Rd3)	D 2-2	McManaman, Rush	21,553
Nov 20	Port Vale	(R)	W 4-1	McManaman, Walters, Houghton, Saunders	18,725
Dec 3	Peterborough	(Rd4)	L 0-1		14,114

UEFA Cup

Sep 18	KUUSYSI LAHTI	(Rd1/1L)	W 6-1	Saunders 4, Houghton 2	17,131
Oct 2	Kuusysi Lahti	(Rd1/2L)	L 0-1		8,435
Oct 23	Auxerre	(Rd2/1L)	L 0-2		16,500
Nov 6	AUXERRE	(Rd2/2L)	W 3-0	Molby (pen), Marsh, Walters	23,094
Nov 27	Swarovski Tyrol	(Rd3/1L)	W 2-0	Saunders 2	12,500
Dec 11	SWAROVSKI TYROL	(Rd3/2L)	W 4-0	Saunders 3, Venison	16,007
Mar 4	Genoa	(Rd4/1L)	L 0-2		40,000
Mar 18	GENOA	(Rd4/2L)	L 1-2	Rush	38,840

League & Cup Appearances

PLAYER	LEAGUE	CUP COMPETITION			TOTAL
		FA CUP	LC	UEFA	
Ablett	13 (1)		2 (1)	6	21 (2)
Barnes	12	4		1	17
Burrows	30	6	5	7	48
Carter				0 (1)	0 (1)
Grobbelaar	37	9	4	5	55
Harkness	7 (4)	1	2 (1)	3 (1)	13 (6)
Hooper	5		1	3	9
Houghton	36	8	3	4	51
Hutchison	0 (3)				0 (3)
Hysen	3 (2)		2		5 (2)
Jones B				0 (1)	0 (1)
Jones R	28	9		2	39
Kozma	3 (2)	0 (2)			3 (4)
Marsh	19 (15)	4 (2)	3 (1)	7 (1)	33 (19)
McMahon	15		4	5	24
McManaman	26 (4)	8	5	8	47 (4)
Molby	25 (1)	5 (1)	3	5	38 (2)
Nicol	34	8	3	7	52
Redknapp	5 (1)	2		1 (1)	8 (2)
Rosenthal	7 (13)	1 (2)	0 (3)	1	9 (18)
Rush	16 (2)	4 (1)	3	5	28 (3)
Saunders	36	8	5	5	54
Tanner	32	2	5	5 (1)	44 (1)
Thomas	16 (1)	5			21 (1)
Venison	9 (4)	1 (2)		0 (3)	10 (9)
Walters	18 (7)	2 (1)	4	4 (1)	28 (9)
Whelan	9 (1)	3			12 (1)
Wright	21	9	1	4	35

Goalscorers

PLAYER	LEAGUE	CUP COMPETITION			TOTAL
		FA CUP	LC	UEFA	
Saunders	10	2 (1)	2	9	23 (1)
Houghton	8	1	1	2	12
McManaman	5	3	3		11
Rush	4	1 (1)	3	1	9 (1)
Walters	3		2	1	6
Molby	3	1		1	5
Thomas	3	2			5
Barnes	1	3 (1)			4 (1)
Rosenthal	3				3
Venison	1			1	2
Burrows	1				1
Hysen	1				1
Marsh				1	1
McMahon	1				1
Nicol	1				1
Redknapp	1				1
Tanner	1				1
Whelan	1				1

Penalty shoot-out goals in brackets.

Final Division One Table

	P	W	D	L	F	A	Pts
1 Leeds U	42	22	16	4	74	37	82
2 Manchester U	42	21	15	6	63	33	78
3 Sheffield W	42	21	12	9	62	49	75
4 Arsenal	42	19	15	8	81	46	72
5 Manchester C	42	20	10	12	61	48	70
6 Liverpool	42	16	16	10	47	40	64
7 Aston Villa	42	17	9	16	48	44	60
8 Nottingham F	42	16	11	15	60	58	59
9 Sheffield U	42	16	9	17	65	63	57
10 Crystal Palace	42	14	15	13	53	61	57
11 QPR	42	12	18	12	48	47	54
12 Everton	42	13	14	15	52	51	53
13 Wimbledon	42	13	14	15	53	53	53
14 Chelsea	42	13	14	15	50	60	53
15 Tottenham H	42	15	7	20	58	63	52
16 Southampton	42	14	10	18	39	55	52
17 Oldham Ath	42	14	9	19	63	67	51
18 Norwich C	42	11	12	19	47	63	45
19 Coventry C	42	11	11	20	35	44	44
20 Luton T	42	10	12	20	38	71	42
21 Notts Co	42	10	10	22	40	62	40
22 West Ham U	42	9	11	22	37	59	38

Season 1992-93

FA Premier League

DATE	OPPONENTS	SCORE	GOALSCORERS	ATTENDANCE
Aug 16	Nottingham Forest	L 0-1		20,038
Aug 19	SHEFFIELD UNITED	W 2-1	Walters, Stewart	33,107
Aug 23	ARSENAL	L 0-2		34,961
Aug 25	Ipswich Town	D 2-2	Walters, Molby (pen)	20,109
Aug 29	Leeds United	D 2-2	Whelan, Molby (pen)	29,597
Sep 1	SOUTHAMPTON	D 1-1	Wright	30,024
Sep 5	CHELSEA	W 2-1	Saunders, Redknapp	34,199
Sep 12	Sheffield United	L 0-1		20,632
Sep 19	Aston Villa	L 2-4	Walters, Rosenthal	37,863
Sep 26	WIMBLEDON	L 2-3	Molby (pen), McManaman	29,574
Oct 3	SHEFFIELD WEDNESDAY	W 1-0	Hutchison	35,785
Oct 18	Manchester United	D 2-2	Hutchison, Rush	33,243
Oct 25	NORWICH CITY	W 4-1	Thomas, Hutchison, Burrows, Walters (pen)	36,318
Oct 31	Tottenham Hotspur	L 0-2		32,917
Nov 7	MIDDLESBROUGH	W 4-1	Rosenthal 2, McManaman, Rush	34,974
Nov 23	Queens Park Rangers	W 1-0	Rosenthal	21,056
Nov 28	CRYSTAL PALACE	W 5-0	McManaman 2, Marsh, Rosenthal, Hutchison	36,380
Dec 7	Everton	L 1-2	Wright	35,826
Dec 13	BLACKBURN ROVERS	W 2-1	Walters 2	43,668
Dec 19	Coventry City	L 1-5	Redknapp	19,779
Dec 28	MANCHESTER CITY	D 1-1	Rush	43,037
Jan 9	ASTON VILLA	L 1-2	Barnes	40,826
Jan 16	Wimbledon	L 0-2		11,294
Jan 31	Arsenal	W 1-0	Barnes (pen)	27,580
Feb 6	NOTTINGHAM FOREST	D 0-0		40,463
Feb 10	Chelsea	D 0-0		20,981
Feb 13	Southampton	L 1-2	Hutchison	17,216
Feb 20	IPSWICH TOWN	D 0-0		36,680
Feb 27	Sheffield Wednesday	D 1-1	Hutchison	33,964
Mar 6	MANCHESTER UNITED	L 1-2	Rush	44,374
Mar 10	QUEENS PARK RANGERS	W 1-0	Rush	30,370
Mar 13	Middlesbrough	W 2-1	Hutchison, Rush	22,463
Mar 20	EVERTON	W 1-0	Rosenthal	44,619
Mar 23	Crystal Palace	D 1-1	Rush	18,688
Apr 3	Blackburn Rovers	L 1-4	Rush	15,032
Apr 10	OLDHAM ATHLETIC	W 1-0	Rush	36,129
Apr 12	Manchester City	D 1-1	Rush	28,098
Apr 17	COVENTRY CITY	W 4-0	Walters 3 (1 pen), Burrows	33,328
Apr 21	LEEDS UNITED	W 2-0	Barnes, Walters (pen)	34,992
May 1	Norwich City	L 0-1		20,610
May 5	Oldham Athletic	L 2-3	Rush 2	15,381
May 8	TOTTENHAM HOTSPUR	W 6-2	Rush 2, Barnes 2, Harkness, Walters (pen)	43,385

FA Cup

Jan 3	Bolton Wanderers	(Rd3)	D 2-2	Winstanley o.g., Rush	21,502
Jan 13	BOLTON WANDERERS	(R)	L 0-2		34,790

League Cup (Coca-Cola Cup)

Sep 29	CHESTERFIELD	(Rd2/1L)	D 4-4	Rosenthal, Hutchison, Walters, Wright	12,533
Oct 6	Chesterfield	(Rd2/2L)	W 4-1	Hutchison, Redknapp, Walters, Rush	10,632
Oct 28	Sheffield United	(Rd3)	D 0-0		17,856
Nov 11	SHEFFIELD UNITED	(R)	W 3-0	McManaman 2, Marsh (pen)	17,654
Dec 1	CRYSTAL PALACE	(Rd4)	D 1-1	Marsh (pen)	18,525
Dec 16	Crystal Palace	(R)	L 1-2	Marsh (pen)	19,622

European Cup-Winners' Cup

Sep 16	APOLLON LIMASSOL	(Rd1/1L)	W 6-1	Stewart 2, Rush 4	12,769
Sep 29	Apollon Limassol	(Rd1/2L)	W 2-1	Rush, Hutchison	8,000
Oct 22	Spartak Moscow	(Rd2/1L)	L 2-4	Wright, McManaman	60,000
Nov 4	SPARTAK MOSCOW	(Rd2/2L)	L 0-2		37,993

Charity Shield

Aug 8	Leeds United	L 3-4*	Rush, Saunders, o.g.	61,201

*Played at Wembley.

MANAGER: Graeme Souness **CAPTAIN:** Mark Wright

TOP SCORER: Ian Rush 22 (14 League)

TRANSFERS IN: Paul Stewart from Tottenham Hotspur, Torben Piechnik from FC Copenhagen, Stig Inge Bjornebye from Rosenborg, Istvan Kozma from Dunfermline, David James from Watford

TRANSFERS OUT: Dean Saunders to Aston Villa

League & Cup Appearances

PLAYER	LEAGUE	CUP COMPETITION			OTHER	TOTAL
		FA CUP	LC	ECWC		
Barnes	26 (1)	2	2			30 (1)
Bjornebyel	11	2				13
Burrows	29 (1)		5	4	1	39 (1)
Charnock			1	0 (1)		1 (1)
Grobbelaar	5		2	2	1	10
Harkness	9 (1)			1 (1)		10 (2)
Hooper	8 (1)	2	3	1		14 (1)
Hutchison	27 (4)	1 (1)	5	3	0 (1)	36 (6)
James	29		1	1		31
Jones	30	2	2 (1)	2		36 (1)
Kozma	0 (1)		0 (1)		0 (1)	0 (3)
Marsh	22 (6)	2	6	4	1	35 (6)
McManaman	27 (4)	1	5	3		36 (4)
Molby	8 (2)		1	2		11 (2)
Nicol	32	1	4	2		39
Piechnik	15 (1)	2	5			22 (1)
Redknapp	27 (2)	1	6	4		38 (2)
Rosenthal	16 (11)	1 (1)	2 (1)	0 (3)	1	20 (16)
Rush	31 (1)	1	4	4	1	41 (1)
Saunders	6				1	7
Stewart	21 (3)	1	3	2	1	28 (3)
Tanner	2 (2)		1 (2)	1 (1)	1	5 (5)
Thomas	6 (2)	2	1	2		11 (2)
Walters	26 (8)	1	5	3	1	36 (8)
Whelan	17				1	18
Wright	32 (1)		2 (2)	3	1	38 (3)

Goalscorers

PLAYER	LEAGUE	CUP COMPETITION			OTHER	TOTAL
		FA CUP	LC	ECWC		
Rush	14	1	1	5	1	22
Walters	11		2			13
Hutchison	7		2	1		10
McManaman	4		2	1		7
Rosenthal	6		1			7
Barnes	5					5
Marsh	1		3			4
Wright	2		1	1		4
Molby	3					3
Redknapp	2		1			3
Stewart	1			2		3
Burrows	2					2
Saunders	1				1	2
Harkness	1					1
Thomas	1					1
Whelan	1					1
Opps' o.gs.		1			1	2

Fact File

Ian Rush's four goals on 16 September 1992 and one on 29 September 1992 v Apollon Limassol made him the leading club goalscorer in the three European competitions with 20 goals.

Final Premier League Table

		P	W	D	L	F	A	Pts
1	Manchester U	42	24	12	6	67	31	84
2	Aston Villa	42	21	11	10	57	40	74
3	Norwich C	42	21	9	12	61	65	72
4	Blackburn R	42	20	11	11	68	46	71
5	QPR	42	17	12	13	63	55	63
6	Liverpool	42	16	11	15	62	55	59
7	Sheffield W	42	15	14	13	55	51	59
8	Tottenham H	42	16	11	15	60	66	59
9	Manchester C	42	15	12	15	56	51	57
10	Arsenal	42	15	11	16	40	38	56
11	Chelsea	42	14	14	14	51	54	56
12	Wimbledon	42	14	12	16	56	55	54
13	Everton	42	15	8	19	53	55	53
14	Sheffield U	42	14	10	18	54	53	52
15	Coventry C	42	13	13	16	52	57	52
16	Ipswich T	42	12	16	14	50	55	52
17	Leeds U	42	12	15	15	57	62	51
18	Southampton	42	13	11	18	54	61	50
19	Oldham Ath	42	13	10	19	63	74	49
20	Crystal Palace	42	11	16	15	48	61	49
21	Middlesbrough	42	11	11	20	54	75	44
22	Nottingham F	42	10	10	22	41	62	40

Season 1993-94

FA Premier League

DATE	OPPONENTS	SCORE	GOALSCORERS	ATTENDANCE
Aug 14	SHEFFIELD WEDNESDAY	W 2-0	Clough 2	44,004
Aug 18	Queens Park Rangers	W 3-1	Nicol, Clough, Rush	19,635
Aug 22	Swindon Town	W 5-0	Ruddock, Whelan, McManaman 2, Marsh	17,017
Aug 25	TOTTENHAM HOTSPUR	L 1-2	Clough	42,456
Aug 28	LEEDS UNITED	W 2-0	Molby (pen), Rush	44,068
Sep 1	Coventry City	L 0-1		16,740
Sep 12	BLACKBURN ROVERS	L 0-1		37,355
Sep 18	Everton	L 0-2		38,157
Sep 25	Chelsea	L 0-1		31,271
Oct 2	ARSENAL	D 0-0		42,750
Oct 16	OLDHAM ATHLETIC	W 2-1	Fowler, Barlow o.g.	32,661
Oct 23	Manchester City	D 1-1	Rush	30,403
Oct 30	SOUTHAMPTON	W 4-2	Rush, Fowler 3	32,818
Nov 6	WEST HAM UNITED	W 2-0	Clough, Martin o.g.	42,254
Nov 21	Newcastle United	L 0-3		36,374
Nov 28	ASTON VILLA	W 2-1	Redknapp, Fowler	38,484
Dec 4	Sheffield Wednesday	L 1-3	Fowler	32,177
Dec 8	QUEENS PARK RANGERS	W 3-2	Molby (pen), Barnes, Rush	24,561
Dec 11	SWINDON TOWN	D 2-2	Wright, Barnes	32,739
Dec 18	Tottenham Hotspur	D 3-3	Redknapp, Fowler 2 (1 pen)	31,394
Dec 26	Sheffield United	D 0-0		22,932
Dec 28	WIMBLEDON	D 1-1	Scales o.g.	32,232
Jan 1	Ipswich Town	W 2-1	Ruddock, Rush	22,355
Jan 4	MANCHESTER UNITED	D 3-3	Ruddock, Clough 2	42,795
Jan 15	Oldham Athletic	W 3-0	Dicks, Redknapp, Fowler	14,573
Jan 22	MANCHESTER CITY	W 2-1	Rush 2	41,872
Feb 5	Norwich City	D 2-2	Barnes, Culverhouse o.g.	19,746
Feb 14	Southampton	L 2-4	Dicks (pen), Rush	18,306
Feb 19	Leeds United	L 0-2		40,053
Feb 26	COVENTRY CITY	W 1-0	Rush	38,547
Mar 5	Blackburn Rovers	L 0-2		20,831
Mar 13	EVERTON	W 2-1	Rush, Fowler	44,281
Mar 19	CHELSEA	W 2-1	Rush, Burley o.g.	38,629
Mar 26	Arsenal	L 0-1		35,556
Mar 30	Manchester United	L 0-1		44,751
Apr 2	SHEFFIELD UNITED	L 1-2	Rush	36,642
Apr 4	Wimbledon	D 1-1	Redknapp	13,819
Apr 9	IPSWICH TOWN	W 1-0	Dicks (pen)	30,485
Apr 16	NEWCASTLE UNITED	L 0-2		44,601
Apr 23	West Ham United	W 2-1	Rush, Fowler	26,096
Apr 30	Norwich City	L 0-1		44,339
May 7	Aston Villa	L 1-2	Fowler	45,347

FA Cup

Jan 19	Bristol City	(Rd3)	D 1-1	Rush	21,718
Jan 25	BRISTOL CITY	(R)	L 0-1		36,720

League Cup (Coca-Cola Cup)

Sep 22	Fulham	(Rd2/1L)	W 3-1	Clough, Fowler, Rush	13,599
Oct 5	FULHAM	(Rd2/2L)	W 5-0	Fowler 5	12,541
Oct 27	IPSWICH TOWN	(Rd3)	W 3-2	Rush 3	19,058
Dec 1	WIMBLEDON	(Rd4)	D 1-1	Molby (pen)	19,290
Dec 14	Wimbledon	(R)	D 2-2*	Ruddock, Segars o.g.	11,343

*After extra time. Score at 90 mins 2-2. Liverpool lost 3-4 on penalties. Scorers: Ruddock, Barnes, Fowler.

MANAGER: Graeme Souness; Roy Evans from February

CAPTAIN: Ian Rush

TOP SCORER: Ian Rush 19 (14 league)

BIGGEST WIN: 5-0, 22 August 1993, v Swindon Town (A) Premier League; 5 October 1993, v Fulham, Coca-Cola Cup

HIGHEST ATTENDANCE: 45,374, 7 May 1994, v Aston Villa (A), Premier League

TRANSFERS IN: Nigel Clough from Nottingham Forest, Neil Ruddock from Tottenham Hotspur, Julian Dicks from West Ham United

TRANSFERS OUT: Ronnie Rosenthal to Tottenham Hotspur, Mike Hooper to Newcastle United, David Burrows to West Ham United, Istvan Kozma to Ujpest Te, Bruce Grobbelaar to Southampton, Torben Piechnik to AGF Aahus, Don Hutchison to West Ham United

League & Cup Appearances

PLAYER	LEAGUE	CUP COMPETITION FA CUP	LC	TOTAL
Barnes	24 (2)	2	2	28 (2)
Bjornebye	6 (3)	0 (1)		6 (4)
Burrows	3 (1)			3 (1)
Clough	25 (2)	2	2	29 (2)
Dicks	24	1	3	28
Fowler	27 (1)	1	5	33 (1)
Grobbelaar	29	2	5	36
Harkness	10 (1)	1	2 (1)	13 (2)
Hutchison	6 (5)	0 (1)	2 (1)	8 (7)
James D	13 (1)			13 (1)
Jones R	38	2	5	45
Marsh	0 (2)			0 (2)
Matteo	11		2	13
McManaman	29 (1)	2	1 (1)	32 (2)
Molby	11		2	13
Nicol	27 (4)	2	2	31 (4)
Piechnik	1			1
Redknapp	29 (6)	2	4	35 (6)
Rosenthal	0 (3)			0 (3)
Ruddock	39	2	5	46
Rush	41 (1)	2	5	48 (1)
Stewart	7 (1)		3	10 (1)
Thomas	1 (6)			1 (6)
Walters	7 (10)	1	0 (2)	8 (12)
Whelan	23			23
Wright	31		5	36

Goalscorers

PLAYER	LEAGUE	CUP COMPETITION FA CUP	LC	TOTAL
Rush	14	1	4	19
Fowler	12		6 (1)	18 (1)
Clough	7		1	8
Redknapp	4			4
Ruddock	3		1 (1)	4 (1)
Barnes	3		(1)	3 (1)
Dicks	3			3
Molby	2		1	3
McManaman	2			2
Marsh	1			1
Nicol	1			1
Whelan	1			1
Wright	1			1
Opps' o.gs.	5		1	6

Penalty shoot-out goals in brackets.

Fact File

Robbie Fowler became the fourth player to score five goals in a competitive game, v Fulham on 5 October 1993, 10 years after Ian Rush did the same thing in a league game v Luton Town.

Final Premier League Table

		P	W	D	L	F	A	Pts
1	Manchester U	42	27	11	4	80	38	92
2	Blackburn R	42	25	9	8	63	36	84
3	Newcastle U	42	23	8	11	82	41	77
4	Arsenal	42	18	17	7	53	28	71
5	Leeds U	42	18	16	8	65	39	70
6	Wimbledon	42	18	11	13	56	53	65
7	Sheffield W	42	16	16	10	76	54	64
8	Liverpool	42	17	9	16	59	55	60
9	QPR	42	16	12	14	62	61	60
10	Aston Villa	42	15	12	15	46	50	57
11	Coventry C	42	14	14	14	43	45	56
12	Norwich C	42	12	17	13	65	61	53
13	West Ham U	42	13	13	16	47	58	52
14	Chelsea	42	13	12	17	49	53	51
15	Tottenham H	42	11	12	19	54	59	45
16	Manchester C	42	9	18	15	38	49	45
17	Everton	42	12	8	22	42	63	44
18	Southampton	42	12	7	23	49	66	43
19	Ipswich T	42	9	16	17	35	58	43
20	Sheffield U	42	8	18	16	42	60	42
21	Oldham Ath	42	9	13	20	42	68	40
22	Swindon T	42	5	15	22	47	100	30

Season 1994-95

FA Premier League

DATE	OPPONENTS	SCORE	GOALSCORERS	ATTENDANCE
Aug 20	Crystal Palace	W 6-1	Rush 2, Molby (pen), McManaman 2, Fowler	18,084
Aug 28	ARSENAL	W 3-0	Fowler 3	30,017
Aug 31	Southampton	W 2-0	Barnes, Fowler	15,190
Sep 10	WEST HAM UNITED	D 0-0		30,907
Sep 17	Manchester United	L 0-2		43,740
Sep 24	Newcastle United	D 1-1	Rush	34,435
Oct 1	SHEFFIELD WEDNESDAY	W 4-1	Rush, McManaman 2, Walker o.g.	31,493
Oct 8	ASTON VILLA	W 3-2	Fowler 2, Ruddock	32,158
Oct 15	Blackburn Rovers	L 2-3	Barnes, Fowler	30,263
Oct 22	WIMBLEDON	W 3-0	Barnes, McManaman, Fowler	31,139
Oct 29	Ipswich Town	W 3-1	Barnes, Fowler 2	22,513
Oct 31	Queens Park Rangers	L 1-2	Barnes	18,295
Nov 5	NOTTINGHAM FOREST	W 1-0	Fowler	33,329
Nov 9	CHELSEA	W 3-1	Fowler 2, Ruddock	32,855
Nov 21	Everton	L 0-2		39,866
Nov 26	TOTTENHAM HOTSPUR	D 1-1	Fowler (pen)	35,007
Dec 3	Coventry City	D 1-1	Rush	21,029
Dec 11	CRYSTAL PALACE	D 0-0		30,972
Dec 18	Chelsea	D 0-0		27,050
Dec 26	Leicester City	W 2-1	Rush, Fowler	21,393
Dec 28	MANCHESTER CITY	W 2-0	Fowler, Phelan o.g.	38,122
Dec 31	Leeds United	W 2-0	Redknapp, Fowler	38,563
Jan 2	NORWICH CITY	W 4-0	Rush, Scales, Fowler 2	34,709
Jan 14	IPSWICH TOWN	L 0-1		32,733
Jan 24	EVERTON	D 0-0		39,505
Feb 4	Nottingham Forest	D 1-1	Fowler	25,418
Feb 11	QUEENS PARK RANGERS	D 1-1	Scales	35,996
Feb 25	Sheffield Wednesday	W 2-1	Barnes, McManaman	31,964
Mar 4	NEWCASTLE UNITED	W 2-0	Rush, Fowler	39,300
Mar 14	COVENTRY CITY	L 2-3	Burrows o.g., Molby	27,183
Mar 19	MANCHESTER UNITED	W 2-0	Bruce o.g., Redknapp	38,906
Mar 22	Tottenham Hotspur	D 0-0		31,988
Apr 5	SOUTHAMPTON	W 3-1	Rush 2, Fowler (pen)	29,881
Apr 9	LEEDS UNITED	L 0-1		37,454
Apr 12	Arsenal	W 1-0	Fowler	38,036
Apr 14	Manchester City	L 1-2	McManaman	27,055
Apr 17	LEICESTER CITY	W 2-0	Rush, Fowler	36,012
Apr 29	Norwich City	W 2-1	Rush, Fowler	21,843
May 2	Wimbledon	D 0-0		12,041
May 6	Aston Villa	L 0-2		40,154
May 10	West Ham United	L 0-3		22,446
May 14	BLACKBURN ROVERS	W 2-0	Barnes, Redknapp	40,014

FA Cup

Jan 7	Birmingham City	(Rd3)	D 0-0		25,326
Jan 18	BIRMINGHAM CITY	(R)	D 1-1*	Redknapp	36,275
Jan 28	Burnley	(Rd4)	D 0-0		20,551
Feb 7	BURNLEY	(R)	W 1-0	Barnes	32,109
Feb 19	WIMBLEDON	(Rd5)	D 1-1	Fowler	25,124
Feb 28	Wimbledon	(R)	W 2-0	Rush, Barnes	12,553
Mar 11	TOTTENHAM HOTSPUR	(Rd6)	L 1-2	Fowler	39,592

*After extra time. Score at 90 mins 1-1. Liverpool won 2-0 on penalties. Scorers: Redknapp, Bjornebye.

League Cup (Coca-Cola Cup)

Sep 21	BURNLEY	(Rd2/1L)	W 2-0	Scales, Fowler	23,359
Oct 5	Burnley	(Rd2/2L)	W 4-1	Clough, Redknapp 2, Fowler	19,032
Oct 25	STOKE CITY	(Rd3)	W 2-1	Rush 2	32,060
Nov 30	Blackburn Rovers	(Rd4)	W 3-1	Rush 3	30,115
Jan 11	ARSENAL	(Rd5)	W 1-0	Rush	36,004
Feb 15	CRYSTAL PALACE	(SF/1L)	W 1-0	Fowler	25,480
Mar 8	Crystal Palace	(SF/2L)	W 1-0	Fowler	18,224
Apr 2	Bolton Wanderers	(F)	W 2-1	McManaman 2	75,595

*Played at Wembley.

MANAGER: Roy Evans

CAPTAIN: Ian Rush

TOP SCORER: Robbie Fowler 31 (25 league)

BIGGEST WIN: 6-1, 20 August 1994, v Crystal Palace (A), Premier League

HIGHEST ATTENDANCE: 75,595, 2 April 1995, v Bolton Wanderers (Wembley), Coca-Cola Cup final

TRANSFERS IN: Phil Babb from Coventry City, John Scales from Wimbledon, Mark Kennedy from Millwall

TRANSFERS OUT: Ronnie Whelan to Southend, Paul Stewart to Burnley, Julian Dicks to West Ham United

League & Cup Appearances

PLAYER	LEAGUE	CUP COMPETITION FA CUP	LC	TOTAL
Babb	33 (1)	6	7	46 (1)
Barnes	38	6	6	50
Bjornebye	31	5 (1)	7	43 (1)
Clough	3 (7)		1	4 (7)
Fowler	42	7	8	57
Harkness	8			8
James D	42	7	8	57
Jones L	0 (1)		0 (1)	0 (2)
Jones R	31	7	8	46
Kennedy	4 (2)			4 (2)
Matteo	2 (5)	1		3 (5)
McManaman	40	7	8	55
Molby	12 (2)		2	14 (2)
Nicol	4		1	5
Redknapp	36 (5)	6	8	50 (5)
Ruddock	37	7	8	52
Rush	36	7	7	50
Scales	35	7	7	49
Thomas	16 (7)	2 (1)	1 (2)	19 (10)
Walters	7 (11)	2 (2)	1	10 (13)
Wright	5 (1)			5 (1)

Goalscorers

PLAYER	LEAGUE	CUP COMPETITION FA CUP	LC	TOTAL
Fowler	25	2	4	31
Rush	12	1	6	19
Barnes	7	2		9
McManaman	7		2	9
Redknapp	3	1 (1)	2	6 (1)
Scales	2		1	3
Molby	2			2
Ruddock	2			2
Bjornebye		0 (1)		0 (1)
Clough			1	1
Harkness	1			1
Opps' o.gs.	4			4

Penalty shoot-out goals in brackets.

Fact File

Manager Roy Evans signed as a professional in October 1965 and played 11 games for the first team between 1969-74. He became reserve team trainer in 1974-75 and steered his side to seven Central League championships in nine seasons. In this, his first full season as manager, Liverpool won the League (Coca Cola) Cup.

Final Premier League Table

		P	W	D	L	F	A	Pts
1	Blackburn R	42	27	8	7	80	39	89
2	Manchester U	42	26	10	6	77	28	88
3	Nottingham F	42	22	11	9	72	43	77
4	Liverpool	42	21	11	10	65	37	74
5	Leeds U	42	20	13	9	59	38	73
6	Newcastle U	42	20	12	10	67	47	72
7	Tottenham H	42	16	14	12	66	58	62
8	QPR	42	17	9	16	61	59	60
9	Wimbledon	42	15	11	16	48	65	56
10	Southampton	42	12	18	12	61	63	54
11	Chelsea	42	13	15	14	50	55	54
12	Arsenal	42	13	12	17	52	49	51
13	Sheffield W	42	13	12	17	49	57	51
14	West Ham U	42	13	11	18	44	48	50
15	Everton	42	11	17	14	44	51	50
16	Coventry C	42	12	14	16	44	62	50
17	Manchester C	42	12	13	17	53	64	49
18	Aston Villa	42	11	15	16	51	56	48
19	Crystal Pal	42	11	12	19	34	49	45
20	Norwich C	42	10	13	19	37	54	43
21	Leicester C	42	6	11	25	45	80	29
22	Ipswich T	42	7	6	29	36	93	27

Season 1995-96

FA Premier League

DATE	OPPONENTS	SCORE	GOALSCORERS	ATTENDANCE
Aug 19	SHEFFIELD WEDNESDAY	W 1-0	Collymore	40,535
Aug 21	Leeds United	L 0-1		35,852
Aug 26	Tottenham Hotspur	W 3-1	Barnes 2, Fowler	31,254
Aug 30	QUEENS PARK RANGERS	W 1-0	Ruddock	37,548
Sep 9	Wimbledon	L 0-1		19,530
Sep 16	BLACKBURN ROVERS	W 3-0	Collymore, Redknapp, Fowler	39,502
Sep 23	BOLTON WANDERERS	W 5-2	Harkness, Fowler 4	40,104
Oct 1	Manchester United	D 2-2	Fowler 2	34,934
Oct 14	COVENTRY CITY	D 0-0		39,079
Oct 22	Southampton	W 3-1	Redknapp, McManaman 2	15,245
Oct 28	MANCHESTER CITY	W 6-0	Rush 2, Redknapp, Fowler 2, Ruddock	39,267
Nov 4	Newcastle United	L 1-2	Rush	36,547
Nov 18	EVERTON	L 1-2	Fowler	40,818
Nov 22	West Ham United	D 0-0		24,324
Nov 25	Middlesbrough	L 1-2	Ruddock	29,390
Dec 2	SOUTHAMPTON	D 1-1	Collymore	38,007
Dec 9	Bolton Wanderers	W 1-0	Collymore	21,042
Dec 17	MANCHESTER UNITED	W 2-0	Fowler 2	40,546
Dec 23	ARSENAL	W 3-1	Fowler 3	39,806
Dec 30	Chelsea	D 2-2	McManaman 2	31,137
Jan 1	NOTTINGHAM FOREST	W 4-2	Collymore, Cooper o.g., Fowler 2	39,206
Jan 13	Sheffield Wednesday	D 1-1	Rush	32,747
Jan 20	LEEDS UNITED	W 5-0	Collymore, Fowler 2, Ruddock 2	40,254
Jan 31	Aston Villa	W 2-0	Collymore, Fowler	39,332
Feb 3	TOTTENHAM HOTSPUR	D 0-0		40,628
Feb 11	Queens Park Rangers	W 2-1	Wright, Fowler	18,405
Feb 24	Blackburn Rovers	W 3-2	Collymore 2, Thomas	33,163
Mar 3	ASTON VILLA	W 3-0	McManaman, Fowler 2	39,508
Mar 13	WIMBLEDON	D 2-2	Collymore, McManaman	34,063
Mar 16	CHELSEA	W 2-0	Wright, Fowler	40,820
Mar 23	Nottingham Forest	L 0-1		29,058
Apr 3	NEWCASTLE UNITED	W 4-3	Collymore 2, Fowler 2	40,702
Apr 6	Coventry City	L 0-1		23,137
Apr 8	WEST HAM UNITED	W 2-0	Collymore, Barnes	40,326
Apr 16	Everton	D 1-1	Fowler	39,022
Apr 27	MIDDLESBROUGH	W 1-0	Collymore	40,782
May 1	Arsenal	D 0-0		38,323
May 5	Manchester City	D 2-2	Lomas o.g., Rush	31,436

FA Cup

Jan 1	ROCHDALE	(Rd3)	W 7-0	McAteer, Collymore 3, Rush, Fowler, Valentine o.g.	28,126
Feb 18	Shrewsbury	(Rd4)	W 4-0	McAteer, Collymore, Fowler, Walton o.g.	7,752
Feb 28	CHARLTON ATHLETIC	(Rd5)	W 2-1	Collymore, Fowler	36,818
Mar 10	Leeds United	(Rd6)	D 0-0		34,632
Mar 20	LEEDS UNITED	(R)	W 3-0	McManaman 2, Fowler	30,812
Mar 31	Aston Villa*	(SF)	W 3-0	Fowler 2, McAteer	39,072
May 11	Manchester United**	(F)	L 0-1		79,007

*Played at Old Trafford. **Played at Wembley.

League Cup (Coca-Cola Cup)

Sep 20	SUNDERLAND	(Rd2/1L)	W 2-0	McManaman, Thomas	25,579
Oct 4	Sunderland	(Rd2/2L)	W 1-0	Fowler	20,560
Oct 25	MANCHESTER CITY	(Rd3)	W 4-0	Scales, Fowler, Rush, Harkness	29,394
Nov 29	NEWCASTLE UNITED	(Rd4)	L 0-1		40,077

UEFA Cup

Sep 12	Spartak Vladikavkaz	(Rd1/1L)	W 2-1	McManaman, Redknapp	43,000
Sep 26	SPARTAK VLADIKAVKAZ	(Rd1/2L)	D 0-0		35,042
Oct 17	Brondby	(Rd2/1L)	D 0-0		37,648
Oct 31	BRONDBY	(Rd2/2L)	L 0-1		35,878

MANAGER: Roy Evans **CAPTAIN:** Ian Rush/John Barnes

TOP SCORER: Robbie Fowler 36 (28 league)

BIGGEST WIN: 7-0, 1 January 1996, v Rochdale (H), FA Cup

HIGHEST ATTENDANCE: 79,007, 11 May 1996, v Manchester United (Wembley), FA Cup final

TRANSFERS IN: Stan Collymore from Nottingham Forest, Jason McAteer from Bolton Wanderers

TRANSFERS OUT: Ian Rush to Leeds United, Mark Walters to Southampton, Jan Molby to Swansea, Nigel Clough to Manchester City

League & Cup Appearances

PLAYER	LEAGUE	CUP COMPETITION			TOTAL
		FA CUP	LC	UEFA	
Babb	28	4	4	4	40
Barnes	36	7	3	4	50
Bjornebye	2				2
Clough	1 (1)				1 (1)
Collymore	30 (1)	7	2 (2)	1 (1)	40 (4)
Fowler	36 (2)	7	4	3 (1)	50 (3)
Harkness	23 (1)	1	4	4	32 (1)
James D	38	7	4	4	53
Jones R	33	7	3	4	47
Kennedy	1 (3)		0 (1)	0 (1)	1 (5)
Matteo	5	0 (1)			5 (1)
McAteer	27 (2)	7	3 (1)		37 (3)
McManaman	38	7	4	4	53
Redknapp	19 (4)	2 (1)	3	4	28 (5)
Ruddock	18 (2)	2	3 (1)	2	25 (3)
Rush	10 (10)	0 (4)	2	2 (1)	14 (15)
Scales	27	7	2	2	38
Thomas	18 (9)	5 (1)	0 (1)	2 (1)	25 (12)
Wright	28	7	3	4	42

Goalscorers

PLAYER	LEAGUE	CUP COMPETITION			TOTAL
		FA CUP	LC	UEFA	
Fowler	28	6	2		36
Collymore	14	5			19
McManaman	6	2	1	1	10
Rush	5	1	1		7
Ruddock	5				5
Redknapp	3			1	4
Barnes	3				3
McAteer		3			3
Harkness	1		1		2
Thomas	1		1		2
Wright	2				2
Scales			1		1
Opps' o.gs.	2	2			4

Fact File

Goalscoring legend Ian Rush played his last club game in the FA Cup final v Manchester United. In his career he scored 346 goals in 658 competitive games including 229 in 469 league appearances. Liverpool were awarded a trophy by the Premier League for the 'Match of the Decade' following the game against Newcastle United on 3 April 1996.

Final Premier League Table

		P	W	D	L	F	A	Pts
1	Manchester U	38	25	7	6	73	35	82
2	Newcastle U	38	24	6	8	66	37	78
3	Liverpool	38	20	11	7	70	34	71
4	Aston Villa	38	18	9	11	52	35	63
5	Arsenal	38	17	12	9	49	32	63
6	Everton	38	17	10	11	64	44	61
7	Blackburn R	38	18	7	13	61	47	61
8	Tottenham H	38	16	13	9	50	38	61
9	Nottingham F	38	15	13	10	50	54	58
10	West Ham U	38	14	9	15	43	52	51
11	Chelsea	38	12	14	12	46	44	50
12	Middlesbrough	38	11	10	17	35	50	43
13	Leeds U	38	12	7	19	40	57	43
14	Wimbledon	38	10	11	17	55	70	41
15	Sheffield W	38	10	10	18	48	61	40
16	Coventry C	38	8	14	16	42	60	38
17	Southampton	38	9	11	18	34	52	38
18	Manchester C	38	9	11	18	33	58	38
19	QPR	38	9	6	23	38	57	33
20	Bolton W	38	8	5	25	39	71	29

Season 1996-97

FA Premier League

DATE	OPPONENTS	SCORE	GOALSCORERS	ATTENDANCE
Aug 17	Middlesbrough	D 3-3	Fowler, Barnes, Bjornebye	30,039
Aug 19	ARSENAL	W 2-0	McManaman 2	38,103
Aug 24	SUNDERLAND	D 0-0		40,508
Sep 4	Coventry City	W 1-0	Babb	23,021
Sep 7	SOUTHAMPTON	W 2-1	McManaman, Collymore	39,189
Sep 15	Leicester City	W 3-0	Berger 2, Thomas	20,987
Sep 21	CHELSEA	W 5-1	Fowler, Barnes, Berger 2, Myers o.g.	40,739
Sep 29	West Ham United	W 2-1	Collymore, Thomas	25,064
Oct 12	Manchester United	L 0-1		55,128
Oct 27	DERBY COUNTY	W 2-1	Fowler 2	39,515
Nov 3	Blackburn Rovers	L 0-3		29,598
Nov 16	Leeds United	W 2-0	McManaman, Ruddock	39,981
Nov 20	EVERTON	D 1-1	Fowler	40,751
Nov 23	WIMBLEDON	D 1-1	Collymore	39,027
Dec 2	Tottenham Hotspur	W 2-0	McManaman, Thomas	32,899
Dec 7	SHEFFIELD WEDNESDAY	L 0-1		39,507
Dec 14	MIDDLESBROUGH	W 5-1	Fowler 4, Bjornebye	39,491
Dec 17	NOTTINGHAM FOREST	W 4-2	Collymore 2, Fowler, Lyttle o.g.	36,126
Dec 23	Newcastle United	D 1-1	Fowler	36,570
Dec 26	LEICESTER CITY	D 1-1	Collymore	40,786
Dec 29	Southampton	W 1-0	Barnes	15,222
Jan 1	Chelsea	L 0-1		28,329
Jan 11	WEST HAM UNITED	D 0-0		40,102
Jan 18	ASTON VILLA	W 3-0	Collymore, Fowler, Carragher	40,489
Feb 1	Derby County	W 1-0	Collymore	18,102
Feb 19	LEEDS UNITED	W 4-0	Collymore 2, Redknapp, Fowler	38,957
Feb 22	BLACKBURN ROVERS	D 0-0		40,747
Mar 2	Aston Villa	L 0-1		39,839
Mar 10	NEWCASTLE UNITED	W 4-3	McManaman, Fowler 2, Berger	40,751
Mar 15	Nottingham Forest	D 1-1	Fowler	29,181
Mar 24	Arsenal	W 2-1	McAteer, Collymore	36.068
Apr 6	COVENTRY CITY	L 1-2	Fowler	40,079
Apr 13	Sunderland	W 2-1	McManaman, Fowler	21,938
Apr 16	Everton	D 1-1	Thomsen o.g.	40,177
Apr 19	MANCHESTER UNITED	L 1-3	Barnes	40,892
May 3	TOTTENHAM HOTSPUR	W 2-1	Collymore, Berger	40,003
May 6	Wimbledon	L 1-2	Owen	20,016
May 11	Sheffield Wednesday	D 1-1	Redknapp	38,943

FA Cup

Jan 4	BURNLEY	(Rd3)	W 1-0	Collymore	33,252
Jan 26	Chelsea	(Rd4)	L 2-4	Collymore, Fowler	27,950

League Cup (Coca-Cola Cup)

Oct 23	Charlton Athletic	(Rd3/1L)	D 1-1	Fowler	15,000
Nov 13	CHARLTON ATHLETIC	(Rd3/2L)	W 4-1	Wright, Fowler 2, Redknapp	20,714
Nov 27	ARSENAL	(Rd4)	W 4-2	McManaman, Fowler 2, Berger	32,814
Jan 8	Middlesbrough	(Rd5)	L 1-2	McManaman	28,670

European Cup-Winners' Cup

Sep 12	MyPa 47	(Rd1/1L)	W 1-0	Bjornebye	5,500
Sep 26	MYPA 47	(Rd1/2L)	W 3-1	Collymore, Barnes, Berger	39,013
Oct 17	FC Sion	(Rd2/1L)	W 2-1	Fowler, Barnes	16,500
Oct 31	FC SION	(Rd2/2L)	W 6-3	McManaman, Bjornebye, Barnes, Fowler 2, Berger	38,514
Mar 6	Brann Bergen	(Rd3/1L)	D 1-1	Fowler	12,700
Mar 20	BRANN BERGEN	(Rd3/2L)	W 3-0	Fowler 2 (1 pen), Collymore	40,326
Apr 10	Paris Saint-Germain	(SF/1L)	L 0-3		35,142
Apr 24	PARIS SAINT-GERMAIN	(SF/2L)	W 2-0	Fowler, Wright	38,984

MANAGER: Roy Evans

CAPTAIN: John Barnes

TOP SCORER: Robbie Fowler 31 (18 league)

BIGGEST WIN: 6-3, 31 October 1996, v FC Sion (H), European Cup-Winners' Cup

HIGHEST ATTENDANCE: 55,128, 12 October 1996, v Manchester United (A), Premier League

TRANSFERS IN: Patrik Berger from Borussia Dortmund, Bjorn Tore Kvarme from Rosenborg

TRANSFERS OUT: John Scales to Tottenham Hotspur, Stan Collymore to Aston Villa

League & Cup Appearances

PLAYER	LEAGUE	CUP COMPETITION			TOTAL
		FA CUP	LC	ECWC	
Babb	21 (1)	1	3	4 (1)	29 (2)
Barnes	34 (1)	2	3	7	46 (1)
Berger	13 (10)	1 (1)	3	6	23 (11)
Bjornebye	38	2	4	8	52
Carragher	1 (1)		0 (1)		1 (2)
Collymore	25 (5)	2		4 (1)	31 (6)
Fowler	32	1	4	7	44
Harkness	5 (2)			3	8 (2)
James D	38	2	4	8	52
Jones L	0 (2)				0 (2)
Jones R	2		1		3
Kennedy	0 (5)	0 (1)	0 (1)	0 (1)	0 (8)
Kvarme	15	1			16
Matteo	22 (4)	2	3	7	34 (4)
McAteer	36 (1)	2	4	8	50 (1)
McManaman	37	2	4	8	51
Owen	1 (1)				1 (1)
Redknapp	18 (5)	1	1	4 (3)	24 (8)
Ruddock	15 (2)		2	2 (1)	19 (3)
Scales	3		1	2 (1)	6 (1)
Thomas	29 (2)	1	4	5 (1)	39 (3)
Thompson	0 (2)				0 (2)
Wright	33	2	3	5	43

Goalscorers

PLAYER	LEAGUE	CUP COMPETITION			TOTAL
		FA CUP	LC	ECWC	
Fowler	18	1	5	7	31
Collymore	12	2		2	16
McManaman	7		2	1	10
Berger	6		1	2	9
Barnes	4			3	7
Bjornebye	2			2	4
Redknapp	2		1		3
Thomas	3				3
Wright			1	1	2
Babb	1				1
Carragher	1				1
McAteer	1				1
Owen	1				1
Ruddock	1				1
Opps' o.gs.	3				3

Fact File

Robbie Fowler's 27th-minute goal (his second of four in the game) v Middlesbrough on 14 December was his 100th club goal, while Michael Owen scored on his first-team debut v Wimbledon on 6 May 1997.

Final Premier League Table

1	Manchester U	38	21	12	5	76	44	75
2	Newcastle U	38	19	11	8	73	40	68
3	Arsenal	38	19	11	8	62	32	68
4	Liverpool	38	19	11	8	62	37	68
5	Aston Villa	38	17	10	11	47	34	61
6	Chelsea	38	16	11	11	58	55	59
7	Sheffield W	38	14	15	9	50	51	57
8	Wimbledon	38	15	11	12	49	46	56
9	Leicester C	38	12	11	15	46	54	47
10	Tottenham H	38	13	7	18	44	51	46
11	Leeds U	38	11	13	14	28	38	46
12	Derby Co	38	11	13	14	45	58	46
13	Blackburn R	38	9	15	14	42	43	42
14	West Ham U	38	10	12	16	39	48	42
15	Everton	38	10	12	16	44	57	42
16	Southampton	38	10	11	17	50	56	41
17	Coventry C	38	9	14	15	38	54	41
18	Sunderland	38	10	10	18	35	53	40
19	Middlesbrough	38	10	12	16	51	60	39
20	Nottingham F	38	6	16	16	31	59	34

Middlesbrough deducted three points for failure to fulfil a fixture on a given date.

Season 1997-98

FA Premier League

DATE	OPPONENTS	SCORE	GOALSCORERS	ATTENDANCE
Aug 9	Wimbledon	D 1-1	Owen	26,106
Aug 13	LEICESTER CITY	L 1-2	Ince	35,007
Aug 23	Blackburn Rovers	D 1-1	Owen	30,187
Aug 26	Leeds United	W 2-0	McManaman, Riedle	39,775
Sep 13	SHEFFIELD WEDNESDAY	W 2-1	Thomas, Ince	34,705
Sep 20	Southampton	D 1-1	Riedle	15,252
Sep 22	ASTON VILLA	W 3-0	McManaman, Fowler, Riedle	34,843
Sep 27	West Ham United	L 1-2	Fowler	25,908
Oct 5	CHELSEA	W 4-2	Fowler, Berger 3	36,647
Oct 18	Everton	L 0-2		40,112
Oct 25	DERBY COUNTY	W 4-0	McManaman, Leonhardsen, Fowler 2	38,017
Nov 1	Bolton Wanderers	D 1-1	Fowler	25,000
Nov 8	TOTTENHAM HOTSPUR	W 4-0	McManaman, Redknapp, Leonhardsen, Owen	38,006
Nov 22	BARNSLEY	L 0-1		41,011
Nov 30	Arsenal	W 1-0	McManaman	38,094
Dec 6	MANCHESTER UNITED	L 1-3	Fowler (pen)	41,027
Dec 13	Crystal Palace	W 3-0	McManaman, Leonhardsen, Owen	25,790
Dec 20	COVENTRY CITY	W 1-0	Owen	39,707
Dec 26	LEEDS UNITED	W 3-1	Fowler 2, Owen	43,854
Dec 28	Newcastle United	W 2-1	McManaman 2	36,702
Jan 10	WIMBLEDON	W 2-0	Redknapp 2	38,011
Jan 17	Leicester City	D 0-0		21,633
Jan 20	NEWCASTLE UNITED	W 1-0	Owen	42,791
Jan 31	BLACKBURN ROVERS	D 0-0		43,890
Feb 7	SOUTHAMPTON	L 2-3	Owen 2	43,550
Feb 14	Sheffield Wednesday	D 3-3	Owen 3	35,405
Feb 23	EVERTON	D 1-1	Ince	44,501
Feb 28	Aston Villa	L 1-2	Owen (pen)	39,372
Mar 7	BOLTON WANDERERS	W 2-1	Ince, Owen	44,532
Mar 14	Tottenham Hotspur	D 3-3	McManaman 2, Ince	30,245
Mar 28	Barnsley	W 3-2	McManaman, Riedle 2	18,648
Apr 10	Manchester United	D 1-1	Owen	55,171
Apr 13	CRYSTAL PALACE	W 2-1	Leonhardsen, Thompson	43,007
Apr 19	Coventry City	D 1-1	Owen	22,721
Apr 25	Chelsea	L 1-4	Riedle	34,639
May 2	WEST HAM UNITED	W 5-0	McAteer 2, Leonhardsen, Ince, Owen	44,414
May 6	ARSENAL	W 4-0	Leonhardsen, Ince 2, Owen	44,417
May 10	Derby County	L 0-1		30,492

FA Cup

Jan 3	COVENTRY CITY	(Rd3)	L 1-3	Redknapp	33,888

League Cup (Coca-Cola Cup)

Oct 15	West Bromwich Albion	(Rd3)	W 2-0	Fowler, Berger	21,986
Nov 18	GRIMSBY TOWN	(Rd4)	W 3-0	Owen 3	28,515
Jan 7	Newcastle United	(Rd5)	W 2-0*	Fowler, Owen	33,207
Jan 27	MIDDLESBROUGH	(SF/1L)	W 2-1	Fowler, Redknapp	33,438
Feb 18	Middlesbrough	(SF/2L)	L 0-2		29,828

*After extra time. Score at 90 mins 0-0.

UEFA Cup

Sep 16	Celtic	(Rd1/1L)	D 2-2	Owen, McManaman	48,526
Sep 30	CELTIC	(Rd1/2L)	D 0-0**		38,205
Oct 21	Strasbourg	(Rd2/1L)	L 0-3		18,813
Nov 4	STRASBOURG	(Rd2/2L)	W 2-0	Fowler (pen), Riedle	32,426

**Liverpool won on away goals rule.

MANAGER: Roy Evans
CAPTAIN: Paul Ince
TOP SCORER: Michael Owen 23 (18 league)
BIGGEST WIN: 5-0, 2 May 1998, v West Ham United (H), Premier League
HIGHEST ATTENDANCE: 55,171, 10 April 1998 v Manchester United (A), Premier League
TRANSFERS IN: Paul Ince from Inter Milan, Oyvind Leonhardsen from Wimbledon, Karlheinz Riedle from Borussia Dortmund
TRANSFERS OUT: John Barnes to Newcastle United, Neil Ruddock to West Ham United, Mark Kennedy to Wimbledon

League & Cup Appearances

PLAYER	LEAGUE	CUP COMPETITION			TOTAL
		FA CUP	LC	UEFA	
Babb	18 (1)		2	1	21 (1)
Berger	6 (16)	0 (1)	2 (1)	1 (1)	9 (19)
Bjornebye	24 (1)		3	4	31 (1)
Carragher	17 (3)		2	1	20 (3)
Fowler	19 (1)	1	4	3	27 (1)
Friedel	11				11
Harkness	24 (1)	1	3 (1)	1	29 (2)
Ince	31	1	4	4	40
James	27	1	5	4	37
Jones R	20 (1)		2	3	25 (1)
Kennedy	0 (1)				0 (1)
Kvarme	22 (1)	1	2	4	29 (1)
Leonhardsen	27 (1)	1	3 (2)	2	33 (3)
Matteo	24 (2)	1	4	2	31 (2)
McAteer	15 (6)	1	3	1	20 (6)
McManaman	36	1	5	4	46
Murphy	6 (10)	0 (1)			6 (11)
Owen	34 (2)		4	3 (1)	41 (3)
Redknapp	20	1	3	2	26
Riedle	18 (7)	1	2 (3)	1 (2)	22 (12)
Ruddock	2		1	1	4
Thomas	10 (1)		1	1	12 (1)
Thompson	1 (4)				1 (4)
Wright	6			1	7

Goalscorers

PLAYER	LEAGUE	CUP COMPETITION			TOTAL
		FA CUP	LC	UEFA	
Owen	18		4	1	23
Fowler	9		3	1	13
McManaman	11			1	12
Ince	8				8
Riedle	6			1	7
Leonhardsen	6				6
Redknapp	3	1	1		5
Berger	3		1		4
McAteer	2				2
Thomas	1				1
Thompson	1				1

Fact File

Robbie Fowler's feat of topping the scoring chart for the last three seasons has now been superseded by Michael Owen who will go on to be leading scorer for four seasons. The record is held by Roger Hunt, leading scorer for eight successive seasons 1961-62 to 1968-69, both in the league and overall.

Final Premier League Table

	P	W	D	L	F	A	Pts
1 Arsenal	38	23	9	6	68	33	78
2 Manchester U	38	23	8	7	73	26	77
3 Liverpool	38	18	11	9	68	42	65
4 Chelsea	38	20	3	15	71	43	63
5 Leeds U	38	17	8	13	57	46	59
6 Blackburn R	38	16	10	12	57	52	58
7 Aston Villa	38	17	6	15	49	48	57
8 West Ham U	38	16	8	14	56	57	56
9 Derby Co	38	16	7	15	52	49	55
10 Leicester C	38	13	14	11	51	41	53
11 Coventry C	38	12	16	10	46	44	52
12 Southampton	38	14	6	18	50	55	48
13 Newcastle U	38	11	11	16	35	44	44
14 Tottenham H	38	11	11	16	44	56	44
15 Wimbledon	38	10	14	14	34	46	44
16 Sheffield W	38	12	8	18	52	67	44
17 Everton	38	9	13	16	41	56	40
18 Bolton W	38	9	13	16	41	61	40
19 Barnsley	38	10	5	23	37	82	35
20 Crystal Pal	38	8	9	21	37	71	33

Season 1998-99

FA Premier League

DATE	OPPONENTS	SCORE	GOALSCORERS	ATTENDANCE
Aug 16	Southampton	W 2-1	Owen, Riedle	15,202
Aug 22	ARSENAL	D 0-0		44,429
Aug 30	Newcastle United	W 4-1	Owen 3, Berger	36,740
Sep 9	COVENTRY CITY	W 2-0	Redknapp, Berger	41,771
Sep 12	West Ham United	L 1-2	Riedle	26,029
Sep 19	CHARLTON ATHLETIC	D 3-3	Fowler 2, Berger	44,526
Sep 24	Manchester United	L 0-2		55,181
Oct 4	CHELSEA	D 1-1	Redknapp	44,404
Oct 17	Everton	D 0-0		40,185
Oct 24	NOTTINGHAM FOREST	W 5-1	McManaman, Owen 4	44,595
Oct 31	Leicester City	L 0-1		21,837
Nov 7	DERBY COUNTY	L 1-2	Redknapp	44,020
Nov 14	LEEDS UNITED	L 1-3	Fowler	44,305
Nov 20	ASTON VILLA	W 4-2	Fowler 3, Ince	39,241
Nov 29	BLACKBURN ROVERS	W 2-0	Owen, Ince	41,753
Dec 5	Tottenham Hotspur	L 1-2	Berger	36,521
Dec 13	Wimbledon	L 0-1		26,080
Dec 19	SHEFFIELD WEDNESDAY	W 2-0	Owen, Berger	40,003
Dec 26	Middlesbrough	W 3-1	Owen, Redknapp, Heggem	34,626
Dec 28	NEWCASTLE UNITED	W 4-2	Owen 2, Riedle 2	44,605
Jan 9	Arsenal	D 0-0		38,107
Jan 16	SOUTHAMPTON	W 7-1	Fowler 3, Owen, Matteo, Carragher, Thompson	44,011
Jan 30	Coventry City	L 1-2	McManaman.	23,056
Feb 6	MIDDLESBROUGH	W 3-1	Owen, Heggem, Ince	44,384
Feb 13	Charlton Athletic	L 0-1		20,043
Feb 20	WEST HAM UNITED	D 2-2	Fowler, Owen	44,511
Feb 27	Chelsea	L 1-2	Owen	34,822
Mar 13	Derby County	L 2-3	Fowler 2	32,913
Apr 3	EVERTON	W 3-2	Fowler 2, Berger	44,852
Apr 5	Nottingham Forest	D 2-2	Owen, Redknapp	28,374
Apr 12	Leeds United	D 0-0		39,451
Apr 17	ASTON VILLA	L 0-1		44,306
Apr 21	LEICESTER CITY	L 0-1		36,019
Apr 24	Blackburn Rovers	W 3-1	McManaman, Leonhardson, Redknapp	29,944
May 1	TOTTENHAM HOTSPUR	W 3-2	McManaman, Redknapp, Ince	44,007
May 5	MANCHESTER UNITED	D 2-2	Redknapp, Ince	44,702
May 8	Sheffield Wednesday	L 0-1		27,383
May 16	WIMBLEDON	W 3-0	Riedle, Berger, Ince	41,902

FA Cup

Jan 3	Port Vale	(Rd3) W 3-0	Fowler, Owen, Ince	16,557
Jan 24	Manchester United	(Rd4) L 1-2	Owen	54,591

League Cup (Worthington Cup)

Oct 27	FULHAM	(Rd3) W 3-1	Morgan o.g., Fowler (pen), Ince	22,296
Nov 10	TOTTENHAM HOTSPUR	(Rd4) L 1-3	Owen	20,772

UEFA Cup

Sep 15	IFC Kosice	(Rd1/1L) W 3-0	Berger, Riedle, Owen	4,500
Sep 29	IFC KOSICE	(Rd1/2L) W 5-0	Redknapp 2, Ince, Fowler 2	23,792
Oct 20	VALENCIA	(Rd2/1L) D 0-0		26,004
Nov 3	Valencia	(Rd2/2L) D 2-2*	McManaman, Berger	49,000
Nov 24	Celta Vigo	(Rd3/1L) L 1-3	Owen	32,000
Dec 8	CELTA VIGO	(Rd3/2L) L 0-1		30,289

*Liverpool won on away goals rule.

MANAGERS: Roy Evans / Gérard Houllier (jointly until November) then Gérard Houllier

CAPTAIN: Paul Ince

TOP SCORER: Michael Owen 23 (18 league)

BIGGEST WIN: 7-1, 16 January 1999, v Southampton (H), Premier League

HIGHEST ATTENDANCE: 55,181, 24 September 1998, v Manchester United (A), Premier League

TRANSFERS IN: Steve Staunton (for second time) from Aston Villa, Vegard Heggem from Rosenborg, Rigobert Song from Salernitana Sport, Djimi Traore from Laval

TRANSFERS OUT: Michael Thomas to Benfica, Steve Harkness to Benfica, Jason McAteer to Blackburn Rovers, B Kvarme to St Etienne

League & Cup Appearances

PLAYER	LEAGUE	CUP COMPETITION			TOTAL
		FA CUP	LC	UEFA	
Babb	24 (1)	1		3 (1)	28 (2)
Berger	30 (2)	2	1	6	39 (2)
Bjornebye	20 (3)	2	2	4	28 (3)
Carragher	34	2	2	6	44
Dundee	0 (3)		0 (1)	0 (1)	0 (5)
Ferri	0 (2)				0 (2)
Fowler	23 (2)	1 (1)	2	5 (1)	31 (4)
Friedel	12		2	1 (1)	15 (1)
Gerrard	4 (8)			1	5 (8)
Harkness	4 (2)	1 (1)	0 (1)	1 (1)	6 (5)
Heggem	27 (2)	1	1	4 (1)	33 (3)
Ince	34	2	2	3	41
James	26	2		5	33
Kvarme	2 (5)			1	3 (5)
Leonhardsen	7 (2)		1	1 (2)	9 (4)
Matteo	16 (4)	1		1 (1)	18 (5)
McAteer	6 (7)	1 (1)	2	3 (2)	12 (10)
McManaman	25 (3)			3	28 (3)
Murphy	0 (1)		1 (1)	0 (1)	1 (3)
Owen	30	2	2	5 (1)	39 (1)
Redknapp	33 (1)	2		4	39 (1)
Riedle	16 (18)	1	0 (1)	2 (2)	19 (21)
Song	10 (3)				10 (3)
Staunton	31	1	2	5 (1)	39 (1)
Thompson	4 (10)		2	2	8 (10)

Goalscorers

PLAYER	LEAGUE	CUP COMPETITION			TOTAL
		FA CUP	LC	UEFA	
Owen	18	2	1	2	23
Fowler	14	1	1	2	18
Redknapp	8			2	10
Berger	7			2	9
Ince	6	1	1	1	9
Riedle	5			1	6
McManaman	4			1	5
Heggem	2				2
Carragher	1				1
Leonhardsen	1				1
Matteo	1				1
Thompson	1				1
Opps' o.gs.			1		1

Fact File

There were 102 substitutions among the 25 players used in the 48 competitive games. Only captain Paul Ince, Jamie Carragher and David James were not used as substitutes but these three were substituted in 2, 2 and 1 game respectively, thus no player completed all the games he was chosen for.

Final Premier League Table

		P	W	D	L	F	A	Pts
1	Manchester U	38	22	13	3	80	37	79
2	Arsenal	38	22	12	4	59	17	78
3	Chelsea	38	20	15	3	57	30	67
4	Leeds U	38	13	13	7	62	34	67
5	West Ham U	38	15	9	13	46	53	57
6	Aston Villa	38	15	10	13	51	46	55
7	Liverpool	38	15	9	14	68	49	54
8	Derby Co	38	13	13	12	40	45	52
9	Middlesbrough	38	12	15	11	48	54	51
10	Leicester C	38	12	13	13	40	46	49
11	Tottenham H	38	11	14	13	47	50	47
12	Sheffield W	38	13	7	18	41	42	46
13	Newcastle U	38	11	13	14	48	54	46
14	Everton	38	11	10	17	42	47	43
15	Coventry C	38	11	9	18	39	51	42
16	Wimbledon	38	10	12	16	40	63	42
17	Southampton	38	11	8	19	37	64	41
18	Charlton Ath	38	8	12	18	41	56	36
19	Blackburn R	38	7	14	17	38	52	35
20	Nottingham F	38	7	9	22	35	69	30

Season 1999-2000

FA Premier League

DATE	OPPONENTS	SCORE	GOALSCORERS	ATTENDANCE
Aug 7	Sheffield Wednesday	W 2-1	Fowler, Camara	34,853
Aug 14	WATFORD	L 0-1		44,174
Aug 21	Middlesbrough	L 0-1		34,783
Aug 23	Leeds United	W 2-1	Camara, Radebe o.g.	39,703
Aug 28	ARSENAL	W 2-0	Fowler, Berger	44,886
Sep 11	MANCHESTER UNITED	L 2-3	Hyypia, Berger	44,929
Sep 18	Leicester City	D 2-2	Owen 2 (1 pen)	21,623
Sep 27	EVERTON	L 0-1		44,802
Oct 2	Aston Villa	D 0-0		39,127
Oct 15	CHELSEA	W 1-0	Thompson	44,826
Oct 23	Southampton	D 1-1	Camara	15,241
Oct 27	WEST HAM UNITED	W 1-0	Camara	44,012
Nov 1	BRADFORD CITY	W 3-1	Camara, Redknapp (pen), Heggem	40,483
Nov 6	DERBY COUNTY	W 2-0	Murphy, Redknapp	44,467
Nov 20	Sunderland	W 2-0	Owen, Berger	42,015
Nov 27	West Ham United	L 0-1		26,043
Dec 5	SHEFFIELD WEDNESDAY	W 4-1	Hyypia, Murphy, Gerrard, Thompson	42,517
Dec 18	COVENTRY CITY	W 2-0	Owen, Camara	44,024
Dec 26	Newcastle United	D 2-2	Owen 2	36,445
Dec 28	WIMBLEDON	W 3-1	Owen, Berger, Fowler	44,107
Jan 3	Tottenham Hotspur	L 0-1		36,004
Jan 15	Watford	W 3-2	Berger, Thompson, Smicer	21,367
Jan 22	MIDDLESBROUGH	D 0-0		44,324
Feb 5	LEEDS UNITED	W 3-1	Hamann, Berger, Murphy	44,793
Feb 13	Arsenal	W 1-0	Camara	38,098
Mar 4	Manchester United	D 1-1	Berger	61,592
Mar 11	SUNDERLAND	D 1-1	Berger (pen)	44,693
Mar 15	ASTON VILLA	D 0-0		43,615
Mar 18	Derby County	W 2-0	Owen, Camara	33,378
Mar 25	NEWCASTLE UNITED	W 2-1	Camara, Redknapp	44,743
Apr 1	Coventry City	W 3-0	Owen 2, Heskey	23,098
Apr 9	TOTTENHAM HOTSPUR	W 2-0	Berger, Owen	44,536
Apr 16	Wimbledon	W 2-1	Heskey 2	26,102
Apr 21	Everton	D 0-0		40,052
Apr 29	Chelsea	L 0-2		34,957
May 3	LEICESTER CITY	L 0-2		43,456
May 7	SOUTHAMPTON	D 0-0		44,015
May 14	Bradford City	L 0-1		18,276

FA Cup

Dec 12	Huddersfield Town	(Rd3) W 2-0	Camara, Matteo	23,678
Jan 10	BLACKBURN ROVERS	(Rd4) L 0-1		32,839

League Cup (Worthington Cup)

Sep 14	Hull City	(Rd2/1L) W 5-1	Murphy 2, Meijer 2, Staunton	10,034
Sep 21	HULL CITY	(Rd2/2L) W 4-2	Murphy, Maxwell, Riedle 2	24,318
Oct 13	Southampton	(Rd3) L 1-2	Owen	13,822

League & Cup Appearances

PLAYER	LEAGUE	CUP COMPETITION FA CUP	LC	TOTAL
Berger	34	1	1 (1)	36 (1)
Camara	22 (11)	2	0 (2)	24 (13)
Carragher	33 (3)	2	2	37 (3)
Fowler	8 (6)			8 (6)
Friedel	2		2	4
Gerrard	26 (3)	2		28 (3)
Hamann	27 (1)	2		29 (1)
Heggem	10 (12)		1 (2)	11 (14)
Henchoz	29	2	2	33
Heskey	12			12
Hyypia	38	2	2	42
Kippe			0 (1)	0 (1)
Matteo	32	1 (1)		33 (1)
Maxwell			1	1
Meijer	7 (14)		3	10 (14)
Murphy	9 (14)	2	2	13 (14)
Newby	0 (1)	0 (2)	0 (1)	0 (4)
Owen	22 (5)	1	2	25 (5)
Redknapp	18 (4)		1	19 (4)
Riedle	0 (1)		1	1 (1)
Smicer	13 (8)	2	2	17 (8)
Song	14 (4)	0 (1)	2	16 (5)
Staunton	7 (5)	1	3	11 (5)
Thompson	19 (8)	0 (1)	3	22 (9)
Traore			2	2
Westerveld	36	2	1	39

Goalscorers

PLAYER	LEAGUE	CUP COMPETITION FA CUP	LC	TOTAL
Owen	11		1	12
Camara	9	1		10
Berger	9			9
Murphy	3		3	6
Fowler	3			3
Heskey	3			3
Redknapp	3			3
Thompson	3			3
Hyypia	2			2
Meijer			2	2
Riedle			2	2
Gerrard	1			1
Hamann	1			1
Heggem	1			1
Matteo		1		1
Maxwell			1	1
Smicer	1			1
Staunton			1	1
Opps' o.gs.	1			1

Fact File

Houllier's team building gathers pace, creating the best defence in the league with Henchoz and Hyypia in the centre, conceding only 30 goals in the league season.

MANAGER: Gérard Houllier **CAPTAIN:** Jamie Redknapp
TOP SCORER: Michael Owen 12 (11 league)
BIGGEST WIN: 5-1, 14 September 1999, v Hull City (A), Worthington Cup
HIGHEST ATTENDANCE: 61,592, 4 March 2000, v Manchester United (A), Premier League
TRANSFERS IN: Sander Westerveld from Vitesse Arnhem, Titi Camara from Marseille, Stephane Henchoz from Blackburn Rovers, Sami Hyypia from Willem II, Vladimir Smicer from Lens, Dietmar Hamann from Newcastle United, Emile Heskey from Leicester City
TRANSFERS OUT: Paul Ince to Middlesbrough, Oyvind Leonhardsen to Tottenham Hotspur, Karlheinz Riedle to Fulham, David James to Aston Villa, Phil Babb to Sporting Lisbon

Final Premier League Table

		P	W	D	L	F	A	Pts
1	Manchester U	38	28	7	3	97	45	91
2	Arsenal	38	22	7	9	73	43	73
3	Leeds U	38	21	6	11	58	43	69
4	Liverpool	38	19	10	9	51	30	67
5	Chelsea	38	18	11	9	53	34	65
6	Aston Villa	38	15	13	10	46	35	58
7	Sunderland	38	16	10	12	57	56	58
8	Leicester C	38	16	7	15	55	55	55
9	West Ham U	38	15	10	13	52	53	55
10	Tottenham H	38	15	8	15	57	49	53
11	Newcastle United	38	14	10	14	63	54	52
12	Middlesbrough	38	14	10	14	46	52	52
13	Everton	38	12	14	12	59	49	50
14	Coventry C	38	12	8	18	47	54	44
15	Southampton	38	12	8	18	45	62	44
16	Derby Co	38	9	11	18	44	57	38
17	Bradford C	38	9	9	20	38	68	36
18	Wimbledon	38	7	12	19	46	74	33
19	Sheffield W	38	8	7	23	38	70	31
20	Watford	38	6	6	26	35	77	24

Season 2000-01

FA Premier League

DATE	OPPONENTS	SCORE	GOALSCORERS	ATTENDANCE
Aug 19	BRADFORD CITY	W 1-0	Heskey	44,183
Aug 21	Arsenal	L 0-2		38,014
Aug 26	Southampton	D 3-3	Owen 2, Hyypia	15,202
Sep 6	ASTON VILLA	W 3-1	Owen 3	43,360
Sep 9	MANCHESTER CITY	W 3-2	Owen, Hamann 2	44,692
Sep 17	West Ham United	D 1-1	Gerrard	25,998
Sep 23	SUNDERLAND	D 1-1	Owen	44,713
Oct 1	Chelsea	L 0-3		34,966
Oct 15	Derby County	W 4-0	Heskey 3, Berger	30,532
Oct 21	LEICESTER CITY	W 1-0	Heskey	44,395
Oct 29	EVERTON	W 3-1	Barmby, Heskey, Berger (pen)	44,718
Nov 4	Leeds United	L 3-4	Hyypia, Ziege, Smicer	40,055
Nov 12	COVENTRY CITY	W 4-1	Heskey 2, Gerrard, McAllister	43,701
Nov 19	Tottenham Hotspur	L 1-2	Fowler	36,036
Nov 26	Newcastle United	L 1-2	Heskey	51,949
Dec 2	CHARLTON ATHLETIC	W 3-0	Fish o.g., Heskey, Babbel	43,515
Dec 10	IPSWICH TOWN	L 0-1		43,509
Dec 17	Manchester United	W 1-0	Murphy	67,533
Dec 23	ARSENAL	W 4-0	Gerrard, Owen, Barmby, Fowler	44,144
Dec 26	Middlesbrough	L 0-1		34,696
Jan 1	SOUTHAMPTON	W 2-1	Gerrard, Babbel	38,474
Jan 13	Aston Villa	W 3-0	Murphy 2, Gerrard	41,336
Jan 20	MIDDLESBROUGH	D 0-0		43,042
Jan 31	Manchester City	D 1-1	Heskey	34,629
Feb 3	WEST HAM UNITED	W 3-0	Smicer, Fowler 2	44,045
Feb 10	Sunderland	D 1-1	Litmanen (pen)	47,533
Mar 3	Leicester City	L 0-2		21,924
Mar 18	DERBY COUNTY	D 1-1	Owen	43,362
Mar 31	MANCHESTER UNITED	W 2-0	Gerrard, Fowler	44,806
Apr 10	Ipswich Town	D 1-1	Heskey	23,504
Apr 13	LEEDS UNITED	L 1-2	Gerrard	44,116
Apr 16	Everton	W 3-2	Babbel, Heskey, McAllister	40,260
Apr 22	TOTTENHAM HOTSPUR	W 3-1	Heskey, Fowler, McAllister	43,547
Apr 28	Coventry City	W 2-0	Hyypia, McAllister	23,063
May 1	Bradford City	W 2-0	Owen, McAllister	22,057
May 5	NEWCASTLE UNITED	W 3-0	Owen 3	44,363
May 8	CHELSEA	D 2-2	Owen 2	43,588
May 19	Charlton Athletic	W 4-0	Fowler 2, Murphy, Owen	20,043

FA Cup

Jan 6	ROTHERHAM UNITED	(Rd3)	W 3-0	Heskey 2, Hamann	30,689
Jan 27	Leeds United	(Rd4)	W 2-0	Barmby, Heskey	37,108
Feb 18	MANCHESTER CITY	(Rd5)	W 4-2	Litmanen (pen), Heskey, Smicer (pen), Babbel	36,231
Mar 11	Tranmere Rovers	(Rd6)	W 4-2	Murphy, Owen, Gerrard, Fowler (pen)	16,334
Apr 8	Wycombe Wanderers*	(SF)	W 2-1	Heskey, Fowler	40,037
May 12	Arsenal**	(F)	W 2-1	Owen 2	74,200

*Played at Villa Park. **Played at the Millennium Stadium, Cardiff.

League Cup (Worthington Cup)

Nov 1	CHELSEA	(Rd3)	W 2-1†	Murphy, Fowler	29,370
Nov 29	Stoke City	(Rd4)	W 8-0	Ziege, Smicer, Babbel, Fowler 3 (1 pen), Hyypia, Murphy	27,109
Dec 13	FULHAM	(Rd5)	W 3-0††	Owen, Smicer, Barmby	20,144
Jan 10	Crystal Palace	(SF/1L)	L 1-2	Smicer	25,933
Jan 24	CRYSTAL PALACE	(SF/2L)	W 5-0	Smicer, Murphy 2, Biscan, Fowler	41,854
Feb 25	Birmingham City	(F)	D 1-1#	Fowler	73,500

†After extra time. Score at 90 mins 1–1. ††After extra time. Score at 90 mins 0–0. #After extra time. Score at 90 mins 1-1. Liverpool won 5-4 on penalties. Scorers: McAllister, Barmby, Ziege, Fowler, Carragher. Played at the Millennium Stadium, Cardiff.

UEFA Cup

Sep 14	Rapid Bucharest	(Rd1/1L)	W 1-0	Barmby	12,000
Sep 28	RAPID BUCHAREST	(Rd1/2L)	D 0-0		37,954
Oct 26	SLOVAN LIBEREC	(Rd2/1L)	W 1-0	Heskey	29,662
Nov 9	Slovan Liberec	(Rd2/2L)	W 3-2	Barmby, Heskey, Owen	6,808
Nov 23	Olympiakos	(Rd3/1L)	D 2-2	Barmby, Gerrard	43,855
Dec 7	OLYMPIAKOS	(Rd3/2L)	W 2-0	Heskey, Barmby	35,484
Feb 15	Roma	(Rd4/1L)	W 2-0	Owen 2	59,718
Feb 22	ROMA	(Rd4/2L)	L 0-1		43,688
Mar 8	Porto	(Rd5/1L)	D 0-0		21,150
Mar 15	PORTO	(Rd5/2L)	W 2-0	Murphy, Owen	40,502
Apr 5	Barcelona	(SF/1L)	D 0-0		90,000
Apr 19	BARCELONA	(SF/2L)	W 1-0	McAllister (pen)	44,203
May 16	Deportivo Alavés	(F)	W 5-4§	Babbel, Gerrard, McAllister (pen), Fowler, Geli o.g.	65,000

§Score at 90 mins 4-4. Liverpool won on golden goals rule in extra time – 116 minutes. Played in Dortmund.

League & Cup Appearances

PLAYER	LEAGUE	CUP COMPETITION			TOTAL
		FA CUP	LC	UEFA	
Arphexad			2		2
Babbel	38	5	4	13	60
Barmby	21 (5)	2 (3)	2 (4)	6 (3)	31 (15)
Berger	11 (3)	0 (1)	1	3 (2)	15 (6)
Biscan	8 (5)	3 (1)	4		15 (6)
Carragher	30 (4)	6	6	12	56 (4)
Diomede	1 (1)			2	3 (1)
Fowler	15 (12)	3 (2)	5	6 (5)	29 (19)
Gerrard	29 (4)	2 (2)	4	9	44 (6)
Hamann	26 (4)	5	2 (3)	13	46 (7)
Heggem	1 (2)			1	2 (2)
Henchoz	32	5	6	10	53
Heskey	33 (3)	3 (2)	3 (1)	9 (2)	48 (8)
Hyypia	35	6	6	11	58
Litmanen	4 (1)	1 (1)	1 (1)	0 (2)	6 (5)
McAllister	21 (9)	4 (1)	2 (3)	4 (5)	31 (18)
Meijer	0 (3)				0 (3)
Murphy	13 (14)	4 (1)	5	6 (4)	28 (19)
Owen	20 (8)	4 (1)	1 (1)	10 (1)	35 (11)
Partridge			1		1
Smicer	16 (11)	4 (1)	5 (1)	6 (5)	31 (18)
Song	3			1	4
Staunton	0 (1)			0 (1)	0 (2)
Traore	8		1	2 (1)	11 (1)
Vignal	4 (2)	0 (1)			4 (3)
Westerveld	38	6	4	13	61
Wright	0 (2)	1	0 (1)		1 (3)
Ziege	11 (5)	2 (1)	1 (3)	6 (3)	20 (12)

Goalscorers

PLAYER	LEAGUE	CUP COMPETITION			TOTAL
		FA CUP	LC	UEFA	
Heskey	14	5	1	3	23
Owen	16	3		4	23
Fowler	8	2	6 (1)	1	17 (1)
Gerrard	7	1		2	10
Murphy	4	1	4	1	10
Barmby	2	1	1 (1)	4	8 (1)
McAllister	5		(1)	2	7 (1)
Smicer	2	1	4		7
Babbel	3	1	1	1	6
Hyypia	3		1		4
Hamann	2	1			3
Berger	2				2
Litmanen	1	1			2
Ziege	1		1 (1)		2 (1)
Biscan			1		1
Carragher			(1)		(1)
Opps' o.gs.	1			1	2

Penalty shoot-out goals in brackets.

Fact File

Liverpool were the first English club to play in every game possible in a season, winning three cups.

Final Premier League Table

		P	W	D	L	F	A	Pts
1	Manchester U	38	24	8	6	79	31	80
2	Arsenal	38	20	10	8	63	38	70
3	Liverpool	38	20	9	9	71	39	69
4	Leeds U	38	20	8	10	64	43	68
5	Ipswich T	38	20	6	12	57	42	66
6	Chelsea	38	17	10	11	68	45	61
7	Sunderland	38	15	12	11	46	41	57
8	Aston Villa	38	13	15	10	46	43	54
9	Charlton Ath	38	14	10	14	50	57	52
10	Southampton	38	14	10	14	40	48	52
11	Newcastle U	38	14	9	15	44	50	51
12	Tottenham H	38	13	10	15	47	54	49
13	Leicester City	38	14	6	18	39	51	48
14	Middlesbrough	38	9	15	14	44	44	42
15	West Ham U	38	10	12	16	45	50	42
16	Everton	38	11	9	18	45	59	42
17	Derby Co	38	10	12	16	37	59	42
18	Manchester C	38	8	10	20	41	65	34
19	Coventry C	38	8	10	20	36	63	34
20	Bradford C	38	5	11	22	30	70	26

Season 2001-02

FA Premier League

DATE	OPPONENTS	SCORE	GOALSCORERS	ATTENDANCE
Aug 18	WEST HAM UNITED	W 2-1	Owen 2	43,935
Aug 27	Bolton Wanderers	L 1-2	Heskey	27,205
Sep 8	ASTON VILLA	L 1-3	Gerrard	44,102
Sep 15	Everton	D 3-1	Owen (pen), Gerrard, Riise	39,554
Sep 22	TOTTENHAM HOTSPUR	W 1-0	Litmanen	44,116
Sep 30	Newcastle United	W 2-0	Murphy, Riise	52,095
Oct 13	LEEDS UNITED	D 1-1	Murphy	44,352
Oct 20	Leicester City	W 4-1	Hyypia, Fowler 3	21,886
Oct 27	Charlton Athletic	W 2-0	Owen, Redknapp	22,887
Nov 4	MANCHESTER UNITED	W 3-1	Owen 2, Riise	44,361
Nov 17	Blackburn Rovers	D 1-1	Owen	28,859
Nov 25	SUNDERLAND	W 1-0	Heskey	43,537
Dec 1	Derby County	W 1-0	Owen	33,289
Dec 8	MIDDLESBROUGH	W 2-0	Berger, Owen	43,674
Dec 12	FULHAM	D 0-0		37,153
Dec 16	Chelsea	L 0-4		41,174
Dec 23	ARSENAL	L 1-2	Litmanen	44,297
Dec 26	Aston Villa	W 2-1	Smicer, Litmanen	42,602
Dec 29	West Ham United	D 1-1	Owen	35,103
Jan 1	BOLTON WANDERERS	D 1-1	Gerrard	43,710
Jan 9	Southampton	L 0-2		31,527
Jan 13	Arsenal	D 1-1	Riise	38,132
Jan 19	SOUTHAMPTON	D 1-1	Owen	43,710
Jan 22	Manchester United	W 1-0	Murphy	67,599
Jan 30	LEICESTER CITY	W 1-0	Heskey	42,305
Feb 3	Leeds United	W 4-0	Heskey 2, Owen, Ferdinand o.g.	40,216
Feb 9	Ipswich Town	W 6-0	Hyypia, Xavier, Heskey 2, Owen 2	25,608
Feb 23	EVERTON	D 1-1	Anelka	44,371
Mar 2	Fulham	W 2-0	Anelka, Litmanen	21,103
Mar 6	NEWCASTLE UNITED	W 3-0	Murphy 2, Hamann	44,204
Mar 16	Middlesbrough	W 2-1	Heskey, Riise	31,253
Mar 24	CHELSEA	W 1-0	Smicer	44,203
Mar 30	CHARLTON ATHLETIC	W 2-0	Smicer, Owen	44,094
Apr 13	Sunderland	W 1-0	Owen	48,335
Apr 20	DERBY COUNTY	W 2-0	Owen 2	43,510
Apr 27	Tottenham Hotspur	L 0-1		36,017
May 8	BLACKBURN ROVERS	W 4-3	Hyypia, Heskey, Anelka, Murphy	40,663
May 11	IPSWICH TOWN	W 5-0	Smicer, Anelka, Owen, Riise 2	44,000

FA Cup

Jan 5	BIRMINGHAM CITY	(Rd3)	W 3-0	Anelka, Owen 2	40,875
Jan 27	Arsenal	(Rd4)	L 0-1		38,092

League Cup (Worthington Cup)

Oct 9	GRIMSBY TOWN	(Rd3)	L 1-2	McAllister	32,672

European Champions League

Aug 8	FC Haka	(QRd/1L)	W 5-0	Hyypia, Heskey, Owen 3	44,940
Aug 21	FC HAKA	(QRd/2L)	W 4-1	Heskey, Fowler, Redknapp, Wilson o.g.	31,602
Sep 11	BOAVISTA	(P1/GB)	D 1-1	Owen	30,015
Sep 19	Borussia Dortmund	(P1/GB)	D 0-0		50,000
Sep 26	DYNAMO KIEV	(P1/GB)	W 1-0	Litmanen	33,513
Oct 16	Dynamo Kiev	(P1/GB)	W 2-1	Murphy, Gerrard	55,000
Oct 24	Boavista	(P1/GB)	D 1-1	Murphy	6,000
Oct 30	BORUSSIA DORTMUND	(P1/GB)	W 2-0	Smicer, Wright	41,507
Nov 20	BARCELONA	(P2/GB)	L 1-3	Owen	41,521
Dec 5	AS Roma	(P2/GB)	D 0-0		57,819
Feb 20	GALATASARAY	(P2/GB)	D 0-0		41,605
Feb 26	Galatasaray	(P2/GB)	D 1-1	Heskey	22,105
Mar 13	Barcelona	(P2/GB)	D 0-0		75,362
Mar 19	AS ROMA	(P2/GB)	W 2-0	Litmanen, Heskey	41,794
Apr 3	BAYER LEVERKUSEN	(QF/1L)	W 1-0	Hyypia	42,454
Apr 9	Bayer Leverkusen	(QF/2L)	L 2-4	Xavier, Litmanen	22,500

Charity Shield

Aug 12	Manchester United**	W 2-1	Owen, McAllister	70,227

**Played at the Millennium Stadium, Cardiff.

European Super Cup

Aug 24	Bayern Munich†	W 3-2	Heskey, Owen, Riise	15,000

†Played in Monaco.

MANAGER: Gérard Houllier **TOP SCORER:** Michael Owen 28 (19 league)
TRANSFERS IN: Jerzy Dudek from Feyenoord, John Arne Riise from Monaco, Milan Baros from Barik Ostrava, Abel Xavier from Everton
TRANSFERS OUT: Robbie Fowler to Leeds United, Sander Westerveld to Real Sociedad, Christian Ziege to Tottenham Hotspur, Gary McAllister to Coventry City – Player/manager

League & Cup Appearances

PLAYER	LEAGUE	CUP COMPETITION FA CUP	LC	ECL	OTHER	TOTAL
Anelka	13 (7)	2				15 (7)
Arphexad	1 (1)			2		3 (1)
Babbel	2			1 (1)	2	5 (1)
Barmby	2 (4)		1	3 (1)	1	7 (5)
Baros				0 (1)		0 (1)
Berger	12 (9)	0 (1)		1 (7)	0 (1)	13 (18)
Biscan	4 (1)			1 (2)	0 (2)	5 (5)
Carragher	33	2	1	15	1 (1)	52 (1)
Diomede				1		1
Dudek	35	2		12		49
Fowler	8 (2)			2 (4)	0 (1)	10 (7)
Gerrard	26 (2)	2		13 (1)	1	42 (3)
Hamann	31	2	1	12	2	48
Henchoz	37	2		15	2	56
Heskey	26 (9)	1 (1)	0 (1)	16	2	45 (11)
Hyypia	37	2	1	15	2	57
Kippe			0 (1)			0 (1)
Kirkland	1		1	2		4
Litmanen	8 (13)	0 (1)	1	4 (5)		13 (19)
McAllister	14 (11)		1	4 (6)	2	21 (17)
Murphy	31 (5)	1 (1)	1	13 (2)	1 (1)	47 (9)
Owen	25 (4)	2		10	2	39 (4)
Redknapp	2 (2)		0 (1)	1 (2)		3 (5)
Riise	34 (4)	2		13 (1)	2	51 (5)
Smicer	13 (9)	1	1	8 (3)		23 (12)
Traore				1		1
Vignal	3 (1)		1	4		8 (1)
Westerveld	1				2	3
Wright	10 (2)	1	1	2 (1)		14 (3)
Xavier	9 (1)			5		14 (1)

Goalscorers

PLAYER	LEAGUE	CUP COMPETITION FA CUP	LC	ECL	OTHER	TOTAL
Owen	19	2		5	2	28
Heskey	9			4	1	14
Murphy	6			2		8
Riise	7				1	8
Litmanen	4			3		7
Anelka	4	1				5
Hyypia	3			2		5
Smicer	4			1		5
Fowler	3			1		4
Gerrard	3			1		4
McAllister			1		1	2
Redknapp	1			1		2
Xavier	1			1		2
Berger	1					1
Hamann	1					1
Wright				1		1
Opps' o.gs.	1			1		2

Fact File

Robbie Fowler's last goals for Liverpool were a hat-trick v Leicester City on 20 October 2001.

Final Premier League Table

		P	W	D	L	F	A	PTS
1	Arsenal	38	26	9	3	79	36	87
2	Liverpool	38	24	8	6	67	30	80
3	Manchester U	38	24	5	9	87	45	77
4	Newcastle U	38	21	8	9	74	52	71
5	Leeds U	38	18	12	8	53	37	66
6	Chelsea	38	17	13	8	66	38	64
7	West Ham U	38	15	8	15	48	57	53
8	Aston Villa	38	12	14	12	46	47	50
9	Tottenham H	38	14	8	16	49	53	50
10	Blackburn R	38	12	10	16	55	51	46
11	Southampton	38	12	9	17	46	54	45
12	Middlesbrough	38	12	9	17	35	47	45
13	Fulham	38	10	14	14	36	44	44
14	Charlton Ath	38	10	14	14	38	49	44
15	Everton	38	11	10	17	45	57	43
16	Bolton W	38	9	13	16	44	62	40
17	Sunderland	38	10	10	18	29	51	40
18	Ipswich T	38	9	9	20	41	64	36
19	Derby Co	38	8	6	24	33	63	30
20	Leicester C	38	5	13	20	30	64	28

Season 2002-03

FA Premier League

DATE	OPPONENTS	SCORE	GOALSCORERS	ATTENDANCE
Aug 18	Aston Villa	W 1-0	Riise	41,183
Aug 24	SOUTHAMPTON	W 3-0	Diouf 2, Murphy	43,058
Aug 28	Blackburn Rovers	D 2-2	Murphy, Riise	29,207
Sep 2	NEWCASTLE UNITED	D 2-2	Owen, Hamann	43,241
Sep 11	BIRMINGHAM CITY	D 2-2	Murphy, Gerrard	43,113
Sep 14	Bolton Wanderers	W 3-2	Baros 2, Heskey	27,328
Sep 21	WEST BROMWICH ALBION	W 2-0	Baros, Riise	43,830
Sep 28	Manchester City	W 3-0	Owen 3	35,131
Oct 6	CHELSEA	W 1-0	Owen	43,856
Oct 19	Leeds United	W 1-0	Diao	40,178
Oct 26	TOTTENHAM HOTSPUR	W 2-1	Owen, Murphy	44,084
Nov 2	WEST HAM UNITED	W 2-0	Owen 2	44,048
Nov 9	Middlesbrough	L 0-1		34,747
Nov 17	SUNDERLAND	D 0-0		43,074
Nov 23	Fulham	L 2-3	Baros, Hamann	18,144
Dec 1	MANCHESTER UNITED	L 1-2	Hyypia	44,250
Dec 7	Charlton Athletic	L 0-2		26,694
Dec 15	Sunderland	L 1-2	Baros	37,118
Dec 22	EVERTON	D 0-0		44,025
Dec 26	BLACKBURN ROVERS	D 1-1	Riise	43,075
Dec 29	Arsenal	D 1-1	Murphy	38,074
Jan 1	Newcastle United	L 0-1		52,147
Jan 11	ASTON VILLA	D 1-1	Owen	43,210
Jan 18	Southampton	W 1-0	Heskey	32,104
Jan 29	ARSENAL	D 2-2	Heskey, Riise	43,668
Feb 2	West Ham United	W 3-0	Baros, Heskey, Gerrard	35,033
Feb 8	MIDDLESBROUGH	D 1-1	Riise	42,247
Feb 23	Birmingham City	L 1-2	Owen	29,449
Mar 8	BOLTON WANDERERS	W 2-0	Owen, Diouf	41,462
Mar 16	Tottenham Hotspur	W 3-2	Owen, Heskey, Gerrard	36,077
Mar 23	LEEDS UNITED	W 3-1	Owen, Murphy, Gerrard	43,021
Apr 5	Manchester United	L 0-4		67,639
Apr 12	FULHAM	W 2-0	Heskey, Owen	42,120
Apr 19	Everton	W 2-1	Owen, Murphy	40,169
Apr 21	CHARLTON ATHLETIC	W 2-1	Hyypia, Gerrard	42,010
Apr 26	West Bromwich Albion	W 6-0	Owen 4, Baros 2	27,128
May 3	MANCHESTER CITY	L 1-2	Baros	44,220
May 11	Chelsea	L 1-2	Hyypia	41,911

FA Cup

Jan 5	Manchester City	(Rd3)	W 1-0	Murphy	28,586
Jan 26	Crystal Palace	(Rd4)	D 0-0		26,054
Feb 5	CRYSTAL PALACE	(R)	L 0-2		35,109

League Cup (Worthington Cup)

Nov 6	SOUTHAMPTON	(Rd3)	W 3-1	Baros, Diouf, Berger	35,870
Dec 4	IPSWICH TOWN	(Rd4)	D 1-1*	Diouf	26,305
Dec 18	Aston Villa	(Rd5)	W 4-3	Baros, Murphy 2, Gerrard	38,530
Jan 8	Sheffield United	(SF/1L)	L 1-2	Mellor	30,095
Jan 21	SHEFFIELD UNITED	(SF/2L)	W 2-0**	Diouf, Owen	43,837
Mar 2	Manchester United†	(F)	W 2-0	Gerrard, Owen	74,500

*After extra time. Liverpool won 5-4 on penalties. Scorers: Baros, Carragher, Diouf, Gerrard, Riise.
**After extra time. Score at 90 mins 1-0. †Played at the Millennium Stadium, Cardiff.

European Champions League

Sep 17	Valencia	(P1/GB)	L 0-2		43,000
Sep 25	FC BASEL	(P1/GB)	D 1-1	Baros	37,634
Oct 2	SPARTAK MOSCOW	(P1/GB)	W 5-0	Hyypia, Heskey 2, Diao, Cheyrou	40,812
Oct 22	Spartak Moscow	(P1/GB)	W 3-1	Owen 3	15,000
Oct 30	VALENCIA	(P1/GB)	L 0-1		41,831
Nov 12	FC Basel	(P1/GB)	D 3-3	Smicer, Owen, Murphy	35,000

UEFA Cup

Nov 28	Vitesse Arnhem	(Rd3/1L)	W 1-0	Owen	28,000
Dec 12	VITESSE ARNHEM	(Rd3/2L)	W 1-0	Owen	23,576
Feb 20	Auxerre	(Rd4/1L)	W 1-0	Hyypia	20,452
Feb 27	AUXERRE	(Rd4/2L)	W 2-0	Owen, Murphy	34,252
Mar 13	Glasgow Celtic	(Rd5/1L)	D 1-1	Heskey	59,759
Mar 20	GLASGOW CELTIC	(Rd5/2L)	L 0-2		44,238

Community Shield

Aug 11	Arsenal††	L 0-1	67,337

††Played at the Millennium Stadium, Cardiff.

Fact File

Michael Owen became the 11th Liverpool player to score 100 league goals, in the 6-0 win v West Bromwich Albion in April.

League & Cup Appearances

PLAYER	LEAGUE	CUP COMPETITION				OTHER	TOTAL
		FA CUP	LC	ECL	UEFA		
Babbel	2		3		1	0 (1)	6 (1)
Baros	17 (10)	0 (1)	2 (2)	2 (3)	1 (3)	0 (1)	22 (20)
Berger	0 (2)		1	0 (1)			1 (3)
Biscan	3 (3)	0 (1)	2 (1)	0 (1)	0 (2)		5 (8)
Carragher	34 (1)	3	3 (2)	6	5		51 (3)
Cheyrou	8 (11)	2	1 (1)	2 (2)	1	0 (1)	14 (15)
Diao	13 (13)	1 (1)	3 (1)	3 (2)	2 (1)		22 (18)
Diouf	21 (8)	3	5	1 (4)	4	1	35 (12)
Dudek	30	1 (1)	2	6	5	1	45 (1)
Gerrard	32 (2)	2	6	5	6	1	52 (2)
Hamann	29 (1)	1	1	5	2 (2)	1	39 (3)
Henchoz	19	2	4	2	4	1	32
Heskey	22 (10)	2 (1)	2 (3)	6	4 (1)	1	37 (15)
Hyypia	36	3	4	6	6	1	56
Kirkland	8	2	4		1		15
Mellor	1 (2)	1	2				4 (2)
Murphy	36	3	4	6	6	0 (1)	55 (1)
Otsemobor			1				1
Owen	32 (3)	2	3 (1)	5 (1)	6	1	49 (5)
Riise	31 (6)	2 (1)	4	6	4 (1)	1	48 (8)
Smicer	10 (11)	1	4 (1)	1 (1)	2 (2)	0 (1)	18 (16)
Traore	30 (2)	2	2 (1)	4 (1)	6	1	45 (4)
Vignal	0 (1)		2	0 (1)			2 (2)
Welsh			0 (1)				0 (1)
Xavier	4		1			1	6

Goalscorers

PLAYER	LEAGUE	CUP COMPETITION				OTHER	TOTAL
		FA CUP	LC	ECL	UEFA		
Owen	19		2	4	3		28
Baros	9		2 (1)	1			12 (1)
Murphy	7	1	2	1	1		12
Heskey	6			2	1		9
Gerrard	5		2 (1)				7 (1)
Diouf	3		3 (1)				6 (1)
Riise	6		(1)				6 (1)
Hyppia	3			1	1		5
Diao	1			1			2
Hamann	2						2
Berger			1				1
Cheyrou				1			1
Mellor			1				1
Smicer				1			1
Carragher			(1)				(1)

Penalty shoot-out goals in brackets.

MANAGER: Gérard Houllier
CAPTAIN: Sami Hyypia
TRANSFERS IN: Bruno Cheyrou from Lille, Salif Diao from Sedan, El-Hadji Diouf from Lens
TRANSFERS OUT: Nick Barmby to Leeds United, Jari Litmanen to Ajax, Jamie Redknapp to Tottenham Hotspur

Final Premier League Table

		P	W	D	L	F	A	Pts
1	Manchester U	38	25	8	5	74	34	83
2	Arsenal	38	23	9	6	85	42	78
3	Newcastle U	38	21	6	11	63	48	69
4	Chelsea	38	19	10	9	68	38	67
5	Liverpool	38	18	10	10	61	41	64
6	Blackburn R	38	16	12	10	52	43	60
7	Everton	38	17	8	13	48	49	59
8	Southampton	38	13	13	12	43	46	52
9	Manchester C	38	15	6	17	47	54	51
10	Tottenham H	38	14	8	16	51	62	50
11	Middlesbrough	38	13	10	15	48	44	49
12	Charlton Ath	38	14	7	17	45	56	49
13	Birmingham C	38	13	9	16	41	49	48
14	Fulham	38	13	9	16	41	50	48
15	Leeds U	38	14	5	19	58	57	47
16	Aston Villa	38	12	9	17	42	47	45
17	Bolton W	38	10	14	14	41	51	44
18	West Ham U	38	10	12	16	42	59	42
19	West Bromwich Alb	38	6	8	24	29	65	26
20	Sunderland	38	4	7	27	21	65	19

The War Years

First World War: Season 1915-16

Lancashire Section Principal Tournament

DATE	OPPONENTS	SCORE	GOALSCORERS	ATTENDANCE
Sep 4	Bolton Wanderers	D 1-1	Pagnam	3,000
Sep 11	MANCHESTER CITY	L 0-1		15,000
Sep 18	Stoke City	D 2-2	Longworth, Pagnam	8,000
Sep 25	BURNLEY	W 5-2	Dawson 2, Henderson, Pagnam, Goddard	15,000
Oct 2	Preston North End	W 2-1	Pagnam, Wadsworth	12,000
Oct 9	STOCKPORT COUNTY	D 0-0		16,000
Oct 16	ROCHDALE	D 2-2	Pagnam2	12,000
Oct 23	Bury	L 1-2	Pagnam	7,000
Oct 30	MANCHESTER UNITED	L 0-2		15,000
Nov 6	Blackpool	L 2-5	Goddard 2 (1 pen)	4,000
Nov 13	SOUTHPORT	W 4-2	Metcalfe, Watson, Pagnam 2 (1 pen)	14,000
Nov 20	Oldham Athletic	W 2-1	Banks 2	4,000
Nov 27	EVERTON	W 4-1	Pagnam 3, Watson	20,000
Dec 4	BOLTON WANDERERS	D 3-3	Banks, Pagnam, Mackinlay	5,000
Dec 11	Manchester City	L 1-2	Watson (pen)	6,000
Dec 18	STOKE CITY	W 2-0	Pagnam 2	7,000
Dec 25	Burnley	D 3-3	Pagnam 2, Watson	15,000
Jan 1	PRESTON NORTH END	L 0-2		8,000
Jan 8	Stockport County	W 3-1	Mackinlay 2, Pagnam	6,000
Jan 15	Rochdale	L 1-3	Mackinlay	4,000
Jan 22	BURY	W 2-1	Pagnam, Watson	16,000
Jan 29	Manchester United	D 1-1	Pinkney	10,000
Feb 5	BLACKPOOL	W 1-0	Pinkney	16,000
Feb 12	Southport	W 5-2	Watson 2, Pagnam 2 (1 pen), Metcalfe	5,000
Feb 19	OLDHAM ATHLETIC	L 0-2		17,000
Feb 26	Everton	W 1-0	Metcalfe	18,000

Playing record: P26 W11 D7 L8 F48 A 42 Points 29 Position 6th

Lancashire Section Supplementary Competition

DATE	OPPONENTS	SCORE	GOALSCORERS	ATTENDANCE
Mar 4	OLDHAM ATHLETIC	W 4-1	Watson, Pagnam 2, Metcalfe	14,000
Mar 11	Manchester City	D 1-1	Watson	15,000
Mar 18	Manchester United	D 0-0		10,000
Mar 25	STOCKPORT COUNTY	W 2-1	Metcalfe, Waine	15,000
Apr 1	Everton	L 0-1		25,000
Apr 8	Oldham Athletic	L 1-2	Watson	2,000
Apr 15	MANCHESTER CITY	L 0-2		12,000
Apr 21	EVERTON	W 5-2	Banks, Pagnam 3 (2 pen), Watson	27,000
Apr 22	MANCHESTER UNITED	W 7-1	Watson 2, Pagnam 3, Pinkney, Wadsworth	18,000
Apr 29	Stockport County	L 1-2	Pagnam	6,000

Playing record: P10 W4 D2 L4 F21 A13 Points 10 Position 4th

Appearances & Goalscorers

	PRIN T		SUPP T		TOTALS	
PLAYERS	APP	G	APP	G	APP	G
Bamber	4		10		14	
Banks	15	3	5	1	20	4
Bradley*	13				13	
Campbell	10		1		11	
Cunliffe*	4		10		14	
Dawson	11	2			11	2
Fairfoul	5				5	
Goddard	20	3	6		26	3
Henderson*	10	1			10	1
Kennedy*			1		1	
Lacey	1				1	
Longworth	22	1	10		32	1
Mackinlay	23	4	6		29	4
McGhie*	4				4	
Metcalf	9	3	6	2	15	5
Middlehurst*	19		8		27	
Molyneux	7				7	
Pagnam	26	21	8	9	34	30
Pinkney*	17	2	7	1	24	3
Richie*	1				1	
Scott	15				15	
Scott	2				2	
Speakman	9		2		11	
Taylor*	1		9		10	
Wadsworth W	12	1	8	1	20	2
Waine*	2		3	1	5	1
Watson*	18	7	10	6	28	13
Williams*	2				2	
Winn*	4				4	

* Indicates guest player.

1916-17

Lancashire Section Principal Tournament

DATE	OPPONENTS	SCORE	GOALSCORERS	ATTENDANCE
Sep 2	BOLTON WANDERERS	W 3-1	Pagnam, Goddard, Bamber	8,000
Sep 9	Burslem Port Vale	D 0-0		10,000
Sep 16	OLDHAM ATHLETIC	W 2-0	Pagnam 2	15,000
Sep 23	Preston North End	W 1-0	Pagnam	4,000
Sep 30	BURNLEY	D 0-0		16,000
Oct 7	Manchester United	D 0-0		8,000
Oct 14	Blackpool	W 1-0	Lewis	8,000
Oct 21	STOCKPORT COUNTY	W 3-1	Metcalfe, Mackinlay, Pagnam	15,000
Oct 28	Bury	W 4-3	Pagnam 2, Longworth, Metcalfe	1,000
Nov 4	STOKE CITY	W 3-1	Pagnam 2, Goddard	15,000
Nov 11	Southport Central	W 3-1	Metcalfe 2, Bamber	3,000
Nov 18	BLACKBURN ROVERS	W 3-1	Metcalfe 2, Lewis	14,000
Nov 25	Manchester City	D 1-1	Metcalfe	15,000
Dec 2	EVERTON	W 2-1	Metcalfe, Bennett	22,000
Dec 9	Rochdale	L 2-3	Bennett 2	8,000
Dec 23	BURSLEM PORT VALE	W 5-1	Bennett 4, Mackinlay	2,000
Dec 30	Oldham Athletic	W 1-0	Bennett	1,500
Jan 6	PRESTON NORTH END	W 3-1	Bennett 2, Bamber	11,000
Jan 13	Burnley	W 1-0	Lewis	7,000
Jan 20	MANCHESTER UNITED	D 3-3	Lewis 2, Bennett	12,000
Jan 27	BLACKPOOL	D 2-2	Lewis, Pagnam	14,000

Appearances & Goalscorers

	PRIN T		SUPP T		TOTALS	
PLAYERS	APP	G	APP	G	APP	G
Ashcroft*	5				5	
Bamber	26	4	5		31	4
Beattie*	1				1	
Bennett	20	17	4	2	24	19
Bradley*	11	1	3		14	1
Butler*	4				4	
Campbell	8		1		9	
Capper*	1				1	
Cunliffe*	29	1	6		35	1
Curtis*	2				2	
Donnachie*	3				3	
Fairhurst*			1		1	
Gee*	1				1	
Goddard	18	2	4	1	22	3
Hannaway*	1				1	
Henderson*	2				2	
Houghton*	2		5		7	
Jenkinson	4				4	
Lee*			1		1	
Lewis	24	10	4	2	28	12

1916-17 continued

DATE	OPPONENTS	SCORE	GOALSCORERS	ATTENDANCE
Feb 3	Stockport County	D 0-0		7,000
Feb 10	BURY	W 4-0	Bradley, Bennett 2, Lewis	15,000
Feb 17	Stoke City	L 0-1		12,000
Feb 24	SOUTHPORT CENTRAL	W 4-2	Hemsley o.g., Lewis, Bennett, Metcalfe (pen)	13,000
Mar 3	Blackburn Rovers	W 2-0	Bennett, Metcalfe	8,000
Mar 10	MANCHESTER CITY	W 3-0	Lewis, Bamber, Wadsworth	20,000
Mar 17	Everton	D 2-2	Bennett, Wadsworth	24,000
Mar 24	ROCHDALE	W 4-0	Lewis, Bennett, Metcalfe, Cunliffe	15,000
Apr 28	Bolton Wanderers	L 0-1		10,000

Playing record: P30 W19 D8 L3 F62 A26 Points 46 Position 1st

Lancashire Section Supplementary Tournament

DATE	OPPONENTS	SCORE	GOALSCORERS	ATTENDANCE
Dec 26	SOUTHPORT	L 0-1		16,000
Mar 31	Stockport County	D 0-0		6,000
Apr 7	Everton	L 0-4		16,000
Apr 9	Southport	W 7-0	Goddard, Pagnam 3, Mackinlay 3	2,000
Apr 14	STOCKPORT COUNTY	W 6-0	Metcalfe, Mackinlay, Lewis 2, Bennett 2	18,000
Apr 21	EVERTON	L 0-5		25,000

Playing record: P6 W2 D1 L3 F13 A10 Points 5 Position 9th

	PRIN T		SUPP T		TOTALS	
PLAYERS	APP	G	APP	G	APP	G
Longworth	28	1	6		34	1
Lowe			1		1	
Lucas	24		5		29	
Mackinlay	29	2	6	4	35	6
Metcalf	24	11	4	1	28	12
Murphy*	1		1		2	
Osbourne*	1				1	
Page T*	1		1		2	
Pagnam	12	10	2	3	14	13
Pinkney*	4				4	
Rigg*	1				1	
Speakman	3				3	
Stansfield*	1				1	
Sutcliffe*	1				1	
Swann*	3				3	
Taylor	8				8	
Wadsworth W	24	2	6		30	2
Waine*	1				1	
Watson*	1				1	
Williams*	1				1	
Opps' o.gs.		1				1

* Indicates guest player.

1917-18

Lancashire Section Principal Tournament

DATE	OPPONENTS	SCORE	GOALSCORERS	ATTENDANCE
Sep 1	Port Vale	W 3-2	Bamber, Bennett J o.g., Bennett T	5,000
Sep 8	PORT VALE	W 4-0	Bennett 2, Lewis, Metcalfe	12,000
Sep 15	Bolton Wanderers	W 3-0	Bennett 2, Metcalfe	5,000
Sep 22	BOLTON WANDERERS	W 6-0	Bennett 3, Lewis 3	15,000
Sep 29	Everton	D 2-2	Bennett, Metcalfe	25,000
Oct 6	EVERTON	W 6-0	Mackinlay, Lewis 4, Bennett	26,000
Oct 13	Preston North End	W 6-0	Metcalfe 2, Waine, Bennett, Lewis, Bamber	4,000
Oct 20	PRESTON NORTH END	D 2-2	Bennett 2	16,000
Oct 27	BLACKPOOL	W 4-1	Bennett, Metcalfe 2, Wadsworth W	12,000
Nov 3	Blackpool	W 6-0	Bennett 2, Metcalfe 2, Wadsworth W, Waine	2,000
Nov 10	MANCHESTER CITY	W 2-0	Bennett 2	18,000
Nov 17	Manchester City	D 1-1	Bennett	20,000
Nov 24	BLACKBURN ROVERS	W 7-0	Bennett, Metcalfe, Lewis 2, Mackinlay, Waine 2	14,000
Dec 1	Blackburn Rovers	W 6-1	Bennett 2, Lewis, Metcalfe, Waine, Mackinlay	7,000
Dec 8	ROCHDALE	W 5-1	Bennett 5	16,000
Dec 15	Rochdale	L 0-1		5,000
Dec 22	OLDHAM ATHLETIC	W 3-0	Lewis 2 (1 pen), Bennett	15,000
Dec 29	Oldham Athletic	D 3-3	Waine, Bennett, Balmer o.g.	10,000
Jan 5	STOCKPORT COUNTY	W 2-1	Schofield, Lewis (pen)	18,000
Jan 12	Stockport County	L 0-1		6,000
Jan 19	MANCHESTER UNITED	W 5-1	Metcalfe 2, Bennett 2, Mackinlay	20,000
Jan 26	Manchester United	W 2-0	Lewis, Metcalfe	10,000
Feb 2	SOUTHPORT	W 6-1	Lewis 2, Bennett 2, Metcalfe, Mackinlay	15,000
Feb 9	Southport	W 3-1	Bennett 2, Lewis	7,000
Feb 16	BURNLEY	W 7-1	Bennett 5, Lewis, Metcalfe	16,000
Feb 23	Burnley	W 3-1	Wadsworth W, Schofield, Green	2,000
Mar 2	STOKE CITY	D 1-1	Lewis (pen)	22,000
Mar 9	Stoke City	L 1-3	Schofield	25,000
Mar 16	BURY	D 1-1	Bennett	15,000
Mar 23	Bury	W 1-0	Metcalfe	5,000

Playing record: P30 W21 D6 L3 F101 A26 Points 48 Position 2nd

Lancashire Section Supplementary Tournament

DATE	OPPONENTS	SCORE	GOALSCORERS	ATTENDANCE
Jan 1	EVERTON	W 4-1	Lewis 2, Waine, Bennett	25,000
Mar 29	Everton	L 2-3	Lewis, Green	28,000
Mar 30	Southport	W 8-0	Bennett 4, Green 3, Schofield	6,000
Apr 6	SOUTHPORT	W 2-0	Bennett, Green	20,000
Apr 13	Stockport County	W 4-1	Green 3, Bennett	2,500
Apr 20	STOCKPORT COUNTY	W 4-2	Green, Lewis 2 (1 pen), Goddard	18,000

Playing record: P6 W5 D0 L1 F24 A7 Points 10 Position 1st

Appearances & Goalscorers

	PRIN T		SUPP T		TOTALS	
PLAYERS	APP	G	APP	G	APP	G
Bamber	30	2	6		36	2
Bennett	29	41	6	7	35	48
Birchall*			1		1	
Butler*	2				2	
Campbell	13		1		14	
Connell*	2		5		7	
Cross*	1				1	
Cunliffe*	8				8	
Goddard			1	1	1	1
Green*	2	1	5	9	7	9
Hayes*			1		1	
Houghton*	7				7	
Hughes*	1				1	
Jenkinson	15		6		21	
Lewis	30	21	5	5	35	26
Longworth	28		4		32	
Lovell*	3				3	
Lucas	10				10	
Mackinlay	29	5	6		35	5
Metcalf	29	17		1	30	17
Neish*	1				1	
Page T*	2		1		3	
Pagnam	1				1	
Rigg*	1				1	
Robertson*			4		4	
Schofield*	21	3	6	1	27	4
Smith*	2				2	
Speakman	5		1		6	
Wadsworth H	1				1	
Wadsworth W	29	3	1		30	3
Waine*	28	6	5	1	33	7
Opps' o.gs.		2				2

* Indicates guest player.

1918-19

Lancashire Section Principal Tournament

DATE	OPPONENTS	SCORE	GOALSCORERS	ATTENDANCE
Sep 7	ROCHDALE	W 4-0	Bennett 2, Lewis, Metcalfe	20,000
Sep 14	Rochdale	W 2-1	Lewis, Green	8,000
Sep 21	PRESTON NORTH END	W 8-0	Metcalfe, Lewis, Wadsworth H, Mackinlay 2, Bennett 3	16,000
Sep 28	Preston North End	W 2-0	Bennett, Lewis	3,000
Oct 5	EVERTON	L 2-4	Metcalfe, Wadsworth H	30,000
Oct 12	Everton	L 2-4	Green, Waring o.g.	35,000
Oct 19	BOLTON WANDERERS	W 6-1	Green 2, Bamber, Metcalfe, Lewis, Wadsworth H	22,000
Oct 26	Bolton Wanderers	D 2-2	Bennett, Mackinlay	8,000
Nov 2	Port Vale	W 2-0	Lewis, Green	5,000
Nov 9	PORT VALE	W 4-0	Green, Bennett, Wadsworth H 2	14,000
Nov 16	Manchester City	W 2-0	Metcalfe, Bennett	30,000
Nov 23	MANCHESTER CITY	W 2-0	Wadsworth H, Bennett.	27,000
Nov 30	Oldham Athletic	W 2-0	Green 2	5,000
Dec 7	OLDHAM ATHLETIC	W 5-1	Wadsworth H, Mackinlay 2, Green 2	18,000
Dec 14	Blackburn Rovers	W 2-1	Metcalfe 2	7,000
Dec 21	BLACKBURN ROVERS	W 1-0	Duckworth F o.g.	16,000
Dec 28	BURNLEY	W 7-0	Miller 2, Lewis 2, Phillips, Mackinlay 2	25,000
Jan 11	SOUTHPORT VULCANS	W 3-0	Lewis, Page T 2	20,000
Jan 18	Southport Vulcans	L 1-2	Matthews	2,000
Jan 25	MANCHESTER UNITED	D 1-1	Matthews	25,000
Feb 1	Manchester United	W 1-0	Wadsworth H	15,000
Feb 8	STOKE CITY	D 1-1	Matthews	25,000
Feb 15	Stoke City	L 1-3	Matthews	20,000
Feb 22	Bury	D 1-1	Miller	6,000
Mar 1	BURY	W 6-0	Lewis (pen), Matthews, Miller 3, Mackinlay	16,000
Mar 8	Blackpool	L 2-3	Miller, Lewis	5,000
Mar 15	BLACKPOOL	W 3-1	Lewis 2, Mackinlay	28,000
Mar 22	Stockport County	L 1-2	Lewis	6,000
Mar 29	STOCKPORT COUNTY	W 3-0	Lewis 2, Longworth	20,000
Apr 7	Burnley	L 3-5	Wadsworth H, Matthews 2	8,500

Playing record: P30 W19 D4 L7 F82 A 33 Points 42 Position 3rd

Lancashire Section Supplementary Tournament

DATE	OPPONENTS	SCORE	GOALSCORERS	ATTENDANCE
Jan 1	EVERTON	W 4-1	Lewis 2, Waine, Bennett	30,000
Apr 5	SOUTHPORT VULCANS	W 4-2	Miller, Lewis, Wadsworth W, Wadsworth H	20,000
Apr 12	Southport Vulcans	W 2-0	Mackinlay, Matthews	10,000
Apr 18	EVERTON	D 1-1	Pearson	36,955
Apr 19	STOCKPORT COUNTY	W 3-1	Mackinlay, Wadsworth H, Miller	18,000
Apr 26	Stockport County	D 1-1	Bamber	5,000

Playing record: P6 W4 D2 LO F13 A6 Points 10 Position 1st

Appearances & Goalscorers

	PRIN T		SUPP T		TOTALS	
PLAYERS	APP	G	APP	G	APP	G
Bamber	29	1	6	1	35	2
Bennett	11	10			11	10
Birchall	1				1	
Bromilow			1		1	
Campbell	3				3	
Checkland	1				1	
Connell	6				6	
Cross*	1		1		2	
Forshaw			2		2	
Green*	12	10			12	10
Jenkinson	28		6		34	
Lewis	30	16	6	2	36	18
Longworth	18	1	3		21	1
Mackinlay	29	9	6	2	35	11
McTavish	1				1	
Matthews	11	7	2	1	13	8
Metcalfe	17	7	1	1	18	8
Miller	14	7	5	2	19	9
Newman*			1		1	
Page J*	1				1	
Page T*	1	2			1	2
Patterson*	1				1	
Pearson	2		5	1	7	1
Penman			1		1	
Phillips*	3	1	1		4	1
Robertson*	6				6	
Schofield*	18				18	
Scott *	21		6		27	
Speakman	11		1		12	
Wadsworth H	28	9	5	2	33	11
Wadsworth W	26		6	1	32	1
Opps' o.gs.		2				2

* Indicates guest player.

Second World War: 1939-40

Football League Division One

DATE	OPPONENTS	SCORE	GOALSCORERS	ATTENDANCE
Aug 26	Sheffield United	L 1-2	McInnes	20,000
Aug 30	MIDDLESBROUGH	W 4-1	Taylor 2, Van Den Berg, Balmer	16,762
Sep 2	CHELSEA	W 1-0	Done	19,386

Normal league football suspended. Re-organised on regional basis.

Football League Western Division

DATE	OPPONENTS	SCORE	GOALSCORERS	ATTENDANCE
Oct 21	Stockport County	W 3-0	Balmer 2, Fagan	5,000
Oct 28	PORT VALE	D 1-1	Balmer	4,000
Nov 11	Tranmere Rovers	W 3-1	Fagan, Nieuwenhuys 2	6,000
Nov 18	MANCHESTER UNITED	W 1-0	Fagan (pen)	5,000
Nov 25	Wrexham	L 1-2	Nieuwenhuys	2,000
Dec 2	EVERTON	D 2-2	Nieuwenhuys, Fagan (pen)	8,000
Dec 9	Stoke City	L 1-3	Fagan	1,300
Dec 23	NEW BRIGHTON	W 6-2	Done 4, Carney, Eastham	2,000
Jan 1	CREWE ALEXANDRA	W 7-3	Nieuwenhuys 3, Liddell, Leadbetter, Busby, Carney	2,000
Jan 6	Manchester City	W 7-3	Liddell 3, Fagan 2, Nieuwenhuys 2	6,000
Jan 20	CHESTER CITY	D 1-1	Nieuwenhuys	1,000
Feb 24	Port Vale	W 8-3	Fagan 4 (1 pen), Van Den Berg 2, Tennant, Liddell	2,000
Mar 16	Manchester United	L 0-1		6,000
Mar 22	Crewe Alexandra	W 6-3	Fagan 3 (2 pens), Carney, Balmer, Liddell	4,300

Appearances & Goalscorers

	DIV 1		WEST L		WC		TOTALS	
PLAYERS	APP	G	APP	G	APP	G	APP	G
Balmer	3	1	7	5	1		11	6
Brown*			4				4	
Busby	3		14	1	2		19	1
Bush	3		7		1		11	
Carney			13	5	2		15	5
Cook*			1				1	
Cooper			9				9	
Doherty*			1	2			1	2
Done	1	1	4	4			5	5
Easdale			3				3	
Eastham S*			9	1	1		10	1
Fagan	3		12	14		1	16	15
Guttridge*			3				3	
Halsall*			2				2	
Hanson*			2	1			2	1
Harley	3		5		1		9	
Kemp	3		4				7	
Kinghorn			1				1	
Lambert			5		2		7	
Leadbetter*			4	1			4	1
Liddell			14	9	2		16	9
Mansley*			6		1		7	
McInnes	3	1	11				14	1
Murphy*			3	1			3	1

1939-40 continued

DATE	OPPONENTS	SCORE	GOALSCORERS	ATTENDANCE
Mar 23	WREXHAM	D 0-0		8,000
Mar 30	Everton	W 3-1	Nieuwenhuys 2, Liddell	12,896
Apr 6	STOKE CITY	L 1-2	Balmer	5,000
May 11	STOCKPORT COUNTY	W 4-3	Nieuwenhuys 3, Van Den Berg	6,000
May 18	Chester City	L 0-4		1,500
May 25	MANCHESTER CITY	W 3-2	Nieuwenhuys, Liddell (pen), Murphy	2,000
May 29	TRANMERE ROVERS	W 8-3	Nieuwenhuys 2, Doherty 2, Carney 2, Liddell, Hanson	5,000
Jun 1	New Brighton	D 0-0		1,500

Playing record: P22 W12 D5 L5 F66 A40 Points 29 Position 2nd

War League Cup

Apr 20	Barrow	L 0-2		5,963
Apr 27	BARROW	L 1-2	Fagan (pen)	9,147

	DIV 1		WEST L		WC		TOTALS	
PLAYERS	APP	G	APP	G	APP	G	APP	G
Nieuwenhuys	3		20	18	2		25	18
Paisley			5		2		7	
Palk			2				2	
Patterson			1				1	
Ramsden	3		11		1		15	
Riley			10		1		11	
Rogers			5		1		6	
Spicer			1				1	
Stuart*			1				1	
Swift*			2				2	
Taylor	2	2	11				13	2
Tennant*			15	1			15	1
Van Den Berg	3	1	13	3	1		17	4
Walton*			1				1	

* Indicates guest player.

1940-41

North Regional League

DATE	OPPONENTS	SCORE	GOALSCORERS	ATTENDANCE
Aug 31	PRESTON NORTH END	D 3-3	Nieuwenhuys, O'Donnell, Fagan	5,000
Sep 7	Blackburn Rovers	W 3-0	Nieuwenhuys, Fagan 2	2,176
Sep 14	BLACKBURN ROVERS	D 1-1	Nieuwenhuys	5,000
Sep 21	Preston North End	L 0-5		3,000
Sep 28	Chester City	W 2-0	Westcott 2	2,500
Oct 5	CHESTER CITY	W 9-1	Westcott 4, Nieuwenhuys 3, Paisley, Drury	5,000
Oct 12	Bury	W 3-0	Drury 2, Nieuwenhuys	5,000
Oct 19	MANCHESTER CITY	L 0-4		8,000
Oct 26	Stockport County	L 0-2		2,000
Nov 2	STOCKPORT COUNTY	W 5-0	Hunt 2, Paisley, Grundy, Nieuwenhuys	1,000
Nov 9	Manchester City	L 1-5	Hunt	2,000
Nov 16	BURY	W 3-0	Hunt, Nieuwenhuys, Atkinson	3,000
Nov 23	MANCHESTER UNITED	D 2-2	Hunt, Fagan	3,000
Nov 30	Manchester United	L 0-2		700
Dec 7	Tranmere Rovers	L 1-3	Grundy	1,500
Dec 14	NEW BRIGHTON	W 6-4	Nieuwenhuys 4, Liddell, Paisley	1,000
Dec 25	EVERTON	W 3-1	Carney 2, Nieuwenhuys	5,000
Dec 28	TRANMERE ROVERS	L 2-3	Carney, Liddell	3,000
Jan 4	EVERTON*	L 1-2	Paisley	3,000
Jan 11	Everton*	L 1-4	Shafto	4,000
Jan 18	Oldham Athletic	W 3-0	Paisley, Search, Collister.	500
Feb 8	EVERTON	L 1-3	Done	3,000
Mar 1	Bury	W 5-2	Liddell 2, Dorsett 2, Done	2,000
Mar 8	WREXHAM	W 7-2	Paisley 3, Dorsett 2, Done, Liddell	1,500
Mar 15	Blackpool	L 4-6	Fagan (2 pens), Paisley, Done	7,000
Mar 22	BLACKPOOL	L 2-6	Dorsett 2	3,000
Mar 29	Bury	W 5-1	Dorsett 2, Pickstock, Done, Liddell	1,500
Apr 5	BURY	W 2-0	Palk, Done	2,000
Apr 12	Blackpool	D 0-0		4,000
Apr 14	Southport	L 0-2		1,500
Apr 26	MANCHESTER UNITED	W 2-1	Done, Liddell	2,000
May 3	Manchester United	D 1-1	Done	1,500
May 17	Wrexham	L 3-4	Paisley, Nieuwenhuys, Liddell	1,200
May 24	Chester City	W 6-1	Done 3, Cole o.g, Cook, Liddell	700
May 31	EVERTON	D 2-2	Liddell, Done	6,000
Jun 2	Everton	L 1-3	Jones o.g.	4,000
Jun 7	Preston North End	L 1-6	Lyon	5,000

Playing record: P37 W15 D6 L16 F91 A82 Points 36 Position 16th

*Also counted as Lancashire Senior Cup.

League War Cup North

Feb 15	SOUTHPORT	(Rd1/1L)	L 2-3	Liddell 2 (1 pen)	3,000
Feb 22	Southport	(Rd1/2L)	D 2-2	Done, Eastham	4,000

Appearances & Goalscorers

	NR L		L CN		TOTALS	
PLAYERS	APP	G	APP	G	APP	G
Balmer	1		1		2	
Bartram*	16				16	
Batey*	12				12	
Britton*	1				1	
Bush	1		1		2	
Cairns*	1				1	
Carney	2	3			2	3
Carter*	1				1	
Collister*	3	1			3	1
Cook DF	12	1	1		13	1
Cook W*	1				1	
Cullis*	8				8	
Done	16	12	1	1	17	13
Dorsett*	5	8	1		6	8
Drury*	4	3			4	3
Eastham S*	7		1	1	8	1
Fagan	19	6			19	6
Fairhurst*	1				1	
Farrow*	1				1	
Fazakerley*	2				2	
Grosvenor*			1		1	
Grundy*	5	2			5	2
Hansen	3				3	
Harley	6				6	
Hobson*	10				10	
Hunt*	7	5			7	5
Iceton*	1				1	
Jackson*	13				13	
Kaye	15				15	
Kinghorn			1		1	
Lambert	37		2		39	
Lewis*	1				1	
Liddell	35	10	2	2	37	12
Longdon*	1				1	
Loran*	1				1	
Lyon*	1	1			1	1
Mansley*	4		2		6	
Massey*	1				1	
Nieuwenhuys	21	15			21	15
O'Donnell*	2	1			2	1
Owens*	4				4	
Paisley	25	10	2		27	10
Palk	21	1			21	1
Patterson	1				1	
Pickstock*	3	1			3	1
Ramsden	1				1	
Robinson*	2				2	
Search*	1	1			1	1
Seddon	8				8	
Shafto	2	1			2	1
Spicer	29		2		31	
Stuart*	14		1		15	
Teasdale*	2				2	
Turner*	10		2		12	
Westcott*	2	6	1		3	6
Woodburn*	3				3	
Yoxon*	1				1	
Opps' o.gs.		3				3

* Indicates guest player.

1941-42

Football League Northern Section, First Period

DATE	OPPONENTS	SCORE	GOALSCORERS	ATTENDANCE
Aug 30	WREXHAM	W 5-2	Palk, Done, Dorsett 2, Hall	5,000
Sep 6	Wrexham	L 3-5	Liddell, Palk, Done	2,500
Sep 13	Manchester City	W 4-3	Done 2, Dorsett, Liddell	3,000
Sep 20	MANCHESTER CITY	W 4-2	Done 3, Dorsett	5,000
Sep 27	NEW BRIGHTON	W 7-2	Done 4, Fagan 2, Liddell	5,000
Oct 4	New Brighton	D 5-5	Done 3, Dorsett 2	3,000
Oct 11	Stockport County	W 2-1	Done, Palk	3,000
Oct 18	STOCKPORT COUNTY	W 6-1	Done 2, Dorsett 2, Ainsley, Liddell	3,000
Oct 25	EVERTON	W 3-2	Liddell 2, Bush	12,989
Nov 1	Everton	L 3-5	Done 2, Liddell	20,000
Nov 8	Chester City	W 4-3	Shafto, Palk, Cook 2	3,000
Nov 15	CHESTER CITY	W 4-2	Liddell, Ainsley, Nieuwenhuys, Palk	4,000
Nov 22	MANCHESTER UNITED	D 1-1	Taylor	10,000
Nov 29	Manchester United	D 2-2	Dorsett, Liddell	3,000
Dec 6	Tranmere Rovers	W 2-1	Dorsett, Ainsley	1,000
Dec 13	TRANMERE ROVERS	W 7-2	McIntosh 3, Dorsett 2, Carney 2	3,000
Dec 20	STOKE CITY	D 1-1	Liddell	5,500
Dec 25	Stoke City	L 3-4	Nieuwenhuys, Palk, Liddell	8,000

Playing record: P18 W11 D4 L3 F66 A 44 Points 26 Position 8th

Football League Northern Section, Second Period

DATE	OPPONENTS		SCORE	GOALSCORERS	ATTENDANCE
Dec 27	BURY*	(QRd)	W 4-0	Ainsley 2, Nieuwenhuys, Liddell	6,000
Jan 3	Bury*	(QRd)	W 3-2	Carney, Liddell, Nieuwenhuys	1,338
Jan 10	Preston North End*	(QRd)	W 2-1	Carney, Palk	5,000
Jan 17	PRESTON NORTH END*	(QRd)	W 2-1	Done 2	10,000
Feb 7	Blackpool*	(QRd)	L 2-6	Done 2	10,000
Feb 14	BLACKPOOL*	(QRd)	L 1-3	Done	14,295
Feb 21	SHEFFIELD UNITED*	(QRd)	W 5-2	Done 2, Liddell 2, Jones	4,600
Feb 28	Sheffield United*	(QRd)	L 1-5	Done	8,000
Mar 14	Rochdale*	(QRd)	W 8-2	Balmer 3, Done 3, Nieuwenhuys 2	3,000
Mar 21	Chester City		W 3-1	Carney, Haycock, Liddell	3,000
Mar 28	ROCHDALE*	(QRd)	W 5-2	Liddell 3, Dorsett, Palk	5,000
Apr 4	Burnley *	(Rd1)	W 3-0	Balmer 2, Liddell (pen)	7,000
Apr 6	BURNLEY*	(Rd1)	W 4-1	Done 3, Taylor	11,253
Apr 11	EVERTON*	(Rd2)	L 0-2		33,445
Apr 18	Everton*	(Rd2)	W 1-0	Balmer	33,780
Apr 25	BLACKBURN ROVERS		D 0-0		4,000
May 9	CHESTER CITY**		W 3-0	Done 3	5,000
May 16	Preston North End		W 2-0	Balmer, Liddell	3,000
May 23	BLACKBURN ROVERS** †		L 2-3	McLaren, Mutch	8,062
May 25	Blackpool		L 2-8	Liddell (pen), Done	4,000
May 30	EVERTON		W 4-1	Done 2, Carney, Wharton	13,761

Playing record: P21 W14 D2 L5 F57 A40 Points 30 Position 4th

*Indicates also League War Cup.
**Indicates also Lancashire Cup. All cups games counted in final league position.
†23 May v Blackburn Rovers, 90 minute score of 2-2 counted as League score.

Appearances & Goalscorers

	NR L		L CN		TOTALS	
PLAYERS	APP	G	APP	G	APP	G
Ainsley*	9	3	2	2	13	5
Balmer	3		9	7	12	7
Batey*	1				1	
Breeze*	1				1	
Busby			1		1	
Bush	3	1	6		9	1
Carney	4	2	8	4	12	6
Cook*	11	2			11	2
Doherty*			1		1	
Done	11	19	18	20	29	39
Dorsett*	13	12	2	1	15	13
Eastham H			1		1	
Eastham S*	1		6		7	
Fagan	2	2	1		3	2
Fazackerley	8		2		10	
Finney			7		7	
Grainger*			1		1	
Guttridge*	7		18		25	
Hall W*	2	1			2	1
Harley	1		3		4	
Haycock*			15	1	15	1
Hobson	17		21		38	
Hulligan*	1		1		2	
Jones W			5	1	5	1
Kaye	17		21		38	
Lambert	18		18		36	
Liddell	17	11	18	11	35	22
McDonald*	1				1	
McInnes	3		1		4	
McIntosh*	4	3	1		5	3
McLaren*			2	1	2	1
Mutch*			1	1	1	1
Nieuwenhuys	4	2	13	4	17	6
O'Donnell*	2				2	
Owen*			3		3	
Owens	1				1	
Palk	13	6	7	2	20	8
Patterson	1		1		2	
Pryde*			1		1	
Ramsden	1		1		2	
Ridge*			1		1	
Seddon	1				1	
Shafto	1	1	2		3	1
Shankly*			1		1	
Spicer	9		1		10	
Taylor	3	1	5	1	8	2
Wharton*			1	1	1	1
Whittaker*	6		3		9	
Woodruff*			1		1	
Young*	1				1	

* Indicates guest player.

1942-43

Lancashire Section Principal Tournament

DATE	OPPONENTS	SCORE	GOALSCORERS	ATTENDANCE
Aug 29	Wrexham	W 4-3	Nieuwenhuys, Palk (pen), Mills, Liddell	2,500
Sep 5	WREXHAM	W 4-0	Done 3, Dorsett	5,000
Sep 12	EVERTON	W 1-0	Mills	17,131
Sep 19	Everton	D 4-4	Done, Dorsett 2, Liddell	17,000
Sep 26	Bury	W 4-1	Mills 2, Done, Liddell	2,310
Oct 3	BURY	W 5-2	Gemmall o.g., Mills, Done 2, Hulligan	8,362
Oct 10	Manchester United	W 4-3	Done 2, Harley, Hulligan	4,000
Oct 17	MANCHESTER UNITED	W 2-1	Fagan, Done	12,788
Oct 24	Manchester City	W 4-1	Done 2, Mills, Balmer	4,000
Oct 31	MANCHESTER CITY	W 3-1	Done 2, Fagan	12,401
Nov 7	CHESTER CITY	W 4-2	Fagan, Balmer, Done, Liddell	11,047
Nov 14	Chester City	W 5-1	Fagan, Balmer 3, Carney	5,000
Nov 21	Southport	L 2-3	Shafto, Done.	10,000
Nov 28	SOUTHPORT	W 6-2	Mills 3, Fagan 2 (1 pen), Dorsett	22,273
Dec 5	Burnley	L 1-3	Dorsett.	3,006
Dec 12	BURNLEY	W 9-2	Done 3, Dorsett 2, Fagan 2, Hulligan, Haycock	10,000
Dec 19	TRANMERE ROVERS	W 6-2	Dorsett 5 (1 pen), Done	4,023
Dec 25	Tranmere Rovers	L 2-3	Fagan, Hall	7,207

Playing record: P18 W14 D1 L3 F70 A34 Points 29 Position 2nd

Appearances & Goalscorers

	FLN 1ST		FLN 2ND		LANC C		TOTALS	
PLAYERS	APP	G	APP	G	APP	G	APP	G
Balmer	8	5	6	6	2	3	16	14
Bush	2		3				5	
Campbell			4	1			4	1
Carney	3	1					3	1
Charlesworth*			9				9	
Done	17	20	20	17	2		39	37
Dorsett*	11	12	3	2			14	14
Eastham H			1				1	
Edelston*			3	1			3	1
Fagan	9	9	17	11	2		28	20
Finney	1						1	
Guttridge*	16		4				20	
Hall W	1	1	3	1			4	2
Harley	2	1					2	1
Haycock*	4	1	5				9	1
Hobson	18		20		2		40	
Hughes			2				2	
Hulligan	9	3	20	13	2		31	16
Jackson*	5		1				6	
Jones W	1		4				5	
Kaye	17		19	2	2		38	2

1942-43 continued

Football League Northern Section, Second Period

Dec 26	WREXHAM*	(QRd) D 2-2	Fagan (pen), Hulligan	12,000
Jan 2	Wrexham*	(QRd) W 1-0	Dorsett	2,000
Jan 9	Everton*	(QRd) W 3-1	Hulligan 2, Shepherd	18,206
Jan 16	EVERTON*	(QRd) W 2-1	Balmer, Done	20,400
Jan 23	SOUTHPORT*	(QRd) W 3-1	Dorsett, Hulligan 2	14,325
Jan 30	Southport*	(QRd) D 2-2	Fagan, Patterson	5,000
Feb 6	Tranmere Rovers*	(QRd) W 5-1	Fagan 3 (1 pen), Done 2	6,958
Feb 13	TRANMERE ROVERS*	(QRd) W 4-1	Hulligan, Done 3	11,365
Feb 20	MANCHESTER CITY*	(QRd) W 4-2	Hulligan 2, Done, Edelston	21,836
Feb 27	Manchester City*	(QRd) L 1-3	Hall	14,795
Mar 6	BURY*	(Rd1/1) L 1-3	Hulligan	17,099
Mar 13	Bury*	(Rd2/1) W 7-2	Done 3, Hulligan 2, Pilling, Griffiths o.g.	10,904
Mar 20	BLACKPOOL*	(Rd2/1) W 3-1	Balmer 2, Kaye.	40,000
Mar 27	Blackpool*	(Rd2/2) L 0-5		22,000
Apr 3	CHESTER CITY**	W 4-1	Balmer, Fagan, Liddell, Done	8,000
Apr 10	Chester City**	W 5-2	Fagan 4, Balmer.	4,000
Apr 17	SOUTHPORT**	W 3-0	Done, Hulligan, Patterson	10,000
Apr 24	Bolton Wanderers**	W 6-3	Welsh 2, Done 2, Kaye Hulligan	4,000
Apr 26	EVERTON***	W 4-1	Fagan (pen), Balmer, Done, Nieuwenhuys	17,000
May 1	BOLTON WANDERERS**	W 4-0	Done 2, Pearson, Campbell	10,000

Playing record: P20 W15 D2 L3 F64 A32 Points 32 Position 1st

*Also League War Cup. **Also Lancashire Cup games.
***Also Liverpool Senior Cup, 1st leg.

Lancashire Cup Final

May 8	MANCHESTER UNITED	L 1-3	Nieuwenhuys	12,117
May 15	Manchester United	D 3-3	Balmer 3	9,196

	FLN 1ST		FLN 2ND		LANC C		TOTALS	
PLAYERS	APP	G	APP	G	APP	G	APP	G
Keen*	17						17	
Kirkby*			1				1	
Lambert	3		6		1		10	
Liddell	13	4	2	1			15	5
Livingstone*			1				1	
Low*			1				1	
Mather*			1		1		2	
McInnes	1		2				3	
Mills*	9	9					9	9
Murphy*					1		1	
Nieuwenhuys	3	1	3	1	1	1	7	3
Pearson*			1	1			1	1
Pilling	14		20	1	2		36	1
Palk	2	1					2	1
Patterson			2	2			2	2
Pope*			1				1	
Rawlings*			1				1	
Rist*			6		2		8	
Seddon			6				6	
Shafto	1	1					1	1
Shepherd			1	1			1	1
Spicer	2						2	
Taylor	1		4				5	
Welsh*			1	2			1	2
Westby*	3		14		2		19	
Williams F*	3		1				4	
Williams S*	1						1	
Wood*	1						1	
Woodruff *			1				1	
Opps' o.gs.	1		1				2	

* Indicates guest player

1943-44

Football League Northern Section, First Period

DATE	OPPONENTS	SCORE	GOALSCORERS	ATTENDANCE
Aug 28	MANCHESTER CITY	W 4-1	Balmer 3, Done	16,000
Sep 4	Manchester City	L 1-2	Hanson	10,229
Sep 11	WREXHAM	W 8-0	Shepherd 6, Balmer, Hanson	10,000
Sep 18	Wrexham	W 5-2	Balmer 3, Shepherd 2	5,100
Sep 25	BURY	W 3-1	Done 2, Shepherd	14,000
Oct 2	Bury	W 2-1	Shepherd, Hulligan	3,000
Oct 9	Everton	W 6-4	Done 4, Harley, Welsh	28,835
Oct 16	EVERTON	W 5-2	Harley, Done, Balmer 2 Nieuwenhuys	25,000
Oct 23	MANCHESTER UNITED	L 3-4	Balmer 2, Welsh	15,000
Oct 30	Manchester United	L 0-1		13,647
Nov 6	Chester City	L 1-3	Welsh	2,500
Nov 13	CHESTER CITY	W 9-0	Done 7, Palk, Beattie	9,000
Nov 20	SOUTHPORT	W 9-0	Beattie 3, Welsh 3, Nieuwenhuys, Done, Campbell	13,600
Nov 27	Southport	W 3-1	Welsh, Done, Balmer	4,000
Dec 4	Burnley	W 1-0	Palk	5,995
Dec 11	BURNLEY	D 1-1	Beattie	11,360
Dec 18	Tranmere Rovers	W 9-2	Gulliver, Beattie 3, Done 3, Balmer, Welsh	3,500
Dec 25	TRANMERE ROVERS	W 2-1	Done 2	17,204

Playing record: P18 W13 D1 L4 F72 A26 Points 27 Position 3rd

Football League Northern Section, Second Period

Dec 27	WREXHAM	(QRd) W 4-0	Hulligan, Balmer 2, Done	20,139
Jan 1	Wrexham	(QRd) L 2-4	Done 2	4,442
Jan 8	Tranmere Rovers	(QRd) W 6-1	Campbell 2, Welsh, Palk, Done 2	6,000
Jan 15	TRANMERE ROVERS	(QRd) W 5-1	Done, Balmer, Black, Campbell, Beattie	13,537
Jan 22	EVERTON	(QRd) L 1-4	Fagan	34,221
Jan 29	Everton	(QRd) W 3-2	Nieuwenhuys, Balmer, Welsh (pen)	45,820
Feb 5	Crewe Alexandra	(QRd) W 3-1	Campbell, Liddell 2	3,000
Feb 12	CREWE ALEXANDRA	(QRd) W 8-0	Done 3, Campbell 2, Balmer, Liddell, Beattie	13,006
Feb 19	CHESTER CITY	(QRd) W 4-2	Done, Nieuwenhuys, Campbell, Liddell	13,355
Feb 26	Chester City	(QRd) L 0-6		6,000
Mar 4	OLDHAM ATHLETIC*	(Rd1) W 8-1	Balmer 4, Taylor 2, Done 2	20,786

Appearances & Goalscorers

	FLN 1ST		FLN 2ND		LANC C		TOTALS	
PLAYERS	APP	G	APP	G	APP	G	APP	G
Balmer	15	13	11	9			26	22
Beattie*	7	8	17	4	1		25	12
Black*			2	1			2	1
Busby			4				4	
Butler*			4				4	
Campbell	9	1	15	9	1		25	10
Done	14	22	21	22	1	1	36	45
Dougal*			1				1	
Fagan			1	1			1	1
Gorman*			1				1	
Gulliver*	15	1	21			1	37	1
Guttridge*	2						2	
Hall W	4		3	1			7	1
Hanson*	11	2					11	2
Harley	3	2					3	2
Hobson	18		21		1		40	
Hughes	18		20		1		39	
Hulligan	2	1	4	4			6	5
Johnstone*					1		1	
Jones JE*			1				1	
Jones W			2				2	
Kaye		15	4				19	
Lambert			3				3	
Liddell	1		5	4			6	4
McCormick*			2	1			2	1
McDonald	1						1	
Nieuwenhuys	3	2	6	4	1		10	6
Palk	5	2	12	2			17	4
Patterson	1						1	
Pilling	18		21		1		40	
Seddon	4						4	
Shafto	2						2	
Shepherd	5	10	2				7	10
Taylor	1		3	2			4	2
Thorpe*	1		1				2	
Welsh*	9	8	8	6	1	2	18	16
Westby*	14		14		1		29	
Whiteside*			1				1	
Opp's o.gs.				1				1

* Indicates guest player.

1943-44 continued

DATE	OPPONENTS	SCORE	GOALSCORERS	ATTENDANCE
Mar 11	Oldham Athletic*	(Rd1) L 0-1		4,955
Mar 18	Manchester City*	(Rd2) D 1-1	Welsh	27,792
Mar 25	MANCHESTER CITY*†	(Rd2) L 2-3	McCormick, Done	41,498
Apr 1	SOUTHPORT**	(Rd1) W 6-2	Done 3, Nieuwenhuys (pen), Hall, Beattie	8,533
Apr 8	Southport**	(Rd1) W 7-4	Done 2, Welsh 2 (1 pen), Beattie, Campbell, Hulligan	4,000
Apr 10	Everton**	L 0-3		40,000
Apr 15	EVERTON**	W 3-0	Hulligan 2, Done ††	25,062
Apr 22	EVERTON**	W 4-2	Done 3 (1 pen), Palk.	24,404
Apr 29	BLACKBURN ROVERS	W 1-0	Welsh (pen).	17,103
May 6	BOLTON WANDERERS**	(F/1L) W 3-1	Nieuwenhuys, Hubbick o.g. Campbell	16,591

Playing record: P21 W14 D2 L5 F71 A38 Points 30 Position 3rd

*Also League War Cup.
**Also Lancashire Senior Cup.
†25 March v Manchester City, 90 minutes score of 2-2 counted as league.
††15 April v Everton after 135 minutes play.

May 13	Bolton Wanderers**	(F/2L) W 3-2	Welsh 2, Done	10,254

LANCASHIRE SENIOR CUP WINNER

1944-45

Football League Northern Section, First Period

DATE	OPPONENTS	SCORE	GOALSCORERS	ATTENDANCE
Aug 26	Stockport County	W 3-2	Done 2, Welsh (pen)	5,300
Sep 2	STOCKPORT COUNTY	W 2-0	Fagan, Done	12,418
Sep 9	MANCHESTER CITY	D 2-2	Done, Nieuwenhuys	24,009
Sep 16	Manchester City	D 2-2	Dix 2 (1 pen)	10,000
Sep 23	Crewe Alexandra	L 1-4	Welsh	4,500
Sep 30	CREWE ALEXANDRA	L 1-4	Eastham	16,894
Oct 7	WREXHAM	L 0-3		17,427
Oct 14	Wrexham	L 1-2	Welsh	7,976
Oct 21	Everton	W 2-0	Smith 2	33,199
Oct 28	EVERTON	D 0-0		26,008
Nov 4	MANCHESTER UNITED	W 3-2	Walsh 2 (1 pen), Roughton o.g.	17,610
Nov 11	Manchester United	W 5-2	Welsh 3, Fagan, Liddell	5,000
Nov 18	Bury	L 0-2		4,415
Nov 25	BURY	W 3-1	Cumner, Nieuwenhuys 2	11,377
Dec 2	CHESTER CITY	W 6-0	Nieuwenhuys 2, Taylor 2, Welsh, Kinghorn	13,609
Dec 9	Chester City	L 2-3	Campbell, Nieuwenhuys	3,500
Dec 16	Tranmere Rovers	W 5-1	Welsh 4 (1 pen), Campbell	4,000
Dec 23	TRANMERE ROVERS	W 3-0	Taylor 2, Baines	10,877

Playing record: P18 W9 D3 L6 F41 A30 Points 21 Position 16th

Football League Northern section, Second Period

DATE	OPPONENTS	SCORE	GOALSCORERS	ATTENDANCE
Dec 25	Southport*	(QRd) W 4-1	Liddell 2, Taylor, Kinghorn	4,000
Dec 26	Everton	D 2-2	Liddell 2	35,226
Dec 30	SOUTHPORT*	(QRd) W 12-1	Campbell 2, Liddell 2, Welsh 6, Hulligan 2	13,673
Jan 6	Stockport County*	(QRd) W 3-2	Welsh 2, Shepherd	3,000
Jan 12	STOCKPORT COUNTY*	(QRd) W 4-1	Taylor 2, Campbell, Welsh	14,357
Feb 3	Everton*	(QRd) L 1-4	Taylor	26,780
Feb 10	EVERTON*	(QRd) W 3-1	Cumner 2, Nieuwenhuys	33,235
Feb 17	Bolton Wanderers*	(QRd) L 1-2	Campbell	11,494
Feb 24	BOLTON WANDERERS*	(QRd) D 1-1	Campbell	20,966
Mar 3	Southport	W 5-0	Taylor 2, Liddell 2, Pilling	5,000
Mar 10	TRANMERE ROVERS*	(QRd) W 3-1	Nieuwenhuys, Hinsley, Taylor	15,102
Mar 17	Tranmere Rovers*	(QRd) W 2-1	Hulligan, Liddell	7,000
Mar 24	EVERTON*	(Rd1) W 1-0	Liddell	39,640
Mar 31	Everton*	(Rd1) W 1-0	Liddell	51,512
Apr 2	EVERTON**	L 1-3	Shannon	22,815
Apr 7	MANCHESTER CITY*	(Rd2) W 3-0	Liddell, Welsh 2	36,131
Apr 14	Manchester City*	(Rd2) W 3-1	Taylor, Welsh 2	24,905
Apr 21	CHESTERFIELD*	(Rd3) D 0-0		35,001
Apr 28	Chesterfield*	(Rd3) L 0-1		27,000
May 5	OLDHAM ATHLETIC	W 3-2	Taylor, Nieuwenhuys, Shannon	2,000
May 9	PRESTON NORTH END	W 5-1	Taylor 2, Shannon 2, Kaye (pen)	35,000
May 12	Oldham Athletic	W 7-0	Westby, Pilling, Kinghorn, Taylor 2, Patterson, Nieuwenhuys	2,000
May 19	BLACKPOOL	W 2-0	Fagan 2	16,807
May 21	Derby County	L 0-1		16,723

Playing record: P24 W16 D3 L5 F67 A26 Points 35 Position 3rd

*Also League War Cup. **Also Liverpool Senior Cup.

Appearances & Goalscorers

	FLN 1ST		FLN 2ND		TOTALS	
PLAYERS	APP	G	APP	G	APP	G
Baines*	1	1			1	1
Balmer	3				3	
Blood*			5		5	
Busby	2		3		5	
Bush	3				3	
Campbell	11	2	19	5	30	7
Cumner	5	1	10	2	15	3
Dix*	6	2			6	2
Done	3	4			3	4
Eastham H	2	1	4		6	1
Fagan	3	2	2	2	5	4
Garner	1				1	
Gulliver*	18		22		40	
Hall H			1		1	
Hall W	2				2	
Harley	8		8		16	
Hinsley*			3	1	3	1
Hobson	14		23		37	
Hughes	17		22		39	
Hulligan	2		5	3	7	3
Jones JE*	1				1	
Jones W			1		1	
Kaye	8		24	1	32	1
Kemp	4				4	
Kinghorn	4	1	5	2	9	3
Liddell	4	1	11	12	15	13
McInnes	7		2		9	
McIntosh*			1		1	
Mulvaney*	1				1	
Nieuwenhuys	12	6	17	4	29	10
Patterson	1		2	1	3	1
Pilling	16		20	2	36	2
Rawcliffe*			1		1	
Seddon	3		2		5	
Shannon			4	4	4	4
Shepherd	2		1	1	3	1
Smith*	2	2			2	2
Spicer			1		1	
Taylor	16	4	21	13	37	17
Thorpe*	1				1	
Welsh*	11	13	10	13	21	26
Westby	3		14	1	17	1
Whalley*	1				1	
Opp's o.gs.		1				1

* Indicates guest player.

1945-46

Football League North

DATE	OPPONENTS	SCORE	GOALSCORERS	ATTENDANCE
Aug 25	Burnley	W 3-1	Liddell 2, Nieuwenhuys	7,481
Aug 29	BOLTON WANDERERS	D 2-2	Taylor, Kippax	17,437
Sep 1	BURNLEY	L 2-3	Balmer, Liddell	25,000
Sep 8	BURY	D 1-1	Balmer (pen)	24,400
Sep 12	EVERTON	W 2-1	Liddell, Shannon	25,446
Sep 15	Bury	L 1-2	Nieuwenhuys	7,218
Sep 22	Blackburn Rovers	W 5-0	Jones, Balmer 2, Fagan 2	3,500
Sep 29	BLACKBURN ROVERS	W 4-0	Paisley, Kaye, Fagan, Balmer	24,713
Oct 6	BRADFORD PARK AVENUE	W 4-1	Kaye 2, Liddell, Balmer	30,000
Oct 13	Bradford Park Avenue	W 2-0	Liddell, Shannon	18,308
Oct 20	Manchester City	L 0-1		23,034
Oct 27	MANCHESTER CITY	L 0-5		34,941
Nov 3	NEWCASTLE UNITED	W 3-0	Fagan 3	33,818
Nov 10	Newcastle United	L 2-6	Nieuwenhuys, Fagan (pen)	49,723
Nov 17	Sheffield Wednesday	W 3-2	Balmer 2, Liddell	20,000
Nov 24	SHEFFIELD WEDNESDAY	L 0-2		33,000
Dec 1	HUDDERSFIELD TOWN	W 4-1	Fagan, Balmer, Liddell 2	30,000
Dec 8	Huddersfield Town	L 1-3	Balmer	10,362
Dec 15	Chesterfield	D 1-1	Taylor	12,000
Dec 22	CHESTERFIELD	D 2-2	Liddell 2	29,274
Dec 25	BARNSLEY	W 5-2	Liddell, Paisley, Priday, Fagan 2	30,000
Dec 26	Barnsley	L 0-1		28,290
Dec 29	Everton	D 2-2	Baron, Liddell	60,926
Jan 12	PRESTON NORTH END	W 4-2	Liddell 2, Fagan, Priday	38,368
Jan 19	Preston North End	L 1-2	Fagan	12,000
Feb 2	Leeds United	L 0-3		10,000
Feb 9	Manchester United	L 1-2	Balmer	33,000
Feb 16	MANCHESTER UNITED	L 0-5		37,000
Feb 23	SUNDERLAND	D 2-2	Liddell, Balmer	37,000
Mar 2	Sunderland	W 2-0	Fagan, Liddell	18,000
Mar 9	Sheffield United	L 1-3	Balmer (pen)	35,000
Mar 16	SHEFFIELD UNITED	L 0-3		47,000
Mar 23	MIDDLESBROUGH	L 1-2	Nieuwenhuys	35,000
Mar 30	Middlesbrough	W 5-2	Done 3, Balmer, Fagan	20,000
Apr 6	Stoke City	W 1-0	Done	9,000
Apr 10	LEEDS UNITED	D 1-1	Fagan	8,000
Apr 13	STOKE CITY	W 4-1	Priday 2, Fagan, Balmer	28,000
Apr 19	GRIMSBY TOWN	W 2-0	Fagan, Nieuwenhuys	38,850
Apr 20	Blackpool	D 1-1	Burke	7,000
Apr 22	Grimsby Town	D 1-1	Done	14,000
Apr 27	BLACKPOOL	W 4-0	Thorpe o.g., Jones, Balmer, Taylor	22,000
Apr 29	Bolton Wanderers	L 0-1		16,000

Playing record: P42 W17 D9 L16 F80 A70 Points 43 Position 11th

FA Cup – this seasons FA Cup results are included on page 239 (1946-47 Season).

Appearances & Goalscorers

	FLN 1ST		FLN 2ND		TOTALS	
PLAYERS	APP	G	APP	G	APP	G
Ashcroft	5				5	
Balmer	34	16	2	1	36	17
Baron	9	1	3		12	1
Burke*	1	1			1	1
Bush	6		1		7	
Campbell	1				1	
Carney	1				1	
Done	9	5			9	5
Easdale	7				7	
Eastham H	3				3	
Fagan	35	17	4	3	39	20
Finney	2		2		4	
Gulliver*	16				16	
Hall H	7				7	
Harley	24		3		27	
Hobson	6		1		7	
Hughes	32		3		35	
Hulligan	2				2	
Jones W	4	2			4	2
Kaye	26	3	1		27	3
Kemp	2				2	
Kippax*	1	1			1	1
Lambert	17		4		21	
Liddell	28	17	2	1	30	18
McInnes	6				6	
Nickson	10		3		13	
Nieuwenhuys	29	5	4	1	33	6
Paisley	25	2	4		29	2
Patterson	3				3	
Pilling	4				4	
Priday	11	4	4		15	4
Ramsden	18		1		19	
Sanders*	3				3	
Seddon	1				1	
Shannon	11	2			11	2
Sidlow	9				9	
Spicer	9		1		10	
Taylor	32	3	1		33	3
Welsh*	2				2	
Westby	11				11	
Opp's o.gs.		1				1

* Indicates guest player.

Complete Players' Career Records

(Records up to and including season 2002-03)

* Played only in the Lancashire League 1892-93. ** Denotes two periods with LFC.
Figures in brackets in goals columns indicates goals scored in a penalty shoot-out.
Totals for each competition in each period are shown with one grand total.

	Year	Year		League			FA Cup			FLC		
Player	**Joined**	**Left**	**To**	**Apps**	**Sub**	**Goals**	**Apps**	**Sub**	**Goals**	**Apps**	**Sub**	**Goals**
Ablett, G.I.	1981	1985	Derby County	103	6	1	16	2		10	1	
A'Court, A.	1952	1964	Tranmere Rovers	354		61	24		2	2		
Aitken, A.L.	1930	1931	Newburn Athletic	1								
Aldridge, J.W.	1987	1989	Real Sociedad	69	14	50	12		8	7	1	3
Allan, G.H.**	1895	1897	Glasgow Celtic }	49		41	7		3			
	1898	1899	Died }	30		8	6		3			
Allman, M.W.	1908	1909	Wrexham	1								
Anderson, E.	1952	1957	Barnsley	73		22	3					
Anelka, N.	2001	2002	Manchester City	13	7	4	2		1			
Armstrong, T.	1920	1920	Preston North End	1								
Arnell, A.J.	1953	1961	Tranmere Rovers	69		33	6		2			
Arnold, S.F.	1970	1973	Rochdale	1	1							
Arphexad, P.M.	2000	2003	Released	1	1					2		
Arrowsmith, A.W.	1960	1968	Bury	42	6	20	6		4			
Ashcroft, C.T.	1945	1955	Ipswich Town	87			2					
Babb, P.A.	1994	2000	Sporting Lisbon	124	4	1	12			16		
Babbel, M.	2000		Still at club	42		3	5		1	7		1
Balmer, J.	1935	1952	Retired	291		99	21		12			
Bamber, J.	1915	1924	Leicester City	72		2	8					
Banks, A.	1956	1961	Cambridge City	8		6						
Banks , W.	1913	1919	Fulham	26		6						
Barkas, H.B.	1930	1932	Not known	5								
Barmby, N.J.	2000	2002	Leeds United	23	9	2	2	3	1	3	4	1(1)
Barnes, J.C.B.	1987	1997	Newcastle United	310	4	84	51		16(1)	26		3(1)
Baron, F.J.	1925	1927	Southend United	20		7						
Baron, K.M.P.	1944	1954	Southend United	141		31	12		1			
Baros, M.	2002		Still at club	17	10	9		1		2	2	2(1)
Barton, H.B.	1928	1934	Sheffield United	103		25	6		4			
Bartrop, W.	1914		Died 1918	3								
Battles, B.**	1896	1897	Glasgow Celtic }	2								
	1898	1898	Glasgow Celtic }	1								
Beadles, G.H.	1921	1924	Cardiff City	17		6						
Beardsley, P.A.	1987	1991	Everton	120	11	46	22	3	11	13	1	1
Becton, F.J.	1895	1898	Sheffield United	70		38	12		4			
Beeby, A.R.	1908	1911	Manchester City	16								
Beglin, J.M.	1983	1989	Leeds United	64		2	10			13		
Bennett, T.S.	1916	1921	Rochdale	1								
Berger, P.	1996	2003	Portsmouth	106	42	28	4	4		9	2	3
Berry, A.**	1907	1909	Fulham (amateur) }	3								
	1912	1912	Northern Nomads }	1								
Bimpson, J.L.	1953	1959	Blackburn Rovers	96		38	6		1			
Biscan, I.	2000		Still at club	15	9		3	2		6	1	1
Bjornebye, S.I.	1992	2000	Blackburn Rovers	132	7	2	11	2	0(1)	16		
Blanthorne, R.	1905	1907	Grimsby Town	2		1						
Blenkinsop, E.	1934	1937	Cardiff City	71								
Blore, R.	1957	1960	Southport	1								
Boersma, P.	1965	1975	Middlesbrough	73	10	17	7	3	1	5	3	3
Bovill, J.M.	1911	1914	Linfield	27		7	2					
Bowen, G.	1901	1902	Wolverhampton W	2								
Bowyer, S.	1907	1912	Bristol City	45		14	3		2			
Bradley, J.E.	1905	1911	Reading	169		5	15		3			
Bradshaw, T.H.	1893	1898	Tottenham Hotspur	118		45	14		5			
Bradshaw, T.	1930	1938	Third Lanark	277		3	14		1			
Bratley, P.W.	1914	1919	Rotherham County	13								
Brierley, K.L.	1948	1953	Oldham Athletic	60		8	1					
Bromilow, T.	1919	1930	Retired	341		11	33					
Brough, J.	1910	1912	Bristol City	11		3						
Brownbill, D.A.	1972	1975	Port Vale	1								
Browning, J.	1934	1939	Renton	19								
Bruton, L.H.R.	1932	1933	Leamington Town	6		1	2					
Buck, F.R.	1903	1904	Plymouth Argyle	13		1						
Bull, B.H.	1895	1896	No known	1		1						
Burkinshaw, K.H.	1953	1957	Workington	1								
Burrows, D.	1988	1993	West Ham United	135	11	3	16	1		16		
Busby, M.	1936	1945	Retired	118		3	7					
Bush, W.T.	1933	1947	Retired	64		1	8					
Byrne, G.	1955	1969	Retired	273	1	2	29			5		
Cadden, J.Y.	1948	1952	Grimsby Town	4			1					
Callaghan, I.R.	1959	1978	Swansea Town	636	4	49	77	2	2	42		7
Camara, A.S.	1999	2000	West Ham United	22	11	9	2		1		2	

League: includes Second Division, First Division and Premier league.
FLC: includes Football League Cup, Milk Cup, Rumbelows Cup, Coca-Cola Cup, Littlewoods Cup and Worthington Cup.
Euro Cup: includes European Cup and Champions League. **ECW Cup:** denotes European Cup-Winners' Cup
Others: includes Lancashire League 1892-93; Test Matches; Sheriff of London/Charity/Community Shields; European Super Cup; World Club Championship; Screen Sport Super Cup and Mercantile Credit Centenary Trophy.
Note: the three league games of the abandoned 1939-40 season are included.
Games from the First and Second World Wars are not included.

E Cup			ECW Cup			UEFA Cup			Others			Total		
Apps	Sub	Goals	Apps	Sub	Goals	Apps	Sub	Goals	Apps	Sub	Goals	Apps	Sub	Goals
						6			3			138	9	1
1												381		63
												1		
									1		2	89	15	63
									4		3	**		
												96		58
												1		
												76		22
												15	7	5
												1		
												75		35
												1	1	
2												5	1	
			1						1			50	6	24
												89		
			4	1		8	1					164	6	1
2	1					13		1	2	1		71	2	6
												312		111
												80		2
												8		6
												26		6
												5		
3	1					6	3	4	1			38	20	8 (1)
			7		3	5			4		2	403	4	108 (2)
												20		7
												153		32
1	7	1					2			1		20	23	12 (1)
												109		29
												3		
									3			**		
												6		
									1			18		6
									5		1	160	15	59
									4			86		42
												16		
3		1							8			98		3
												1		
1	8		6		2	10	3	2		1		136	60	35
												**		
												4		
												102		39
1	3						2			2		25	19	1
			8		2	8						175	9	4(1)
												2		1
												71		
												1		
1	1		4		2	8	5	6	1		1	99	22	30
												29		7
												2		
												48		16
									1			185		8
									6		3	138		53
												291		4
												13		
												61		8
									1			375		11
												11		3
												1		
												19		
												8		1
												13		1
												1		1
												1		
			4			7			3			181	12	3
												125		3
												72		1
7		1	9			6			3		1	332	1	4
												5		
30		3	17		1	40	1	6	8		0(1)	850	7	68 (1)
												24	13	10

Player	Year Joined	Year Left	To	League Apps	League Sub	League Goals	FA Cup Apps	FA Cup Sub	FA Cup Goals	FLC Apps	FLC Sub	FLC Goals
Cameron, J.	1892	1893	Not known				2		1			
Cameron, James	1894	1895	Not known	4								
Campbell, D.	1950	1958	Crewe Alexandra	47		2	1					
Campbell, K.	1911	1920	Partick Thistle	125			17					
Campbell, R.J.	1954	1961	Wigan Athletic	24		2				1		
Carlin, J.	1902	1907	Preston North End	32		8	3					
Carlin, W.	1958	1962	Halifax Town	1								
Carney, L.F.	1939	1948	Retired	6		1						
Carr, L.L.	1933	1936	Newport County	31		8	2					
Carragher, J.L.D.	1996		Still at club	182	12	2	15			16	3	0(2)
Carter, J.W.C.	1991	1991	Arsenal	2	3		2					
Case, J.R.	1972	1981	Brighton & Hove Albion	170	16	23	20	2	7	21	1	3
Chadburn, J.	1903	1904	Plymouth Argyle	2								
Chadwick, E.W.	1902	1904	Blackpool	43		7	2					
Chalmers, W.G.	1923	1925	Tranmere Rovers	2								
Chambers, H.	1915	1928	West Bromwich Albion	310		135	28		16			
Charlton, J.B.	1929	1932	Derry City	3								
Charnock, P.A.	1993	1996	Crewe Alexandra							1		
Checkland, F.J.	1918	1923	Tranmere Rovers	5								
Cheyrou, B.	2002		Still at club	8	11		2			1	1	
Childs, A.R.	1952	1956	South Liverpool	2								
Chisnall, J.P.	1964	1967	Southend	6		1						
Chorlton, T.	1904	1912	Manchester United	117		8	4					
Christie, F.	1949	1951	East Fife	4								
Clark, J.R.	1928	1931	Nottingham Forest	39		11	3					
Cleghorn, T.	1896	1899	Portsmouth	56			10		1			
Cleland, J.W.	1895	1895	Not known									
Clemence, R.N.	1967	1981	Tottenham Hotspur	470			54			55		
Clough, N.H.	1993	1996	Manchester City	29	10	7	2			3		2
Cockburn, W.C.	1924	1928	Queens Park Rangers	63			4					
Cohen, A.	1979	1981	Maccabi Tel Aviv	16	2	1	2			1		
Collins, J.H.	1936	1937	Cardiff City	7								
Collymore, S.V.	1995	1997	Aston Villa	55	2	26	9		7	2	2	
Colvin, R.	1897	1898	Glossop	3								
Cooper, T.	1934	1940	Died	150			10					
Cormack, P.B.	1972	1976	Bristol City	119	6	21	14		2	20		1
Cotton, C.	1903	1904	West Ham United	12								
Cox, J.	1898	1909	Blackpool	327		73	33		8			
Craik, H.C.	1903	1904	Not known	1								
Crawford, E.C.	1932	1933	Clapton Orient	8		4						
Crawford, R.S.	1909	1915	Not known	108		1	6					
Crossley, R.	1947	1954	Shrewsbury Town	68			5					
Cunliffe, F.D.	1897	1898	New Brighton Tower	14		6	4		1			
Cunningham, W.	1920	1923	Barrow	3								
Curran, J.	1894	1895	Hibernian	20		3	3					
Dabbs, B.E.	1932	1938	Watford	54			2					
Dalglish, K.M.	1977	1991	Retired	342	13	118	37		13	57	2	27
Davidson, D.L.	1928	1930	Newcastle United	58		2	4					
Davies, J.M.	1900	1903	Blackpool	9			1					
Dawson, J.	1912	1916	Not known	13		3	1					
Devlin, W.A.	1927	1927	Heart of Midlothian	19		15						
Dewhurst, G.P.	1894	1894	Corinthians	1								
Diao, S.A.	2002		Still at club	13	13	1	1	1		3	1	
Dick, D.C.	1893	1894	Third Lanark	11		2						
Dicks, J.A.	1993	1994	West Ham United	24		3	1			3		
Dickson, J.J.M.	1952	1958	Headington United	6		4						
Dines, J.	1912	1912	Ilford	1								
Diomede, B.T.N.	2000	2003	Ajaccio	1	1							
Diouf, E-H	2002		Still at club	21	8	3	3			5		3(1)
Doig, J.E.	1904	1908	St Helens Rec's	51			2					
Done, C.C.	1938	1952	Tranmere Rovers	96		33	15		5			
Done, R.	1926	1935	Reading	147		13	8					
Donnelly, W.	1896	1898	Clyde	6			2					
Drummond, J.	1894	1895	Barnsley St Peters	14			3		1			
Dudek, J.	2001		Still at club	65			3	1		2		
Dundee, S.	1998	1999	Stuttgart		3						1	
Dunlop, W.T.P.	1894	1909	Retired	325		2	36					
Durnin, J.P.	1986	1989	Oxford United							1	1	
Easdale, J.	1937	1948	Stockport County	2								
Eastham, H.	1936	1948	Tranmere Rovers	62		3	6		1			
Edmed, R.A.	1926	1932	Bolton Wanderers	160		44	10		2			
English, S.	1933	1935	Queen of the South	47		24	3		2			
Evans, A.W.	1968	1972	Aston Villa	77	2	21	9	2	3	7		2
Evans, J.W.	1953	1957	Colchester	97		49	10		4			
Evans , R.Q.E.	1965	1974	Retired	9						1		
Fagan, C.J.	1970	1971	Tranmere Rovers	1							1	
Fagan, W.	1937	1952	Belfast Distillery	161		47	24		10			
Fairclough, D.	1970	1983	Lucerne	64	34	34	10	5	14	7	14	10
Fairfoul, T.	1913	1916	Not known	62			9					

Euro Cup Apps	Euro Cup Sub	Euro Cup Goals	ECW Cup Apps	ECW Cup Sub	ECW Cup Goals	UEFA Cup Apps	UEFA Cup Sub	UEFA Cup Goals	Others Apps	Others Sub	Others Goals	Total Apps	Total Sub	Total Goals
									7		4	9		5
												4		
												48		2
												142		
												25		2
												35		8
												1		
												6		1
												33		8
22						23			1	1		259	16	2 (2)
							1					4	4	
19	3	7				7	2	5	8		1	245	24	46
												2		
												45		7
												2		
									1			339		151
												3		
				1								1	1	
												5		
3	2	1								1		14	15	1
												2		
1		1	1							1		8	1	2
												121		8
												4		
												42		11
									4			70		1
									1			1		
33			8			36			9			665		
												34	10	9
												67		
2	1											21	3	1
												7		
			4	1	2	1	1					71	10	35
												3		
												160		
1			1	2	1	13	1	1	1		0(1)	169	9	26 (1)
												12		
									1			361		81
												1		
												8		4
												114		1
												73		
												18		7
												3		
									1			24		
												56		
46	1	10							16	1	4	498	17	172
												62		2
												10		
												14		3
												19		15
												1		
5	2	1					1					22	18	2
												11		2
												28		3
												6		4
												1		
1						2						4	1	
2	4					3			1			35	12	6 (1)
												53		
												111		38
												155		13
												8		
									1			18		1
19						4			1			94	1	
							1						5	
									2			363		2
									1			2	1	
												2		
												68		4
												170		46
												50		26
			2	1	1	9	1	6	1			105	6	33
												107		53
						1						11		
												1	1	
												185		57
5	6	3				2	3	1	3		3	92	62	55
												71		

Player	Year Joined	Year Left	To	League Apps	League Sub	League Goals	FA Cup Apps	FA Cup Sub	FA Cup Goals	FLC Apps	FLC Sub	FLC Goals
Ferguson, R.	1912	1915	Not known	92		1	11		1			
Ferns, P.	1958	1965	Bournemouth	27		1	1					
Ferri, J-M	1998	1999	Sochaux		2							
Finnerhan, F.P.	1897	1898	Bristol City	5		1	3					
Finney, F.	1941	1947	South Liverpool				2					
Fitzpatrick, H.J.	1907	1908	Chesterfield	4		2						
Fitzsimmons, M.J.	1936	1939	Ipswich Town	1								
Fleming, G.	1901	1906	Retired	79		5	4		1			
Forshaw, R.	1919	1927	Everton	266		117	21		7			
Fowler, R.B.	1990	2001	Leeds United	210	26	120	21	3	12	32		27 (2)
Foxall, A.	1899	1900	Queens Park Rangers	1								
Friedel, B.H.	1997	2000	Blackburn Rovers	25						4		
Furnell, J.	1962	1963	Arsenal	28								
Gardner, T.	1928	1931	Grimsby Town	5								
Garner, J.A.	1922	1926	Southport	5								
Garside, J.A.	1904	1906	Accrington Stanley	5								
Gayle, H.A.	1974	1983	Birmingham City	3	1	1						
Geary, F.	1895	1899	Retired	39		14	5					
Gerhardi, H.	1952	1953	Retired	6								
Gerrard, S.G.	1995		Still at club	117	19	16	8	2	1	10		2(1)
Gilhespy, T.W.C.	1921	1925	Bristol City	19		3						
Gillespie, G.T.	1983	1991	Glasgow Celtic	152	4	14	21	2		22		2
Gilligan, S.A.	1910	1913	Gillingham	40		16						
Givens, J.	1894	1895	Paisley Abercorn	10		3						
Glassey, R.J.	1934	1936	Stoke City	9		4						
Glover, J.W.	1900	1903	Small Heath	58			1					
Goddard, A.M.	1902	1914	Cardiff City	387		72	27		5			
Goldie, A.	1895	1900	New Brighton Tower	125		1	20					
Goldie, W.G.	1897	1904	Fulham	158		6	16					
Goode, B.J.	1908	1910	Wrexham	7		1						
Gordon, P.	1893	1894	Blackburn Rovers	26		7	3					
Gorman, J.	1905	1908	Leaicester Fosse	19			4		1			
Gracie, T.	1912	1914	Heart of Midlothian	33		5	1					
Graham, R.	1960	1972	Coventry City	97	6	31	7	3	4	7	1	2
Gray, W.J.	1926	1930	Exeter City	1								
Grayer, F.	1912	1914	Retired	1								
Green, T.	1901	1903	Swindon Town	7		1						
Griffin, M.R.	1907	1907	Crystal Palace	4								
Griffiths, H.	1905	1908	Chesterfield	6								
Grobbelaar, B.D.	1981	1994	Southampton	440			62			70		
Gunson, J.H.	1930	1934	Swindon Town	81		24	6		2			
Hafekost, C.H.	1914	1918	Hartlepool	1								
Haigh, J.	1949	1952	Scunthorpe United	11		3						
Hall, B.W.	1965	1976	Plymouth Argyle	140	15	15	17	2	3	12	1	1
Hamann, D.	1999		Still at club	113	6	6	10		1	4	3	
Hancock, E.	1931	1933	Burnley	10		2						
Hannah, A.B.	1892	1895	Rob Roy	40		1	6					
Hannah, D.	1894	1897	Dundee	31		11	2		1			
Hansen, A,D.	1977	1991	Retired	434		8	57	1	2	68		1
Hanson, A.J.	1931	1938	Chelsea	166		50	11		2			
Hardy, S.	1905	1912	Aston Villa	219			20					
Harkness, S.	1989	1999	Benfica	90	12	3	5	1		11	4	1
Harley, J.	1934	1948	Retired	118			16					
Harrington, J.C.	1920	1921	South Liverpool	4								
Harrop, J.	1908	1912	Aston Villa	133		4	6					
Harrower, J.	1958	1961	Newcastle United	96		21	6		1	3		
Harston, E.	1937	1939	Ramsgate Town	5		3						
Hartill, W.J.	1936	1936	Bristol Rovers	4								
Hartley, A.	1897	1898	Southampton	7		1	5					
Hateley, A.	1967	1968	Coventry City	42		17	7		8	2		
Heggem, V.	1998	2003	Released	38	16	3	1			2	2	
Heighway, S.D.	1970	1981	Minnesota Kicks	312	19	50	33	3	8	38		7
Henchoz, S.	1999		Still at club	117			11			12		
Henderson, A.	1931	1933	Clapton Orient	5								
Henderson, D.	1893	1894	Partick Thistle	20		10	2		2			
Henderson , H.	1894	1895	Not Known	2								
Henderson, J.R.	1893	1895	Not Known	1								
Heskey, E.W.I.	2000		Still at club	93	22	32	6	4	5	5	5	
Hewitt, C.W.	1907	1908	West Bromwich Albion	16		6						
Hewitt, J.	1904	1910	Bolton Wanderers	152		69	11		2			
Heydon, J.	1948	1953	Millwall	63			4					
Hickson, D.	1959	1961	Cambridge City	60		37	4			3		1
Hignett, A.J.	1962	1966	Chester City	1								
Hignett, A.	1903	1908	Not Known	1								
Hoare, J.H.	1903	1904	Southampton	7								
Hobson, A.**	1936	1938	Chester City	26			1					
	1944	1946	South Liverpool				1					
Hodgson, D.J.	1982	1984	Sunderland	21	7	4	3		1	6	3	3
Hodgson, G.	1925	1936	Aston Villa	358		233	19		8			

Euro Cup Apps	Euro Cup Sub	Euro Cup Goals	ECW Cup Apps	ECW Cup Sub	ECW Cup Goals	UEFA Cup Apps	UEFA Cup Sub	UEFA Cup Goals	Others Apps	Others Sub	Others Goals	Total Apps	Total Sub	Total Goals
												103		2
												28		1
													2	
												8		1
												2		
												4		2
												1		
												83		6
									1			288		124
2	4	1	7		7	17	7	4	1			289	41	171 (2)
												1		
						1	1					30	1	
												28		
												5		
												5		
												5		
	1											3	2	1
									1			45		14
												6		
18	1	1				16		2	2			171	22	22 (1)
												19		3
2	1								8	2		205	9	16
												40		16
												10		3
												9		4
												59		
									1			415		77
									4			149		1
												174		6
												7		1
									1		1	30		8
												23		1
												34		5
3		1	3			7	2	4	1			125	12	42
												1		
												1		
												7		1
												4		
												6		
30			2			5			19			628		
												87		26
												1		
												11		3
2	1	1	7			18	7	1	2		0(1)	198	26	21(1)
17	1					15	1		3			162	11	7
												10		2
									23			69		1
												33		12
42	1	3							17			618	2	14
												177		52
									1			240		
			4	1		9	2					119	20	4
												134		
												4		
												139		4
												105		22
												5		3
												4		
												12		1
						5		3				56		28
						5	1					46	19	3
22	4	4	8		2	30		5	5	1		448	27	76
21						10			3			174		
												5		
									1			23		12
												2		
												1		
22		6				13	3	4	3		1	142	34	48
												16		6
									1			164		71
												67		
												67		38
												1		
												1		
												7		
												**		
												28		
3	4	2								2		33	16	10
												377		241

Player	Year Joined	Year Left	To	League Apps	League Sub	League Goals	FA Cup Apps	FA Cup Sub	FA Cup Goals	FLC Apps	FLC Sub	FLC Goals
Holden, R.	1911	1914	Tranmere Rovers	2								
Holmes, J.	1895	1898	Burton Swifts	42			2					
Hood, W.J.	1937	1938	Derry City	3								
Hooper, M.D.	1985	1993	Newcastle United	50	1		5			10		
Hopkin, F.	1921	1931	Darlington	335		10	24		2			
Houghton, R.J.	1987	1992	Aston Villa	147	6	28	26	1	4	14		3
Howe, F.	1935	1938	Manchester City	89		36	5					
Howell, R.	1897	1901	Preston North End	59			8					
Hughes, E.W.	1967	1979	Wolverhampton W	474		35	62		1	46		3
Hughes, Jas.	1904	1907	Crystal Palace	14			1					
Hughes, John	1903	1906	Plymouth Argyle	31		2	1					
Hughes, L.	1942	1960	Retired	303		1	23					
Hughes, W.	1893	1894	Not Known	1								
Hunt, R.	1959	1969	Bolton Wanderers	401	3	245	44		18	10		5
Hunter, J. (S)	1899	1902	Heart of Midlothian	37		10	8		3			
Hunter, T.J.	1899	1902	Preston North End	5								
Hunter, W.	1908	1909	Sunderland	1								
Hutchison, D.	1990	1994	West Ham United	33	12	7	1	2		7	1	2
Hysen, G.I.	1989	1992	GAIS	70	2	2	13			6		1
Hyypia, S.	1999		Still at club	146		11	13			13		1
Ince, P.E.C.	1997	1999	Middlesbrough	65		14	3		1	6		1
Ireland, R.J.	1929	1931	St. Johnstone	1								
Irvine, A.J.	1986	1987	Dundee United		2			1			1	
Irwin, C.T.	1974	1981	Swansea Town	26	3	3	4			6		
Jackson, B.H.	1951	1958	Port Vale	126		11	7					
Jackson, J.	1925	1933	Retired	212		2	12					
James, D.B.	1992	1999	Aston Villa	213	1		19			22		
James, N.L.	1929	1933	Bradford City	8								
Jenkinson, W.	1919	1921	Wigan Borough	13								
Johnson, D.E.	1976	1982	Everton	128	21	55	17	2	6	15	4	9
Johnson, R.K.	1920	1925	Stoke City	77		28	5		2			
Johnson, T.C.F.	1934	1936	Darwen	36		8	2					
Johnston, C.P.	1981	1988	Retired	165	25	30	14	6	4	32	3	3
Jones, A.P.	1955	1963	Brentford	5								
Jones, B.	1989	1992	Wrexham									
Jones, H.	1947	1954	Rhyl Athletic	1								
Jones, J.H.	1924	1925	Llandudno Town	4								
Jones, J.M.	1951	1953	Scunthorpe United	4			1					
Jones, J.P.	1975	1978	Wrexham	72		3	9			4		
Jones , P.L.	1992	1997	Tranmere Rovers		3						1	
Jones, R.	1991	1999	Retired	182	1		27			21	1	
Jones, R.M.	1938	1945	Not known	5		1						
Jones, W.H.	1938	1954	Ellesmere Port	256		17	21					
Jowitt, C.H.	1896	?1897	Not known	1								
Kane, S.	1935	1937	Not known	6								
Kaye, G.H.	1941	1947	Swindon Town	1			1					
Keech, W.	1895	1896	Barnsley St Peters	6								
Keegan, J.K.	1971	1977	Hamburg SV	230		68	28		14	23		6
Keetley, J.F.	1923	1925	Wolverhampton W	9		2						
Kelly, *	1892	1893	Not known									
Kelso, J.*	1892	1893	Not known									
Kelvin, A.W.*	1892	1893	Kilmarnock				2					
Kemp, D.J.	1936	1946	Retired	30			3					
Kennedy, A.P.	1978	1985	Sunderland	249	2	15	21			45		2
Kennedy, M.	1995	1998	Queens Park Rangers	5	11			1			2	
Kennedy, R.	1974	1982	Swansea City	272	3	51	28		3	35		6
Kerr, N.	1894	1895	Nottingham Forest	12		3						
Kettle, B.	1973	1980	Wigan Athletic	3								
Kewley, J.K.	1972	1978	Dallas Tornado		1							
Kinghorn, W.J.D.	1938	1945	Not known	19		4						
Kippax, F.P.	1949	1950	Preston North End	1								
Kippe, F.P.	1999	2002	Lillestrom		2							
Kirkland, C.E.	2001		Still at club	9			2			5		
Kozma, I.	1992	1993	Ujpest TE	3	3			2			1	
Kvarme, B.T.	1997	1999	St Etienne	39	6		2			2		
Kyle, P.	1899	1900	Leicester Fosse	4			1					
Lacey, W.	1912	1924	New Brighton	230		18	28		11			
Lambert, R.	1936	1956	Retired	308		2	33					
Lane, F.	1971	1975	Notts County	1						1		
Lathom, G.	1902	1909	Southport	18			1					
Lawler, C.	1959	1975	Portsmouth	406		41	47		4	27		5
Lawrence, T.J.	1957	1971	Tranmere Rovers	306			42			6		
Lawrenson, M.T.	1981	1988	Retired	233	8	11	24		2	49	1	2
Lawson, H.S.R.	1924	1925	Airdrieonians	12			4					
Leavey, H.J.	1910	1911	Barnsley	5								
Lee, S.	1975	1986	Queens Park Rangers	190	7	13	17			39		2
Leishman, T.	1959	1963	Hibernian	107		6	9			2		1
Leonhardsen, O.	1997	1999	Tottenham Hotspur	34	3	7	1			4	2	
Lester, H.	1911	1913	Oldham Athletic	2								

Euro Cup			ECW Cup			UEFA Cup			Others			Total		
Apps	Sub	Goals	Apps	Sub	Goals	Apps	Sub	Goals	Apps	Sub	Goals	Apps	Sub	Goals
												2		
												44		
												3		
			1			3			2	1		71	2	
									1			360		12
						4		2	4		1	195	7	38
												94		36
												67		
22		1	8		2	45		6	8		13(1	665		61 (1)
												15		
												32		2
												326		1
												1		
14		10	7		2	8	2	5	3		1	487	5	286
												45		13
												5		
												1		
			3		1					1		44	16	10
									2			91	2	3
21		3				17		1	3			213		16
						7		1				81		17
												1		
													4	
4	1											40	4	3
												133		11
												224		2
			9			13						276	1	
												8		
												13		
14	6	8							3	3		177	36	78
												82		30
												38		8
13	4	2							8	1	1	232	39	40
												5		
							1						1	
												1		
												4		
												5		
11						1			3			100		3
													4	
			2			9						241	2	
												5		1
												277		17
												1		
												6		
												2		
												6		
12		4	6		1	22		7	2			323		100
												9		2
									3			3		
									1			1		
									4			6		
												33		
34		3(1)							8			357	2	20 (1)
				1			1					5	16	
32		6	4		2	10		4	9			390	3	72
												12		3
						1						4		
													1	
												19		4
												1		
													2	
3												19		
										1		3	7	
						5						48	6	
												5		
									1			259		29
												341		2
												2		
												19		
16		3	15		5	35		3	3			549		61
14			9			10			3			390		
26	1	2							14		1	346	10	18
												16		
												5		
33		4							9			288	7	19
												118		7
						3	2					42	7	7
												2		

Player	Year Joined	Year Left	To	League Apps	League Sub	League Goals	FA Cup Apps	FA Cup Sub	FA Cup Goals	FLC Apps	FLC Sub	FLC Goals
Lewis, H.	1916	1923	Hull City	59		10	11		2			
Lewis, K.	1960	1963	Huddersfield Town	72		39	8		3	2		2
Liddell, W.B.	1938	1961	Retired	492		215	42		13			
Lindsay, A.	1969	1977	Stoke City	168	2	12	22		1	23		1
Lindsay, J.	1928	1930	Swansea Town	14		2	2		1			
Lipsham, J.R.	1906	1907	Chester City	3								
Litmanen, J.O.	2001	2002	Ajax	12	14	5	1	2	1	2	1	
Livermore, D.E.	1965	1970	Norwich City	13	3					1		
Livingstone, G.T.	1902	1903	Manchester City	31		4	1					
Lloyd, L.V.	1969	1974	Coventry City	150		4	16			20		
Lock, F.W.	1953	1955	Watford	41			1					
Longworth, E.	1910	1928	Retired	342			28					
Low, N.H.	1933	1936	Newport County	13								
Lowe, H.C.	1911	1921	Nottingham Forest	122		2	13					
Lowry, T.	1963	1966	Crewe Alexandra	1								
Lucas, T.	1916	1933	Clapton Orient	341		3	25					
Lumsden, J.	1897	1898	Glossop	6		2	2					
MacDonald, K.D.	1984	1989	Coventry City	29	11	1	9		1	1	3	1
Mackinlay, D.	1910	1929	Prescot Cables	393		33	40		1			
Maloney, J.J.	1951	1954	Shrewsbury Town	12								
Marsh, M.A.	1987	1993	West Ham United	42	27	2	6	2		13	1	3
Marshall, R.G.	1897	1899	Portsmouth	20		2	1					
Marshall, W.H.	1901	1902	Not known	1								
Matteo, D.	1989	2000	Leeds United	112	15	1	6	2	1	9		
Matthews, R.W.	1918	1922	Bristol City	9		4						
Maxwell, L.J.	1997	2001	Cardiff City	1		1						
McAllister, G.	2000	2002	Coventry City	35	20	5	4	1		3	3	1(1)
McAteer, J.W.	1995	1999	Blackburn Rovers	34	16	3	11	1	3	12	1	
McAvoy, D.H.	1947	1949	Queen of the South	2								
McBain, N.	1928	1928	Watford	12								
McBride, J.	1892	1894	Manchester City	30		3	5					
McCallum, D.	1901	1903	Greenock Morton	2								
McCann, W.	1894	1895	Not known	15			2					
McCartney, J.	1892	1898	New Brighton Tower	124		4	18		1			
McConnell, J.M.	1909	1912	Aberdeen	50		1	3					
McCowie, A.	1896	1899	Woolwich Arsenal	33		11	2					
McDermott, T.	1974	1982	Newcastle United	221	11	54	23		4	36		5
McDevitt, W.	1923	1925	Exeter City	4								
McDonald, J.	1909	1912	Newcastle United	78		4	3					
McDougall, J.	1928	1938	South Liverpool	338		12	18					
McDougall, R.	1913	1920	Falkirk	7		1	1					
McFarlane, J.	1928	1930	Halifax Town	2								
McGuigan, A.	1900	1902	Middlesbrough	32		14	5					
McInnes, J.S.	1938	1946	Retired	48		2	3					
McKenna, J.	1905	1907	Not known	1								
McKinney, P.	1920	1923	New York Giants	3		1						
McLaughlin, J.T.	1967	1976	Barrow	38	2	2	4		1	3		
McLean, D.	1892	1895	St Bernards, Edinburgh	51		5	8					
McLean, J.	1903	1904	Not known	4								
McLean, J.C.	1894	1897	Grimsby Town	26			2					
McLeod, T.	1945	1951	Chesterfield	7								
McMahon, S.	1985	1991	Manchester City	202	2	29	30		7	27		13
McManaman, S.	1987	1999	Real Madrid	258	14	46	28	1	5	32	1	10
McMullan, D.	1925	1928	Belfast Distillery	31			4					
McNab, J.S.	1919	1928	Queens Park Rangers	200		6	21					
McNamara, A.	1957	1958	Crewe Alexandra	9		3	1					
McNaughton, H.	1920	1921	Not known	1								
McNulty, T.	1954	1958	Hyde United	36								
McOwen, W.A.	1892	1894	Blackpool (amateur)	23			3					
McPherson, A.	1929	1934	Sheffield United	130		18	3		1			
McPherson, W.	1906	1908	Glasgow Rangers	48		15	7		1			
McQue, J.	1892	1898	Third Lanark	103		10	16		2			
McQueen, H.	1892	1895	Derby County	39		11	5		2			
McQueen, M.	1892	1899	Retired	77		2	8					
McRorie, D.M.	1930	1933	Millwall	33		6	2					
McVean, M.	1892	1897	Burnley	89		25	11		6			
Meijer, E.	1999	2000	Hamburg SV	7	17		3		2			
Melia, J.J.	1954	1964	Wolverhampton W	268		77	18		2			
Mellor, N.	2002		Still at club	1	2		1			2		1
Metcalf, A.	1912	1919	Stockport County	52		23	11		5			
Michael, W.	1895	1897	Heart of Midlothian	19		5	4					
Millar, W.	1928	1930	Barrow	3		2						
Miller, J.*	1892	1893	The Wednesday				3		3			
Miller, J.	1919	1921	Aberdeen	8								
Miller, T.	1912	1920	Manchester United	127		50	19		6			
Milne, G.	1960	1967	Blackpool	234	2	17	28		1			
Minshull, R.	1946	1951	Southport	28			3					
Mitchell, F.W.G.	1921	1923	Tranmere Rovers	18								
Molby, J.	1984	1996	Swansea Town	195	23	44	24	4	4	25	3	9

Euro Cup			ECW Cup			UEFA Cup			Others			Total		
Apps	Sub	Goals	Apps	Sub	Goals	Apps	Sub	Goals	Apps	Sub	Goals	Apps	Sub	Goals
												70		12
												82		44
												534		228
3			6		1	22		3	2		0(1)	246	2	18(1)
												16		3
												3		
4	5	3					2					19	24	9
												14	3	
												32		4
4			4			23		1	1			218		5
												42		
									1			371		
												13		
												135		2
												1		
												366		3
												8		2
3									7	1	2	49	15	5
									1			434		34
												12		
			4			7	1	1	1			70	31	6
												21		2
												1		
			7			3	1					137	18	2
												9		4
												1		1
4	6					4	5	2	2		1	52	35	9(1)
			8			4	2					119	20	6
												2		
												12		
									21		4	56		7
												2		
												17		
									23		1	165		6
												53		1
												35		11
30	1	12							7		6	317	12	81
												4		
												81		4
												356		12
												8		1
												2		
												37		14
												51		2
												1		
												3		1
1						7						53	2	3
									23		1	82		6
												4		
									1			29		
												7		
						5			11		1	275	2	50
			11		2	19		3				348	16	66
												35		
									1			222		6
												10		3
												1		
												36		
									1			27		
												133		19
												55		16
									23		2	142		14
									17		3	61		16
									18		5	103		7
												35		6
									26		9	126		40
												10	17	2
												286		79
												4	2	1
												63		28
												23		5
												3		2
									21		22	24		25
												8		
												146		56
10			6						2			280	2	18
												31		
												18		
			2			5		1	9	2	3	260	32	61

Player	Year Joined	Year Left	To	League Apps	League Sub	League Goals	FA Cup Apps	FA Cup Sub	FA Cup Goals	FLC Apps	FLC Sub	FLC Goals
Molyneux, J.A.	1955	1962	Chester City	229		2	17		1	3		
Molyneux, W.S.	1963	1967	Oldham Athletic	1								
Money, R.	1977	1982	Luton Town	12	2		1			1		
Mooney, B.	1983	1987	Preston North End		1							
Moran, R.	1949	1968	Retired	342		15	32		2			
Morgan, H.	1898	1900	Blackburn Rovers	59		15	9		3			
Morris, F.W.	1958	1960	Crewe Alexandra	47		14	1					
Morris, R.	1902	1906	Grimsby Town	38		5	1					
Morrison, T.K.	1928	1935	Sunderland	240		4	14					
Morrissey, J.J.	1955	1962	Everton	36		6	1					
Muir, A.J.	1947	1949	South Liverpool	4								
Murdoch, W.R.	1955	1959	Barrow	17		5	2		2			
Murphy, D.B.	1997		Still at club	95	44	20	10	3	2	13	1	9
Murray, D.B.	1904	1905	Leeds City	15								
Murray, W.T.	1927	1930	Barrow	4		1						
Neal, P.G.	1974	1985	Bolton Wanderers	453	2	41	45		3	66		4
Neill, R.S.G.	1895	1897	Glasgow Rangers	22		2	4		1			
Newby, J.P.R.	1997	2001	Bury		1			2			1	
Nicholl, J.	1914	1915	Not known	52		12	7		2			
Nicholson, J.P.	1957	1961	Port Vale	1								
Nickson, H.W.	1945	1946	Not known				3					
Nicol, S.	1981	1995	Notts County	328	15	36	50		3	42		4
Nieuwenhuys, B.	1933	1947	Retired	239		74	21		5			
Ogrizovic, S.	1977	1982	Shrewsbury Town	4								
Ogston, J.K.	1965	1968	Doncaster Rovers	1								
Orr, R.	1908	1912	Raith Rovers	108		36	4		3			
Otsemobor, J.	1995		Still at club							1		
Owen, M.J.	1996		Still at club	164	23	102	11	1	7	12	2	9
Oxley, C.	1925	1928	Southend United	31		6	3					
Pagnam, F.	1914	1919	Arsenal	37		28	2		2			
Paisley, R.	1939	1954	Retired	252		10	25		2			
Palk (not Polk), S.	1940	1948	Port Vale	13								
Parkinson, J.A.	1899	1900	Blackpool	1								
Parkinson, J.	1901	1914	Bury	200		125	19		5			
Parr, S.V.	1948	1955	Exeter City	20								
Parry, E.H.	1921	1926	Walsall	13								
Parry, M.P.	1900	1909	Partick Thistle	207		4	14					
Partridge, R.J.	1995		Still at club							1		
Patterson, G.L.	1937	1946	Swindon Town	2			1		1			
Payne, J.B.	1944	1957	Everton	222		38	21		5			
Peake, E.H.	1908	1914	Third Lanark	51		5	4		1			
Pearson*	1892	1893	Not known									
Pearson, A.V.	1919	1921	Port Vale	43		4	8					
Penman, J.	1919	1921	Lochgelly United	1								
Peplow, S.T.	1964	1970	Swindon Town	2								
Perkins, W.H.	1898	1903	Northampton Town	107			10					
Perry, F.N.	1954	1957	Sittingbourne	1								
Peters, K.	1936	1940s	Retired	1								
Piechnik, T.	1992	1994	AGF Aarhus	16	1		2			5		
Pither, G.B.	1926	1928	Crewe Alexandra	12		1						
Platt, P.	1902	1905	Luton Town	44			1					
Pratt, D.	1923	1927	Bury	77		1	8					
Price, J.G.	1954	1957	Aston Villa	1								
Priday, R.H.	1945	1949	Blackburn Rovers	34		6	6		1			
Pursell, R.R.	1911	1920	Port Vale	99			13					
Race, H.	1927	1930	Manchester City	43		18						
Raisbeck, A.G.	1898	1909	Partick Thistle	312		18	28		2			
Ramsden, B.	1933	1948	Sunderland	60			6					
Rawlings, A.	1924	1926	Walsall	63		8	4		2			
Raybould, S.F.	1900	1907	Sunderland	211		119	14		9			
Redknapp, J.F.	1991	2002	Tottenham Hotspur	207	30	30	17	1	2(1)	26	1	5
Reid, T.J.	1925	1929	Manchester United	51		30	4					
Richardson*	1892	1893	Not known									
Riedle, K.	1997	1999	Fulham	34	26	11	2			3	4	2
Riise, J.A.	2001		Still at club	65	10	13	4	1		4		(1)
Riley, A.J.	1925	1945	Retired	322			16					
Roberts, J.E.	1933	1934	Wigan Athletic	1								
Roberts, S.	1931	1937	Shrewsbury Town	58		10	4		3			
Robertson, J.T.	1900	1902	Southampton	42			5					
Robertson, T.	1898	1902	Heart of Midlothian	126		31	15		3			
Robinson, M.J.	1983	1984	Queens Park Rangers	26	4	6	2		1	11	1	4
Robinson, R.S.	1904	1912	Tranmere Rovers	254		63	17		1			
Rogers, F.	1933	1940	Retired	70			5					
Rogers, T.	1907	1912	Tranmere Rovers	38			2					
Rosenthal, R.	1990	1994	Tottenham Hotspur	32	42	21	5	3		2	7	1
Ross, I.	1963	1972	Aston Villa	42	6	2	9	1	1	3		
Ross, J.D.	1894	1897	Burnley	73		37	7		3			
Ross, S.H.*	1892	1893	Not known				3					
Rowley, A.A.	1951	1954	Wrexham	11								

Euro Cup			ECW Cup			UEFA Cup			Others			Total		
Apps	Sub	Goals	Apps	Sub	Goals	Apps	Sub	Goals	Apps	Sub	Goals	Apps	Sub	Goals
												249		3
												1		
1												15	2	
													1	
4									1			379		17
												68		18
												48		14
												39		5
												254		4
												37		6
												4		
												19		7
19	2	3				12	5	2	1	2		150	57	36
												15		
												4		1
57		10(1)				12		1	15			648	2	59 (1)
									1			27		3
													4	
												59		14
												1		
												3		
8	2	2	2			7			14		1	451	17	46
												260		79
									1			5		
												1		
												112		39
												1		
15	1	9				24	3	10	3		2	229	30	139
												34		6
												39		30
												277		12
												13		
												1		
									1			220		130
												20		
												13		
									1			222		4
												1		
												3		1
												243		43
												55		6
									1			1		
												51		4
												1		
						1						3		
												117		
												1		
												1		
												23	1	
												12		1
												45		
												85		1
												1		
												40		7
												112		
												43		18
									1			341		20
												66		
												67		10
									1			226		128
1	2	1	8	3		11	1	3				270	38	41 (1)
												55		30
									1			1		
						3	4	2				42	34	15
19	1					4	1		3		1	99	13	14 (1)
												338		
												1		
												62		13
												47		
												141		34
6	1	2							1			46	6	13
												271		64
												75		
												40		
				3		1			1	1		41	56	22
			3	1		2	2	1				59	10	4
									5			85		40
									18			21		
												11		

Player	Year Joined	Year Left	To	League Apps	Sub	Goals	FA Cup Apps	Sub	Goals	FLC Apps	Sub	Goals
Rowley, A.C.	1953	1958	Tranmere Rovers	60		38	3		1			
Ruddock, N.	1993	1998	West Ham United	111	4	11	11			19	1	1(1)
Rudham, K.R.	1954	1960	Johan'burg Ramblers	63			3					
Rush, I.J.**	1980	1986	Juventus	224		139	25		20	47		25
	1986	1996	Leeds United	223	22	90	30	6	19(1)	31		23
Russell, C.	1978	1982	Huddersfield Town		1							
Rylands, D.R.	1970	1974	Hereford United	1								
Salisbury, W.	1928	1929	Bangor City	16		2	1		1			
Sambrook, J.H.	1922	1923	Stockport County	2								
Satterthwaite, C.O.	1899	1902	New Brompton	45		12						
Saul, P,	1906	1909	Coventry City	75		1	8		1			
Saunders, D.N.	1991	1992	Aston Villa	42		11	8		2(1)	5		2
Saunders, R.	1948	1959	Swansea Town	134		1	12					
Savage, R.E.	1931	1937	Manchester City	100		2	5					
Scales, J.R.	1994	1996	Tottenham Hotspur	65		2	14			10		2
Scott, A.	1929	1932	Swindon Town	3		2	1					
Scott, E.	1912	1934	Belfast Celtic	430			37					
Scott, J.	1910	1915	Dumbarton	10								
Scott, T.	1925	1928	Bristol City	17		4	1					
Seagraves, M.	1983	1986	Norwich City				1			1		
Sealey, A.J.	1962	1966	Chester City	1		1						
Shafto, J.	1936	1944	Retired	17		6	3		1			
Shannon, L.	1941	1949	Burnley	11		1						
Shears, A.E.	1924	1930	Tranmere Rovers	16								
Sheedy, K.M.	1978	1982	Everton	1	2		2		2			
Sheldon, J.	1913	1922	Retired	129		17	18		3			
Shepherd, J.W.	1945	1952	Wigan Athletic	54			4					
Shield, J.G.	1935	1937	Retired	1								
Shields, S.M.	1949	1951	Airdrieonians	1								
Shone, D.	1921	1928	West Ham United	76		23	5		3			
Sidlow, C.	1946	1952	New Brighton	149			16					
Slater, R.	1959	1962	Dundee	99			9			3		
Sloan, D.	1908	1909	Belfast Distillery	6								
Smicer, V.	1999		Still at club	53	38	7	8	1	1	12	2	4
Smith, A.	1937	1939	Crewe Alexandra	1								
Smith, J.T.	1929	1932	Tunbridge Wells Rangers	61		38	1					
Smith, J.T.	1951	1954	Torquay United	57		14	2					
Smith, J.*	1892	1893	The Wednesday				2					
Smith, S.W.	1903	1904	Southport Central	2		1						
Smith, T.	1960	1978	Swansea City	467		36	52		2	30		2
Smyth, S.	1952	1955	Bangor City	44		20						
Song, R.	1999	2000	West Ham United	27	7			1		2		
Souness, G.J.	1978	1984	Sampdoria	246	1	38	24		2	45		9
South, A.W.	1954	1956	Halifax Town	6		1	1					
Spackman, N.J.	1987	1989	Queens Park Rangers	39	12		5			6	1	
Speakman, J.	1909	1913	Not known	8		1						
Speakman, S.	1912	1920	South Liverpool	25			1					
Speedie, D.R.	1991	1991	Blackburn Rovers	8	4	6	1	1				
Spicer, E.W.	1937	1954	Retired	158		2	10					
Staniforth, F.W.	1913	1914	Not known	3								
Staunton, S.**	1986	1991	Aston Villa	55	10		14	2	1	6	2	4
	1998	2000	Aston Villa	38	6		2			5		1
Steel, W.G.	1931	1935	Birmingham	120			8					
Stevenson, W.	1898	1900	Barnsley	21			1					
Stevenson, W.	1962	1967	Stoke City	188		15	24		1			
Stewart, J.M.	1909	1914	Hamilton Academicals	61		26	2					
Stewart, P.A,	1992	1996	Sunderland	28	4	1	1			6		
St. John, I.	1961	1971	Hellenic FC	334	2	95	48	1	12	6		1
Storer, H.	1895	1901	Retired	102			15					
Storton, T.G.	1972	1974	Chester City	5			1			4		
Stott, J.	1893	1894	Grimsby Town	15		14	2					
Strong, G.H.	1964	1970	Coventry City	150	5	30	23		1	4		
Stuart, W.	1910	1914	Not known	3		1	2					
Stubbins, A.	1946	1953	Ashington	159		75	19		8			
Tanner, N.	1988	1994	Bath City	36	4	1	2			6	2	
Taylor, H.	1932	1937	Not known	70		6	2					
Taylor, P.H.	1936	1954	Retired	314		34	31					
Tennant, J.W.	1933	1936	Bolton Wanderers	39			3					
Thomas, M.L.	1991	1998	Benfica	96	28	9	15	2	2	7	3	1
Thompson, C.	1929	1931	Blackpool	5			1					
Thompson, D.A.	1994	2000	Coventry City	24	24	5		1		5		
Thompson, M.S.	1974	1978	Blackpool	1								
Thompson, P.H.	1963	1974	Bolton Wanderers	317	5	41	37	1	5	9		2
Thompson, P.B.	1971	1985	Sheffield United	337	3	7	36			42	1	1
Thomson, R.	1962	1965	Luton Town	7			1					
Tomley, F.W.	1953	1955	Chester City	2								
Toshack, J.B.	1970	1978	Swansea City	169	3	74	24		8	13		3
Tosswill, J.S.	1912	1913	Southend United	11		1						
Traore, D.	1999		Still at club	38	2		2			5	1	

Euro Cup Apps	Euro Cup Sub	Euro Cup Goals	ECW Cup Apps	ECW Cup Sub	ECW Cup Goals	UEFA Cup Apps	UEFA Cup Sub	UEFA Cup Goals	Others Apps	Others Sub	Others Goals	Total Apps	Total Sub	Total Goals
												63		39
			2	1		3						146	6	12 (1)
												66		
24	1	14(1)							10		9	**		
			4		5	7	1	1	5		1	630	30	346 (2)
													1	
												1		
												17		3
												2		
												45		12
												83		2
						5		9	1		1	61		25 (1)
												146		1
												105		2
			2	1		2						93	1	4
												4		2
									1			468		
												10		
												18		4
												2		
												1		1
												20		7
												11		1
												16		
												3	2	2
												147		20
												58		
												1		
												1		
												81		26
												165		
												111		
												6		
11	5	2				6	6			1		90	53	14
												1		
												62		38
												59		14
									10		5	12		5
												2		1
26		1	16		2	41		5	5	1	0(1)	637	1	48 (1)
												44		20
						1						30	8	
35	1	6(1)							7			357	2	55 (1)
												7		1
												50	13	
												8		1
												26		
												9	5	6
												168		2
												3		
												**		
						5	2		1		1	126	22	7
												128		
												22		
14		1	9			2	1		3		1	240	1	18
												63		26
			2		2				1			38	4	3
13		7	9		2	8	2	1	2			420	5	118
									4			121		
						1	1					11	1	
												17		14
7			4		2	5	1		2			195	6	33
												5		1
												178		83
			1	1		5	1		1			51	8	1
												72		6
												345		34
												42		
			7	1		3	1					128	35	12
												6		
						2						31	25	5
							1					1	1	
13		1	9	2	1	18	2	4	2			405	10	54
30	2		1		2	13	1	2	11		1	470	7	13
												8		
												2		
8		2	1	3		21	3	8	1		1	237	9	96
												11		1
5	1					8	1		1			59	5	

Player	Year Joined	Year Left	To	League Apps	Sub	Goals	FA Cup Apps	Sub	Goals	FLC Apps	Sub	Goals
Twentyman, G.	1953	1960	Ballymena United	170		18	14		1			
Underwood, E.D.	1953	1956	Watford	45			5					
Uren, H.J.	1907	1912	Everton	42		2	3					
Van Den Berg, H.H.C.	1937	1940	Retired	22		4						
Venison, B.	1986	1992	Newcastle United	103	7	1	16	5		14	3	
Vignal , G.	2002		Still at club	7	4			1		3		
Waddle, A.R.	1973	1977	Leicester City	11	5	1	2			3		
Wadsworth, H.	1919	1924	Leicester City	55		3						
Wadsworth, W.	1912	1926	Bristol City	217		7	23		1			
Walker, J.	1898	1902	Glasgow Rangers	109		30	11		1			
Walker, W.	1897	1898	Leith Athletic	12		2						
Wall, T.P.	1966	1970	Crystal Palace	31			6			2		
Wallace, G.H.	1960	1967	Crewe Alexandra	20		3						
Walsh, J.A.	1922	1928	Hull City	69		24	8		3			
Walsh, P.A.	1984	1988	Tottenham Hotspur	63	14	25	6	2	3	10	2	4
Walters, M.E.	1991	1996	Southampton	58	36	14	6	3		10	2	4
Wark, J.	1984	1988	Ipswich Town	64	6	28	11	2	6	6	4	3
Watkinson, W.W.	1946	1951	Accrington Stanley	24		2						
Watson, A.F.	1985	1991	Bournemouth	3	1		1	1		1	1	
Welfare, J.H.	1912	1913	Rio de Janeiro	4		1						
Welsh, J.	2002		Still at club								1	
West, A.**	1903	1909	Reading }	124		5	11		1			
	1910	1911	Notts County }	4			1					
Westerveld, S.	1999	2001	Real Sociedad	75			8			5		
Wheeler, J.E.	1956	1962	Retired	164		21	10		2	3		
Whelan, R.A.	1979	1994	Southend United	351	11	46	40	1	7	46	4	14
White, R.	1955	1962	Doncaster Rovers	203			11		1	3		
White, W.	1901	1902	Dundee	6		1						
Whitehead, J.	1894	1894	Not known	2								
Whitehurst, A.J.	1928	1929	Bradford City	8		2						
Whitham, J.	1970	1974	Cardiff City	15		7				1	1	
Whitworth, G.G.	1950	1953	Not known	9								
Wilkie, T.J.	1895	1899	Portsmouth	57		1	6		1			
Wilkinson, G.B.	1953	1960	Bangor City	78			1					
Williams, R.B.	1945	1953	South Liverpool	31		5	3					
Wilson, C.	1897	1905	Retired	84		3	7					
Wilson, D.	1899	1900	Not known	2								
Wilson, D.C.	1967	1968	Preston North End		1							
Woan, D.	1950	1951	Leyton Orient	2								
Worgan, A.	1893	1895	Chester City	2		2						
Wright, D.	1930	1934	Hull City	93		35	7					
Wright, E.V.	1934	1937	Plymouth Argyle	81		31	4		2			
Wright, M	1991	1998	Retired	156	2	5	18			14	2	2
Wright, S.J.	1997	2002	Sunderland	10	4		2			1	1	
Wylie, T.G.*	1892	1893	Bury				3		5			
Xavier, A.L.D.C	2002	2003	Galatasaray	13	1	1				1		
Yeats, R.	1961	1971	Tranmere Rovers	357	1	13	50			7		
Younger, T.	1956	1959	Falkirk	120			7					
Ziege, C.	2000	2001	Tottenham Hotspur	11	5	1	2	1		1	3	1(1)

Bibliography

All these books, magazines and websites were useful in researching this book:

The Anfield Encyclopedia, Stephen Kelly, Mainstream
Back Page Football, Stephen Kelly, Queen Anne Press
The Complete Book of The World Cup, Cris Freddi, Collins Willow
Daily Telegraph Football Chronicle, Norman Barrett, Stanley Paul
England Football Fact Book, Chris Freddi, Guinness
England: The Complete Post-War Record, Mike Payne, Breedon
The Essential History of Everton, Mark Platt, WHSmith
Football Managers, Dennis Turner and Alex White, Breedon
Goodison Glory, Ken Rogers, Breedon
The Great Derby Matches: Liverpool Versus Everton, Michael Heatley and Ian Welch, Dial House
Liverpool Player By Player, Ivan Ponting, Hamlyn
My Autobiography, Kevin Keegan, Little Brown
The Official Illustrated History of the FA Cup, Bryon Butler, Headline Book Publishing

Euro Cup			ECW Cup			UEFA Cup			Others			Total		
Apps	Sub	Goals	Apps	Sub	Goals	Apps	Sub	Goals	Apps	Sub	Goals	Apps	Sub	Goals
												184		19
												50		
												45		2
												22		4
							3	1	6		1	139	18	3
4	1											14	6	
	1											16	6	1
												55		3
									1			241		8
												120		31
												12		2
						3						42		
1		2							1		1	22		6
												77		27
6		3							7	2	2	92	20	37
			3			4	1	1	1			82	42	19
9		5							4	2		94	14	42
												24		2
									1			6	3	
												4		1
													1	
									1			**		
												141		6
						13			2			103		
												177		23
22	1	6							16	1		475	18	73
												217		1
												6		1
									1			3		
												8		2
							1					16	2	7
												9		
									1			64		2
												79		
												34		5
												91		3
												2		
													1	
												2		
												2		2
												100		35
												85		33
			8		2	9			1			206	4	9
2	1	1										15	6	1
									22		11	25		16
5		1							1			20	1	2
14		1	9			13		1	3		1	453	1	16
												127		
						6	3					20	12	2(1)

The Official Liverpool Fans' Guide, David Walmsley, Carlton
The Official Liverpool FC Illustrated History, Jeff Anderson, Carlton
100 Seasons of League Football, Bryon Butler, Queen Anne Press
Pictorial History of English Football, Robert Jeffrey, Dempsey Parr
Rothmans Book of Football Records, Jack Rollin, Headline Book Publishing
Rothmans Football Yearbook, eds Glenda Rollin and Jack Rollin, Headline Book Publishing
Ian Rush: An Autobiography, Ebury
Shankly, Bill Shankly, Book Club Associates
Shanks, Dave Bowler, Orion
Shanks For The Memory, John Keith, Robson
The Story of Liverpool, CL Lamb and E Smallpage, Lamb
Sunday Times Illustrated History of Football, Chris Nawrat and Steve Hutchings, Hamlyn
Talking Shankly, Tom Darby, Mainstream
Total Football magazine
Wembley, The First Time, Mick Blakeman, Yore
www.guardian.co.uk
www.soccerbase.com

WHS

OTHER TITLES IN THE SERIES

The Essential History of...

Football		
Arsenal	Rab MacWilliam/Kevin Connolly	*0 7553 1267 8*
Blackburn Rovers	Mike Jackman	*0 7553 1022 5*
Celtic	Graham McColl/George Sheridan	*0 7553 1141 8*
Charlton Athletic	Paul Clayton	*0 7553 1020 9*
England	Andrew Mourant/Jack Rollin	*0 7553 1142 6*
Everton	Mark Platt	*0 7553 1274 0**
Leeds United	Andrew Mourant	*0 7553 1170 1**
Leicester City	Tony Matthews	*0 7553 1023 3*
Manchester City	Ian Penney	*0 7553 1168 X**
Manchester United	Ivan Ponting/Cliff Butler	*0 7553 1269 4*
Middlesbrough	Richard Jones	*0 7553 1143 4*
Newcastle United	Paul Joannou/Bill Swann/Steve Corke	*0 7553 1270 8*
Rangers	Stephen Halliday	*0 7553 1145 0*
West Bromwich Albion	Gavin McOwan	*0 7553 1146 9*
West Ham United	Kirk Blows/Tony Hogg	*0 7553 1169 8**
Rugby Union		
England	Ian Malin/John Griffiths	*0 7553 1271 6*
Scotland	Nick Oswald/John Griffiths	*0 7553 1272 4*
Wales	Steve Lewis/John Griffiths	*0 7553 1273 2*

** Trade paperback editions*

Please contact your local WHSmith store for details about ordering any of these titles.